Presenting

The Graphic Story
of the
AMERICAN
PRESIDENTS

The Graphic Story
of the
AMERICAN
PRESIDENTS

by David C. Whitney

EDITED BY THOMAS C. JONES

Published by

J. G. Ferguson Publishing Company / Chicago

DISTRIBUTED TO THE BOOK TRADE BY DOUBLEDAY & COMPANY, INC.

Lithographed in the United States of America
by Photopress, Inc., Broadview, Illinois

Foreword

No PLAYWRIGHT ever conceived a work so filled with drama, suspense, tragedy, and unexpected turns of fate as that played out on the stage of the White House. No director ever chose such a fascinatingly heterogeneous group of stars as the thirty-seven men who have performed the lead role in American history. And no actors ever dared to rewrite their parts to fit their own talents and ambitions as have the Presidents.

When created nearly two centuries ago, the office of the President of the United States was unique—a ruler to be elected and to be judged by his electors every four years; a ruler combining the powers of a king, a prime minister, and a commanding general. The statesmen of Europe, wise in the politics of royal courts, knowingly winked at each other and predicted that the peculiar American experiment would last a few years at the most—that a strong President would refuse to bow to the wishes of the electors and would make himself king for life, or that a weak President would be cast out of office by revolution before his four years were up. They were wrong. And the reasons why they were wrong can only be understood by studying the lives of the Presidents and their part in the evolution of American political democracy.

The American system of government—with its checks and balances, its constitutional restrictions of power, and its unwritten complexities of two-party politics—is exceedingly complicated. But at the heart of the system lies a simple idea—that the people have the right to change their leaders at regular intervals. Every four years the people can retain or remove the President. And every two years they can pass judgment on his policies by supporting or rejecting the congressional candidates of his party. Congress, moreover, has the power to remove the President if he is guilty of treason, bribery, or "other high crimes and misdemeanors." One day a man can hold the most powerful office in the world, and the next he can be out of office with no more power than that held by any other private citizen. The universal acceptance of this simple idea, first demonstrated by George Washington when he turned the presidency over to John Adams, has given the American system a resilient vitality, enabling the people to tolerate a President they merely dislike in the knowledge that they do not have long to wait until they can be rid of him.

Of even more importance has been the acceptance of the idea that both the President and his party can be turned out of office and replaced with a new leader *and* a new party by means of an election instead of an insurrection. The first such "election revolution" took place when liberal Thomas Jefferson and his Democratic-Republican followers won out over conservative John Adams and his Federalists. At the time, doom-sayers forecast that blood would run in the streets if the Democratic-Republicans were allowed to assume control of the government. But when Adams peacefully stepped down and Jefferson demonstrated that an opposition party could assume power in a responsible manner, the tradition of revolution by election was established.

Throughout the early days, however, the election of the President was by no means in the hands of the man-in-the-street voter. From Washington to John Quincy Adams, presidential candidates were chosen by caucuses of senators and congressmen. In turn, state legislatures indirectly chose the President by appointing electors to the Electoral College. Because of this system, the early Presidents did not have to strive for great popular appeal with the masses of voters, but instead were more concerned with staying in the good graces of Congress and the state legislatures. Presidential political campaigns in the modern sense were unknown. And the Presidents themselves—Washington, Adams, Jefferson, Madison, and Monroe—were able to emphasize their roles as statesmen rather than as popular politicians.

The disputed election of 1824 broke this pattern. None of the candidates had a majority of votes in the Electoral College, so the President was chosen by the House of Representatives. Although Andrew Jackson had received the largest number of electoral votes, the supporters of John Quincy Adams and Henry Clay united to award the presidency to Adams—who in turn appointed Clay as his Secretary of State. Jackson's followers cried "foul!"

By the time of the election of 1828, the power to name the presidential electors had been taken out of the hands of the state legislatures in all states except South Carolina and had been given directly to the voters. When Jackson soundly defeated Adams in their return engagement in 1828, he became the first President to be popularly elected in the modern sense. Members of the older order were horrified when Jackson rewarded his backwoods followers by opening the doors of the White House to them and by cutting them in on the "political spoils" of victory.

Jackson next broke the power of the congressional caucus to name presidential candidates. The first national convention of the Democratic party in 1832, which brought together local politicians from all states, renominated Jackson for President and ratified his choice of Martin Van Buren for Vice President.

The whoop-and-holler style of national political campaigns came into its own in 1840 when the Whigs learned the importance of appealing to the common man by portraying their candidate, William Henry Harrison, as a national hero who had been born in a log cabin. Torchlight processions, campaign slogans, and campaign songs roused the electorate and brought 40% more voters to the polls than in the previous election.

From that time on, the major political parties began to choose their presidential candidates for their popular appeal as much as for their abilities. Candidates campaigned more and more aggressively, trying to be seen and heard by as many voters as possible. Eventually radio and television carried the presidential campaigns directly into the voters' homes.

After Jackson had demonstrated that a man did not need to be a member of the aristocracy or even a college graduate in order to be elected President, it became the American dream of most mothers that their sons would "grow up to be President." And many later Presidents were to attribute their success to their mothers' encouragement.

With few if any exceptions, the men who have been President have wanted the office very badly, and they have worked hard to get it. Some were rich men who devoted their lives to public service. Some were poor boys who struggled to the top in the Horatio Alger tradition. Others were men who won their fame on the battlefield. The majority have been lawyers—the law profession being a natural entrée to local politics. Almost all held lesser political offices before climbing to national stature.

The men who have been our most successful Presidents have had the ability both to administer the government as statesmen and to lead their political parties as politicians.

DAVID C. WHITNEY

Contents

Vital Facts About the Presidents of the United States

	Name	Born	Birthplace	Died	Age at Death
1.	George Washington	Feb. 22, 1732	Westmoreland County, Va.	Dec. 14, 1799	67
2.	John Adams	Oct. 30, 1735	Braintree, Mass.	July 4, 1826	90
3.	Thomas Jefferson	Apr. 13, 1743	Albemarle County, Va.	July 4, 1826	83
4.	James Madison	Mar. 16, 1751	Port Conway, Va.	June 28, 1836	85
5.	James Monroe	Apr. 28, 1758	Westmoreland County, Va.	July 4, 1831	73
6.	John Quincy Adams	July 11, 1767	Braintree, Mass.	Feb. 23, 1848	80
7.	Andrew Jackson	Mar. 15, 1767	Waxhaw, S. C.	June 8, 1845	78
8.	Martin Van Buren	Dec. 5, 1782	Kinderhook, N. Y.	July 24, 1862	79
9.	William H. Harrison	Feb. 9, 1773	Berkeley, Va.	Apr. 4, 1841	68
10.	John Tyler	Mar. 29, 1790	Greenway, Va.	Jan. 18, 1862	71
11.	James K. Polk	Nov. 2, 1795	Pineville, N. C.	June 15, 1849	53
12.	Zachary Taylor	Nov. 24, 1784	Orange County, Va.	July 9, 1850	65
13.	Millard Fillmore	Jan. 7, 1800	Locke, N. Y.	Mar. 8, 1874	74
14.	Franklin Pierce	Nov. 23, 1804	Hillsboro, N. H.	Oct. 8, 1869	64
15.	James Buchanan	Apr. 23, 1791	Mercersburg, Pa.	June 1, 1868	77
16.	Abraham Lincoln	Feb. 12, 1809	Hardin County, Ky.	Apr. 15, 1865	56
17.	Andrew Johnson	Dec. 29, 1808	Raleigh, N. C.	July 31, 1875	66
18.	Ulysses S. Grant	Apr. 27, 1822	Point Pleasant, O.	July 23, 1885	63
19.	Rutherford B. Hayes	Oct. 4, 1822	Delaware, O.	Jan. 17, 1893	70
20.	James A. Garfield	Nov. 19, 1831	Orange, O.	Sept. 19, 1881	49
21.	Chester A. Arthur	Oct. 5, 1830	Fairfield, Vt.	Nov. 18, 1886	56
22.	Grover Cleveland	Mar. 18, 1837	Caldwell, N. J.	June 24, 1908	71
23.	Benjamin Harrison	Aug. 20, 1833	North Bend, O.	Mar. 13, 1901	67
24.	Grover Cleveland	Mar. 18, 1837	Caldwell, N. J.	June 24, 1908	71
25.	William McKinley	Jan. 29, 1843	Niles, O.	Sept. 14, 1901	58
26.	Theodore Roosevelt	Oct. 27, 1858	New York City	Jan. 6, 1919	60
27.	William H. Taft	Sept. 15, 1857	Cincinnati, O.	Mar. 8, 1930	72
28.	Woodrow Wilson	Dec. 28, 1856	Staunton, Va.	Feb. 3, 1924	67
29.	Warren G. Harding	Nov. 2, 1865	Morrow County, O.	Aug. 2, 1923	57
30.	Calvin Coolidge	July 4, 1872	Plymouth Notch, Vt.	Jan. 5, 1933	60
31.	Herbert Hoover	Aug. 10, 1874	West Branch, Ia.	Oct. 20, 1964	90
32.	Franklin D. Roosevelt	Jan. 30, 1882	Hyde Park, N. Y.	Apr. 12, 1945	63
33.	Harry S Truman	May 8, 1884	Lamar, Mo.	Dec. 26, 1972	88
34.	Dwight D. Eisenhower	Oct. 14, 1890	Denison, Tex.	Mar. 28, 1969	78
35.	John F. Kennedy	May 29, 1917	Brookline, Mass.	Nov. 22, 1963	46
36.	Lyndon B. Johnson	Aug. 27, 1908	Gillespie County, Tex.	Jan. 22, 1973	64
37.	Richard Nixon	Jan. 9, 1913	Yorba Linda, Calif.		
38.	Gerald R. Ford	July, 14, 1913	Omaha, Nebr.		

	Burial Place	Served	Age on Taking Office	Party	Vice-President
1.	Mount Vernon, Va.	1789-1797	57	Federalist	John Adams
2.	Quincy, Mass.	1797-1801	61	Federalist	Thomas Jefferson
3.	Monticello, Va.	1801-1809	57	Democratic-Republican	Aaron Burr George Clinton
4.	Montpelier, Va.	1809-1817	57	Democratic-Republican	George Clinton Elbridge Gerry
5.	Richmond, Va.	1817-1825	58	Democratic-Republican	Daniel D. Tompkins
6.	Quincy, Mass.	1825-1829	57	Democratic-Republican	John C. Calhoun
7.	Hermitage, Tenn.	1829-1837	61	Democratic	John C. Calhoun Martin Van Buren
8.	Kinderhook, N. Y.	1837-1841	54	Democratic	Richard M. Johnson
9.	North Bend, O.	1841	68	Whig	John Tyler
10.	Richmond, Va.	1841-1845	51	Whig	
11.	Nashville, Tenn.	1845-1849	49	Democratic	George M. Dallas
12.	Louisville, Ky.	1849-1850	64	Whig	Millard Fillmore
13.	Buffalo, N. Y.	1850-1853	50	Whig	
14.	Concord, N. H.	1853-1857	48	Democratic	William R. King
15.	Lancaster, Pa.	1857-1861	65	Democratic	John C. Breckinridge
16.	Springfield, Ill.	1861-1865	52	Republican	Hannibal Hamlin Andrew Johnson
17.	Greeneville, Tenn.	1865-1869	56	Democratic	
18.	New York City	1869-1877	46	Republican	Schuyler Colfax ; Henry Wilson
19.	Fremont, O.	1877-1881	54	Republican	William A. Wheeler
20.	Cleveland, O.	1881	49	Republican	Chester A. Arthur
21.	Albany, N. Y.	1881-1885	50	Republican	
22.	Princeton, N. J.	1885-1889	47	Democratic	Thomas A. Hendricks
23.	Indianapolis, Ind.	1889-1893	55	Republican	Levi P. Morton
24.	Princeton, N. J.	1893-1897	55	Democratic	Adlai E. Stevenson
25.	Canton, O.	1897-1901	54	Republican	Garret A. Hobart Theodore Roosevelt
26.	Oyster Bay, N. Y.	1901-1909	42	Republican	Charles W. Fairbanks
27.	Arlington, Va.	1909-1913	51	Republican	James S. Sherman
28.	Washington, D.C.	1913-1921	56	Democratic	Thomas R. Marshall
29.	Marion, O.	1921-1923	55	Republican	Calvin Coolidge
30.	Plymouth, Vt.	1923-1929	51	Republican	Charles G. Dawes
31.	West Branch, Ia.	1929-1933	54	Republican	Charles Curtis
32.	Hyde Park, N. Y.	1933-1945	51	Democratic	John N. Garner Henry A. Wallace Harry S Truman
33.	Independence, Mo.	1945-1953	60	Democratic	Alben W. Barkley
34.	Abilene, Kan.	1953-1961	62	Republican	Richard M. Nixon
35.	Arlington, Va.	1961-1963	43	Democratic	Lyndon B. Johnson
36.	Stonewall, Tex.	1963-1969	55	Democratic	Hubert H. Humphrey
37.		1969-1974	56	Republican	Spiro Agnew ; Gerald Ford
38.		1974-	61	Republican	Nelson A. Rockefeller

Political Control of Congress: 1789-1975

Congress	Years	PRESIDENT AND PARTY	HOUSE OF REPRESENTATIVES			SENATE		
			Majority Party	Minority Party	Other	Majority Party	Minority Party	Other
1st	1789-91	George Washington . . . . Federalist	Fed-38	A-F-26	. . .	Fed-17	A-F-9	. . .
2nd	1791-93	George Washington . . . . Federalist	Fed-37	DR-33	. . .	Fed-16	DR-13	. . .
3rd	1793-95	George Washington . . . . Federalist	DR-57	Fed-48	. . .	Fed-17	DR-13	. . .
4th	1795-97	George Washington . . . . Federalist	Fed-54	DR-52	. . .	Fed-19	DR-13	. . .
5th	1797-99	John Adams . . . . Federalist	Fed-58	DR-48	. . .	Fed-20	DR-12	. . .
6th	1799-1801	John Adams . . . . Federalist	Fed-64	DR-42	. . .	Fed-19	DR-13	. . .
7th	1801-03	Thomas Jefferson . . Democratic-Republican	DR-69	Fed-36	. . .	DR-18	Fed-13	. . .
8th	1803-05	Thomas Jefferson . . Democratic-Republican	DR-102	Fed-39	. . .	DR-25	Fed-9	. . .
9th	1805-07	Thomas Jefferson . . Democratic-Republican	DR-116	Fed-25	. . .	DR-27	Fed-7	. . .
10th	1807-09	Thomas Jefferson . . Democratic-Republican	DR-118	Fed-24	. . .	DR-28	Fed-6	. . .
11th	1809-11	James Madison . . . . Democratic-Republican	DR-94	Fed-48	. . .	DR-28	Fed-6	. . .
12th	1811-13	James Madison . . . . Democratic-Republican	DR-108	Fed-36	. . .	DR-30	Fed-6	. . .
13th	1813-15	James Madison . . . . Democratic-Republican	DR-112	Fed-68	. . .	DR-27	Fed-9	. . .
14th	1815-17	James Madison . . . . Democratic-Republican	DR-117	Fed-65	. . .	DR-25	Fed-11	. . .
15th	1817-19	James Monroe . . . . . Democratic-Republican	DR-141	Fed-42	. . .	DR-34	Fed-10	. . .
16th	1819-21	James Monroe . . . . . Democratic-Republican	DR-156	Fed-27	. . .	DR-35	Fed-7	. . .
17th	1821-23	James Monroe . . . . . Democratic-Republican	DR-158	Fed-25	. . .	DR-44	Fed-4	. . .
18th	1823-25	James Monroe . . . . . Democratic-Republican	DR-187	Fed-26	. . .	DR-44	Fed-4	. . .
19th	1825-27	John Quincy Adams . . . . Coalition	Co-105	Ja-97	. . .	Co-26	Ja-20	. . .
20th	1827-29	John Quincy Adams . . . . Coalition	Ja-119	Co-94	. . .	Ja-28	Co-20	. . .
21st	1829-31	Andrew Jackson . . . . Democrat	D-139	NR-74	. . .	D-26	NR-22	. . .
22nd	1831-33	Andrew Jackson . . . . Democrat	D-141	NR-58	14	D-25	NR-21	2
23rd	1833-35	Andrew Jackson . . . . Democrat	D-147	AM-53	60	D-20	NR-20	8
24th	1835-37	Andrew Jackson . . . . Democrat	D-145	W-98	. . .	D-27	W-25	. . .
25th	1837-39	Martin Van Buren . . . . Democrat	D-108	W-107	24	D-30	W-18	4
26th	1839-41	Martin Van Buren . . . . Democrat	D-124	W-118	. . .	D-28	W-22	. . .
27th	1841-43	William H. Harrison . . . . Whig John Tyler . . . . Whig	W-133	D-102	6	W-28	D-22	2
28th	1843-45	John Tyler . . . . Whig	D-142	W-79	1	W-28	D-25	1
29th	1845-47	James K. Polk . . . . Democrat	D-143	W-77	6	D-31	W-25	. . .
30th	1847-49	James K. Polk . . . . Democrat	W-115	D-108	4	D-36	W-21	1
31st	1849-51	Zachary Taylor . . . . Whig Millard Fillmore . . . . Whig	D-112	W-109	9	D-35	W-25	2
32nd	1851-53	Millard Fillmore . . . . Whig	D-140	W-88	5	D-35	W-24	3
33rd	1853-55	Franklin Pierce . . . . Democrat	D-159	W-71	4	D-38	W-22	2
34th	1855-57	Franklin Pierce . . . . Democrat	R-108	D-83	43	D-40	R-15	5
35th	1857-59	James Buchanan . . . . Democrat	D-118	R-92	26	D-36	R-20	8
36th	1859-61	James Buchanan . . . . Democrat	R-114	D-92	31	D-36	R-26	4
37th	1861-63	Abraham Lincoln . . . . Republican	R-105	D-43	30	R-31	D-10	8
38th	1863-65	Abraham Lincoln . . . . Republican	R-102	D-75	9	R-36	D-9	5
39th	1865-67	Abraham Lincoln . . . . Unionist Andrew Johnson . . . . Unionist	U-149	D-42	. . .	U-42	D-10	. . .
40th	1867-69	Andrew Johnson . . . . Unionist	R-143	D-49	. . .	R-42	D-11	. . .
41st	1869-71	U. S. Grant . . . . Republican	R-149	D-63	. . .	R-56	D-11	. . .
42nd	1871-73	U. S. Grant . . . . Republican	R-134	D-104	5	R-52	D-17	5
43rd	1873-75	U. S. Grant . . . . Republican	R-194	D-92	14	R-49	D-19	5
44th	1875-77	U. S. Grant . . . . Republican	D-169	R-109	14	R-45	D-29	2
45th	1877-79	Rutherford B. Hayes . . . . Republican	D-153	R-140	. . .	R-39	D-36	1
46th	1879-81	Rutherford B. Hayes . . . . Republican	D-149	R-130	14	D-42	R-33	1
47th	1881-83	James A. Garfield . . . . Republican Chester A. Arthur . . . . Republican	R-147	D-135	11	R-37	D-37	1
48th	1883-85	Chester A. Arthur . . . . Republican	D-197	R-118	10	R-38	D-36	2
49th	1885-87	Grover Cleveland . . . . Democrat	D-183	R-140	2	R-43	D-34	. . .
50th	1887-89	Grover Cleveland . . . . Democrat	D-169	R-152	4	R-39	D-37	. . .

Congress	Years	PRESIDENT AND PARTY	HOUSE OF REPRESENTATIVES			SENATE		
			Majority Party	Minority Party	Other	Majority Party	Minority Party	Other
51st	1889-91	Benjamin Harrison............Republican	R-166	D-159	...	R-39	D-37	...
52nd	1891-93	Benjamin Harrison............Republican	D-235	R-88	9	R-47	D-39	2
53rd	1893-95	Grover Cleveland................Democrat	D-218	R-127	11	D-44	R-38	3
54th	1895-97	Grover Cleveland................Democrat	R-244	D-105	7	R-43	D-39	6
55th	1897-99	William McKinley.............Republican	R-204	D-113	40	R-47	D-34	7
56th	1899-1901	William McKinley.............Republican	R-185	D-163	9	R-53	D-26	8
57th	1901-03	{ William McKinley.............Republican Theodore Roosevelt...........Republican	R-197	D-151	9	R-55	D-31	4
58th	1903-05	Theodore Roosevelt...........Republican	R-208	D-178	...	R-57	D-33	...
59th	1905-07	Theodore Roosevelt...........Republican	R-250	D-136	...	R-57	D-33	...
60th	1907-09	Theodore Roosevelt...........Republican	R-222	D-164	...	R-61	D-31	...
61st	1909-11	William H. Taft...............Republican	R-219	D-172	...	R-61	D-32	...
62nd	1911-13	William H. Taft...............Republican	D-228	R-161	1	R-51	D-41	...
63rd	1913-15	Woodrow Wilson................Democrat	D-291	R-127	17	D-51	R-44	1
64th	1915-17	Woodrow Wilson................Democrat	D-230	R-196	9	D-56	R-40	...
65th	1917-19	Woodrow Wilson................Democrat	D-216	R-210	6	D-53	R-42	...
66th	1919-21	Woodrow Wilson................Democrat	R-240	D-190	3	R-49	D-47	...
67th	1921-23	Warren G. Harding............Republican	R-301	D-131	1	R-59	D-37	...
68th	1923-25	{ Warren G. Harding............Republican Calvin Coolidge................Republican	R-225	D-205	5	R-51	D-43	2
69th	1925-27	Calvin Coolidge................Republican	R-247	D-183	4	R-56	D-39	1
70th	1927-29	Calvin Coolidge................Republican	R-237	D-195	3	R-49	D-46	1
71st	1929-31	Herbert Hoover.................Republican	R-267	D-163	1	R-56	D-39	1
72nd	1931-33	Herbert Hoover.................Republican	D-218	R-216	1	R-48	D-47	1
73rd	1933-35	Franklin D. Roosevelt...........Democrat	D-310	R-117	5	D-60	R-35	1
74th	1935-37	Franklin D. Roosevelt...........Democrat	D-319	R-103	10	D-69	R-25	2
75th	1937-39	Franklin D. Roosevelt...........Democrat	D-331	R-89	13	D-76	R-16	4
76th	1939-41	Franklin D. Roosevelt...........Democrat	D-261	R-164	4	D-69	R-23	4
77th	1941-43	Franklin D. Roosevelt...........Democrat	D-268	R-162	5	D-66	R-28	2
78th	1943-45	Franklin D. Roosevelt...........Democrat	D-218	R-208	4	D-58	R-37	1
79th	1945-47	{ Franklin D. Roosevelt...........Democrat Harry S. Truman...............Democrat	D-242	R-190	2	D-56	R-38	1
80th	1947-49	Harry S. Truman...............Democrat	R-245	D-188	1	R-51	D-45	...
81st	1949-51	Harry S. Truman...............Democrat	D-263	R-171	1	D-54	R-42	...
82nd	1951-53	Harry S. Truman...............Democrat	D-234	R-199	1	D-49	R-47	...
83rd	1953-55	Dwight D. Eisenhower........Republican	R-221	D-211	1	R-48	D-47	1
84th	1955-57	Dwight D. Eisenhower........Republican	D-232	R-203	...	D-48	R-47	1
85th	1957-59	Dwight D. Eisenhower........Republican	D-233	R-200	...	D-49	R-47	...
86th	1959-61	Dwight D. Eisenhower........Republican	D-283	R-153	...	D-64	R-34	...
87th	1961-63	John F. Kennedy...............Democrat	D-263	R-174	...	D-65	R-35	...
88th	1963-65	{ John F. Kennedy...............Democrat Lyndon B. Johnson..............Democrat	D-258	R-177	...	D-67	R-33	...
89th	1965-67	Lyndon B. Johnson..............Democrat	D-295	R-140	...	D-68	R-32	...
90th	1967-69	Lyndon B. Johnson..............Democrat	D-247	R-187	...	D-64	R-36	...
91st	1969-71	Richard M. Nixon..............Republican	D-243	R-192	...	D-57	R-43	...
92nd	1971-73	Richard M. Nixon..............Republican	D-254	R-180	...	D-54	R-44	2
93rd	1973-75	{ Richard M. Nixon..............Republican Gerald R. Ford.................Republican	D-243	R-192	...	D-56	R-42	2
94th	1975-77	Gerald R. Ford.................Republican	D-291	R-144	...	D-61	R-37	2

Political party abbreviations:
A-F—Anti-Federalist; AM—Anti-Masonic; Co—coalition;
D—Democrat; DR—Democratic-Republican; Fed—Federalist; Ja—Jacksonian; NR—National Republican;
R—Republican; U—Unionist; W—Whig.

Major Candidates' Popular and Electoral Vote

Year	Winner and Loser	Popular Vote and Percentage	Electoral Vote
1789	George Washington (No party) No opposition	Unknown	69
1792	George Washington (F) No opposition	Unknown	132
1796	John Adams (F)	Unknown	71
	Thomas Jefferson (DR)	Unknown	68
1800	Thomas Jefferson[1] (DR)	Unknown	73
	Aaron Burr (DR)	Unknown	73
	John Adams (F)	Unknown	65
	Charles C. Pinckney (F)	Unknown	64
1804	Thomas Jefferson (DR)	Unknown	162
	Charles C. Pinckney (F)	Unknown	14
1808	James Madison (DR)	Unknown	122
	Charles C. Pinckney (F)	Unknown	47
1812	James Madison (DR)	Unknown	128
	De Witt Clinton (F)	Unknown	89
1816	James Monroe (DR)	Unknown	183
	Rufus King (F)	Unknown	34
1820	James Monroe (DR)	Unknown	231
	John Quincy Adams (No party)	Unknown	1
1824	John Quincy Adams[2] (No party)	108,740 — 30.6%	84
	Andrew Jackson (No party)	153,544 — 43.1%	99
	William H. Crawford (No party)	46,618 — 13.1%	41
	Henry Clay (No party)	47,136 — 13.2%	37
1828	Andrew Jackson (D)	647,286 — 56.0%	178
	John Quincy Adams (NR)	508,064 — 44.0%	83
1832	Andrew Jackson (D)	687,502 — 56.5%	219
	Henry Clay (NR)	530,189 — 43.5%	49
1836	Martin Van Buren (D)	765,483 — 50.9%	170
	William H. Harrison (W)	549,567 — 41.8%	73
1840	William H. Harrison (W)	1,274,624 — 53.1%	234
	Martin Van Buren (D)	1,127,781 — 46.9%	60
1844	James K. Polk (D)	1,338,464 — 49.6%	170
	Henry Clay (W)	1,300,097 — 48.1%	105
1848	Zachary Taylor (W)	1,360,967 — 47.3%	163
	Lewis Cass (D)	1,222,342 — 42.5%	127
1852	Franklin Pierce (D)	1,601,117 — 50.9%	254
	Winfield Scott (W)	1,385,453 — 44.1%	42
1856	James C. Buchanan (D)	1,832,955 — 45.3%	174
	John C. Frémont (R)	1,339,932 — 33.1%	114
	Millard Fillmore (A)	871,731 — 21.6%	8
1860	Abraham Lincoln (R)	1,865,593 — 39.8%	180
	Stephen A. Douglas (D)	1,382,713 — 29.5%	12
	John C. Breckinridge (D)	848,356 — 18.1%	72
	John Bell (CU)	592,906 — 12.6%	39
1864	Abraham Lincoln (R)	2,206,938 — 55.0%	212
	George McClellan (D)	1,803,787 — 45.0%	21
1868	Ulysses S. Grant (R)	3,013,421 — 52.7%	214
	Horatio Seymour (D)	2,706,829 — 47.3%	80
1872	Ulysses S. Grant (R)	3,596,745 — 55.6%	286
	Horace Greeley (D)[3]	2,843,446 — 44.0%	66
1876	Rutherford B. Hayes (R)	4,036,572 — 48.0%	185
	Samuel J. Tilden (D)	4,284,020 — 51.0%	184
1880	James A. Garfield (R)	4,453,295 — 48.5%	214
	Winfield S. Hancock (D)	4,414,082 — 48.1%	155
1884	Grover Cleveland (D)	4,879,507 — 48.5%	219
	James G. Blaine (R)	4,850,293 — 48.2%	182
1888	Benjamin Harrison (R)	5,447,129 — 47.9%	233
	Grover Cleveland (D)	5,537,857 — 48.6%	168
1892	Grover Cleveland (D)	5,555,426 — 46.0%	277
	Benjamin Harrison (R)	5,182,690 — 43.0%	145
	James Weaver (P)	1,029,846 — 8.5%	22
1896	William McKinley (R)	7,102,246 — 51.0%	271
	William J. Bryan (D)	6,492,559 — 46.7%	176
1900	William McKinley (R)	7,218,491 — 51.7%	292
	William J. Bryan (D)	6,356,734 — 45.5%	155

Year	Winner and Loser	Popular Vote and Percentage	Electoral Vote
1904	Theodore Roosevelt (R)	7,628,461 — 56.4%	336
	Alton B. Parker (D)	5,084,223 — 37.6%	140
1908	William H. Taft (R)	7,675,320 — 51.6%	321
	William J. Bryan (D)	6,412,294 — 43.1%	162
1912	Woodrow Wilson (D)	6,296,547 — 41.9%	435
	Theodore Roosevelt (Pr)	4,118,571 — 27.4%	88
	William H. Taft (R)	3,486,720 — 23.2%	8
1916	Woodrow Wilson (D)	9,127,695 — 49.4%	277
	Charles E. Hughes (R)	8,533,507 — 46.2%	254
1920	Warren G. Harding (R)	16,143,407 — 60.4%	404
	James M. Cox (D)	9,130,328 — 34.2%	127
1924	Calvin Coolidge (R)	15,718,211 — 54.0%	382
	John W. Davis (D)	8,385,283 — 28.8%	136
	Robert M. La Follette (Pr)	4,031,289 — 16.6%	13
1928	Herbert C. Hoover (R)	21,391,993 — 58.2%	444
	Alfred E. Smith (D)	15,016,169 — 40.9%	87
1932	Franklin D. Roosevelt (D)	22,809,638 — 57.4%	472
	Herbert C. Hoover (R)	15,758,901 — 39.7%	59
1936	Franklin D. Roosevelt (D)	27,752,869 — 60.8%	523
	Alfred Landon (R)	16,674,665 — 36.5%	8
1940	Franklin D. Roosevelt (D)	27,307,819 — 54.8%	449
	Wendell Willkie (R)	22,321,018 — 44.8%	82
1944	Franklin D. Roosevelt (D)	25,606,585 — 53.5%	432
	Thomas E. Dewey (R)	22,014,745 — 46.0%	99
1948	Harry S Truman (D)	24,105,812 — 49.5%	303
	Thomas E. Dewey (R)	21,970,065 — 45.1%	189
	J. Strom Thurmond (SR)	1,169,063 — 2.4%	39
	Henry A. Wallace (Pr)	1,157,172 — 2.4%	0
1952	Dwight D. Eisenhower (R)	33,936,234 — 55.1%	442
	Adlai E. Stevenson (D)	27,314,992 — 44.4%	89
1956	Dwight D. Eisenhower (R)	35,590,472 — 57.4%	457
	Adlai E. Stevenson[4] (D)	26,022,752 — 42.0%	73
1960	John F. Kennedy[5] (D)	34,227,096 — 49.7%	303
	Richard M. Nixon (R)	34,108,546 — 49.5%	219
1964	Lyndon B. Johnson (D)	43,129,484 — 61.1%	486
	Barry M. Goldwater (R)	27,178,188 — 38.5%	52
1968	Richard M. Nixon (R)	31,785,480 — 43.4%	301
	Hubert H. Humphrey (D)	31,275,165 — 42.7%	191
	George C. Wallace (AI)	9,906,473 — 13.5%	46
1972	Richard M. Nixon[6] (R)	47,169,911 — 60.7%	520
	George S. McGovern (D)	29,170,383 — 37.5%	17
	John G. Schmitz (AI)	1,098,482 — 1.4%	0

In those years where the percentages do not add up to 100%, votes for minor candidates have not been included in the table.

1. Elected by the House of Representatives due to a tie electoral vote.
2. Elected by the House of Representatives, no candidate having polled a majority.
3. Horace Greeley died November 29, 1872. His 66 electoral votes were split as follows: Thomas A. Hendricks, 42; B. Gratz Brown, 18; Charles J. Jenkins, 2; David Davis, 1.
4. Democrats elected 74 electors but one from Alabama refused to vote for Stevenson, voted for Walter B. Jones.
5. Senator Harry F. Byrd (D-Va) received 15 electoral votes; 6 from unpledged Alabama Democrats, 8 from unpledged Mississippi Democrats, and 1 from a defecting Oklahoma Republican elector.
6. One Virginia Republican elector switched his vote from President Nixon to a minor party candidate, reducing Nixon's total from 521 to 520.

Political party abbreviations used in the table:

A...American; AI...American Independent; CU...Constitutional Union;
D...Democratic; DR...Democratic-Republican; F...Federalist;
NR...National Republican; P...Populist; Pr...Progressive;
R...Republican; SR...States' Rights Democratic; W...Whig.

Vice-Presidents of the United States

	Name	Birthplace	Served Under	Took Office
1.	John Adams (F) (1735–1826)	Braintree, Mass.	Washington	1789
2.	Thomas Jefferson (R) (1743–1826)	Shadwell, Va.	J. Adams	1797
3.	Aaron Burr (R) (1756–1836)	Newark, N.J.	Jefferson	1801
4.	George Clinton (R) (1734–1812)	Little Britain, N.Y.	Jefferson Madison	1805
5.	Elbridge Gerry (R) (1744–1814)	Marblehead, Mass.	Madison	1813
6.	Daniel D. Tompkins (R) (1774–1825)	Fox Meadows, N.Y.	Monroe	1817
7.	John C. Calhoun (R) (1782–1850)	Abbeville District, S.C.	J. Q. Adams Jackson	1825
8.	Martin Van Buren (D) (1782–1862)	Kinderhook, N.Y.	Jackson	1833
9.	Richard M. Johnson (D) (1780–1850)	Beargrass, Ky.	Van Buren	1837
10.	John Tyler (W) (1790–1862)	Charles City County, Va.	W. H. Harrison	1841
11.	George M. Dallas (D) (1792–1864)	Philadelphia, Pa.	Polk	1845
12.	Millard Fillmore (W) (1800–74)	Cayuga County, N.Y.	Taylor	1849
13.	William R. King (D) (1786–1853)	Sampson Co., N.C.	Pierce	1853
14.	John C. Breckinridge (D) (1821–75)	Lexington, Ky.	Buchanan	1857
15.	Hannibal Hamlin (R) (1809–91)	Paris, Me.	Lincoln	1861
16.	Andrew Johnson* (1808–75)	Raleigh, N.C.	Lincoln	1865
17.	Schuyler Colfax (R) (1823–85)	New York, N.Y.	Grant	1869
18.	Henry Wilson (R) (1812–75)	Farmington, N.H.	Grant	1873
19.	William A. Wheeler (R) (1819–87)	Malone, N.Y.	Hayes	1877
20.	Chester A. Arthur (R) (1830–86)	Fairfield, Vt.	Garfield	1881
21.	Thomas A. Hendricks (D) (1819–85)	Muskingum Co., Ohio	Cleveland	1885
22.	Levi P. Morton (R) (1824–1920)	Shoreham, Vt.	B. Harrison	1889
23.	Adlai E. Stevenson (D)† (1835–1914)	Christian Co., Ky.	Cleveland	1893
24.	Garret A. Hobart (R) (1844–99)	Long Branch, N.J.	McKinley	1897
25.	Theodore Roosevelt (R) (1858–1919)	New York, N.Y.	McKinley	1901
26.	Charles W. Fairbanks (R) (1852–1918)	Unionville Center, Ohio	T. Roosevelt	1905
27.	James S. Sherman (R) (1855–1912)	Utica, N.Y.	Taft	1909
28.	Thomas R. Marshall (D) (1854–1925)	N. Manchester, Ind.	Wilson	1913
29.	Calvin Coolidge (R) (1872–1933)	Plymouth Notch, Vt.	Harding	1921
30.	Charles G. Dawes (R) (1865–1951)	Marietta, Ohio	Coolidge	1925
31.	Charles Curtis (R) (1860–1936)	Topeka, Kan.	Hoover	1929
32.	John N. Garner (D) (1868–1967)	Red River Co., Texas	F. Roosevelt	1933
33.	Henry A. Wallace (D) (1888–1966)	Adair Co., Iowa	F. Roosevelt	1941
34.	Harry S Truman (D) (1884–1972)	Lamar, Mo.	F. Roosevelt	1945
35.	Alben W. Barkley (D) (1877–1956)	Graves Co., Ky.	Truman	1949
36.	Richard M. Nixon (R) (1913–)	Yorba Linda, Calif.	Eisenhower	1953
37.	Lyndon B. Johnson (D) (1908–73)	Near Stonewall, Texas	Kennedy	1961
38.	Hubert H. Humphrey (D) (1911–)	Wallace, S.D.	Johnson	1965
39.	Spiro T. Agnew (R) (1918-)	Baltimore, Md.	Nixon	1969
40.	Gerald R. Ford (R) (1913-)	Omaha, Nebr.	Nixon	1973
41.	Nelson A. Rockefeller (R) (1908-)	Bar Harbor, Maine	Ford	1974

* Andrew Johnson: A Democrat nominated by Republicans and elected with Lincoln on the National Union ticket.
† Adlai E. Stevenson: 23d Vice-President. Grandfather of the Democratic candidate for President, 1952 and 1956.

Aaron Burr, Vice-President under President Thomas Jefferson.

—From an engraving by E. G. Williams & Brothers

John C. Breckinridge, Vice-President under President James Buchanan.

—From an engraving by A. B. Walter

Vice-President Hubert Humphrey *(left)* and Senator Eugene McCarthy chatting at the "Solidarity Day" rally of the Poor People's Campaign at the Lincoln Memorial, Washington, D. C., June 19. 1968.

Wives of the Presidents

Name	Birthplace	Married	Children
Washington, Martha (Dandridge) Custis (1731–1802)	New Kent Co., Va.	1759	—
Adams, Abigail Smith (1744–1818)	Weymouth, Mass.	1764	5
Jefferson, Martha (Wayles) Skelton (1748–1782)	Charles City Co., Va.	1772	6
Madison, Dorothea "Dolley" (Payne) Todd (1768–1849)	Guilford Co., N.C.	1794	—
Monroe, Elizabeth Kortright (1768–1830)	New York, N.Y.	1786	3
Adams, Louisa Catherine Johnson (1775–1852)	London, England	1797	4
Jackson, Rachel (Donelson) Robards (1767–1828)	Halifax Co., Va.	1791	—
Van Buren, Hannah Hoes (1783–1819)	Kinderhook, N.Y.	1807	4
Harrison, Anna Symmes (1775–1864)	Morristown, N.J.	1795	10
Tyler, Letitia Christian (1790–1842)	Cedar Grove, Va.	1813	8
Tyler, Julia Gardiner (1820–1889)	Gardiner's Is., N.Y.	1844	7
Polk, Sarah Childress (1803–1891)	Murfreesboro, Tenn.	1824	—
Taylor, Margaret Smith (1788–1852)	Calvert Co., Md.	1810	6
Fillmore, Abigail Powers (1798–1853)	Stillwater, N.Y.	1826	2
Fillmore, Caroline (Carmichael) McIntosh (1813–1881)	Morristown, N.J.	1858	—
Pierce, Jane Means Appleton (1806–1863)	Hampton, N.H.	1834	3
Lincoln, Mary Todd (1818–1882)	Lexington, Ky.	1842	4
Johnson, Eliza McCardle (1810–1876)	Leesburg, Tenn.	1827	5
Grant, Julia Dent (1826–1902)	St. Louis, Mo.	1848	4
Hayes, Lucy Ware Webb (1831–1889)	Chillicothe, Ohio	1852	8
Garfield, Lucretia Rudolph (1832–1918)	Hiram, Ohio	1858	7
Arthur, Ellen Lewis Herndon (1837–1880)	Fredericksburg, Va.	1859	3
Cleveland, Frances Folsom (1864–1947)	Buffalo, N.Y.	1886	5
Harrison, Caroline Lavinia Scott (1832–1892)	Oxford, Ohio	1853	2
Harrison, Mary Scott (Lord) Dimmick (1858–1948)	Honesdale, Pa.	1896	1
McKinley, Ida Saxton (1847–1907)	Canton, Ohio	1871	2
Roosevelt, Alice Hathaway Lee (1861–1884)	Chestnut Hill, Mass.	1880	1
Roosevelt, Edith Kermit Carow (1861–1948)	Norwich, Conn.	1886	5
Taft, Helen Herron (1861–1943)	Cincinnati, Ohio	1886	3
Wilson, Ellen Louise Axson (1860–1914)	Savannah, Ga.	1885	3
Wilson, Edith (Bolling) Galt (1872–1961)	Wytheville, Va.	1915	—
Harding, Florence (Kling) DeWolfe (1860–1924)	Marion, Ohio	1891	—
Coolidge, Grace Anna Goodhue (1879–1957)	Burlington, Vt.	1905	2
Hoover, Lou Henry (1875–1944)	Waterloo, Iowa	1899	2
Roosevelt, Anna Eleanor Roosevelt (1884–1962)	New York, N.Y.	1905	6
Truman, Elizabeth "Bess" Wallace (1885–)	Independence, Mo.	1919	1
Eisenhower, Mamie Geneva Doud (1896–)	Boone, Iowa	1916	2
Kennedy, Jacqueline Lee Bouvier (1929–)	Southampton, N.Y.	1953	3
Johnson, Claudia Alta Taylor (1912–)	Marshall, Texas	1934	2
Nixon, Thelma Patricia "Pat" Ryan (1912–)	Ely, Nevada	1940	2
Ford, Elizabeth "Betty" (Bloomer) Warren (1918–)	Chicago, Ill.	1948	4

Martha Washington

Names in parentheses are maiden names of formerly married women.
Children by previous marriages are not included.
Includes children who died in infancy.

Mrs. Hubert Humphrey; nominee for Vice-President, Hubert Humphrey; Mrs. Lyndon Johnson; and President Johnson, after their nomination, August 26, 1964.

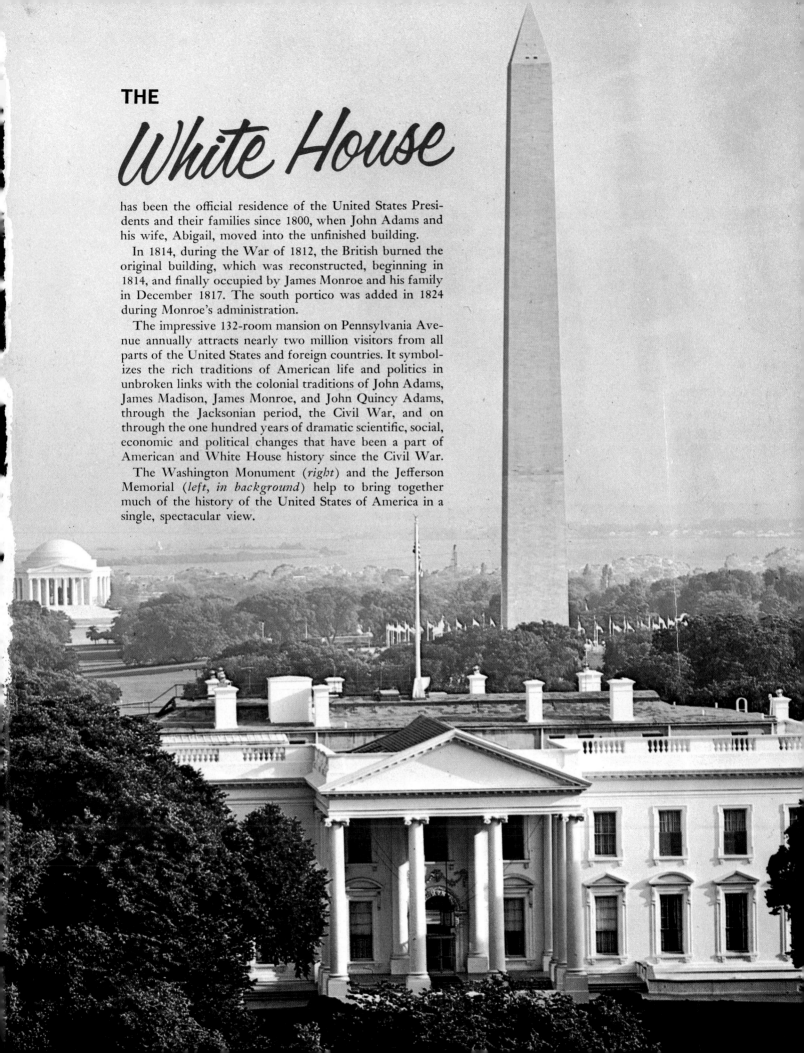

THE
White House

has been the official residence of the United States Presidents and their families since 1800, when John Adams and his wife, Abigail, moved into the unfinished building.

In 1814, during the War of 1812, the British burned the original building, which was reconstructed, beginning in 1814, and finally occupied by James Monroe and his family in December 1817. The south portico was added in 1824 during Monroe's administration.

The impressive 132-room mansion on Pennsylvania Avenue annually attracts nearly two million visitors from all parts of the United States and foreign countries. It symbolizes the rich traditions of American life and politics in unbroken links with the colonial traditions of John Adams, James Madison, James Monroe, and John Quincy Adams, through the Jacksonian period, the Civil War, and on through the one hundred years of dramatic scientific, social, economic and political changes that have been a part of American and White House history since the Civil War.

The Washington Monument (*right*) and the Jefferson Memorial (*left, in background*) help to bring together much of the history of the United States of America in a single, spectacular view.

The front lawn of the Executive Mansion at 1600 Pennsylvania Avenue, Washington, D.C., a national showplace, with magnificent landscaping, fountains, and other interesting details.

(Right)
The North portico, featuring Ionic columns and facing Pennsylvania Avenue, the main entrance to the building.

Color photographs of the Presidential Seal, the Oval Office, the Blue Room, the Red Room, the south grounds and portico as well as the night scene of the White House by courtesy of Ollie Atkins, personal photographer to President Nixon. Other color photographs in this section by courtesy of the National Park Service, Department of the Interior.

The East Room, the largest room in the building (45 by 87½ feet), with its magnificent crystal chandeliers, is a gracious place for state occasions — receptions, balls, weddings, and even funerals.

The State Dining Room, featuring a portrait of Abraham Lincoln by George P. A. Healy, is the scene of official banquets given by the President.

The Green Room as it appeared during the Eisenhower administration, with the famous portrait of Benjamin Franklin painted in 1767 by David Martin in London, and the rug with the Presidential Seal which was in the room at that time.

(Left) Another view of the Green Room, which shows several interesting paintings, including a portrait of former President Dwight D. Eisenhower.

(Right)
The Oval Office
photographed with
a wide-angle lens.

The Diplomatic Reception Room, on the ground floor under the south portico,
is very colorfully decorated with murals of various scenes from American history.

VIEWS OF THE WHITE HOUSE AS IT APPEARED DURING THE EISENHOWER ADMINISTRATION

1. When the White House was renovated during the Truman administration, an intensive search for an original cornerstone—perhaps with the above inscription by John Adams—was made without success. The quotation is from a letter by John Adams and was later carved on the mantel of the State Dining Room.

2. The family dining room.

3. Ground floor main hall.

4. Top floor hall.

5. Second floor hall.

6. First floor library.

7. Executive office.

8. The Fish Room in the West Wing.

The Blue Room

The Red Room

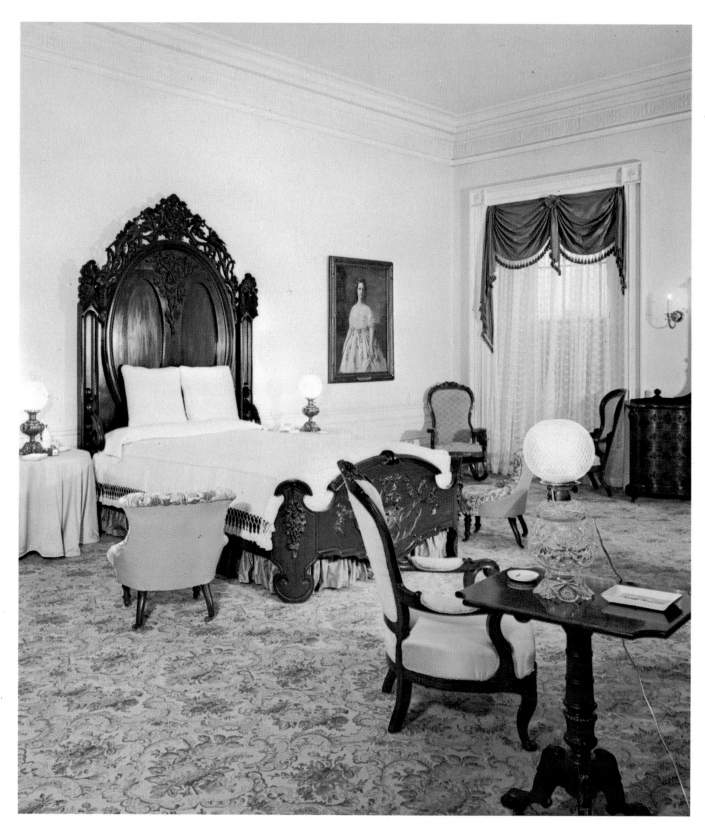

The Lincoln Bedroom, featuring furniture of that period.

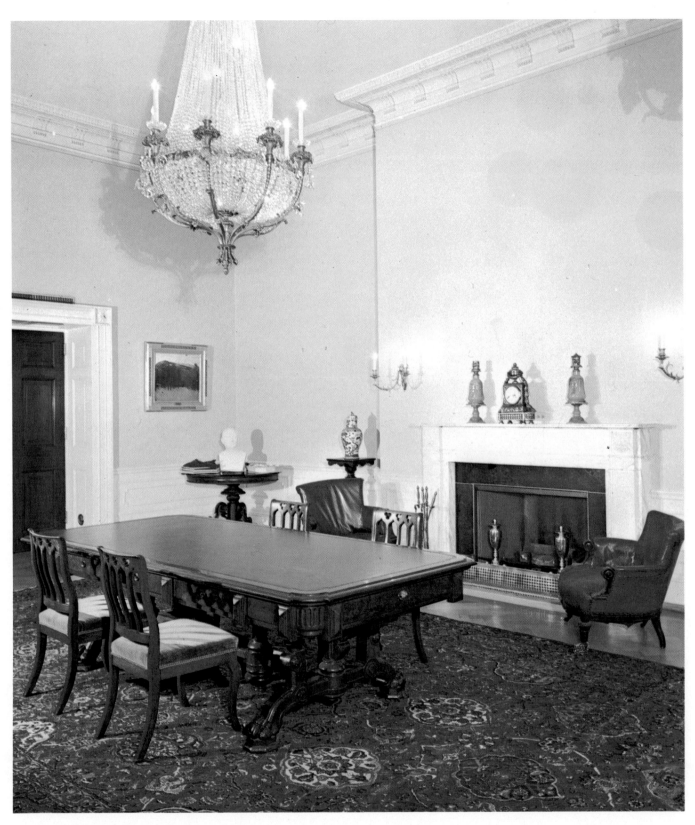

The Treaty Room, which was chosen by President Andrew Johnson for his Cabinet Room and continued to serve as such until 1902—now used as a waiting room or meeting room for the President.

EARLY DAYS IN THE WHITE HOUSE (circa 1890)

1. The East Room in 1893.
2. The State Dining Room, elegantly adorned, with table ornaments from the days of James Monroe.
3. A White House mounted messenger "boy."
4. A cluttered, dingy White House office.
5. This confusion of wiring and furniture of the period is a stark contrast to the White House offices of today.
6. Members of the White House staff in 1893.
7. The East Room used as a Reception Hall.
8. The President's Bedroom in 1893.
9. The "situation room" in the White House offices of another era.

*Frances Benjamin Johnson photographs
by courtesy of The Library of Congress*

The lovely south grounds and portico of the White House, showing the gardens, fountains, and shrubbery which help to make this sixteen-acre estate one of the nicest of its kind in the world.

The **38**th President
of the UNITED STATES

Gerald R. Ford

xviii   GERALD R. FORD

Gerald Rudolph Ford

The Thirty-eighth President of the United States
1974 –

1913 (July 14) Born in Omaha, Nebraska.

1915 Moved with mother to Grand Rapids, Michigan, where he grew up.

1935 Graduated from the University of Michigan; named to College All-Stars football team.

1935–41 Assistant football coach at Yale University.

1941 Received law degree from Yale University.

1941–42 Practiced law in Grand Rapids, Michigan, in partnership with Philip Buchen.

1942–46 Served in U.S. Navy during World War II, rising from ensign to lieutenant commander.

1946–48 Practiced law in Grand Rapids, Mich.

1948 (October 15) Married Elizabeth Bloomer Warren.

1949–73 U.S. Representative from Michigan.

1965–73 Minority leader for the Republican Party in the U.S. House of Representatives.

1973 (December 6) Sworn in as the fortieth Vice President of the United States under President Nixon, the first person ever appointed to the office.

1974 (August 9) Sworn in as thirty-eighth President of the United States upon the resignation of President Nixon.

Leading Officials in Ford's Administration

Office	Name	Years Served
Chief Justice	Warren Earl Burger	1969-
Vice President	Nelson A. Rockefeller	1974-
Secretary of State	Henry A. Kissinger	1973-
Secretary of the Treasury	William E. Simon	1974-
Secretary of Defense	James R. Schlesinger	1973-
Attorney General	William B. Saxbe	1974-1975
	Edward Hirsch Levi	1975-
Secretary of the Interior	Rogers C. B. Morton	1971-
Secretary of Agriculture	Earl L. Butz	1971-
Secretary of Commerce	Frederick B. Dent	1973-
Secretary of Labor	Peter J. Brennan	1973-1975
	John T. Dunlop	1975-
Secretary of Health, Education, and Welfare	Caspar W. Weinberger	1973-
Secretary of Housing and Urban Development	James T. Lynn	1973-1975
	Carla Anderson Hills	1975-
Secretary of Transportation	Claude S. Brinegar	1973-1975
	William T. Coleman, Jr.	1975-

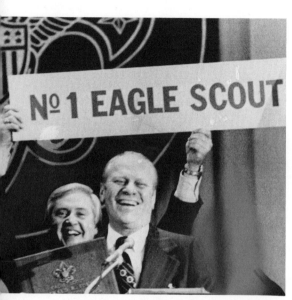

As Vice President, Gerald Ford was designated honorary No. 1 Eagle Scout, after addressing a Boy Scout potluck dinner at Cobo Hall in Detroit, Michigan, in February 1974. —*UPI Compix*

The first chief executive to reach the White House by the route of appointment rather than the elective process, 61-year-old Gerald R. Ford became President at the climax of a constitutional crisis in 1974 over the Watergate scandals that had caused his predecessor, Richard Nixon, to resign in disgrace. A determinedly honest and deeply religious Episcopalian, Ford promised upon being sworn in that "our long national nightmare is over." He also asked for prayers for the former President.

The people of the United States, weary and disillusioned by the almost daily revelations of government corruption during the past two years, welcomed Ford's accession with a sigh of relief. As the first Eagle Scout to become President, he was sure to restore honesty to the nation's highest office, they felt. For the first time since Franklin D. Roosevelt had moved into the White House during the Great Depression, Americans eagerly anticipated giving a chief executive their full support. But the honeymoon was short-lived.

Seriously misjudging the nation's sense of forgiveness, Ford made a surprise announcement only a month after taking office that he had granted Nixon a "full, free and absolute pardon for all offenses" committed during his administration. At the same time he revealed that Nixon eventually would be allowed to destroy the tapes of conversations that played an important part in his downfall.

Outraged that Nixon would be allowed to escape indictment and trial while his associates went to prison, the American people recalled President Lyndon Johnson's sarcastic comment: "Jerry Ford is a nice guy, but he played too much football with his helmet off." More seriously, congressional leaders called the pardon a "misuse of power"—an impeachable offense. Questions were raised as to the constitutionality of granting a pardon prior to conviction in a court of law, and speculation was widely voiced that the pardon was part of a political "deal" by which Ford had attained the presidency.

Defending his action, Ford declared:

"There was no understanding, no deal between me and the former President . . . I am absolutely convinced, when dealing with the reality in this very, very difficult situation that I made the right decision in an effort, an honest conscientious effort, to end the discussions and turmoil in the United States."

Boyhood in Michigan

The future President was born on July 14, 1913, in Omaha, Nebraska, Named Leslie Lynch King at birth, he was the son of Dorothy Gardner King and Leslie King, a wool trader. When his parents were divorced in 1915, he and his mother returned to her hometown, Grand Rapids, Michigan. There his mother met and soon married a young paint salesman by the name of Gerald Rudolf Ford. His new stepfather formally adopted the boy, renaming him Gerald Rudolph Ford, Jr.

Growing up in Grand Rapids, the boy was called "Junie," short for Junior. The elder Ford had dropped out of high school and had little interest in reading, so there were few books in the Fords' comfortable middle-class home. Unlike some other Presidents who were avid readers in boyhood, young Ford was more interested in outdoor activities and

The first residence in Grand Rapids, Michigan, of the future President, where he lived for seven years.　　　*—UPI Compix*

Gerald Ford at the age of three, with "man's best friend," a Boston bull terrier.　　*—UPI Compix*

competitive sports. As soon as he was old enough, he joined the Boy Scouts and doggedly accumulated merit badges until he finally attained the coveted honor of Eagle Scout. By the time he was fourteen, he had three younger half brothers: Thomas, Richard, and James.

In the 1920s the Ford paint-selling business prospered. The family made vacation trips to Florida in their open touring car. In 1929 the elder Ford formed a paint manufacturing corporation, and the family moved to a more fashionable neighborhood in East Grand Rapids. Young Ford was able to buy his own car—a $75 seven-year-old Model T.

But, like millions of other Americans, the Fords were hard hit by the stock-market crash of 1929 and the ensuing depression. Unable to meet the mortgage payments on their new home, the Fords were forced to move to a more modest house. A more personal disaster struck 16-year-old Jerry, then a high school junior, when his cherished Model T burned up because he had carelessly covered the hood with a blanket on a cold night when the engine still was hot.

At 17 Ford had an even more traumatic experience. He had not known he was an adopted child, his mother and stepfather having concealed the information because child guidance experts of the 1920s advised it was harmful for a child to be told. So it was a shock one day, while he was working to earn pocket money in the malt shop across from his high school when a stranger approached and said, "Leslie, I'm your father." Disbelieving, young Ford heard for the first time the story of his parents' divorce. He confirmed it later that day when he confronted his mother and stepfather. Loyal to them, the boy directed his resentment at his obviously well-to-do real father for failing to offer financial help to the hard-pressed Fords.

As a student at Grand Rapids' South High School, Jerry Ford became a football star. Big for his age, he played center, a bruising position that called for great strength and stamina, especially in those days when a player was expected to play a full sixty minutes on both offense and defense. Determined to do his best, Ford helped lead his team to a state championship in his senior year. He was chosen center on Grand Rapids' "All-City" team three years in a row. Contradicting the stereotype of football players, Ford was a conscientious student, earning mostly B grades with a scattering of A's.

College Athlete, Law Student,
and Assistant Coach

UPON Ford's graduation from high school in 1931, the country still was sliding deeper into the Great Depression. His family had no money to spare for a college education. But the boy's athletic ability won him a scholarship to the University of Michigan, where he helped work his way with jobs as a dishwasher, janitor, and waiter. As a sophomore he joined Delta Kappa Epsilon fraternity. Two fraternity brothers later were to play major roles in his life. Jack Stiles would manage his first successful campaign for Congress. Philip Buchen would become his law partner and much later his chief legal counsel as President.

Although during his sophomore and junior years in 1932 and 1933 the University of Michigan won honors as the best college football team in the country, Ford's athletic career languished. He was second best to Michigan's all-American center, Chuck Bernard. After Bernard's graduation, Ford became the first-string center in his senior year. But 1934 was a disastrous season for Michigan. The team defeated only Georgia Tech in its eight-game schedule.

Ford, however, received recognition for his football skill, being chosen to play in the East-West game in San Francisco on January 1, 1935, and in the College All-Stars game in Chicago the following August. His performance in these games won him professional football offers, but they had slight appeal because in those days there was little glamour and less money for the pros.

While football was his first love, Ford had not neglected his studies. He graduated from Michigan in 1935 with a B average, having received four A's during his four years—in American government, organized labor, European history, and in an economics course on money and credit.

Ready to center the ball with the 1934 Wolverines of the University of Michigan, Gerald Ford (number 48) played center well enough to be selected on several all-star teams and excelled in several sports. —*UPI Compix*

(*Left*) One of the President's favorite means of relaxing and keeping fit—a few laps in the pool. (*Right*) An enthusiastic skiier on the slopes of Vail, Colorado. **—*UPI Compix***

Jobs were hard to come by in 1935. Ford counted himself lucky when Yale's football coach, Raymond "Ducky" Pond, offered him a $2,400-a-year position as assistant football line coach and boxing coach. Even though he knew next to nothing about boxing, Ford accepted the job, which was to begin in September. That summer he worked at the family paint factory and in his spare time went to the YMCA three times a week to take boxing lessons from a former amateur boxing champion, Stanley Levandoski. For the next six years Ford coached at Yale.

While at Yale it was convenient for Ford to make frequent weekend trips to New York City. There he dated a beautiful model, Phyllis Brown, of whom he later said, "I almost married that girl." She persuaded Ford to put up $1,000 to go into partnership with a friend of hers, Harry Conover, to form a model agency. Blond and handsome, Ford himself posed with Phyllis for pictures that appeared in *Look* magazine and on the cover of *Cosmopolitan*. After a financial disagreement, Ford later withdrew from the agency partnership.

Partly at the urging of his stepfather, Ford applied for entrance to the Yale law school. The faculty tried to discourage him, pointing to his undistinguished academic record at Michigan and warning him that a majority of the Yale law students were Phi Beta Kappas. Then in 1938 the law professors relented sufficiently to let Ford take two courses as a trial. When he completed them satisfactorily, he was allowed to begin a full-time law schedule the following semester. While continuing to work as a coach, he studied at night and on weekends, determined to succeed. He finally received his law degree from Yale in 1941, graduating in the upper third of his class. Significantly, his highest grade—an A plus—was for a course in legal ethics.

Home for Christmas in 1944 at the peak of World War II, Lieutenant Ford explains to his mother, the former Dorothy Ayer Gardner, where he had been in the Pacific.
—*UPI Compix*

*War Years and
Entrance into Politics*

RETURNING to Grand Rapids in 1941, Ford was admitted to the Michigan bar and began law practice in partnership with his college friend Philip Buchen. In the next few months he became active in a political reform group, the Republican Home Front, formed by a local dentist with the object of wresting control from the local GOP boss, Frank D. McKay. But the Japanese attack on Pearl Harbor in December 1941 interrupted the young lawyer's political ambitions.

The 28-year-old Ford volunteered for service in the U.S. Navy, receiving a direct commission as ensign on April 20, 1942. Assigned as a physical-education instructor to the naval air cadet training program, he spent his first year of war at Chapel Hill, North Carolina. Chafing for a more active role in the war, Ford applied for sea duty. After receiving gunnery training at Norfolk, Virginia, he was assigned to the *USS Monterey*, a new light aircraft carrier being readied for sea at Camden, New Jersey.

The *Monterey* joined the Pacific fleet in 1943, taking part in the island-hopping campaign to Japan. One of the worst moments of the war for Ford and his ship came during the typhoon that struck the fleet in December 1944, sinking three destroyers and severely damaging many other ships. At the height of the storm the *Monterey's* planes caught fire and the ship's engine rooms had to be abandoned. As 100-mile-an-hour winds battered the ship, Ford lost his footing on the flight deck and narrowly escaped being blown overboard. In all he took part in ten battles. He rose to the rank of lieutenant commander.

When the war was over Ford came home to Grand Rapids in December 1945 with seventy days of accumulated leave. He resumed his law practice and his interest in politics, aided by his stepfather who meanwhile had won election as Kent County Republican chairman with the backing of the Home Front reform group. At first Jerry Ford concentrated his efforts on helping organize a veterans committee that pressured local officials into making possible the building of low-cost housing for returning GIs.

Counting on assistance from the reform Home Front group, Jerry Ford decided to run for Congress in Michigan's Fifth District. The district had been represented since 1940 by Bartel J. Jonkman, a 64-year-old Dutchman, who was backed by McKay's regular Republican organization. The reactionary Jonkman had alienated many of the district's young veterans of World War II. As a senior member of the House Foreign Affairs Committee Jonkman had repeatedly attacked President Truman's foreign policy, especially the multibillion-dollar Marshall Plan for aid to Europe. To win a congressional seat, Ford's first task was to defeat Jonkman in the Republican primary.

With his college fraternity brother Jack Stiles as his campaign manager, Jerry Ford worked hard to make himself better known to the voters throughout the summer of 1948. One of his problems as a candidate was that, while many remembered him as a high school and college football star, questions were raised as to whether he was smart enough to be a Congressman. When voters asked his stand on issues with which he was unfamiliar, the handsome young candidate disarmed them by candidly admitting he did not know the answers but would find out. To woo the large number of Dutch farmers in the district, Ford went out into their fields and helped with their chores while asking for their support. Jonkman, who was counting on the help of the regular Republican organization, made few appearances in Grand Rapids during the campaign and refused to debate Ford on the issues. In the primary election on September 14, 1948, Ford won with a 62.2% majority, garnering 23,632 votes to 14,341. Ford's victory almost assured him of a seat in Congress because the district had not sent a Democrat to Washington since 1910.

Now confident that he would become a Congressman, Ford went ahead with plans to marry Betty Bloomer Warren, a 30-year-old former Martha Graham dancer, who in 1947 had divorced her husband, William C. Warren, a furniture salesman, on grounds of incompatibility. But because the district had a large number of Dutch Calvinists who opposed divorce, Ford kept his October 15, 1948, marriage secret during the remainder of the election campaign. The marriage was a happy one with four children born in following years: Michael Gerald in 1950, John Gardner in 1952, Steven Meigs in 1956, and Susan Elizabeth in 1957.

In the November election Ford defeated the Democratic candidate, Fred J. Barr, Jr., by 74,191 to 46,972—a majority of 61%. Many of Ford's fellow Republicans were not so lucky, because in that election President Truman upset Republican Thomas E. Dewey and the Democrats took control of Congress.

Vice President and Mrs. Ford relaxing at their home in Alexandria, Virginia.   —*UPI Compix*

Quarter of a Century as a Congressman

DURING the next quarter of a century Ford won reelection a dozen times, never with less than 60% of the vote.

Ford took his seat in Congress in 1949 as a junior member of the minority party, a situation that was not conducive to the building of a brilliant legislative reputation. He was satisfied with honestly and conscientiously representing his constituents in Grand Rapids. This meant keeping a low profile, promptly answering requests from back home, maintaining a good record of attendance, and voting as the Republican leadership decided.

During his first term Ford became acquainted with another young Navy veteran, Richard M. Nixon, then a U.S. Representative from California. But Ford made no effort to emulate his new friend's publicity-garnering tactics as a Communist hunter.

In his second term Ford became a member of the powerful House Appropriations Committee, which controls all bills for expenditures by the federal government. He became a specialist on defense budgets, winning friends among the generals and admirals for his consistent support of increased armed forces spending. As part of this assignment Ford made trips abroad on military planes, receiving appropriately friendly receptions at the facilities he visited.

In 1952 Ford turned down an offer to run for the Senate. He felt that he was well on his way toward building the seniority necessary to eventually become Speaker of the House—his long-term goal. Like other Republicans Ford achieved improved status when Dwight D. Eisenhower won the presidential election in 1952, helping the GOP regain control of Congress. However, Ford still did not have sufficient seniority to chair a committee. After the Republicans lost their majority in the House two years later, he had no further opportunities to become a congressional committee chairman.

After fourteen years in Congress, Ford first began to win national attention in 1963 when the "young Turks" of the GOP elected him chairman of the House Republican caucus, replacing long-term conservative Iowa Representative Charles B. Hoeven.

Ford was appointed by President Johnson in December 1963 as a member of the seven-man Warren Commission to investigate the assassination of President Kennedy. In turn Ford named to the commission staff his old college friend and manager of his first election campaign, Jack Stiles. After the commission reported its findings, Stiles and Ford in 1965 coauthored a book on the subject, *Portrait of the Assassin*.

The 51-year-old Ford achieved the next-to-last rung on his climb toward Speaker of the House when he was elected in 1965 as Republican minority leader of the House, defeating Representative Charles A. Halleck of Indiana. In this internal party fight Ford was aided by three close friends: Representatives Robert Griffin of Michigan, Melvin R. Laird of Wisconsin, and Charles E. Goodell of New York. With Senate Minority Leader Everett M. Dirksen of Illinois, Ford began appearing on a GOP television series, *The Ev and Jerry Show*, which presented the Republican congressional views on current issues.

Although Ford preferred to call himself a "moderate on domestic issues," his voting record was that of a conservative on most of the major legislation proposed by President Johnson. He opposed increased aid to education, establishment of a "war on poverty," and Medicare for social security recipients.

In 1967 Ford made one of his rare speeches on the floor of the House to attack President Johnson's handling of the Vietnam War. He urged increased Air Force bombing of communist forces and a blockade of North Vietnam. "Why are we pulling our best punches in Vietnam?" he asked.

A portrait of Representative Ford in 1960.　　　*—UPI Compix*

In 1969, as a Republican congressman, Gerald Ford met with Senator Dirksen and President Nixon to discuss strictly enforcing the cutoff of federal funds to students who create campus disorders.

—UPI Compix

Members of the Senate Rules Committee hear Representative Ford testify on his qualifications to be Vice President. The Senators *(front row left to right)* are: Claiborne Pell (D-R.I.); Howard Cannon (D-Nev.) chairman; Marlow Cook (R-Ky.); Robert Griffin (R-Mich.); and Mark Hatfield (R-Ore.). —*UPI Compix*

Confirmed as the 40th Vice President of the United States, and the first one not elected, Gerald Ford displays the Vice Presidential Commission. —*UPI Compix*

40th Vice President of the United States

As Republican minority leader of the House throughout President Nixon's first term, Ford was noted for his loyal support of White House measures. He often arranged behind-the-scenes coalitions with Southern Democrats to pass administration proposals.

Ford raised the hackles of liberals in 1970 when he called on the House to impeach Associate Justice of the Supreme Court William O. Douglas. He charged Douglas among other things with defending the civil disobedience of youthful anti-Vietnam War protestors, of supporting the publication of pornography, and of accepting money from a private foundation. In his speech in the House, Ford made one statement that later was to be widely quoted: "An impeachable offense is whatever the House of Representatives considers it to be at a given moment in history."

After President Nixon won reelection in 1972 by one of the greatest landslides in history, yet was unable to lead Republicans to majority control of Congress, Ford saw his chances of becoming Speaker of the House go glimmering. He began to think of retiring from politics while there was still time left to resume a private career as a lawyer. Neither he nor anyone else could predict the onrush of events that within less than two years would propel him into the highest office in the land.

WHEN Vice President Spiro Agnew resigned in 1973, accepting conviction for income tax violations rather than face trial on bribery charges, the door to high office suddenly swung open for Ford. Amendment 25 to the United States Constitution, which had been ratified in 1967, came into use for the first time. It provided that a vacancy in the office of Vice President could be filled by nomination of the President and confirmation by both houses of Congress.

President Nixon, suffering from the twin blows of the Watergate scandals and the Agnew bribery charges, began a frantic scramble to find someone to fill the vacancy. This someone had to exude honesty to be acceptable to the public. He had to have unquestioned loyalty to the President. And he had to be someone whom Congress would quickly approve. Who else could fit this bill of particulars except Jerry Ford?

Democratic Speaker of the House Carl Albert of Oklahoma took credit for being the first to suggest to Nixon that Ford be nominated. Albert, who stood next in succession to the presidency after Agnew's resignation, had no desire to become President himself, and he was afraid that just might happen if the vice presidency remained vacant very long.

In the glare of TV lights Ford's nomination as Vice President was announced by President Nixon on October 12, 1973, to the enthusiastic applause of congressional leaders of both parties. In accepting, Ford promised to "do my utmost to the best of my ability to serve this country well and to perform those duties that will be my new assignment as effectively and efficiently and with as much accomplishment as possible."

In the next two months Ford underwent a searching investigation to determine his fitness for the office. The critical nature of his nomination was heightened late in October when the House Judiciary Committee formally began proceedings to determine whether President Nixon should be impeached. About the worst thing the confirmation hearings turned up on Jerry Ford was that he had associated with lobbyists, and the members of Congress knew that was unavoidable. His net assets were disclosed as $256,378, mostly in the value of three homes in Grand Rapids, Michigan, Alexandria, Virginia, and Vail, Colorado. Even his handful of political enemies were unable to find any proof he ever had committed an illegal act. However, he again made a statement that in light of future events was to prove all too true. In reply to a question about whether he would have the power to pardon President Nixon should he resign, Ford replied: "I do not think the public would stand for it." The Senate approved his nomination 92 to 3 on November 27, and the House voted approval by 387 to 35 on December 6. An hour after the House vote Ford was sworn in as the 40th Vice President.

In the eight months Ford occupied the nation's second highest office he was a man dancing on a tightrope. He had to continue to exhibit loyalty to the President, even while public confidence in Nixon rapidly eroded with each new revelation in the Watergate scandals. At the same time Ford had to maintain his own credibility with the public as a leader who could be trusted.

Vice President Ford stumped the country traveling about 100,000 miles to 40 states, speaking to conventions, to university convocations, and to almost any other large group that would invite him. His success was demonstrated by public opinion polls that showed his popularity steadily rising.

AFTER President Nixon resigned on August 9, 1974, Ford took the presidential oath of office at noon in the East Room of the White House while the nation watched on TV. As his wife held the Bible on which

Vice President Gerald Ford accepting a silver replica of the Old North Church lantern from the Middlesex Club in Boston after speaking at its 107th annual dinner in acknowledgment of its Man-of-the-Year Award, March 11, 1974.
—*UPI Compix*

President Ford's Administration

Gerald Ford taking the oath of office as the 38th President from Chief Justice Warren E. Burger, at the White House August 9, 1974.—*UPI Compix*

President Ford addresses the assembled guests and the nation in the East Room of the White House after taking the oath of office.

—All photographs UPI Compix

(Left) President Ford in the Oval Office during his first, busy week in office. (Below) Mrs. Ford leaving the White House after a tour of living quarters before moving in.

Two former football players, actor John Wayne and Gerald Ford at the sixteenth annual Hall of Fame banquet December 4, 1973. *(Right)* Vice President Ford accepting the Frank Leahy All-American Award from George Halas, University of Illinois and Chicago Bears football hero, February 15, 1974.

—*All photographs UPI Compix*

Wearing his golf cap and carrying some odds and ends, the President hurriedly leaves his Alexandria home for a golf date.

With a group of congresswomen and Mrs. Ford looking on, President Ford signed a proclamation declaring Women's Equality Day August 26, 1974. The viewers *(left to right)* are: Marjorie S. Holt (R-Md.); Leonor K. Sullivan (D-Mo.); Betty Ford; Cardiss Collins (D-Ill.); Corinne C. Boggs (D-La.); Margaret M. Heckler (R-Mass.); and Bella S. Abzug (D-N.Y.).

A meeting with the Joint Chiefs of Staff on August 14, 1974. Clockwise from President Ford are: Secretary of Defense James Schlesinger; White House Chief of Staff Alexander Haig; Air Force Chief of Staff General David Jones; Army Chief of Staff the late Creighton Abrams; General George Brown, chairman of the Joint Chiefs; Major General Brent Scowcroft, deputy assistant to the President for National Security Affairs, and Secretary of State Henry Kissinger.

Ford rested his left hand, Chief Justice Warren E. Burger administered the oath. Ford then made perhaps his most moving address:

"The oath that I have taken is the same oath that was taken by George Washington and by every President under the Constitution.

"But I assume the Presidency under extraordinary circumstances never before experienced by Americans. This is an hour of history that troubles our minds and hurts our hearts.

"Therefore, I feel it is my first duty to make an unprecedented compact with my countrymen. Not an inaugural address, not a fireside chat, not a campaign speech—just a little straight talk among friends. And I intend it to be the first of many.

"I am acutely aware that you have not elected me as your President by your ballots, and so I ask you to confirm me as your President with your prayers. And I hope that such prayers will also be the first of many.

"If you have not chosen me by secret ballot, neither have I gained office by any secret promises. I have not campaigned either for the Presidency or the Vice Presidency. I have not subscribed to any partisan platform. I am indebted to no man, and only to one woman—my dear wife—as I begin this very difficult job.

"I have not sought this enormous responsibility, but I will not shirk it. Those who nominated and confirmed me as Vice President were my friends and are my friends. They were of both parties, elected by all the people and acting under the Constitution in their name. It is only fitting then that I should pledge to them and to you that I will be the President of all the people.

"Thomas Jefferson said the people are the only sure reliance for the preservation of our liberty. And down the years, Abraham Lincoln renewed this American article of faith asking, 'Is there any better way or equal hope in the world?'

"I intend, on Monday next, to request of the Speaker of the House of Representatives and the President pro tempore of the Senate the privilege of appearing before the Congress to share with my former colleagues and with you, the American people, my views on the priority business of the Nation and to solicit your views. And may I say to the Speaker and the others, if I could meet with you right after these remarks, I would appreciate it.

"Even though this is late in an election year, there is no way we can go forward except together and no way anybody can win except by serving the people's urgent needs. We cannot stand still or slip backwards. We must go forward now together.

"To the peoples and the governments of all friendly nations, and I hope that could encompass the whole world, I pledge an uninterrupted and sincere search for peace. America will remain strong and united, but its strength will remain dedicated to the safety and sanity of the entire family of man, as well as to our own precious freedom.

"I believe that truth is the glue that holds government together, not only our Government, but civilization itself. That bond, though strained, is unbroken at home and abroad.

"In all my public and private acts as your President, I expect to follow my instincts of openness and candor with full confidence that honesty is always the best policy in the end.

"My fellow Americans, our long national nightmare is over.

"Our Constitution works; our great Republic is a Government of laws and not of men. Here the people rule. But there is a higher power, by

Gerald Ford in his first news conference as President, August 28, 1974.　　　　—*UPI Compix*

At an early cabinet meeting, *(left to right)* Interior Secretary Rogers C. B. Morton, Secretary of State Henry Kissinger, the President, and Secretary of Defense James Schlesinger. *(Right)* President Ford presenting his Vice Presidential choice, former New York Governor Nelson Rockefeller, to a nationwide television audience on August 20, 1974.   —*UPI Compix*

whatever name we honor Him, who ordains not only righteousness but love, not only justice but mercy.

"As we bind up the internal wounds of Watergate, more painful and more poisonous than those of foreign wars, let us restore the golden rule to our political process, and let brotherly love purge our hearts of suspicion and of hate.

"In the beginning, I asked you to pray for me. Before closing, I ask again your prayers, for Richard Nixon and for his family. May our former President, who brought peace to millions, find it for himself. May God bless and comfort his wonderful wife and daughters, whose love and loyalty will forever be a shining legacy to all who bear the lonely burdens of the White House.

"I can only guess at those burdens, although I have witnessed at close hand the tragedies that befell three Presidents and the lesser trials of others.

"With all the strength and all the good sense I have gained from life, with all the confidence my family, my friends, and my dedicated staff impart to me, and with the good will of countless Americans I have encountered in recent visits to 40 states, I now solemnly reaffirm my promise I made to you last December 6: to uphold the Constitution, to do what is right as God gives me to see the right, and to do the very best I can for America.

"God helping me, I will not let you down."

The new President asked all members of the Cabinet and the heads of government agencies to remain with him indefinitely in his administration.

Ford announced on August 20, 1974, his nomination for Vice President: 66-year-old Nelson Aldrich Rockefeller, one of the world's wealthiest men, who had served four terms as governor of New York from 1958 to 1973. After extensive congressional hearings, Rockefeller was confirmed and sworn in as Vice President on December 19, 1974.

DURING Ford's first month in office, public opinion polls showed that only 3 percent of the people disapproved of the job he was doing as President—as close to universal approval as any President is ever likely

End of the Honeymoon

President Ford walks back to the White House with Dr. Kissinger after escorting King Hussein of Jordan to his limousine following a meeting.

Mrs. Nelson Rockefeller and Mrs. Gerald Ford on the balcony of the White House August 22, 1974.

—All photographs UPI Compix

Meeting with UAW President Leonard Woodcock August 29, 1974. *(Left)* President Ford and AFL-CIO President George Meany in a meeting August 13, 1974.

to get. However, this was to be the peak of his popularity.

On a quiet Sunday morning in Washington, on September 8, 1974, when the President returned to the White House from attending church services, he called in the handful of newsmen then on duty. He proceeded to drop a bombshell—the announcement of unconditional pardon of former President Nixon. Ford's press secretary, J.H. terHorst, expressed the disapproval felt by millions of Americans by immediately resigning. TerHorst, a Michigan newsman who had supported Ford since his first campaign for Congress, felt his candor had been undermined because he previously had assured newsmen that Ford was standing by his 1973 statement about a possible Nixon pardon that "I do not think the public would stand for it."

Ford, who at his swearing-in speech a month earlier had promised "openness and candor," was deluged by phone calls, telegrams, and letters denouncing his action. Members of Congress of both parties were angered both by the pardon and at not having been consulted in advance. A few days later, when the White House indicated Ford was considering pardons for everyone connected with the Watergate scandals, the Senate quickly voted 55 to 24 for a resolution that the President should not pardon anyone prior to conviction.

Eight days after the Nixon pardon, Ford announced an offer of conditional amnesty for the thousands of young men who had opposed the Vietnam War by evading the draft or by deserting the armed forces. The amnesty was conditioned on the youths agreeing to two years of service in low-paying public service jobs. Ford's new action did little to revive his popularity. Those who had supported the Vietnam War thought his action too generous, those who had opposed the war believed the amnesty should have been unconditional. In ensuing months few resisters turned themselves in to accept the conditional amnesty.

Bewildered that he should have become the center of a storm of controversy for actions that he regarded as humanitarian, Ford could only repeat to critics that the pardon and the conditional amnesty both were "my honest and conscientious effort to heal the wounds."

To allay suspicions that he had made a "deal" with Nixon, such as promising the pardon in order to obtain the Presidency. Ford took the unprecedented step of appearing before a congressional subcommittee and answering the members' questions about the pardon. His formal testimony before the House judiciary subcommittee on October 17, 1974, was the first time a sitting President ever had given up claims of executive privilege and appeared in person to submit to a congressional inquiry. As television carried the proceedings into home living rooms across the nation, Ford answered every question put to him with confidence and candor.

"I want to assure you," he said, "members of this subcommittee, members of Congress, and the American people, there was no deal."

Political analysts unanimously predicted a Democratic landslide in the November 1974 congressional elections with voters punishing the Republicans for the Watergate affair and the Nixon pardon. In the weeks before the election, President Ford did his best in trying to stem the tide, barnstorming by plane from coast to coast and warning the voters not to give the Democrats such a substantial majority that they would create a "veto-proof" Congress. When the election results were tabulated, the Democrats had increased their majority control of both houses of the 94th Congress, but not by the landslide proportions they had achieved in the 1964 election of Lyndon B. Johnson.

With a portrait of President Lincoln in the background, President Ford signs the order of conditional amnesty for Vietnam draft evaders and military deserters September 16, 1974. —*UPI Compix*

President Ford greets the Japanese people after leaving the Akasaka Palace where he met Emperor Hirohito.

Recession and Worsening Relations with Congress

WHEN Ford took office a raging inflation was pushing up prices at a higher rate than at any time since the post-World War II period. In his first address to a joint session of Congress on August 12, 1974, Ford named inflation as "domestic enemy NO. 1." After calling a "summit conference" of economists and representatives of various segments of the economy in September to discuss ways of combating inflation, he again addressed a joint session of Congress on October 8. He called on Congress to enact a variety of measures to combat inflation, including a 5 percent tax surcharge on incomes above $7,500.

At the same time he called on Americans to join in a mobilization of volunteers to be called WIN to "whip inflation now." He urged consumers to buy less and save more. "Only two of my predecessors have come in person to call upon Congress for a declaration of war," Ford said, "and I shall not do that. But I say to you with all sincerity, that our inflation, our public enemy NO. 1, will, unless whipped, destroy our country, our homes, our liberties, our property, and finally our national pride, as surely as any well-armed wartime enemy."

The President's call for a tax increase, coming four weeks before the November congressional elections, received less than an enthusiastic response from Congress. However, consumers, already hard-pressed by high prices, heeded the President's urging to buy less.

The automobile industry was almost immediately hit by slumping sales that sagged by one-third or more compared to the previous year. Auto makers began closing their plants in November and December 1974, throwing hundreds of thousands of employees out of work.

By December the nation was in a deepening recession as unemployment climbed to 7.1 percent with more than 6.5 million persons unable to find a job. Investors suffered losses as stock values fell to their lowest level in a dozen years.

(*At top*) President Ford and Emperor Hirohito share a toast during a dinner at the Emperor's Palace, November 19, 1974. (*Above*) Friendly handshakes are exchanged as President Ford goes down the diplomatic receiving line during ceremonies outside the Akasaka Palace in Japan, November 19, 1974. Built in Tokyo in 1906 as the residence of the Crown Prince, the palace is now the State Guest House. (*Right*) President Ford toasts members of the parliament of Japan during a reception in Japan, November 20, 1974.

At the same time President Ford was suffering from a deteriorating relationship with Congress. In his first five months in office Ford vetoed twenty-four legislative measures, and Congress overrode his veto four times with huge bipartisan majorities. This was the poorest showing by a President in confrontation with Congress since President Franklin Pierce lost five out of nine veto fights in the 1850s.

TURNING to foreign affairs in an effort to revive his flagging leadership, President Ford went on a week-long trip to the Far East in late November 1974. He made the first visit of an American President to Japan, emphasizing the friendship developed since Japan's defeat in World

Atomic Arms
Limitation Agreement with
the Soviet Union

In South Korea, President Ford views Intra-Divisional Championship Competition of Tae Kwon Do with Camp Casey servicemen, November 22, 1974.

On leaving the army base in South Korea, the President signals to Camp Casey servicemen that they are number one, second to none.

The leaders of the United States and the U.S.S.R. reach across the table for a toast in the midst of S.A.L.T. talks in Vladivostok, November 24, 1974.

War II. He then traveled to South Korea, where he reaffirmed continued American support to preserve that nation's independence.

As the main objective of his Far Eastern tour, President Ford flew to the Soviet Union on November 23 for his first summit meeting with Communist leader Leonid Brezhnev. In the talks held at Vladivostok, Ford and Brezhnev reached agreement on the basic terms of a new treaty limiting the production and deployment of atomic weapons for the period 1977 to 1986.

In a report to the American people on December 2, Ford declared that the agreement "put a firm ceiling on the strategic arms race which has heretofore eluded us since the nuclear age began." Revealing details of the agreement, he said each side agreed to a 2,400 limit on the number of intercontinental ballistic missiles, submarine-launched missiles, and heavy bombers. Of each side's total of 2,400, only 1,320 could be armed with multiple warheads.

"What we have done," President Ford said, "is to set firm and equal limits on the strategic forces of each side, thus preventing an arms race with all its terror, instability, war-breeding tension and economic waste. We have in addition created the solid basis from which future arms reductions can be—and hopefully will be—negotiated."

President Ford, during his visit to the Soviet Union, with Soviet General Secretary Brezhnev, November 23, 1974.

En route to the airport from Vladivostok, President Ford and Secretary of State Kissinger chat in the dining car on the train, November 23, 1974.

THE economy continued to slide in 1975. Although the stock market bounced back in January, unemployment rose to 8.2 percent or 7.5 million unemployed. President Ford addressed a joint session of the new 94th Congress on January 15 in the annual presidential report on the state of the Union, which he summed up bluntly:

"I must say to you that the state of the Union is not good.

"Millions of Americans are out of work. Recession and inflation are eroding the money of millions more. Prices are too high, and sales are too slow."

Reversing the appeal he had made for tax increases only three months earlier, the President now asked Congress to approve an immediate tax reduction of $16 billion, with $12 billion in rebates to taxpayers on their 1974 payments and $4 billion in liberalized investment tax credits to business. He also proposed that future income taxes be reduced by $16.5 billion by cutting tax rates for low and middle income taxpayers. He estimated the federal budget deficit as a result would be about $30 billion in 1975 and $45 billion in 1976.

Blaming the economic disruptions of the world and of the United States on the quadrupling of the world price of petroleum in 1974, President Ford proposed a program to make the United States independent of foreign energy imports. He said:

"I have set the following national energy goals to assure that our future is as secure and as productive as our past:

"—First, we must reduce oil imports by 1 million barrels per day by the end of this year and by 2 million barrels per day by the end of 1977.

"—Second, we must end vulnerability to economic disruption by foreign suppliers by 1985.

"—Third, we must develop our energy technology and resources so that the United States has the ability to supply a significant share of the energy needs of the free world by the end of this century."

To force American consumers to use less gasoline and fuel oil, he announced that he was using his presidential powers to increase the import fees on foreign oil by $3 a barrel by April 1, 1975, and that on that date he would decontrol the price of domestic crude oil. He urged Congress to enact a windfall profits tax by that date "to ensure that oil producers do not profit unduly."

President Ford said that if the increased prices of gasoline and oil did not achieve his goals of reducing oil imports he would use his presidential authority to limit the amount that could be imported.

"I want you to know," he said, "that before deciding on my energy conservation program, I considered rationing and higher gasoline taxes as alternatives. In my judgment, neither would achieve the desired results and both would produce unacceptable inequities."

To further reduce gasoline and oil consumption and "to make the United States invulnerable to foreign disruption," he proposed that Congress enact legislation that would:

1. Make heat insulation standards mandatory for all new buildings in the United States.

2. Provide a tax credit of up to $150 for homeowners who install insulation equipment.

3. Establish an energy conservation program to help low income families purchase insulation supplies.

4. Modify and defer automotive pollution standards for five years to

President Ford delivering his State of the Union address to Congress on January 15, 1975. —*UPI Compix*

A family group in the White House August 9, 1974, including *(left to right)* sons, Jack, 22, and Steve, 18, Mrs. Betty Ford, the President, daughter Susan, 17, daughter-in-law Gayle and her husband Mike, 24.

enable manufacturers to improve automobile gas mileage by 40 percent by 1980.

5. Provide emergency standby legislation and a strategic storage program of 1 billion barrels of oil for domestic needs and 300 million barrels for national defense purposes.

To increase energy production in the United States, the President said that his program envisioned in the next ten years:

—200 major nuclear power plants,

—250 major new coal mines,

—150 major coal-fired power plants,

—30 major new oil refineries,

—20 major new synthetic fuel plants,

—the drilling of many thousands of new oil wells,

—the insulation of 18 million homes, and

—the manufacturing and sale of millions of new automobiles, trucks, and buses that use much less fuel.

"I happen to believe that we can do it," President Ford said. "In another crisis—the one in 1942—President Franklin D. Roosevelt said this country would build 50,000 military aircraft. By 1943, production in that program had reached 125,000 aircraft annually. They did it then. We can do it now."

Because of the huge impending deficits in federal government spending, President Ford urged Congress to adopt restraints on government benefit programs and limit federal pay increases in 1975 to 5 percent.

President Ford with a copy of the budget for fiscal 1976. —*UPI Compix*

He further warned that he would veto any new spending programs adopted by Congress, except for energy production.

"Part of our trouble is that we have been self-indulgent," he said. "For decades, we have been voting ever-increasing levels of government benefits, and now the bill has come due. We have been adding so many new programs that the size and the growth of the federal budget has taken on a life of its own.

"One characteristic of these programs is that their cost increases automatically every year because the number of people eligible for most of the benefits increases every year. When these programs are enacted, there is no dollar amount set. No one knows what they will cost. All we know is that whatever they cost last year, they will cost more next year.

"It is a question of simple arithmetic. Unless we check the excessive growth of federal expenditures or impose on ourselves matching increases in taxes, we will continue to run huge inflationary deficits in the federal budget."

Summarizing his program, President Ford said:

"America needs a new direction, which I have sought to chart here today—a change of course which will:

"—put the unemployed back to work;

"—increase real income and production;

"—restrain the growth of Federal Government spending;

"—achieve energy independence; and

"—advance the cause of world understanding.

"We have the ability. We have the know-how. In partnership with the American people, we will achieve these objectives.

"As our 200th anniversary approaches, we owe it to ourselves, and to posterity, to rebuild our political and economic strength. Let us make America once again and for centuries more to come what it has so long been—a stronghold and a beacon-light of liberty for the whole world."

President Ford seized the initiative from Congress on January 23, 1975, and imposed higher tariffs on imported oil to launch his anti-recession and energy program. Watching the signing of the proclamation at the White House are *(left to right)* Frank Zarb, Federal Energy administrator; Alan Greenspan, chairman of the Council of Economic Advisers, and William Seidman, assistant to the President for Economic Affairs. —*UPI Compix*

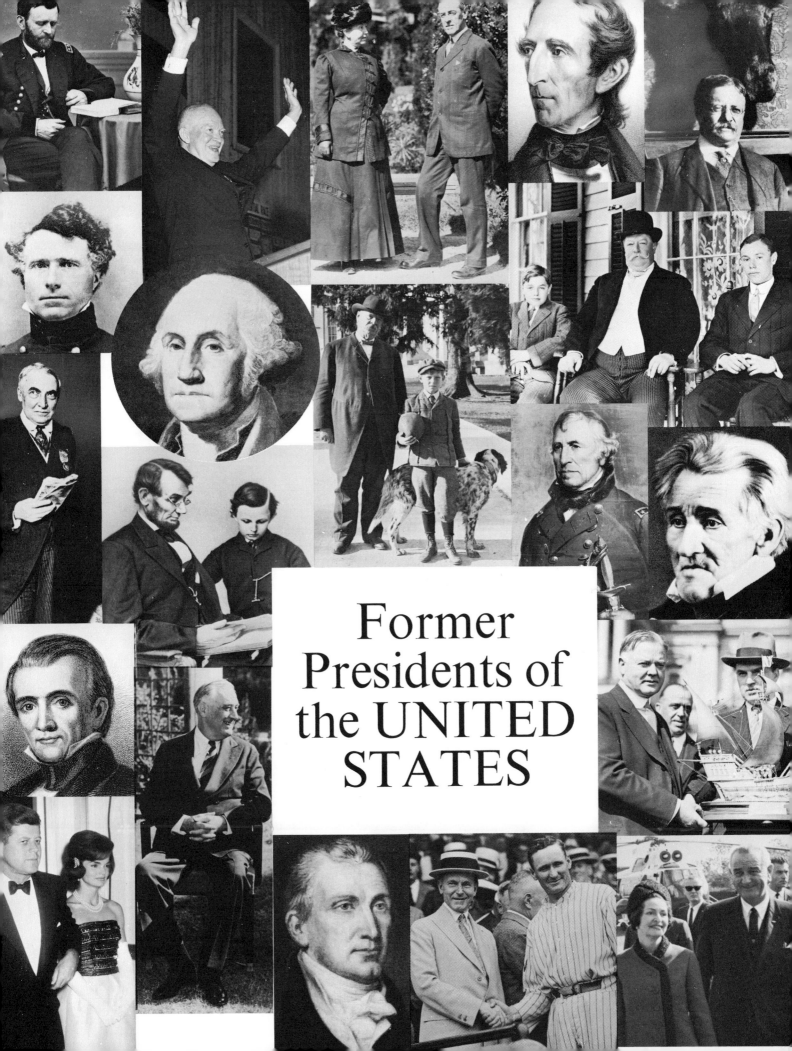

Former Presidents of the UNITED STATES

2   RICHARD NIXON

Richard Nixon

The Thirty-seventh President of the United States
1969 – 74

1913 (January 9) Born in Yorba Linda, California.

1934 Graduated from Whittier (California) College.

1937 Received law degree from Duke University in Durham, North Carolina.

1937–41 Practiced law in Whittier, California.

1940 (June 21) Married Thelma Patricia (Pat) Ryan.

1942 Attorney in the Office of Price Administration in Washington, D.C.

1942–46 Served in U.S. Navy during World War II, rising from lieutenant (junior grade) to lieutenant commander.

1947–50 U.S. Representative from California.

1950–53 U.S. Senator from California.

1953–61 Thirty-sixth Vice President of the United States under President Eisenhower.

1960 As Republican nominee for President, defeated in election by John F. Kennedy.

1962 As Republican candidate for governor of California, defeated in election by Governor Pat Brown.

1963–68 Practiced law in New York City.

1969–74 Thirty-seventh President of the United States.

1974 (August 9) Resigned as President to avoid impeachment and trial by Congress.

Leading Officials in Nixon's Administration

Office	Name	Years Served
Chief Justice	Earl Warren	1953-1969
	Warren Earl Burger	1969-
Vice-President	Spiro Agnew	1969-1973
	Gerald R. Ford	1973-1974
Secretary of State	William P. Rogers	1969-1973
	Henry A. Kissinger	1973-
Secretary of the Treasury	David M. Kennedy	1969-1971
	John B. Connally, Jr.	1971-1972
	George P. Shultz	1972-1974
	William E. Simon	1974-
Secretary of Defense	Melvin R. Laird	1969-1973
	Elliot L. Richardson	1973
	James R. Schlesinger	1973-
Attorney General	John N. Mitchell	1969-1972
	Richard G. Kleindienst	1972-1973
	Elliot L. Richardson	1973
	William B. Saxbe	1974-1975
Postmaster General*	Winton M. Blount	1969-1971
Secretary of the Interior	Walter J. Hickel	1969-1971
	Rogers C. B. Morton	1971-
Secretary of Agriculture	Clifford M. Hardin	1969-1971
	Earl L. Butz	1971-
Secretary of Commerce	Maurice H. Stans	1969-1972
	Peter G. Peterson	1972-1973
	Frederick B. Dent	1973-
Secretary of Labor	George P. Shultz	1969-1970
	James D. Hodgson	1970-1973
	Peter J. Brennan	1973-1975
Secretary of Health, Education, and Welfare	Robert H. Finch	1969-1970
	Elliot L. Richardson	1970-1973
	Caspar W. Weinberger	1973-
Secretary of Housing and Urban Development	George W. Romney	1969-1973
	James T. Lynn	1973-1975
Secretary of Transportation	John A. Volpe	1969-1973
	Claude S. Brinegar	1973-1975

*Abolished as Cabinet post in 1971.

A family portrait of Hannah and Frank Nixon with three of their sons—Harold *(left)*, Donald on his mother's lap, and three-year-old Richard. —*UPI photograph*

The first President to resign to avoid impeachment and conviction by Congress for misuse of power, Richard Nixon left a stain on the office of the presidency unequaled by any of his predecessors. His first term as chief executive from 1969 to 1973 was marked by foreign policy achievements that brought improved relations with the Soviet Union and Communist China and ended United States participation in the unpopular Vietnam War—the longest and one of the costliest in United States history. But his second term was wrecked and aborted by the Watergate scandals that ultimately forced him to leave the White House.

After a fourteen-year career as a Republican Congressman, U.S. Senator, and Vice President, Nixon lost his first bid for the presidency to John F. Kennedy in a close election in 1960. Eight years later he made a surprising political comeback by winning the 1968 presidential election over Vice President Hubert H. Humphrey. He followed this with a triumphant reelection landslide in 1972 over Senator George S. McGovern of South Dakota. However, illegal actions, many stemming from the 1972 reelection campaign, led to Nixon's downfall and the conviction of many of his close associates and campaign supporters.

Throughout the five years and six and a half months of his administration, Nixon faced a politically hostile Congress. For the first time a President twice won election for himself while being unable to lead his party to a victory in either house of Congress. As a result Nixon's administration was marked by constant conflict with Congress. The President found it difficult to get legislative proposals enacted and he repeatedly impounded and refused to spend money on projects for which Congress had appropriated funds.

Nixon had promised during his campaign for the presidency in 1968 that he had a plan for ending the Vietnam War, which had severely divided the nation. As President he gradually brought home most of the half-million American fighting men from South Vietnam while strengthening the army of that country so it could defend itself from the forces of Communist North Vietnam. The President's chief foreign policy advisor, Henry A. Kissinger, worked tirelessly to negotiate a settlement of the war. Finally, a week after President Nixon was inaugurated for his second term, a cease-fire was signed. American prisoners of war were released by the Communists, and remaining American servicemen in Vietnam came home.

President Nixon also made progress in creating what he called "a new structure of peace" in the world. When he first took office, the world still was split by the Cold War between Communist and anti-Communist nations, causing many to fear that an atomic war between the two sides might blaze forth at any moment. Although throughout his previous political career Nixon had built a reputation as a hard-line anti-Communist, he reversed the twenty-year-old official policy of the United States that had refused to recognize the Communist rule of China. He helped Communist China gain membership in the United Nations, and then flew to Peking to dramatize America's new friendship. Next, he traveled to Moscow, where he signed agreements with the Soviet Union providing for the first limitations on the production and deployment of atomic weapons. This was followed by later summit meetings in the United States and the Soviet Union that officially brought an end to the Cold War.

THE second of five brothers, Richard Milhous Nixon was born on January 9, 1913, at Yorba Linda, California, where his father raised lemons. His mother was, as he later described her, "a gentle, Quaker mother, with a passionate concern for peace." She reared Dick as a Quaker and imbued him with peaceful ideals. When Dick was nine years old, his father moved the family to Whittier, California. There his father opened a combination gasoline station and general store where the boys of the family worked when they were not in school.

In school Dick Nixon took part in many activities and made excellent grades as well. He was a leading member of the debate teams both in high school and college. He won prizes for public speaking. He acted in plays. He played the organ in the Quaker meeting house and the piano at parties. He was elected to various school offices, including president of the college student body. And, when he graduated from Whittier College in 1934, he stood second in his class.

Years later Nixon attributed his drive to do well in school to efforts to please his father, who had been forced to leave school after the sixth grade in order to earn his living. "Never a day went by when he did not tell me and my four brothers how fortunate we were to be able to go to school. I was determined not to let him down. My biggest thrill in those years was to see the light in his eyes when I brought home a good report card . . . ."

He received a tuition scholarship to the law school at Duke University in Durham, North Carolina. To help pay his way through school he did research for the dean of the school for thirty-five cents an hour. When he graduated from Duke in 1937, he was third in his class.

Nixon returned to California, passed the state bar examination, and joined a law firm in Whittier. One of his outside activities was acting in an amateur theater group. There he was introduced to Pat Ryan, a red-haired high school typing teacher. He proposed the same night he met her. But she put off saying "Yes" for two years. They were both twenty-seven when they married on June 21, 1940. They later had two daughters, Patricia and Julie. After Nixon had been elected President in 1968, his daughter Julie married David Eisenhower, the grandson of President Eisenhower. Tricia, as his other daughter was nicknamed, married law student Edward Cox in a gala White House wedding in June 1971.

After the Japanese attack on Pearl Harbor in December, 1941, Nixon decided to take part in the war effort. He went to Washington and obtained a $61-a-week job doing legal work in the Office of Price Administration. But after a few months with the OPA he decided that despite his Quaker background he should help more directly to fight the war.

He applied for and received a Navy commission as a lieutenant (j.g.) in September, 1942. The next year he was sent to the South Pacific as operations officer for a Navy air transport unit. After fifteen months on islands and coral atolls, he returned to shore duty in the United States. By the time the war was over, he had advanced to the rank of lieutenant commander.

WHILE Nixon was awaiting release from the Navy in November, 1945, a banker friend suggested that he should enter politics. He pointed out that a committee of California Republicans had unsuccessfully advertised for a Congressional candidate. The friend suggested that Nixon apply. He did. And the committee agreed to back him in a campaign

Student, Lawyer, and Navy Officer

Mrs. Richard M. Nixon, the former Thelma Patricia Ryan of Ely, Nevada. —*UPI photograph*

Congressman and Senator

Julie Nixon and David Eisenhower after their wedding rehearsal, with Mrs. Nixon in the background, at Marble Collegiate Church, New York, where they were married on December 22, 1968. —*UPI photograph*

Richard M. Nixon, as a member of the House of Representatives Un-American Activities Committee in 1948, with Robert Stripling, chief investigator for the committee, examining microfilms of government papers which were discovered in a hollowed-out pumpkin on Whittaker Chambers' farm in Maryland. —*UPI photograph*

against Democratic Representative Jerry Voorhis, who had represented California's 12th District for ten years.

During the 1946 campaign the politically unknown Nixon made himself known by getting Voorhis to agree to a series of face-to-face debates. Nixon attacked Voorhis as a left-wing socialist and ridiculed his record in Congress. Because Nixon had no record to attack, Voorhis was forced on the defensive. In the November election the thirty-three-year-old Nixon rode to victory as part of a nationwide Republican landslide.

Nixon became one of the youngest members of the Republican-controlled 80th Congress, which President Truman came to label the "Do-Nothing Congress." He was assigned to the Education and Labor Committee, where he became acquainted with another freshman Congressman, John Kennedy. The main effort of this committee was directed toward writing the Taft-Hartley Act, called the "slave labor law" by unions. Long before they or anyone else suspected that someday they might run against each other for President, Nixon and Kennedy were called upon to debate the Taft-Hartley Act before a meeting in McKeesport, Pennsylvania. Nixon said later of this debate: "I was for the bill; Kennedy was against it. And we both presented our points of view as vigorously as we could. As far as the audience was concerned, I probably had the better of the argument because most of those present, as employers, tended to be on my side in the first place." Nixon helped pass the Taft-Hartley Act over President Truman's veto.

The Cold War between the United States and Russia was developing in intensity in 1947 and 1948 with the United States becoming aware that Russia had no intent of freeing the countries of Eastern Europe that it had "liberated" during World War II. It was against this background that Nixon received two other committee appointments that shaped his future career.

Nixon was named as a member of the Congressional Herter Committee to investigate the need for the Marshall Plan. He traveled to Europe with the other members of the committee. And he came back convinced that economic aid was needed to prevent the war-torn countries of Western Europe from falling to communism. He became an ardent supporter of foreign aid, a stance that in later years conservative members of his party criticized as being too liberal.

But it was Nixon's assignment to the Un-American Activities Committee that brought him to national prominence and set the stage for his becoming Vice President and ultimately President. The committee was holding many hearings trying to pin down the extent of communist infiltration into the government, into the motion picture industry, and other areas of American life. Nixon put his skills as a lawyer and a debater to work in questioning witnesses called before the committee. He seemed to have a sixth sense as to when a witness was telling less than the full truth.

Early in August, 1948, a witness before the Un-American Activities Committee, Elizabeth Bentley, testified that thirty-two government officials had delivered information to her to pass on to a communist spy ring. Then a few days later Whittaker Chambers, a senior editor for *Time* magazine, named seven more officials and former officials as members of the Communist Party or fellow travelers. Among those named was Alger Hiss, a former State Department officer who had organized the UN Charter meeting in San Francisco. Two days later Hiss appeared before the committee and denied he had ever been a communist or had even known a person named Whittaker Chambers. Hiss made such a convincing appearance that newspapers and prominent persons attacked the committee for besmirching the name of Hiss, who was then president of the Carnegie Endowment and had taken that job at the request of its board chairman, John Foster Dulles.

The majority of members of the committee were ready at this point to drop the entire Hiss-Chambers affair, but Nixon was not. He argued the committee into carrying on the investigation in the face of public criticism. So Nixon was appointed head of a subcommittee to pursue the matter. At a press conference in Washington President Truman dismissed the charges against Hiss as a "red herring."

Throughout August, 1948, Nixon, Hiss, and Chambers made the newspaper headlines. Nixon brought the two together at a closed subcommittee meeting on August 17. Hiss was quite shaken because on the same day newspapers reported the death by a heart attack of Harry Dexter White, a former assistant Secretary of the Treasury who had been named by Chambers as a "fellow traveler." After much hesitation, Hiss admitted he had known Chambers thirteen years earlier under the name "George Crosley," but continued to deny he ever had been a communist. The confrontation between Hiss and Chambers was repeated in a televised public hearing on August 25. When Chambers repeated his charges on a TV show, Hiss sued for libel.

The national election campaign was going on during this period, so for the next several weeks Nixon devoted himself to politics. He easily won re-election to Congress, although the Democrats took control of Congress and President Truman defeated his Republican opponent, Thomas Dewey. Nixon felt Dewey had not hit hard enough at the "communists-in-government" issue.

In November Chambers produced secret documents that he said had been given to him by Hiss and by White as part of a communist spy ring. These papers became known as the "pumpkin papers," because some were on microfilm that Chambers had hidden in a hollowed-out pumpkin on his farm.

In December Nixon made new headlines by charging that the Democratic administration intended to sweep the Hiss-Chambers affair under the carpet by prosecuting Chambers for perjury instead of Hiss. A few days later a New York grand jury indicted Hiss for perjury. Hiss' first trial ended in a hung jury in July, 1949. He was found guilty in a second trial that ended in January, 1950, and he was sentenced to five years in prison. Nixon and the House Un-American Activities Committee had been vindicated.

Nixon's drive to expose communist infiltration in the government received a new boost in the spring of 1950 when the FBI revealed that communists had stolen the secret of the atomic bomb. Several Americans were arrested and convicted as part of the communist A-bomb spy ring.

Riding high on the crest of his fame as a communist hunter, Nixon ran for the U.S. Senate in 1950 against Democratic Congresswoman Helen Gahagan Douglas. Nixon hit hard at Mrs. Douglas' record in Congress, claiming she had supported communist policy against the best interests of the United States. Earl Warren, who was at that time the popular Republican governor of California, refused to campaign with Nixon. But in the November election Nixon won by a plurality of nearly 700,000 votes.

At thirty-seven, Nixon became the youngest Republican U.S. Senator.

Ex-Communist Whittaker Chambers, Richard Nixon, and Robert Stripling in 1948, studying a newspaper report of the mutual interest of Chambers and Alger Hiss with regard to the possible purchase of a Maryland farm in 1936.
—UPI photograph

Though not noted as a fisherman, Richard Nixon tried to outwit the wily trout at President Eisenhower's Colorado retreat.
—UPI photograph

7

But, as a freshman Republican Senator in a Democratic-controlled Senate, Nixon had little opportunity for important assignments. His popularity still was growing, however, and during 1951 he appeared as a speaker at many meetings across the country. On a trip to Europe he met with General Dwight Eisenhower and became a supporter of his campaign to win the Republican presidential nomination.

*Vice President
of the United States*

At the Republican National Convention in July, 1952, in Chicago, Eisenhower easily won the nomination. Then he invited Nixon to be his vice-presidential running mate. "No one has done more to put the fear of God into those who would betray their country," said one of the speakers who supported Nixon's candidacy.

But in September it looked for a time as though Nixon would be forced to drop out of the race. The New York *Post* ran a front page story accusing Nixon of using a secret $18,000 fund collected by a "millionaire's club" for his personal expenses. Demands flooded in to Eisenhower asking him to remove Nixon from the ticket. Eisenhower replied that Nixon would have to prove that he was "as clean as a hound's tooth." On September 23, five days after the story had broken, Nixon went on a nationwide TV show with his wife at his side to explain the fund. The largest TV audience to that time—some sixty million persons—watched and listened as Nixon explained that the fund had been used entirely to aid his political campaigning and had not been used for personal expenses. He listed all of his assets. And he told his viewers that although someone had given his children a small dog called Checkers he didn't believe he should take the dog away from them just because he was a public figure. "I don't believe I ought to quit, because I am not a quitter," he said. He appealed to the audience to send in their views as to what he should do. Millions of letters and phone calls poured in during the next several days. The response was overwhelmingly pro-Nixon. It was a great triumph over his detractors.

Richard Nixon playing with Checkers, the cocker spaniel given to his children by a friend. The dog later became nationally famous when mentioned in Nixon's disclosure of his finances on nationwide TV. *—UPI photograph*

As the campaign proceeded, Nixon pulled no punches in attacking Adlai Stevenson, the Democratic nominee for President. He particularly denounced Stevenson for once having given testimony upholding Alger Hiss' character, and for failing to recognize the threat of communist subversion in the United States. In the election, the Eisenhower-Nixon ticket won by a landslide, as it later did again in the election of 1956.

During his eight years as Vice President, from 1953 to 1961, Nixon took a more active role in the government than had any previous holder of the office. However, he later described the vice-presidency as ". . . a

The confident smiles of General Dwight D. Eisenhower *(right)* and Senator Richard M. Nixon of California, Republican candidates for President and Vice President, prophetically reflect their victory in the election of November, 1952. *—UPI photograph*

hollow shell—the most ill-conceived, poorly defined position in the American political system." During Eisenhower's absences from Washington, Nixon presided over nineteen meetings of the President's Cabinet and over twenty-six meetings of the National Security Council. The U.S. Senate was evenly divided between Republicans and Democrats in 1953 to 1954, but Nixon as presiding officer was called upon to decide only eight tie votes.

Nixon was one of the first to stir up a public controversy over Vietnam. In 1954, when it became apparent that the French were about to pull their forces out of that communist-torn country, Nixon openly advocated sending American troops to Vietnam if necessary to prevent the entire country from falling to communism.

In the early years of the Eisenhower administration, Senator Joseph McCarthy was in his heyday, claiming that all communists still had not been rooted out of government jobs. At first Nixon acted as an intermediary between Eisenhower and McCarthy, warding off a head-to-head fight. But Nixon broke with McCarthy in 1954 when the senator openly attacked the Eisenhower administration and held a long series of hearings probing the Army's handling of security risks. During the Congressional election of 1954, Nixon criss-crossed the country assuring voters that the administration had "fired the communists and fellow travelers and security risks by the thousands." But the Democrats won control of Congress and held it for the last six years of the Eisenhower-Nixon administration.

When President Eisenhower was incapacitated by a heart attack in 1955, by an intestinal disorder in 1956, and by a stroke in 1957, Nixon kept the executive branch of the government running smoothly. As he later explained: "My role was to absorb some of the more routine duties of the President, relieving the burden on him, and yet not to appear to be stepping into his shoes."

Eisenhower frequently called upon Nixon to make good-will trips to foreign countries, and in the course of these assignments he visited fifty-four other nations. On a tour of South America in 1958, communist-led mobs jeered Nixon, spat on him, and tried to overturn his car and kill him. He showed great courage in the face of these attacks, increasing his popularity in the United States because of his cool-headed actions. On a visit to Russia in 1959, Nixon engaged in a series of informal public debates with the Russian dictator, Nikita Khrushchev, on the merits of democracy versus communism. Most Americans felt Nixon came out ahead.

During his tour of the Soviet Union in July 1959, Vice President Nixon engaged in an impromptu debate with Premier Nikita Khrushchev, which later served to increase Nixon's popularity at home. *—UPI photograph*

By late 1959 it was generally accepted that Nixon and Kennedy were likely to be the opposing candidates in the next presidential election. Nixon was heartened because public opinion polls showed him leading Kennedy in popularity by a margin of 53% to 47%. Nixon entered and won all the state Republican preferential primaries unopposed. Kennedy also won in the primaries, beating his strongest opponent, Senator Hubert Humphrey of Minnesota. When the primaries were over, Kennedy led Nixon in the public opinion polls by a percentage of 52 to 48.

Nixon's main opponent for the Republican presidential nomination in 1960 was Nelson Rockefeller, who had won the governorship of New York in 1958 despite Republican losses all across the nation. Rockefeller was critical of the Eisenhower administration and was demanding a more liberal GOP party platform. Nixon went to New York and in a meeting

Losing Two Big Elections

with Rockefeller reached agreement on the wording of the platform.

With the backing of President Eisenhower, Nixon won by acclamation the Republican presidential nomination at the Chicago convention in July. He chose as his running mate Henry Cabot Lodge, Jr., the U.S. Ambassador to the UN. "I believe in the American dream," Nixon told the convention in his acceptance speech, "because I have seen it come true in my own life." In the weeks that followed he campaigned tirelessly in every one of the fifty states.

Nixon reluctantly agreed to a series of four public debates with Kennedy on TV. "I knew from long experience," Nixon said, "that in debate the man who can attack has a built-in advantage that is very hard to overcome." On the other hand, he felt obligated to take part in the debates. "Had I refused the challenge, I would have opened myself to the charge that I was afraid to defend the Administration's and my own record."

Political commentators have generally agreed that the Nixon-Kennedy debates were an important factor in Nixon's losing the election. Nixon later believed he made a serious mistake in not using TV makeup to improve his appearance before the cameras. He realized it when his mother phoned him from California after the first debate to ask if he was "feeling all right." She was one of an estimated eighty million viewers.

The results of the November election were very close. There were indications of fraud in the vote count in Illinois and Texas, both of which went to Kennedy by small margins. But Nixon decided not to fight for a recount, feeling that it would do "incalculable and lasting damage throughout the country." He conceded the election and sent Kennedy his best wishes.

After his term as Vice President was completed, Nixon returned to California where he joined the law firm of Adams, Duque & Haseltine of Los Angeles. There he enjoyed a considerably larger income than he ever had earned in political life. During the next year he wrote the book Six Crises, which detailed the highlights of his career to date. It was published in March, 1962. In it he indicated why he would not give up politics:

". . . probably the greatest magnet of all is that those who have known great crisis—its challenge and tension, its victory and defeat—can never become adjusted to a more leisurely and orderly pace. They have drunk too deeply of the stuff which really makes life exciting and worth living to be satisfied with froth."

Eleven months after his defeat in the presidential election, Nixon announced that he would run for governor of California in 1962. He fought a hard campaign against Democratic Governor Edmund G. (Pat) Brown. But Brown easily won with 53.6% of the vote. At a news conference after the election, Nixon lost his temper, blaming his defeat on what he believed was biased coverage of the campaign by newsmen. After that, almost everyone believed Nixon was absolutely finished as a politician.

Historic Comeback to Win the Presidency

But, as Nixon had told sixty million TV viewers in 1952 at the time of the "fund scandal," he was not a quitter. He changed his base of operations in 1963 by moving to New York City, where he became a partner in the law firm of Nixon, Mudge, Rose, Guthrie, Alexander & Mitchell. He made no effort to win the Republican presidential nom-

During the campaign of 1956, Vice President Nixon being greeted by Senator Joseph R. McCarthy upon his arrival in Milwaukee October 1.

—UPI photograph

ination in 1964, but hit the campaign trail to support the party's nominee, Barry Goldwater. After Goldwater's disastrous loss to Lyndon Johnson, Nixon helped rebuild the shattered forces of the Republican party. He campaigned vigorously to aid local candidates throughout the nation in the elections of 1965 and 1966. By 1967 he was again a leading contender for the presidency, and public opinion polls in November of that year showed he was more popular than President Johnson.

The Democratic party was bitterly divided in 1968 over President Johnson's policy of massive U.S. intervention in the Vietnam War. Senator Eugene McCarthy of Minnesota launched a campaign for the Democratic presidential nomination as a peace candidate. He won a surprisingly large vote in the first presidential primary of 1968 in New Hampshire. Shortly after, Senator Robert Kennedy of New York, the late President's brother, announced his candidacy in opposition to Johnson. Then on March 31 Johnson announced a halt to the bombing of much of North Vietnam and at the same time said he would not be a candidate for re-election in order to devote full time toward trying to obtain peace in Vietnam. Vice President Humphrey then entered the race with Johnson's backing. Calling for the country to "move in a different direction," Kennedy seemed to be winning the most popular support for the nomination. But, shortly after midnight on June 5, just as he had finished a victory speech upon winning the crucial California primary, an assassin's bullet struck down Kennedy. The sorrowing followers of Kennedy refused to join McCarthy in a stop-Humphrey drive. At the Democratic Convention in Chicago, a further pall was thrown over the party by violence that broke out in the streets between police and peace demonstrators, many of whom were McCarthy supporters. Humphrey easily won the presidential nomination. He chose as his running mate Senator Edmund Muskie of Maine.

Nixon, meanwhile, had proved he still was a vote-getter in the Republican primaries. He knocked out Governor George Romney of Michigan in the New Hampshire primary in March. And he smothered Governor Nelson Rockefeller of New York in the Oregon primary in May. At the Republican National Convention in Miami, he easily won the presidential nomination on the first ballot. He named Governor Spiro Agnew of Maryland as his choice for Vice President.

The election campaign was complicated by the entrance of a third party—the American Independent Party. It was formed by George Wallace, a former governor of Alabama who was a symbol of the Deep South's antagonism to the liberalization of civil rights for Negroes.

At the start of the campaign, public opinion polls indicated that Nixon would be a sure winner. Nixon campaigned in a more relaxed manner than ever before. His posters used the bland slogan, "Nixon's the One." He refrained from making the Vietnam War an issue. And he avoided any TV debates with Humphrey.

Five days before the election, President Johnson announced that he was ordering a halt to all bombing of North Vietnam. Peace advocates, such as McCarthy, had been calling for such action for months. McCarthy, who had refused to support Humphrey, now joined in the closing days of the campaign to aid the Democratic nominee. Public opinion polls indicated that Humphrey was rapidly overtaking Nixon's lead and might even win.

On election night, November 5, it appeared for some time that Nixon was about to lose again. Humphrey took an early lead in the East, win-

Rival vice-presidential nominees—Senator Edmund Muskie, Democrat (*left*), shaking hands with Spiro T. Agnew, Republican, Vice-President in the Nixon administration.   —*UPI photograph*

Running mates on the American Independent Party ticket in 1968—presidential candidate George C. Wallace (*right*) and vice-presidential candidate, retired Air Force General Curtis LeMay.
    —*UPI photograph*

ning such states as Connecticut and New York by large majorities. Then Nixon began to pick up strength, winning many Southern states, most of the states of the Midwest, and all the Western states except Washington and Hawaii. In the final count Nixon won in thirty-two states with 301 electoral votes, Humphrey won thirteen states with 191 electoral votes, and Wallace took five states with 46 electoral votes. The popular vote was much closer, with Nixon leading Humphrey by only seven-tenths of one percent in more than seventy-two million votes.

The 56-year-old Nixon was sworn into office as the thirty-seventh President less than a month after American astronauts had accomplished man's first triumphal flight around the moon. Referring to this in his inaugural address, Nixon drew an ironic parallel: "We find ourselves rich in goods, but ragged in spirit; reaching with magnificent precision for the moon, but falling into raucous discord on earth." He called for unity and an end to the strife that had divided America on the issues of the Vietnam War and expanded civil rights for Negroes, saying, "To go forward at all is to go forward together."

Above all else, Nixon dedicated his administration to seek world peace:

"I have taken an oath today in the presence of God and my conscience: To uphold and defend the Constitution of the United States. And to that oath, I now add this sacred commitment: I shall consecrate my office, my energies and all the wisdom I can summon, to the cause of peace among nations."

Early Years of the Nixon Administration

In the first months of Nixon's administration, the country adopted a wait-and-see attitude. Vietnam peace talks had begun in Paris in January 1969 among the United States, North Vietnam, South Vietnam, and the Viet Cong. For some time public hope remained high that a breakthrough for peace might take place at the conference table, but in the spring of 1969 new antiwar protests broke out among draft-age students at many college campuses. In answer Nixon announced in June that, although there had been no progress in the Paris talks or in secret negotiations, he planned to begin the gradual withdrawal of American forces from the war zone with the first 25,000 troops due home by September. He made continued withdrawal contingent (1) upon what he termed the "Vietnamization" of the war—the increased capability of South Vietnamese soldiers to take over the defense of their country, and (2) upon the exercise of restraint by the North Vietnamese in not increasing their attacks on the remaining U.S. forces in Vietnam.

A temporary lift to American spirits took place in July 1969 when American Astronauts Neil A. Armstrong and Edwin E. Aldrin of the Apollo 11 flight became the first men to land on the moon. Uncounted millions of people watched as television cameras sent back pictures to earth of the historic feat. President Nixon talked by radio-telephone to the astronauts from 200,000 miles away, saying, "For one priceless moment in the whole history of man all the people on this earth are truly one— one in their pride in what you have done and one in our prayers that you will return safely to earth." Subsequently, the flight of Apollo 12 in November 1969 gave two more astronauts, Charles Conrad, Jr. and Alan L. Bean, an opportunity to explore the moon's surface. Both flights brought back rocks that indicated the moon was four billion years old, but the astronauts found no signs of life, past or present, on the moon. Another moon flight, Apollo 13 in April 1970, nearly ended in disaster when the spacecraft experienced a power failure deep in space near the moon, but

Richard Nixon and Mrs. Nixon after it became apparent that he had been elected President, November 6, 1968.

—UPI photograph

emergency procedures brought the crew safely back to earth. Four more successful moon trips took place—two in 1971 and two in 1972.

ALTHOUGH the space flights to the moon clearly showed America's technological advancement to the rest of the world, many persons raised questions as to why such complicated scientific achievements could be accomplished while seemingly simpler problems, such as poverty, hunger, inadequate education, and other social ills, remained unsolved. Partly in response to such criticism, President Nixon reduced the budget for future space explorations, although he pledged that the program would continue in the 1970's with a "grand tour" of all the planets in the solar system by unmanned spacecraft and with the development of an atomic-powered spaceship.

The Supreme Court became embroiled in greater political controversy than at any time since Franklin D. Roosevelt's attempt to "pack" the Court with liberals in the late 1930's. In the waning months of President Johnson's administration, 77-year-old Chief Justice Earl Warren had announced his desire to retire. Johnson attempted to fill the position by nominating Associate Justice Abe Fortas. But opposition to the appointment developed in the Senate when doubt was cast on Fortas' ethics, for accepting a teaching fee and for jeopardizing Constitutional separation of powers by acting as an advisor to Johnson while sitting on the Supreme Court. Consequently, Fortas withdrew his name and Warren continued as Chief Justice into the early months of the Nixon administration. Controversy continued to swirl about Fortas as it was revealed he had accepted a $20,000 fee from the family foundation of a financier who had been convicted of stock swindling. Although Fortas declared he had returned the money and had not been guilty of misconduct, he resigned in May 1969—the first Associate Justice ever to quit the Court under fire.

SHORTLY after Fortas' resignation, Nixon named a new Chief Justice, Warren E. Burger, a conservative federal judge from Minnesota. The nomination was quickly confirmed. Then new controversy broke as Nixon, in an effort to repay debts to Southern political leaders who had helped him win the Presidency, attempted to fill Fortas' chair with a Southern conservative. He first nominated Federal Judge Clement F. Haynsworth, Jr. of South Carolina. But a Senate investigation revealed that Haynsworth had dealt in the stock of companies whose cases he had heard as a federal judge, and the Senate rejected his nomination. Then Nixon named another Southern conservative, Federal Judge G. Harrold Carswell of Florida. This time evidence was turned up that Carswell had run for the Georgia legislature many years earlier as a white supremacy racist. Again the Senate rejected the nomination. Angered by these rebuffs to his judgment, Nixon declared that it was obvious that the Senate would never approve a Southerner to the Court. He then nominated Federal Judge Harry A. Blackmun of Minnesota, a childhood friend of Chief Justice Burger. The Senate confirmed this nomination unanimously in May 1970, and Fortas' seat finally was filled after having remained vacant for more than a year.

In 1971 the retirement of two Associate Justices of the Supreme Court enabled Nixon to appoint two additional conservatives: Lewis F. Powell, Jr., a Virginian, and William H. Rehnquist of Arizona. The appointments gave the Supreme Court a conservative majority for the first time in more than three decades.

Domestic Problems Require Attention

Astronaut Edwin E. Aldrin, Jr., walking on the surface of the moon near a leg of the lunar module during the successful Apollo 11 lunar landing July 20, 1969. -*NASA*

Difficulty Filling Supreme Court Vacancies

An anti-Vietnam War demonstration May 9, 1970, with the south portico of the White House in the background. —*UPI photograph*

Nationwide antiwar protests calling for an immediate end to the Vietnam War were organized by students who had been supporters of Senator Eugene McCarthy's presidential candidacy. Many prominent officials spoke at rallies on Vietnam Moratorium Day, October 15, 1969. But Nixon maintained silence after observing that he would "under no circumstances whatever" be affected by the protests. However, Vice-President Spiro Agnew answered for the administration four days later by saying, "A spirit of national masochism prevails, encouraged by an effete corps of impudent snobs who characterize themselves as intellectuals." Agnew later criticized TV and newspaper coverage of administration policies as biased against the President. Nixon broke his self-imposed silence on November 3 with an appeal on television for support from "the great silent majority." Public opinion polls substantiated that some sixty percent of the country supported his efforts to end the war.

Protests reached a new climax when more than 300,000 demonstrators gathered in Washington, D.C. on November 15-16. They participated in a "March Against Death," carrying the names of the more than 40,000 American servicemen who had died in the war. Police and U.S. Army troops guarded the White House as the march took place, while the President remained inside watching a televised football game to indicate he would not be influenced by the protestors. Antiwar sentiment heightened with the revelation in November that U.S. troops had massacred hundreds of Vietnamese civilians in the village of My Lai on March 16, 1968. In March 1971, after a court-martial that lasted four months, Lieutenant William Calley was found guilty of premeditated murder in the massacre. Many persons charged that the army had made Calley a scapegoat while higher officers were only given reprimands. President Nixon intervened personally in the case to save Calley from going to prison pending his appeal of the court-martial finding. His conviction was overturned in 1974 and he was released from prison.

Environmental Concerns and Race Relations

In an effort to divert national attention to a noncontroversial issue that might bring greater unity, Nixon made the theme of his first State of the Union Address in January 1970 the need to rescue the natural environment from pollution, which he said "may well become the major concern of the American people in the decade of the seventies." He proposed a $10 billion program to clean the nation's rivers and lakes.

"Restoring nature to its natural state, the President said, "is a cause beyond party and beyond factions. It has become a common cause of all the people of this country. It is the cause of particular concern to young Americans because they, more than we, will reap the grim consequences of our failure to act on the programs which are needed now, if we are to prevent disaster later—clean air, clean water, open spaces. These should once again be the birthright of every American. If we act now they can be. . . . Through our years of past carelessness we incurred a debt to nature and now that debt is being called."

Nixon enraged white liberals and black leaders by pursuing a policy of "benign neglect" on the issue of race relations. This policy had been recommended to him by one of his close advisors, Daniel P. Moynihan, who wrote in a confidential memo to the President: "The time may have come when the issue of race could benefit from a period of 'benign neglect.' The subject has been too much talked about. The forum has been too much taken over by hysterics, paranoids and boodlers on all sides. We may need a period in which Negro progress continues and racial rhetoric fades." As it became apparent in 1970 that the administration had slowed down the drive to integrate whites and blacks in previously segregated public schools, unrest developed within the administration, with many protests and resignations in the Department of Health, Education and Welfare. This culminated in the shifting of HEW Secretary Robert H. Finch from the Cabinet to a position as a White House advisor and the firing of U.S. Commissioner of Education James E. Allen, Jr., a strong advocate of school integration.

THE Vietnam War took a new turn in the spring of 1970, after military leaders overthrew the pro-communist chief of state of Cambodia, Prince Norodom Sihanouk. The new Cambodian government appealed for military supplies and assistance as North Vietnamese communist troops began moving toward the Cambodian capital. After Secretary of State William Rogers had assured Congressional leaders that the United States had no intention of sending U.S. troops to the aid of Cambodia, President Nixon surprised the nation on April 30 by announcing that U.S. and South Vietnamese troops were marching into Cambodia in an effort to capture North Vietnamese troops and supplies. He promised that the action would be of short duration and that all American troops would be withdrawn by June 30. Senators and Congressmen of both major political parties protested Nixon's move, pointing out that under the Constitution only Congress has the power to declare war on another country. On June 30, the day on which all American ground forces were removed from Cambodia, the Senate, in a major rebuff to Nixon's war policies, voted fifty-eight to thirty-seven for the Cooper-Church amendment, which would cut off all funds for the support of any further American military operations in Cambodia. Three years later, in 1973, a Senate investigation revealed that the U.S. Air Force had bombed Communist forces in Cambodia since 1969, while concealing the bombing from Congress and the American public.

The nation was thrown into new turmoil in May, when National Guard troops fired into a crowd of student protestors on the campus of Kent State University in Ohio, killing four students. Again, thousands of students and antiwar protestors descended on Washington, D.C. to demonstrate against the Cambodian operation and the Kent State killings. This time President Nixon indicated his concern by making a predawn visit to students camped near the Lincoln Memorial, but he gave no evidence of changing his mind about his policies to pursue the Vietnam War.

Early in June the President again took to television to defend his sending American troops into Cambodia, terming it "the most successful operation of this long and very difficult war." He showed movies of captured enemy arms and supplies, reminded his listeners that 110,000 American troops already had been brought home from the fighting, reiterated a previous pledge that 150,000 more American troops would be withdrawn from Vietnam in the ensuing twelve months, and reaffirmed that all American troops would be removed from Cambodia by June 30.

"There is one commitment yet to be fulfilled," President Nixon said. "I pledged to end this war. And I shall keep that promise. But I am determined to end the war in a way that will promote peace rather than conflict throughout the world. . . . Peace is the goal toward which we are working. And peace is the goal this Government will pursue until the day we reach it."

In June 1970 Congress passed and President Nixon signed into law an act lowering the voting age from twenty-one to eighteen, although he ex-

Invasion of Cambodia and New Student Unrest

This demonstration on May 20, 1970, by the "hard-hats" (construction workers) in the Wall Street financial district was a reaction in support of the Nixon war policy in Indochina.
—UPI photograph

15

pressed doubt that the measure was constitutional. A year later, in June 1971, constitutional doubts were erased when Amendment 26 to the Constitution was ratified by the states, lowering the voting age to eighteen in all elections, both federal and local.

Congressional Elections and the Pentagon Papers

In the Congressional elections of 1970, Nixon and Agnew personally campaigned throughout the nation in an effort to purge representatives and senators that they called "radical-liberals" and replace them with conservatives who would support administration-backed legislation. The Vietnam War did not play a significant role in the mid-term campaign issues. Nixon, Agnew, and the Republican candidates largely emphasized their qualifications to deal with student violence and preserve law and order. On the other hand, Democratic candidates for Congress pointed to rising unemployment and worsening economic conditions under the Nixon administration. When the votes were counted in November, Republicans made some slight gains in the Senate, lost a handful of seats in the House of Representatives, and failed to gain a majority in either house of Congress. Nixon was left in the position of having to continue to try to work with a Democrat-controlled Congress to achieve his legislative aims.

In June 1971 the Democratic-controlled Senate passed, as an amendment to the draft extension bill, a measure calling for all American troops to be withdrawn from Vietnam within nine months. Shortly after, the Vietcong proposed at the peace talks in Paris that if the United States would withdraw all forces from Vietnam by the end of 1971, the communists would release all their war prisoners simultaneously. They further proposed that as soon as a withdrawal date had been set, a cease-fire could be agreed upon. Opponents of President Nixon accused him of trying to prolong the Vietnam War so that he could bring it to an end in 1972—an election year—and thus help himself win re-election.

Attempts by the Nixon administration to restrict the freedom of the press reached a climax in June 1971 when, for the first time in the nation's history, the federal government obtained injunctions to prevent the *New York Times* and other newspapers from publishing documents about the Vietnam War that the government contended would endanger the national security. The Supreme Court by a 6 to 3 vote upheld the newspapers' right to publish the documents, called the *Pentagon Papers*, which were part of a history of the Vietnam War compiled by the Department of Defense and classified as "top secret." The documents, which had been provided to the newspapers by Daniel Ellsberg, a former government employee who opposed the war, showed that the government had concealed much vital information from the public during the course of the American build-up in Vietnam.

Daniel Ellsberg *(left)* and Anthony Russo *(right)* were indicted and arrested on charges of espionage for giving the Pentagon Papers to newspapers. Their trial was dismissed in 1973 as the result of government activities revealed during the investigation of the Watergate scandals.

—UPI photograph

During the early years of Nixon's administration the nation's economy slid into a recession. Prices of consumer products rose at a rate of about 10 percent a year while labor unions continued to win large wage increases. At the same time the production of goods declined and unemployment increased to 6 percent. For more than two years President Nixon relied on high interest rates and reduced government spending to try to adjust the economy. He repeatedly refused to institute wage and price controls to halt inflation or to increase government spending in order to reduce unemployment. Then, on August 15, 1971, President Nixon dramatically reversed himself, announcing in a 20-minute nationwide telecast a "new economic policy" which called for controls on prices and wages to halt inflation, a new 10 percent tax on most imported goods, a reduction in the number of federal employees, reduced spending on foreign aid, and devaluation of the dollar by suspending its convertibility into gold.

After Nixon ended wage and price controls in 1973, inflation resumed unchecked for the rest of his administration.

Opening the Door to China

As part of his plan to bring about a "generation of peace," President Nixon culminated a period of careful diplomatic preparation by flying to Communist China in February 1972 for an eight-day visit to open the way toward normalization of relations, cultural exchanges, and trade with the world's largest nation. For more than two decades, the United States had refused official recognition of the Communist government of China. As Senator, Vice President, and presidential candidate, Nixon himself had been one of the foremost advocates of containing Communist China. Therefore, the policy reversal had almost as many personal overtones as it did international implications and warranted the President's own assessment that "This was the week that changed the world."

The stage for the China trip had begun to be set nearly two years earlier. In 1970, the journalist Edgar Snow reported that, in a conversation he had had with Communist Party Chairman Mao Tse-tung, the Chinese leader had expressed interest in a visit by the American President. Next, the Bamboo Curtain that had separated China from the Western World throughout the period of the Cold War parted widely enough to permit an American table tennis team to visit mainland China, where they were treated with friendliness. Then, in July 1971, Dr. Henry Kissinger, assistant to the President for national security affairs, flew to China for secret meetings with China's Premier Chou En-lai, ensuring that a summit meeting between the leaders of the two nations would have positive results. Shortly after, President Nixon was able to surprise the world with a television announcement of the impending China trip. In October, the United States withdrew its opposition to China's membership in the United Nations, and Communist China promptly was admitted to the UN while Nationalist China was expelled.

To make sure that all the drama of the first journey in history of an American President to China would be brought into the homes of the American public, a special TV communications satellite was launched to hover 23,000 miles over the mid-Pacific. An American advance party set up a portable TV station in China to beam instant coverage to the United States. An estimated sixty million Americans watched the pomp and ceremony of the visit, most getting their first look behind the Bamboo Curtain.

Upon his return, the President could state with conviction that the trip had been a success: "We entered into agreements to expand cultural, educational and journalistic contacts between the Chinese and the American people. We agreed to work to begin and broaden trade between our two countries. We have agreed that the communications that have now been established between our Governments will be strengthened and expanded. Most important, we have agreed on some rules of international conduct which will reduce the risk of confrontation and war in Asia and in the Pacific.

"We agreed that we are opposed to domination of the Pacific area by any one power. We agreed that international disputes be settled without the use of the threat of force, and we agreed that we are prepared to

The President and Mrs. Nixon with Premier Chou En-lai at the Shanghai Industrial Exhibition during their visit to the Chinese People's Republic "the week that changed the world."

—UPI photograph

President Nixon toasting Soviet leaders Podgorny, Brezhnev, and Gromyko in the U.S.S.R. at the signing ceremony of the second agreement, May 24, 1972, in his quest for a lasting peace.

apply this principle to our mutual relations. . . . We've agreed that we will not negotiate the fate of other nations behind their back and we did not do so in Peking. There were no secret deals of any kind."

Ending the Cold War
with the Soviet Union

President Nixon with Dr. Henry A. Kissinger, who became Secretary of State succeeding William P. Rogers.

PLANS for a U.S.-Soviet Union summit meeting in Moscow—the first state visit by an American President to the Russian capital—had been made public in the fall of 1971, when progress in the Strategic Arms Limitation Talks (SALT) had convinced both sides that solid achievements would be possible at a meeting of the top leaders. Trip preparations proceeded through the spring of 1972, despite a sharp escalation of fighting in Vietnam when Hanoi committed most of its main-force army to a full-scale invasion of South Vietnam.

But early in May 1972, following North Vietnam's rejection of renewed American initiatives for a negotiated settlement, the President decided new measures were needed to counter the threat to the remaining U.S. forces in Vietnam. North Vietnamese ports would be mined, he announced May 8 in a TV address to the nation, and air bombing of other supply routes would be stepped up.

Would the result be a military confrontation with the Soviet Union—main supplier of war materials to North Vietnam—or a cancellation of the forthcoming Moscow visit? President Nixon made clear that the action was not directed at the Soviet Union and that he was looking forward to better relationships with the Moscow leaders. Moscow agreed. Plans for the trip went forward.

The President and his official party arrived in Moscow on May 22. During the next eight days' ceaseless round of talks and ceremonies, a new spirit of good will formed between the leaders of the world's two most powerful nations. On Sunday, May 28, President Nixon was invited to make the first direct address on TV to the Russian people by an American chief of state. The President keynoted his message with these words: "As great powers, we shall sometimes be competitors, but we need never be enemies."

In all, nine agreements and treaties were signed during the summit meeting, the most important of which were those restricting atomic weapons. Other agreements were concerned with environmental protection, medicine, space, science and technology, the prevention of incidents at sea between military ships and planes, the creation of a joint trade commission, and a 12-point declaration of guidelines to provide "peaceful coexistence" between the two nations.

Soviet leader Leonid I. Brezhnev flew to the United States in June 1973 for more summit meetings that were hailed as bringing an official end to the quarter century of Cold War between the world's two superpowers. Brezhnev, in a TV address to the American people, praised the new spirit of cooperation and world peace. Nine more agreements were signed for U.S.-Soviet cooperation in agriculture, transportation and other areas.

A final summit meeting between Brezhnev and Nixon in Moscow in June 1974 failed to make substantive progress on further limitations on atomic armament, but was hailed by both leaders as having been successful as an expression of continuing friendly relations.

PRESIDENT Nixon's 1972 diplomatic triumphs with China and the Soviet Union were accomplished while Democratic presidential aspirants battled each other in preferential primaries. In July Democrats chose Senator George McGovern of South Dakota as their presidential candidate and Senator Thomas Eagleton of Missouri as his running mate. When newspapers disclosed that Eagleton had a record of hospitalization for "nervous exhaustion," McGovern asked him to withdraw and chose Sargent Shriver, brother-in-law of President Kennedy, as the Democratic vice presidential candidate.

Republicans meeting at Miami Beach on August 22-23 nominated Nixon and Agnew for a second term by acclamation. Nixon called on Democrats and new 18- to 21-year-old voters to join in forming a "new majority."

On October 26, twelve days before the election, Presidential advisor Kissinger announced in a White House press conference that "peace is at hand" in the Vietnam War. He explained he had reached substantial agreement in secret negotiations with North Vietnamese diplomats in Paris, even though a cease-fire had not yet been signed.

In the ensuing election a record 77,718,554 voters went to the polls, giving the Nixon-Agnew ticket a landslide victory. They captured 60.7 percent of the votes to 37.5 percent for McGovern-Shriver. However, the Republicans again failed to win either house of Congress.

The 1972 Presidential Elections

AFTER the election, Kissinger resumed negotiations in Paris with North Vietnam's chief negotiator, Le Duc Tho. The talks went poorly. In mid-December Kissinger announced the talks had been suspended because Tho had tried to change previously agreed-upon matters.

Two days later, on December 18, President Nixon ordered the beginning of the heaviest bombing attacks of the war against North Vietnam. The intense bombing continued for nearly two weeks, despite protests about their severity from many of America's allies, including Canada. Then, on December 30, the White House announced that peace negotiations would resume in Paris, and that bombing of North Vietnam's capital and main seaport would be halted. As the renewed peace talks showed progress, the President halted all bombing of North Vietnam on January 15, 1973.

In his second inauguration address, on January 20, the President said: "We stand on the threshold of a new era of peace in the world." Three days later he announced that an agreement had been reached "to end

End of the Vietnam War

the war and bring peace with honor in Vietnam and Southeast Asia." The formal signing of the agreements took place in Paris on January 27, and the next day the cease-fire began in Vietnam. As provided in the agreement during the next sixty days the remaining 25,000 American troops were withdrawn from South Vietnam and the Communists released 590 American prisoners of war. But, after a brief respite, fighting resumed between South Vietnamese and North Vietnamese forces.

Watergate Scandals and White House Horrors

Former White House aides, E. Howard Hunt *(above)* and G. Gordon Liddy *(below)* arriving at the U.S. District Court on January 8, 1973, for the opening of the Watergate bugging trial.
—*UPI photographs*

THE WATERGATE scandals began to transcend all other domestic concerns soon after President Nixon began his second term. The affair had its origin in the 1972 Presidential election campaign in which the Republicans collected a record sum of over $60 million and ended with a surplus of more than $4 million. But as investigations of the scandals developed and expanded during 1973, many "White House horrors" extending back into the President's first term were exposed: The term "White House horrors" itself was coined by Nixon's former law partner, campaign manager, and Attorney General of the United States, John Mitchell, who was among those subsequently indicted in the scandals, and who used the term in describing those actions by the administration that he conspired to keep secret to ensure Nixon's re-election.

The scandals got their name from the Watergate office-hotel buildings in Washington, D.C. There, on the night of June 17, 1972, five burglars were captured in the offices of the Democratic national headquarters, carrying with them telephone wiretapping equipment and spy cameras. One of the burglars turned out to be James McCord, a former CIA agent and security chief of the Committee to Re-Elect the President (CREEP), the political organization conducting Nixon's campaign. Mitchell, then chairman of CREEP, immediately denied that his committee had anything to do with the burglary. A White House press spokesman called it a "third-rate burglary attempt." And, five days after the burglary, President Nixon told a press conference, "There is no involvement by the White House."

In the face of these denials, the Democrats were unable to stir public opinion to regard the burglary as much more than a minor political escapade. Public apathy continued even after Washington newspapers exposed in August that $114,000 in Nixon campaign checks had been deposited to the bank account of one of the burglars, especially when the President declared on August 29, 1972: "I can say categorically that . . . investigation indicates that no one in the White House staff, no one in this Administration, presently employed, was involved in this very bizarre incident." Two weeks later the five burglars were indicted along with two other men: G. Gordon Liddy, an attorney for Nixon's campaign finance committee, who was said to have been fired because he refused to answer FBI questions, and E. Howard Hunt, a former White House consultant and former CIA secret agent.

All seven indicted men remained silent. But an eighth member of the bugging-burglary team, Alfred C. Baldwin, a former FBI agent, agreed to be a government witness against the others in return for immunity from prosecution. On October 4 the *Los Angeles Times* published Baldwin's story in which he said CREEP officials were involved, and that he had transcribed wiretapped conversations of Democratic Party officials, delivering them to CREEP headquarters. On October 10 the *Washington Post* reported the Republicans were sabotaging the campaigns of Democratic candidates and named Donald Segretti as head of the operation.

On October 23 *Time* magazine reported that Segretti had been employed for the political sabotage work by Dwight Chapin, the President's appointments secretary, and had been paid by Herbert Kalmbach, the President's personal lawyer. On October 25 the *Washington Post* named H. R. "Bob" Haldeman, one of President Nixon's top two assistants in the White House, as being one of a group controlling a special White House fund of half a million dollars used for political espionage.

There were other similar stories. But, largely because the Nixon administration had for years hammered at the press, usually through speeches by Vice President Agnew claiming that the press was anti-Nixon, the public generally seemed to feel the news stories were politically inspired. By their overwhelming vote for President Nixon on November 7 the American people clearly indicated their disbelief in the statement by Sen. George McGovern that Nixon's administration was "the most corrupt in history."

The trial of the seven-man Watergate bugging-burglary team began on January 8, 1973. Hunt and four others pleaded guilty. Liddy and McCord stood trial and were found guilty on January 30. All the men refused to tell what they knew about the Watergate affair. The judge postponed sentencing until March 23 in hopes one of the convicted men might talk in order to get a reduced sentence.

During the presidential election campaign, the Justice Department had urged Congress not to conduct an investigation of Watergate so as not to impede the trial of the burglars. The House Banking and Currency Committee had voted on October 3, 1972, not to probe the Nixon campaign finances, even though the government's General Accounting Office had discovered several violations of the Federal Election Campaign Act of 1971. The GAO investigation had led to an indictment of the Nixon re-election finance committee, and a fine of $8,000 had been levied by a federal district court against the committee on January 26, 1973, after the committee did not contest the charges.

Public interest in these matters had not been great, because they had been overshadowed by the events leading to the end of the Vietnam War and by the ceremonies surrounding the President's inauguration to his second term. But now, with all these events in the past, the Senate voted unanimously on February 7, 1973, to establish a seven-member select committee chaired by Democratic Senator Sam J. Ervin of North Carolina, to conduct a year-long investigation of the Watergate incident and the 1972 presidential election campaign. Other investigations of Watergate also were proceeding: a Washington grand jury was continuing to hear testimony on the Watergate burglary, a New York grand jury was exploring the campaign financing, and depositions were being taken in several civil damage suits in connection with the campaign and the Watergate incident.

While promising to cooperate with the Senate investigating committee, the White House said that the constitutional doctrine of separation of powers or executive privilege would prevent members of the administration from testifying before the committee under oath, but that they might give informal testimony. Senator Ervin declared: "That is not executive privilege. That is executive poppycock."

New and startling disclosures began to be revealed almost daily. A court deposition in New York on February 27 disclosed that a $200,000 cash contribution by a financier under investigation by the Securities and Exchange Commission (SEC) had been made to CREEP. Nixon cam-

Following a closed session with a special Senate investigating panel, March 28, 1973, convicted Watergate conspirator James M. McCord, Jr. (*at left*) remained silent while his attorney, Bernard Fensterwald (*right*) answered the questions of reporters.
—*UPI photograph*

Members of the Senate Watergate Committee—(*seated, left to right*) Senators Howard Baker (R-Tenn.) and Sam Ervin (D-N.C.), chairman—(*standing, left to right*) Senators Lowell Weicker (R-Conn.); Daniel Inouye (D-Hawaii); Herman Talmadge (D-Ga.); and Edward Gurney (R-Fla.).
—*UPI photograph*

Former Attorney General John Mitchell leaves his car at the Pensacola Federal Building, April 25, 1973, on his way to appear at a pre-trial hearing for eight Vietnam Veterans Against the War.
—*UPI photograph*

Sam Dash, chief counsel of the Senate Watergate Committee, arrives at the U.S. District Court, June 8, 1973, to seek immunity for Jeb Stuart Magruder and John Dean. Fred Thompson, the committee's minority counsel, is in the background.　　—*UPI photograph*

paign officials had concealed the contribution that had been made in April 1972 and said they had given it back to the financier, Robert L. Vesco, in January 1973. Later, on May 10, a New York grand jury indicted Mitchell and former Secretary of Commerce Maurice H. Stans on charges of perjury and conspiracy in the Vesco case. (In April 1974, after a 10-week trial, a New York jury ruled that neither was guilty.)

On February 28, 1973, the Senate Judiciary Committee began hearings on President Nixon's nomination of L. Patrick Gray, III, to become director of the FBI. Gray confirmed earlier newspaper stories about the political sabotage activities of Kalmbach, Chapin, and Segretti. (All three later were sent to prison.) Gray revealed that he had been ordered not to discuss the Watergate scandals by Attorney General Richard G. Kleindienst, but on March 22 told the committee that President Nixon's chief legal counsel, John W. Dean, III, "probably" had lied in answering FBI questions during the agency's investigation of the Watergate incident.

On March 23, when the Watergate burglars were brought up for sentencing, McCord told the judge he was ready to tell who was behind the affair. Five days later, in a closed session of the Senate Watergate investigating committee, McCord named Mitchell as the "over-all boss" and named various White House aides as conspirators.

President Nixon withdrew Gray's nomination as FBI director on April 5. Then, on April 17, Nixon announced he had uncovered "major developments" in the Watergate case and was reversing his stand on executive privilege, ordering his staff members to testify before the Senate inquiry. The White House withdrew previous statements about having "full confidence" in Dean, and on April 19 Dean issued a statement that no one would succeed in making him a "scapegoat" in the Watergate scandals. That same day Attorney General Kleindienst announced his withdrawal from the Watergate investigation because of "personal and professional relationships." On April 26 newspapers reported that acting FBI director Gray had admitted to friends he destroyed secret Watergate files. The next day Gray resigned.

On April 27 the *Washington Post* reported that Dean had told federal prosecutors that the President's two top assistants, Haldeman and John D. Ehrlichman, were involved in the Watergate scandals. That same day the judge in the trial of Daniel Ellsberg in Los Angeles, who was being tried for having disclosed to newspapers the secret documents about the Vietnam War called the *Pentagon Papers,* revealed that two of the convicted Watergate burglars, Liddy and Hunt, had in 1971 broken into the office of Ellsberg's psychiatrist seeking evidence against him.

President Nixon, in an emotional TV address on April 30, announced the resignations of his top aides, Ehrlichman, Haldeman, Dean, and Kleindienst. He named Secretary of Defense Elliot L. Richardson to succeed Kleindienst as Attorney General, giving him power to appoint a special prosecutor in the Watergate case—a step the Democrats had been urging since the previous summer. The President asked his audience "for your prayers to help me in everything that I do," saying that facts about the unfolding scandal had been concealed from him as well as from the public.

In the days immediately following the President's address, newspapers disclosed that Liddy and Hunt had been part of what was called the "plumbers" unit in the White House, using illegal methods to discover "leaks" of information that the administration wanted kept secret. On May 7 it was disclosed that the President's former White House counsel

Charles W. Colson had used the "plumbers" to forge cables to show to newsmen to make them believe President Kennedy had ordered the assassination of South Vietnamese President Ngo Dinh Diem during the Vietnam War. (In 1974 Colson pleaded guilty to charges in relation to activities of the "plumbers" and began serving a 1 to 3 year prison sentence.)

On May 11, 1973, the judge dismissed the Pentagon Papers trial in Los Angeles because secret wiretaps of telephone conversations of Ellsberg could not be found by the FBI. Three days later the missing wiretap documents were found in a safe in Ehrlichman's White House office along with other secret wiretaps the plumbers had made on the phones of newsmen and government officials. The same day, May 14, the Senate Armed Services Committee heard testimony that the White House had tried to enlist the CIA in illegal domestic spy activity, and two days later heard the deputy CIA director tell of White House attempts to use the CIA to cover up the Watergate scandal.

THE Senate Watergate investigating committee began televised public hearings on May 17, 1973—hearings that for the next several months were to bring home to millions of Americans a real-life soap opera with the names, faces, places, and events of the unfolding scandals. On May 18 McCord told the Senators that he had been offered executive clemency in the name of President Nixon if he would refuse to talk. That same day the White House announced that President Nixon had no intention of resigning as had been suggested by defeated Democratic Vice-Presidential candidate Sargent Shriver. The next day, Mrs. Martha Mitchell, wife of the former Attorney General, told newsmen that her husband had been protecting President Nixon, and that the President should resign rather than wait to be impeached.

On June 15 Jeb Stuart Magruder, former deputy director of the CREEP group, spent five hours before the televised Senate investigation detailing how he and other high administration officials financed the Watergate break-in and then conspired to cover up the scandal with perjury and payments to the accused burglars. His testimony implicated Ehrlichman, Haldeman, Mitchell, Dean, and others. (Magruder later became the first to plead guilty in the conspiracy and in 1974 began serving a prison term of 10 months to 4 years.)

During the week of June 17-23 the Senate investigators suspended their hearings while Soviet leader Leonid I. Brezhnev attended a summit meeting in the United States.

The Senate hearings resumed on June 25 with a full week of testimony by former White House counsel Dean who shocked listeners with charges that President Nixon had misled the nation by denying involvement in the Watergate cover up. He accused the President of telling him that raising a million dollars to pay "hush money" to the Watergate defendants was no problem. Dean also revealed a White House list of "political enemies" and told of efforts to get the Internal Revenue Service and other government departments to harass these people. (Dean began serving a prison term of one to four years in 1974 after pleading guilty in the conspiracy.)

The President refused on July 7, 1973 a request by the Senate investigators to turn over presidential papers to the committee and said that he would refuse on constitutional grounds to appear before the committee. Mitchell, testifying before the Senators in July, denied authorizing the

The Senate Watergate Investigation

Richard G. Kleindienst tells a news conference at the Justice Department, April 30, 1973, that he resigned as Attorney General because he did not feel he was fulfilling a useful role for President Nixon. *—UPI photograph*

Jeb Stuart Magruder, former deputy director of the 1972 Nixon campaign, testifying before the Senate Watergate Committee, June 14, 1973. *—UPI photograph*

Watergate burglary, but admitted being present at meetings where it was discussed. He claimed that his central role in the conspiracy was one of trying to protect the President from finding out about the scandals, fearing that if the President learned the details he would have destroyed his chances for re-election by disclosing them to the public.

On July 16 the Senate investigators heard testimony, and the White House confirmed, that all conversations and phone calls in the President's offices had been automatically taped since 1971. Sure that these tapes would provide important evidence in the investigation, both the Senate committee and the Justice Department's Watergate prosecutors served subpoenas on the White House to obtain the recordings. On July 26 the President announced he would refuse to honor the subpoenas. However, a few days later, Haldeman, while testifying before the Senate investigators, revealed that the President had allowed him to take several of the tapes home. Haldeman said that what he remembered from listening to the recordings indicated the President was not involved in the cover up of the Watergate scandals. Not satisfied with this, the Senators moved ahead with efforts to get the courts to force the President to release the taped conversations.

A Vice Presidential Resignation and Appointment

Spiro T. Agnew was the first Vice President to resign to avoid trial on criminal charges.

THE PROBLEMS of the Nixon administration were further compounded in August 1973 when newspapers revealed that U.S. attorneys in Baltimore were investigating charges that Vice President Agnew had accepted bribes from contractors both before and after he became Vice President. Agnew held a televised press conference at which he admitted he was under investigation for a possible criminal indictment, but denounced the charges as "damned lies" and said that news reports that he had taken bribes were "false, scurrilous and malicious."

Late in September a Baltimore grand jury began hearing testimony from former associates of the Vice President. Agnew filed suit to try to stop the investigation.

Suddenly Agnew announced on October 10, 1973, at what had been expected to be a routine court appearance in Baltimore, that he had resigned as Vice President. He pleaded no contest to a charge of evading federal income taxes and was sentenced to three years probation and a fine of $10,000. The government made public evidence supporting charges that Agnew had accepted bribes of more than $100,000 as governor of Maryland and as Vice President. Agnew continued to deny that he was guilty of any wrongdoing, claiming he resigned only to save the Nixon administration the embarrassment of a public trial.

Two days after Agnew's resignation, President Nixon used Amendment 25 to the Constitution for the first time to nominate a new Vice President: Gerald R. Ford, a Republican Congressman from Michigan who had been minority leader of the House of Representatives since 1965. Both houses of Congress held lengthy televised hearings into Ford's background before confirming the nomination. Finally, Ford was sworn in as the nation's 40th Vice President on December 6, 1973.

Confrontations with Congress

THROUGHOUT President Nixon's administration he repeatedly vetoed measures passed by Congress that would have expanded U.S. funding of education and social programs. Although both houses of Congress were controlled by Democrats, the President usually had sufficient support to uphold his vetoes. He also impounded, or refused to spend, funds voted by Congress for programs he did not support. But by 1973 opposition to any further U.S. military action in Indochina was so widespread and the

President's authority had sunk so low because of the Watergate scandals that Congress began to override his vetoes.

After the Vietnam cease-fire in January 1973, the U.S. continued to bomb communist forces in Cambodia in an effort to make them join in the cease-fire. In May Congress voted to cut off all funds for the Cambodian bombing. Nixon vetoed the measure, and the House upheld.

However, Congress passed new legislation in June 1973 to halt all funds for military action in Indochina, including the Cambodian bombing. In an effort to force the President to accept it, Congress attached the measure to a bill needed to fund all federal activities beyond July 1. For a time a complete breakdown of U.S. government operations appeared imminent when Nixon vetoed the legislation on June 27 and the House again upheld his veto. Two days later the crisis was averted after Republican congressional leaders prevailed on the President to accept new legislation to end all U.S. military action in Indochina on August 15, 1973.

Fears of U.S. future involvement in another prolonged conflict like the Vietnam War caused Congress to approve legislation limiting the President's war-making powers. When Nixon vetoed the measure in November 1973, both houses of Congress overrode his veto. The law requires the President to consult with Congress before committing U.S. armed forces in hostilities and requires termination of such military activities within 60 days unless Congress declares war or otherwise approves continuation of U.S. participation.

When the fourth Arab-Israeli War in three decades broke out in October, 1973, the U.S. rushed military supplies to aid Israel. In retaliation, Arab nations placed a six-month embargo on oil shipments to the U.S. and other nations friendly to Israel. The embargo brought a shortage of gasoline and fuel oil in the winter months of 1973-1974. President Nixon ordered restrictions on the use of fuel, but resisted demands for gasoline rationing. He called on Congress to support his plans for Project Independence, to make the U.S. self-sufficient in energy by the 1980s.

Archibald Cox, special Watergate prosecutor.   —*UPI photograph*

Impeachment Proceedings and New Revelations

THE WATERGATE scandals reached a new crescendo in what was called the "Saturday Night Massacre" on October 20, 1973. In an effort to prevent the disclosure of damaging evidence in the scandals, the President had ordered special Watergate prosecutor Archibald Cox to drop his efforts to subpoena White House tapes of presidential conversations relating to Watergate. When Cox refused, the President ordered Attorney General Elliot Richardson to fire Cox. Richardson and Deputy Attorney General William Ruckelshaus immediately resigned rather than carry out the order. Cox then was fired by the new Acting Attorney General, Robert Bork.

These high-handed actions by the President brought a public outcry and new demands for his resignation or impeachment. The House of Representatives instituted impeachment proceedings with the House Judiciary Committee collecting evidence and holding hearings to determine whether impeachment was warranted. The President refused to cooperate with the committee and would not honor committee subpoenas for White House tapes and documents.

In the next several months new events and revelations steadily worsened the President's position. He made unsuccessful efforts to regain public confidence by such measures as a TV address on November 17, 1973, in which he declared, "I am not a crook."

H. R. "Bob" Haldeman, former White House Chief of Staff, takes the oath prior to testifying before the Committee, July 30, 1973. His attorney, John Wilson, is at the left.　　　—*UPI photograph*

After newspaper articles accused the President of improprieties in the handling of his personal income taxes, the White House revealed in December 1973 that he had become a millionaire since taking office but had paid only $1,670.84 in income taxes for the years 1970 and 1971. After a Congressional investigation of the matter, the President announced in April 1974 that he would pay $432,787.13 in back income taxes for 1969-72.

During 1973 and 1974 there were many reports of large sums having been spent by the government as "security measures" to improve estates owned by President Nixon in California and Florida. A House subcommittee in March 1974 reported that these government improvements had totaled $17 million The White House denied the report as distorted.

A new special Watergate prosecutor, Leon Jaworski, had been appointed in November 1973. He continued Cox's efforts to obtain White House tapes and documents as evidence, receiving some but being denied others. On March 1 Jaworski obtained grand jury indictments of Nixon's former two top assistants, Haldeman and Ehrlichman, of former Attorney General Mitchell, and of several others on charges of involvement in a conspiracy to cover up the Watergate affair. (On January 1, 1975, after a three-month trial. Haldeman, Ehrlichman, Mitchell, and Robert Mardian, an assistant to Mitchell, all were found guilty, by a jury, of conspiracy and obstruction of justice in the Watergate cover-up.)

In a further futile effort to defend himself, President Nixon on April 30, 1974, made public transcripts of some of the White House tapes of conversations that had previously been made available to the Watergate grand jury. The President claimed these tapes would prove his innocence of involvement in the Watergate cover-up. Published in paperback editions for newsstand sale, the Watergate tape transcripts became instant best sellers. They were widely interpreted as proving the President had approved the payment of "hush money" to Watergate burglars to ensure their silence.

The Watergate grand jury was revealed on June 6, 1974, to have named the President as an unindicted co-conspirator in the Watergate cover-up. The grand jury forwarded its evidence to the House Judiciary Committee considering the President's impeachment. Another blow at the integrity of President Nixon's administration was delivered the next day when former Attorney General Richard G. Kleindienst accepted conviction and a suspended sentence for having misled a Senate committee—the first cabinet officer convicted of a crime since the days of the Harding administration's Teapot Dome scandal.

The President's position further eroded in July 1974. A staff report of the Senate Watergate investigating committee indicated Nixon had used campaign funds to buy his wife diamond earrings and pay for improvements to his Florida estate. His former chief domestic advisor, John D. Ehrlichman, was convicted with several others of conspiracy in the "plumbers'" break-in of a psychiatrist's office to obtain evidence for the *Pentagon Papers* trial of Daniel Ellsberg. Ehrlichman was sentenced to 20 months to 5 years in prison. Former Secretary of the Treasury John B. Connally, a contender for the 1976 Republican presidential nomination, was indicted by the Watergate grand jury on charges of accepting a $10,000 bribe from a dairy cooperative to influence an increase in milk prices.

Before a huge nationwide television audience, the House Judiciary Committee began debate on articles of impeachment of the President on

July 24, 1974. Six Republicans joined 21 Democrats on the committee on July 27 to vote for impeachment of President Nixon for obstructing justice in the Watergate cover-up, with the final vote 27 to 11. By an even larger bipartisan vote of 28 to 10, the committee on July 29 approved a second article of impeachment charging the President with violating the Presidential Oath of Office. A third article of impeachment was approved 21 to 17 on July 30 for the President's defiance of committee subpoenas.

CLAIMING "executive privilege," the President had for months fought to prevent release to the special Watergate prosecutor of an additional 64 White House tapes and other documents. However, on July 24, 1974, the Supreme Court had ruled unanimously by an 8 to 0 vote that the President must comply with the prosecutor's subpoenas.

Admitting that his impeachment by the House was "virtually a foregone conclusion," President Nixon on August 5 made public parts of the additional tapes he now was required to turn over to the courts. They revealed that less than a week after the Watergate break-in in 1972 the President had instructed his then chief of staff, H. R. Haldeman, to obstruct the FBI investigation of the affair.

Almost all support for the President now collapsed. Republican congressional leaders reported to the President that not only would he be impeached by the House but that the Senate was sure to convict him.

Nixon became the first President ever to resign on August 9, 1974. In a televised speech the night before he did so, the 61-year-old Nixon announced he had decided to resign because, "It has become evident to me that I no longer have a strong enough political base in the Congress" to justify continued efforts to remain in office. He did not mention his impending impeachment, nor did he admit any guilt to the charges that had been leveled against him. Nixon's resignation became effective while he was flying West to retirement at his home in San Clemente, California.

A month after Nixon's resignation, his successor, President Gerald R. Ford, on September 8, 1974, surprised and shocked the nation by granting the former President a "full, free, and absolute pardon" for all offenses committed during his administration. By this action Ford saved Nixon from the possibility of criminal indictment and trial. In accepting the pardon, Nixon again made no admission of guilt. He said:

"Looking back on what is still in my mind a complex and confusing maze of events, decisions, pressures, and personalities, one thing I can see clearly now is that I was wrong in not acting more decisively and more forthrightly in dealing with Watergate, particularly when it reached the stage of judicial proceedings and grew from a political scandal into a national tragedy.

"No words can describe the depths of my regret and pain at the anguish my mistakes over Watergate have caused the nation and the Presidency, a nation I so deeply love and an institution I so greatly respect.

"I know that many fair-minded people believe that my motivation and actions in the Watergate affair were intentionally self-serving and illegal. I now understand how my own mistakes and misjudgments have contributed to that belief and seemed to support it. This burden is the heaviest one of all to bear.

"That the way I tried to deal with Watergate was the wrong way is a burden I shall bear for every day of the life that is left to me."

Nixon's Resignation and Pardon

Sen. Sam Ervin, chairman of the Committee, administers the oath to John D. Ehrlichman, a former top aide to President Nixon, July 24, 1973.   *—UPI photograph*

28   LYNDON BAINES JOHNSON

Lyndon Baines Johnson

The Thirty-sixth President of the United States
1963–1969

1908 (August 27) Born near Stonewall, Texas.

1924 Graduated from Johnson City, Texas, high school.

1927–30 Attended Southwest Texas State Teachers College, graduating with a bachelor of science degree.

1930–31 Taught public speaking and debate in Sam Houston High School in Houston, Texas.

1932–35 Secretary to U.S. Representative Richard M. Kleberg of Texas.

1934 (November 17) Married Claudia "Lady Bird" Taylor.

1935–37 Director of the National Youth Administration in Texas.

1937–48 U.S. representative from Texas.

1941–42 Served on active duty during World War II as a lieutenant commander in the U.S. Navy.

1949–60 U.S. senator from Texas; majority leader of the Senate, 1955–60.

1961–63 Vice President of the United States.

1963–69 Thirty-sixth President of the United States.

1973 (January 22) Died at his ranch in Johnson City, Texas.

Leading Officials in Johnson's Administration

Office	Name	Years Served
Chief Justice	Earl Warren	1953-1969
Vice-President	Hubert Humphrey	1965-1969
Secretary of State	Dean Rusk	1961-1969
Secretary of the Treasury	C. Douglas Dillon	1961-1965
	Henry H. Fowler	1965-1969
Secretary of Defense	Robert S. McNamara	1961-1968
	Clark Clifford	1968-1969
Attorney General	Robert F. Kennedy	1961-1964
	Nicholas deB. Katzenbach	1964-1966
	Ramsey Clark	1967-1969
Postmaster General	John A. Gronouski, Jr.	1963-1965
	Lawrence Francis O'Brien	1965-1968
	W. Marvin Watson	1968-1969
Secretary of the Interior	Stewart Lee Udall	1961-1969
Secretary of Agriculture	Orville Lothrop Freeman	1961-1969
Secretary of Commerce	Luther H. Hodges	1961-1964
	John T. Connor	1965-1967
	Alexander B. Trowbridge	1967-1968
	C. R. Smith	1968-1969
Secretary of Labor	W. Willard Wirtz	1962-1969
Secretary of Health, Education, and Welfare	Anthony J. Celebrezze	1962-1965
	John William Gardner	1965-1968
	Wilbur J. Cohen	1968-1969
Secretary of Housing and Urban Development	Robert C. Weaver	1966-1969
Secretary of Transportation	Alan S. Boyd	1966-1969

The eighth Vice President to succeed to the nation's highest office on the death of a President, Lyndon Baines Johnson was far better prepared to do so than any of his seven predecessors. Under President Kennedy he had been given greater responsibility and had been kept better informed of the inner workings of the government than had any previous Vice President. Moreover, he was a master politician in his own right, having served in Congress for twenty-four years—twelve years as a representative and twelve as a senator, the last several as majority leader.

Upon Kennedy's death, Johnson pledged to press forward the New Frontier program that had become bogged down in legislative inaction. He did so. Then in the election of 1964 he won the presidency in his own right, topping all previous records by receiving over 43 million popular votes. Calling his own program the "Great Society," Johnson obtained passage of sweeping new civil rights laws, tax reductions to stimulate the economy, a multi-billion-dollar anti-poverty program, federal aid for all aspects of education, and increased social security benefits that included medical care for the aged.

Johnson met with considerably less success in foreign affairs. When he sent American troops into the Dominican Republic to prevent Communists from taking over the government, he aroused Latin American fears of a new United States interventionist policy. But these fears eased when the American troops were made part of an inter-American force commanded by a Brazilian general. Even more disastrous was the Vietnam War, in which he escalated American participation in an effort to prevent a Communist take-over of South Vietnam, but succeeded only in making it America's costliest war and in severely dividing the American people. Ultimately, the Vietnam situation and unrest at home forced him to withdraw from seeking a second elected term as President.

The six-foot-three-inch Texan made it clear that he regarded himself as a Southwesterner rather than a Southerner. He often spoke in a more folksy manner than his Harvard-educated predecessor. In describing his vision of a "Great Society" in his inaugural address in 1965 he said:

"I do not believe that the Great Society is the ordered, changeless and sterile battalion of the ants. It is the excitement of becoming—always becoming, trying, probing, falling, resting and trying again—but always trying and always gaining. In each generation—with toil and tears—we have had to earn our heritage again."

From Texas Ranch to New Deal Washington

LYNDON BAINES JOHNSON was born on a ranch in the bleak hill country near Stonewall, Texas, on August 27, 1908. He was the first of five children of Samuel and Rebekah Johnson. Both his mother and father had been teachers, so they helped him learn to read even before he started to school. As his father and both his grandfathers had been members of the Texas legislature, young Lyndon grew up hearing the inside story of politics.

At the age of five, Lyndon moved with his family to Johnson City, Texas—named for his grandfather—and started to public school the same year. Like most families in the small town, the Johnsons had barely enough money to live on, so as he grew older Lyndon earned spending money for movies and other entertainment by such odd jobs as shining

The fifth, sixth, and seventh grades of the Cotulla, Texas grammar school in 1928, with their teacher, Lyndon Johnson (second row center).

UPI photograph

shoes and picking cotton. At the age of fifteen, he was graduated from high school.

Tired of study and books, Lyndon decided to make his own way in the world with no further education. He and some friends bummed their way to California, where he lived the life of a hobo, picking oranges, washing dishes for meals, and finding out how hard it was to earn money in the period of farm depression then underway.

After nearly a year he returned to Johnson City where he got a job on a road gang. It was hard manual labor, but he stubbornly stuck to it for about a year despite the urging by both his parents that he continue his education. When he was eighteen, he finally changed his mind, borrowed $75 from the Johnson City bank, and enrolled in Southwest State Teachers College, in San Marcos, Texas.

Johnson earned his way through college. He worked for a while as a janitor and then as an office helper for the college president. He dropped out of school one year to earn extra money by teaching Mexican children in a tiny school in the town of Cotulla—where he spent a good part of his small salary buying playground equipment for his poverty-stricken students. Then he went back to college, graduating in 1930 at the age of twenty-one.

After teaching debate and public speaking for a year in a Houston high school, the opportunity came that drew Johnson into politics. U.S. Representative Richard Kleberg, one of the owners of the million-acre King ranch, invited Johnson to come to Washington with him as his secretary

31

Mrs. Lyndon B. Johnson, daughter of a Texas rancher, popularly known as "Lady Bird," an active and gracious First Lady.

at $3000 a year. From 1932 to 1935—in the last months of the Hoover administration and in the exciting first years of the Roosevelt administration—Johnson learned just how Congress worked.

On a trip home to Texas in 1934 Johnson met twenty-year-old Claudia Alta Taylor, called Lady Bird by her family and friends. The twenty-six-year-old Johnson conducted a whirlwind courtship, and they were married on November 17, 1934—just two months after they had first been introduced. Several years later, using money she had inherited from her mother, Mrs. Johnson bought a small radio station in Austin and with great business skill pyramided her investment into a multimillion-dollar fortune. The Johnsons had two daughters.

When President Roosevelt established the National Youth Administration (NYA) in 1935 as a program to help unemployed young people earn money and go to school, Johnson applied for a job with the new organization. At twenty-six he was appointed NYA administrator for Texas—the youngest of the state directors. He swiftly organized projects that employed tens of thousands of youths.

IN 1937, Representative James P. Buchanan of Johnson's Texas congressional district, died, and a special election was called to fill the vacancy. Johnson was one of ten men who entered as candidates, but he was the only one who forthrightly supported the policies of President Roosevelt. Many of the young people whom he had helped in the NYA pitched in to work in his campaign, and in the election he received almost twice as many votes as the next nearest candidate.

President Roosevelt heard of this young man who had run and won as his supporter. He invited Johnson to ride on his special train, and offered him his help in obtaining assignment to important congressional committees. Johnson also had another influential friend in Washington—Sam Rayburn, the majority leader of the House of Representatives, who had once been a fellow state legislator with Johnson's father in Texas.

In his early years in Congress, Johnson devoted much of his effort to pushing the building of federally-supported electrical services for farmers. He also was a supporter of public housing to clean up city slums and was an active member of the Naval Affairs Committee. He did such a good job for his home congressional district that he was not opposed for re-election in 1938, 1940, and 1942.

When one of the senators from Texas, Morris Sheppard, died in April 1941, Johnson ran as a candidate to fill the remainder of the term. Although he campaigned hard throughout Texas, he lost to conservative Governor W. Lee O'Daniel by the narrow margin of 1311 votes out of nearly 600,000 cast. Disappointed but not discouraged, he returned to Washington to resume his duties in the House of Representatives.

A few months later the Japanese bombed Pearl Harbor. As soon as he heard the news, Johnson asked for active duty as a member of the Naval Reserve, in which he had served for several years and had the rank of lieutenant commander. He was the first member of Congress to go on active military duty in World War II. In May 1942, President Roosevelt sent Johnson on a special fact-finding mission in the South Pacific. During this tour one bomber in which he was flying was shot up by Japanese fighter planes. Another time he was aboard a plane that crash-landed in Australia. General Douglas MacArthur decorated him with the Silver Star for gallantry under enemy fire. In July, President Roosevelt ordered Johnson and all other members of Congress to return to their legislative posts in Washington.

In 1948 the thirty-nine-year-old Johnson decided to try again to win a seat in the U.S. Senate. He was one of eleven candidates to enter the Democratic primary. Using a helicopter, a kind of flying machine few people in Texas had seen at that time, Johnson hopped about the state campaigning. In the July vote he came in second to Governor Coke Stevenson with 405,617 votes to Stevenson's 477,077. The nine other candidates combined received 320,000. Since neither Johnson nor Stevenson had a clear majority, a runoff election was required. After another hard-fought campaign the vote was taken. This time Johnson won by an eyelash—with 494,191 to Stevenson's 494,104—a difference of only 87 votes. Stevenson contested the election, but the courts and the state Democratic party's executive committee upheld Johnson. Although Stevenson supported the Republican candidate who opposed Johnson in the November election, Johnson won the Senate seat by a 2-to-1 vote.

As a senator, Johnson began to win national attention in the 1950s as chairman of the Preparedness Investigating Subcommittee. This was a successor to the investigating committee that had been headed by Harry S Truman during World War II. It was estimated that during the Korean War Johnson's committee saved the nation more than $5 billion by ex-

UPI photograph

On November 17, 1934, Lyndon B. Johnson and Claudia Alta Taylor were married and went to Mexico on their honeymoon.

33

In December, 1960, Vice-President-elect Lyndon Johnson greeting Mrs. Franklin D. Roosevelt, an old friend from his earliest days in Washington. · *UPI photograph*

posure of wasteful practices.

In 1951 Johnson took an important step toward party leadership when his fellow Democratic senators elected him party whip—or assistant leader of the Senate Democrats. In this post he was responsible for seeing to it that Democratic members were on the floor of the Senate whenever a crucial vote was taken.

In the presidential election of 1952 many Texas Democrats, including the then governor, Allan Shivers, supported the Republican candidacy of Dwight Eisenhower against Democrat Adlai Stevenson. But Johnson backed Stevenson and campaigned with him throughout Texas. Johnson's efforts were not enough to stem the Eisenhower tide, and Texas placed its electoral votes in the Republican column. But his party loyalty stood Johnson in good stead. The Democratic leader of the Senate, Ernest McFarland of Arizona, lost his seat in the Eisenhower sweep, and when the new Congress met in January 1953, the Democratic senators elected Johnson their leader. This made him, at forty-four, the youngest man ever elected Senate floor leader by either the Democrats or the Republicans.

As minority leader of the Senate, Johnson was determined that the Democrats should not indulge in obstruction of Republican measures for the mere sake of obstruction. He said, "When we are forced by our convictions to oppose Administration proposals, our opposition will be based on principle and will be expressed in a principled manner." To strengthen his influence with new Democratic senators who had just been elected, he persuaded the more senior members of his party to relax seniority rules to the extent that each freshman senator received at least one important committee assignment. One of these freshman senators who was to remember with gratitude this action was John F. Kennedy, newly elected senator from Massachusetts.

Following what he called "politics of responsibility," Johnson saw to it that Senate Democrats accumulated a record of supporting the President on many issues in which the majority of conservative Republican senators

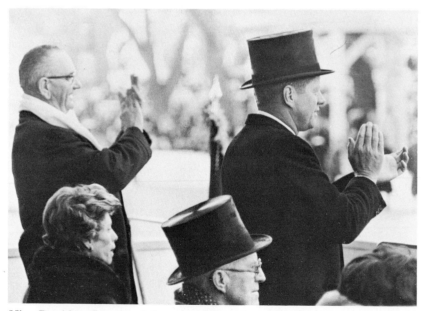

Vice-President Lyndon Johnson and President John F. Kennedy *(right)* in the reviewing stand in front of the White House applauding the inaugural parade, with the President's sister, Mrs. Sargent Shriver, and his father, Joseph P. Kennedy *(in foreground)*. *UPI photograph*

opposed him. Johnson was up for re-election in 1954, but he did not leave Washington to campaign in the Democratic primary in Texas. Nevertheless, he defeated his one opponent by a vote of nearly 3 to 1.

In the congressional election campaign of 1954 Johnson made speeches throughout the western states, hitting hard at the theme that a Democratic Congress would help Eisenhower more than would a Republican Congress. The theme paid off, for the Democrats again won control of both houses—a majority control they would continue to hold through the remainder of Eisenhower's administration.

When the Eighty-fourth Congress met in January 1955, the forty-six-year-old Johnson was the youngest man ever to have served as majority leader of the Senate. An astute politician, he now wielded great power of persuasion to bring together senators of divergent viewpoints. He became known for his expression, "Let us reason together." Senator Hubert Humphrey of Minnesota, who years later was to be Johnson's Vice President, said of him at the time that Johnson was "a genius in the art of the legislative process."

Although the tall, thin Johnson seemed easy-going and calm as he directed the Senate, he was working harder than he ever had. He paid the consequences when he was struck down by a heart attack on the Fourth of July weekend in 1955. "It was as bad an attack as a man could have and still live," Johnson said later. His doctors made him give up cigarette smoking—he had been a chain smoker—and he was forced to rest for six months. But in January 1956, he resumed his work as majority leader of the Senate.

Johnson's greatest accomplishments during his remaining time in the Senate were the passage of civil rights acts in 1957 and 1960. These measures, designed to help Negroes achieve equal voting rights with whites, were the first pieces of civil rights legislation to be approved by Congress since the period of Reconstruction. Johnson also gave personal leadership in Congress to efforts to vitalize the American space program after Russia surprised the world by beating the United States to the launching of the first successful man-made satellite in 1957.

As the 1960 presidential election approached, Johnson hoped that he would be chosen as the Democratic nominee. But he did not enter the presidential preferential primaries to compete with John F. Kennedy, and he did not announce his candidacy for the nomination until shortly before the National Convention met in Los Angeles in July. By that time Kennedy had the nomination sewed up. On the first ballot Kennedy won with 806 votes to Johnson's 409. When Kennedy asked Johnson to become his running mate, the Texas senator accepted and the convention delegates nominated him for Vice President by acclamation.

In the election campaign Johnson concentrated his efforts on the Southern and Western states, helping bring back into the Democratic column the electoral votes of Texas, Louisiana, New Mexico, and Nevada. In the close-fought election the combined vote of these states was enough to provide the margin of victory.

After taking office as Vice President in January 1961, Johnson continued to work hard. President Kennedy gave him greater responsibilities than ever before had been given a Vice President. Johnson was a regular member of the Cabinet and the National Security Council. He also served as chairman of the National Aeronautics and Space Council, the President's Committee on Equal Employment Opportunities, and the Peace Corps Advisory Council. He traveled widely throughout the world as the President's good-will ambassador—going to Africa, South Asia, the Far East, the Middle East, Europe, and Latin America.

As a Texas rancher, President Johnson appearing in a pasture with some of his Hereford cattle on his ranch.

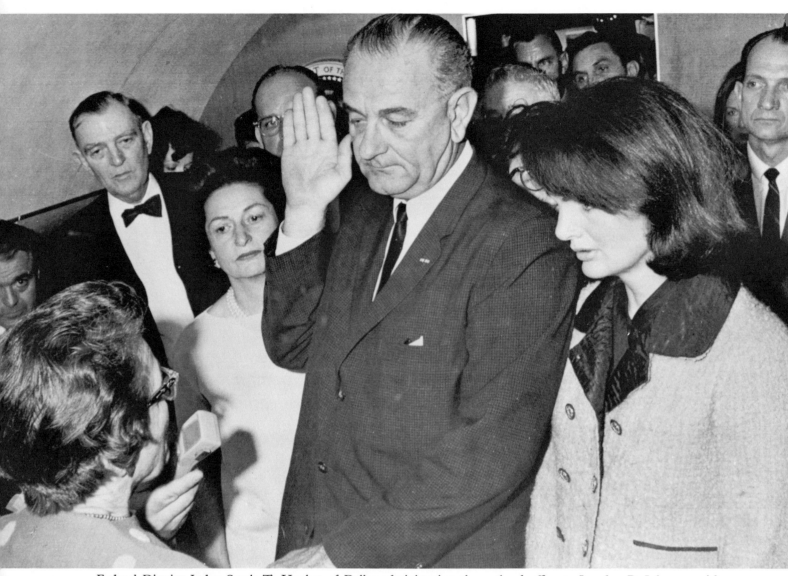

Federal District Judge Sarah T. Hughes of Dallas administering the oath of office to Lyndon B. Johnson, with Mrs. Johnson *(left)* and Mrs. John F. Kennedy *(right)* aboard the Presidential plane in Dallas, November 22, 1963, after the assassination of President John F. Kennedy.   *UPI photograph*

Johnson's Administration

ON November 22, 1963, in the fatal cavalcade at Dallas, Vice President Johnson rode in a car a short distance back of President Kennedy's. When the shots rang out, the Secret Service man assigned to Johnson threw him to the floor of the car and flung himself on top to protect the Vice President. Johnson's car then followed the President's at high speed to a hospital where the President was pronounced dead.

At 2:39 P.M., less than two hours after the assassination, the fifty-five-year-old Johnson was sworn in as President aboard the presidential plane. The oath was administered by Federal Judge Sarah T. Hughes, the first time a woman had ever sworn in a President. Then Johnson issued his first presidential order, "Now, let's get airborne."

A few hours later, while millions of Americans watched on television, the presidential jet landed in Washington. With Mrs. Johnson at his side, President Johnson stepped to a microphone at the airport and addressed his first words to reassure the people of the United States: "I will do my best. That is all I can do. I ask your help, and God's."

Johnson purposely stayed in the background for the next several days as the people expended their grief in the funeral ceremonies for Kennedy. Then five days after the assassination—on the day before Thanksgiving—Johnson addressed a special joint session of Congress. He called on the senators and representatives to honor Kennedy's memory by carrying forward the dead President's New Frontier program, saying, "Let us continue."

He asked for early passage of a new civil rights bill "to eliminate from this nation every trace of discrimination and oppression that is based upon race or color." He asked for passage of Kennedy's tax revision measure "to provide insurance against recession." And he appealed, "Let us here highly resolve that John Fitzgerald Kennedy did not live—or die—in vain."

Johnson knew and respected the members of Kennedy's Cabinet, so he retained them, including the late President's brother, Attorney General Robert Kennedy. The next year Kennedy became the first to leave the Cabinet when he resigned in order to run successfully for the U.S. Senate in New York.

In his first State of the Union address to Congress on January 8, 1964, Johnson repeated his call for action to fulfill Kennedy's program, saying:

"Let this session of Congress be known as the session which did more for civil rights than the last hundred sessions combined; as the session which enacted the most far-reaching tax cut of our time; as the session which declared all-out war on human poverty and unemployment in these United States; as the session which finally recognized the health needs of all of our older citizens; as the session which reformed our tangled transportation and transit policies; as the session which achieved the most effective, efficient foreign aid program ever; and as the session which helped

Attorney General Robert F. Kennedy, brother of John F. Kennedy, congratulating President Johnson, November 27, 1963, after the latter addressed Congress. *UPI photograph*

The parade on Pennsylvania Avenue on the occasion of the Inauguration of President Lyndon B. Johnson.   *UPI photograph*

to build more homes and more schools and more libraries and more hospitals than any single session of Congress in the history of our Republic."

Congress responded to Johnson's appeal by passing all of the laws which he asked for except medical care for the aged. To head his new poverty program, Johnson appointed Sargent Shriver, Kennedy's brother-in-law who had successfully directed the Peace Corps.

In July 1964, the Republican National Convention named Senator Barry Goldwater of Arizona as its candidate for President. He was leader of the conservative wing of the party, and his nomination represented the first time in forty years—since the days of Calvin Coolidge—that conservatives had controlled the Republican Convention. Goldwater had voted against the Civil Rights Act of 1964, and in his acceptance speech he appealed to ultra-rightist organizations with the phrases "extremism in the defense of liberty is no vice" and "moderation in the pursuit of justice is no virtue." His vice-presidential running mate was Representative William E. Miller of New York.

On July 2, 1964, President Johnson in a televised ceremony, a few hours after the House of Representatives approved Senate amendments to the Civil Rights Act of 1964, addressed the nation and signed the Bill in the presence of leaders of the House and Senate including the late Senator Robert F. Kennedy of New York *(third from the left, and continuing left to right)*, Senator Everett Dirksen of Illinois, Senator Hubert Humphrey of Minnesota, Representative Charles Halleck of Indiana, and *(right, one row to the rear)* the late Dr. Martin Luther King.

The Democratic National Convention that met in Atlantic City, New Jersey, in August adopted a platform plank that denounced "extremism" and named such organizations as the Communist party, the Ku Klux Klan, and the John Birch Society as examples of extremist groups. By acclamation the delegates nominated Johnson as their choice for President. Johnson flew to the convention while his nomination was underway, and minutes after it had been accomplished asked the delegates to nominate for Vice President Senator Hubert Humphrey of Minnesota as the man most fitted to succeed him. The delegates approved Humphrey without opposition.

In November the Johnson-Humphrey ticket won by one of the greatest landslides in American history, receiving 61.1% of the popular vote. Johnson won 43,129,484 votes to Goldwater's 27,178,188, and 486 electoral votes to Goldwater's 52. Johnson lost only in Alabama, Georgia, Louisiana, Mississippi, South Carolina, and Arizona. In addition the Democrats won increased majorities in both houses of Congress.

A conference, January 8, 1964, with the Joint Chiefs of Staff at the Johnson ranch in Johnson City, Texas, where the President grew up and has his private residence. *UPI photograph*

Holding the signed "Poverty" Bill, President Johnson stated that this legislative enactment on August 20, 1964 would mark the beginning of a new era in the United States' approach to the problems of the lower income groups, as Attorney General Robert Kennedy *(left)* held a discussion.

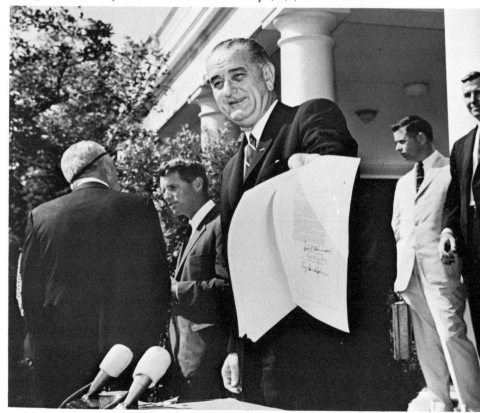

The President and his Lady enjoy a social function.

A cabinet meeting attended, among others, by *(clockwise)* Postmaster General John Gronouski, Ambassador to the United Nations Adlai Stevenson, Vice-President Hubert Humphrey, Secretary of Defense Robert McNamara, Secretary of Agriculture Orville Freeman, Secretary of Labor Willard Wirtz, Secretary of Health, Education and Welfare Anthony J. Celebrezze, Secretary of Commerce John T. Connor, Attorney General Nicholas Katzenbach, President Johnson, Secretary of the Interior Stewart Udall, with special assistants, Jack Valenti, Bill Moyer, and McGeorge Bundy *(in background at right)*.

Greetings from the home folks at San Marcos, Texas, were received by President Johnson, November 8, 1965, as he arrived for an inspection tour of the Gary Job Corps Training Center, after which he traveled to his alma mater, the Southwest Texas State College, to sign into law the Education Bill.

UPI photograph

President Johnson, in a ceremony at the Statue of Liberty in New York City, signed a bill abolishing the United States immigration quota system, October 3, 1965.

At Cam Ranh Bay, South Vietnam, President Johnson reviewing the troops during a visit to the huge supply base in November, 1966.

Unidentified GI in silent prayer over the grave of his fallen comrade, somewhere in Vietnam.

In his inaugural address on January 20, 1965, Johnson expressed his ideals and his hopes for the future:

"On this occasion, the oath I have taken before you—and before God—is not mine alone, but ours together. We are one nation and one people. Our fate as a nation and our future as a people rests not upon one citizen but upon all citizens. That is the majesty and the meaning of this moment. For every generation, there is a destiny. For some, history decides. For this generation, the choice must be our own. Even now, a rocket moves toward Mars. It reminds us that the world will not be the same for our children, or even for ourselves in a short span of years. The next man to stand here will look out on a scene that is different from our own, because ours is a time of change—rapid and fantastic change, baring the secrets of nature, multiplying the nations, placing in uncertain hands new weapons for mastery and destruction, shaking old values and uprooting old ways.

"Our destiny in the midst of change will rest on the unchanged character of our people—and on their faith. They came here—the exile and the stranger, brave but frightened—to find a place where a man could be his own man. They made a covenant with this land. Conceived in justice, written in liberty, bound in union, it was meant one day to inspire the hopes of all mankind. And it binds us still. If we keep its terms, we shall flourish. . . ."

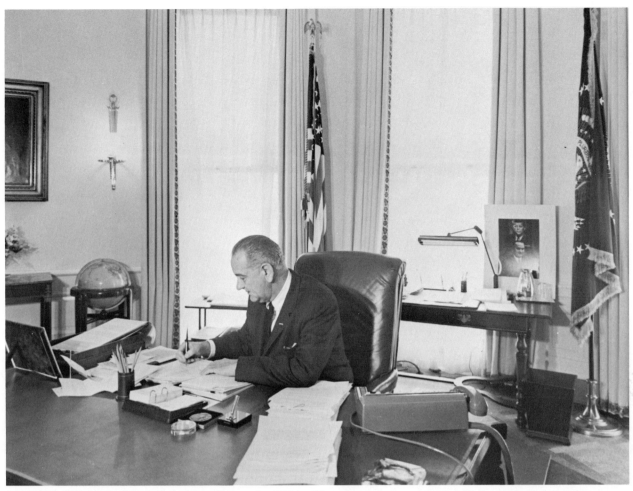

President Johnson at his desk in his office at the White House.

On June 11, 1968 Senator Eugene McCarthy of Minnesota, candidate for the Democratic nomination for the Presidency, visited the White House and was briefed by President Johnson on world conditions.

President Johnson and Premier Kosygin of Soviet Russia at their historic meeting in Glassboro, New Jersey, June 23, 1967.   *UPI photograph*

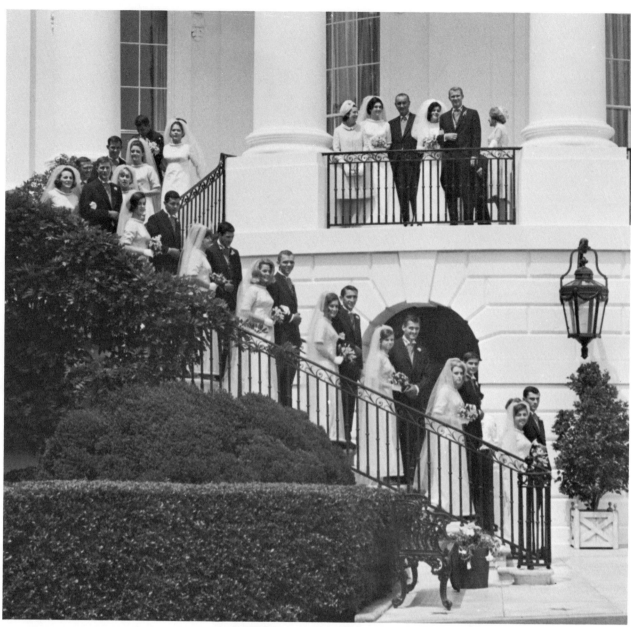

The White House social schedule was brightened by the wedding of Luci Johnson, the President's younger daughter, to Patrick Nugent, on August 6, 1966, as shown here on the south portico of the White House.

As President in his own right, Johnson met continued success in dealing with Congress for implementation of his Great Society domestic program. The Eighty-ninth Congress approved a multi-billion-dollar federal-aid-to-education program to improve schools and libraries at all grade levels. The social security system was expanded to provide medical care for persons over sixty-five. The anti-poverty program was expanded. A new civil rights bill was approved to insure the rights of blacks to register to vote. A new cabinet-level Department of Housing and Urban Development was created in 1966 to aid cities in attacking their problems of housing and planning. And in 1967 a new Department of Transportation was established.

However, blacks did not feel that progress was being made fast enough in the implementation of civil rights legislation. Riots broke out in the black slum areas of many cities throughout Johnson's second term. In 1968 after the assassination of black civil rights leader Martin Luther King Jr., federal troops had to be called out to restore order in the nation's capital itself.

In foreign affairs Johnson received considerable criticism for his handling of crises in the Dominican Republic and in Vietnam. In April 1965, when a revolt broke out in the Dominican Republic, Johnson sent 20,000 U.S. troops to intervene, explaining that he was preventing Communists from taking over the government as had occurred in Cuba. Later the American troops were placed under supervision of the Organization of American States, and elections were held in 1966 to permit the Dominican Republic to choose a new government.

In Vietnam, President Johnson faced a more complex problem. Under Presidents Eisenhower and Kennedy military supplies and advisers had been sent to help the South Vietnamese preserve their freedom in a guerrilla war with Communists from North Vietnam. Then in 1964 U.S. destroyers in the Gulf of Tonkin were attacked by North Vietnamese torpedo boats. On Aug. 7, 1964, Congress approved the "Tonkin resolution" giving the President authority "to prevent further aggression." Johnson ordered bombing attacks on North Vietnam and sent U.S. troops to fight side by side with the South Vietnamese soldiers. By 1968 more than half a million U.S. soldiers were fighting in Vietnam. But the South Vietnamese themselves, with no tradition of democracy, seemed incapable of finding a government of their own that could inspire a unified effort.

The Vietnam War seriously divided the United States. Critics of the war demanded that Johnson unconditionally end the bombing of North Vietnam and were supported in this demand by Secretary General U Thant of the United Nations. But President Johnson insisted that the United States should not stop the bombing unless North Vietnam also reduced its war efforts. Some critics of the administration urged young men of draft age to refuse to fight in Vietnam and some did so. On the other hand, other groups called on Johnson to step up the war and win a clear-cut victory over North Vietnam.

In the Congressional elections of 1966, the Democratic party retained its control of both the Senate and the House of Representatives, but with greatly reduced majorities. Public opinion polls showed that Johnson had lost much of his popularity with the voters, largely because of the growing anti-war sentiment.

Johnson had repeatedly sent messages to North Vietnam asking for negotiations to end the fighting. But the North Vietnamese rejected these messages, insisting that the United States end its bombing of North Vietnam and withdraw its forces from South Vietnam. Finally, in a dramatic television address to the American people on March 31, 1968, President Johnson announced that he was calling a partial halt to the bombing in an effort to show America's seriousness of intention in wanting negotiations. At the same time, to remove all possibility that his move might be interpreted as promoting his own political fortune, Johnson unexpectedly announced that he would not be a candidate for another term as President. North Vietnam responded favorably, and in May face-to-face negotiations began between American and North Vietnamese emissaries in Paris.

The Vietnam peace talks dragged on through the summer of 1968 with the North Vietnamese insisting that all bombing of North Vietnam must

A second romance blossomed during the Johnson Presidency — that of Lynda Johnson and Marine Corps Captain Charles Robb.

U.S. Marines at Khe Sanh, South Vietnam, using their helmets to block the deafening roar of helicopters.   *UPI photograph*

President Johnson bidding good-bye to his Secretary of State, Dean Rusk, at a State Department reception honoring the President on January 16, 1969.

—UPI photograph

be halted before any agreements could be reached. Then on October 31 President Johnson announced that he was ordering an end to all bombing of North Vietnam and that the Paris peace talks would be expanded to include representatives of the South Vietnam government and the Vietcong, the communist rebels of South Vietnam. But subsequent resistance by the South Vietnamese to sitting down with their communist enemies delayed resumption of the talks despite the bombing halt.

In deciding not to run for another term, Johnson followed the historic precedent that no "accidental" President ever had been twice elected to the presidency. All those before him had either not tried or had failed if they did try, including John Tyler, Millard Fillmore, Andrew Johnson, Chester Arthur, Theodore Roosevelt, Calvin Coolidge, and Harry S Truman. And, in fact, only one Vice-President ever had been twice elected President—Thomas Jefferson, who had served as Vice-President under John Adams.

After Johnson's withdrawal from the 1968 political race, one of the leading contenders for the Democratic presidential nomination became New York Senator Robert F. Kennedy, who had served as Attorney General both under his brother, John F. Kennedy, and under Johnson. Kennedy strongly opposed the Vietnam War and spoke out for greater efforts to help blacks and the poor. Early in June he had just won the important California Democratic primary when he was shot down by an assassin just as his brother had been.

The nation became deeply concerned by the violence in the United States that had seen six assassinations in less than five years—those of the Kennedy brothers, of King and two other black leaders, Medgar Evers and Malcolm X, and of American Nazi leader George Lincoln Rockwell. Johnson appointed a presidential commission to study all aspects of violence in American society and at the same time urged Congress to put stricter controls on the sale and ownership of guns.

In the 1968 presidential campaign, Johnson helped Vice President Humphrey win the Democratic presidential nomination. He was disappointed when Humphrey was narrowly defeated by the Republican nominee, former Vice President Richard Nixon. But he received some satisfaction in that the Republicans were unable to win a majority in either house of Congress.

Johnson had been an ardent supporter of the nation's space program from its outset when he was a senator. So it gave him great pleasure in the last month of his administration—in Christmas week 1968—when three American astronauts in the Apollo 8 spaceship successfully made man's first deep flight into space, spectacularly orbiting the moon ten times before returning safely to earth.

When Johnson won the presidency by a landslide in 1964 and as he ramrodded through Congress his liberal legislative program in 1965 and 1966, it had seemed he might go down in history as one of the nation's great Presidents. But his inability to bring the Vietnam War to a successful conclusion and the spirit of discontent and domestic violence that developed in the latter years of his administration doomed him to a place in history as a President who was something less than great.

Johnson himself summarized the difficulties he had faced with public opinion:

". . . a President must do what he thinks is right. He must think in terms of the national interest and the Nation's security—even if this means stirring up some segments of public opinion, no matter how vocif-

Lyndon Baines Johnson, September 18, 1972

—Frank Wolfe

erous. I confess that on the home front it is easier for the public to understand what an administration is planning to do. They see that some of our schools are overcrowded, that we must do something to help our Negro citizens, that we are rapidly outgrowing our cities, and they are responsive to programs that seek remedies. But when the President takes an extremely serious step in foreign matters, then it is really a more difficult proposition for people to grasp."

On his last full day in office, Sunday, January 19, 1969, President Johnson composed a prayer that expressed his hopes for the nation and the world. The prayer, which was read to the congregation of Washington's National City Christian Church that Johnson and his family attended, said in part:

"Blind our eyes to the colors of men's skins, close our hearts against hate and violence, and will our souls with a love of justice and compassion. May we, as a nation, deserve no enemies, and be worthy of all our friends, striving without ceasing for a day when mankind shall not know war anymore."

After leaving the Presidency, Johnson lived quietly at his LBJ Ranch at Johnson City, Texas, making few public appearances. On January 22, 1973, less than a month after the death of former President Truman, the sixty-four-year-old Johnson died of a heart attack at his ranch. Ironically, his death came just one day before an agreement was initialed in Paris to end the Vietnam War, for which he had sacrificed his political career. However, it was disclosed that shortly before his death, he had been informed by phone by President Nixon of the impending peace agreement.

Johnson's body was flown to Washington for memorial services in the same plane aboard which he had been sworn in as President nine years earlier. After the services in the nation's capital, his body was flown back to Texas and buried in a family graveyard a few hundred feet from his birthplace in Stonewall, Texas.

When he learned of Johnson's death, President Nixon said:

"No man had greater dreams for America than Lyndon Johnson. Even as we mourn his death, we are grateful for his life, which did so much to make those dreams into reality. And we know that so long as this nation lives, so will his dreams and his accomplishments."

The Johnsons and their dog, Yukie, at the LBJ Ranch at Johnson City, Texas, November 6, 1972.
—*Frank Wolfe*

The Lyndon Baines Johnson Library on the University of Texas campus in Austin, opened in 1971.   —*The Lyndon Baines Johnson Library*

48 JOHN FITZGERALD KENNEDY

John Fitzgerald Kennedy

The Thirty-fifth President of the United States
1961–63

1917 (May 29) Born in Brookline, Massachusetts.

1935 Attended Princeton University.

1936–40 Attended Harvard University, graduating *cum laude.*

1940 Published his first book, *Why England Slept,* which became a best seller.

1940–41 Attended Stanford University graduate business school.

1941–45 Served in World War II in the U.S. Navy, rising from seaman to lieutenant (senior grade).

1945 Worked as a newspaper reporter.

1947–52 U.S. representative from Massachusetts.

1953–60 U.S. senator from Massachusetts.

1953 (September 12) Married Jacqueline Lee Bouvier.

1956 Published *Profiles in Courage,* a best-selling book that won Kennedy a Pulitzer prize.

1961–63 Thirty-fifth President of the United States.

1963 (November 22) Assassinated in Dallas, Texas.

Leading Officials in
Kennedy's Administration

Office	Name	Years Served
Chief Justice	Earl Warren	1953-1969
Vice-President	Lyndon B. Johnson	1961-1963
Secretary of State	Dean Rusk	1961-1969
Secretary of the Treasury	C. Douglas Dillon	1961-1965
Secretary of Defense	Robert S. McNamara	1961-1968
Attorney General	Robert F. Kennedy	1961-1964
Postmaster General	J. Edward Day	1961-1963
	John A. Gronouski, Jr.	1963-1965
Secretary of the Interior	Stewart L. Udall	1961-1969
Secretary of Agriculture	Orville L. Freeman	1961-1969
Secretary of Commerce	Luther H. Hodges	1961-1964
Secretary of Labor	Arthur J. Goldberg	1961-1962
	W. Willard Wirtz	1962-1969
Secretary of Health, Education, and Welfare	Abraham A. Ribicoff	1961-1962
	Anthony J. Celebrezze	1962-1965

One of the buildings of the Choate School in Wallingford, Connecticut, where John Kennedy, as a prep school student, developed an early interest in history and economics.　　　　　　　　　　*—UPI photograph*

The first President born in the twentieth century, John Fitzgerald Kennedy captured the imagination of the nation's youth with his vigorous and idealistic "New Frontier" program. At forty-three he was the youngest man ever elected President—symbolizing, in his own words, "renewal as well as change" in taking over the White House from the oldest President who had ever served. In his inaugural address Kennedy prophetically warned that his far-reaching program would not be completed "in the life of this Administration, nor even perhaps in our lifetime on this planet." And to the grief and horror of the nation these words came true when an assassin killed him after he had served in office only two years and ten months.

As the first Roman Catholic to become President, Kennedy won out over the religious bigotry that had helped defeat Al Smith thirty years earlier. His election victory over Republican Vice President Richard M. Nixon also was hailed as a triumph for the modern communication marvel of television, because he overshadowed his better-known opponent in a series of TV debates during the political campaign. But Kennedy's plurality was the smallest in history—only .2% of the popular vote. This narrow victory margin made it difficult for him to lead Congress during his short administration.

The focus of attention throughout most of Kennedy's presidency was on foreign affairs. Both Russia and the United States increased the pace of their nuclear arms race, stockpiling hydrogen bombs, building more and more sophisticated long-range guided missiles, and increasing the sizes of their armies. The Cold War reached a climax in October 1962, when Russia secretly began arming Cuba with atomic missiles. Kennedy coolly ordered a naval blockade of the island. For several days Russia and the United States stood "eyeball to eyeball," in the words of Secretary of State Dean Rusk, and then Russia backed down, removing the missiles from Cuba. Tension was further eased in August 1963, when the United States, Great Britain, and Russia signed a treaty ending the testing of atomic weapons in the earth's atmosphere.

In the speech which he had prepared for delivery on the day that he was killed, Kennedy had written:

"We in this country, in this generation, are, by destiny rather than choice, the watchmen on the walls of world freedom. We ask, therefore, that we may be worthy of our power and responsibility, that we may exercise our strength with wisdom and restraint, and that we may achieve in our time and for all time the ancient vision of 'peace on earth, good will toward men.' That must always be our goal—and the righteousness of our cause must always underlie our strength. For as was written long ago: 'Except the Lord keep the city, the watchman waketh but in vain.'"

LIKE Theodore Roosevelt and Franklin D. Roosevelt, John Kennedy was the son of wealthy parents. Born on May 29, 1917, in Brookline, Massachusetts, he was the second of nine children of Joseph and Rose Kennedy. His father, one of the wealthiest men in the United States, served in various important government posts in Franklin Roosevelt's administration. His mother was the daughter of a former mayor of Boston.

While Jack was in elementary school, his father moved the family to New York, where they lived first in Riverdale, and then in Bronxville, an exclusive suburb north of New York City. After completing sixth grade in the Bronxville public schools, the thirteen-year-old Jack Kennedy was sent first to Canterbury School in New Milford, Connecticut, a Roman Catholic private school, then to Choate, a non-sectarian private school, in Wallingford, Connecticut. Although an average student, with a scholastic rank barely in the upper half of his class, he was recognized by his classmates as "most likely to succeed."

As they grew up, Jack and his brothers and sisters led an active life in vacation periods when they were all together. In winter they vacationed in Palm Beach, Florida, and in summers lived at Hyannis Port, Massachusetts, on Cape Cod. There was much swimming, tennis, boating, touch football, and other sports and games.

The summer after graduating from Choate, eighteen-year-old Jack went to England to study under socialist professor Harold Laski at the London School of Economics, but an attack of jaundice caused him to drop out of this school. Returning to the United States, he matriculated at Princeton, but after two months a recurrence of jaundice again forced him to drop his studies.

After recovering his health, Jack entered Harvard, his father's alma mater. For the first three years his grades were mostly "C's," but in his senior year he blossomed as he concentrated on courses in economics and political science. A thesis that he wrote discussing the British and French appeasement of Hitler at Munich won such faculty praise that he was graduated with honors in 1940.

Encouraged by the praise he had received for his thesis, the twenty-three-year-old Kennedy decided to expand it and try to get it published as a book. Under the title *Why England Slept*, the book became a best seller soon after it was published in the summer of 1940.

In the winter of 1940–41, while his father had a falling out with President Roosevelt and was forced to resign as ambassador to England because of anti-British statements, Jack Kennedy attended graduate business school at Stanford University. In the spring of 1941 he signed up for an enlistment in the Army, but was turned down because of a back injury he had received playing football. After taking a strenuous course of exercises, he passed a Navy physical and was accepted as a seaman in September 1941.

For more than a year, even after the Japanese attack on Pearl Harbor, Kennedy's military duties were routine desk jobs. Finally, he asked his father to use his influence to get him sea duty. He soon was assigned to

PT-boat training, received a commission as a lieutenant (j.g.), and in March 1943, was given command of his own torpedo boat in the South Pacific.

In the early morning darkness of August 2, 1943, a Japanese destroyer sliced through Kennedy's PT 109 west of New Georgia island. Two of the crew were killed, but Kennedy and ten others clung to the wreckage. After fifteen hours in the water they reached a tiny island. Kennedy kept up the men's courage and for four days they swam from island to island until they found some natives who took a message carved on a coconut to the nearest Navy base. When rescued, Kennedy discovered he and his crew had been given up as lost and their families had been notified of their deaths.

Sick with malaria and a recurrence of his old back injury, Kennedy was returned to the United States. He was in a Navy hospital near Boston when word came that his older brother, Joe, had been killed while flying a bomber in Europe. Discharged from the Navy early in 1945 because of his physical condition, Kennedy covered the United Nations organizational meeting in San Francisco as a reporter for the Hearst newspapers. Later that year he reported the British elections for Hearst, and then dropped newspaper work to try his hand at politics.

Winning the Presidency

KENNEDY later explained that he entered politics "because Joe died"—his elder brother having been counted on as the member of the family most likely to go far in politics. At twenty-eight, gray-eyed, curly-headed John Kennedy took up residence in Boston and began a campaign to win the Democratic nomination for Congress in the Eleventh District. Most of the members of the Kennedy family plunged in to help the campaign, hundreds of house parties were held for voters, and when the primary election was held in June 1946, "the poor little rich kid"—as one opponent called him—beat out the nine other candidates for the nomination. In November he easily overcame his Republican opponent in the normally Democratic district. He repeated his congressional election victory twice, in 1948 and in 1950.

During his six years as a U.S. representative from Massachusetts, Kennedy lived the carefree life of a bachelor. He supported most of President Truman's "Fair Deal" program against the combination of conservative Republicans and Southern Democrats that opposed it. When the leaders of the American Legion opposed a bill he had introduced for federal funds for slum clearance and low-cost housing, Kennedy denounced them as having "not had a constructive thought for the benefit of this country since 1918." As a congressman he insisted that federal aid to education must be for both parochial and public schools, contributing to the defeat of federal aid to education at that time. From time to time he attacked President Truman's foreign policy, particularly the loss of China to the Communists, the reduction of U.S. forces in Europe during the Korean War, and the huge expenditures of money in foreign aid to other parts of the world.

In the spring of 1952 the thirty-five-year-old Kennedy began a campaign for U.S. senator from Massachusetts against Republican Henry Cabot Lodge, Jr., who had held the office since 1936 except for a period of military service in World War II. As his campaign manager, Kennedy chose his twenty-seven-year-old brother, Robert, who directed the spending of about $500,000 on the contest. Again, all the Kennedys pitched in to help, holding receptions and coffee parties for voters, knocking on doors, and asking everyone to vote for Jack. On election day he beat Lodge with a plurality of 70,000 votes, although the Republicans won the state governorship and Eisenhower carried the state by more than 200,000. This made Kennedy the leading Democrat in Massachusetts, and an important figure nationally.

Two years earlier Kennedy had met Jacqueline Lee Bouvier, an attractive co-ed at George Washington University. Kennedy was thirty-six and Jackie, an inquiring photographer for the Washington *Times-Herald*, was twenty-four when they were married on September 12, 1953. They had three children, one of whom died shortly after birth.

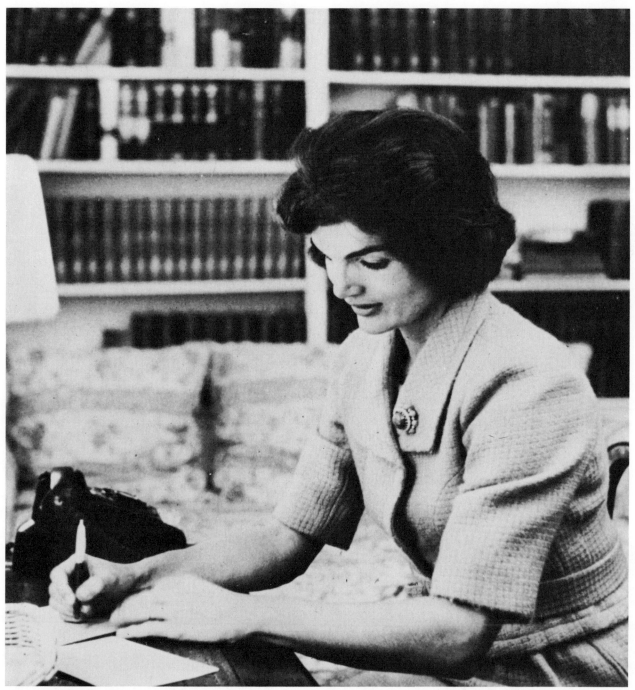

Mrs. John F. Kennedy (Jacqueline Lee Bouvier), whose grace and charm made her a national heroine during the presidential campaign of 1960, the three years of the Kennedy administration, and during the sad days following the assassination.

Dexter School's first football team, of which Joseph *(circle)*, the oldest of the Kennedy brothers, and John *(lower right)* were members, in 1926.

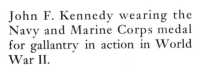

John F. Kennedy wearing the Navy and Marine Corps medal for gallantry in action in World War II.

Joseph P. Kennedy arriving in New York at Christmas time on a visit from Great Britain with his son, John Kennedy—a happy young man of twenty-one in 1938.

On the eve of Election Day, nominee for President, Senator John F. Kennedy, Mrs. Kennedy, and Caroline, awaiting the returns at their Hyannis Port home, November 8, 1960.

Caroline Kennedy's pony, Macaroni, grazing on the White House lawn, March 16, 1962.

(Right) At Hyannis Port, Massachusetts, shortly after announcing their engagement in 1953, John Kennedy and Jacqueline Lee Bouvier were a happy couple.

(Left) John Kennedy, Jr.'s famous farewell salute to his father.

Baptism of John F. Kennedy, Jr. by Father Martin Casey in the chapel of Georgetown Hospital, on December 8, 1960, with his parents watching. Mr. and Mrs. Charles L. Bartlett were godmother and acting godfather (for Prince Stanislaus Radziwill).

The Kennedy brothers in September, 1959—Robert *(left)* and John *(right)*, discussing the Rackets Hearing with their youngest brother, Edward (Ted), a graduate of the University of Virginia Law School.

Senator John F. Kennedy looking toward his mother and sister Pat, as he listened to the applause, after being named Democratic candidate for the Presidency, July 13, 1960.

Enthusiastic crowds greeted President Kennedy wherever he traveled, as demonstrated during his visit to Cork, Ireland, in June, 1963.

Robert Kennedy, a key member of the Kennedy team, relaxing for a moment during the hectic intra-party struggle for the Democratic nomination for President in 1960.

All photographs on this double-spread courtesy of UPI

President Kennedy, who spoke to an enthusiastic crowd in Berlin in July, 1963, inspecting the Berlin Wall.

In 1946, at the age of twenty-nine, John Kennedy ran for Representative to Congress from the Eleventh Congressional District of Massachusetts.

Mrs. John F. Kennedy looking on, as the 1960 rivals for the Presidency shook hands at Midway Airport, Chicago. *—UPI photograph*

The freshman senator from Massachusetts was first assigned to two committees, the Labor and Public Welfare Committee, and the Government Operations Committee, the chairman of which was Senator Joseph McCarthy of Wisconsin. John's younger brother Robert worked for the McCarthy committee as an attorney. By 1954 McCarthyism—the charges of Communism and pro-Communism against public officials—had become one of the central issues of American politics. John Kennedy attempted to sit on the fence between those who admired and those who loathed the

—UPI photograph

During the last big campaign rally before the election, held at the New York Coliseum, November 5, 1960, Mrs. Franklin Roosevelt appeared with candidates John F. Kennedy and Lyndon B. Johnson *(left and right, respectively)*.

McCarthy investigations, and when the Senate voted to censure Mc-Carthy, was in a hospital recovering from surgery to correct his old back ailment.

While there he filled in his time writing *Profiles in Courage,* a series of biographies of senators who had taken courageous stands throughout American history. Published in 1956 the book became a best seller, and won Kennedy the Pulitzer Prize for biography. It also won him considerable popularity among literary liberals.

After returning to the Senate in 1955, Kennedy took the leadership in a fight to prevent a constitutional amendment to change the Electoral College system. This amendment, sponsored by conservatives, would have made it possible for losing candidates to receive a proportion of a state's electoral vote—in effect it would have reduced the political effectiveness of minority groups that sometimes swing an entire state's vote to one candidate. Kennedy again picked up liberal support by helping defeat the amendment.

With the approach of the 1956 presidential campaign, Kennedy made an effort to win the vice-presidential nomination on the ticket with Adlai Stevenson. At the Chicago convention, Kennedy was chosen to place Adlai Stevenson in nomination for President. After Stevenson won the presidential nomination on the first ballot, a fight for the vice-presidential nomination developed between Kennedy and Senator Estes Kefauver of Tennessee. On the first ballot Kefauver led, on the second ballot Kennedy jumped into the lead, but on the third ballot Kefauver won. Kennedy went on to help campaign for the Stevenson-Kefauver ticket, making speeches in twenty-six states.

When Kennedy was appointed to the Senate Foreign Relations Committee in 1957, he began to be listened to more and more on foreign affairs. He created a particular furor when he recommended that the United States support Algerian nationalists to obtain freedom from France. He also began to speak about the "missile gap" between the United States and Russia—warning that President Eisenhower had weakened national defense so much that Russia was moving ahead in the production of intercontinental ballistic missiles with which to wage an atomic war.

With an eye to the Democratic presidential nomination in 1960, Kennedy's voting record in the Senate became increasingly liberal. He supported the compromise civil rights legislation in 1957—the first such measure since Reconstruction days, spoke widely throughout the country, and wrote many articles for magazines. Public opinion polls showed him as the leading contender for the next presidential nomination by his party. In his re-election for senator in 1958 he proved his power as a vote getter, receiving the largest plurality ever given a candidate in Massachusetts to that time—a record 875,000 votes more than his Republican opponent.

The efforts of all the Kennedy family concentrated for the next two years on winning Jack the presidential nomination. Robert Kennedy managed the campaign, as he had his brother's previous successes. To show his political strength, Kennedy went into presidential preference primaries in seven states and won them all. After defeating Senator Hubert Humphrey of Minnesota in the hotly contested West Virginia primary, Humphrey withdrew from the race. This left as Kennedy's main opponents Senator Lyndon Johnson of Texas, the majority leader of the Senate; Senator Stuart Symington of Missouri, formerly Secretary of the Air Force under President Truman; and Adlai Stevenson.

By the time the delegates met at the Democratic Convention in Los Angeles in July, Kennedy had the nomination all but wrapped up. He

When John F. Kennedy's name was put in for nomination as Democratic presidential candidate, this huge papier-mâché likeness of Kennedy was paraded around the hall. *—UPI photograph*

Former President Truman and President Kennedy at the White House the day after the inauguration, January 21, 1961.

Kennedy's Administration

Senator Eugene McCarthy of Minnesota at the rostrum as he nominated Adlai Stevenson for the Presidency at the Democratic National Convention, July, 1960.

won on the first ballot with 806 votes to Johnson's 409, Symington's 86, and Stevenson's 79½, and topped off his triumph by persuading Johnson to accept the vice-presidential nomination.

The Republicans met at Chicago shortly thereafter to nominate Vice President Richard M. Nixon. As their vice-presidential nominee they chose Henry Cabot Lodge, Jr., U.S. delegate to the United Nations.

The highlight of the political campaign was the series of four televised debates between Kennedy and Nixon—the first time in history that most of the American people were able to see and hear both major party candidates state their views and question each other face-to-face. The Democratic platform on which Kennedy and Johnson ran was the most liberal ever presented up to that time by a political party. It promised greatly expanded civil rights for minorities and an enlarged social security program. Nixon and Lodge ran largely on the record of the Eisenhower administration.

In the election the vote was so close that the result was in doubt until the next day. Kennedy received 34,227,096 votes to Nixon's 34,108,546, and 303 electoral votes to Nixon's 219.

A BLIZZARD had filled the streets of Washington with snow on January 20, 1961, when the forty-three-year-old Kennedy was sworn in as President. His inspirational inaugural address was aimed primarily at the youth of the country. In it he said:

". . . Let the word go forth from this time and place, to friend and foe alike, that the torch has been passed to a new generation of Americans, born in this century, tempered by war, disciplined by a hard and bitter peace, proud of our ancient heritage, and unwilling to witness or permit the slow undoing of those human rights to which this nation has always been committed, and to which we are committed today at home and around the world.

"Let every nation know, whether it wishes us well or ill, that we shall pay any price, bear any burden, meet any hardship, support any friend, oppose any foe to assure the survival and the success of liberty.

". . . In the long history of the world, only a few generations have been granted the role of defending freedom in its hour of maximum danger. I do not shrink from this responsibility; I welcome it. I do not believe that any of us would exchange places with any other people or any other generation. The energy, the faith, the devotion which we bring to this endeavor will light our country and all who serve it, and the glow from that fire can truly light the world.

"And so, my fellow Americans, ask not what your country can do for you; ask what you can do for your country. . . ."

In his State of the Union address less than two weeks later, Kennedy told a joint session of Congress:

". . . No man entering upon this office, regardless of his party, regardless of his previous service in Washington, could fail to be staggered upon learning, even in this brief ten-day period, the harsh enormity of the trials through which we must pass in the next four years. Each day the crises multiply. Each day their solution grows more difficult. Each day we draw nearer the hour of maximum danger, as weapons spread and hostile forces grow stronger."

Breaking precedent, President Kennedy appointed his younger brother Robert, to his Cabinet as Attorney General. He relied heavily on "Bobby" as an adviser on all critical policy decisions. In 1962 his youngest brother, Edward, was elected U.S. senator from Massachusetts. This was the first time that three members of the same family ever had held such high

President Kennedy being greeted by Vice-President Johnson on the White House lawn, April 7, 1961.
—*UPI photograph*

Premier Nikita S. Khrushchev of Soviet Russia and President John F. Kennedy conversing at the Russian Embassy in Vienna on June 4, 1961, at a time when the relations between the two countries were unusually strained. —*UPI photograph*

Two former Presidents, Harry Truman and Dwight Eisenhower, and President John Kennedy, attending the burial of the Speaker of the House, Sam Rayburn, in Bonham, Texas, on November 18, 1962. —*UPI photograph*

A gathering on the south lawn of the White House in April, 1962, with Mrs. John Kennedy in the foreground.

President and Mrs. Kennedy *(foreground)* surrounded by hundreds of foreign students on the White House lawn. Viewing the proceedings from the balcony *(indicated by arrow in left photo)* is three-year-old Caroline Kennedy *(in the close-up at the right)*.

—UPI photograph

President John F. Kennedy's extreme popularity with foreigners was demonstrated during his visit to Mexico City, June 29, 1962.
—UPI photograph

A concert on the south lawn of the White House in August, 1962, typifying the Kennedys' encouragement of all types of cultural activity.

President Kennedy on the occasion of his signing of the Douglas Bill, September 5, 1962.

The President applauding the First Lady following a speech she delivered on November 29, 1962, with Vice-President Johnson applauding on the left.

President Kennedy congratulating Astronaut Alan B. Shepard, Jr., first U.S. man in space, on his historic feat.　　　　　　—*NASA*

positions at the same time in the federal government. Naturally, there was considerable discussion of the Kennedy family influence by the President's opponents, but he shrugged off all criticism.

During his first several months in office Kennedy sent many messages to Congress outlining in detail the legislation that he wanted to carry out his "New Frontier" program. However, the Eighty-seventh Congress was slow to act, and a coalition of conservative Democrats and Republicans blocked the passage of many of his proposals.

In the political campaign and in his State of the Union message Kennedy had called for the establishment of a peace corps "enlisting the services of all those with the desire and capacity to help foreign lands meet their urgent needs for trained personnel." This program, which appealed especially to college students, was passed by Congress in March 1961. Kennedy appointed one of his brothers-in-law, Sargent Shriver, to direct the Peace Corps, which became one of the Kennedy administration's most successful achievements.

The next month Kennedy suffered his greatest defeat in foreign relations. On April 17 an army of Cuban exiles attempted to invade Cuba to overthrow the government of dictator Fidel Castro. The exiles had been trained by the CIA, the U.S. government's top intelligence agency, but the invasion of the Bay of Pigs failed miserably with more than 1000 of the exiles taken prisoner. Kennedy took personal responsibility for the failure, although the project had been started under the Eisenhower administration.

A new Kennedy-sponsored foreign-aid program to Latin America was launched in 1961 under the name Alliance for Progress. The program called for a ten-year plan to develop the resources of Latin American countries.

In Europe, relations with Russia continued to deteriorate. Kennedy flew to Vienna in June 1961 to confer for two days with Russian Prime Minister Khrushchev about Russian threats that Communist East Germany would be given control of supply routes to West Berlin. No agreements were reached at the meeting. In August the Communists built a high wall to seal off West Berlin from East Berlin in order to prevent the escape of East Berliners to the West. Kennedy later said of it: ". . . the wall is the most obvious and vivid demonstration of the failures of the Communist system . . ."

When Kennedy became President the economy had been undergoing a mild recession for several months, but by the end of his first year in office he was able to report that the country was "on the highroad of recovery and growth." The minimum hourly wage had been raised to $1.25. In the Trade Expansion Act, Congress had given Kennedy new powers to reduce tariffs. Defense spending had been increased, and the number of nuclear submarines and intercontinental ballistic missiles had been expanded. But Congress failed to act on Kennedy's requests for improved civil rights measures, medical care for the aged financed by social security, or broad federal aid to education. Even after the Democrats won the mid-term congressional elections of 1962, Kennedy continued to have difficulty getting Congress to go along with his proposals for major domestic legislation.

Kennedy won great praise for his handling of the crisis over Cuba in 1962 that came close to starting World War III. Dictator Fidel Castro of Cuba had revealed in December 1961 that he was a Communist and that he was aligning Cuba with Russia and China. Russia began supplying military aid to Cuba. Then, in October 1962, U.S. aerial photos of Cuba showed that missiles were being installed that could launch atomic war-

Obviously enjoying the occasion, President Kennedy faces the press at the State Department.

Early in his administration President Kennedy sustained his only real reverse, as a result of the abortive effort of the Cuban exiles to overturn the Cuban communist regime of Castro. Although not involved in the planning of the invasion, he acknowledged that, as President, he could have stopped it but did not. After months of negotiations, he succeeded in getting back more than twelve hundred of the prisoners captured by the Communists. These are scenes at the Orange Bowl in Florida, December 29, 1962, when the President and Mrs. Kennedy greeted some 35,000 Cuban exiles. —*UPI photographs*

On the occasion of the unveiling of Leonardo da Vinci's "Mona Lisa," on loan from the Louvre, President Kennedy, Mrs. Malraux, André Malraux, France's minister of cultural affairs, Mrs. John F. Kennedy, and Vice-President Johnson visited the National Gallery of Art, Washington, D. C., to commemorate the opening, January 8, 1963.

President and Mrs. Kennedy passing the old State Department building during a parade in honor of a visit by the King of Morocco, March 27, 1963.

Adlai Stevenson, former United States Ambassador to the United Nations and twice Democratic nominee for President, with President Kennedy *(left, foreground)*, speaking on the occasion of the issuance of a stamp honoring the late Mrs. Franklin D. Roosevelt. One of her sons, Representative James Roosevelt of California, and her grandson Hall Delano Roosevelt are behind the speaker *(at the left).*   *—UPI photograph*

heads at the United States or Latin America. Kennedy ordered a blockade of Cuba and insisted that Russia dismantle the missile bases and remove the missiles. Although he did not directly say so, Kennedy implied that the United States would bomb the bases if U.S. demands were not met. When Russian Premier Khrushchev ordered the missiles withdrawn, the threat of war was averted.

Under President Eisenhower, Russia and the United States had reached an unofficial understanding ending the testing of atomic weapons because of the danger of contaminating the earth's atmosphere with radiation. But in September 1961, Russia resumed such testing, and Kennedy ordered the resumption of U.S. atomic tests shortly after. Kennedy then initiated discussions with Russia that led to the signing of a treaty on August 5, 1963, banning nuclear tests in the earth's atmosphere. The United States, Russia, and Great Britain originally signed the treaty and other nations subscribed to it later.

Many persons saw the nuclear test ban treaty as the basis for hope that further agreements might be reached with Russia to reduce the possibility of nuclear war. To such persons, Kennedy said, "Let us always make clear our willingness to talk, if talk will help, and our readiness to fight, if fight we must. Let us resolve to be the masters, not the victims, of our history, controlling our own destiny without giving way to blind suspicion and emotion. . . ."

The revolutionary drive for Negro civil rights continued under President Kennedy, who sent federal marshals to Montgomery, Alabama, in 1961, when riots grew out of a Negro boycott of a bus line. Federal troops had to intervene in riots at the University of Mississippi in 1962 when Negro James Meredith insisted on his right to enroll at that previously all white school. In 1963 Kennedy twice had to call the National Guard into federal service in Alabama to protect Negroes seeking to integrate schools. In August 1963, about 200,000 Negro and white civil rights demonstrators came to Washington on a "Freedom March," demanding action on civil rights legislation Kennedy had sent to Congress. In a television address to the American people, he said, "One hundred years of delay have passed since President Lincoln freed the slaves, yet their heirs, their grandsons, are not fully free. They are not yet freed from the bonds of injustice. They are not yet freed from social and economic oppression, and this

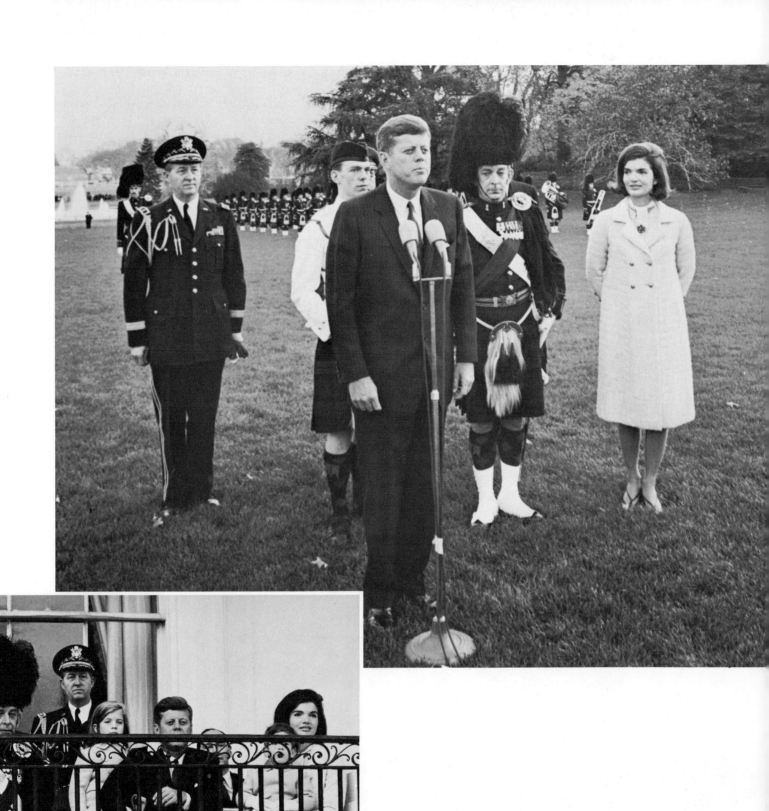

On November 13, 1963, the Kennedys reviewed Scotland's Black Watch drill team performing on the White House lawn.

nation, for all its hopes and all its boasts, will not be fully free until all its citizens are free. . . ."

Throughout his administration Kennedy pressed the nation's scientists to step up the race with Russia for the mastery of outer space. In April 1961, the Russians had sent the first man into space, and the next month the United States had sent up its first astronaut. Kennedy promised that the United States would be the first to land a man on the moon. He said, "We choose to go to the moon in this decade, and do the other things, not because they are easy but because they are hard; because that goal will serve to organize and measure the best of our energies and skills; because that challenge is one that we are willing to accept, one we are unwilling to postpone, and one which we intend to win . . ."

The Assassination

In November 1963, Kennedy went on a speaking trip to Texas. He dedicated a new Aero-Space Medical Health Center at Brooks Air Force Base, spoke at a dinner in Houston, and next day at a breakfast in Fort Worth. At noon on November 22 he was scheduled to speak at a luncheon in Dallas.

While driving in a motorcade through the streets of Dallas, Kennedy was struck in the head and neck by rifle bullets fired by an assassin and died a few minutes later. The governor of Texas, John B. Connally, who was riding with him also was seriously wounded, but later recovered. Lee Harvey Oswald, an emotionally unbalanced former U.S. Marine who believed in communism and had once renounced his U.S. citizenship to live in Russia, was arrested as the assassin after he killed a Dallas policeman while trying to evade arrest. Two days later, as millions of Americans watched in shocked horror on television, Oswald himself was shot dead by a Dallas nightclub owner, Jack Ruby. Ten months later a commission headed by Chief Justice Earl Warren certified Oswald's guilt, but without being able to establish a motive other than his "deep-rooted resentment of all authority." In succeeding years many persons claimed Oswald was part of a larger conspiracy against Kennedy.

President Kennedy, in the presence of many legislators and other dignitaries, signing the Nuclear Test Ban Treaty, considered one of the great accomplishments of his administration.

Foreign dignitaries leaving the White House to walk behind the caisson en route to St. Matthew's Cathedral for the funeral services of President John F. Kennedy—*(front row, left to right)* Dr. Heinrich Luebke, President of West Germany; President Charles de Gaulle of France; Queen Frederika of Greece; King Baudouin of Belgium; Emperor Haile Selassie of Ethiopia; Diosdado Macapagal, President of the Philippines; and Chung Hee Park, President-elect of Korea. —*UPI photograph*

The body of forty-six-year-old President Kennedy was flown to Washington on the evening of the day of assassination. His wife, who had been riding with him, escorted his body back to the White House still wearing a dress stained with his blood. Lyndon Johnson, who had been in the motorcade, was sworn in as President aboard the airplane before it took off. On Monday, November 25, millions of grieving Americans watched the presidential funeral on TV. Kennedy was buried in Arlington National Cemetery and an eternal flame was lighted over his grave. Two days later President Johnson addressed a joint session of Congress, emphasizing the need to carry out President Kennedy's program:

"All I have I would have given gladly not to be standing here today.

"The greatest leader of our time has been struck down by the foulest deed of our time. Today John Fitzgerald Kennedy lives on in the immortal words and works that he left behind. He lives on in the mind and memories of mankind. He lives on in the hearts of his countrymen.

"No words are sad enough to express our sense of loss. No words are strong enough to express our determination to continue the forward thrust of America that he began.

"The dream of conquering the vastness of space—the dream of partnership across the Atlantic—and across the Pacific as well—the dream of a Peace Corps in less-developed nations—the dream of education for all of our children—the dream of jobs for all who seek them and need them—the dream of care for our elderly—the dream of an all-out attack on mental illness—and above all, the dream of equal rights for all Americans, whatever their race or color—these and other American dreams have been vitalized by his drive and by his dedication.

"And now the ideas and ideals which he so nobly represented must and will be translated into effective action. . . ."

On the first anniversary of the assassination of President Kennedy, Senator-elect Robert F. Kennedy placing a flower near the eternal flame on his brother's grave. —*UPI photograph*

69

70   DWIGHT DAVID EISENHOWER

Dwight David Eisenhower

The Thirty-fourth President of the United States
1953–61

1890 (October 14) Born in Denison, Texas.

1892 Moved with family to Abilene, Kansas.

1909 Graduated from Abilene High School.

1911–15 Attended U.S. Military Academy at West Point, graduating with commission as second lieutenant.

1916 (July 1) Married Mamie Geneva Doud; promoted to first lieutenant.

1917–18 Commander of tank training school at Camp Colt, Gettysburg, Pennsylvania, advanced to lieutenant colonel (temporary rank).

1932–35 Senior aide to General Douglas MacArthur, chief of staff of the U.S. Army.

1935–39 Senior military assistant to General MacArthur as military adviser to the Philippines government.

1941 Chief of staff of the Third Army, headquartered in San Antonio, Texas; advanced to brigadier general.

1942 Appointed commanding general of U.S. forces in Europe.

1943–45 Supreme Commander of Allied Expeditionary Forces in Europe.

1945–48 Chief of staff of the U.S. Army.

1948–50 President of Columbia University.

1951–52 Supreme commander of NATO forces in Europe.

1953–61 Thirty-fourth President of the United States.

1969 (March 28) Died in Washington, D.C.

Leading Officials in Eisenhower's Administration

Office	Name	Years Served
Chief Justice	Frederick M. Vinson	1946-1953
	Earl Warren	1953-1969
Vice-President	Richard M. Nixon	1953-1961
Secretary of State	John Foster Dulles	1953-1959
	Christian A. Herter	1959-1961
Secretary of the Treasury	George M. Humphrey	1953-1957
	Robert B. Anderson	1957-1961
Secretary of Defense	Charles E. Wilson	1953-1957
	Neil H. McElroy	1957-1959
	Thomas S. Gates, Jr.	1959-1961
Attorney General	Herbert Brownell, Jr.	1953-1957
	William P. Rogers	1957-1961
Postmaster General	Arthur E. Summerfield	1953-1961
Secretary of the Interior	Douglas McKay	1953-1956
	Fred A. Seaton	1956-1961
Secretary of Agriculture	Ezra Taft Benson	1953-1961
Secretary of Commerce	Sinclair Weeks	1953-1958
	Lewis L. Strauss	1958-1959
	Frederick H. Mueller	1959-1961
Secretary of Labor	Martin P. Durkin	1953
	James P. Mitchell	1953-1961
Secretary of Health, Education, and Welfare	Oveta Culp Hobby	1953-1955
	Marion B. Folsom	1955-1958
	Arthur S. Flemming	1958-1961

Of all the previous Presidents, Dwight D. Eisenhower had the most in common with Ulysses S. Grant. He and Grant were the only two West Point graduates to become President. Both had been commanding generals of victorious armies, and neither had had any political experience or ever been elected to a lesser public office. Perhaps most surprising, they were the only two Republican Presidents to serve out two complete four-year terms.

Hero-worshipped as the commander of the allied armies that defeated Germany in World War II, Eisenhower was elected and re-elected by huge majorities in 1952 and 1956. But although the people were happy to chant "We Like Ike," they did not like his party, so he had to work with a Congress controlled by the opposition through six of his eight years in office.

The Space Age began during Eisenhower's administration with the launching of earth-circling satellites by Russia and the United States. Atomic energy plants were first used to produce electricity, and an International Atomic Energy Agency was organized at Eisenhower's suggestion to control the peaceful uses of atomic energy. The United States grew to fifty states with the admission of Alaska and Hawaii.

As in the Truman administration, the Cold War between the Communist nations and the Western democracies dominated the times. Communism gained its first foothold in the Western Hemisphere when Fidel Castro overthrew the government of Cuba.

Eisenhower sought to organize the presidency in the style of a commanding general. He tried to have a staff which would keep him informed and provide him with alternate courses of action, although the ultimate responsibility remained his. He did not see himself as the leader of a political party, in the old-fashioned sense, as evidenced by a note written in his diary a few days before his first inauguration in which he commented that he hoped "that I will be compelled to have a little to do, during the next four years, with the distribution of Federal patronage."

A Career Soldier

DWIGHT DAVID EISENHOWER was born in Denison, Texas, October 14, 1890, the third of seven brothers, one of whom died as a baby. The Eisenhowers lived only briefly in Texas, having gone there following the failure of a general store the elder Eisenhower had managed in Hope, Kansas. Before Dwight was two, they had moved back to Kansas and settled in Abilene, where the father worked in a creamery.

With many mouths to feed and little income, the Eisenhowers had to struggle to make ends meet. As soon as each boy became old enough he worked in the family garden to help grow vegetables for the table, and when he became a little older usually began working at odd jobs. Dwight worked in the creamery after school and on vacations.

Eisenhower's parents, members of a Protestant sect called the River Brethren, brought up their children in an old-fashioned atmosphere of puritanical morals. Prayer and Bible reading were a daily part of their lives. Violence was forbidden, though in a family of six boys the edict was a bit hard to enforce.

As he was growing up, Dwight had a narrow escape. When he developed blood poisoning in his leg from a scratch, the family doctor ad-

Mrs. Dwight D. Eisenhower, the former Mamie Geneva Doud of Denver.
—*Harris & Ewing*

vised amputation. Dwight and his older brothers resisted the doctor, and the leg healed.

In school Dwight, whose favorite subject was history, particularly enjoyed reading about military heroes of the past. When he graduated from Abilene High School in 1909, the class prophecy predicted that he would "wind up as a professor of history at Yale."

But the Eisenhowers could not afford to send Dwight to college. Temporarily he took a full-time job at the creamery, but he was determined to go to college and a year later applied for admittance to the U.S. Naval Academy at Annapolis. When he went to Topeka to take the examination, he found the same exam was being given for both Annapolis and West Point. He passed with flying colors, and was jubilant when he was appointed to West Point.

Five feet, ten and a half inches tall, the twenty-year-old Eisenhower was bigger and older than most of the others in his class at the Point in 1911. For a time it looked as though Ike would become one of Army's great football stars, but he injured his knee in the 1912 season and after that became a member of the cheerleading squad. An average student, Eisenhower ranked sixty-first in his class of 168 when he graduated in 1915.

As a second lieutenant, Eisenhower's first duty post was with the 19th Infantry at Fort Sam Houston in San Antonio, Texas. While there he met and became engaged to Mamie Geneva Doud, the nineteen-year-old daughter of a well-to-do Denver businessman. They were married on July 1, 1916, the day he received his promotion to first lieutenant. They had two sons, one of whom died as a baby. The other, John Eisenhower, followed his father's career as an officer in the U.S. Army.

During World War I, Eisenhower was kept in the United States as an instructor at various military camps. In the spring of 1918 he was given command of the Tank Training Center at Camp Colt, near Gettysburg, Pennsylvania. Although he did not have any tanks until after the war had ended, he trained his troops in the theory of operating tanks, and rose to the temporary rank of lieutenant colonel.

After the war Ike was reduced to his permanent rank of captain. For two years he was assigned to duty in the Panama Canal Zone, and then after several routine assignments was sent to the Army General Staff School in Leavenworth, Kansas, in 1926. He knew that if he did well in this school it would mark him for eventual command, so with hard work he managed to graduate first in his class of 275 officers. As a result, Ike was picked to attend the War College in Washington, D.C.

In the early years of the Depression, Major Eisenhower served on the staff of the Assistant Secretary of War. In 1932 he was appointed aide to General Douglas MacArthur, at that time chief of staff of the U.S. Army. Two years later, when MacArthur was assigned to help the Filipinos build an army, Eisenhower went along to the Philippines as his assistant. In the four years he spent in the islands, Eisenhower was advanced to the permanent rank of lieutenant colonel. He also learned to fly while helping train the Philippine Air Force.

When Eisenhower returned to duty in the United States in 1940, there were fewer than 50,000 foot soldiers in the U.S. Army. During the peaceful years since World War I the Army had dwindled to a point where regulars like Eisenhower were beginning to wonder if there was going to be anything left. But in the spring of 1940 Hitler's troops swept through Europe, causing the United States to begin a hasty build-up of its armed forces with the first draft of civilians since World War I.

By the spring of 1941 Eisenhower had been promoted to colonel and assigned as chief of staff of the Third Army in San Antonio, Texas. That summer Eisenhower distinguished himself in the big maneuvers held in Louisiana by the Second and Third Armies and won promotion to brigadier general.

Crusader in Europe

FIVE days after the Japanese attack on Pearl Harbor, Eisenhower received orders from Chief of Staff General George Marshall to report for duty with the War Department in Washington, D.C. Ike's long experience in the Philippines was needed to help plan American strategy in the Pacific. In March 1942, Eisenhower was appointed by Marshall as chief of the Operations Division of the War Department General Staff with the temporary rank of major general. In his new position Eisenhower and his staff developed the strategy for opening a "second front" with the invasion of German-occupied France. When Eisenhower reported to Marshall in June 1942 that the plans were ready for execution, Marshall asked, "When can you leave?"

The dizzying rise from lieutenant colonel to commanding general of the European Theater of Operations in a little more than two years had advanced Eisenhower over more than 350 senior general officers. During the next two years he won an increasing reputation as an organizer, a planner, and a man who could bring into agreement diverse leaders with conflicting views. He commanded the successful Allied invasions of French North Africa in November 1942, and of Sicily and Italy in the late summer of 1943. Then, in December 1943, President Roosevelt appointed Eisenhower Supreme Commander of all Allied forces in Europe,

Noon mess for General Eisenhower in Tunisia in March 1943.
—*U.S. Army photograph*

General Dwight D. Eisenhower decorating Lieutenant General George S. Patton, American tank corps specialist in North Africa in 1943.
—*Bureau of Publications, War Dept.*

General Eisenhower and French General Giraud at the ceremonies for the formal turnover of American equipment to the new French Army in North Africa, May 8, 1943.
—*U.S. Army photograph*

On the eve of the invasion of France, June 6, 1944, General Eisenhower talking with a paratroop unit.
—*U.S. Army photograph*

At the port of Cherbourg, France, in 1945, General Eisenhower encouraging the troops.

French General De Gaulle and General Eisenhower in Normandy, August 22, 1944.

With another Allied General, the noted General Montgomery of Great Britain, General Eisenhower reviewing the action, July 26, 1944.

A meeting at staff level, with *(left to right)* Field Marshal Sir Alan Brooke, Chief of the English Imperial Staff; General Dwight Eisenhower, Supreme Allied Commander; English Prime Minister Winston Churchill; and Air Chief, Marshal Sir Arthur Tedder, November 14, 1944.

The city of London welcoming General Eisenhower, June 12, 1945.

In the taproom of the Raleigh Tavern at Williamsburg, Virginia, in 1947, *(left to right)* John D. Rockefeller III, Sir Maitland Wilson, Chief of Staff, British Army, Colgate Darden, ex-Governor of Virginia, Sir Winston Churchill, and General Dwight Eisenhower.

Colonial Studio by Frank Dementi—Copyright 1947

with the particular task of directing nearly three million troops in the invasion of France.

On Eisenhower's order the D-Day cross-channel assault on Normandy —the greatest amphibian invasion in history—was launched on June 6, 1944. He then directed the triumphant series of battles that freed Europe from Hitler's control, culminating in the German surrender in May 1945.

With victory achieved in Europe, Eisenhower was hailed as America's No. 1 hero, and in December 1945, President Truman called him to Washington as Chief of Staff of the U.S. Army. In this post, which he held for more than two years, Eisenhower supervised the demobilization of the Army. He also worked with President Truman in an effort to unify the armed forces under a single command, resulting in the organization of the Department of Defense in 1947. He wrote *Crusade in Europe,* an account of his World War II service, which was published in 1948 and instantly became a best seller.

In May 1948, Eisenhower retired from active duty to become President of Columbia University. Besieged by both Democrats and Republicans to run for President, he repeatedly rejected all offers, and did not even disclose his political identity as a Democrat or a Republican.

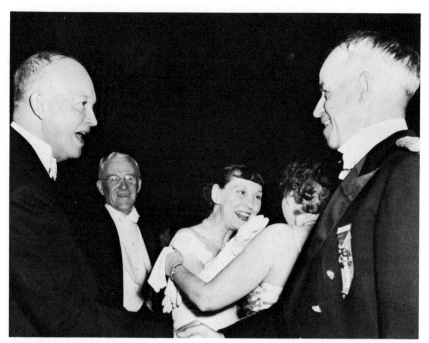

The Eisenhowers as guests at the Truman Inaugural Ball in 1949, with General Eisenhower greeting a fellow officer and West Point classmate, General Omar Bradley. *UPI photograph*

In 1950, at President Truman's invitation, he returned to active military duty as Supreme Commander of NATO. Going to Europe in the spring of 1951, he welded together a powerful unified military force.

As the presidential election of 1952 approached, politicians of both parties again began to make overtures to Eisenhower. Then, Governor Thomas E. Dewey of New York, the Republican presidential nominee in 1944 and 1948, publicly threw his support to Eisenhower. Dewey represented the liberal wing of the Republican party and was determined to prevent the nomination of Senator Robert Taft of Ohio, leader of the conservative elements. In January 1952, Eisenhower disclosed that he was a Republican. He was nominated on the first ballot at the Republican National Convention. Senator Richard M. Nixon of California was chosen as his vice-presidential running mate.

The Democrats nominated Governor Adlai E. Stevenson of Illinois, and as his running mate picked Senator John J. Sparkman of Alabama.

The contest was an unequal one because Stevenson was little known outside his own state, while Eisenhower was the hero who had brought victory in World War II. At the climax of the campaign, Eisenhower said he would personally go to Korea to bring the war there to an end—a pledge that won him wide support. Eisenhower won by a tremendous margin with 33,936,234 votes to Stevenson's 27,314,992, and with 442 electoral votes to 89.

In the interval before assuming office Eisenhower made good on his promise to fly to Korea and take a firsthand look at conditions there. A truce agreement ending the Korean War was signed several months later—on July 27, 1953.

EISENHOWER had joined the Presbyterian church after his election, and on the morning of Inauguration Day he and his family attended an early morning communion service. Afterwards he wrote a short prayer with which he began his inaugural address:

At the 1952 Republican Convention "I Like Ike" was a popular slogan of the Eisenhower backers.
UPI photograph

Eisenhower's Administration

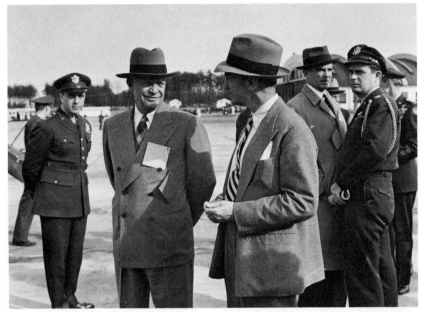

General Eisenhower and Secretary of Defense Forrestal having a visit.

General Eisenhower, candidate for President, at the American Legion Convention in the old Madison Square Garden, New York, in August, 1952. *UPI photograph*

"Almighty God, as we stand here at this moment my future associates in the Executive branch of government join me in beseeching that Thou will make full and complete our dedication to the service of the people in this throng, and their fellow citizens everywhere.

"Give us, we pray, the power to discern clearly right from wrong, and allow all our words and actions to be governed thereby, and by the laws of this land. Especially we pray that our concern shall be for all the people regardless of station, race or calling.

"May cooperation be permitted and be the mutual aim of those who, under the concepts of our Constitution, hold to differing political faiths; so that all may work for the good of our beloved country and Thy glory. Amen."

In the heart of his address he called for the removal of "the causes of mutual fear and distrust among nations," and he declared that "we must be ready to dare all for our country. For history does not long entrust the care of freedom to the weak or timid . . ."

In closing, he said: "The peace we seek, then, is nothing less than the practice and fulfillment of our whole faith. . . . It signifies much more than the stilling of guns, easing the sorrow of war. More than an escape from death, it is a way of life. More than a haven for the weary, it is a hope for the brave."

In the field of domestic policy Eisenhower established himself as a "middle of the roader," calling his program "Modern Republicanism" or "Dynamic Conservatism." He supported a huge highway-building program including the far-sighted Interstate Highway System. He approved expansion of social security and the increase of the national minimum wage to one dollar an hour.

The domestic revolution that was to bring increased civil rights to Negroes had its beginning during the Eisenhower administration, when in 1954 the Supreme Court, headed by Eisenhower appointee Earl Warren, ruled that compulsory segregation in public schools was unconstitutional. Later, Eisenhower sent federal troops to Arkansas to protect Negro students when a high school in Little Rock was integrated for the first time in 1957.

In the area of foreign relations, the death of Premier Stalin of Russia raised hopes that some new working accord might be reached with the new leaders of the Soviet Union. In 1955 Eisenhower attended a "summit meeting" with the leaders of Russia, France, and Great Britain in Geneva, but was unable to reach agreement on means to reduce Cold War tensions.

During his first year in office, Eisenhower made a dramatic appearance before the United Nations General Assembly in which he called on the world organization to plan for peaceful uses of atomic energy. This resulted in 1957 in the formation of the International Atomic Energy Agency.

Senator Joseph McCarthy of Wisconsin continued to fan hysteria against Communists and Communist sympathizers in the government during Eisenhower's first two years in office. After McCarthy accused the State Department of carrying Communist and pro-Communist books in overseas libraries, a number of books from these libraries were burned by U.S. officials. Eisenhower spoke out against these book burnings, but seemed unable to exert sufficient leadership to enforce his views. Finally, when McCarthy attacked the U.S. Army as being infiltrated by Communists, pro-Administration senators succeeded in passing a resolution censuring McCarthy for his activities.

Although the country experienced a continued high level of prosperity and public-opinion polls showed that Eisenhower retained his popularity with the people, the Republican party lost control of Congress in the elections of 1954. For the next six years Eisenhower exercised his skill of conciliation, working with the leaders of the opposition party in order to keep the business of the government going. In this he was particularly

At Cambridge, Massachusetts, on October 22, 1952, Harvard students engulfed the Eisenhower cavalcade.   *UPI photograph*

aided by Senator Lyndon Johnson of Texas, the Democratic majority leader of the Senate.

Eisenhower had three serious attacks of illness while President. In September 1955, he had a heart attack while vacationing in Colorado, but returned to duty in Washington three months later. In June 1956, an inflammation of his small intestine required an emergency operation from which he recovered rapidly. Then in November 1957, he had a mild stroke that for a time affected his speech.

In the 1956 election, Eisenhower again faced Adlai E. Stevenson as his Democratic opponent, and won, but by an even larger majority than in 1952. He received 35,590,472 popular votes to Stevenson's 26,022,752, and 457 electoral votes to 73. Amazingly, the Republicans failed to win either house of Congress—the first time this had occurred in a presidential election since that of Zachary Taylor in 1848. Obviously, the victory was a personal one for Ike.

Two crises in foreign affairs took place shortly before the 1956 election. On October 23, the people of Hungary revolted against their Communist rulers, appealing to the United States for help. A few days later France, Great Britain, and Israel invaded Egypt, apparently in an effort to recover the Suez Canal, which Egypt had nationalized. The United States joined Russia in condemning the action, and aided the United Nations in arranging a cease-fire. Meantime, Russian tanks crushed the Hungarian rising. In both cases, the United States was accused in some circles of failing to back its friends.

In September, 1955, President Eisenhower was stricken by a coronary thrombosis, from which he is shown here recovering at Fitzsimons Army Hospital, Denver, Colorado.   *UPI photograph*

Senator Everett Dirksen of Illinois (*extreme left*) on the speaker's platform at the 1952 Republican Convention.

"Peace and Prosperity," the old slogan of the Republican Party, was featured on posters at the 1956 Republican Convention at the Cow Palace in San Francisco.

President Eisenhower greeting Prime Minister Jawaharlal Nehru of India on the White House porch in December, 1956.

A year later, on October 4, 1957, Russia startled the world by launching *Sputnik*, the first man-made space satellite. The Space Age had begun. American prestige suffered throughout the world from this unexpected Soviet technological triumph, and the American press and public began a long-term debate as to whether something was wrong with the country's educational system if Soviet scientists had been able to forge ahead so spectacularly. But the first successful American earth satellite, *Explorer I*, was put in orbit in January 1958, and though Russia held its initial lead, the "space race" between the two countries became a reality.

At the request of the President, Congress in 1957 had approved a new foreign-policy posture which came to be called the "Eisenhower Doctrine." This authorized the President to use armed force to aid any nation or group of nations "requesting assistance against armed aggression from any country controlled by international communism." When the government of Lebanon requested such assistance in 1958, Eisenhower sent the U.S. Marines to protect that tiny Middle Eastern country.

When Communist China threatened to invade Formosa in September 1958, and began shelling islands between Formosa and the Chinese mainland, Eisenhower ordered the U.S. Navy to provide protection for Chinese Nationalist ships supplying military outposts on the islands. In the face of this strong stand, the Chinese Communists backed down.

After the death of Secretary of State John Foster Dulles in 1959, President Eisenhower became visibly more active in directing American foreign policy, hopeful that he could ease the tensions between the United States and Communist Russia. In 1959, Eisenhower entertained Russian

The Eisenhower farm at Gettysburg, Pennsylvania, was the scene for launching a "crusade" with fried chicken the feature of the day, during the 1956 campaign.   *UPI photograph*

President Eisenhower preparing to throw out the traditional first ball of opening day of the baseball season, with Representative Charles Halleck of Indiana, Senator Lyndon Johnson of Texas, Chief Justice Earl Warren, Representative Joseph Martin of Massachusetts, and Vice-President Richard Nixon *(left to right)*.

Premier Khrushchev on a visit to the United States. In turn, Khrushchev invited Eisenhower to visit Russia and a second "summit conference" was scheduled in Paris.

However, world hopes for accord were dashed in May 1960, just before the planned meeting in Paris, when Russia shot down an American U-2 high-altitude reconnaissance plane and Eisenhower admitted that "spy" flights over Russia had been going on for four years. Khrushchev broke up the Paris summit meeting with a demand that Eisenhower personally apologize for the spy flights. When the President refused, Khrushchev withdrew the invitation for Eisenhower to visit Russia.

Prevented from consideration of a third term by the Twenty-second Amendment, Eisenhower gave his support for the Republican presidential nomination in 1960 to Vice President Richard M. Nixon. Though Eisenhower did not campaign vigorously for Nixon, he was disappointed by the narrow election defeat to Democratic Senator John F. Kennedy of Massachusetts: "I felt as though I had been hit in the solar plexus with a ball bat—as though eight years of work had been for naught. It was a low moment . . ."

The United States suffered one further setback in foreign affairs in the closing days of Eisenhower's administration. In 1959, in Cuba, Fidel Castro overthrew the dictatorship of Fulgencio Batista and moved steadily leftward, finally revealing himself openly as a Communist. Early in January 1961, the Eisenhower administration broke off diplomatic relations with Cuba.

By the time he left office Eisenhower was seventy—the oldest man ever to be President. He made an unusual farewell address by radio and television to the American people, warning them of the dangers that lay ahead and of the necessity for moderation:

". . . threats, new in kind or degree, constantly arise. I mention two only. . . . we have been compelled to create a permanent armaments industry of vast proportions. Added to this, three and a half million men and women are directly engaged in the defense establishment. We annually spend on military security more than the net income of all United States corporations.

"This conjunction of an immense military establishment and a large arms industry is new in American experience. The total influence—economic, political, even spiritual—is felt in every city, every state house, every office of the federal government. We recognize the imperative need for this development. Yet we must not fail to comprehend its grave implications. . . .

"In the councils of government, we must guard against the acquisition of unwarranted influence, whether sought or unsought, by the military-industrial complex. The potential for the disastrous rise of misplaced power exists and will persist.

"We must never let the weight of this combination endanger our liberties or democratic processes. . . .

"Akin to, and largely responsible for the sweeping changes in our industrial-military posture, has been the technological revolution during recent decades.

"In this revolution, research has become central; it also becomes more formalized, complex, and costly. A steadily increasing share is conducted for, by, or at the direction of, the federal government. . . .

"The prospect of domination of the nation's scholars by federal employment, project allocations, and the power of money is ever present and is gravely to be regarded.

"Yet, in holding scientific research and discovery in respect, as we

President Eisenhower signing the Hawaiian statehood bill in the presence of various Congressional leaders.

should, we must also be alert to the equal and opposite danger that public policy could itself become the captive of a scientific-technological elite. . . .

"Down the long lane of the history yet to be written America knows that this world of ours, ever growing smaller, must avoid becoming a community of dreadful fear and hate, and be, instead, a proud confederation of mutual trust and respect.

"Such a confederation must be one of equals. The weakest must come to the conference table with the same confidence as do we, protected as

The Eisenhowers as proud grandparents, with the children of their son, John.

Former President Eisenhower with Nelson Rockefeller at Syracuse in 1962 at a Republican fundraising function.

we are by our moral, economic, and military strength. That table, though scarred by many past frustrations, cannot be abandoned for the certain agony of the battlefield.

"Disarmament, with mutual honor and confidence, is a continuing imperative. Together we must learn how to compose differences, not with arms, but with intellect and decent purpose. Because this need is so sharp and apparent I confess that I lay down my official responsibilities in this field with a definite sense of disappointment. As one who has witnessed the horror and the lingering sadness of war—as one who knows that another war could utterly destroy this civilization which has been so slowly and painfully built over thousands of years—I wish I could say tonight that a lasting peace is in sight.

"Happily, I can say that war has been avoided. Steady progress toward our ultimate goal has been made. But, so much remains to be done. As a private citizen, I shall never cease to do what little I can to help the world advance along that road. . . .

"To all the peoples of the world, I once more give expression to America's prayerful and continuing aspiration:

"We pray that peoples of all faiths, all races, all nations may have their great human needs satisfied; that those now denied opportunity shall come to enjoy it to the full; that all who yearn for freedom may experience its spiritual blessings; that those who have freedom will understand, also, its heavy responsibilities; that all who are insensitive to the needs of others will learn charity; that the scourges of poverty, disease, and ignorance will be made to disappear from the earth, and that, in the goodness of time, all peoples will come to live together in a peace guaranteed by the binding force of mutual respect and love. . . ."

After leaving the presidency, Eisenhower retired to his farm near Gettysburg, Pennsylvania. There he wrote two volumes of memoirs of his two terms as President. At the age of seventy-eight he died of congestive heart failure on March 28, 1969, at Walter Reed General Hospital in Washington, D.C. His body was buried at his boyhood home in Abilene, Kansas. Though in general Eisenhower had expressed satisfaction with his eight years in office, he also voiced his greatest disappointment:

"One of my major regrets is that as we left the White House I had to admit to little success in making progress in global disarmament or in reducing the bitterness of the East-West struggle. . . . I think no one can justifiably charge the bleak record to any lack of striving on our part. . . . But though, in this, I suffered my greatest disappointment, it has not destroyed my faith that in the next generation, the next century, the next millennium these things will come to pass."

A Christmas scene at the White House with the Eisenhowers and their son, John, and his family, and the traditional Christmas tree and crèche.

90   HARRY S TRUMAN

Harry S Truman

The Thirty-third President of the United States
1945–53

1884 (May 8) Born in Lamar, Missouri.

1890–1901 Attended public school in Independence, Missouri.

1906–17 Farmed near Grandview, Missouri.

1917–19 Commanded an artillery battery in World War I, rising to rank of major.

1919 (June 28) Married Elizabeth "Bess" Wallace.

1919–22 Partner in men's clothing store in Kansas City.

1923–24 County judge of Jackson County, Missouri.

1927–34 Presiding judge of Jackson County.

1935–45 U.S. senator from Missouri.

1945 Vice President of the United States.

1945–53 Thirty-third President of the United States.

1972 (December 26) Died in Kansas City, Missouri.

Leading Officials in
Truman's Administration

Office	Name	Years Served
Chief Justice	Harlan Fiske Stone	1941-1946
	Frederick M. Vinson	1946-1953
Vice-President	Alben W. Barkley	1949-1953
Secretary of State	Edward R. Stettinius, Jr.	1944-1945
	James F. Byrnes	1945-1947
	George C. Marshall	1947-1949
	Dean G. Acheson	1949-1953
Secretary of the Treasury	Henry Morgenthau, Jr.	1934-1945
	Frederick M. Vinson	1945-1946
	John W. Snyder	1946-1953
Secretary of War	Henry L. Stimson	1940-1945
	Robert P. Patterson	1945-1947
	Kenneth C. Royall	1947
Secretary of Defense	James V. Forrestal	1947-1949
	Louis A. Johnson	1949-1950
	George C. Marshall	1950-1951
	Robert A. Lovett	1951-1953
Attorney General	Francis Biddle	1941-1945
	Thomas C. Clark	1945-1949
	J. Howard McGrath	1949-1952
	James P. McGranery	1952-1953
Postmaster General	Frank C. Walker	1940-1945
	Robert E. Hannegan	1945-1947
	Jesse M. Donaldson	1947-1953
Secretary of the Navy	James V. Forrestal	1944-1947
Secretary of the Interior	Harold L. Ickes	1933-1946
	Julius A. Krug	1946-1949
	Oscar L. Chapman	1949-1953
Secretary of Agriculture	Claude R. Wickard	1940-1945
	Clinton P. Anderson	1945-1948
	Charles F. Brannan	1948-1953
Secretary of Commerce	Henry A. Wallace	1945-1946
	W. Averell Harriman	1946-1948
	Charles Sawyer	1948-1953
Secretary of Labor	Frances Perkins	1933-1945
	Lewis B. Schwellenbach	1945-1948
	Maurice J. Tobin	1948-1953

The first President to take office in the midst of a war, Harry S Truman said at the time that he felt "like the moon, the stars and all the planets had fallen on me." The nation and the world wondered if he was a big enough man to fill Roosevelt's shoes. His background and even his appearance were unpromising. He was the first President in fifty years without a college education. He spoke the language of a Missouri dirt farmer and World War I artilleryman—both of which he had been. Instead of looking like a statesman, he looked like a bank clerk or haberdasher—both of which he also had been. And, worst of all, everyone knew that for more than twenty years he had been a lieutenant of Tom Pendergast, one of the most corrupt political bosses in the country.

What most people didn't know was that he was an unswervingly honest man who knew his own mind and one of the most knowledgeable students of history ever to enter the White House. He understood the powers of the President, and he knew why some men had been strong Chief Executives and others had been weak ones.

He ordered the atomic bomb dropped because he was sure it would save American lives and end World War II quickly. It did not bother him in later years that intellectuals questioned whether one man should have made such an awesome decision. He knew he had been right.

When World War II had been won, Truman helped shift the nation smoothly from a war footing to a peacetime economy—the first time in its history that the United States did not suffer a depression as an aftermath of war. When the former New Dealers in his Cabinet sneered at him, Truman fired them, so the liberals decided he was too conservative. When he called for extended social welfare and sweeping civil rights measures in his domestic Fair Deal program, Southern Democrats and conservative Republicans fought him because he was too liberal.

Despite opposition by isolationists who felt the United States should bring home all its troops and forget the problems of the war-torn countries, Truman upheld America's newly won responsibilities as the world's most powerful nation. He brought to fruition Wilson's dream of bringing the United States into a world peace-keeping organization—the United Nations. He helped rebuild Europe. And he launched a gigantic foreign-aid program in which the United States underwrote the cost of helping underprivileged nations improve themselves.

When Communist Russia and Communist China challenged America in the Cold War, Truman held them back with the stubbornness of a Missouri mule. To prevent the Russians from overrunning Europe, he helped organize the North Atlantic Treaty Organization with troops of the United States and Western Europe under a unified command. On the other side of the world, when Communist troops invaded South Korea, Truman instantly dispatched American armed forces to repel the aggressors.

Despite his accomplishments on the world scene, Truman had made so many enemies at home among New Dealers, Southern Democrats, conservative Republicans, and liberal intellectuals, that when he ran for a second term in 1948 everyone expected him to be defeated. But the common people trusted Truman, ignored the political prophets, and gave him a substantial victory.

"I wasn't one of the great Presidents," Truman said after leaving the White House, "but I had a good time trying to be one, I can tell you that." Winston Churchill went much further, declaring to Truman:

"You, more than any other man, have saved Western Civilization."

THE son of a mule-trader, Harry S Truman was born in a small house in Lamar, Missouri, on May 8, 1884. Because his family could not agree on a middle name for him, his middle initial "S" does not stand for a name. Mule-trading was not a particularly prosperous business, so the Trumans moved about to various Missouri towns until settling down in Independence when Harry was six.

Before he started school at eight, Harry had been outfitted with thick-lensed glasses because of an eye condition called hyperopia. Because of his glasses, the boy was excluded from much of the rough-and-tumble play of his friends and spent a good deal of his time reading the Bible, biographies, and history. He also took piano lessons.

At sixteen he had his first experience with politics when he obtained a job as a page at the Democratic National Convention held in Kansas City in 1900. He was particularly impressed at hearing William Jennings Bryan speak. The next year he was graduated from high school in a ceremony in which his friend Charlie Ross was the class valedictorian.

Because his father had had business reverses, Harry had to go to work to help support his younger brother and sister. He worked for about a year as a timekeeper with a railroad work gang, then obtained a $7-a-week job in the mailroom of the Kansas City *Star*. Next, he became a bank clerk, then a bookkeeper. For a time he roomed in a boardinghouse with a fellow bank clerk named Arthur Eisenhower who had a younger brother named Dwight.

In 1906, when Truman was twenty-two, his father asked him to come to Grandview, Missouri, and run his grandmother's 600-acre farm. For the next eleven years he lived the life of a dirt farmer, raising corn, hogs, and cattle—which he did with success.

His father died in 1914, and Harry was named to succeed him in a minor political job, that of road overseer in Jackson County. The next year he was appointed postmaster of Grandview, and began going into Kansas City regularly to attend meetings of a Democratic political club that was part of the party machine of the city's boss, T. J. Pendergast.

Shortly after the United States entered World War I in 1917, Truman joined a National Guard artillery company as a lieutenant. In August it was taken into the Regular Army as the 129th Field Artillery of the 35th Division. While the troops trained at Fort Sill, Oklahoma, Truman acted as canteen officer. Under his management the post store earned a profit of $15,000 in six months.

Truman landed in France in April 1918. A few weeks later he was promoted to captain, and in July was given command of Battery D of the Second Battalion of the 129th. He first saw action in September when his battery laid down a barrage of gas shells on the German lines in the Vosges Mountains. Later in the same month he and his men took part in the heavy fighting in the Argonne Forest. In October, Truman and his artillery battery advanced with the 35th Division on Verdun—he was firing on the German-held city of Metz when the war ended in November. Truman arrived back in the United States in the spring of 1919, and after being promoted to the rank of major was mustered out of the Army in May.

The thirty-five-year-old Truman gave up bachelorhood on June 28, 1919, when he married Elizabeth "Bess" Wallace, an Independence,

A Missouri Farmer

Harry Truman as a member of the National Guard after the United States became involved in World War I

As a captain of artillery in France during World War I, Harry Truman served with the 129th Field Artillery. —*UPI photograph*

Missouri, girl who had gone through school with him from fifth grade and to whom he had become engaged shortly before joining the Army. He and his wife lived at his mother-in-law's home in Independence, while he and an army friend opened a men's clothing store in Kansas City. At first the store prospered, but as farm prices fell during the Harding administration business slacked off. He and his partner finally had to close the store in 1922, Truman losing about $30,000. It took him more than fifteen years to pay off his debts, but he refused to declare himself bankrupt.

In 1922 Truman decided to make politics his career. With the help of his wartime buddies and the Pendergast political machine, he was elected one of the three "judges" of Jackson County—the county that includes Kansas City and Independence. Despite its title, the position was non-judicial and was largely concerned with road and bridge building and maintenance. During the two years he was in this office, Truman decided to improve his education and attended night classes at the Kansas City Law School, but did not attain a law degree.

Two major events took place in 1924. His only child, a daughter named Mary Margaret, was born. And he was defeated for re-election, largely because of the opposition of the Ku Klux Klan, which mistakenly believed he was part-Jewish because one of his grandfathers was named Solomon Young. For the next two years he earned a living in a variety of jobs, from selling auto-club memberships to being a partner in a small bank that failed.

In 1926 Truman was elected presiding judge of Jackson County—a position that controlled hundreds of patronage jobs important to the Pendergast machine. He held this office for eight years, winning re-election in 1930, and during this time controlled public works projects totaling more than $50 million—which involved a sizable amount of concrete bought from Tom Pendergast's Ready Mixed Concrete Company. But despite the well-merited reputation of the Pendergast machine, no suspicion of dishonesty ever fell on Truman.

In 1934 Pendergast was having trouble with his own machine as well as with rival factions in the Missouri Democratic party. Desperate for a candidate for the U.S. Senate, he finally hit on the obscure Truman, who surprisingly won a three-cornered race for the Democratic nomination in August, and went on to capture the Senate seat in November with a plurality of more than 260,000 votes. With astounding suddenness, fifty-year-old Harry Truman was launched in big-time politics.

One of thirteen new Democratic senators who took office in January 1935, he soon became a good friend of Vice President John Nance Garner and frequently was chosen by Garner to stand in for him in presiding over the Senate. Truman voted consistently for Roosevelt's New Deal program and made a bit of a name for himself by conducting subcommittee hearings of the Senate Interstate Commerce Committee, looking into dubious practices in railroad financing. Truman was genuinely shocked in 1939 when political boss Tom Pendergast was indicted for bribery, pleaded guilty, and was sent to prison, leaving the machine in the hands of his nephew Jim Pendergast.

When Truman ran for re-election for senator in 1940, the feeling was that with the Pendergast power broken he stood little chance. Once more he proved a skillful and indefatigable campaigner, battling two strong rivals in the primary: Lloyd Stark, the governor, and Maurice Milligan, the U.S. attorney who had prosecuted Pendergast. Truman won the primary by the narrow plurality of 8000 votes. In the fall election he

President Franklin D. Roosevelt, Vice-President Harry Truman, and former Vice-President Henry Wallace, returning to the White House from the inauguration in 1945.

defeated his Republican opponent with a plurality of nearly 45,000 votes, even though the Republicans captured the governorship.

During his second term as senator, Truman became nationally prominent as chairman of a committee that investigated war profiteering. By the end of the war Truman estimated that the work of this committee had saved the government about $15 billion. In the spring of 1944 a survey of Washington newspapermen showed that they regarded Truman second only to Roosevelt as the man in government who had contributed most to the successful prosecution of the war.

As the Democratic National Convention of 1944 approached, Truman's name was repeatedly mentioned as a possible running mate for Roosevelt in place of Henry Wallace, who had alienated party leaders by his too exuberant liberalism. Democratic National Committee Chairman Robert Hannegan, a St. Louis political leader, persuaded Roosevelt to designate Truman as his choice. Truman, heading the Missouri delegation to the convention, believed that Senator James F. Byrnes of South Carolina was the President's choice and had even agreed to make the nomination speech for Byrnes. Hannegan persuaded Byrnes to withdraw and convinced Truman that Roosevelt really wanted him. When the convention began to vote for its vice-presidential choice, Henry Wallace led Truman on the first ballot by more than a hundred votes. On the second ballot Truman was nominated.

After Roosevelt's fourth-term victory over Thomas E. Dewey, the sixty-year-old Truman was sworn in as Vice President on January 20, 1945.

Harry Truman taking the oath of office in the White House April 12, 1945, with Mrs. Truman and daughter, Margaret, on his immediate left.

During the subsequent eighty-two days that Truman was Vice President, he met with the Cabinet a few times and had a half dozen conversations with the President, but he was not filled in on many details of Roosevelt's problems largely because the President was not in Washington most of the period.

Truman's First Term

TRUMAN had just finished presiding over a session of the Senate on April 12, 1945, when he received a phone call from the White House asking him to come at once. When he reached there at 5:25 P.M., Mrs. Roosevelt greeted him with the words, "Harry, the President is dead." By shortly after seven o'clock most of the members of the Cabinet had been assembled, and Truman was sworn in as President by Chief Justice Harlan Stone.

The swearing-in ceremony had hardly been completed when he was asked to make his first presidential decision. Would the organizational meeting of the United Nations still be held in San Francisco as planned on April 25? Yes, came the answer. "I did not hesitate a second," he explained later. "It was of supreme importance that we build an organization to help keep the future peace of the world."

Truman had been President only twenty-five days when Germany surrendered, and he was able to proclaim his sixty-first birthday, May 8, as Victory-in-Europe Day. In June the United Nations Charter was agreed to and Truman flew to San Francisco to give the delegates his personal congratulations. Early in July he sailed for Europe aboard the cruiser U.S.S. *Augusta* to meet with Churchill and Stalin at Potsdam, Germany.

At the Potsdam conference, the five-foot-ten-inch Truman was surprised to find that both Churchill and Stalin were shorter than he was, and that they preferred to stand a step higher when having their pictures

A happy day in history, August 14, 1945, with (left to right) James F. Byrnes, Secretary of State, Cordell Hull, former Secretary of State, and President Truman celebrating the announcement of the Japanese surrender. —*International News photograph*

A close-up of the Truman family—President and Mrs. Truman and their daughter, Margaret.

American leaders of World War II and the years following, including (left to right) Averell Harriman, General George C. Marshall, President Truman, Dean Acheson, and General Omar Bradley (at extreme right).

John L. Lewis, leader of the United Mine Workers of America, was a familiar figure in Washington during and immediately after World War II.

taken with him. The conference lasted from the middle of July into early August. Terms for the occupation of Germany were agreed upon and an ultimatum was sent to Japan calling for that country's unconditional surrender. During the meeting, Churchill's conservative party was defeated in a general election in Great Britain, and he was replaced by Prime Minister Clement Attlee.

While at Potsdam, Truman had received word of the first successful atomic bomb test and had authorized its use against Japan to hasten the end of the war. On his way home across the Atlantic, he was informed that the first A-bomb had been dropped on Hiroshima with devastating results on August 5. Four days later a second A-bomb was dropped on Nagasaki. On August 14 Japan surrendered.

With the end of World War II, Truman now turned his attention to the problems of converting the American economy to a peacetime status. On September 6, he sent Congress a 21-point message outlining his Fair Deal program. He said later this date "symbolizes for me my assumption of the office of President in my own right." The heart of the message was the request for legislation to ensure full employment for all Americans regardless of race, religion, or color. In December, the President called for an extension of his powers to regulate prices and rents in peacetime to prevent a runaway inflation. Truman vetoed the first legislation passed by Congress to extend these controls, declaring that it was worse than no bill at all. On June 30, 1946, price controls expired, and in the next two weeks prices zoomed upward 25%. Congress finally acted and on July 25, 1946, Truman signed new price controls into law. Meanwhile, Congress had passed in February 1946 the full-employment act that Truman had requested.

Although Truman intended to carry out Roosevelt's policies, he was determined to be President in his own right. He had replaced most of Roosevelt's Cabinet with men of his own choosing by the end of 1945. Then in 1946 he fired both Harold Ickes and Henry Wallace from their cabinet posts.

The labor unions demanded that government controls on wages be lifted, and an epidemic of strikes broke out across the country in late 1945 and 1946. When railroad unions called a strike in May 1946, Truman seized the railroads in the name of the government. Then he went before Congress and asked for legislation to draft the workers into the Army so they could be made to go back to work. Just as he was concluding his address, the unions capitulated and returned to their jobs. When coal miners called a national strike, Truman took over the mines and operated them under the Department of the Interior.

In the congressional elections in November 1946, the Republicans won control of both houses of Congress. This Eightieth Congress devoted much of its time to harassing and trying to embarrass Truman. Its investigative subcommittees sought "scandals" to prove that the President's appointees were corrupt, and it passed scores of conservative laws that Truman vetoed. Over Truman's veto, Congress passed a tax reduction bill for persons with incomes over $5000, and followed this with the Taft-Hartley Labor Act, also passed over his veto, which placed stringent curbs on the rights of labor unions.

In the area of foreign policy, Communist Russia had repeatedly gone back on its agreements made at Yalta and Potsdam, making it clear that the Communists intended to try to rule the world. To combat Russia, the President announced the "Truman Doctrine" in a speech to Congress in March 1947. He said: "I believe that it must be the policy of the United States to support free peoples who are resisting attempted subjugation by armed minorities or by outside pressures." Congress responded to his call and voted money that was used to save Greece and Turkey from being taken over by the Communists.

In June 1947, Secretary of State George Marshall in a speech at Harvard announced plans to extend the Truman Doctrine to reconstruct war-torn Europe. The following March, Congress approved the multi-billion-dollar Marshall Plan.

Truman brought consternation to the ranks of Southern Democrats when, in February 1948, he sent a message to Congress calling for a ten-point civil rights program to end religious and racial discrimination of all aspects.

When the British ended their World War I mandate over Palestine in May 1948, Truman immediately recognized the new Israel government, bringing him praise from Jewish leaders and sneers from Arab countries.

Just before the 1948 national political conventions, Truman went on a cross-country speaking tour in which he made dozens of off-the-cuff speeches denouncing the Republican Congress. Shortly after he returned to Washington late in June, he was faced with a major international crisis. The Russians had cut off all ground transportation to Berlin and seemed to be on the point of trying to push American forces out of the former German capital. Truman was determined to resist the Russian intimidation, ordering the Air Force to break the blockade with the "Berlin Airlift." This round-the-clock air supply continued for the next eleven months, until the Russians backed down.

In the spring of 1948 Truman's domestic political fortunes appeared to be at a low ebb. The polls showed his popular support to be so poor that

The crowd gathered in Lafayette Park on Pennsylvania Avenue across from the White House to celebrate the end of World War II.

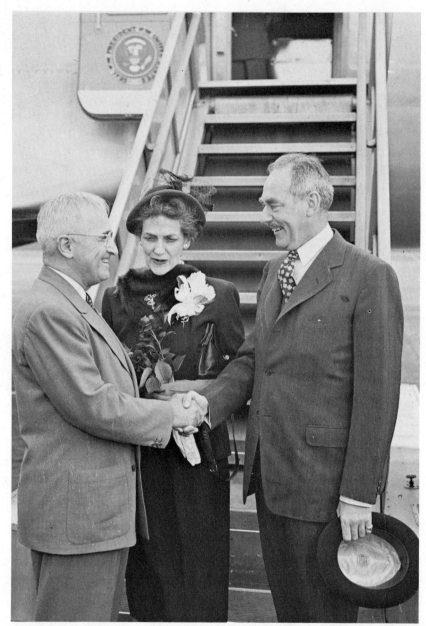

President Truman greeting Dean Acheson, Secretary of State, and Mrs. Acheson.

many Democrats talked of drafting General Eisenhower as their party's candidate. Southern Democrats threatened to bolt the party over civil rights, and former Vice President Wallace's ultra-liberal following planned a third-party ticket. Despite the formidable odds, Truman resolved to run for re-election. He picked Senator Alben Barkley of Kentucky, veteran majority leader of the Senate, as his running mate and roused the delegates at Philadelphia with a fighting speech.

The Republicans, confident of victory though harmed somewhat by their own intra-party conflicts, united behind Governor Thomas E. Dewey of New York, who had run vigorously against Roosevelt in 1944. The threatened defections on both the right and left of the Democratic party materialized in the form of the "Dixiecrat" candidacy of Governor Strom Thurmond of South Carolina and the "Progressive" candidacy of Henry Wallace.

(Right) At a news conference aboard his campaign train, October 16, 1945, Harry Truman answering questions for the reporters. —*Acme photograph*

Harry Truman in Cincinnati's Union Terminal at 10 p.m. on November 4, 1948, en route to Washington, D. C., after a vigorous whistle-stop campaign that brought victory. —*Russell Manuel photograph*

(Right) At Superior, Wisconsin, President Truman spoke to a large and enthusiastic audience during the campaign, in October 1948. *International News photograph*

(Below) In Reading, Pennsylvania, October 7, 1948, Harry Truman called for the election of a Democratic Congress to eradicate the effects of the "awful 80th Congress." —*International News photograph*

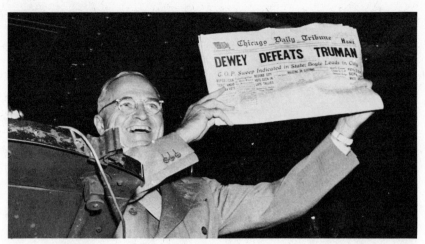

One of the famous news photographs of history, showing President Truman displaying the early edition of the Chicago Tribune, which had jumped to the erroneous conclusion that Truman had been defeated by Dewey.

—*UPI photograph*

In an ingenious piece of campaign strategy, Truman outraged the Republicans by calling a special session of Congress on July 26, immediately after the conventions, challenging the GOP to carry out its platform promises to pass expanded social legislation. When the session adjourned after eleven days without passing any of the legislation, Truman could effectively claim that the Republicans were not serious about their platform promises.

Public opinion polls, newspapers, and magazines almost unanimously predicted Truman's defeat. Undaunted, Truman set out on a "whistle-stop" campaign that ran from Labor Day to Election Day, traveling thousands of miles by train and making hundreds of speeches before large and small crowds. He addressed himself to the common people, tirelessly denouncing the "do-nothing" Republican Eightieth Congress. His homey appearance—Bess and Margaret accompanied him—and his sincerity and seriousness won the crowds.

Yet so certain were the experts of the outcome that when the first count of returns showed Truman leading, political commentators shrugged it off, and maintained that Dewey was bound to win. But the pattern of the astounding upset continued throughout the night, and Dewey finally conceded defeat at eleven o'clock the next morning. The jubilant Truman returned to Washington from his Independence home happily waving to crowds a copy of the Republican Chicago *Tribune* that carried the banner: DEWEY DEFEATS TRUMAN. The final count gave Truman 303 electoral votes and 24,105,812 popular votes to Dewey's 189 and 21,970,065; Thurmond's 39 and 1,169,063; and Wallace's 0 and 1,156,103.

Truman's Second Term

In his inaugural address on January 20, 1949, Truman announced a significant new concept in foreign relations. This was "Point Four" in his listing of foreign policy aims, which he described as "a bold new program for making the benefits of our scientific advances and industrial progress available for the improvement and growth of underdeveloped areas." A year later Congress approved $25 million to start this program.

Of perhaps greater immediate importance was the signing of the treaty for the North Atlantic Treaty Organization (NATO) that took place in Washington on April 4, 1949. The Russians still were blockading Berlin,

Leaving Blair House on January 20, 1949, for the inauguration, *(from the left)* Mrs. Truman, Margaret Truman, Mrs. Max Truitt, Vice-President Alben Barkley, and President Truman. —*UPI photograph*

The inaugural parade moving along Constitution Avenue, January 20, 1949, with the Cadet Corps from West Point in the foreground. —*UPI photograph*

President Truman, accompanied by Carlos Romulo, President of the UN General Assembly, and New York's Mayor William O'Dwyer, in a motorcade along 34th Street in New York, en route to the United Nations General Assembly, where, in a speech, Truman stated that no one nation can always have its own way and asked for arms and atomic energy control, better living conditions for all, and respect for human rights.

Addressing the UN General Assembly at the ceremonies marking the laying of the cornerstone of the United Nations Secretariat Building, President Truman shared the platform with (left to right) Wallace K. Harrison, Director of Planning; M. C. de Freitas Valle, Brazilian Ambassador; Dr. Tingfu F. Tsiang of China; M. Chauvel of France; Mohammed Zafrulla Khan of Pakistan; and Governor Thomas E. Dewey.

Arriving at Fulton, Missouri, March 5, 1946, Winston Churchill and Harry Truman, just before the former great Prime Minister of England delivered the speech in which the phrase, *iron curtain*, was first used.

—International News photograph

Bess Truman and Mamie Eisenhower greeting each other at the White House.

President Truman and Governor Thomas Dewey, adversaries in the 1948 election, greeting each other at the White House.

Former President Herbert Hoover visiting with President Harry Truman.

Blair House, across from the White House, which served as the official residence of the Trumans during the restoration of the White House, at the time of an attempt to assassinate President Truman. In 1973, General Secretary Leonid Brezhnev of the U.S.S.R. and his party stayed here.

and the threat of war hung over Europe. NATO joined the United States with Great Britain, France, Canada, and eight other nations in a mutual defense agreement with a single commander in charge of military units of all twelve nations. General Eisenhower was named as the first NATO commander.

Although the Democrats had won control of Congress in the 1948 election, Truman soon discovered that he still could not get his Fair Deal legislation past the coalition of conservative Southern Democrats and Republicans. Only one major part of his program was approved in 1949, a public housing act.

During most of his second term as President, Truman did not live in the White House. He and his family moved across the street to Blair House, while the presidential residence was completely renovated. An attempt on Truman's life was made on November 1, 1950, by two fanatical Puerto Rican nationalists who tried to shoot their way in. One of the assassins and a Secret Service agent were killed. The President was not harmed.

Truman's enormous energy enabled him to work harder than had many earlier Presidents. He retained the early rising habits of a dirt farmer, usually getting up at 5:30 A.M. and going for a walk of a mile or two, followed by a short swim before breakfast. Newspaper reporters often joined him in these early morning walks and had to trot to keep up with his fast pace.

Although Truman pushed for international control of atomic energy, the Russians thwarted any effective agreement. After Russia exploded its first A-bomb in September 1949, Truman authorized the development of the larger and more awesome hydrogen bomb—the first of which was tested late in his administration in November 1952.

Truman's worst set-back in foreign relations was the loss of China to communism. Missions headed by General Marshall and General Wedemeyer failed to prevent a civil war in which the Nationalist side, headed by Generalissimo Chiang Kai-shek, and backed by the United States, was defeated. Late in 1949, Chiang fled to Formosa, and the Communists triumphantly held all the Chinese mainland.

Fear of Communist subversion in the United States was whipped to a hysterical pitch by congressional investigations throughout Truman's administration. Two of the most prominent figures in these investigations were Representative Richard Nixon of California and Senator Joseph McCarthy of Wisconsin. In 1950, Alger Hiss, a former State Department official under Roosevelt and Truman, was convicted of perjury for denying that he had been part of a Communist spy ring in the 1930s. In the 1950s McCarthy claimed that there were more than two hundred Communists working in the State Department and that Secretary of State Dean Acheson was "soft on Communism." Truman denounced McCarthyism, but it remained an important issue.

In June 1950, Truman was faced with what he later said was the most difficult decision of his presidency. On June 25, Communist North Korean troops invaded American-supported South Korea. After the United Nations Security Council—with Russia absent—denounced the North Koreans as aggressors and called on UN members to send aid to South Korea, Truman on June 28 ordered U.S. armed forces into action. The fighting was to last more than three years, and more than 54,000 American servicemen were to die in the struggle. When UN forces under the command of General Douglas MacArthur were on the point of winning the war in October 1950, powerful Chinese Communist forces entered the conflict on the side of the North Koreans and inflicted a serious defeat on the UN Army. In the succeeding months MacArthur repeatedly disagreed with the Truman administration's policy of not widening the war to include fighting in China. His patience worn thin, Truman finally relieved MacArthur of his command on April 11, 1951.

On the home front, the Korean War caused a fresh burst of inflation before Congress voted powers to reinstitute price and wage controls. In April 1952, after wage negotiations between steelworkers and steel mill owners had broken down, Truman seized the steel industry. In June the Supreme Court ruled that the seizure was unconstitutional. A seven-week strike resulted before settlement was reached.

In the spring of 1952 Truman announced that he would not run for re-election. The Republican Congress had approved the Twenty-second Constitutional Amendment limiting the President to two full terms, but this amendment, which had been written largely in vindictiveness against Roosevelt's four terms, did not apply to Truman, who had less than two full terms. The President chose as his successor Governor Adlai Stevenson of Illinois. He helped Stevenson obtain the nomination, but was disappointed when Stevenson seemed deliberately to refuse to defend Truman's record in the campaign.

The Republicans nominated General Eisenhower and campaigned on issues that included the Korean War, the graft scandals in which some Truman subordinates had been involved, and accusations that the Truman administration was "soft on Communists in government." When Eisenhower won by a large majority, Truman expressed some personal regrets that he had decided not to run for re-election.

The Trumans, Margaret and Clifton Daniel, and Clifton's parents at the Truman home in Independence, Missouri, at the time of Margaret Truman's marriage to Clifton Daniel, in 1956. *—Harry Barth*

President Truman visiting with Democratic Presidential nominee, Adlai Stevenson, and Senator John Sparkman of Alabama, the Vice-Presidential nominee for 1952.

—International News photograph

President Truman presenting the highest award for Meritorious Service to the United States to General Eisenhower.

The historic signing of the Unification Bill, August 10, 1949, creating the Department of Defense, with (left to right) Senator Richard Russell; Secretary of Defense Louis Johnson; Air Force Chief of Staff, General Hoyt Vandenberg; Representative Dewey Short; and Representative Carl Vinson.

—UPI photograph

AFTER Eisenhower's inauguration, Truman returned to his home in Independence. For the next several years he devoted considerable time to writing the two-volume memoirs of his presidency, *Year of Decisions*, published in 1955, and *Years of Trial and Hope*, published in 1956. The Harry S Truman Library, dedicated in Independence in 1957, was built by contributions of his friends to house his presidential papers and provide office space for the former President.

In 1960 the seventy-six-year-old Truman gave a series of lectures to Columbia University students, elucidating the problems of his presidency. These lectures were later published under the title *Truman Speaks*. In them he especially denounced the Twenty-second Amendment, which he said "made a lame duck" out of every President serving a second term. He recalled that the amendment could not apply to him, and jokingly announced that: "I'm going to run again when I'm ninety."

He was pleased when the Democrats returned to power under President John F. Kennedy in 1961, and were continued in power with President Lyndon Johnson's election in 1964. He was particularly honored when President Johnson flew to Independence to sign into law the Medicare Act providing medical assistance for the aged—legislation that first had been proposed as part of Truman's Fair Deal.

At the age of eighty-eight, Truman died on December 26, 1972, at the Research Hospital and Medical Center in Kansas City, Missouri, where he had been fighting for his life for twenty-two days from a respiratory infection and failing body systems. After a simple funeral attended mostly by old friends, the former President's body was buried in the courtyard of the Truman Library in Independence, Missouri.

Former President Lyndon B. Johnson, who himself was to die less than a month later, said at Truman's death: "A 20th century giant is gone. Few men of any times ever shaped the world as did the man from Independence."

President Nixon said: "Our hopes today for a generation of peace rest in large measure on the firm foundation that he laid."

—Harry Barth

(*At left*) Mrs. Harry Truman, Mrs. Franklin Roosevelt, Chief Justice Earl Warren, former President Hoover, Basil O'Connor, and former President Truman at the Truman Library, July 6, 1957. (*Below*) The Harry S. Truman Library in Independence, Missouri, opened in 1957 as part of the National Archives.

—Truman Library

110   FRANKLIN DELANO ROOSEVELT

Franklin Delano Roosevelt

The Thirty-second President of the United States
1933–45

1882 (January 30) Born in Hyde Park, New York.

1896–1900 Attended Groton School in Massachusetts.

1900–04 Attended Harvard University, graduating in 1903.

1904–07 Attended Columbia University Law School.

1905 (March 17) Married Eleanor Roosevelt.

1907 Admitted to the bar to practice law.

1911–12 Senator in the state legislature of New York.

1913–20 Assistant Secretary of the Navy under President Wilson.

1920 Ran unsuccessfully as the Democratic nominee for Vice President.

1921 Crippled by an attack of polio.

1929–32 Governor of New York.

1933–45 Thirty-second President of the United States.

1945 (April 12) Died at Warm Springs, Georgia.

Leading Officials in Roosevelt's Administration

Office	Name	Years Served
Chief Justice	Charles Evans Hughes	1930-1941
	Harlan Fiske Stone	1941-1946
Vice-President	John Nance Garner	1933-1941
	Henry A. Wallace	1941-1945
	Harry S Truman	1945
Secretary of State	Cordell Hull	1933-1944
	Edward R. Stettinius, Jr.	1944-1945
Secretary of the Treasury	W. H. Woodin	1933-1934
	Henry Morgenthau, Jr.	1934-1945
Secretary of War	George H. Dern	1933-1936
	Harry H. Woodring	1936-1940
	Henry L. Stimson	1940-1945
Attorney General	Homer S. Cummings	1933-1939
	Frank Murphy	1939-1940
	Robert H. Jackson	1940-1941
	Francis Biddle	1941-1945
Postmaster General	James A. Farley	1933-1940
	Frank C. Walker	1940-1945
Secretary of the Navy	Claude A. Swanson	1933-1940
	Charles Edison	1940
	Frank Knox	1940-1944
	James Forrestal	1944-1947
Secretary of the Interior	Harold L. Ickes	1933-1946
Secretary of Agriculture	Henry A. Wallace	1933-1940
	Claude R. Wickard	1940-1945
Secretary of Commerce	Daniel C. Roper	1933-1938
	Harry L. Hopkins	1938-1940
	Jesse H. Jones	1940-1945
	Henry A. Wallace	1945-1946
Secretary of Labor	Frances Perkins	1933-1945

With a jaunty smile, a soothing voice, and supreme self-confidence, Franklin D. Roosevelt rallied a fear-ridden nation to overcome the Great Depression, and then mustered the mightiest military host the world had ever seen to free the enslaved people of three continents. Singing his campaign song, "Happy Days Are Here Again," the people of the United States elected him President four times—a greater honor and trust than ever given any other man.

With his New Deal—a program of social justice more sweeping than ever dreamed of by Theodore Roosevelt or Woodrow Wilson—he brought security to the aged, relief to the unemployed, and shorter hours and higher wages to workingmen. He remade the federal government, adding scores of new agencies and services. And he reshaped the principles of his Democratic party, casting aside the long-standing commitment to states' rights and forcing acceptance of Hamilton's belief in a strong central government.

No obstacle short of death could stop him. At thirty-nine an attack of polio crippled both his legs for life, but this did not deter him from becoming governor of New York and then President. To put through his New Deal he put down conservative businessmen, reactionary senators, and even recalcitrant Supreme Court justices. Foreseeing the inevitable clash of America with the power-mad dictators of Germany, Italy, and Japan, he armed the nation despite the opposition of die-hard isolationists. And, after Japan's sneak attack at Pearl Harbor had shattered the U.S. fleet, he guided the strategy that ultimately brought victory in World War II.

As President, his creed was a simple one. He said he believed that the role of any President was ". . . to preserve under the changing conditions of each generation a people's government for the people's good."

A Wealthy Background

THE only son of a railroad executive, Franklin Delano Roosevelt was born on his father's estate in Hyde Park, New York, on January 30, 1882. His mother Sara, who was twenty-six years younger than his father, played a dominant role in his life—still treating him as a small boy even after he had become President.

He never attended an American public school as he was growing up, receiving most of his early education from governesses and tutors. But his education was a broad one, for his family took him on trips to Europe almost every year.

When he was fourteen, young Roosevelt was enrolled at Groton, a private preparatory school in Massachusetts, where he spent four years. Like his cousin Theodore Roosevelt, he attended Harvard University, where he majored in history and received his degree in three years. He then took an additional year of graduate study. But at Harvard he was at least as interested in extra-curricular activities as he was in studies. He led an active social life and felt that one of his greatest accomplishments was becoming editor of the *Harvard Crimson*, the campus newspaper.

While still at Harvard, Roosevelt became engaged to a distant cousin, Eleanor Roosevelt, who was two years younger than himself. Despite mild opposition by his mother, they were married on March 17, 1905. They had six children, one of whom died as a baby.

Meanwhile, Roosevelt began attending classes at Columbia University Law School. He found the study of law dull, just as Theodore Roosevelt

Mrs. Franklin D. Roosevelt (Anna Eleanor Roosevelt) was a sixth cousin of her husband and a niece of Theodore Roosevelt, who exerted a strong influence upon Franklin in choosing a career in public service.

Franklin Roosevelt as a senator in the New York State legislature in 1910, when he was twenty-eight years old.

had, and did not graduate, but he learned sufficient law to pass a bar examination in 1907.

When Roosevelt was twenty-eight, he entered politics. Though the famous name he bore was associated with the GOP, his own branch of the family was Democratic. He made a substantial contribution to the Democratic campaign fund in 1910 and was pleasantly surprised when the state convention nominated him as the Democratic candidate for the state senate from Dutchess County. This may have been considered a joke by the machine politicians, because no Democrat had been elected in Dutchess County in half a century. But Roosevelt took it seriously, used an automobile to travel to every rural by-way, and so impressed the farmers with his integrity that he was elected with a majority of more than a thousand votes.

Again emulating his cousin Theodore, Roosevelt led a revolt against the political bosses that dominated the state government. He received some national notice when he and his friends forced the party leaders to dump their choice for U.S. senator and substitute a man with better qualifications. Re-elected to the state senate in 1912, he shortly thereafter received an appointment by President Wilson as Assistant Secretary of the Navy. In 1914 he made an unsuccessful attempt to win the Democratic nomination for U.S. senator in New York, but lost to a Tammany-supported candidate. He continued his work in the Navy Department, writing at the height of World War I:

"When the United States entered the war, I found that I would have to decide between doing my bit in keeping the Navy at the highest point of efficiency, and neglecting important work to keep run of matters political. . . . I have literally not given the slightest thought or attention to anything but the work immediately before me since."

In 1920 the Democratic National Convention met in San Francisco in June and nominated James Cox of Ohio for President and Roosevelt for Vice President. Roosevelt campaigned strenuously, making speeches in almost every state in support of the major campaign issue—the League of Nations. But the Republican ticket of Harding and Coolidge won by a landslide. "I am not really much surprised at the result," Roosevelt wrote, "because I have felt all along that we are in the middle of a kind

As Assistant Secretary of the Navy, Franklin Roosevelt began a long career in the public eye, in 1913.   —*Clinedinst photograph*

The Wilson Cabinet in 1917, doing calisthenics as a part of wartime physical fitness, with Roosevelt in the center foreground.

The office of the Assistant Secretary of the Navy, December 13, 1917, showing (from the left) Walter Lippmann, noted reporter, columnist, and author, Franklin Roosevelt, and William Blackman.

The last conference of bureau chiefs of the Navy Department attended by Roosevelt as Assistant Secretary of the Navy in 1920.

Franklin Roosevelt and two of his sons working on a model sailboat—one of his favorite hobbies—in 1920.

A memorable photograph taken at the Army-Navy football game of 1920, including (left to right) General Peyton C. March; Newton D. Baker, Secretary of War; General John J. Pershing; Josephus Daniels, Secretary of the Navy; Franklin Roosevelt, Assistant Secretary of the Navy; Admiral Scales, Superintendent of the U.S. Naval Academy; and General John A. Lejeune, Commandant of the United States Marines.

of tidal flow of discontent and destructive criticism, as a result of the tremendous efforts of the war."

In August 1921, the thirty-nine-year-old Roosevelt was vacationing at the family's summer home on Campobello Island, in Canada, when he suffered an attack of poliomyelitis that crippled both his legs. He never again was to regain the use of his legs, but in the following months he learned to get about by the use of crutches, leg braces, and a wheelchair, greatly strengthening his arms and shoulders.

Roosevelt discovered that swimming gave him an opportunity to exercise his legs, and began vacationing at Warm Springs, Georgia, where he could swim in a pool of warm spring water. In 1927 he founded the Georgia Warm Springs Foundation to provide inexpensive treatment for polio victims.

Meanwhile, Roosevelt continued his interest in national politics. He made a dramatic entrance at the Democratic National Convention in New York City's Madison Square Garden in June 1924, where from a wheelchair he rose and walked to the speaker's rostrum on crutches to deliver a nomination speech for Al Smith, whom he called "the 'Happy Warrior' of the political battlefield." Smith did not win the nomination, but the delegates remembered Roosevelt's courage.

Four years later at the 1928 Democratic National Convention in Houston, Texas, Roosevelt again nominated Smith, and this time Smith received the nomination to run against Herbert Hoover. In October the Democratic New York state convention selected Roosevelt to run for governor. Roosevelt campaigned vigorously throughout the state speaking out against the "vile thing" of religious intoleration that had been introduced because of Smith's Roman Catholicism. In the November vote Roosevelt carried the state by a small margin, although Smith lost.

The new governor pushed the legislature to grant tax relief to farm communities in economic difficulty. He also promoted a plan for "old age secured against want," declaring "the first duty of a State, and by that I mean Government, is to promote the welfare of the citizens of that state." Thus Roosevelt already had something of a reputation for social reform when the stock market crashed. Though he had no more inkling than anyone else of the magnitude of the economic disaster, when he was re-elected in the Democratic landslide of 1930 he called the legislature into special session to provide $20 million in relief to the unemployed—the first direct unemployment aid by any state.

When the Democratic National Convention nominated Roosevelt for President in 1932, he dramatically flew to Chicago to become the first nominee ever to deliver his acceptance speech in person. He said, in part, "Never before in modern history have the essential differences between the two major American parties stood out in such striking contrast . . . I pledge you, I pledge myself, to a *new deal* for the American people."

President Hoover, campaigning for re-election, warned that if Roosevelt were elected "the grass will grow in the streets" and "weeds will overrun the fields of millions of farms." But the people blamed the Great Depression on the Republican party and on Hoover, and reacted by electing Roosevelt by a landslide, giving him 22,809,638 popular votes to Hoover's 15,758,901, and 472 electoral votes to 59.

In the interval before taking office, Roosevelt narrowly escaped death when a mentally deranged man fired shots at him in Miami, Florida. His automobile companion, Mayor Anton Cermak of Chicago, was killed.

Overcoming a Handicap

James M. Cox of Ohio, Democratic candidate for President, with his running mate, Franklin D. Roosevelt, in 1920.

In October 1929, Franklin D. Roosevelt, as Governor of New York, greeting skating champion, Jack Shea.

Mrs. Roosevelt, as she appeared in 1933, at the beginning of her husband's first term as President.

WHEN the fifty-one-year-old Roosevelt took office on March 4, 1933, the nation had never before been in such desperate economic plight. There were millions of unemployed, thousands of farmers with mortgages foreclosed. Thousands of banks had gone bankrupt, and virtually all those still operating were closed by state governors to head off further failures. The nation listened via radio as Roosevelt, a fine speaker, brought an accent of hope to the stricken country.

"This is preeminently the time to speak the truth, the whole truth, frankly and boldly . . .

"First of all, let me assert my firm belief that the only thing we have to fear is fear itself—nameless, unreasoning, unjustified terror which paralyzes needed efforts to convert retreat into advance. In every dark hour of our national life a leadership of frankness and vigor has met with that understanding and support of the people themselves which is essential to victory. I am convinced that you will again give that support to leadership in these critical days. . . .

"The money changers have fled from their high seats in the temple of civilization. We may now restore that temple to the ancient truths. . . . The measure of the restoration lies in the extent to which we apply social values more noble than mere monetary profits. . . .

"Our greatest primary task is to put people to work . . . Finally, in our progress toward a resumption of work we require two safeguards against a return of the evils of the old order; there must be a strict supervision of all banking and credits and investments, so that there will be an end to speculation with other people's money; and there must be provision for an adequate but sound currency. . . .

"I am prepared under my constitutional duty to recommend the measures that a stricken Nation in the midst of a stricken world may require. These measures, or such other measures as the Congress may build out of its experience and wisdom, I shall seek, within my constitutional authority, to bring to speedy adoption. . . .

"But in the event that Congress shall fail to take one of these two courses, and in the event that the national emergency is still critical, I shall not evade the clear course of duty that will then confront me. I shall ask the Congress for the one remaining instrument to meet the crisis— broad Executive power to wage a war against the emergency, as great as the power that would be given to me if we were in fact invaded by a foreign foe. . . .

"We do not distrust the future of essential democracy. The people of the United States have not failed. In their need they have registered a mandate that they want direct, vigorous action. They have asked for discipline and direction under leadership. They have made me the present instrument of their wishes. In the spirit of the gift I take it."

In the next hundred days Roosevelt put the federal government through the greatest upheaval it had ever known in peacetime. He called a special session of Congress to meet on March 9. Meanwhile, on March 6 he declared a national "bank holiday" that closed all the banks in the United States until they could be inspected to insure their soundness. He called a conference of state governors on March 6 and warned them that the federal government would step in to prevent starvation if the local and state governments failed to act. On March 12 he gave the first of his "fireside chat" radio addresses, in which he reassured the nation about the reasons for the bank holiday. On March 13 the banks that were sound were permitted to reopen. The Agricultural Adjustment Act (AAA) was passed to bring the farmers more purchasing power and limit their production of agricultural surpluses. The National Industrial Recovery Act

President and Mrs. Roosevelt with Vice-President Henry Wallace and Mrs. Wallace, on the observation platform of a Pennsylvania train.

At his charming best, President Roosevelt enjoying a laugh upon his arrival at Union Station, Washington, D. C., with Marvin McIntyre, the President's secretary, August 12, 1938.   *—UPI photograph*

Roosevelt was a favorite subject of cartoonists because people felt so strongly in favor of him or were so violently opposed to him.

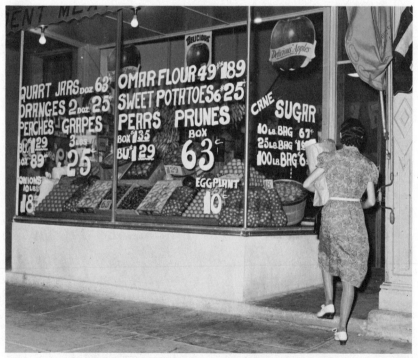

A Saturday night shopper in Grundy Center, Iowa, in September of 1939, with a drastically different level of pricing than that of today.

—*Rothstein photograph*

(NIRA) was an ambitious attempt to regulate business. The Tennessee Valley Authority (TVA) was created to develop the hydroelectric resources of the destitute Tennessee valley. Home Owners Loan Corporation (HOLC) provided assistance to home owners threatened with foreclosures. By executive order Roosevelt took the country off the gold standard to preserve its gold reserves. A Federal Emergency Relief Administration was set up with Harry Hopkins as administrator to make direct grants to states for relief to the unemployed. The Civilian Conservation Corps (CCC) was organized to provide work for unemployed youth. At the conclusion of the congressional session in June, Roosevelt wrote:

"I am certain that this Special Session of Congress will go down in the history of our country as one which, more than any other, boldly seized the opportunity to right great wrongs, to restore clearer thinking and more honest practices, to carry through its business with practical celerity and to set our feet on the upward path."

In the field of foreign relations, Roosevelt restored diplomatic relations with Russia that had been broken off since the Russian Revolution.

In the succeeding years of his first term Roosevelt led Congress in developing many other new agencies of the federal government, including the Federal Communications Commission, the Securities Exchange Commission, the Federal Housing Administration, a National Resources Board, and the Rural Electrification Administration. In 1935, at Roosevelt's urging, Congress passed social security measures to provide old age pensions, unemployment insurance, aid to dependent children, and health services.

In 1936 Roosevelt was re-elected to a second term, defeating the Republican candidate, Governor Alfred M. Landon of Kansas, in a landslide giving him a higher percentage of the popular and electoral votes

—Rothstein photograph

Crowds in Bismarck, North Dakota, waiting for Roosevelt in August 1936.

than he had received four years earlier. The popular vote gave him 27,752,869 to Landon's 16,674,665. The electoral vote was 523 to 8, Landon carrying only Maine and Vermont.

Roosevelt's Second Term

IN his second inaugural address, on January 20, 1937, Roosevelt frankly admitted that the nation had not yet reached the "happy valley" that he envisioned at the beginning of his first term. But he pledged himself to continue to work to relieve the poverty of "one third of a nation ill-housed, ill-clad, ill-nourished."

Starting in 1935 the Supreme Court of the United States had been causing trouble for Roosevelt's New Deal by declaring such important pieces of legislation as the NIRA and the AAA unconstitutional. Most of the justices of the Supreme Court were conservatives who had been appointed by Presidents Taft, Harding, Coolidge, and Hoover—six of the nine justices were over seventy years old. Roosevelt proposed legislation to require retirement by justices at the age of seventy, declaring that he wanted "a modernized judiciary that would look at modern problems through modern glasses." When Congress balked at Roosevelt's plan, calling it an effort to "pack the Supreme Court," Roosevelt made a new "fireside chat" defending the need for changing the personnel of the Court.

Suddenly, without any court reform legislation having been passed, the Supreme Court took on a more liberal tone, upholding the right of states to fix a minimum wage, and reporting that the federal social security laws were constitutional under the "general welfare" clause. As time wore on and death intervened among the members of the Court, Roosevelt had the opportunity to appoint a new Chief Justice and eight associate justices, all of a more liberal background.

But meantime the historical focus was shifting to the war clouds in Europe. The Axis powers of Germany, Italy, and Japan grew stronger and more aggressive during the late 1930s, attacking and conquering one weak neighbor after another. Roosevelt warned Hitler and Mussolini that if they started a general war, history would "hold them accountable." At Roosevelt's urging, Congress revised the nation's neutrality laws in 1939 to make it possible for the United States to sell supplies to friendly nations fighting the Axis powers.

When Hitler's army marched into Poland in September 1939, starting World War II, Roosevelt addressed the nation in a fireside chat: ". . . I have said not once, but many times, that I have seen war and that I hate war. I say that again and again. I *hope* that the United States will keep out of this war. I *believe* that it will. And I give you assurance and reassurance that every effort of your Government will be directed toward that end." Nevertheless, it was at Roosevelt's request that Congress revised neutrality laws to permit sale of arms to the Western Allies.

The following year the Democratic Convention met at the moment of France's fall, with Britain standing alone and beleaguered, and the Nazi peril at its flood height. Despite a formal disclaimer of third-term ambitions, Roosevelt was renominated unanimously. The Republicans nominated a political newcomer, Wendell L. Willkie of Indiana.

The campaign was carried on before the darkening backdrop of the war in Europe. In September, Roosevelt negotiated a deal with Britain whereby fifty old U.S. destroyers were lent to the British in return for naval bases on British West Indies islands. He lashed out strongly at the Republican party, which he said had obstructed his attempts to strengthen the military defense of the United States. In the election he again won by a large majority, though not as large as before: 27,307,819 votes to Willkie's

Queen Elizabeth of England and Mrs. Roosevelt.

22,321,018, and 449 electoral votes to 82.

In his State of the Union message to Congress in January 1941, Roosevelt said:

"In the future days, which we seek to make secure, we look forward to a world founded upon four essential human freedoms.

"The first is freedom of speech and expression—everywhere in the world.

"The second is freedom of every person to worship God in his own way—everywhere in the world.

"The third is freedom from want—which, translated into world terms, means economic understanding which will secure to every nation a healthy peacetime life for its inhabitants—everywhere in the world.

"The fourth is freedom from fear—which, translated into world terms, means a world-wide reduction of armaments to such a point and in such a thorough fashion that no nation will be in a position to commit an act of physical aggression against any neighbor—anywhere in the world."

In August 1941, Roosevelt met with Prime Minister Winston Churchill aboard a cruiser in the North Atlantic to draft a document subsequently called the "Atlantic Charter," which set forth an eight-point agreement on the common principles which they believed should be part of any future peace.

The United States had cut off trade with Japan because of repeated Japanese aggression in Southeast Asia. Relations soon became tense. In December 1941, a special Japanese envoy had arrived in Washington to confer with the American government. On December 7, without warning, the Japanese bombed Pearl Harbor, the U.S. Navy base in Hawaii, and launched an attack on the Philippines. Calling this "a date which will live in infamy," Roosevelt asked Congress for a declaration of war against Japan. A few days later war was declared between the United States and Germany and Italy.

Roosevelt's Third and Fourth Terms

The original draft of Franklin D. Roosevelt's speech to Congress on December 8, 1941, declaring war on Japan. —*UPI photograph*

During World War II, in 1943, President Roosevelt visited French Morocco to discuss the war with leaders in the field, including (left to right) Lieutenant General Mark Clark; President Roosevelt, Harry Hopkins (back to camera); and General George S. Patton, Jr.

—*U. S. Army Air Forces—Office of War Information*

F.D.R. and General Eisenhower at Castelvetrano, Sicily, December 8, 1943.

Wendell Willkie, the Republican candidate for President in 1940, who was defeated by Roosevelt.

In February 1945, President Roosevelt addressed Congress, reporting on the historic Yalta Conference, the full report of which was made ten years later, March 16, 1955. —*UPI photograph*

A dinner scene during the Yalta Conference in February 1945, with Edward R. Stettinius, Jr., former Secretary of State, offering a toast while Russia's foreign Commisar, Vyacheslav Molotov, (extreme right) studies the menu. Across the table (left to right) are Joseph Stalin, Russian Premier; Franklin Roosevelt, United States President; and Winston Churchill, Prime Minister of England. —*UPI photograph*

Mrs. Roosevelt and Fiorello La Guardia, former mayor of New York City.

Under Roosevelt's leadership the country went all out for victory, with rigid controls on prices and wages, hundreds of billions in appropriations, massive conscription of manpower. Censorship was imposed. All strikes and lockouts were forbidden. One major effort was successfully concealed from the general public and the enemy: the development of the atomic bomb.

On New Year's Day, 1942, twenty-six countries subscribed to the principles of the Atlantic Charter and agreed to fight until victory could be won over the Axis powers. At Roosevelt's suggestion the Allies called themselves the "United Nations." This formed the basis for the UN organization created at the end of the war.

During the course of the war Roosevelt conferred several times with Churchill and other allied leaders, planning the grand strategy of the war. After such a conference in Casablanca, Morocco, in 1943, he and Churchill announced that the war would be waged until the Axis had been forced to an unconditional surrender.

By 1943 more than ten million Americans had been inducted into the armed forces, and the Allies had begun to push back the Axis powers. At a press conference late in the year Roosevelt acknowledged that the New Deal had been ended by the war. But he hastened to add, ". . . it seems pretty clear that we must plan for, and help bring about, an expanded economy which will result in more security, more employment, more recreation, for our citizens so that the conditions of 1932 and the beginning of 1933 won't come back."

Allied troops under General Dwight Eisenhower invaded France in June 1944. That same month the Republican National Convention met and nominated Thomas E. Dewey as its candidate for President. In July, Roosevelt announced, "If the Convention should . . . nominate me for the Presidency, I shall accept. If the people elect me, I will serve." Again Roosevelt, this time with Harry S Truman, senator from Missouri, as his running mate, won by a large majority, although by a smaller margin than in his three previous elections. He received 25,606,585 votes to Dewey's 22,014,745, and 432 electoral votes to 99.

The Little White House at Warm Springs, Georgia, where President Franklin Roosevelt died in 1945 from a sudden stroke.

The Roosevelt family burial plot, in the cemetery adjacent to St. James Episcopal Church in Hyde Park, New York.　　　*—Acme photograph*

In his fourth inaugural address in January 1945, Roosevelt declared, "We can gain no lasting peace if we approach it with suspicion and mistrust—or with fear. We can gain it only if we proceed with the understanding and the confidence and courage which flow from conviction."

In February 1945, Roosevelt traveled to Yalta in southwestern Russia to discuss plans for peace with Churchill and Joseph Stalin, the dictator of Russia. He reported to Congress that plans had been agreed to for an organizational meeting of the United Nations on April 25, 1945. He said, "There, we all hope, and confidently expect, to execute a definite charter of organization under which the peace of the world will be preserved and the forces of aggression permanently outlawed. . . . No one can say exactly how long any plan will last. Peace can endure only so long as humanity really insists upon it, and is willing to work for it—and sacrifice for it."

Upon his return from Yalta, Roosevelt looked tired and older than his sixty-three years. Late in March he went to Warm Springs, Georgia, for a rest. On April 12, 1945, he was working at his desk while an artist painted his portrait when he suddenly complained of "a terrific headache." A few hours later, at 4:45 P.M., he died of a cerebral hemorrhage. After services in Washington, his body was buried at his birthplace in Hyde Park. The last words that he had written on the day of his death were:

"The only limit to our realization of tomorrow will be our doubts of today. Let us move forward with strong and active faith."

128   HERBERT CLARK HOOVER

Herbert Clark Hoover

The Thirty-first President of the United States
1929–33

1874 (August 10) Born in West Branch, Iowa.

1884 Moved to Oregon to live with relatives after the death of his father (1880) and mother (1883).

1891–95 Attended Stanford University, graduating with an A.B. degree in engineering.

1897–98 Managed gold mining operations in Australia.

1899 (February 10) Married Lou Henry in Monterey, California.

1899–1900 Chief engineer of China's bureau of mines.

1901 General manager of the Chinese Engineering and Mining Company.

1901–08 Partner in a British engineering firm, traveling throughout the world.

1908–14 Headed own engineering firm supervising projects in many countries.

1914–17 Chairman of the Commission for Relief in Belgium.

1917–19 United States Food Administrator.

1921–28 Secretary of Commerce under Harding and Coolidge.

1929–33 Thirty-first President of the United States.

1946–49 Headed various government commissions appointed by President Truman.

1953–55 Headed a commission on reorganization of the federal government, appointed by President Eisenhower.

1964 (October 20) Died in New York City.

Leading Officials in Hoover's Administration

Office	Name	Years Served
Chief Justice	William Howard Taft	1921-1930
	Charles Evans Hughes	1930-1941
Vice-President	Charles Curtis	1929-1933
Secretary of State	Frank B. Kellog	1925-1929
	Henry L. Stimson	1929-1933
Secretary of the Treasury	Andrew W. Mellon	1921-1932
	Ogden L. Mills	1932-1933
Secretary of War	James W. Good	1929
	Patrick J. Hurley	1929-1933
Attorney General	William D. Mitchell	1929-1933
Postmaster General	Walter F. Brown	1929-1933
Secretary of the Navy	Charles Francis Adams	1929-1933
Secretary of the Interior	Ray Lyman Wilbur	1929-1933
Secretary of Agriculture	Arthur M. Hyde	1929-1933
Secretary of Commerce	Robert P. Lamont	1929-1932
	Roy D. Chapin	1932-1933
Secretary of Labor	James J. Davis	1921-1930
	William N. Doak	1930-1933

Birthplace of Herbert Hoover in West Branch, Iowa.

No other President came to the White House
with more dazzling visions of achievements and left with more shattered
illusions than did Herbert Hoover. It was his first and last elective office—
and therein lies one of the major causes for his failure. As former President Taft commented: "Hoover does not speak the language of the politicians . . ."

Hoover's personal story is one of rags to riches, while the history of the
nation during his administration was one of riches to rags. The first
President born west of the Mississippi River, Hoover was an orphan who
became a highly successful mining engineer, and a millionaire by forty.

During and after World War I, Hoover won a reputation as a great
humanitarian by his efficient administration of war relief in Europe.

A liberal Republican, he supported Wilson in the 1918 elections, and
both Republicans and Democrats began to talk of him as a possible candidate for the presidency. After serving under both Harding and Coolidge
as Secretary of Commerce, he won the 1928 presidential election in a
campaign that promised "a chicken in every pot and a car in every garage."

When the stock market crashed seven months after he took office in
1929, Hoover was automatically doomed to the same obloquy—or worse—
that Van Buren faced in the first national depression nearly a century
earlier. By the time he left office the economic life of the country was
nearing a standstill and his limited measures to meet the crisis appeared
catastrophically inadequate. Eighteen years later he still believed he had
followed the right course, writing:

"I am so immodest as to believe that had we been continued in office
we would have quickly overcome the depression and approached economic
and social problems from the point of view of correcting marginal abuse
and not of inflicting a collectivist economy on the country."

A Self-Made Engineer

THE son of a blacksmith, Herbert Hoover was born in the middle of the
horse-and-buggy age August 10, 1874, in West Branch, Iowa. By the time
he was eight his father and mother had both died, leaving him, his brother,
and his sister to be parceled out among Quaker relatives.

At ten, Herbert was sent to Newberg, Oregon, to live with an aunt and
uncle. His uncle was a country doctor who had helped found a Quaker
secondary school called Newberg College. Here Herbert received the
initial basis of what was to be one of the best formal educations of any
President.

The Herbert Hoover family (from left to right, seated) Herbert Hoover
and Mrs. Lou Henry Hoover (standing) Herbert, Jr., his wife Margaret,
and Allan.

—Underwood & Underwood

At the age of fifteen, he left Newberg College to become a $15-a-month office boy in a real-estate business founded by his uncle in Salem, Oregon. At night he attended a small business college where he learned algebra and geometry. At the real-estate office he met several engineers and fell in love with the profession. Hearing about plans to open a new engineering school, Stanford University in California, Hoover traveled to Portland, Oregon, to take entrance exams. His mathematical talent so impressed the examiners despite the deficiency of his general background that he was recommended for admission.

At Stanford, Hoover worked his own way via a variety of jobs. In addition he took part in many activities—managing the baseball and football teams and taking an active role in student politics on the side of the independents versus the fraternity men. When he graduated in 1895 he had only his degree, $40, and no visible prospects. Unable to find work as an engineer, he took a $2-a-day job as a gold miner's helper in Nevada City, Nevada. When he had saved $100, he decided to go to San Francisco where his brother was working as a linotype operator to support their younger sister. While there he visited the office of Louis Janin, a leading mining engineer, and, when told there were no engineering jobs available, accepted work as a typist. Soon Janin appointed him as an engineering assistant at $150 a month. From that day, as Hoover later wrote, he "never again had to ask for or look for an engineering job of any kind."

At the age of twenty-three, Hoover was hired by a British engineering firm to manage their Australian gold-mining operations. So successful was he that by the time he left two years later he was earning $10,000 a year and was part owner of a profitable gold mine.

In 1899 the Chinese government offered him an appointment as chief engineer of China's bureau of mines. Before going there he returned to the United States where he married his college sweetheart, Lou Henry. They spent their honeymoon on a steamship bound for China.

The Hoovers were in Tientsin when the Boxer Rebellion broke out in 1900. Hoover directed construction of barricades and assumed charge of the water and food supply of the beleaguered foreign quarter. When the rebellion ended, they sailed for London, but returned to China in 1901. Later that year he accepted a lucrative offer of a partnership in the British engineering firm for which he was working.

Hoover on vacation with his fishing catch and (right) enjoying a shore lunch.

The twenty-seven-year-old Hoover and his wife arrived back in London in November 1901. As a 20% owner of the reorganized British firm, Hoover was well on his way to becoming wealthy only five years after leaving college. For the next dozen years he traveled to every continent except Antarctica, planning and supervising major engineering projects, making them profitable, and often sharing in their profits. As a hobby during this period, he turned to writing, preparing a textbook called *Principles of Mining*. In addition, he and his wife spent five years producing the first English translation from the Latin of the sixteenth-century classic work on mining, Agricola's *De Re Metallica*.

THE guns of World War I abruptly ended Hoover's career as an engineer by opening a new one for him as a humanitarian and public servant. In London he organized a committee that helped more than a hundred thousand stranded Americans get back to the United States. That done, he took on an even bigger job—chairman of the Commission for Relief in Belgium. Through this agency he conveyed food and supplies to German-occupied Belgium.

Shortly after the United States declared war on Germany in 1917, President Wilson appointed Hoover as United States Food Administrator.

A Practical Humanitarian

The first President to appear in talking movies—Hoover during a rehearsal.   *—Herbert French photograph*

Hoover's favorite cartoon.
—*Underwood & Underwood*

In this job he was responsible for stabilizing food prices and insuring that food be distributed to those who needed it. One of the measures he recommended to hold prices down was the first excess-profits tax. Hoover himself recommended the title "administrator" for the job—creating an important new organizational title in the federal government; previously, boards or commissions had been appointed to handle the work of such independent agencies, but Hoover insisted that he be given power as an individual rather than as chairman of a committee.

When the war was nearing its conclusion in 1918, Hoover became chairman of the Allied Food Council, handling millions of tons of food for civilians in war-ravaged areas. He directed not only relief but reconstruction, and by the time he returned to the United States in 1919 he was hailed as "the great humanitarian" and was regarded as one of the most important living Americans.

Hoover made a number of statesmanlike speeches supporting the League of Nations, and unsuccessfully tried to persuade Wilson that it would be better to accept certain reservations demanded by various senators than to have American participation in the League rejected altogether.

Democrats and Republicans alike began to talk of Hoover as a possible presidential candidate in 1920. However, he quickly made clear that he was a Republican of long standing, although he had supported Theodore Roosevelt in 1912 and had called for the election of a pro-Wilson Congress in 1918. He did not campaign actively for the 1920 Republican presidential nomination, although his name was entered in several primaries as a representative of the progressive wing of the party. After Harding was nominated, Hoover supported him in the belief that Harding would favor American membership in the League of Nations.

Harding first offered Hoover the post of Secretary of the Interior in his Cabinet, but Hoover said he would prefer to be Secretary of Commerce. Although the conservative wing of the party opposed Hoover's appointment, Harding pushed it through, telling Hoover that he had informed the conservatives that they must accept Hoover if they wanted Andrew Mellon named as Secretary of the Treasury.

Hoover was unscathed by the subsequent scandals in the Harding administration and continued to serve as Secretary of Commerce throughout most of Coolidge's administration, even though Coolidge had little regard for him. During his seven and a half years in the Harding and Coolidge Cabinets, Hoover reorganized the Department of Commerce, worked to improve child health and eliminate child labor, helped reduce the working day from twelve to eight hours, and in general supported the cause of social welfare. He also did a great deal to develop dams, flood control, and hydroelectric projects on the river systems of the nation.

After Coolidge issued his equivocal "I do not choose to run" statement in the summer of 1927, hundreds of Hoover's friends urged him to seek the Republican presidential nomination in 1928. When he asked Coolidge if it would be all right to enter some of the Republican primaries, Coolidge replied, "Why not?" By the time the convention met in Kansas City in June, Hoover had more than 400 of the 1084 delegates pledged to him. Despite a "Stop Hoover" campaign launched by the old guard members of the party, Hoover was nominated on the first ballot with 837 votes. Senator Charles Curtis of Kansas was given the vice-presidential nomination to mollify the senators and machine politicians who had opposed Hoover.

In the 1928 campaign against Democratic nominee Governor Al Smith of New York, Hoover made only a few speeches, leaving most of the grass-roots campaigning to his supporters. Some of his remarks in these speeches

Campaigning in Louisville aboard a sidewheeler in the Ohio River.

later were to come back to haunt him. For example, of America's economic system he said: "We in America are nearer to the final triumph over poverty than ever before in the history of any land. . . . We have not yet reached the goal, but, given a chance to go forward with the policies of the last eight years, we shall with the help of God be in sight of the day when poverty will be banished from the nation . . ."

The Democrats made the repeal of Prohibition a major issue of the campaign, denouncing it as a law that had not worked. Hoover supported Prohibition and called it "a great social and economic experiment, noble in motive and far-reaching in purpose."

Herbert Hoover with Secretary of State Henry L. Stimson at the 1932 Republican Convention.

Calvin Coolidge and Herbert Hoover leaving the White House for the Capitol for the 1929 inauguration.

Herbert Hoover with Charles Curtis of Kansas, Vice-President during his administration.
—Underwood & Underwood

Because Smith was a Catholic, the forces of bigotry, particularly in the South, introduced the issue of religion in the campaign. Hoover denounced the use of religious intolerance by his supporters.

The election results gave Hoover the White House by a landslide. In the popular vote he received 21,391,993 to Smith's 15,016,169, and in the electoral vote he won 444 to 87—the largest electoral vote margin since the election of Grant.

HOOVER'S inaugural address reflected the rosy optimism in which America was then bathed. He proposed to pursue the goals of ". . . the preservation of self-government and its full foundations in local government; the perfection of justice whether in economic or in social fields; the maintenance of ordered liberty; the denial of domination by any group or class; the

Hoover's Administration

General view of the Capitol plaza, February 22, 1932, on the occasion of the 200th anniversary of the birth of George Washington.
—Underwood & Underwood

The traditional parade down Pennsylvania Avenue in Washington, D. C. on the rainy day of Hoover's inauguration.

President Hoover with Mrs. Hoover and friends attending services at Christ Church in Alexandria, Virginia, where Washington worshiped and from which he was buried. —*Underwood & Underwood*

A White House meeting of business leaders February 6, 1932 for the purpose of ending hoarding of money. In front row (left to right) Jesse Jones and Wilson McCarthy of the RFC, Secretary of Commerce Robert P. Lamont, President Hoover, Charles G. Dawes, Assistant Secretary of Commerce Julius Klein, and Secretary of the Treasury Ogden Mills.

—*Underwood & Underwood*

Mrs. Herbert Hoover, honorary President of Girl Scouts, with various Scout executives October 9, 1932.

—Underwood & Underwood

President Hoover greeting delegates of the National Education Association, February 24, 1932.

—Underwood & Underwood

Boy Scouts presenting President Hoover with a fishing tackle bag.

President Hoover shaking hands with Bucky Harris, manager of the Washington Senators baseball team.

building up and preservation of equality of opportunity; the stimulation of initiative and individuality; absolute integrity in public affairs; the choice of officials for fitness to office; the direction of economic progress toward prosperity and the further lessening of poverty; the freedom of public opinion; the sustaining of education and of the advancement of knowledge; the growth of religious spirit and the tolerance of all faiths; the strengthening of the home; the advancement of peace. . . ." It was a program to put the final finishing touches on a near-perfect society.

Yet, as Hoover wrote later, he recognized that "there was urgent need for reform in our social and business life. . . . Little had been done by the federal government in the fields of reform or progress during the fourteen years before my time. After 1914 the Wilson administration had been absorbed mostly in problems of war. The Harding and Coolidge administrations had been concerned with economic reconstruction after the war. Mr. Coolidge was reluctant to undertake much that either was new or cost money. And by 1929 many things were already fourteen years overdue. . . ." Thus Hoover intended his administration to be a progressive, reform regime.

Totally unforeseen, seven months later the stock market crash of October 1929 turned this dream into a nightmare. At first neither Hoover nor anyone else had any notion of how bad the Great Depression was to be. Very soon more than twelve million Americans were out of work and businesses were going bankrupt by the thousand.

Hoover tried hard to do something about the Depression. Unfortunately, neither he nor his advisers, nor the orthodox economists of the country knew what to do. He launched new public works programs, hoping that the building industry could absorb the unemployed. He also asked for and received from Congress a substantial reduction in income tax rates, hoping this would stimulate the economy. Both were small steps in the right direction. But he opposed direct federal relief to the mass of unemployed, and his Republican Congress in February 1931 had to pass over his veto the Bonus Act giving almost a billion dollars to veterans.

The temper of the country had already been shown in the congressional elections of 1930, the Democrats winning control of the House of Representatives and reducing the Republican majority in the senate to one vote. But owing to the archaic "lame duck" congressional organization, this Seventy-second Congress did not meet until December 1931. In his message to Congress, Hoover called for the establishment of a Reconstruction Finance Corporation with a "reasonable capital" to aid businesses and home owners with loans. When Congress capitalized the RFC with two billion dollars, Hoover vetoed the measure saying that it would make the RFC a "gigantic banking and pawnbroking business." But by July 1932, he signed a new measure enlarging the loan power of the RFC to 3.3 billion dollars.

In the spring of 1932 thousands of World War I veterans marched on Washington as a "Bonus army," and they and their families camped in ramshackle huts on the outskirts of Washington in what was called "Hooverville." When Congress adjourned in July without giving the veterans all that they had asked in bonus payments, they continued to live on in their huts. Late in July, Hoover ordered the Army to move the veterans out of Washington, and troops under General Douglas MacArthur herded the veterans and their families out of Washington while the huts were burned.

No one was surprised at the results of the national election in 1932 in which Hoover was defeated for re-election by the Democratic presidential nominee, Franklin Delano Roosevelt, in a landslide of equal proportions

President Hoover presenting National Geographic Society gold medal to Amelia Earhart Putnam in recognition of her nonstop solo flight across the Atlantic Ocean.

to the one by which Hoover had come into office. The country had completely reversed its view of Hoover and was impatient that it had to wait four months until his successor could be inaugurated. This impatience helped bring about the "Lame Duck" Twentieth Amendment to the Constitution that advanced the new President's inauguration to January 20 and the opening of the new Congress to January 3. This amendment did not go into effect until December 1933.

President Hoover relaxing astride his favorite horse.

In the months between the election and the inauguration of the new President, Hoover endeavored to obtain the co-operation of the President-elect. But Roosevelt was as cautious as Lincoln had been in a similar situation when Buchanan had urged him to help solve the nation's problems before taking office. The depression continued to worsen.

Busy Later Years

AFTER leaving the White House in March 1933, Hoover and his wife retired to their home in Palo Alto, California, near the Stanford University campus. For a while he devoted considerable time to the Hoover Library that he had founded at the university, then he began to take a more active role in national politics again as a critic of President Roosevelt's New Deal programs. After his wife's death in 1944, he lived much of his time in an apartment in New York City.

Members of the National Automobile Chamber of Commerce meeting with President Hoover on May 2, 1929 to confer on the program for the expansion of world trade and plans to complete a federal system of roads, as well as an inter-American highway. This remarkable gathering included (left to right) Edsel Ford, President of Ford Motor Company, F. A. Seiberling, President of Seiberling Rubber Company, Alfred H. Swayne, Vice-President of General Motors, Walter P. Chrysler, President of the Chrysler Corporation, A. R. Erskine, President of Studebaker Corporation, F. D. Chapin, Chairman of the Board of Hudson Motors, President Hoover, C. W. Nash, President of Nash Motor Company, Alvan Macauley, President of Packard Motor Company, F. J. Haynes, President of Durant Motors, John Willys, President of Willys Overland, H. H. Rice, Assistant to the President of General Motors, A. J. Brosseau, President of Mack Trucks, and Alfred Reeves, General Manager, National Automobile Chamber of Commerce.

Herbert Hoover in Warsaw viewing the ruins after World War II.

Hoover wrote many books including his own three-volume memoirs. In 1938 he published *The Ordeal of Woodrow Wilson*—the first book by a former President about a President.

President Truman recalled Hoover to public life after World War II. He first served as chairman of the Famine Emergency Commission, an organization to prevent starvation of Europeans in the wake of the war, and in 1947, accepted Truman's appointment as chairman of the Commission on Organization of the Executive Branch of the Government. This group became known as the "Hoover Commission" and recommended many important structural changes in the federal government. President Eisenhower in 1953 appointed Hoover as head of another such commission that recommended further changes in the federal structure.

The ninety-year-old former President died in New York City on October 20, 1964. After funeral ceremonies in New York City and in Washington, D.C., he was buried near his birthplace in West Branch, Iowa. In his memoirs Hoover had summed up his attitude toward the presidency:

"I had felt deeply that no President should undermine the independence of legislative and judicial branches by seeking to discredit them. The constitutional division of powers is the bastion of our liberties and was not designed as a battleground to display the prowess of Presidents. They just have to work with the material that God—and the voters—have given them."

A portrait of Herbert Hoover on the occasion of his 90th birthday.
—*UPI photograph*

—Ruband

144   CALVIN COOLIDGE

Calvin Coolidge

The Thirtieth President of the United States
1923–29

1872 (July 4) Born in Plymouth Notch, Vermont.

1884–90 Attended Black River Academy in Ludlow, Vermont.

1891–95 Attended Amherst College, graduating *cum laude*.

1897 Admitted to the bar to practice law in Massachusetts.

1899–1900 Member of city council of Northampton, Mass.

1900–02 City solicitor of Northampton.

1905 (October 4) Married Grace Anna Goodhue.

1907–08 Member of Massachusetts house of representatives.

1910–11 Mayor of Northampton.

1912–15 Member of Massachusetts state senate, president 1914–15.

1916–18 Lieutenant governor of Massachusetts.

1919–20 Governor of Massachusetts.

1921–23 Vice President of the United States.

1923–29 Thirtieth President of the United States.

1933 (January 5) Died in Northampton, Massachusetts.

*Leading Officials in
Coolidge's Administration*

Office	Name	Years Served
Chief Justice	William Howard Taft	1921-1930
Vice-President	Charles G. Dawes	1925-1929
Secretary of State	Charles Evans Hughes	1921-1925
	Frank B. Kellog	1925-1929
Secretary of the Treasury	Andrew W. Mellon	1921-1932
Secretary of War	John W. Weeks	1921-1925
	Dwight F. Davis	1925-1929
Attorney General	Harry M. Daugherty	1921-1924
	Harlan F. Stone	1924-1925
	John G. Sargent	1925-1929
Postmaster General	Harry S. New	1923-1929
Secretary of the Navy	Edwin Denby	1921-1924
	Curtis D. Wilbur	1924-1929
Secretary of the Interior	Hubert Work	1923-1928
	Roy O. West	1928-1929
Secretary of Agriculture	Henry C. Wallace	1921-1924
	Howard M. Gore	1924-1925
	William M. Jardine	1925-1929
Secretary of Commerce	Herbert Hoover	1921-1928
	William F. Whiting	1928-1929
Secretary of Labor	James J. Davis	1921-1930

Plymouth Notch, Vermont, the birthplace of Calvin Coolidge and his home for many years.

A Puritan in Babylon," as Calvin Coolidge was aptly described in the title of William Allen White's biography, presided over the White House during the Roaring Twenties. The red-haired, freckle-faced Coolidge with his sharp nose and Vermont twang somehow represented the almost-forgotten moral conscience of a nation preoccupied with bootleg booze, sex, and getting-rich-quick.

The first New Englander elected since Franklin Pierce, Coolidge had less aptitude for the presidency than Pierce, but he made more of a success of the job—largely because he had fewer important decisions to make than did Pierce.

As President, Coolidge assiduously followed the maxim that the government that governs least governs best. He made political capital of two traits uncommon for a President—he was naturally tight-lipped as well as tight-fisted. After reporters and comedians told exaggerated stories about these characteristics of an otherwise colorless man, Coolidge joined the game with witty, brief, and unsmiling repartee. He enjoyed the jokes about himself and relished the nickname "Silent Cal." Shortly before leaving the White House in 1929, he gave President-elect Herbert Hoover his best advice on how to get rid of the visitors who would call upon him:

"If you keep dead still they will run down in three or four minutes."

Vermont Farm Boy

THE only President to be born on Independence Day, John Calvin Coolidge entered the world on July 4, 1872, in the crossroads village of Plymouth Notch, Vermont. His father ran the local general store, which was attached to the house where the Coolidge family lived. Young Cal—he dropped the name "John" while still a boy—received a forty-acre farm as a present from his grandfather when he was only six. His grandfather taught him all he knew about farming, and the boy learned early the importance of hard work and saving ways.

His mother, an invalid, died when he was twelve. "The greatest grief that can come to a boy came to me," he said later. For the rest of his life, Coolidge carried his mother's picture in the back of his watch.

From the time he was thirteen until he was seventeen, young Coolidge attended Black River Academy at Ludlow, Vermont, twelve miles from his home. His lonely father drove the distance in a horse-drawn wagon almost every weekend to be with him.

When he failed to pass the entrance examinations for Amherst College in 1890, he went to St. Johnsbury Academy for a term, then gained admittance to Amherst. In his scholastic work in college he was an average student, making mostly B's and a few C's, but was graduated in 1895 *cum laude*. More important to him than his studies, he had learned to debate and make speeches, and a humorous oration that he delivered as part of the closing festivities of his college days was a highlight of his years at Amherst.

The next fall, after spending the summer in Plymouth Notch, Coolidge went off on his own to Northampton, Massachusetts, a few miles from Amherst, and with a friend's help got a job as a law clerk so that he could become a lawyer. Two years later, in 1897, he was admitted to the bar.

He set up his own law office in Northampton and began to take an active part in Republican politics. His willingness to work hard for the party was rewarded. At twenty-six he was elected to the city council, became city solicitor two years later, was re-elected once, and then was defeated for re-election in 1902.

In 1905 the shy young lawyer-politician surprised Northampton by winning for his wife one of the most attractive girls in town, Grace Anna Goodhue, a teacher at a school for the deaf. She was twenty-six and he was thirty-three. They had two sons.

A young lawyer in Northampton, Massachusetts, Coolidge, as he appeared early in his career.

The Coolidge family on the White House lawn (left to right) Calvin, Jr., who died during the Coolidge presidency, Mrs. Coolidge, President Coolidge, and John.

President and Mrs. Coolidge in Philadelphia for the President's Independence Day address in 1926.

The year after his marriage, Coolidge was elected to the state legislature, serving two years in the lower house. At the age of thirty-nine, he was elected mayor of Northampton for two years, following this with election to the state senate in 1912, to which he was returned three times. He established a reputation as a party regular and won enough friends to be elected president of the senate in 1914. Another small boost up the political ladder came in 1915 when he was elected lieutenant governor. He was re-elected to this office twice.

Finally, Coolidge's long persistence in sticking doggedly to the task of taking only one rung at a time in his climb to political power paid off when he captured the Republican nomination for governor of Massachusetts in 1918. That fall he was elected by a majority of less than 17,000 votes.

A strike by the police of Boston in 1919 brought Coolidge national fame. The police had struck because they were not allowed to form an American Federation of Labor union. Rioting and looting broke out when the police failed to report for duty, and the mayor was unable to control the situation. Coolidge called out the state militia to restore order, then, when the head of the AFL, Samuel Gompers, protested that the police were being treated unfairly, Coolidge fired off this reply to him: "There is no right to strike against the public safety by anybody, anywhere, any time!" In a period when there were widespread labor troubles throughout the country, Coolidge's remark caught the fancy of many people because it made him seem to be more fearless and forthright than he actually was.

During his first term as governor, Coolidge undertook a task that he considered required more courage than his actions during the police strike. This was a reorganization of the state government necessitated by an amendment to the state constitution that had been passed during the previous administration. In this reorganization, Coolidge had to reduce the number of departments in the state government from 144 to 20—in effect demoting 122 important job holders.

Coolidge was re-elected governor in 1919 by a large majority. Although he was always a conservative, he sponsored some legislation during his second term that was praised by progressives. He was particularly interested in housing and helped put through laws preventing rent increases of more than 25% a year and prohibiting a landlord from evicting a tenant with less than thirty days' notice.

When the Republican National Convention met in Chicago in 1920, Coolidge was the favorite son of the Massachusetts delegation, receiving 34 votes on the first ballot. The Senate leaders who had decided that Harding would be a "safe" man for the presidency had chosen as his running mate Senator Irvine L. Lenroot of Wisconsin. The Republican leaders sent out the word to the delegates, and Lenroot's vice-presidential nomination was supposed to be unchallenged. But when a delegate from Oregon nominated Coolidge, the convention suddenly revolted against the dictates of their leaders and nominated Coolidge as the Republican vice-presidential candidate with 674 votes to Lenroot's 146.

At the age of forty-eight, Coolidge became Vice President of the United States.

He did a good job of presiding over the Senate, having a knowledge of parliamentary procedure from his years of experience in the Massachusetts legislature. He also was the first Vice President to be invited to sit reguarly at cabinet meetings.

Coolidge's Administration

COOLIDGE was at his birthplace in Vermont, where he and his family had been spending the summer, when he was awakened shortly after midnight on August 3, 1923, by a telegraph messenger bringing word that President Harding had died in San Francisco. After dressing, he had his storekeeper father, who was a notary public, swear him in—the only President ever to take the oath of office from his own father. Then with characteristic calm he went back to bed—he gained the reputation in succeeding years of getting more rest than any other President because of his ability to go to sleep quickly whenever he wanted a nap.

Immediately upon moving into the White House, Coolidge restored some of the dignity it had lost under Harding. There were no more drinking and card parties, but he retained Harding's Cabinet and made few changes in offices. He made his philosophy clear in a talk he gave during the first year in office in which he said "the business of America is business."

The scandals of the Harding administration began to rock the country shortly after Coolidge took office, but they did not touch Coolidge himself. Early in 1924 he accepted the resignation of Secretary of the Navy Denby and forced the resignation of Attorney General Daugherty. To deal with the scandals he appointed two future Supreme Court Justices: Owen J. Roberts as special prosecutor and Harlan F. Stone as Attorney General. In a press conference, he summed up, "Let the guilty be punished."

In the spring of 1924 Coolidge vetoed a bonus bill for veterans of

An artist's sketch of Coolidge taking the oath of office August 3, 1923 in the living room of his father's house in Plymouth Notch, Vermont.

President Coolidge arriving at Wicker Memorial Park, Hammond, Indiana, June 14, 1927.

Coolidge and his sons, Calvin, Jr. (left) and John.

World War I, but Congress passed the measure over his veto. Next, he vetoed a measure granting a general increase to the pensions of veterans of all wars, and this veto was upheld.

Although Coolidge and the Republican leaders of Congress were not in complete harmony, by the time the Republican National Convention met in Cleveland in June 1924, Coolidge firmly controlled the machinery of the party. This convention, the first nationally broadcast by radio, was dull in comparison to previous conventions, as Coolidge received the presidential nomination on the first ballot with only token opposition. The President had indicated he wanted Senator William Borah of Idaho as his running mate, but Borah refused. The convention then nominated former governor Frank Lowden of Illinois for Vice President, but Lowden also refused to accept the office. Finally, the convention again balloted for the vice-presidential nomination, and this time gave it to budget director Charles G. Dawes.

Coolidge was assured of winning the election when the Democratic party became bitterly divided in its convention in New York City. The two leading Democratic contenders were Governor Al Smith of New York and former Secretary of the Treasury William G. McAdoo. Southerners backing McAdoo included members of the Ku Klux Klan, and they were determined that the Roman Catholic Smith should not be nominated. More than one hundred ballots were taken before a compromise candidate, John W. Davis of Virginia, a former ambassador to Great Britain, was given the nomination. Liberals who were dissatisfied with the conservatism of the candidates of both national parties revived Teddy Roosevelt's Progressive party and nominated for President Robert La Follette of Wisconsin.

In November, Coolidge won election to a full term in his own right, though not by as large a majority as Harding had received four years earlier. The results gave him 15,718,211 popular votes to Davis's 8,385,283 and La Follette's 4,031,289. Coolidge won 382 electoral votes to 136 for Davis and 13 for La Follette.

Coolidge's victory was clouded by the death of his youngest son, sixteen-year-old Calvin, Jr., who had developed blood poisoning from a blister while playing tennis on the White House lawn. Later, in his *Autobiography,* Coolidge wrote: "When he went, the power and glory of the Presidency went with him. . . . I don't know why such a price was exacted for occupying the White House."

In his inaugural address on March 4, 1925, Coolidge dealt largely in generalities, concluding on a high religious-patriotic note: "America seeks no earthly empire built on blood and force. No ambition, no temptation, lures her to thought of foreign dominions. The Legions which she sends forth are armed, not with the sword, but with the cross. The higher state to which she seeks the allegiance of all mankind is not of human, but of divine origin. She cherishes no purpose save to merit the favor of Almighty God."

Soon after his inauguration Coolidge learned that he was faced with a coalition of Progressive Republicans and Democrats that had enough power in Congress to make his life difficult. In March 1925, this coalition blocked Coolidge's appointment of a conservative Michigan attorney, Charles Warren, as Attorney General. The defeat was made more irritating to Coolidge in that the Senate was evenly divided on the nomination, but Vice President Dawes was at his hotel taking a nap at the time of the vote and was not present to cast the deciding vote in favor of the appointment.

The Coolidge Cabinet (from left to right, back row)
James J. Davis, Henry C. Wallace, Herbert Hoover,
Hubert Work, (front row) Harry S. New, John W.
Weeks, Charles E. Hughes, Calvin Coolidge, Andrew
Mellon, Harlan F. Stone, Curtis D. Wilbur.

Joie Ray, American miler (left) and Paavo Nurmi,
the immortal Finnish distance runner (right) with
President Coolidge on the White House lawn February 21, 1925.   —UNDERWOOD & UNDERWOOD

A smiling President and Mrs. Coolidge, with one of
their favorite collies.

Mrs. Coolidge and son John, student at Amherst College, strolling near the White House with the old State Department building in the background.

A historic photograph of President Coolidge with renowned baseball commissioner, Judge K. M. Landis; former great manager of the New York Giants, John McGraw; and Bucky Harris, manager of the Washington Senators (left to right).

TRIM
WHEREVER
YOU CAN
C.C.

Calvin Coolidge, idol of American
business, on the White House
lawn.

Domestically, the Coolidge administration practiced economy in government, substantially reducing the national debt. In the field of foreign affairs, Coolidge's Secretary of State, Frank B. Kellogg, won the 1929 Nobel Peace Price for negotiating the Kellogg-Briand Pact outlawing war. It is significant that where Theodore Roosevelt and Woodrow Wilson, both strong Presidents, won Nobel prizes in their own right for their work in international affairs, Coolidge left such matters to his Secretary of State.

While Coolidge had regular visits from the financiers of Wall Street and gave encouraging words to the continuing industrial boom, he turned a deaf ear to the problems of the American farmer, who was not sharing in the general prosperity of the 1920s. Coolidge twice vetoed measures intended to bring relief to the farmers by permitting the government to buy surplus crops and send them abroad.

Because he had served only one full term, the Republican machine of Massachusetts prepared to press Coolidge's renomination. But in August 1927, while vacationing in the Black Hills, the President dropped a bombshell. He handed out to reporters a ten-word statement: "I do not choose to run for President in 1928." He refused to amplify the statement in any way. Its ambiguity worried the politicians because it could be interpreted to mean that he would be willing to run if he were forced to do so by a draft at the next convention.

Coolidge had a reputation for contributing to the stock-market boom by issuing optimistic statements that buoyed up the confidence of investors, and later it was said, though never proved, that he took himself out of the 1928 campaign because he foresaw a depression.

With Coolidge apparently withdrawing, Herbert Hoover, the Secretary of Commerce, became the front runner for the Republican nomination. Coolidge's friends hoped that the convention in Kansas City would deadlock and that the President would be drafted. Coolidge himself seemed to hope that this would happen. But Hoover, whom Coolidge sarcastically called the "wonduh boy," received the nomination on the first ballot.

Coolidge did little to help Hoover's campaign and did not evidence

The President when mourning the loss of his son, Calvin, Jr.

An interesting view of the styles of the day as worn by Mrs. Coolidge (left) and a friend.

any particular pleasure when the latter won. Shortly before the inauguration he told a friend: "The best thing I can do for the Hoover administration is to keep my mouth shut." Coolidge and his wife left by train for their home in Massachusetts on the evening of inauguration day.

Retirement to Northampton

ALTHOUGH Coolidge regularly went to his law office in Northampton, he did not resume practicing law. With the proceeds of his *Autobiography* he bought a large mansion called "The Beeches" near Northampton, where he and his wife lived in seclusion. He also accepted appointment as a member of the board of directors of the New York Life Insurance Company, and began writing a syndicated newspaper column of political observations.

With the stock market crash of 1929 and the deepening depression of the early 1930s, Coolidge seemed to become even more withdrawn than usual. If he blamed himself for the economic disaster that had overtaken the country, he did not say so. When Hoover ran for re-election in 1932, Coolidge gave some help to the campaign with a speech in Madison Square Garden in New York. After Hoover's defeat, a friend asked Coolidge if he would consider running for the presidency again in 1936. He answered: "Nothing would induce me to take office again."

On January 5, 1933, the sixty-year-old Coolidge unexpectedly died of a heart attack while shaving in the bathroom of his Northampton home. He was buried in the graveyard of his birthplace in Vermont. Years later, Herbert Hoover wrote:

"Mr. Coolidge was a real conservative, probably the equal of Benjamin Harrison. The country was prosperous and I suspect that he enjoyed the phrase 'Coolidge prosperity' more than any other tag which the newspapers and the public pinned on him. . . . Any summation of Mr. Coolidge's services to the country must conclude that America is a better place for his having lived in it."

A gathering August 20, 1924 at Plymouth Notch, Vermont, including (left to right) Harvey S. Firestone, Calvin Coolidge, Henry Ford, Thomas A. Edison, Russell Firestone, Mrs. Coolidge, and Colonel John Coolidge, father of the President.

—Harris & Ewing

158   WARREN GAMALIEL HARDING

Warren Gamaliel Harding

The Twenty-ninth President of the United States
1921–23

1865 (November 2) Born on a farm in Morrow County, Ohio.

1883 Graduated from Ohio Central College.

1884 Became editor and publisher of daily *Marion Star*.

1891 (July 8) Married Florence Kling DeWolfe.

1900–04 State senator in Ohio legislature.

1904–06 Lieutenant governor of Ohio.

1909 Defeated as Republican candidate for governor.

1915–20 U.S. senator from Ohio.

1921–23 Twenty-ninth President of the United States.

1923 (August 2) Died in San Francisco.

Leading Officials in
Harding's Administration

Office	Name	Years Served
Chief Justice	Edward D. White	1910-1921
	William Howard Taft	1921-1930
Vice-President	Calvin Coolidge	1921-1923
Secretary of State	Charles Evans Hughes	1921-1925
Secretary of the Treasury	Andrew W. Mellon	1921-1932
Secretary of War	John W. Weeks	1921-1925
Attorney General	Harry M. Daugherty	1921-1924
Postmaster General	Will H. Hays	1921-1922
	Hubert Work	1922-1923
	Harry S. New	1923-1929
Secretary of the Navy	Edwin Denby	1921-1924
Secretary of the Interior	Albert B. Fall	1921-1923
	Hubert Work	1923-1928
Secretary of Agriculture	Henry C. Wallace	1921-1924
Secretary of Commerce	Herbert Hoover	1921-1928
Secretary of Labor	James J. Davis	1921-1930

The brief, scandal-ridden presidential administration of Warren G. Harding stands as a black mark in American history. The road to the nation's highest office was opened for Harding when politicians meeting in a Chicago hotel room chose him as a compromise candidate to break a deadlock in the 1920 Republican National Convention. The Ohio senator's handsome face and genial personality won him wide support from a war-weary electorate seeking a return to "normalcy." But his death three years later came opportunely, some believed *too* opportunely, saving him from extreme embarrassment in the governmental crime and corruption that soon was revealed.

The first man to move directly from the U.S. Senate to the presidency, Harding received over 16,000,000 votes, nearly twice as many as any previous presidential candidate. Many of these votes came from women, voting nationally for the first time under the woman suffrage amendment to the Constitution. Under Harding the nation plunged into the Jazz Age with its mixed morals that brought public support for prohibition while bootleg whisky continued to flow freely, even in the White House. The nation also entered the Radio Age as station KDKA in Pittsburgh made the first broadcasts of election returns on the Harding victory.

Harding's Boyhood

THE first of eight children of George and Phoebe Harding, the future President was born on November 2, 1865, on a farm in Morrow County in north-central Ohio. His early years were like those of most farm boys of the time, filled with day-to-day chores that he did not particularly enjoy. When Harding was eight, his father completed a quick course in homeopathic medicine in Cleveland, and after that the boy sometimes accompanied him on horse-and-buggy calls.

But young Harding's interests soon fixed on newspaper work. His father had become part-owner of an intermittently published weekly, the *Caledonia Argus,* where Harding became a printer's devil, learning to set type, run the press, and clean ink from press rollers. At fourteen, his family sent him to little Ohio Central College, where he played the alto horn, edited the school yearbook, and was graduated in 1883. The seventeen-year-old Harding took up teaching in a country school, but quit the $30-a-month job after one term because he found trying to educate big farm boys a difficult process.

Harding's never-successful father had moved to Marion, Ohio, in 1882, hoping to improve the family's fortunes, and the boy followed the family there after he quit teaching. He tried studying law and selling insurance, but preferred shooting pool and playing poker with the town sports. His greatest early success came with helping organize the Citizen's Cornet Band of Marion, which won third place in a state band festival.

Newspaperman and Politician

ALMOST nineteen, Harding became a $1-a-week reporter for the weekly *Marion Democratic Mirror,* but this job lasted only a few weeks. Harding was an enthusiastic supporter of Republican presidential candidate James G. Blaine in the 1884 national election, and this did not sit well with the Democratic owner of the *Mirror,* who fired him.

His love for newspaperwork undampened, Harding persuaded two unemployed friends, John Sickel and Jack Warwick, to join him in scraping up $300 to take over a bankrupt daily newspaper, the *Marion Star.*

The first edition of the revived newspaper rolled off the press on November 26, 1884, with an offer of a weekly subscription to readers for ten cents. First Sickel, then Warwick, dropped out of the enterprise, but Harding stuck to the job and kept the paper in business.

Although Harding proclaimed that the daily *Star* was independent politically, he cleverly started a separate *Weekly Star* that openly supported Republican candidates, to obtain a share of politically dispensed county government advertising. Battling with two other local papers for the advertising dollars, the tobacco-chewing Harding joined in the rough-and-tumble journalism of the times that disregarded laws of libel in mud-slinging at rivals. In one of these printer's-ink engagements a competing newspaper hinted that Harding was part-Negro—an unproved rumor that cropped up in subsequent political campaigns.

When Harding was twenty-five, he married Florence Kling DeWolfe, a thirty-year-old divorcée who was the daughter of the richest man in Marion. Flossie, as she was called by her friends, had been deserted by her husband and disowned by her father. At the time of her marriage to Harding, she was struggling to support herself and her child by giving piano lessons. She soon took over the business side of running the *Marion Star* and became a driving force behind Harding's business and political career. Because of her domineering manner, Harding jokingly called her "Duchess."

Harding's first attempt to win public office ended in defeat, when in 1892 he lost overwhelmingly in the race for county auditor. After the election, he commented wryly in the *Star* that the opposition Democrat won because he "had an easy mark for an opponent."

By the end of the 1890s, the *Star* had become a financial success and an influential voice in Republican party affairs. Its editor made regular appearances as a speaker in political campaigns. His oratory and handsome appearance made politicians think of him as a likely candidate for office, and at the 1899 state Republican convention, Harding was awarded nomination for the state senate. This time he won the election.

In his first term in the legislature, Harding proved himself a loyal supporter of the party leaders. He sought and won personal popularity with his fellow-lawmakers, also working to compromise differences between the two main factions of the state party led by Joseph Benson Foraker of Cincinnati and Mark Hanna of Cleveland.

Because of Harding's services to the party, the Republicans suspended a long-standing rule against renominating a state senator for re-election in his district, and Harding easily won a second term. In 1903, with the backing of the Cincinnati political machine, he won the nomination for lieutenant governor and went on to win the election.

At the end of his term as lieutenant governor, Harding temporarily abandoned elective office to return to his newspaper career in Marion. Perhaps he foresaw the defeat that came to the state Republican ticket in the next election, or perhaps he decided he should wait for a chance at a higher office.

In 1909 Harding won the Republican nomination for governor. His campaign was managed by Harry M. Daugherty, a small-town lawyer who was to figure importantly in Harding's later career. Although Harding worked hard to win the governorship, he was badly beaten in the election, largely because of a split in the Republican party between reform and machine factions that even Harding's skill could not reconcile.

National honor first came to Harding in 1912 when he was chosen to place President William Howard Taft's name in nomination for a second term at the Republican National Convention. Harding's eloquent oratory

Warren Harding and his wife, Florence.

President Harding with his political manager and Attorney General, Harry M. Daugherty.

brought favorable comment from his fellow politicians, but he was gravely disappointed when Taft went down to election defeat with the national party torn apart by Theodore Roosevelt's Bull Moosers.

Senator from Ohio

DISCOURAGED by the ebb in his political fortunes, Harding at first refused to consider a proposal by Harry Daugherty that he run for the United States Senate in 1914. But Daugherty's persuasiveness and the ambition of Mrs. Harding overcame his doubts. He won the Republican nomination in Ohio's first direct primary, then went on to soundly beat the Democratic candidate, although the Cleveland *Plain Dealer* labeled him a "spokesman of the past."

Harding thoroughly enjoyed his term as a U.S. senator, entering enthusiastically into the club-like spirit of the Senate. He continued to seek popularity, never openly criticizing his colleagues of either party, not even when they occasionally made him the butt of their ill-humor.

As in the state legislature, Harding's record as a lawmaker was undistinguished. Almost half the time he failed to answer roll calls. He introduced no measures of great significance, and displayed few convictions other than those established by his party. On the two great domestic issues of the period on which no legislator could avoid taking a stand, he voted for prohibition, although he personally liked to drink, and he voted for woman suffrage, although he doubted the wisdom of letting women vote. In both cases he voted against his own beliefs to curry favor with important voting blocs. During World War I, he loyally supported President Woodrow Wilson's efforts to win the war. But when the fighting was over, he joined with Henry Cabot Lodge to thwart Wilson's plan for American participation in the League of Nations.

It was during Harding's term as senator that he established a liaison with Nan Britton, a Marion, Ohio blonde who was thirty years his junior. Her book about the affair, *The President's Daughter,* created a sensation when it was published in 1927. It describes how Harding obtained a job for her in New York, how they met frequently in New York and Washington, and how she accompanied him on trips as his "niece." After Harding's death, Miss Britton unsuccessfully sued for a share of his estate for herself and her child who she claimed was Harding's daughter. More than forty years after Harding's death love letters were discovered that detailed another illicit romance between the President and a Marion matron.

Meanwhile, Harding's political career continued to move forward under the management of Daugherty. The tireless Ohio politician engineered the selection of Harding as keynote speaker of the 1916 Republican National Convention that nominated Charles Evans Hughes. Although the keynote address did not rouse huge enthusiasm in the lethargic delegates, it did help win Harding the permanent chairmanship of the convention. His noble appearance and lofty words impressed the delegates—they remembered him in 1920.

The Smoke-Filled Room

BECAUSE he liked the life of a senator and because he recognized his own limitations, Harding was not enthusiastic about Daugherty's urgings that he run for President. He did not think he could win either the nomination or the election, and refused to act until Daugherty told him that by not announcing his presidential candidacy he was jeopardizing his chances of returning to the Senate for a second term. Finally, in December 1919, in a letter to a Republican committee in Ohio that had urged his candidacy, he agreed to seek the presidential nomination.

Daugherty entered his candidate in three preferential primaries: Ohio, Indiana, and Montana. Harding won the Ohio primary over General Leonard Wood by a slim majority, but he lost the Indiana primary by a landslide and received only a handful of votes in the Montana primary. Harding believed he should quit the race, but his wife and Daugherty urged him to continue, hoping that a deadlock would develop at the convention between the two favorites, General Wood and Governor Frank Lowden of Illinois. It did. With Wood and Lowden each more than 200 votes short of a winning majority, the Chicago convention adjourned till morning.

The night was filled with politics. Messengers came and went among the busy candidates and their managers. Strings were pulled. Offers were made. But the most important meeting took place in a room at the Blackstone Hotel, attended by a group of influential Republican senators who wanted neither Wood nor Lowden. After canvassing all possibilities, they decided to offer to swing their support to Harding. Apparently there was some suspicion of the prospective dark horse's private life, because he was called to the hotel and asked bluntly if he had anything in his life or background that might embarrass the party. He was left alone to con-

A picnic dinner served in a tent in July 1921, with President and Mrs. Harding facing the camera, Thomas A. Edison to the left of Mrs. Harding, and Henry Ford second to the right of the President.

Politics seems to change little through the years, as indicated in this campaign poster of 1920 showing Harding and Coolidge as candidates.

President Wilson and Harding en route to the Harding inauguration in March 1921.

sider the question, and after a few minutes' communion with himself, Harding assured the group that his past was an open record. In turn, the group assured him of the nomination.

Next day, Wood and Lowden continued to hold first and second place through eight ballots, but Harding's voting strength slowly climbed. On the ninth ballot he moved into the lead, and on the tenth ballot he won the nomination with 692½ of the convention's 984 votes. Harding's comment as quoted by the *Literary Digest* was typical: "I feel like a man who goes in on a pair of eights and comes out with aces full."

As Harding's running mate, the convention chose Governor Calvin Coolidge of Massachusetts. Coolidge had enthusiastic support in the Republican party because of his firm stand in the Boston police strike of the previous year.

To oppose Harding, the Democratic Convention nominated James M. Cox, governor of Ohio. As their vice-presidential candidate, the Democrats chose Franklin D. Roosevelt, Assistant Secretary of the Navy under President Wilson.

The campaign was dull. For most of the time, Harding remained in Marion conducting a "front porch" campaign. He greeted thousands of well-wishers and spoke informally to them, sticking to bland expressions of his love of humanity, his patriotism, and his belief in the Republican party. In the fall, he climbed aboard a campaign train and made a series of speeches filled with generalities that could be interpreted by his listeners as they wished. The Democrats endeavored to make American participation in the League of Nations an issue, but Harding's position was obscure largely because he had no strong feelings on the matter, other than a determination to preserve the Senate's constitutional right to pass on foreign treaties.

When the voters went to the polls in November, the politicians learned that the campaign had not mattered. The people were so tired of the government restrictions and hardships imposed by the war that they wanted a complete change in administrations to bring back the old days when America did not have to look beyond its own borders. Harding received 16,152,200 popular votes to 9,147,353 for Cox. In the Electoral College he won 404 votes to 127. It is interesting, if futile, to speculate on what might have happened if the two other women in Harding's life had been discovered during the campaign.

BETWEEN the election and the inauguration Harding chose his Cabinet, carefully balancing its membership. Some were close political friends; others represented various leading factions in the Republican party. It had a surprising number of distinguished men, including Secretary of State Charles Evans Hughes, a former governor of New York, Supreme Court justice, and candidate for President in 1916; Secretary of Agriculture Henry C. Wallace of Iowa, editor of a leading farm journal; and Secretary of Commerce Herbert Hoover, an eminent engineer and war-relief administrator. Secretary of the Treasury Andrew W. Mellon was a multimillionaire Pittsburgh banker, who was chosen at the behest of the Republican political machine of Pennsylvania. Secretary of War John W. Weeks of Massachusetts had served in the U.S. Senate with Harding. Postmaster General Will H. Hays of Indiana had been chairman of the Republican National Committee during the Harding presidential campaign.

Secretary of the Navy Edwin Denby was a Detroit, Michigan, lawyer who had made a fortune in the automobile business and had served as a congressman from Michigan.

Harding's Administration

Mr. and Mrs. Albert Einstein with President Harding on April 25, 1921, shortly after Harding's inauguration.

Secretary of the Interior Albert B. Fall of New Mexico, another ex-senatorial colleague, was a friend of Western oilmen who had contributed heavily to the presidential campaign fund.

Secretary of Labor James J. Davis of Pennsylvania had been a steelworker and director of the Loyal Order of Moose.

Finally, Harry Daugherty, the man who had masterminded Harding's rise to the White House, was Attorney General.

This was the formal Cabinet. But much of the real business of Harding's administration took place at the evening poker and drinking parties in the White House. These were regularly attended by Daugherty and Fall, by Jesse Smith, a Harding friend of dubious repute, and various other cronies and hangers-on.

Friends and acquaintances of Harding and Daugherty flocked from Ohio to Washington for jobs. Headquarters of the "Ohio Gang" as they were soon called, was the "Little Green House" at 1625 K Street. Government favors and appointments were bought and sold at this headquarters, but there never has been any evidence to show that Harding himself knew of these transactions. His friends merely knew that he would agree with their suggestions in order to please them.

On the international stage, Harding won the respect of other nations by calling the Washington Conference for the Limitation of Armament in 1921. At this conference the United States urged the end of the arms race between nations and the actual destruction of existing machines of war. Although the treaties designed by this conference were not ratified by the Senate until after Harding's death, the President's reputation as a man of peace was assured in foreign capitals.

Because the Senate disapproved of the Versailles Peace Treaty ending World War I, separate treaties with Germany and its allies were arranged in 1921 that excluded United States participation in the League of Nations.

Perhaps the most lasting contribution of Harding's administration was his establishment of the system of preparing a national budget. For the job of director of the budget, he made one of his best appointments, Charles G. Dawes of Chicago, who proceeded to place the fiscal affairs of the government on a businesslike basis.

In the field of labor, Harding appealed to the steel industry to abolish the twelve-hour working day, which was then the standard in the industry. Although he was rebuffed several times on the matter, he persisted in his efforts. Shortly after his death, the steel firms agreed to shorten the workday.

With Harding's approval, Congress increased protective tariffs to new highs with the Fordney-McCumber Act of 1922. But when Congress passed a huge soldier's bonus bill for the veterans of World War I, the President courageously vetoed it, pointing out that the bill did not provide for necessary additional revenues to pay the bonus.

In the elections of 1922, the Republican majority was reduced in both houses of Congress. This may have been partly caused by a depression in the economy, but Harding worried that the election results showed a loss in confidence in his administration. He resolved to go on a nationwide speaking tour in 1923 to strengthen his popularity.

LATE in 1922, Harding began to learn of irregularities in the Veterans' Bureau. Huge amounts of war surplus materials had been disposed of far below their value to favored purchasers without competitive bidding. In turn new supplies had been purchased above their normal cost. Harding was shocked, because the head of the Veterans' Bureau, Charles R. Forbes, a Medal of Honor war hero, was one of his poker-playing intimates. In January 1923, Forbes was allowed to leave on a trip to Europe. Then Harding announced Forbes' resignation and the appointment of Brigadier General Frank T. Hines to replace him. Harding received a second shock in March 1923 with the suicide of Charles F. Cramer, the attorney for the Veterans' Bureau, who had purchased the Washington house where Harding had lived as a senator.

Apparently Harding was aware that further scandals were in the offing, because he ordered another close friend, Jesse Smith, to leave Washington. Smith had shared a Washington apartment with Attorney General Daugherty, and had been one of the most powerful members of the Ohio Gang in dispensing jobs and favors. But on the night of May 29, Smith returned to Washington and shot himself to death in Daugherty's apartment.

Harding was a badly worried man when he set out from Washington in a special train on June 20, 1923, on what he called a "voyage of understanding." The trip was to take him across the continent and to Alaska. When Harding reached Kansas City, he was visited in his hotel suite by Mrs. Albert B. Fall, whose husband had resigned as Secretary of the Interior a few months earlier. Harding was visibly shaken by the secret conversation, in which he almost surely learned something of Fall's dealings with oil companies over Navy-reserved oil fields. When he reached Alaska in July, Harding received a long code message that had been flown to him from Washington. It, too, must have revealed more about the impending scandals, because he repeatedly muttered comments about friends who had betrayed him.

After returning to the United States from Alaska, Harding was stricken on July 27 in Seattle with what his physician, Surgeon General Charles E. Sawyer, at first diagnosed as indigestion caused by crab meat. It later was believed this may have been a heart attack. Although further

Death and Scandals

Warren G. Harding and Calvin Coolidge (left and center) with Will Hays, Chairman of the Republican National Committee, in June 1920, before they were nominated for the offices of President and Vice-President, respectively.

On the porch of the White House, President Harding with Grantland Rice and Ring Lardner, well known sports writers, and Henry P. Fletcher (left to right).

President Harding and Secretary of War John Weeks with Brigadier General Douglas MacArthur at West Point, September 15, 1921.

An interesting view of President Harding and General John J. Pershing at Camp Meade, Maryland, June 18, 1921.

Marine Major General John A. Lejeune with President Harding throwing out the first baseball at a benefit game for disabled veterans of the American Legion, on August 27, 1921.

President Harding with some of the leading tennis stars of that era, including Watson Washburn (left), Molla Mallory (third from left), Marian Jessup, to the right of the President, Karl Behr, and R. Norris Williams.

President Harding in a relaxed moment with pet and youngster, with Charles G. Dawes, prominent Republican and Vice-President under Calvin Coolidge.

public appearances were canceled, the President seemed to be recovering when he arrived in San Francisco on July 29. Then pneumonia struck. Distinguished physicians were called in, including Ray Lyman Wilbur, president of Stanford University. Again the President passed the crisis and seemed to be recovering. Then, at 7:35 P.M., on August 2, Harding died in bed while being read to by Mrs. Harding. The doctors, believing that a blood clot had been carried to the President's brain, asked for permission to perform an autopsy, but Mrs. Harding refused to allow it. Because the exact cause of the President's death remained in doubt, there later was much speculation that the President might have been poisoned to prevent his testifying against friends.

The public, not yet aware of anything wrong with Harding's administration, crowded the tracks by the thousands to watch the presidential funeral train pass by on its journey back to Washington. Services were held in Washington on August 8, attended by the new President, Calvin Coolidge, and by former Presidents Wilson and Taft. Then Harding's body was escorted back to his hometown of Marion for burial. Eight years later a memorial tomb was dedicated in Marion and there were laid to final rest the bodies of Harding and his wife, who died in 1924.

Even before Harding's death, Senator Thomas J. Walsh of Montana had been growing suspicious of manipulations by Secretary of the Interior Fall that had opened up to private oil companies two huge oil fields that had been held in reserve for future naval needs. Control of the fields, Elk Hills in California and Teapot Dome in Wyoming, had been transferred from the Navy Department to the Department of the Interior in 1921 with Harding's approval. Suspicions of bribery were aroused by the fact that Fall had made lavish improvements on his New Mexico ranch with no sufficient visible source of income.

As Walsh's investigation progressed, it became clear that Fall had received bribes of more than $400,000 from oil millionaires E. L. Doheny and Harry F. Sinclair. After many hearings and court cases, the oil leases of the reserves were canceled in 1927 by the United States Supreme Court. In 1929 Fall was convicted of bribery and sent to prison. Doheny and Sinclair both were brought to trial, but were freed of charges of conspiracy or bribery, although Sinclair was sentenced to jail for six months for contempt of court.

Meanwhile, a Senate investigation of the Veterans' Bureau was launched. Evidence was turned up that hundreds of millions of dollars had been spent for overpriced materials, land sites, and construction. Harding's friend, former director of the Veterans' Bureau Charles R. Forbes, was brought to trial in 1924 for bribery and conspiracy, along with John W. Thompson, an official of one of the firms with which he had been doing business. Both were convicted, fined $10,000 apiece, and sentenced to two years in prison.

Next, the Senate began an investigation of Attorney General Daugherty to determine why he had not prosecuted the central figures in the oil and Veterans' Bureau scandals. Senator Burton K. Wheeler of Montana served as counsel for the committee and dug up masses of testimony about Daugherty's associations with the late Jesse Smith and other members of the Ohio Gang. When Daugherty refused to appear before the Senate committee and would not deliver records to it, President Coolidge asked for his resignation from the Cabinet.

Daugherty and Alien Property Custodian Thomas W. Miller were brought to trial in 1924 on charges of conspiracy growing out of a transaction in which the federal government had turned over nearly $7 million as payment of a claim for a German-owned company that had been

The funeral cortege of President Harding leaving the White House.

confiscated during the war. There was evidence indicating that more than $400,000 had been used to bribe government officials to grease the way for the settlement. Daugherty refused to testify in his own defense on grounds that he might tend to incriminate himself. He and his attorney also implied that his testimony might incriminate the dead President. Miller was convicted and sentenced to prison, but a hung jury could not agree on Daugherty's innocence or guilt. Daugherty was retried and again there was a hung jury. Then the case was dropped.

How much President Harding knew of the corruption among his friends and associates will never be known. After his death, Mrs. Harding burned his papers and correspondence, making a diligent effort to recover and destroy even personal letters that he had written to others. As a result, historians have been thwarted in their search for facts about Harding.

At the dedication of the Harding tomb in Marion in 1931, President Herbert Hoover epitomized the tragedy of the man in whose Cabinet he had served:

"Here was a man whose soul was seared by a great disillusionment. We saw him gradually weaken, not only from physical exhaustion, but also from mental anxiety. Warren Harding had a dim realization that he had been betrayed by a few of the men whom he had believed were his devoted friends. That was the tragedy of the life of Warren Harding."

Newspaper announcements of Presidents who died in office before Harding.

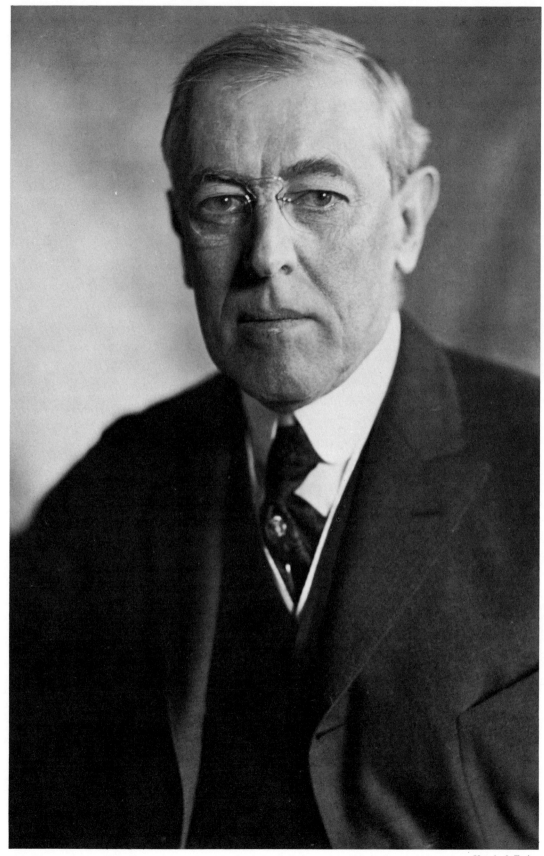

174   WOODROW WILSON

Woodrow Wilson

The Twenty-eighth President of the United States
1913–21

1856 (December 28) Born in Staunton, Virginia.

1879 Graduated from Princeton University.

1879–81 Attended University of Virginia law school.

1882–83 Practiced law in Atlanta, Georgia.

1883–85 Attended Johns Hopkins University, earning Ph.D.

1885 (June 24) Married Ellen Louise Axson.

1885–88 Associate professor of history at Bryn Mawr College.

1888–90 Professor of history and politics at Wesleyan University.

1890–1902 Professor of jurisprudence and politics at Princeton University.

1902–10 President of Princeton University.

1911–13 Governor of New Jersey.

1913–21 Twenty-eighth President of the United States.

1915 (December 18) Married Edith Bolling Galt.

1924 (February 3) Died in Washington, D.C.

Leading Officials in Wilson's Administration

Office	Name	Years Served
Chief Justice	Edward D. White	1910-1921
Vice-President	Thomas R. Marshall	1913-1921
Secretary of State	William Jennings Bryan	1913-1915
	Robert Lansing	1915-1920
	Bainbridge Colby	1920-1921
Secretary of the Treasury	William G. McAdoo	1913-1918
	Carter Glass	1918-1920
	David F. Houston	1920-1921
Secretary of War	Lindley M. Garrison	1913-1916
	Newton D. Baker	1916-1921
Attorney General	James C. McReynolds	1913-1914
	Thomas W. Gregory	1914-1919
	A. Mitchell Palmer	1919-1921
Postmaster General	Albert S. Burleson	1913-1921
Secretary of the Navy	Josephus Daniels	1913-1921
Secretary of the Interior	Franklin K. Lane	1913-1920
	John B. Payne	1920-1921
Secretary of Agriculture	David F. Houston	1913-1920
	Edwin T. Meredith	1920-1921
Secretary of Commerce	William C. Redfield	1913-1919
	Joshua W. Alexander	1919-1921
Secretary of Labor	William B. Wilson	1913-1921

Woodrow Wilson's birthplace, Staunton, Virginia.   —S. J. Collins

Many parallels can be found between Woodrow Wilson and Abraham Lincoln. Like Lincoln, Wilson was elected President with less than a majority of the popular vote because of a split in the opposition party. Like Lincoln, he had the ability to speak in simple meaningful words that inspired the people of the nation and of the world to a deeper belief in democracy. And, like Lincoln, he became a great wartime President, directing America's effort in World War I.

But he also was the opposite of Lincoln in many ways. He was the most highly educated man ever to become President, having received more than a dozen college degrees and having written many scholarly books before entering the White House. He had a cold, austere appearance, lacking the personal magnetism or "common touch" of most successful politicians. And, unlike Lincoln, he did not die at the height of his popularity. At the end of his administration he suffered as the Senate revolted against his leadership, rejecting his plea for participation in the League of Nations —just as Lincoln, if he had lived, likely would have experienced a congressional revolt against his liberal plans for Reconstruction of the South.

As a university graduate student in his twenties, Wilson wrote: "The President is at liberty, both in law and conscience, to be as big a man as he can." A quarter of a century later, when he himself filled the office, President Wilson successfully followed his own earlier advice.

A Southern Boy in the Reconstruction Period

THE oldest son of a Presbyterian minister, Thomas Woodrow Wilson was born on December 28, 1856, in Staunton, Virginia. He later dropped his first name, but throughout his boyhood he was called "Tommie." He had two older sisters, and a younger brother born in 1866. When Tommie was two, his family moved to Augusta, Georgia, where his father, Joseph Ruggles Wilson, became pastor of the First Presbyterian Church.

In later years, Wilson said that his earliest recollection as a child was of a man standing at the gate to his father's house and shouting: "Mr. Lincoln's elected. There'll be war!" He had a few other scattered memories of the war years—of having once stood and looked up to General Robert E. Lee, of staring at the wounded Confederate soldiers brought to his father's church when it was used as a temporary hospital, and at the end of the war of seeing Confederate President Jefferson Davis as a prisoner of Union soldiers.

Southern schools had been disrupted by the war, so Tommie was nine before he started school, and was eleven before he could read very well. When the boy was thirteen, Joseph Wilson moved his family to Columbia, South Carolina, where he became a professor in a theological seminary, as well as minister of the local Presbyterian church. In 1873, when he was sixteen, the bespectacled young Wilson was sent to Davidson College near Charlotte, North Carolina, to prepare himself for the ministry. He withdrew from the school the next spring because of poor health. Later that year, 1874, the Wilsons moved again, this time to Wilmington, N.C., where the elder Wilson again had a new pastorate.

A Rising Young Scholar

AFTER a year and a half spent nursing his health and reading, the eighteen-year-old Wilson went North in 1875 to attend the Presbyterian College of New Jersey at Princeton, where he took part in many student activities and was managing editor of the campus newspaper in his senior year. He helped found the Liberal Debating Club, but refused to compete for a prize when he drew the affirmative for a debate defending the protective tariff, in which he did not believe. Most important in his time at Princeton, he decided not to follow his parents' wishes that he become a minister.

Young Wilson, who had made up his mind to become a statesman, decided first to take up law, entering the best law school in the South—the University of Virginia at Charlottesville in the fall of 1879. He soon

Woodrow Wilson as a young man (third from the right, front row), a student at Princeton University, with other members of the Alligators Club.

Mrs. Woodrow Wilson (Ellen Louise Axson), who died during Wilson's first term, in August 1914.

found that studying law was "as monotonous as . . . Hash," but he enjoyed taking part in debates and polished his writing style with essays for the campus magazine. Early in 1881 illness again forced him to drop out of school. He returned to his family home in Wilmington, and while recovering his health continued with his studies. In 1882 he received a law degree *in absentia* from the University of Virginia and was admitted to the bar.

Wilson formed a law partnership with a friend in Atlanta, Georgia, and from 1882 to 1883 tried to make a living as a lawyer. However, the Georgia capital was filled with lawyers who had better family and political connections, so he decided to return to school to prepare himself to teach.

The twenty-six-year-old Wilson entered the graduate school of Johns Hopkins University at Baltimore in the fall of 1883, and soon after began work on his first book, a study of how Congress rules the American government when a weak President holds office. Under the title *Congressional Government,* it received favorable attention among students of government.

When he completed his studies at Johns Hopkins, he accepted a $1500-a-year position as associate professor at the opening session of a new women's college, Bryn Mawr, in Pennsylvania. As soon as he had accepted the position, he married twenty-five-year-old Ellen Louise Axson, a Presbyterian minister's daughter whom he had wooed for two years. While teaching at Bryn Mawr in 1886 he persuaded the Johns Hopkins faculty to grant him his Ph.D. degree without having to take the oral examinations. From 1888 to 1890 he served as professor of history and politics at Wesleyan University at Middletown, Connecticut, also coaching the Wesleyan football team in a victorious season.

In 1890 Wilson received an appointment as professor of jurisprudence and history at Princeton University, an achievement that he regarded as "a crowning success." By this time the Wilsons had three daughters, and they needed the added income from the Princeton professorship as much as the honor. He was a popular lecturer and indefatigable researcher, a familiar campus sight riding a bicycle to class while working in every spare minute on a tremendous five-volume *History of the American People,* for which he received $12,000 from its publisher.

His remarkable personal qualities are evident in the fact that when the president of Princeton University resigned in 1902 in a dispute with the trustees, the forty-five-year-old Wilson was unanimously chosen as the new president. Among the trustees voting for him was former President Grover Cleveland. As swiftly as possible Wilson forced new standards of scholarship on the university, temporarily causing a drop in enrollment as students who did not want to work turned elsewhere. In 1905 he introduced what was called the preceptoral plan, which provided for adding fifty bright young teachers to the staff to live in the student dormitories and act as tutors.

Although Wilson's educational reforms had been widely hailed as lending a new vigor to Princeton, he met defeat from the alumni in 1907 when he proposed to abolish the students' private eating clubs and substitute college dining halls. But although the plan was voted down, Wilson's stock rose with the public because the newspapers played him up as a fighter for democracy against the privileges of the rich.

In the spring of 1910 Wilson made a speech to Princeton alumni in Pittsburgh that made headlines throughout the nation. In it he denounced private universities for neglecting "opportunities to serve the people," and said that Lincoln would never have been as important a President if he had attended a private university. He accused the Protestant churches of "serving the classes and not the masses," and said they had "more regard for pew rents than for men's souls." And as a crescendo he predicted a revolution with "fields of blood" if the United States could not find "the leadership of men who know her needs."

The Pittsburgh speech did not sit well with the conservative elements of the Princeton alumni. Moreover, Wilson had lost face in a squabble with the dean of the graduate college of the university. There was open speculation that Wilson would leave Princeton for political office if the right opportunity presented itself.

SHORTLY after the spring graduation exercises at Princeton in 1910, Wilson was called to a meeting with George Harvey, the New York publisher of Wilson's books; James "Sugar Jim" Smith, the Democratic political boss of New Jersey; and Colonel Henry Watterson, the Louisville, Kentucky, editor who was a power in the national Democratic party. These men confided to Wilson that they wanted to make him President, and that as the first step Smith would arrange to get him the party's nomination for governor of New Jersey. After receiving assurances that if he won the governorship he would not be interfered with by the Democratic machine, Wilson accepted the invitation.

College President
Turns Politician

The Wilson family—his wife Ellen and Woodrow Wilson (seated) and their three daughters (left to right) Margaret, Eleanor, and Jessie, in 1912.
—Pach Brothers

Wilson as President of Princeton University in 1902.

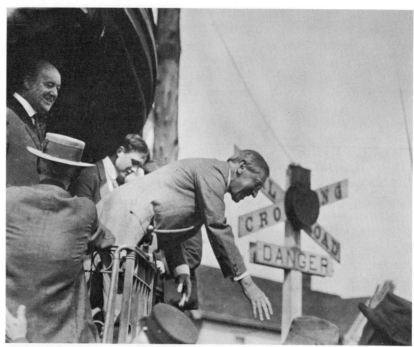

Wilson greeting a crowd from the observation platform of his campaign train in Marion, Indiana, in October 1912.

Wilson was playing golf when word came to him in September that the Democratic state convention had nominated him for governor on the first ballot. He hurried to the convention still wearing his golf clothes and accepted the nomination with a speech that he had prepared well in advance. At the request of the Princeton trustees he resigned as president of the university in October.

The Republicans who had controlled the state government for fourteen years attacked Wilson as a man who pretended to be progressive but was in reality a stooge of the Democratic boss system. To this Wilson replied: "If elected I shall not, either in the matter of appointments to office or assent to legislation, or in shaping any part of the policy of my administration, submit to the dictation of any person or persons, special interest or organization." The voters listened, because on election day he won by a majority of more than 50,000.

Even before he was inaugurated, Wilson was put to the test. Smith announced that he wished to be elected U.S. senator by the Democratic legislature that had come into office on Wilson's coat-tails. Wilson remonstrated with Smith privately, and when the boss refused to withdraw, the governor-elect stumped the state in support of an opposing candidate. When the legislature voted down Smith's candidacy in January, the newspapers reported that the "long-haired bookworm of a professor" had "licked the gang to a frazzle."

As governor, Wilson guided, cajoled, and forced the legislature to pass one reform measure after another. These included the substitution of direct primaries to prevent behind-the-scenes selection of party candidates, electoral reforms to prevent ballot-box stuffing, regulation of public utilities to fix rates and set service standards, a workmen's compensation law, a pure food law, a regulation of the laboring conditions of women and children, and local option to adopt the commission form of government in cities. The Republicans won control of both houses of the legislature in 1912, and after that Wilson was unable to obtain passage of further reform legislation. In the 1912 session of the legislature he vetoed about 10% of all the bills that were passed.

From 1911 on, Wilson openly sought the Democratic presidential nomination, but the machine politicians felt that the more conservative Champ Clark of Missouri, Speaker of the House of Representatives, would be a safer candidate. When the Democratic Convention opened in Baltimore in June 1912, a week after the Republicans had rejected Teddy Roosevelt and re-nominated Taft, Clark had won pledges from almost twice as many delegates as had Wilson, although he still did not have the necessary 726 votes needed to secure the nomination. The convention was deadlocked between these two leading candidates, neither of whom would withdraw. Up to the thirtieth ballot Clark consistently led, but from the fourteenth ballot, on which William Jennings Bryan switched from Clark to Wilson, the New Jersey governor steadily gained support, finally going ahead of Clark on the thirtieth roll call. At last on the forty-sixth ballot, Wilson won the nomination. Throughout the nerve-racking days and nights of the voting from June 27 until the final ballot on July 2, Wilson firmly refused to let his managers make any political deals or promise any political offices, saying, "not a single vote can be or will be obtained by means of a promise."

When former President Roosevelt accepted the presidential nomination of the new Progressive party early in August, this split the Republican party and nearly assured Wilson's election. Wilson and Roosevelt each campaigned strenuously for the progressive vote, while Taft, convinced that he would be defeated, did almost no campaigning. Both Wilson's "New Freedom" and Roosevelt's "New Nationalism" were principally attacks on Big Business, along two divergent lines: Roosevelt emphasized

Familiar Pennsylvania Avenue in Washington, D. C. on the occasion of Wilson's first inauguration, March 4, 1913.

the necessity for regulation, while Wilson advocated breaking up monopolies to the advantage of small business. The count of the popular vote gave Wilson 6,296,547, Roosevelt 4,118,571, and Taft 3,486,720; in the electoral votes Wilson had 435, Roosevelt 88, and Taft 8. To Princeton students who came to cheer him on election night Wilson said: "I myself have no feeling of triumph tonight. I have a feeling of solemn responsibility."

Wilson's First Term

As Wilson took the oath of office on a bright, spring-like March 4, 1913, no one had any premonition of the coming war in Europe, destined to overshadow all other questions in the next several years. Wilson delivered a memorable inaugural address, full of idealism and reform, couched in language not heard since Lincoln's day, and meriting citation at some length:

"No one can mistake the purpose for which the Nation now seeks to use the Democratic party. It seeks to use it to interpret a change in its own plans and point of view. Some old things with which we had grown familiar, and which had begun to creep into the very habit of our thought and of our lives, have altered their aspect. . . . Some new things, as we look frankly upon them . . . have come to assume the aspect of things long believed in and familiar, stuff of our own convictions. We have been refreshed by a new insight into our own life.

"We see that in many things . . . life is very great. It is incomparably great in its material aspects, in its body of wealth, in the diversity and sweep of its energy, in the industries which have been conceived and built up by the genius of individual men and the limitless enterprise of groups of men. It is great, also, very great, in its moral force. Nowhere else in the world have noble men and women exhibited in more striking forms the beauty and energy of sympathy and helpfulness and counsel in their efforts to rectify wrong, alleviate suffering, and set the weak in the way of strength and hope. We have built up, moreover, a great system of government, which has stood through a long age as in many respects a model for those who seek to set liberty upon foundations that will endure against fortuitous change, against storm and accident. Our life contains every great thing, and contains it in rich abundance.

"But the evil has come with the good, and much fine gold has been corroded. With riches has come inexcusable waste. We have squandered a great part of what we might have used, and have not stopped to conserve the exceeding bounty of nature, without which our genius for enterprise would have been worthless and impotent, scorning to be careful, shamefully prodigal as well as admirably efficient. We have been proud of our industrial achievements, but we have not hitherto stopped thoughtfully enough to count the human cost, the cost of lives snuffed out, of energies overtaxed and broken, the fearful physical and spiritual cost to the men and women and children upon whom the dead weight and burden of it all has fallen pitilessly the years through. The groans and agony of it all had not yet reached our ears, the solemn, moving undertone of our life, coming up out of the mines and factories and out of every home where the struggle had its intimate and familiar seat. With the great Government went many deep secret things which we too long delayed to look into and scrutinize with candid, fearless eyes. The great Government we loved has too often been made use of for private and selfish purposes, and those who used it had forgotten the people.

"At last a vision has been vouchsafed us of our life as a whole. We see the bad with the good, the debased and decadent with the sound and vital. With this vision we approach new affairs. Our duty is to cleanse,

Governor Wilson of New Jersey and Champ Clark, Democratic representative and speaker of the House of Representatives, at Sea Girt, New Jersey, where Wilson was notified of his nomination.

to reconsider, to restore, to correct the evil without impairing the good, to purify and humanize every process of our common life without weakening or sentimentalizing it. There has been something crude and heartless and unfeeling in our haste to succeed and be great. Our thought has been 'Let every man look out for himself, let every generation look out for itself,' while we reared giant machinery which made it impossible that any but those who stood at the levers of control should have a chance to look out for themselves. We had not forgotten our morals. We remembered well enough that we had set up a policy which was meant to serve the humblest as well as the most powerful, with an eye single to the standards of justice and fair play, and remembered it with pride. But we were very heedless and in a hurry to be great.

"We have come now to the sober second thought. The scales of heedlessness have fallen from our eyes. We have made up our minds to square every process of our national life again with the standards we so proudly set up at the beginning and have always carried at our hearts. Our work is a work of restoration.

"We have itemized with some degree of particularity the things that ought to be altered and here are some of the chief items: A tariff which cuts us off from our proper part in the commerce of the world, violates the just principles of taxation, and makes the Government a facile instrument in the hands of private interests; a banking and currency system based upon the necessity of the Government to sell its bonds fifty years ago and perfectly adapted to concentrating cash and restricting credits; an industrial system which, take it on all its sides, financial as well as administrative, holds capital in leading strings, restricts the liberties and limits the opportunities of labor, and exploits without renewing or conserving the natural resources of the country; a body of agricultural activities never yet given the efficiency of great business undertakings or served as it should be through the instrumentality of science taken directly to the farm, or afforded the facilities of credit best suited to its practical needs;

Woodrow Wilson and President Taft leaving the White House for the Wilson inauguration.

President Wilson working at his desk.

President Wilson delivering his first inaugural address March 4, 1913.

watercourses undeveloped, waste places unreclaimed, forests untended, fast disappearing without plan or prospect of renewal, unregarded waste heaps at every mine. We have studied as perhaps no other nation has the most effective means of production, but we have not studied cost or economy as we should either as organizers of industry, as statesmen, or as individuals.

"Nor have we studied and perfected the means by which government may be put at the service of humanity, in safeguarding the health of the Nation, the health of its men and its women and its children, as well as their rights in the struggle for existence. This is no sentimental duty. The firm basis of government is justice, not pity. These are matters of justice. There can be no equality or opportunity, the first essential of justice in the body politic, if men and women and children be not shielded in their lives, their very vitality, from the consequences of great industrial and social processes which they can not alter, control, or singly cope with. Society must see to it that it does not itself crush or weaken or damage its own constituent parts. The first duty of law is to keep sound the society it serves. Sanitary laws, pure food laws, and laws determining conditions of labor which individuals are powerless to determine for themselves are intimate parts of the very business of justice and legal efficiency.

"These are some of the things we ought to do, and not leave the others undone, the old-fashioned, never-to-be-neglected, fundamental safeguarding of property and of individual right. This is the high enterprise of the new day: To lift everything that concerns our life as a Nation to the light that shines from the hearthfire of every man's conscience and vision of the right. It is inconceivable that we should do this as partisans; it is inconceivable we should do it in ignorance of the facts as they are or in blind haste. We shall restore, not destroy. We shall deal with our economic system as it is and as it may be modified, not as it might be if we had a clean sheet of paper to write upon; and step by step we shall make it what it should be, in the spirit of those who question their own wisdom and seek counsel and knowledge, not shallow self-satisfaction or the excitement of excursions whither they can not tell. Justice, and only justice, shall always be our motto.

"And yet it will be no cool process of mere science. The Nation has been deeply stirred, stirred by a solemn passion, stirred by the knowledge of wrong, of ideals lost, of government too often debauched and made an instrument of evil. The feelings with which we face this new age of right and opportunity sweep across our heartstrings like some air out of God's own presence, where justice and mercy are reconciled and the judge and the brother are one. We know our task to be no mere task of politics but a task which shall search us through and through, whether we be able to understand our time and the need of our people, whether we be indeed their spokesmen and interpreters, whether we have the pure heart to comprehend and the rectified will to choose our high course of action.

"This is not a day of triumph; it is a day of dedication. Here muster, not the forces of party, but the forces of humanity. Men's hearts wait upon us; men's lives hang in the balance; men's hopes call upon us to say what we will do. Who shall live up to the great trust? Who dares fail to try? I summon all honest men, all patriotic, all forward-looking men, to my side. God helping me, I will not fail them, if they will but counsel and sustain me!"

Less than two weeks after his inauguration Wilson called the first regularly scheduled press conference because he believed the people had a right to know regularly from the President the state of affairs of the nation.

Because all his life Wilson had been an admirer of liberal British prime ministers and felt that the British parliamentary system in which the head of the government led the legislature brought cohesiveness to national government, he seized the opportunity of a special session of Congress in April 1913 to address a joint session of the two houses—a precedent-shattering event that had not occurred since the administration of John Adams. In all the more than a hundred intervening years Presidents had sent their messages to be read to Congress. But Wilson was determined to lead, not follow. He told the joint session: "I am very glad indeed to have this opportunity . . . to verify for myself the impression that the President of the United States is a person, not a mere department of the Government hailing Congress from some island of jealous power, sending messages, not speaking naturally and with his own voice—that he is a human being trying to cooperate with other human beings in a common service."

Wilson had called Congress into special session to enact a tariff reform law. The tariff bill was quickly passed by the House, but bogged down in the Senate, where so many tariff reform bills of the past had died or been

President Wilson at his second inauguration with his second wife, Edith Bolling Galt.

emasculated. Wilson appealed directly to the people to help defeat the business lobbies working against the measure. He declared that never before had there been "so insidious a lobby." He said "money without limit is being used to sustain this lobby . . . Only public opinion can check and destroy it." Senators were deluged by letters, and on October 3, 1913, the measure was signed into law by Wilson, removing tariffs on wool, sugar, iron, food, and generally reducing tariffs by about 25%. The law also provided for the first income tax under the Sixteenth Amendment to the Constitution.

Wilson went before Congress a second time, on June 23, 1913, to ask for legislation to reform the nation's banking and currency laws. "We must have a currency, not rigid as now, but readily, elastically responsive to sound credit . . . Our banking laws must mobilize reserves . . . And the control of the system of banking and of issue . . . must be vested in the Government itself, so that the banks may be the instruments, not the masters, of business and of individual enterprise and initiative." The result, despite the opposition of the banking interests, was the Federal Reserve Act of 1913—regarded by many as the most important piece of domestic legislation of Wilson's administration.

He helped push through Congress the most far-reaching series of laws concerned with social justice of any President to that time. This legislation included the establishment of the Federal Trade Commission to regulate business, the Clayton Anti-trust Law to strengthen the government's power to prevent monopolies, and the Seamen's Act to provide greater safety for sailors and greater freedom for them in their relations with ship owners. Later in his administration he helped forward child labor legislation and government loans to farmers.

Perhaps Wilson's greatest failure in the area of social justice was his unwillingness to aid the Negro to achieve equality. Booker T. Washington and other Negro leaders were distressed and angered that Wilson did nothing to prevent the imposition of segregation rules in federal departments and agencies as Southern Democrats came to power.

Wilson was dismayed in the congressional elections of 1914 when the Democrats lost forty-eight seats in the House of Representatives, retaining their majority by only twenty-five seats. But after consideration he determined to proceed with his program for the New Freedom as strongly as ever.

But foreign affairs soon demanded his attention. Trouble loomed first in Mexico, where civil war broke out and forced Wilson to order the Navy to occupy Vera Cruz. The Mexican bandit-patriot Francisco Villa briefly invaded New Mexico in 1916, and American troops fruitlessly pursued him across the Rio Grande. Wilson was momentarily on the verge of asking for a declaration of war with Mexico in 1916, but decided to withdraw the troops.

Far more important, though seeming more remote, was the war that broke out in Europe in July 1914. On August 4, Wilson issued a Neutrality Proclamation spelling out in detail the means by which the United States would avoid participation. In succeeding months his patience wore thin as both Germany and the Allies repeatedly ignored American neutrality. Wilson tried hard to keep the United States out of the conflict while trying to protect American lives and property. But Germany's violation of the neutrality of Belgium and the attacks by German submarines on passenger ships created a strong pro-Allied public opinion in the United States.

Meantime personal tragedy struck with the death of Mrs. Wilson in August 1914. For a time Wilson was a sad and lonely man, then, in 1915,

President Wilson finds the Washington Monument a good vantage point.

he met Mrs. Edith Bolling Galt, an attractive Washington widow. Nine months after their first meeting Wilson married the forty-three-year-old Mrs. Galt in a quiet ceremony at her Washington home.

When the Republican National Convention met in June 1916, the delegates rejected the candidacy of former President Roosevelt and nominated Charles Evans Hughes, an associate justice of the Supreme Court and a former governor of New York.

In the summer of 1916 the railroad unions threatened a nationwide strike unless the railroads granted an eight-hour working day. Wilson intervened and got the unions to accept arbitration, but the presidents of the railroad companies arrogantly refused. A week before the strike deadline Wilson called a joint session of Congress and pleaded for legislation for an eight-hour day. Congress acted swiftly and Wilson signed the measure into law.

The Republican presidential candidate, Hughes, denounced Wilson's action as a surrender to the unions, "the most shameful proceeding that has come to my attention since I have observed public life." But Wilson won new support from progressive and labor circles.

Yet the overriding issue of 1916 was war. The Democrats campaigned with the slogan, "He kept us out of war," and they cited Theodore Roosevelt's demands for intervention as proof that if the Republicans won office the nation would be drawn into the European conflict.

Election returns on the evening of November 7 showed that Hughes had won almost every Eastern state, and the Democratic New York *World* conceded Hughes' victory. Wilson went to bed in the White House believing he had been defeated, but the next day returns from the West showed that Wilson had done better there than had been expected. He carried California by about 4000 votes, winning that state's critical 13 votes—enough to give him victory. The final count of popular votes gave Wilson 9,127,695 and Hughes 8,533,507. In the electoral votes it was Wilson 277 and Hughes 254.

For the remainder of his first term Wilson busied himself with efforts to bring about a settlement of the war in Europe. In January 1917, he addressed the Senate, calling on the European nations to accept "peace without victory." But a few days later the German government, having decided that war with the United States was inevitable, announced that starting February 1, 1917, its submarines would sink without warning any ship, including any American ship, engaged in trade with the Allies. On February 3, Wilson spoke to a joint session of Congress, announcing the breaking off of diplomatic relations with Germany, but expressing his continuing hope for peace. These hopes were further blasted when at the end of February a message between Germany and Mexico was intercepted in which Mexico was promised the recovery of Texas, Arizona, and New Mexico if it joined in war on the United States. Wilson kept this note secret, but immediately went before Congress again to ask for power to arm American merchant ships. When Congress appeared loath to grant this authority, Wilson revealed the Germany-Mexico note on March 1. Although the House passed a bill giving the authority the same day, action was blocked in the Senate until the Sixty-fourth Congress expired on March 4.

Golfer Woodrow Wilson examining his golf ball.

PROMPTLY after his second inauguration, Wilson announced that even without special congressional approval he intended on his own authority to arm American merchant ships. When German submarines sank without warning three U.S. merchantmen on March 18, influential persons throughout the country joined former President Roosevelt in calling for

Wilson's Second Term

Campaign headquarters of Wilson for his second presidential campaign featuring his slogan, "Peace and Prosperity."

Who is this Wilson?

an immediate declaration of war. Two days later Wilson called for a special session of Congress to meet on April 2, and he began drafting a war message.

Addressing Congress on April 2, Wilson asked for a declaration of war: "There are, it may be, many months of fiery trial and sacrifice ahead of us. It is a fearful thing to lead this great peaceful people into war . . . but the right is more precious than peace, and we shall fight for the things which we have always carried nearest our hearts,—for democracy, for the right of those who submit to authority to have a voice in their own Government, for the rights and liberties of small nations, for a universal dominion of right by . . . a concert of free peoples . . ." After action by the Senate and House, Wilson signed the declaration of war on Germany.

Wilson showed the same strength of leadership in war as he had in peace. He directed the mobilization of America's economic and manpower resources, and perhaps most important, he voiced the moral ideals and objectives that the peoples of the world might hope for. When the Bolshevik Revolution broke out in Russia in 1917, the new government published secret treaties among Britain, France, and Czarist Russia which cast a dubious light on Allied war aims. The American President was the logical man to counter these disclosures by stating public war aims to which liberals and idealists could give their adherence, and for which America's power furnished a guarantee. Accordingly, Wilson delivered a major address to Congress on January 8, 1918, setting forth "Fourteen Points" as "the only possible program" for peace from the American viewpoint. The Fourteen Points included open instead of secret treaties; freedom of the seas; removal of tariff barriers; disarmament; colonial adjustments; evacuation of Russian, Belgian, French, and Balkan territory by the Germans; return of Alsace-Lorraine to France; self-determination for the subject peoples of Austria-Hungary and Turkey; an independent Poland; and finally, as the Fourteenth Point, "a general association of nations must be formed under specific covenants for the purpose of affording mutual guarantees of political independence and territorial integrity to great and small states alike."

American troops and supplies poured into Europe, turning the tide of war against Germany. Eleven months later Germany asked for an armistice.

In an effort to insure that his Fourteen Points would truly be the basis of settlement in Europe, Wilson decided to head the American peace delegation—the first trip to Europe by an American President while holding office. He arrived in France in December 1918 and was received triumphantly everywhere. But at the peace conference Wilson found himself forced to give up on one point after another in order to preserve his idea of a League of Nations.

When Wilson brought the Treaty of Versailles back to the United States in July 1919, he found that great opposition had built up to it. He had made the tactical mistake of not including a representative of the U.S. Senate or a representative of the Republican party in his peace delegation. The Republicans had won control of Congress in the 1918 election, and now they were determined to embarrass Wilson.

Trying to rally public opinion to his side, Wilson went on an 8000-mile speaking tour throughout the Midwest and to the Pacific Coast. On the night of September 25, 1919, after speaking at Pueblo, Colorado, he collapsed from exhaustion. Canceling the rest of his engagements, he returned to Washington, where on October 3 he had a stroke that paralyzed his left side. Suddenly he was an invalid, hardly able to quit his bed or wheel chair.

The Wilson funeral procession February 6, 1924.

Wilson refused to accept reservations that Republican senators insisted on adding to the Treaty of Versailles, and instructed Democratic senators to vote against the treaty unless the Republicans withdrew their amendments. As a result the treaty was voted down twice in the Senate, in November 1919, and in March 1920. Confident that the public still would come to the support of the League of Nations, Wilson insisted that this should be the central issue of the presidential campaign of 1920. His hopes were crushed when Republican Warren G. Harding was elected President overwhelmingly in the race with Democratic candidate James M. Cox. But international faith in his leadership was reaffirmed when Wilson was awarded the Nobel Peace Prize in December 1920 for his efforts in seeking a just peace and in supporting the idea of the League of Nations.

Three important amendments to the United States Constitution were proclaimed during Wilson's presidency. The Seventeenth, in 1913, provided for the direct election of senators by the people instead of by the state legislatures. The Eighteenth, in 1919, prohibited the manufacture, sale, or transportation of intoxicating beverages. And the Nineteenth, in 1920, gave women the right to vote.

BROKEN in health, though not in spirit, Wilson retired with his wife to a small house on S Street in Washington. He joined in a law partnership with Bainbridge Colby, his last Secretary of State, but did not take an active part in the affairs of the firm. To the end he was confident that his belief in the League of Nations as the salvation of the world would be vindicated. At the age of sixty-seven he died in his sleep on February 3, 1924, and his body was buried in the National Cathedral in Washington.

A Prophecy

Two decades later the world would remember his prophecy made during the national tour that led to his collapse:

"There will come sometime . . . another struggle in which, not a few hundred thousand fine men from America will have to die, but many millions . . . to accomplish the final freedom of the peoples of the world."

190 WILLIAM HOWARD TAFT

William Howard Taft

The Twenty-seventh President of the United States
1909–13

1857 (September 15) Born in Cincinnati, Ohio.

1878 Graduated from Yale University.

1880 Received law degree from Cincinnati College and admitted to the bar to practice law.

1882–83 Tax collector, appointed by President Arthur.

1886 (June 19) Married Helen Herron.

1887–90 Judge of the superior court of Cincinnati.

1890–92 Solicitor General of the United States, appointed by President Harrison.

1892–1900 U.S. Circuit Judge, appointed by President Harrison.

1896–1900 Professor and dean of the law department of the University of Cincinnati.

1900 President of the U.S. Philippine Commission.

1901–04 First civil governor of the Philippine Islands, appointed by President McKinley.

1904–08 Secretary of War, appointed by President Roosevelt.

1909–13 Twenty-seventh President of the United States.

1913 Appointed professor of law at Yale University.

1918–19 Joint chairman of the National War Labor Board, appointed by President Wilson.

1921–30 Chief Justice of the United States, appointed by President Harding.

1930 (March 8) Died in Washington, D.C.

Leading Officials in Taft's Administration

Office	Name	Years Served
Chief Justice	Melville W. Fuller	1888-1910
	Edward D. White	1910-1921
Vice-President	James Schoolcraft Sherman	1909-1912
Secretary of State	Philander C. Knox	1909-1913
Secretary of the Treasury	Franklin MacVeagh	1909-1913
Secretary of War	Jacob M. Dickinson	1909-1911
	Henry L. Stimson	1911-1913
Attorney General	George W. Wickersham	1909-1913
Postmaster General	Frank H. Hitchcock	1909-1913
Secretary of the Navy	George von Lengerke Meyer	1909-1913
Secretary of the Interior	Richard A. Ballinger	1909-1911
	Walter L. Fisher	1911-1913
Secretary of Agriculture	James Wilson	1897-1913
Secretary of Commerce and Labor	Charles Nagel	1909-1913

The Taft family, with daughter Helen (left), Charles, President Taft, Robert, who became a leading Republican Senator from Ohio, and Mrs. Taft.

Anyone who followed Teddy Roosevelt as President was bound to seem dull, but the six-foot two-inch William Howard Taft with his walrus mustache and 300-pound girth was so ponderous and slow-moving that he appeared to be the very antithesis of his active predecessor. Prodded into the presidency by his ambitious wife, he said he found it "the lonesomest place in the world." A judge both by profession and temperament, Taft achieved his greatest distinction as the only former President to be appointed Chief Justice of the United States.

Before becoming President, Taft had occupied a succession of appointive positions, such as Governor of the Philippines and Secretary of War. Like most other men who became Chief Executive without working their way along the elective stepping-stones of politics, he was ill-equipped to cope with political bosses, patronage, and pleasing the public. Worse, he committed the error of angering Roosevelt—the man who had singlehandedly put him in the White House. And T.R. wrecked the Republican party to prevent "Big Bill" Taft from having a second term.

"I was a man of straw," Taft said of himself, during his last year in the White House.

Born on September 15, 1857, in Cincinnati, Ohio, William Howard Taft, or "Willie" as he was called as a boy, was the son of a prominent attorney, Alphonso Taft. Although Willie came close to being killed at the age of nine when a horse ran away with the carriage in which he was riding, his comfortable childhood was relatively uneventful.

By the time he entered high school he had reached his full height, and his powerful physique had won him a reputation as a wrestler and fighter to be feared. His father even boasted to heavyweight champion John L. Sullivan that he believed "My Will is a better man." And young Taft took as easily to books as he did to sports, usually ranking first in his class.

In 1874 he enrolled at Yale University, where he continued to distinguish himself in his studies. During his college years his father served in President Grant's Cabinet, first as Secretary of War and then as Attorney General. When Will graduated in 1878 at the age of twenty, his parents were somewhat disappointed that he ranked only second in his class of 191.

Returning home he studied for two years at the Cincinnati Law School and received his law degree and admission to the bar in 1880. His father's political connections won him appointment as assistant prosecuting attorney of Hamilton County in 1881, and the following year he was appointed by President Arthur as tax collector for the first district. At about the same time Arthur appointed the elder Taft ambassador to Austria-Hungary. In 1883, Will Taft resigned as tax collector, spent a few months in Europe visiting his parents at the court of the Hapsburgs in Vienna, and then joined his father's law firm.

After several years of courtship, the twenty-eight-year-old Taft married twenty-five-year-old Helen "Nellie" Herron on June 19, 1886. He was deeply in love with her, but it also was an advantageous marriage because she was the daughter of a law partner of former President Rutherford B. Hayes. They had two sons and a daughter. Their oldest son, Robert Alphonso Taft, became a leading U.S. senator, and their youngest, Charles Phelps Taft II, mayor of Cincinnati.

In 1887 the Republican governor of Ohio appointed Taft a judge of the superior court, and the following year he was elected to the court for a five-year term. To accept an appointment by President Harrison as U.S. Solicitor General, he resigned from the judgeship in 1890. He established a good record during his two years in court, winning a high percentage of the cases he handled, including an important anti-trust suit. This brief sojourn in Washington also gave him the opportunity to become acquainted with Theodore Roosevelt, then serving on the Civil Service Commission.

At the age of thirty-four, Taft was appointed by President Harrison as judge of the U.S. Sixth Circuit Court of Appeals, over which he presided from 1892 to 1900, establishing a reputation as a strict interpreter of the law. During most of this time he served as a professor of law and dean of the law department at the University of Cincinnati.

His fellow Ohioan President McKinley appointed him President of the U.S. Philippine Commission in 1900.

Upon arriving in Manila with his wife and children, he and his fellow commissioners set about establishing the basis for a civil government while U.S. troops still were putting down the revolution that had broken out in opposition to American occupation. When Taft remarked that the Filipinos were his "little brown brothers," American soldiers who were fighting them composed the verse:

> "He may be a brother of Big Bill Taft,
> But he ain't no friend of mine."

President Taft marking his golf score card.

A view of the styles of the day in 1908, as a crowd listens to a Taft campaign speech in De Witt, Nebraska.

Taft soon came to the conclusion that the Filipinos were not well enough educated to the idea of democracy to be able to administer their own government, so in 1901 he accepted an appointment by McKinley as the island's first civil governor.

In 1902 Taft became seriously ill with an internal abscess that necessitated three operations over a period of several months. He was called back briefly to Washington for Senate hearings on the Philippines, and while there became better acquainted with Roosevelt, now President, concerning whom he wrote privately: "I wish he would not think out loud so much." He returned to the Philippines by way of Europe, where he stopped in Rome as a special envoy from Roosevelt to Pope Leo XIII to request that the Roman Catholic Church give up the hundreds of thousands of acres of farm land it owned in the islands.

When Roosevelt offered to appoint him to the Supreme Court—an office for which he had expressed repeated longing—Taft turned down the opportunity, feeling that there remained too much important work to be done in the Philippines. But his wife and brothers also advised against his taking the judicial position because they felt it would block any possibility of his becoming President.

Washington Bound   IN 1904 Taft accepted appointment by Roosevelt as Secretary of War, but not until he had obtained the approval of his brothers along with their assurance that they would give him a special allowance to help him meet the high cost of entertaining in Washington. Because the administration of the Philippines came under the War Department, Taft continued to have a strong influence on efforts to improve conditions in the islands.

As Secretary of War, Taft became the most widely-traveled American of the times. He repeatedly made trips to Panama to supervise the work on the Panama Canal, and in 1905 he was sent to Japan to encourage that nation to accept American mediation in the Russo-Japanese War. In 1906 he went to Cuba to intervene in a threatened revolution against the weak government of the former Spanish colony. Roosevelt sent him the next year on a 24,000-mile trip around the world that included a stop in Japan to allay fears of war with that country.

All his life Taft's vice was over-eating. But even he became alarmed when his weight reached 314 pounds in 1905. He went on a rigid diet for a few months that dropped him to 255, but in later years his weight and his girth continued to expand.

From 1906 on, it became clear that Roosevelt had chosen Taft as his successor. Taft's mother gave him no encouragement, writing: "I do not want my son to be President. His is a judicial mind and he loves the law." But his wife urged him on toward the White House.

At the Republican Convention in Chicago in 1908 Taft won the presidential nomination by acclamation on the first ballot. James S. Sherman, a New York congressman, was chosen as the vice-presidential nominee. For Taft's opponent the Democrats again chose William Jennings Bryan, who had previously been defeated by McKinley in 1896 and 1900. With Roosevelt urging him, "Hit them hard, old man!" Taft campaigned throughout the country. Issues were few and relatively unimportant. When the voters went to the polls they elected Taft with 7,675,320 popular votes to Bryan's 6,412,294, and with an electoral vote of 321 to 162.

"I ALWAYS said it would be a cold day when I got to be President of the United States," Taft joked to Roosevelt when a winter storm descended on Washington on Inauguration Day in 1909. Taft's inaugural address covered many subjects. He gave special emphasis to the need for a revision

Taft's Administration

William H. Taft and President Roosevelt driving to the Capitol for the inauguration, one of the most blizzardy inaugurals in history, March 2, 1909, the day Taft became President.

Formation of cavalry awaiting the inaugural ceremony on the approach to the Capitol.

of tariffs and announced that he was calling a special session of Congress for March 15 to reduce the tariff rates. He also said he planned to submit proposals for amendments to the Constitution to regulate trusts and interstate commerce.

In June he sent a special message to Congress urging an amendment to the Constitution that would authorize an income tax. He said such a measure was needed to overcome the deficit in government spending. This measure ultimately became law in 1913.

Taft suffered a major legislative defeat by the Republican Congress in August 1909, when it passed the Payne-Aldrich Tariff Act that kept tariff rates high. Although he disliked the measure, Taft did not veto it. As a consequence he, more than Congress, was blamed by the public for the continuing high prices. He publicly declared: "I am bound to say that I think the Payne tariff bill is the best tariff bill that the Republican party ever passed," which might be construed as faint praise.

Taft's administration had many positive accomplishments. Postal savings and parcel post services were established. Arizona and New Mexico were admitted to the Union, bringing the total number of states to forty-eight. And about twice as many anti-trust suits were prosecuted by the federal government under Taft as had been under Roosevelt.

Nevertheless liberal Republicans felt that Taft was falling too much under the influence of millionaires and corporation lawyers. They rallied around Roosevelt, who called for a "New Nationalism" and actively campaigned to win delegates for the 1912 presidential nomination. Taft was bewildered that Roosevelt had turned on him, and then became bitter, writing to his aunt: "I have a sense of wrong in the attitude of Theodore Roosevelt toward me which I doubt if I can ever get over. But I have

President and Mrs. Taft returning to the White House along Pennsylvania Avenue after leaving the Capitol following the inauguration.

President Taft at Helena, Montana, September 27, 1909.

The Taft procession leaving San Antonio, Texas.

Taft as Chief Justice and Miss Mabel Boardman, former secretary of the American Red Cross, in 1921.

President Taft in Clinton, Iowa, in June 1912.

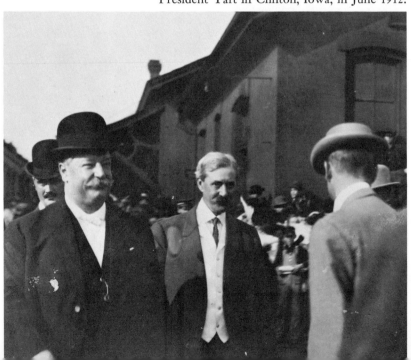

an abiding confidence . . . in the eventual justice of the American people, and I am quite sure that in the end the hypocrisy, the insincerity, the selfishness, the monumental egotism . . . that possesses Theodore Roosevelt will make themselves known to the American people in such a way that his place in history will be accurately defined."

The regulars in the Republican party stuck with Taft and helped him win the presidential nomination in 1912, but Taft was dismayed when Roosevelt organized the Progressive party and became its candidate for President. The Democrats nominated Woodrow Wilson, then governor of New Jersey. Taft made campaign speeches in nearly five hundred towns and cities, but he knew he could not win the three-cornered race. He wrote: "If I cannot win I hope Wilson will." When the election came in November, Taft ran behind Wilson and Roosevelt—the worst defeat ever suffered by a President running for re-election.

Chief Justice

Upon leaving the White House, the fifty-five-year-old Taft accepted an appointment as a law professor at Yale. He became immensely popular with the students and found fun in the campus activities for eight years. During World War I he served on the War Labor Board.

Taft supported Warren G. Harding's campaign for the presidency— Harding had made Taft's nomination speech at the Republican Convention in 1912—and was pleased when his friend won, partly because he was hopeful that he might finally achieve his lifelong ambition of an appointment to the Supreme Court. When Chief Justice Edward D. White died shortly after Harding's inauguration, Taft was swiftly appointed to fill the vacancy.

His last nine years were the happiest of his life. His geniality brought a spirit of harmony to the Supreme Court. He avoided writing any dissenting opinions, noting: "I would not think of opposing the views of my brethren if there is a majority against my own."

In February 1930, at the age of seventy-two, Taft resigned as Chief Justice because of heart trouble. A month later, on March 8, 1930, he died in Washington and was buried in Arlington National Cemetery.

President Taft as Chief Justice of the Supreme Court (seated in center).

200 THEODORE ROOSEVELT

Theodore Roosevelt

The Twenty-sixth President of the United States
1901–09

1858 (October 27) Born in New York City.

1880 Graduated from Harvard College.

1880 (October 27) Married Alice Hathaway Lee.

1882–84 Representative in the New York state legislature.

1886 Unsuccessful candidate for mayor of New York City.

1886 (December 2) Married Edith Kermit Carow.

1889–95 Member of U.S. Civil Service Commission.

1895–97 President of board of police commissioners of New York City.

1897–98 Assistant Secretary of the Navy.

1898 Colonel of the "Rough Riders" volunteer cavalry regiment in the Spanish-American War.

1899–1900 Governor of New York.

1901 Vice President of the United States.

1901–09 Twenty-sixth President of the United States.

1912 Defeated in presidential election as candidate of the "Bull Moose" party, or Progressive party.

1913–14 Explored the River of Doubt in Brazil.

1919 (January 6) Died in Oyster Bay, New York.

Leading Officials in Roosevelt's Administration

Office	Name	Years Served
Chief Justice	Melville W. Fuller	1888-1910
Vice-President	Charles W. Fairbanks	1905-1909
Secretary of State	John Hay	1898-1905
	Elihu Root	1905-1909
	Robert Bacon	1909
Secretary of the Treasury	Lyman J. Gage	1897-1902
	Leslie M. Shaw	1902-1907
	George B. Cortelyou	1907-1909
Secretary of War	Elihu Root	1899-1904
	William H. Taft	1904-1908
	Luke E. Wright	1908-1909
Attorney General	Philander C. Knox	1901-1904
	William H. Moody	1904-1906
	Charles J. Bonaparte	1906-1909
Postmaster General	Charles E. Smith	1898-1902
	Henry C. Payne	1902-1904
	Robert J. Wynne	1904-1905
	George B. Cortelyou	1905-1907
	George von L. Meyer	1907-1909
Secretary of the Navy	John D. Long	1897-1902
	William H. Moody	1902-1904
	Paul Morton	1904-1905
	Charles J. Bonaparte	1905-1906
	Victor H. Metcalf	1906-1908
	Truman H. Newberry	1908-1909
Secretary of the Interior	Ethan A. Hitchcock	1898-1907
	James R. Garfield	1907-1909
Secretary of Agriculture	James Wilson	1897-1913
Secretary of Commerce and Labor	George B. Cortelyou	1903-1904
	Victor H. Metcalf	1904-1906
	Oscar S. Straus	1906-1909

The first new President of the twentieth century and the youngest man ever to hold the office, Theodore Roosevelt brought a vim, vigor, and vitality to the White House that swept away the cobwebs of the nineteenth century. He did not wait for history to make him great, but plunged ahead doing what he felt was best for the nation and the world. With his slogan of "Speak softly and carry a big stick," he carried forward McKinley's ambitions to make the United States a world power—winning for himself the first Nobel Peace Prize awarded to an American while doing so. But he did not speak so softly in tilting against the "invisible government" of business and finance that had dominated the federal government since the days of the Civil War. He skillfully played upon the power of public opinion to help force an unwilling Congress to give the people a "Square Deal" by curbing the power of the barons of Wall Street.

An apostle of "The Strenuous Life," Roosevelt climbed the Matterhorn, hunted in Africa, explored Brazil, led cavalry charges in the Spanish-American War, and worked as a cowboy in the Dakotas. While in the White House, he practiced boxing and judo as well as taking his weary Cabinet on long hikes. After leaving the White House he became the first President, or former President, to ride in an airplane. He also found time to write more than thirty books and tens of thousands of letters.

While many of the Presidents found the chores of office a burden and expressed relief when they had completed their terms, Roosevelt loved every minute of it. He said:

"No President has ever enjoyed himself as much as I have enjoyed myself, and for the matter of that I do not know any man of my age who has had as good a time . . ."

A Born New Yorker

THE second of four children of a wealthy New York City banker, Theodore Roosevelt was born on October 27, 1858—the only President ever born in New York City. A pale, sickly boy, "Teedie," as he was called, was given to fits of asthmatic coughing. He led the pampered life of a rich man's son with private tutors, several trips to Europe with his family, and whatever books and presents he asked for.

When "Teedie" was thirteen, he was given his first gun. And it was when he could not hit the bullseye with it that his parents discovered he was nearsighted and needed glasses. About this same time he had an unhappy experience of being teased by four other boys throughout a stagecoach ride to Maine and was unable to fight them because he was so puny. With his father's encouragement, young Roosevelt determined to improve his body. He began a vigorous program of exercise in a gymnasium his father built on the second floor of their New York City home. For the rest of his life Roosevelt seemed to try to outdo everyone else with his energy and strength.

When Roosevelt was eighteen he entered Harvard College, but was not particularly popular with his classmates because he was trying to learn, while most of them were merely trying to get by. He continued boxing at Harvard, as a lightweight, but he was not very successful because he found it difficult to see his opponents without his glasses. While he was a small boy Roosevelt had developed an intense interest in natural science,

Alice Hathaway Lee Roosevelt, whom Roosevelt married on his twenty-second birthday, when she was nineteen.

and he continued this at Harvard with many science courses. His excellent grades won him election to Phi Beta Kappa. He was graduated in 1880 at the age of twenty-one.

After spending the summer on an extended hunting trip in Iowa and Minnesota with his brother Elliott, Roosevelt returned to Boston to marry Alice Hathaway Lee, the daughter of a socially prominent Boston family, whom he had ardently courted in college. The marriage took place on Roosevelt's twenty-second birthday. The blue-eyed, brown-haired bride was nineteen.

During the winter of 1880–81, Roosevelt attended Columbia Law School, but found legal studies dull. Being a man of means in his own right, his father having died three years earlier, Roosevelt decided to take his bride on a tour of Europe in the summer of 1881. While there, he collected information for his first book, *The Naval War of 1812*, which he had begun while a senior at Harvard. He also climbed the Matterhorn in Switzerland during this trip.

When Roosevelt returned from Europe in the fall of 1881 he found himself suddenly propelled into a political campaign. He had joined a local Republican club that had met over a saloon the previous year, and now a rebellious group within the club asked him to become their nominee for the state legislature. He was given the nomination on October 28, and twelve days later at the age of twenty-three was elected to the New York assembly.

Roosevelt took his seat in the legislature in Albany in 1882, and that same year his book on the War of 1812 was published with favorable reviews in the New York newspapers. At first Roosevelt's fellow legislators treated him as a joke, because of his Harvard accent and the fact that he dressed like a "dude," wearing his eyeglasses at the end of a long silk cord. Roosevelt soon made a name for himself as a fearless legislator by calling for an investigation of corruption involving railroad magnate Jay Gould and a state supreme court justice. He was re-elected by a large majority in 1882—a year in which the Democrats, headed by Grover Cleveland running for governor, drove many Republicans out of Albany. With the Democrats holding a majority of assembly seats in 1883, the Republicans put up the twenty-four-year-old Roosevelt for the office of Speaker— knowing he would lose. The following year when the Republicans won back control of the assembly the party leaders refused to let him have the office. Although a reformer, Roosevelt was generally conservative in outlook and was particularly opposed to labor legislation. He voted against a bill to reduce the working day of streetcar employees to twelve hours, and opposed raising the pay of New York City firemen to $1200 a year.

Tragedy hit Roosevelt a double blow on February 14, 1884, when both his wife and his mother died on the same day from unrelated diseases. His mother died of typhoid fever, his wife of Bright's disease following the birth of their only child. "When my heart's dearest died," Roosevelt wrote, "the light went from my life for ever."

Roosevelt garbed in a buckskin suit, out west in 1885.   —*Bain photograph*

Teddy Roosevelt was an enthusiastic and talented horseman.

To try to overcome his grief, Roosevelt plunged even harder into work. He completed his term at Albany, attended the Republican National Convention that nominated James Blaine to oppose Grover Cleveland for President, and campaigned for Blaine in the election, although he had opposed Blaine's nomination.

After the election, still suffering from his personal tragedy, Roosevelt went West to make a new life for himself as a cattle rancher in the Bad Lands of Dakota. For three years he shuttled back and forth from East to West. In the Dakotas he lived the life of a cowboy, became a deputy sheriff, captured some thieves, and was challenged to a duel. He also found time to write many magazine articles. After most of his cattle were lost in blizzards in the winter of 1886–87, he gave up the experiment and returned to the East.

IN OCTOBER 1886, Roosevelt agreed to run for mayor of New York City as the Republican candidate. Although the Republicans regularly lost this office, Roosevelt had some hope of winning because this time it was a three-cornered race, in which he was opposed by Henry George, the Socialist philosopher, who was running as an independent, and by Abram S. Hewitt, a wealthy Democrat. When Hewitt easily won the contest with the help of Tammany Hall and Roosevelt came in third behind George, everyone agreed that Roosevelt's political future looked black. The humor magazine *Puck* commented in a mocking letter: "You are not the timber of which Presidents are made."

A month after his election defeat, Roosevelt married again; this time to Edith Kermit Carow, three years younger than himself, who had been a childhood playmate in New York. The ceremony took place in London

Political Defeat and Remarriage

The second Mrs. Theodore Roosevelt, the former Edith Kermit Carow, whom he had known since his childhood.

on December 2, 1886. The young couple remained in Europe until the spring of 1887.

Roosevelt campaigned for the election of Benjamin Harrison as President in 1888, and was rewarded the next year by his appointment to the U.S. Civil Service Commission. He served in this office for six years, being re-appointed by President Cleveland in 1893.

When a reform mayor, William Strong, was elected in New York City on a fusion ticket, Roosevelt was invited to become commissioner of the corruption-ridden police force. He accepted with alacrity, resigning his civil service post. He forced the resignation of the chief of the uniformed police, a man who explained that his $300,000 fortune had been made in stock speculation with the aid of Jay Gould. Roosevelt adopted the practice of prowling the streets at night in a black cape, on the lookout for policemen not doing their duty. These nocturnal strolls made good newspaper copy, and there was even talk that the energetic police commissioner would be a good man to run for President. But his popularity dimmed with many of the citizens of New York City when he insisted on enforcing the Sunday blue laws closing saloons. New Yorkers were glad to see him go in 1897, when he accepted President McKinley's appointment as Assistant Secretary of the Navy.

The thirty-seven-year-old Roosevelt soon began to overshadow the Secretary of the Navy, John D. Long. A forceful orator, Roosevelt was in frequent demand as a speaker. He used the opportunities to call for a more powerful Navy and to hint that the United States should intervene in the Cuban revolution against Spain. He made such jingoistic comments as, "No triumph of peace is quite so great as the supreme triumphs of war." When the *Maine* was sunk in Havana Harbor, Roosevelt denounced it as "an act of dirty treachery" on the part of the Spaniards, even though no proof of Spanish complicity appeared. Privately he told friends that McKinley had "no more backbone than a chocolate eclair" in not going to war at once.

WITHIN two weeks after Congress declared war against Spain in April 1898, Roosevelt had resigned from the Navy department to accept a commission as lieutenant colonel, second in command to Leonard Wood, in the Volunteer 1st Cavalry. The outfit quickly became known as Roosevelt's Rough Riders, as cowboys from the West and polo players from the East joined up to train at the unit's camp in San Antonio, Texas.

Roosevelt's regiment finally reached Cuba at the end of June, but without its horses, which were left in the United States. A few days after arriving, Roosevelt was promoted to colonel and Wood was advanced to commander of the brigade. On July 1 Roosevelt achieved glory when he led the Rough Riders in a charge up San Juan Hill in the face of in-

The Rough Riders in Cuba

Colonel Theodore Roosevelt of the Rough Riders, in 1898.

A Roosevelt family scene showing Ethel holding the dog, Archie on the arm of his dad's chair, Theodore Roosevelt, Kermit, Theodore, Jr., Mrs. Roosevelt, and Alice.

tense enemy fire, losing a quarter of his men. Two days later the U.S. Navy destroyed the Spanish fleet at Santiago, and two weeks after that the fighting in Cuba was over. When American troops began to fall ill of yellow fever, Roosevelt pulled strings to get his Rough Riders shipped back to the United States as quickly as possible and by mid-August they were home. "San Juan was the great day of my life," Roosevelt still said twenty years later.

Certainly San Juan made his political career. On the strength of it, Roosevelt immediately won the Republican nomination for governor of New York. In November he beat the Tammany-supported Democratic candidate by the slim plurality of 17,800 votes. After taking office in 1899, he alienated the leaders of the Republican party by forcing the legislature to pass a tax on corporation franchises. It was in his dealings with the Republican state machine that Roosevelt commented: "I have always been fond of the West African proverb: 'Speak softly and carry a big stick, you will go far.'"

By early 1900 it had become apparent that the Republicans of New York would like to get rid of this young governor that they could not control. They began to talk of pushing him upstairs into the vice presidency. Promptly, in February 1900, Roosevelt issued a statement: ". . . under no circumstances could I or would I accept the nomination for the Vice-Presidency."

At the Republican National Convention in Philadelphia in June, Roosevelt was a sensation in his Rough Rider campaign hat. When he made one of the seconding speeches for the renomination of McKinley, the convention went wild and nominated him as McKinley's running mate by acclamation, although Mark Hanna, the Republican national chairman, was not pleased. "Don't any of you realize that there's only one life between this madman and the White House?" he warned.

Roosevelt did the lion's share of the campaigning against Democratic candidate William Jennings Bryan, while McKinley stayed quietly at home. The energetic vice-presidential nominee toured the country making hundreds of speeches, and in November, McKinley and Roosevelt were elected by a huge majority.

After Roosevelt was inaugurated as Vice President on March 4, 1901, he presided over the Senate for five days in a special session called to approve presidential appointments. This completed his official duties as Vice President until Congress convened in December. He busied himself with plans to resume his law studies, and spent a good deal of time at his summer home, Sagamore Hill, in Oyster Bay, Long Island, romping with his six children.

Roosevelt was on a hunting and fishing excursion in Vermont when he received word that President McKinley had been seriously wounded by an assassin at Buffalo, New York. He hurried to McKinley's bedside, but assured that the President would recover, he left to join his family on a vacation in the Adirondacks.

On September 13, 1901, Roosevelt was coming down from a mountain-climbing expedition when he was met by a messenger carrying word that the President was dying. By the time Roosevelt could reach a railroad the next day, he learned that McKinley was dead. He hurried on to Buffalo, and, in the house where McKinley's body lay, the forty-three-year-old Roosevelt was sworn in as the youngest President in the history of the United States.

The stock-manipulators and trust-builders of Wall Street worried about what this hotheaded young upstart would do in the White House. Roosevelt's friends cautioned him to behave conservatively or he might start a financial panic that would plunge the country into a new depression. So for several months Roosevelt repeatedly said he intended to carry out McKinley's policies. He retained all the members of McKinley's Cabinet, even though he did not respect them. And he even made friends with Senator Mark Hanna, who had once called him a "madman."

But Wall Street learned its fears had been justified when Roosevelt sent his first message to Congress in December. He warned:

"There is a widespread conviction in the minds of the American people that the great corporations known as trusts are in certain of their features and tendencies hurtful to the general welfare. . . . Corporations engaged in interstate commerce should be regulated if they are found to exercise a license working to the public injury. It should be as much the aim of those who seek for social betterment to rid the business world of crimes of cunning as to rid the entire body politic of crimes of violence."

He went on to call for a new cabinet post of Secretary of Commerce and Industries, and for the right of the government to inspect the books and records of corporations engaged in interstate commerce. "What further remedies are needed in the way of governmental regulation, or taxation, can only be determined after publicity has been obtained . . ."

The lengthy message called for important new efforts toward improving the conservation of natural resources. He asked for a stronger Navy, and urged that a canal be built at once to connect the Atlantic and Pacific Oceans.

The warm-hearted Roosevelt unwittingly created Southern antagonism early in his administration when he invited the distinguished Negro educator Booker T. Washington to have dinner with him at the White

Roosevelt's Administration

Colonel Roosevelt as an officer in the army in 1898.

The President's dream of a successful hunt.

A typical pose of a crusading president, Theodore Roosevelt, in 1907.

A colorful scene in Fort Worth, Texas, as Teddy greeted old soldiers in 1905.

Speaking to the crowd was a favorite activity of Roosevelt, as shown here in 1907.

A crowd greeting Roosevelt at the Alamo in San Antonio, Texas, in 1905.

The President in Panama.

A scene with almost the quality of a movie set showing Teddy on a western tour by train.

House. When it was learned that for the first time in history a President had sat down to dinner with a Negro, Southern newspapers fulminated, one calling the dinner "the most damnable outrage ever."

Meanwhile, Roosevelt moved quietly to carry out some of the threats to Wall Street that he had hinted at in his message to Congress. Without even letting his Cabinet know that he was doing so, he had Attorney General Philander Knox prepare an anti-trust suit against the Northern Securities Company, a giant railroad trust organized by J. P. Morgan. No anti-trust suits had been successful under the McKinley administration, but Roosevelt was determined to get the Supreme Court to uphold the law. After two years of litigation, the Supreme Court reversed its previous opinions and upheld the Sherman Anti-trust Act, deciding on March 14, 1904, that the Northern Securities Company should be dissolved.

In May 1902, 140,000 members of the United Mine Workers union went on strike for higher wages and better working conditions in the anthracite mines of Pennsylvania. These miners were earning an average yearly wage of less than $600 a year, and most of that went to pay grocery bills to company-owned stores and rent for company-owned houses. Coal-mine owners refused to negotiate with the union, and the strike dragged on into the fall with coal prices rising and stocks of coal disappearing. By October many schools and hospitals had been forced to close because of lack of fuel. Determined to get the mines back into operation before winter, Roosevelt privately threatened the owners that he would take over the mines if they would not agree to arbitration—even though he had no legal power to do so. In the face of this threat, the owners agreed to let Roosevelt appoint an arbitration commission, which ended the strike with the miners eventually winning a 10% wage increase.

Roosevelt always regarded the building of the Panama Canal as his most important contribution as President, and six months after he urged the project in his first message to Congress, he had signed the Spooner Act authorizing the government to negotiate for construction of the canal. At that time Panama was a province of Colombia, and in the subsequent negotiations the government of Colombia resisted giving up some of its sovereign rights in Panama unless the United States was willing to pay more than Roosevelt was willing to offer. With encouragement from Roosevelt, a revolt was organized in Panama on November 3, 1903, the rebels declaring Panama's independence from Colombia. Roosevelt immediately recognized the new government, and U.S. warships stood off both coasts of Panama. Soon a treaty was concluded with the upstart government, and the construction of the canal got under way. "I took Panama without consulting the Cabinet," Roosevelt candidly wrote later in his *Autobiography*.

In June 1904, the Republican National Convention nominated Roosevelt for President by acclamation and gave the vice-presidential nomination to Senator Charles W. Fairbanks of Indiana. The Democrats named Judge Alton B. Parker of New York for President and Henry G. Davis of West Virginia for Vice President. Roosevelt won by an even greater margin than McKinley had achieved in 1900—7,628,461 to 5,084,223 popular votes and 336 to 140 electoral votes.

Elected President in his own right, Roosevelt began to act with an even bolder hand than before. In his annual message to Congress in December 1904, he announced an expansion of the concept of the Monroe Doctrine that became known as the Roosevelt Corollary. He said: ". . . in the Western Hemisphere the adherence of the United States to the Monroe Doctrine may force the United States, however reluctantly, in flagrant cases of such wrongdoing or impotence, to the exercise of an international police power." Shortly after announcing it, Roosevelt used this new power to intervene in the island country of Santo Domingo (now the Dominican Republic). Because this small Latin American country was not making good on its payment of foreign debts, Roosevelt had American officials seize the customs office of the Dominican government to collect taxes and make payments on the debts. This arrangement continued for more than two years until the country's foreign finances were straightened out.

The Russo-Japanese War had been going on for more than a year when Roosevelt began efforts in 1905 to act as a mediator. He succeeded in bringing representatives of the two nations together in August in Portsmouth, New Hampshire, where agreement was reached on terms for peace. His role as peacemaker won recognition the next year when he was awarded the Nobel Peace Prize.

A temporary coolness developed between Japan and the United States as a result of Portsmouth. Japan had been pressured by Roosevelt to forego a demand for a large indemnity from Russia; relations between the two countries were made worse when the San Francisco school board barred Japanese children from public schools. Roosevelt put pressure on the school board to reverse its decision, and when the U.S. "Great White Fleet" visited Japan on a round-the-world cruise, American sailors were greeted with friendship.

Roosevelt put on a determined fight to obtain federal regulation of the railroads. The Interstate Commerce Act of 1887 had proven ineffective in controlling the abuses of the railroads in rate-fixing and rebates to favored customers. By March 1906, Roosevelt had put enough pressure on Congress to obtain passage of the Hepburn Act that gave the Interstate Commerce Commission increased powers over transportation.

Although Roosevelt had obtained congressional approval to establish a Department of Commerce and Labor in 1903, he did not press too vigorously to break up the large trusts. A brilliant group of journalists—Lincoln Steffens, Ida Tarbell, Upton Sinclair, and others—were directing atten-

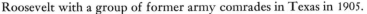

Roosevelt with a group of former army comrades in Texas in 1905.

Roosevelt on a hunting expedition in Africa with Kermit in 1914.

tion to the evils of politics and business. Roosevelt coined the epithet *muckraker* to describe them, but nevertheless was influenced by them. In 1906 he was inspired by Sinclair's *The Jungle*, an exposé of sordid conditions in the packing industry, to force the passage of legislation requiring federal inspection of packing houses. That same year Roosevelt obtained the Pure Food Act, providing regulation of the food industry.

Roosevelt was away from Washington on a bear hunt in October 1907, when a financial panic hit Wall Street sending stock prices tumbling and forcing the collapse of some large investment companies. Depression followed. In a special message to Congress in January 1908, he made his strongest speech denouncing "gambling in the stock market" and dishonesty in the business world. He also criticized the use of injunctions to stop strikes, and boldly proclaimed: ". . . if it were true that to cut out rottenness from the body politic meant a momentary check to an unhealthy seeming prosperity, I should not for one moment hesitate to put the knife to the corruption."

During his last two years in office Roosevelt had little success in obtaining the passage of legislation. There was a large Republican majority in both houses of Congress, but the representatives and senators knew that Roosevelt was not going to run for office again, so they paid little attention to his recommendations.

Roosevelt used what remaining power he had to obtain the Republican nomination for President in 1908 for William Howard Taft, believing that Taft would carry on his policies. He worked hard to achieve Taft's nomination, which came on the first ballot. And he continued to labor in the campaign that followed, offering advice at every step of the way until Taft had been elected.

The Bull Moose

ONLY fifty years old when he left the White House for the last time, Roosevelt was determined to continue to lead the strenuous life that he loved. Within three weeks after turning the presidency over to Taft, he sailed for Africa with his twenty-year-old son Kermit to hunt big game, one of the first Americans to do so. At the end of the year-long adventure he listed nearly three hundred animals that he had bagged, including nine lions, five elephants, thirteen rhinoceroses, and seven hippopotamuses.

Teddy Roosevelt's frustrations during World War I.

Rue de la Paix decorated for Theodore Roosevelt's visit to Paris in 1910.

He and his wife then went on a triumphal tour of Europe, where he was wined and dined by kings and queens and cheered by the masses.

When Roosevelt returned home to New York in June 1910, he was soon made aware of the fact that Taft was not carrying forward progressive policies but had succumbed to the influence of the business forces that Roosevelt had fought. In the summer of 1910 he made a political speaking tour to the West and Southwest, where he was greeted by crowds as large as those that had gathered while he was still President. When he

A close-up of Teddy Roosevelt in 1910.

stopped at St. Louis he took a ride in an airplane piloted by Arch Hoxsey. But such dramatic incidents to exhibit his fearlessness were subordinate to his theme of the New Nationalism in which "every man holds his property subject to the general right of the community to regulate its use to whatever degree the public welfare may require it." He made another speaking tour into the South in October, campaigned for the Republican candidate for New York, and helped edit the political-opinion magazine *Outlook.*

Early in 1912 Roosevelt declared in a talk in Cleveland that "My hat is in the ring" to win the Republican presidential nomination. But at the National Convention that met in Chicago in June, the party's National Committee was ruled by Taft-supporters who refused to seat many delegates pledged to Roosevelt. Consequently, Taft was nominated to run for a second term, but 344 delegates refused to vote. That night these and other Roosevelt supporters met with Roosevelt and pledged him their support for an independent campaign. He told them: "If you wish me to make the fight, I will make it."

In July the Democratic National Convention nominated Woodrow Wilson and some of Roosevelt's followers deserted him to join Wilson.

A meeting of 10,000 Roosevelt boosters in Chicago in August formed the Progressive party and nominated Roosevelt for President. Hiram

Visiting Roosevelt, Arizona, in 1911, riding in the touring cars of that day.

Johnson of California was the new party's candidate for Vice President. The platform called for the enactment of a wide range of political and social reforms, including woman suffrage.

In the midst of the campaign, on October 14, just before a speech in Milwaukee, a deranged assassin fired a bullet into Roosevelt's chest. Although the bullet had actually entered his lung and Roosevelt did not know whether or not he was dying, he insisted on going ahead with his speech, saying: "I have a message to deliver and will deliver it as long as there is life in my body." After completing the address he was rushed to a hospital. Wilson and Taft called a halt to the campaign until Roosevelt recovered, but within two weeks the robust ex-Rough Rider was well enough to address a crowd of 12,000 in Madison Square Garden in New York City.

Roosevelt had not expected to win, so he was well pleased with the results in which he came in second to Wilson with Taft trailing as a poor third.

During the winter of 1913–14 Roosevelt went to South America on an even more strenuous expedition than his earlier African big-game hunt. He and his son Kermit explored a Brazilian waterway called the River of Doubt, later renamed the Roosevelt. He seriously injured his leg on this trip and also came down with a tropical fever, but his brimming good health pulled him through.

A Progressive party convention again nominated Roosevelt as its candidate for President in 1916, but this time he declined to run, throwing his support to the Republican candidate, Charles Evans Hughes. Roosevelt campaigned bitterly against Wilson, whom he denounced for not doing enough to protect American lives and ships in the World War then raging in Europe.

Immediately after the United States declared war on Germany in April 1917, Roosevelt hurried to Washington to plead with Wilson to let him form a "Roosevelt Division" and lead it to France. But Wilson rejected the offer. A year later he aged visibly after his youngest son, Quentin, was killed while flying in battle in France.

His own death came suddenly and unexpectedly. On the evening of January 5, 1919, at his Oyster Bay home, he dictated an article for the Kansas City *Star*, and then retired. Early on the morning of January 6, he succumbed to an arterial blood clot.

Roosevelt himself provided perhaps the best description of his effect upon the presidency:

"While President I have *been* President, emphatically; I have used every ounce of power there was in the office and I have not cared a rap for the criticisms of those who spoke of my 'usurpation of power'; for I knew that the talk was all nonsense and that there was no usurpation. I believe that the efficiency of this Government depends upon its possessing a strong central executive, and wherever I could establish a precedent for strength in the executive . . . I have felt not merely that my action was right in itself, but that in showing the strength of, or in giving strength to, the executive, I was establishing a precedent of value. I believe in a strong executive; I believe in power; but I believe that responsibility should go with power, and that it is not well that the strong executive should be a perpetual executive. Above all and beyond all I believe as I have said before that the salvation of this country depends upon Washington and Lincoln representing the type of leader to which we are true."

Roosevelt greeting his good friend, the beloved Cardinal Gibbons.

218 WILLIAM McKINLEY

William McKinley

The Twenty-fifth President of the United States
1897–1901

1843 (January 29) Born in Niles, Ohio.

1859 Attended Allegheny College in Meadville, Pennsylvania.

1860 Taught in a country school and clerked in the post office.

1861–65 Served in the Union Army in the Civil War, rising from private to major.

1867 Admitted to the bar to practice law.

1869–71 Prosecuting attorney of Stark County, Ohio.

1871 (January 25) Married Ida Saxton.

1877–91 U.S. representative from Ohio.

1892–96 Governor of Ohio.

1897–1901 Twenty-fifth President of the United States.

1901 (September 6) Shot by an assassin in Buffalo, New York.

1901 (September 14) Died of wounds in Buffalo.

Leading Officials in
McKinley's Administration

Office	Name	Years Served
Chief Justice	Melville W. Fuller	1888-1910
Vice-President	Garret A. Hobart	1897-1899
	Theodore Roosevelt	1901
Secretary of State	John Sherman	1897-1898
	William R. Day	1898
	John Hay	1898-1905
Secretary of the Treasury	Lyman J. Gage	1897-1902
Secretary of War	Russell A. Alger	1897-1899
	Elihu Root	1899-1904
Attorney General	Joseph McKenna	1897-1898
	John W. Griggs	1898-1901
	Philander C. Knox	1901-1904
Postmaster General	James A. Gary	1897-1898
	Charles E. Smith	1898-1902
Secretary of the Navy	John D. Long	1897-1902
Secretary of the Interior	Cornelius N. Bliss	1897-1899
	Ethan A. Hitchcock	1898-1907
Secretary of Agriculture	James Wilson	1897-1913

The birthplace of William McKinley in Niles, Ohio.

A kind gentle man, William McKinley loved everyone and wanted everyone to love him. Most did. He was re-elected to a second term as President with a larger plurality of popular votes than Lincoln or any other previous Chief Executive. When he was struck down by an assassin's bullet, his first thought was of others, crying out to protect his assailant, "Don't let them hurt him!" The third President to be killed by an assassin, he was as deeply and elaborately mourned as were Lincoln and Garfield. A biography issued immediately after his death described the mood of the country: "An universal spasm of grief passed from end to end of the land. . . . Never was there a crime more without purpose, more without possible good effect."

Yet history has not been kind to McKinley's memory. Today his name is used as a symbol for nineteenth-century backward-looking conservatism. He is recalled for his sponsorship of high tariffs and for weakly letting the country be pushed into the Spanish-American War. It is generally forgotten that he led the nation onto the world stage and made the historic declaration:

"Isolation is no longer possible or desirable."

From Mess Sergeant to President

THE seventh in a family of nine children, William McKinley was born in Niles, Ohio, on January 29, 1843. When he was nine his family moved to nearby Poland, Ohio, where he and his brothers and sisters attended a small private school called Union Seminary. He took an early interest in oratory and became president of the local debating society. He also became a member of the Methodist church, giving his mother hope that he might become a minister. When he was seventeen, McKinley attended Allegheny College in Meadville, Pennsylvania, for a year, but was forced to drop out because of illness.

The eighteen-year-old McKinley was clerking in the Poland post office when the Civil War began. In the tradition of his great-grandfather who fought in the Revolutionary War and his grandfather who fought in the War of 1812, he enlisted in the 23d Ohio Volunteer Infantry in June 1861. A major of the regiment was Rutherford B. Hayes, who also was to become President. Young McKinley was made commissary (mess) sergeant, and in the battle of Antietam, distinguished himself by serving a hot meal to troops under fire. Given a battlefield commission as second lieutenant, he shortly became brigade quartermaster on Hayes' staff. In 1864 the young officer's gallantry in battle advanced him to captain. He was successively transferred to the staffs of Generals George Crook and Winfield S. Hancock. In March 1865, he was promoted to major for his bravery in the battles of Opequan, Cedar Creek, and Fishers Hill.

When the war was over, Major McKinley was only twenty-two. His years of hard life in the field had changed him from the pale sickly boy who had volunteered for army duty into a healthy, robust young man. After turning down an invitation to remain in the Army, he decided to begin studying law. Following two years in the office of a prominent attorney in Youngstown, Ohio, he entered law school in Albany, New York, and was admitted to the bar the next year.

In 1867 he settled in Canton, Ohio, to practice, largely because his elder sister, Anna, was teaching school there. He at once began to take part in Republican party affairs and was welcomed by the politicians for his forensic ability. When McKinley was nominated for prosecuting attorney of Stark County in 1869, even his friends did not think he had a chance because the Democrats regularly won all the county elections. But his vigorous campaigning brought him victory, though two years later the opposition mustered its forces and beat him by 45 votes.

While still prosecuting attorney, McKinley had married Ida Saxton, the blue-eyed daughter of Canton's leading banker, on January 25, 1871. The marriage was a tragic one, for both their daughters died, one as an infant, the other at the age of four, while Mrs. McKinley became a lifelong invalid. The sincere affection that McKinley showered on his wife won him sympathy in his subsequent political career.

William McKinley and his wife, Ida, who for many years was an invalid.

The home of William McKinley in Canton, Ohio, as it appeared in 1896. 　　　　—*Courtney photograph*

William McKinley in his study, which shows typical furnishings of the late nineteenth and early twentieth centuries.

McKinley (third from the right) and a group of his friends visiting his farm in 1901, shortly before his assassination.

In 1876, when his old commanding officer Hayes ran for President, the thirty-three-year-old McKinley was elected to Congress. He was repeatedly re-elected, serving almost continuously for fifteen years. In the House of Representatives, McKinley was sometimes compared to Napoleon because of his short stature and general appearance, including his habit of putting one hand inside his coat while speaking.

In the first Congress in which he sat, McKinley surprisingly voted with the Democratic majority to pass free silver legislation for "cheap" money over the veto of President Hayes.

But the issue on which McKinley won his principal reputation as a congressman was his support of high protective tariffs. He came by his convictions naturally because his father had been a small iron manufacturer, and McKinley had been imbued from childhood with the importance of protective tariffs for American industry. As author of the McKinley Tariff Act in 1890, he forced tariffs to new highs. But the high retail prices that the legislation caused brought a backlash at the polls, and Republican congressmen, including McKinley, lost their seats.

In 1891 the Ohio Republicans nominated McKinley for governor. For three months he campaigned harder than he ever had in his life, making several speeches a day—130 in all—and appearing in almost every one of the state's eighty-eight counties. He was elected with a narrow plurality of 21,000 votes. Two years later he was re-elected with a plurality of nearly

81,000 votes, indicating a successful administration. In the hard times brought by the depression of 1893, McKinley sent carloads of provisions for the relief of the unemployed in Ohio. His own modest fortune of $20,000 was wiped out by the business failure of a financial partner, leaving him with more than $100,000 in debts. But wealthy friends contributed to a fund that paid his debts and returned him the money he had lost.

While governor, McKinley became famous for his devotion to his invalid wife. Every afternoon at exactly three o'clock he would interrupt whatever business he was engaged in to step to the window of his office and wave his handkerchief to his wife, who awaited this greeting from their hotel suite across the street. And each morning after leaving the hotel he would pause outside, remove his hat, and bow to her window, before proceeding to his office.

Our Destiny

Where our artisans have the admitted capacity to excel, where our inventive genius has initiated many of the grandest discoveries of these later days, and where the native resources of our land are as limitless as they are valuable to supply the world's needs, it is our province, as it should be our earnest care, to lead in the march of human progress, and not rest content with any secondary place.

Copyright, 1900, by F. M. Buckles & Co.

A quotation from one of McKinley's speeches.

McKinley had received 182 votes in the 1892 Republican National Convention that renominated Harrison. The former's industrialist friends, led by Cleveland millionaire Mark Hanna, were determined to help him win the presidency in 1896. To achieve national support, his friends financed a 10,000-mile trip through seventeen states in which he made nearly four hundred speeches in eight weeks. The McKinley boom was so successful that by the time the Republican National Convention met in St. Louis in June 1896, McKinley was nominated on the first ballot. Garret A. Hobart of New Jersey was chosen as the vice-presidential candidate.

Although McKinley was prepared to campaign on the issue of tariffs, the nomination by the Democrats of thirty-six-year-old William Jennings

William McKinley and President Grover Cleveland leaving the White House for the Capitol for the McKinley inauguration.

Bryan of Nebraska, an ardent free-silver advocate, changed the central issue. McKinley dropped his advocacy of silver coinage and came out strongly for the gold standard and "sound" money. In doing so he won the support of President Cleveland and many other conservative Democrats. Mark Hanna and his friends raised the largest campaign fund up to that time in American politics, more than three million dollars, by frightening bankers and businessmen with the specter of inflation and federal controls on business. Workmen were told that factories would be closed if Bryan won, and banks informed farmers that their payments would be extended at lower rates of interest if McKinley were elected. In the November election, McKinley received 7,102,246 votes to Bryan's 6,492,559, and 271 to 176 electoral votes.

McKinley made a partial payment of his political debt to Hanna by appointing the feeble seventy-three-year-old Senator John Sherman of Ohio

William McKinley and his running mate, Garret A. Hobart of New Jersey, and the slogan of their campaign —"Protection (meaning tariffs) and Sound Money."

The inaugural platform prior to McKinley's address, showing his wife and his mother awaiting the beginning of the ceremonies.

as Secretary of State. This created an opening in the Senate to which the Ohio legislature elected Hanna, a maneuver which drew some caustic criticism.

McKinley's Administration

WHILE his aged mother and invalid wife looked on, the fifty-four-year-old McKinley was inaugurated President on a mild, spring-like March 4, 1897. In a long, wordy inaugural address he reviewed the problems of the depression that still gripped the country, but noted the need to "make haste slowly" in grappling with the situation. He called for higher tariffs to increase revenues and stop the climb of the national debt. "Legislation helpful to producers is beneficial to all," he said.

McKinley's long experience in Congress aided him in knowing how to bring pressure to bear in getting the legislation he wanted. He often called recalcitrant members of Congress to the White House and reasoned with them to prevent the introduction of legislation he opposed or to win their support. As a result he was forced to use the veto only fourteen times during his administration. Illinois Senator Shelby Cullom commented, "We have never had a President who had more influence with Congress than Mr. McKinley."

The special session of Congress that McKinley called in March 1897 completed its work by July, passing the higher tariffs that he had requested. Whether as a result of this legislation or the natural course of economic events, an upturn followed.

As recovery set in, the nation's attention turned in a new direction—Cuba. A revolution had begun against Spanish rule of the island in 1895, but President Cleveland had skillfully avoided any American involvement. Popular sympathy was with the Cuban rebels, but McKinley's approach was cautious. In May 1897, he asked Congress to appropriate $50,000 for the relief of Americans stranded on the island. Two rival New York newspaper publishers, William Randolph Hearst and Joseph Pulitzer, began using the Cuban revolution to build circulation. They sent

McKinley delivering his inaugural address.

reporters to the scene, and played up lurid stories of atrocities by the Spaniards. At the same time influential men revived the expansionist fever of Polk's administration, repeating that it was the "manifest destiny" of the United States to expand beyond its existing borders. McKinley hoped that he could intervene and act as a mediator between the Cubans and the Spanish.

Two events in February 1898 moved the United States closer to intervention in Cuba. On February 9, Hearst's *Journal* printed the contents of a private letter sent by the Spanish minister in Washington to a friend. In it the Spaniard expressed an insulting opinion of the American President, saying that "McKinley is weak and a bidder for the admiration of the crowd, besides being a would-be politician who tries to leave a door open behind himself while keeping on good terms with the jingoes of his party." Less than a week later, on February 15, the U.S. battleship *Maine* was mysteriously blown up and sunk in Havana Harbor, killing most of the crew and setting off a storm of popular reaction across the United States. While an American commission investigated the explosion, McKinley quietly asked Congress to pass a fifty-million-dollar national defense appropriation. The bill was hurried through and by March 9 had become law.

The nation rushed headlong toward war, and the force of events swept McKinley along with it. Even though on April 10 the American ambassador in Spain cabled word that Spain was ready to suspend hostilities in Cuba and grant the Cubans self-government, McKinley did not feel that he could any longer withstand American demands for war. On April 11 he sent a message to Congress asking that he be empowered to use the Army and Navy to intervene in Cuba. Nine days later Congress granted the power, but with an amendment forbidding the annexation of Cuba. On April 25, McKinley asked Congress for a declaration of war against Spain. It was approved the same day.

In the declining years of the horse-and-buggy days, this small town American scene was repeated again and again, as the train carrying McKinley's body traveled to Washington for his funeral.

The electric ambulance which carried the martyred President from the Temple of Music in Buffalo, New York, where he was shot, to the hospital.

The Spanish-American War itself lasted less than four months. On May 1, Commodore George Dewey destroyed a Spanish fleet in Manila Harbor; on June 10, U.S. Marines landed in force at Guantánamo Bay, Cuba; on July 3, the Spanish Caribbean fleet was destroyed at Santiago, Cuba. American troops landed in Puerto Rico on July 25, and the war ended with the unconditional surrender of the Philippines on August 15. In the entire war, the U.S. Army and Navy reported a total of 1941 combat casualties, with 298 killed. Some 5000 others died of disease.

By the time McKinley made his second annual address to Congress in December 1898, he was able to report that most of the troops mustered for the war had already been released from service, and that the American flag was flying over Cuba, Puerto Rico, and the Philippines. Also during the short war, on July 7, 1898, McKinley had signed the congressional resolution approving the annexation of Hawaii. But the new empire was not to be as easily controlled as it had been won. The Filipinos revolted against American rule and a prolonged struggle ensued.

Now a confirmed "sound money" man, McKinley repeatedly urged Congress to settle the issue of gold-vs.-silver by making gold the basis of the country's monetary system. Congress acceded to his wishes in 1900 by passing the Gold Standard Act.

When a secret revolutionary society called the Boxers started a rebellion in China in 1900, with the intent of driving all foreigners out of the country, McKinley ordered U.S. Marines to join an international relief expedition with seven other nations. These troops captured the Chinese capital in August 1900, and the Chinese government was later forced to pay indemnities to each of the foreign powers. The United States returned its share to China, which used the money to educate Chinese students at American universities.

McKinley received the unanimous nomination for a second term as President from the Republican National Convention in Philadelphia in June 1900. Governor Theodore Roosevelt of New York was nominated for Vice President. The Democrats again chose Bryan as their standard bearer, and as his running mate nominated Adlai E. Stevenson, who had served as Vice President during Cleveland's second administration.

The Democrats sought new campaign issues to add to the tariff and free silver. They accused the McKinley administration of being the tool of big business and demanded legislation to control the trusts. They also accused McKinley of a new imperialism, pointing to the use of American troops in the Philippines to quell the uprising of the Filipinos. McKinley spent most of the campaign at his home in Canton, confident of victory. His confidence was justified, for in the election he rolled up the impressive total of 7,218,491 votes to Bryan's 6,356,734 and an electoral vote of 292 to 155.

The first months of his second term of office were pleasantly uneventful. McKinley left Washington on April 29, 1901, for a transcontinental tour that was supposed to last six weeks. However, his wife became ill in California, and after she recovered he decided to spend the rest of the summer in Canton. He left from there to make a promised address on September 5 at the Pan-American Exposition in Buffalo, New York.

McKinley had spent many days preparing what proved to be his last speech. In it he looked forward, forecasting the growing importance of the United States in the world. He said:

"Isolation is no longer possible or desirable. . . . Our capacity to produce has developed so enormously, and our products have so multiplied, that the problem of more markets requires our urgent and immediate attention. Only a broad and enlightened policy will keep what we have. . . . The period of exclusiveness is past. . . . A policy of good will and friendly trade relations will prevent reprisals. Reciprocity treaties are in harmony with the spirit of the times; measures of retaliation are not. If, perchance, some of our tariffs are no longer needed for revenue or to encourage and protect our industries at home, why should they not be employed to extend and promote our markets abroad? . . ."

Thus, in his last public address, McKinley turned away from the ever-higher protectionist tariffs that had first made him a national figure.

On September 6, 1901, the day after his address, the President stood in the Exposition's Temple of Music shaking hands with a long line of well-wishers, when a man approached with his right hand wrapped in a handkerchief. As McKinley extended his hand, two shots were fired from a pistol concealed under the handkerchief. As the wounded McKinley was helped to a chair, he gasped to his secretary: "Be careful about my wife. Do not tell her." Then he cautioned that his assassin should not be hurt.

McKinley was removed to a private residence, and after several days seemed to be recovering. Then he took a turn for the worse. Shortly before his death early on the morning of September 14, he whispered to his wife: "Good-by all, good-by. It is God's way. His will be done."

The assassin, a neurotic young anarchist by the name of Leon F. Czolgosz, who explained that he had shot the President because he wanted to kill a "ruler," was tried and electrocuted.

The nation went into deepest mourning. Millions lined the railroad tracks as the funeral train bore the coffin from Buffalo to Washington for a state funeral and then to Canton for burial.

Former President Grover Cleveland said of McKinley:

"All our people loved their dead President. His kindly nature and lovable traits of character, and his amiable consideration for all about him will long live in the minds and hearts of his countrymen."

"The little savings bank in the home means more for the future of the children of a family, ··· than all the advice in the world. It gives them the right start." WILLIAM McKINLEY

230 GROVER CLEVELAND

Grover Cleveland

The Twenty-fourth President of the United States
The Twenty-second President of the United States
1893–97; 1885–89

1837 (March 18) Born in Caldwell, New Jersey.

1851–52 Grocery clerk in Fayetteville, New York.

1853–55 Worked in New York Institution for the Blind in New York City.

1855–62 Studied law and worked as a law clerk in Buffalo, New York.

1859 Admitted to the bar to practice law.

1863–65 Assistant district attorney of Erie County, New York.

1871–73 Sheriff of Erie County.

1882 Mayor of Buffalo, New York.

1883–84 Governor of New York.

1885–89 Twenty-second President of the United States.

1886 (June 2) Married Frances Folsom.

1893–97 Twenty-fourth President of the United States.

1908 (June 24) Died in Princeton, New Jersey.

Leading Officials in
Cleveland's Administrations

Office	Name	Years Served
Chief Justice	Morrison R. Waite	1874-1888
	Melville W. Fuller	1888-1910
Vice-President	Thomas A. Hendricks	1885
	Adlai E. Stevenson	1893-1897
Secretary of State	Thomas F. Bayard	1885-1889
	Walter Q. Gresham	1893-1895
	Richard Olney	1895-1897
Secretary of War	William C. Endicott	1885-1889
	Daniel S. Lamont	1893-1897
Secretary of the Treasury	Daniel Manning	1885-1887
	Charles S. Fairchild	1887-1889
	John G. Carlisle	1893-1897
Attorney General	Augustus H. Garland	1885-1889
	Richard Olney	1893-1895
	Judson Harmon	1895-1897
Postmaster General	William F. Vilas	1885-1888
	Don M. Dickinson	1888-1889
	Wilson S. Bissel	1893-1895
	William L. Wilson	1895-1897
Secretary of the Navy	William C. Whitney	1885-1889
	Hilary A. Herbert	1893-1897
Secretary of the Interior	Lucius Q. C. Lamar	1885-1888
	William F. Vilas	1888-1889
	Hoke Smith	1893-1896
	David R. Francis	1896-1897
Secretary of Agriculture	Norman J. Colman	1889
	Julius Sterling Morton	1893-1897

The birthplace of Grover Cleveland at Caldwell, New Jersey.

He is the kind of man who would rather do something badly for himself than have somebody else do it well."

That description of Grover Cleveland by his friend Samuel J. Tilden went far toward explaining how Cleveland achieved the distinction of being the only President to serve one term, lose an election, and then make a comeback for a second term.

A short, jolly, blue-eyed fat man, who was descriptively called "Uncle Jumbo" by young relatives, he was the first Democrat to be elected President after the Civil War. Among other unusual claims to fame, he was the only President who had ever hanged a man—while serving as sheriff in Buffalo, New York. And he was the only President to be married in the White House.

As Chief Executive, Cleveland brought the country no unusual theories of government; but he did restore to the presidency much of the prestige eroded by Congress during the Reconstruction Era. Above all, he exemplified honesty, even when it lost him the support of powerful interests in his party. He fought the corruption of New York City's Democratic Tammany organization. He argued for a low tariff against the Eastern industrialists' pleas for protection, but fought the Western free silver interests and defended "sound money" as strenuously as his Republican predecessors. He supported government controls on the railroad robber barons, but he also clamped down hard on the rising labor movement. Essentially he was a conservative. In his battles with Congress, he exercised the veto power more times than had all previous Presidents combined. He fittingly summed up his life on his deathbed with these words:

"I have tried so hard to do right."

A Minister's Son

ONE of a family of nine children of a Presbyterian minister, Stephen Grover Cleveland was born in Caldwell, New Jersey, on March 18, 1837. He attended schools in Fayetteville and Clinton, New York, as his father moved from pastorate to pastorate, and ended his formal education at the age of fourteen to help support the family. Young Grover ran errands and clerked in a grocery store in Fayetteville for one dollar a week.

When he was sixteen, his father died. Joining his eldest brother, William, a teacher at the New York Institution for the Blind, Grover worked as an assistant and odd-job helper for two years, regularly sending his meager pay home to his mother.

At eighteen, in the spring of 1855, Grover decided to head West to make his fortune. When he paused in Buffalo, New York, to visit relatives, he was offered a job helping on his uncle's farm and decided to stay. Before the year was up, Cleveland's uncle obtained the boy a clerkship in a local law firm where he could study law while earning his keep at five dollars a week.

Four years later, in 1859, Cleveland was admitted to the bar, and promoted to chief clerk in the same law firm at a wage of $600 a year, with the promise of a $100 raise each year. He needed the steady income to help support his younger brothers and sisters.

The young lawyer began to take an interest in the Democratic party, and he worked especially hard in the successful gubernatorial campaign of Horatio Seymour in 1862. As a political reward, Cleveland was appointed assistant district attorney of Erie County, an office he held throughout the Civil War. Partly because he was an anti-war Democrat and partly because his family depended on him, Cleveland hired a substitute for $300 when his name came up in the draft.

In 1865 Cleveland lost his first election. He ran for district attorney of Erie County, but was defeated by his roommate, Lyman K. Bass, the Republican candidate. After this he established himself in private law practice in Buffalo.

Cleveland tried for public office again in 1870, this time running for sheriff and winning. The thirty-three-year-old sheriff soon made a name for himself as an honest public official, exposing crooked contractors who had been delivering short measures of food and fuel to the county jail. When it came time to hang two convicted murderers, Cleveland sprang the trap himself, explaining that he could not ask his deputies to do a job just because he didn't want to do it himself. By the time his term was up in 1873, Cleveland had saved $20,000 from his salary and fees, and for the first time in his life was out of debt.

For nine years he prospered as a lawyer, while continuing to be active in the local Democratic party inner circle. As a bachelor, he led a happy-go-lucky life, frequenting the local saloons and enjoying extended hunting and fishing trips with his cronies.

In 1881 Cleveland accepted the nomination to run as a reform candidate for mayor, to clean up corruption in the city government of Buffalo. He won by 15,000 votes to his opponent's 11,500, and soon became known as the "veto mayor," turning down one crooked measure after another that had been voted by his corrupt city council.

When the Democratic state convention met in the fall of 1882 to choose a candidate for governor, Cleveland's name was on the lips of many Western delegates who wanted to overturn the power of the Eastern bloc of the party. Cleveland's friends captured the nomination for him with the aid of New York's Tammany machine, but he made no promises to the New York City politicians. The Republican candidate for governor, Charles J. Folger, was serving as President Arthur's Secretary of the Treasury, and was known as the favored candidate of the corrupt millionaire Jay Gould. Consequently, reform-minded Republicans joined the Democrats in voting for Cleveland in the November election, and he received the largest plurality of any governor up to that time—with 535,000 votes to Folger's 342,000.

To their chagrin, the leaders of the Tammany machine learned that Cleveland meant what he said about reform. In his two years as governor, Cleveland refused to go along with measures designed to feather the nests of Tammany's friends. Cleveland read every word of every law passed by the legislature before he would sign or veto it—even if it meant he had to stay up all night to get the job done.

"*Thrift and carefulness of expend. ture among the people tend to secur a thrifty government.*"

GROVER CLEVELAND

A poster of the period of Cleveland's first term showing him with the previous United States Presidents.

As the national election of 1884 approached, the Republican party chose as its presidential candidate James G. Blaine, who as Speaker of the House under President Grant had been deeply involved in the railroad scandals. Many prominent members of the GOP angrily declared they would not support such a candidate, and they urged the Democrats to choose a reform candidate.

When the Democratic National Convention met in July 1884, Cleveland's reputation for honesty made him the favorite. The New York City bosses made a last-ditch effort to derail Cleveland's nomination by spreading the story that he was anti-labor, anti-Catholic, and anti-Irish. It was easy for Cleveland's friends to disprove these charges, and on the second ballot the delegates nominated "Grover the Good," as he was somewhat fatuously dubbed, with Governor Thomas A. Hendricks of Indiana as his running mate.

Just ten days later the most sensational bombshell in campaign history exploded. Under the headline "A Terrible Tale," a Buffalo newspaper revealed that eleven years earlier Cleveland had fathered a son by a woman he did not marry. The charge was true and Cleveland refused to deny it. His partisans, without his consent, hit back with a story that Blaine's first son had been born less than three months after he had married his wife. They also made free use of charges of corruption, the evidence for which appeared strong despite Blaine's denials. Republican torchlight parades marched to the chant:

> Blaine! Blaine! James G. Blaine!
> Plum-ed Knight from the State of Maine!

To which the Democrats retorted:

> Blaine! Blaine! James G. Blaine!
> Continental liar from the State of Maine!

The Republicans converted their own favorite theme, Cleveland's illicit paternity, into a memorable chant:

> Ma, ma, where's my Pa?
> Gone to the White House, ha ha ha!

As the most scurrilous campaign in U.S. history drew to a close, Blaine appeared to have the edge. His home state of Maine, voting early as was its custom, gave him the largest victory the Republicans had ever achieved in the state. Blaine was favored to capture the crucial New York electoral vote because of the Tammany disaffection with Cleveland and the effect of the paternity scandal on Irish Catholic voters. But six days before the election a delegation of Protestant clergymen made a courtesy call on Blaine at his New York hotel, and their spokesman referred to the Democrats as the party of "rum, Romanism and rebellion." Blaine neglected to disavow the remark, which was instantly seized on by the Democrats, printed, and distributed outside Catholic churches Sunday morning. Cleveland carried New York by 1149 votes out of a million cast, and with it the election. Blaine himself attributed his defeat to the unhappy phrase of his supporter. Nationally, Cleveland received 4,874,986 votes to Blaine's 4,851,981.

The victorious Democrats came up with a last triumphant jingle:

> Hurrah for Maria,
> Hurrah for the kid,
> We voted for Grover
> And we're damn glad we did.

THE forty-seven-year-old Cleveland stood confidently with one hand behind his back and delivered his inaugural address without notes on the spring-like March 4, 1885. A huge crowd listened as the first Democrat to be elected President in a quarter of a century spoke:

"The people demand reform in the administration of the Government and the application of business principles to public affairs. As a means to this end, civil-service reform should be in good faith enforced. Our citizens have the right to protection from the incompetency of public employees who hold their places solely as the reward of partisan service, and from the corrupting influence of those who promise and the vicious methods of those who expect such rewards; and those who worthily seek public employment have the right to insist that merit and competency shall be recognized instead of party subserviency or the surrender of honest political belief."

Nevertheless, Democrats from all parts of the country descended on Washington expecting to be rewarded with the more than 100,000 jobs that Cleveland had it in his power to fill. In letters to friends, Cleveland called the problem "a nightmare." He wrote, "This dreadful, frightful, damnable office seeking hangs over me and surrounds me . . ." He refused to remove Republicans from office just because they were Republicans, and insisted that for anyone to be removed from office it was necessary to bring charges of incompetence or corruption. Throughout the nation Republican newspapers attacked Cleveland for the charges that were being brought against Republican office holders, while Democratic papers attacked him for not putting good Democrats in office. These attacks brought from the President one of the most sweeping denunciations ever made against the press:

"I don't think there ever was a time when newspaper lying was so general and mean as the present, and there never was a country under the sun where it flourished as it does in this. The falsehoods daily spread before the people in our newspapers, while they are proofs of the mental ingenuity of those engaged in newspaper work, are insults to the American love for decency and fair play of which we boast . . ."

In one of his last acts as President, Arthur had provided for the opening of the Indian Territory (now Oklahoma) for settlement. This would have robbed the Indians of thousands of acres of land they had been promised. So within a week after taking office, Cleveland issued a proclamation canceling the opening of the lands and warning all intruders that they would be removed by troops if necessary.

Throughout his first administration, Cleveland ruthlessly vetoed special-interest legislation, running up a total of more than 300 vetoes during his four years in office, compared to a total of 132 vetoes by the previous twenty-one Presidents.

In his first annual message to Congress, Cleveland called for a reduction in tariffs, pointing out that the federal revenues were "in excess of the actual needs of an economical administration of the Government." He said that the seventy-million-dollar surplus of revenues over expenses would merely tempt Congress to pass money-wasting laws. He also asked for an end to the coinage of silver dollars, warning that gold was being hoarded and that the country's fiscal system was in danger.

Early in 1886 there were hundreds of railroad strikes throughout the country as the new Knights of Labor union demanded higher wages and an eight-hour workday. Recognizing the importance of the growing labor movement, Cleveland sent a special message to Congress in April—the first by any President devoted exclusively to the problems of labor. In it he

Frances Folsom, the attractive daughter of a former law partner, who became the wife of President Cleveland in a White House ceremony June 2, 1886.

The home in Princeton, New Jersey to which Cleveland retired after his second term as President.

asked for the creation of a three-member commission to settle labor-management disputes. The critical nature of the labor situation was emphasized two weeks later by the Haymarket riot in Chicago, in which seven persons were killed and more than fifty injured in a battle between strikers and police. Two years later Congress passed and Cleveland signed legislation creating the Department of Labor.

Cleveland brought a unique social event to the White House on June 2, 1886, by marrying twenty-one-year-old Frances Folsom, the daughter of one of his former law partners. It remains the only marriage of a President in the White House. The Clevelands had five children. Their second daughter, Esther, born during his second administration, was the first child of a President born in the White House.

The first federal controls on business were enacted in 1887, when Congress passed, with Cleveland's approval, the Interstate Commerce Act. For years the powerful railroads had thwarted attempts by the states to regulate them in such matters as the setting of discriminatory freight rates that could make or break a company or a local community. Largely by executive order, Cleveland also recovered more than eighty million acres of public land grants from the railroads and from the cattle ranchers.

Several of Cleveland's actions antagonized the powerful GAR (Grand Army of the Republic)—the organization of Civil War veterans. He vetoed a pension measure that would have given $12 a month to unemployed veterans, calling it a fraud and a raid on the public treasury. Then in an effort to further heal remaining wounds between the North and South, he ordered the captured Southern battle flags to be returned to

Augustus Saint-Gaudens, Irish born sculptor, whose work in the United States changed the style of American sculpturing, working on a bas-relief of his model, Mrs. Grover Cleveland, at Marion, Massachusetts.

the Southern states. This raised such a hue and cry by veteran groups that even Cleveland had to back down and rescind the order.

Despite the antagonism of the many special interest groups, the Democratic National Convention in June 1888 nominated him by acclamation for a second term, with Allen G. Thurman, a former senator from Ohio, as his running mate. To oppose Cleveland, the Republicans nominated Benjamin Harrison, a grandson of President William H. Harrison, who had served as a general in the Civil War and as a senator from Indiana.

Cleveland knew that the Tammany machine of New York City was determined to beat him this time, and without the electoral votes of New York he knew he would lose. When the votes were counted in November, Cleveland received nearly 100,000 more votes than Harrison; but, as he had anticipated, he lost New York by 13,000 votes, and thus lost the election with only 168 electoral votes to Harrison's 233. When his term ended on March 4, 1889, Cleveland commented that there was "no happier man in the United States" than himself, but young Frances Cleveland cautioned the White House staff to take good care of the furnishings because they would be back in four years.

Preparing for a Comeback

THE Clevelands settled down in New York City where he joined the law firm of Bangs, Stetson, Tracy, and McVeagh. They lived in a four-story house at 816 Madison Avenue, and the former President rode to work each day on a streetcar.

Under President Harrison the Republican-controlled Congress imposed new higher tariffs, increased veterans pensions, stepped up the coinage of

"A Business Administration—No Time for Nonsense" was the topic of this cartoon by G. Y. Coffin.

General Adlai E. Stevenson of Bloomington, Illinois (grandfather of Adlai E. Stevenson, former governor of Illinois, Democratic candidate for President, and U.S. ambassador to the United Nations) and Grover Cleveland as they appeared on campaign posters.

silver, and passed so many appropriations measures that it became known as the "Billion-Dollar Congress." Cleveland attacked the spending program, the new McKinley high tariff, and inflationary silver coinage, getting his views known to the public by having them printed and distributed to the newspapers. In the congressional elections of 1890, the Democrats won a landslide victory with nearly half the Republican members of the House losing their seats.

The Republican National Convention met in Minneapolis in June 1892 and re-nominated Harrison to run for a second term. As his running mate the Republicans chose Whitelaw Reid, the publisher of the New York *Tribune*.

Cleveland's Tammany enemies, who had lost him the election in 1888, were determined to prevent him from being nominated in 1892. When the Democratic Convention met in Chicago late in June, Tammany controlled the entire New York delegation, and actively fought Cleveland. But despite the fact that he did not receive a single vote from his home state, Cleveland won the nomination on the first ballot. The Democrats chose as their vice-presidential candidate Adlai E. Stevenson, a former congressman from Illinois.

The campaign of 1892 was one of the quietest in the history of American politics with neither Cleveland nor Harrison actively campaigning. Most interest was stirred by the left-wing Populist party, which nominated General James B. Weaver of Iowa for President and campaigned for the free coinage of silver, a graduated income tax, and the establishment of postal savings banks. The Populists were so strong in the West that the Democrats did not even enter a slate in Colorado, Idaho, Kansas, North Dakota, and Wyoming. And no one was more surprised than Cleveland when he won with the huge electoral vote margin of 277 to Harrison's 145 and Weaver's 22. The Populists had drawn more than a million votes, and many of them obviously had been taken from the Republicans. Cleveland received 5,555,426 popular votes to Harrison's 5,182,690 and Weaver's 1,029,846.

CLEVELAND'S first administration had seen four of the most prosperous years in the nation's history and this prosperity had continued throughout the Harrison administration. But by the time Cleveland took office on a snowy March 4, 1893, there were many signs that the country was in for some serious economic trouble. Gold had been draining out of the country at the rate of about $50 million a year, farm prices were falling, and only

*Cleveland's
Second Administration*

An invitation to the Cleveland inaugural ball and reception.

a few days before the inauguration the large Philadelphia & Reading Railroad had gone bankrupt with debts of about $125 million. The fifty-five-year-old Cleveland warned in his inaugural address:

"It can not be doubted that our stupendous achievements as a people and our country's robust strength have given rise to heedlessness of those laws governing our national health which we can no more evade than human life can escape the laws of God and nature.

"Manifestly nothing is more vital to our supremacy as a nation and to the beneficent purposes of our Government than a sound and stable currency. Its exposure to degradation should at once arouse to activity the most enlightened statesmanship, and the danger of depreciation in the purchasing power of the wages paid to toil should furnish the strongest incentive to prompt and conservative precaution."

By May, the Panic of 1893 gripped the nation. The stock market collapsed, large companies went bankrupt, silver became a drug on the market. In June, Cleveland called Congress to meet in special session in August "to the end that the people may be relieved through legislation from present and impending danger and distress."

On the same day that he issued the call for the special congressional session, the President hurried to New York and boarded a yacht for a secret operation. It had been discovered that he had a cancer on the roof of his mouth that must be removed immediately, and the President, fearing that the news would heighten the economic panic, decided to have the

The Cleveland family in 1907—Esther, Francis, Mrs. Cleveland, Marion, Richard, and Grover Cleveland (left to right).

Grover Cleveland in his study in 1906.

Mrs. Cleveland at her desk, showing an accumulation of knickknacks and the frilly dress of the early twentieth century.

operation aboard the yacht so that the public would not know about it. On July 1 the operation was successfully performed with the removal of most of his upper jaw. An artificial upper jaw of rubber was made for him, and since there were no external scars the facts of the operation remained a secret until long after Cleveland left office.

When the special session of Congress met, it received a message from Cleveland asking for the repeal of the Sherman Silver Purchase Act of 1890 which required the Treasury to buy 4,500,000 ounces of silver each month and pay for them with notes redeemable in either gold or silver. A bill repealing the measure was the subject of bitter debate, the Democratic senators from the West and South resisting. In the end Cleveland achieved passage only with the support of Republican senators.

In the field of foreign affairs, Cleveland managed to antagonize public opinion by thwarting the annexation of Hawaii. During Harrison's administration, the U.S. minister in Hawaii had taken part in a bloodless revolution that had overthrown the government of Queen Liliuokalani with the aid of U.S. Marines. A treaty of annexation to the United States had been hastily prepared and sent to the Senate for ratification. Since the Senate had not yet acted when Cleveland took office, he withdrew the treaty and after an investigation concluded that the actions of the U.S. minister had not been honorable. In a special message to Congress in December 1893, he asked for congressional help in finding some way to restore the Queen to power in a manner "consistent with American honor, integrity, and morality." Although he was denounced by many newspapers for not expanding the United States possessions into the Pacific, Cleveland stood firm on what he believed was right.

In 1894 economic conditions continued to grow worse. In May about 400 unemployed arrived in Washington, a part of the "army" marching from Massillon, Ohio, under the leadership of "General" Jacob S. Coxey. They asked for Congress to pass a bill establishing a 500-million-dollar road-building program to create jobs. For trespassing on White House grounds, Coxey was arrested and sent to jail for twenty days. Even more serious labor troubles erupted in Illinois that same month when the Pullman Company fired about 5000 workers for protesting a wage cut.

In June the American Railway Union, the most powerful labor union in the United States at that time, called a sympathy strike for the Pullman workers by refusing to handle any train hauling Pullman cars. Because this interfered with the movement of mail, the federal government obtained an injunction against the strike on July 2. In retaliation a mob derailed a mail train outside of Chicago the next day. On July 3, Cleveland ordered federal troops to preserve order in Illinois, even though the governor of Illinois insisted this was not necessary. On July 6 a mob stoned a train, killing the engineer and injuring many passengers. Cleveland then issued an order on July 8 that all persons in Illinois engaged in mob activity must return to their homes. The next day he extended the order to nine other Western states. Eugene Debs, the Socialist leader of the American Railway Union, was arrested for conspiracy and for violating the federal injunction. He later was sentenced to six months in jail. Most strikers had returned to work by the second week in July, and federal troops were withdrawn on July 19.

While Cleveland was battling with the unruly labor unions, he also was engaged in combat with Congress over the keystone of his economic plans—the reduction of tariffs. In January 1894, the House had passed a tariff act to his liking, greatly reducing most import duties and in addition calling for the levy of a 2% income tax on all incomes over $4000. But the tariff bill received rough treatment in the Senate. It was amended

Eugene Debs, socialist labor leader.
—*Wilshire's Magazine*

more than six hundred times before the upper house finally passed it by a vote of 39 to 33 in August 1894. Cleveland was disgusted with the measure because the tariff reductions were now so small as to be almost meaningless. He considered vetoing it, but finally allowed the bill to become law without his signature because he was persuaded it was better than nothing. The failure was made even more complete the next year when the Supreme Court ruled that the provision for an income tax was unconstitutional.

Economic conditions continued to grow worse during 1894—farm prices fell and unemployment rose. In the congressional elections of 1894, the Republicans achieved a landslide of even greater proportions than the Democrats had four years earlier.

By January of 1895 only about $40 million in gold remained in the United States Treasury. If something could not be done to replenish the supply it seemed likely that the nation would have to abandon the gold standard, with damaging effect on the government's credit and possibly far-reaching economic effects. To save the situation Cleveland arranged with a syndicate of New York bankers headed by J. P. Morgan to purchase a new issue of bonds for gold and reverse the flow of gold out of the country. The bankers, with a serious stake in keeping money "sound," made good on their promise and delivered more than $65 million in gold to the U.S. Treasury.

In 1895 Cleveland regained some of his waning public support by a vigorous application of the Monroe Doctrine against Great Britain. The British had been engaged in a dispute with Venezuela over the boundary of British Guiana. Cleveland sent a strongly worded message to Congress calling for the appointment of a commission to determine the boundary. He asserted that the United States should "resist by every means in its power, as a willful aggression upon its rights and interests" any attempt by Britain to take any more than the land awarded by the American commission. Congress appropriated money for the commission and war fever spread. Luckily the British reacted reasonably and the dispute was settled.

But jingoism could not solve the country's economic problems, and the Democrats of the West were losing patience with Cleveland's cautious gold-standard conservatism. When the Democratic National Convention met in Chicago in July 1896, the delegates by a 2 to 1 vote adopted a platform repudiating Cleveland's policies and accepting a free silver plank written by Nebraskan William Jennings Bryan. Bryan electrified the convention with his famous "cross of gold" speech in which he said: "Having behind us the producing masses of the nation and the world, the laboring interests and the toilers everywhere, we will answer their demand for a gold standard by saying to them: 'You shall not press down upon the brow of labor this crown of thorns—you shall not crucify mankind upon a cross of gold!'" The convention proceeded to nominate Bryan as its candidate for President—a greater humiliation for Cleveland than even the platform.

Cleveland refused to support Bryan in the ensuing campaign, but he also refused nomination for a third term by the Gold-Democrats, or the National Democratic party as the conservatives called themselves. He rejoiced when the Republican nominee, William McKinley, a "sound money" man, defeated Bryan in the November election. After McKinley's inauguration, Cleveland commented: "I envy him today only one thing, and that was the presence of his own mother at the inauguration. I would have given anything in the world if my mother could have been at my inauguration."

Grover Cleveland on his front porch at Princeton with his favorite English setter.

An interesting view of ladies' dress during Cleveland's administration showing Mrs. Cleveland and the wives of the Cabinet members.

AFTER leaving the presidency for the second time, Cleveland settled with his family in Princeton, New Jersey. He had saved about a third of a million dollars and this was sufficient to live in retirement without further income. He took a close interest in Princeton University and became a trustee in 1901. He also gave lectures from time to time to the students.

As the years passed and the free silver movement died, Cleveland came to be regarded with greater and greater respect. In 1905 when the huge Equitable Life Assurance Society came under investigation, Cleveland accepted appointment as one of a board of trustees to reorganize the company. In 1907 he became head of the Association of Presidents of Life Insurance Companies, an organization to lobby against restrictive government regulation of insurance companies.

In his last years, he suffered with heart and kidney ailments as well as gout. Finally, on June 24, 1908, the seventy-one-year-old former President died in his bed at his home in Princeton. A verse written about Cleveland by James Russell Lowell in 1889 perhaps states most clearly the reason he has been more honored for his efforts than for his accomplishments:

The Sage of Princeton

> Let who has felt compute the strain
> Of struggle with abuses strong,
> The doubtful course, the helpless pain
> Of seeing best intents go wrong;
> We, who look on with critic eyes
> Exempt from action's crucial test,
> Human ourselves, at least are wise
> In honoring one who did his best.

248   BENJAMIN HARRISON

Benjamin Harrison

The Twenty-third President of the United States
1889–93

1833 (August 20) Born at North Bend, Ohio.

1852 Graduated from Miami University, Oxford, Ohio.

1853 (October 20) Married Caroline Lavinia Scott.

1854 Began practicing law in Indianapolis, Indiana.

1860 Elected reporter of the Supreme Court of Indiana.

1862–65 Commanded the 70th Indiana Regiment of Volunteers during the Civil War.

1876 Defeated as Republican candidate for governor of Indiana.

1881–87 U.S. senator from Indiana.

1889–93 Twenty-third President of the Unites States.

1893–94 Lectured on law at Leland Stanford Jr. University.

1896 (April 6) Married Mary Scott Lord Dimmick.

1899 Counsel for Venezuela in boundary dispute with British Guiana.

1901 (March 13) Died in Indianapolis.

Leading Officials in
Harrison's Administration

Office	Name	Years Served
Chief Justice	Melville W. Fuller	1888-1910
Vice-President	Levi P. Morton	1889-1893
Secretary of State	James G. Blaine	1889-1892
	John W. Foster	1892-1893
Secretary of War	Redfield Proctor	1889-1891
	Stephen B. Elkins	1891-1893
Secretary of the Treasury	William Windom	1889-1891
	Charles Foster	1891-1893
Attorney General	William H. H. Miller	1889-1893
Postmaster General	John Wanamaker	1889-1893
Secretary of the Navy	Benjamin F. Tracy	1889-1893
Secretary of the Interior	John W. Noble	1889-1893
Secretary of Agriculture	Jeremiah M. Rusk	1889-1893

Benjamin Harrison as a young man.

Every successful Republican presidential candidate, from the end of the Civil War to 1900, served as an officer in the Union Army and was born in Ohio. Benjamin Harrison had these two qualifications for the presidency, if few others. Before being elected President he had won a popular election to only one other office—that of reporter to the Supreme Court of Indiana. He had been defeated as Republican candidate for governor of Indiana in 1876, and he had served an undistinguished term as U.S. senator from Indiana (elected by the state legislature) under Presidents Garfield, Arthur, and Cleveland.

A cold, austere little man whose hair was prematurely white, he was known as "Little Ben" by his troops in the Civil War, and was nicknamed "Kid Gloves" Harrison by the Democrats of Indiana. Because his grandfather, William Henry Harrison, had also been President, the Republicans campaigned in 1888 with a song, "Grandfather's Hat Fits Ben." But the Democrats countered with cartoons showing that it took a microscope to find Ben under his grandfather's hat.

As President he did not endeavor to exert personal leadership, and allowed Congress to dictate policies. When Congress pushed tariffs to new highs and lavishly appropriated money for special-interest projects, the public turned against "Little Ben" and he lost in his bid for re-election.

Born at North Bend, Ohio, on August 20, 1833, Benjamin Harrison was named for his great-grandfather, who had been a signer of the Declaration of Independence and a governor of Virginia. Young Ben was one of nine children of John Scott Harrison, whose farm was five miles down the Ohio River from that of Ben's grandfather, the hero of Tippecanoe. The boy was seven years old when his grandfather was elected President.

Lawyer, Soldier, and Politician

Because the Harrisons lived too far from any town to send their children to regular schools, John Scott Harrison built a one-room log schoolhouse on his farm and hired a teacher each winter to drill his children in reading, writing, and arithmetic. When Ben was fourteen, he was sent to a college preparatory school called Farmer's College, near Cincinnati. After two years there, he transferred to Miami University at Oxford, Ohio, where he studied hard and took a particular interest in debate. When he graduated at the age of eighteen, in 1852, he ranked fourth in his class of sixteen boys.

From school he went directly into a law office in Cincinnati, where he studied for his future profession. Before completing his law studies, he married his college sweetheart, Caroline Lavinia Scott, the daughter of the president of a girls' school in Oxford, Ohio. They were married October 20, 1853, when Harrison was nineteen and his wife was twenty. They had two children.

After completing his law studies, Harrison decided to set up his law practice in Indianapolis, Indiana. He and his wife moved there in March 1854, taking a room in a boardinghouse while Ben got his first job, as crier of the federal court at a salary of $2.50 a day. He quickly became acquainted with most of the lawyers in town, and they began to give him small legal errands. The next year one of them, William Wallace, invited the young man to go into partnership with him.

Harrison entered politics at the age of twenty-seven, when he became the Republican candidate for the office of reporter to the Supreme Court

General Harrison as an officer of the Union Army.

of Indiana. He proved an able speaker, and won handily with a majority of more than 9000.

In 1862 Governor Oliver Morton offered Harrison command of a regiment of Indiana volunteers, to be recruited by Harrison. The young lawyer set to work energetically, raised the necessary complement of men, and received his commission as colonel. His regiment, the 70th Indiana Volunteers, saw heavy fighting, especially in Georgia in 1864, where "Little Ben" several times led infantry charges against Confederate positions. General Hooker recommended him for promotion to brigadier general, an advancement he received in March 1865.

At the end of the war, young General Harrison returned to Indianapolis and resumed his office as clerk of the state supreme court, having been re-elected while still at the front in 1864. He declined renomination at the next election in order to return to private law practice, forming a new law firm with former Governor Porter as a partner. Aided by his natural gifts, his war record, and his political contacts he became one of the leading figures of the state in law and politics.

In 1876 Harrison reluctantly accepted the Republican nomination for governor. His opponent, a tall gangling farmer who resembled Abraham Lincoln, was known as Jimmy "Blue Jeans" Williams because of the overalls he wore for all occasions. In contrast, the dapper five-foot-six-inch Harrison received the nickname "Kid Gloves." When the votes were tabulated, Harrison had lost by 5000 votes out of more than 434,000 cast.

Harrison led the Republican delegation of Indiana to the National Convention in 1880 where after supporting Blaine through thirty ballots, his switch to Garfield helped decide the nomination. After Garfield's election he was offered a cabinet post, but declined because the Indiana legislature had elected him to the office of U.S. senator.

In the Senate from 1881 to 1887, Harrison played an unobtrusive role, siding with the leaders of his party on most questions. He supported increases in tariff duties, voted for civil service reform, opposed President Cleveland's vetoes of pension bills, and urged increasing the size of the Navy.

When the Republican National Convention met in Chicago in June 1888, another deadlock developed, this time between John Sherman of Ohio and Walter Q. Gresham of Indiana. James Blaine cabled from Scotland: "Take Harrison." So on the eighth ballot Harrison was given the nomination, largely because he was "safe" and would be easy to control. His later appointment of Blaine as Secretary of State indicated that his nomination was achieved as the result of a familiar type of political deal.

In the campaign against President Cleveland, Harrison remained in Indianapolis addressing influential groups who called on him. Cleveland had antagonized so many people during his first term that the Republicans figured that they could win with a soft-pedal campaign. Actually Harrison received fewer votes than Cleveland—5,447,129 to Cleveland's 5,537,857; but the distribution of the votes—above all Harrison's narrow victory in New York—gave Harrison an Electoral College victory with 233 votes to Cleveland's 168.

In a lengthy inaugural address on a rainy March 4, 1889, Harrison spoke largely in generalities, but he also called for the traditional Republican high protective tariff, the revision of the naturalization laws to restrict Oriental immigration, and the liberalization of veterans' pensions. He opened the door to an increase in federal spending:

Harrison's Administration

". . . There is nothing in the condition of our country or of our people to suggest that anything presently necessary to the public prosperity, security, or honor should be unduly postponed. It will be the duty of Congress wisely to forecast and estimate these extraordinary demands, and, having added them to our ordinary expenditures, to so adjust our revenue laws that no considerable annual surplus will remain. . . ."

The Republicans were firmly in control of both houses of Congress with a 47 to 37 majority in the Senate and 173 to 156 in the House. To please Western farmers and mine owners, the Sherman Silver Purchase Act substantially increased the amount of silver the Treasury was required to purchase each month. Since this silver was paid for with notes that could be redeemed for gold, a drain on the government's gold supply resulted; this contributed directly to the Panic of 1893. Also to please Western farm organizations, the Sherman Anti-trust Act was passed, outlawing trusts or business combines that interfered with commerce. Congress voted pensions to any Civil War veteran who could not work, even if his disability was not service-connected, nearly doubling the amount of money paid for pensions. And the McKinley Tariff Act, sponsored by the congressman from Ohio who later was to become President, raised duties on imports to new highs. When the Democrats dubbed it the "Billion-Dollar Congress," Speaker of the House Thomas B. Reed retorted that "This is a billion-dollar country!"

But when merchants began marking up prices following passage of the McKinley Tariff Act in 1890, hard-pressed laboring people and farmers went to the polls in the mid-term congressional elections with blood in their eyes. They "threw the rascals out," giving the Democrats a majority in the House of 235 to 88 Republicans.

Harrison pursued a vigorous foreign policy. His Secretary of State was James G. Blaine, the smooth politician who had put both Garfield and Harrison in the White House but missed in his own bid. Harrison and Blaine pushed American claims to Samoa, for a time almost causing naval hostilities with Germany. In 1889 the first Pan-American conference met in Washington, presaging better relations among the nations of the Western Hemisphere.

The most important development of Harrison's administration was the continuing growth of the United States. Six new states were admitted—Washington, Idaho, Montana, Wyoming, North Dakota, and South Dakota—bringing the total number to forty-four. The country's population reached nearly 63 million in 1890, an increase of more than 25% in a single decade. And the Bureau of the Census reported in 1890 that the Western frontier no longer existed—the country was settled from coast to coast.

Scientific and technical progress was equally impressive. Electric lights were installed in the White House, although the Harrisons continued to use gaslight much of the time.

In 1892, despite a bid by Blaine, Harrison won renomination on the first ballot. But he lost the election to former President Cleveland, partly because the people were dissatisfied with the high prices brought on by the McKinley Tariff Act, and partly because the new Populist party drew many Western votes away from the Republican ticket.

Less than three weeks before leaving office, Harrison sent to the Senate a treaty for the annexation of Hawaii. "I do not deem it necessary to discuss at any length the conditions which have resulted in this decisive action," Harrison told the Senate. "Prompt action upon this treaty is very desirable." However, the Senate delayed, and after Cleveland entered

Benjamin Harrison's inauguration in March 1889.

office the new President withdrew the treaty on grounds the U.S. representative had not acted honorably in aiding the overthrow of the Hawaiian government in order to achieve annexation.

FIFTY-NINE years old when he left the White House, Harrison accepted an invitation to deliver a series of law lectures at Stanford University in 1893–94. Then he returned to Indianapolis to practice law.

A Second Marriage

The home of Benjamin Harrison in Indianapolis, Indiana.

Benjamin Harrison and his wife, Carrie.

Mothers and children in the White House nursery—Mrs. Mary Harrison McKee, daughter of President Harrison; Mary McKee; Marthena Harrison, daughter of Russell Harrison, son of the President; Mrs. Russell Harrison; and another McKee child.

He had lost his first wife a few days before the election of 1892, and in 1896, at the age of sixty-two, married her niece, thirty-seven-year-old Mrs. Mary Scott Lord Dimmick. They had one child, a daughter.

In 1897 Harrison wrote a book on the government of the United States titled *This Country of Ours*. He was employed as counsel for the government of Venezuela in the boundary dispute with Great Britain and in 1899 ably upheld the Venezuelan case before an international arbitration tribunal.

On March 13, 1901, at the age of sixty-seven, Harrison died in his home in Indianapolis. In announcing the death of his predecessor, President McKinley said of Harrison:

"The country has been deprived of one of its greatest citizens. A brilliant soldier in his young manhood . . . a leader of the bar . . . an orator and legislator . . . he displayed extraordinary gifts as administrator and statesman. In public and in private life he set a shining example for his countrymen."

258 CHESTER A. ARTHUR

Chester A. Arthur

The Twenty-first President of the United States
1 8 8 1 – 8 5

1830 (October 5) Born in Fairfield, Vermont.

1848 Graduated from Union College.

1853 Admitted to bar to practice law in New York City.

1859 (October 29) Married Ellen Lewis Herndon.

1861–62 Served on New York governor's staff with rank of brigadier general helping supply troops for Civil War.

1871–79 Collector of the Port of New York.

1881 Vice President of the United States.

1881–85 Twenty-first President of the United States.

1886 (November 18) Died in New York City.

Leading Officials in Arthur's Administration

Office	Name	Years Served
Chief Justice	Morrison R. Waite	1874-1888
Secretary of State	James G. Blaine	1881
	Frederick T. Frelinghuysen	1881-1885
Secretary of War	Robert T. Lincoln	1881-1885
Secretary of the Treasury	William Windom	1881
	Charles J. Folger	1881-1884
	Walter Q. Gresham	1884
	Hugh McCulloch	1884-1885
Attorney General	Wayne MacVeagh	1881
	Benjamin H. Brewster	1881-1885
Postmaster General	Thomas L. James	1881
	Timothy O. Howe	1881-1883
	Walter Q. Gresham	1883-1884
	Frank Hatton	1884-1885
Secretary of the Navy	William H. Hunt	1881-1882
	William E. Chandler	1882-1885
Secretary of the Interior	Samuel J. Kirkwood	1881-1882
	Henry M. Teller	1882-1885

Chester A. Arthur never in his entire life won election to a public office on his own (unless one counts his tag-along election to the vice presidency). Even the professional military men who became President had the experience of earning election to that office. But Arthur, known as "The Gentleman Boss" of the Republican party in New York City, was always a behind-the-scenes politician, building the party organization and managing the election campaigns of others.

The nation was shocked when Arthur succeeded to the presidency upon the death of Garfield. The word "politician" had become synonymous with "corrupt." Only two years earlier President Hayes had made Arthur the very symbol of the evils of patronage by dismissing him as Collector of the Port of New York—an action hailed as a triumph of reform. No wonder that even a leading Republican exclaimed: "Chet Arthur President of the United States! Good God!"

But the nation was agreeably surprised when Arthur turned out to be an honest, conscientious Chief Executive. In fact, he was so honest and conscientious that his party refused to give him a chance to run for the office on his own when his term was up.

The Rise of a Boss

THE son of a Baptist clergyman, Chester Alan Arthur was born in Fairfield, Vermont, on October 5, 1830. Later, some of his political enemies claimed he was disqualified from becoming President because he actually had been born in Canada, where his Irish-immigrant father had lived a few years earlier, and that he had adopted the birthplace and birthdate of a younger brother who had died as a baby—but this rather frivolous charge was never proved.

Young Chet attended local schools in various towns in New York where his father preached. At the age of fifteen he entered Union College in Schenectady and joined one of the early college social fraternities, Psi Upsilon. An excellent student, he was one of six in his class of one hundred admitted to the national honor fraternity, Phi Beta Kappa. He graduated in 1848 at the age of eighteen.

For a time Arthur interspersed semesters of law school at Ballston Spa, New York, with periods of teaching school. In 1853 he became a student in the law office of Erastus D. Culver in New York City and later the same year was admitted to the bar to practice law, becoming a member of Culver's firm.

The son of an ardent abolitionist, Arthur often undertook the defense of fugitive slaves and other persecuted Negroes. In one famous case, he helped six slaves obtain their freedom from their Virginia owner who had made the mistake of thinking that he could transport them through the free state of New York. In another case that caused much publicity, he obtained $500 damages from a transit company for a Negro woman named Lizzie Jennings, who had been thrown off a New York City horse-car because of her color.

The young Abolitionist lawyer attended the first Republican state convention at Saratoga, New York, and campaigned for Frémont for President in 1856.

In 1859 the twenty-eight-year-old Arthur married Ellen Lewis Herndon, the twenty-two-year-old daughter of a U.S. Navy officer. They had two sons and a daughter, although the eldest boy died in infancy. After twenty

Ellen Lewis Herndon, who became Mrs. Chester Arthur in 1859.

years of marriage, Mrs. Arthur died—the year before her husband became President.

Arthur worked hard to help Republican Governor Edwin D. Morgan win re-election in 1860. As a reward, Morgan appointed Arthur to the honorary post of state engineer-in-chief, with the rank and uniform of a brigadier general. When the Civil War began, the governor appointed him acting quartermaster general to help supply the volunteer troops being organized in the state. The following year, the governor gave Arthur the title of state inspector general of militia, again with the rank of brigadier general. When Morgan was succeeded as governor by Democrat Horatio Seymour in 1863, Arthur returned to his law practice, but continued to use the title "General" for the rest of his life.

Persevering at his work in the Republican party organization, Arthur rose to be recognized as the No. 2 man in the state Republican machine of Senator Roscoe Conkling. He furthered his political fortunes as chairman of the New York club that worked for General Grant's nomination and election in 1868.

Grant rewarded Arthur in 1871 with appointment as Collector of the Port of New York. This was considered the most important federal job in that city because the collector controlled the appointment of more than 1000 employees of the New York Custom House. In his first year as collector, Arthur was said to have received a personal income of more than

Chester Arthur (left) leaving a resort hotel, dressed as usual in the latest fashion of the day.

$40,000. Holding the position for eight years, he used it to build a loyal political machine. President Hayes incurred the eternal wrath of Conkling and Arthur when he removed the "General" from the post in 1879 as part of his reform effort to eliminate politics from the civil service.

At the Republican National Convention in Chicago in 1880, Arthur was a member of the New York delegation of Stalwarts, supporting the nomination of Grant for a third term. When James G. Blaine's Half-Breeds switched the convention to nominate Garfield for President, Arthur was given the vice-presidential nomination in order to insure Stalwart support for the national ticket.

After taking office as Vice President in 1881, Arthur found himself in an unusually influential position because the Democrats and Republicans in the Senate were evenly divided, thirty-seven to thirty-seven. As presiding officer he was often called upon to cast a deciding vote. He and Garfield openly broke when the President appointed one of Blaine's friends to Arthur's old job of Collector of the Port of New York without consulting either Arthur or Conkling.

After Garfield was shot, Arthur made no effort to assume the duties of the presidency in the eighty-day period while the President hovered near death. He particularly hesitated to make any such move in light of the assassin's declaration that the motive for the crime was to make Arthur President and put the Stalwarts in control of patronage.

WHEN Arthur received word of Garfield's death, he took the oath of office as President on September 20, at his home in New York City, before a New York Supreme Court judge. Two days later the oath was adminis-

Arthur's Administration

President Arthur taking the oath of office at his private residence on September 20, 1881.

tered to him again in the Vice President's room in the Capitol by Chief Justice Morrison R. Waite. In his inaugural address, Arthur said:

"For the fourth time in the history of the Republic its Chief Magistrate has been removed by death. All hearts are filled with grief and horror at the hideous crime which has darkened our land, and the memory of the murdered President, his protracted sufferings, his unyielding fortitude, the example and achievements of his life, and the pathos of his death will forever illumine the pages of our history.

"For the fourth time the officer elected by the people and ordained by the Constitution to fill a vacancy so created is called to assume the Executive chair. . . . Men may die, but the fabrics of our free institutions remain unshaken. No higher or more assuring proof could exist of the strength and permanence of popular government than the fact that though the chosen of the people be struck down his constitutional successor is peacefully installed without shock or strain except the sorrow which mourns the bereavement."

As President, Arthur encouraged American participation in international, political, cultural, and scientific conferences. He called an international conference that helped resolve the chaos in communities depending on local sun time, by establishing standard time zones. He called a meeting of all the countries of the Western Hemisphere to seek ways to prevent war. He suggested that all the countries of North and South America agree to use the same currency system in order to facilitate trade. And he negotiated a treaty, turned down by the Senate, to build an inter-ocean canal through Nicaragua.

More striking than any of these proposals was one Arthur put forward in his first annual message to Congress in December 1881—reform of the civil service system. His own well-known patronage background notwithstanding, he pledged himself to approve any reasonable merit system Congress thought practical. And he made good his word by signing into law, in January 1883, the Pendleton Civil Service Act.

Arthur never had the full co-operation of Congress during his administration, particularly after the Democrats again won control of the House in the mid-term elections of 1882. He used his veto power sparingly. The two most important measures that he vetoed were passed over his veto— a measure excluding Chinese immigration and a nineteen-million-dollar rivers-and-harbors bill that Arthur felt had too many special-interest ramifications.

Many suggestions made by Arthur in his annual messages to Congress were never acted upon. He appealed for federal aid to education, suggesting that the government distribute money to the states on a ratio based on the amount of illiteracy in each state. He suggested that since the country was so prosperous, that all internal revenue taxes be abolished except those on tobacco and alcoholic beverages. He also asked Congress to draw up legislation to clarify the conditions of "inability" under which a Vice President should assume the powers of the presidency.

Arthur had hopes of winning the presidency on his own merits in the election of 1884, but though his good record pleased the country it did not entirely please the politicians of his party. In the Republican National Convention, his political enemy James G. Blaine captured the nomination. Arthur was not too unhappy to see Blaine defeated in the November election by Democrat Grover Cleveland.

One of the last public ceremonies in which Arthur took part before leaving the White House was the dedication of the Washington Monument on February 21, 1885. And on the day before leaving office he sent a note to the Senate asking that the impoverished former President Grant

Chester Arthur (right) and a friend
picnicking at Alexandria Bay
on the St. Lawrence River
in New York in 1882.

A day of fishing on the St. Lawrence River for Chester Arthur
(standing at left).

be restored to the retired list of the Army with full pay as a general.

After Cleveland's inauguration, Arthur returned to New York and re-
sumed his law practice, but soon was forced to retire because of illness.
On November 18, 1886, the fifty-six-year-old Arthur died in his New
York home.

"I am but one in fifty-five million," Mark Twain said, "still in the opinion
of this one-fifty-five-millionth of the country's population, it would be hard
to better President Arthur's administration."

266   JAMES A. GARFIELD

James A. Garfield

The Twentieth President of the United States

1 8 8 1

1831 (November 19) Born at Orange, Ohio.

1856 Graduated from Williams College.

1857–61 President of Hiram Eclectic Institute (now Hiram College).

1858 (November 11) Married Lucretia Rudolph.

1859–61 Member of Ohio state senate.

1861–63 Rose from lieutenant colonel to major general in Union Army in Civil War.

1863–80 U.S. representative from Ohio.

1880 Elected to U.S. Senate.

1881 Twentieth President of the United States.

1881 (July 2) Wounded by assassin in Washington, D.C.

1881 (September 19) Died of wounds at Elberon, New Jersey.

Leading Officials in Garfield's Administration

Office	Name	Years Served
Chief Justice	Morrison R. Waite	1874-1888
Vice-President	Chester A. Arthur	1881
Secretary of State	James G. Blaine	1881
Secretary of War	Robert T. Lincoln	1881-1885
Secretary of the Treasury	William Windom	1881
Attorney General	Wayne MacVeagh	1881
Postmaster General	Thomas L. James	1881
Secretary of the Navy	William H. Hunt	1881-1882
Secretary of the Interior	Samuel J. Kirkwood	1881-1882

An artist's concept of Garfield's birthplace in Orange, Ohio.

The second President to be killed by an assassin, James A. Garfield served only two hundred days as Chief Executive, and for eighty of those days he lay near death with a bullet through his spine. The six-foot blue-eyed Garfield brought unquestioned talents to the White House, but he had little opportunity to demonstrate whether they would be used more for the benefit of his country or for the benefit of his party.

The last President to be born in a log cabin, he was a self-made man in the tradition of Horatio Alger (who was then at the height of his popularity). Garfield worked as a canalboat tow boy at seventeen, became a college president at twenty-six, was the youngest general in the Union Army at thirty, and in seventeen years in Congress became leader of the Republican party in the House and one of the finest orators of his day.

President Hayes, who felt that the nomination of his friend and fellow-Ohioan was a vindication of his own administration, wrote glowingly of Garfield in his diary:

"The truth is no man ever started so low that accomplished so much in all our history. Not Franklin or Lincoln even. . . . He is the ideal candidate because he is the ideal self-made man."

A Log-Cabin Boyhood

THE youngest of five children, James Abram Garfield was born in a crude one-room log cabin on his father's frontier farm in Orange township, Ohio, on November 19, 1831. The boy was only a year and a half old when his father, Abram, died of a throat infection coupled with exhaustion from fighting a forest fire. Although left deeply in debt, his mother, Eliza Ballou Garfield, was determined to keep her small family together. She sold fifty acres of the farm, paid the debts, and with her children's help worked the remaining thirty acres, barely eking out a living.

From the time he was three years old, Garfield attended local schools, developing a great love for reading and an ambition to go to college. At seventeen he decided to become a sailor, but soon found that life aboard a Great Lakes freighter was not as romantic as he had thought. He next got a job as a "tow boy," driving horses and mules pulling boats on the Ohio Canal. He fell off the narrow tow path many times, and, as he later said, "had fourteen almost miraculous escapes from drowning."

Early in 1848 his mother gave him $17 that she had managed to save, and he and two cousins set out to attend Geauga Seminary in Chester, Ohio. Discovering that he could not afford the $1.50-a-week for room and board at the academy, he and his cousins rented a room in a farmhouse and cooked their own meals while attending school. He earned extra money on Saturdays as a carpenter's helper.

At eighteen he dropped out of the Geauga Seminary for a semester to earn $48 teaching at a country school. He proved he was qualified for the job in true Horatio Alger style, by thrashing the local bully who had driven away the last schoolteacher. He then returned to Chester to complete his preparation for college.

In August 1851, he entered Hiram Eclectic Institute (later Hiram College), a school founded by the Disciples of Christ, to which Garfield and his family belonged. In his three years at Hiram, Garfield became especially proficient in the Greek and Latin languages and paid his expenses by tutoring other students—including his future wife.

A benefactor loaned him money to attend Williams College in Williamstown, Massachusetts, which he entered as a junior in 1854. While there, he taught school one winter at North Pownal, Vermont, where, by a curious coincidence, the previous teacher had been Chester A. Arthur, his future successor as President. While at Williams, Garfield received the special attention of its president, the famous educator Mark Hopkins. This led to Garfield's later description of what he regarded as a perfect school: ". . . a simple bench, Mark Hopkins on one end and I on the other . . ."

After graduating from Williams with honors in 1856, Garfield returned to Hiram, where he was appointed professor of Latin and Greek. During

The schoolhouse in Orange Township, Ohio, where James A. Garfield attended school. *—Underwood & Underwood*

the following year, at the age of twenty-six, he was made president of the school.

In 1858 he married Lucretia Rudolph, a farmer's daughter who had been a fellow student both in Chester and in Hiram. He and his wife "Crete," as he called her, had seven children, one of whom, James Rudolph Garfield, became Secretary of the Interior under President Theodore Roosevelt.

The energetic Garfield, not content with being merely the president of a small college, devoted considerable time to acting as a lay preacher for the Disciples of Christ—an activity that polished his oratory. He also diligently studied to become a lawyer. Entering politics in 1859, he was elected a Republican member of the state senate.

Civil War General and Politician

At the outbreak of the Civil War the students of Hiram College formed a company that was attached to the 42d Ohio Infantry Volunteers. The men elected Garfield lieutenant colonel, and he soon was promoted to colonel in command of the regiment. Early in 1862 he led a brigade that drove Confederate forces out of eastern Kentucky, and was rewarded at the age of thirty with the commission of brigadier general. After taking part in the battles of Shiloh and Corinth, he was assigned as a member of the court-martial that found Major General Fitz John Porter guilty of disobeying orders at the second battle of Bull Run.

Returning to battlefront duty, Garfield became chief of staff to Major General William Rosecrans. He distinguished himself at the battle of Chickamauga in September 1863, when, even though his horse was shot from under him, he safely delivered a message that saved the Army of the

Mrs. James Garfield (Lucretia Rudolph), who met Garfield at a school in Chagrin Falls, Ohio, as one of his pupils.

James Garfield as a Major General in the Union Army in 1863.

A Garfield family scene, as shown in a reproduction of a lithograph by Restein.

President Garfield photographed in a theatrical pose.

Cumberland from disaster. For his bravery, he was given a battlefield promotion to major general.

While on active duty in 1862, Garfield was elected to Congress, and in December of 1863, yielding to an urgent request by President Lincoln, resigned his commission and took his seat in the House of Representatives. This began an unbroken period of seventeen years in Congress—a record for any President-to-be, and testimony to his popularity, for during this time many fellow Republicans went down to defeat in Ohio elections, including his friend Rutherford B. Hayes.

In Congress, Garfield sided with the Radical Republicans in pressing for the Reconstruction Acts and the impeachment of President Johnson. His feelings against the South remained strong to the end of his life—at the Chicago convention that nominated him for President, he declared there was only one condition for restoring friendship with the South, "that it shall be admitted, forever and forever more, that in the war for the Union, we were right and they were wrong."

During Grant's administration, Garfield became chairman of such important House committees as Military Affairs, Banking and Currency, and Appropriations. He was also one of the congressmen accused of taking bribes for political favors, but the charges against him were never conclusively proved. In 1877 he was a member of the Electoral Commission named to decide the disputed Hayes-Tilden election, and helped arrange the bargain that brought Hayes to the presidency. While the Democrats held a majority in the House under Hayes, Garfield served as minority leader of the Republicans. In January 1880, the Ohio legislature elected him to the U.S. Senate, but he never served in that office.

At the Republican National Convention in Chicago in June 1880, the party was split into two factions—the "Stalwarts," headed by New York

Senator Roscoe Conkling, and the "Half-Breeds," led by Maine Senator James G. Blaine. The Stalwarts were determined to win the nomination for former President Grant, while the Half-Breeds were equally determined to win it for Blaine. As head of the Ohio delegation, Garfield avoided taking either side and placed in nomination his fellow Ohioan, Secretary of the Treasury John Sherman. For 33 ballots the Stalwarts and Half-Breeds stalemated each other. On the thirty-fourth ballot Wisconsin swung its votes to Garfield. Blaine gave his support to Garfield, and on the thirty-sixth ballot the presidential nomination was accorded the former canalboat tow boy—the first time a President-to-be was present at his own nomination. To reconcile the Stalwarts, the convention chose for its vice-presidential candidate Chester A. Arthur, the political hack who had been ousted by President Hayes as Collector for the Port of New York.

Upon returning to Washington, Garfield, a superstitious man, told President Hayes of two omens bearing on his nomination, which Hayes noted in his diary of June 15: "As he entered the Convention the day of his nomination a man distributing leaves of the New Testament handed him a leaf which he (Garfield) put in his pocket. Long after the nomination, emptying his pockets the leaf was found. The verse that was uppermost as it was folded read 'The Stone which the builders reject etc. etc.' At one o'clock p.m., the hour of the nomination, an Eagle lit on Garfield's house in Washington and sat there several minutes and was seen by many persons."

Garfield conducted a front-porch campaign from his home at Mentor, Ohio. The Democrats, who had given their presidential nomination to

The Republican Convention in Chicago, June 2, 1880, while Garfield was delivering his acceptance speech as the Republican nominee for the presidency.

INDEPENDENT AMERICA.—The home of the freeman, where the humblest citizen can attain the highest honors in the gift of her people.

The inaugural parade in 1881, beginning the Garfield administration.

Major General Winfield Scott Hancock, a hero of the battle of Gettysburg and a man with no political experience, revived the charges of bribery that had been hurled at Garfield during the Grant administration. Perhaps the most important issue of the campaign was the protective tariff, supported by the Republicans and opposed by the Democrats. Times were prosperous, President Hayes had helped dispel the shadow of corruption that had fallen on the Republican party, and Garfield narrowly won the election. The popular votes were almost a tie, with 4,454,416 for Garfield and 4,444,952 for Hancock, but Garfield received 214 electoral votes to Hancock's 155.

Garfield's Administration and Assassination

AFTER being sworn in on the Capitol steps on March 4, 1881, the forty-nine-year-old Garfield's first act was to turn and kiss his aged mother—the first time a President's mother had been present at an inauguration. In his address, Garfield placed particular emphasis on the need for civil service reform:

"The civil service can never be placed on a satisfactory basis until it is regulated by law. For the good of the service itself, for the protection of those who are intrusted with the appointing power against the waste of time and obstruction to the public business caused by the inordinate pressure for place, and for the protection of incumbents against intrigue and wrong, I shall at the proper time ask Congress to fix the tenure of the minor offices of the several Executive Departments and prescribe the grounds upon which removal shall be made during the terms for which incumbents have been appointed."

To pay off his political debt to the Half-Breeds, Garfield appointed Blaine Secretary of State and replaced the politically important Collector of the Port of New York. These moves stirred considerable resentment among the Stalwarts, but no one was prepared for the tragedy that suddenly struck.

On the morning of July 2, 1881, Garfield and Blaine were entering the Baltimore and Potomac railroad station where the President was to board a train to attend the twenty-fifth reunion of his class at Williams College, when a mentally disturbed and disaffected office seeker named Charles J. Guiteau fired two shots. One struck the President in the arm and the other in the back. Guiteau shouted: "I am a Stalwart! Arthur is now President!"

The wounded Garfield was carried to the White House where he lingered near death week after week, the physicians unable to locate and remove the bullet (the X ray was fourteen years in the future). In September the President asked to be removed from the heat of Washington, and he was taken to a seaside cottage at Elberon, New Jersey, where he died on September 19, 1881. After a trial, at which it was shown that the assassin was not acting as part of a conspiracy by the Stalwarts, Guiteau was hanged on June 30, 1882.

An artist's sketch of the assassination of Garfield, as he was about to board a train for Williamstown, Massachusetts, to attend the twenty-fifth reunion of his class at Williams College, on July 2, 1881, in the Baltimore and Potomac Railroad station in Washington, D. C.

276   RUTHERFORD B. HAYES

Rutherford B. Hayes

The Nineteenth President of the United States
1877–81

1822 (October 4) Born in Delaware, Ohio.

1842 Graduated from Kenyon College.

1843–45 Studied law at Harvard University.

1845 Began the practice of law in Ohio.

1852 (December 30) Married Lucy Ware Webb.

1858–61 City solicitor of Cincinnati, Ohio.

1861–65 Served as an officer in the Union Army in the Civil War, rising to the rank of brevet major general.

1865–67 U.S. representative from Ohio.

1868–72; 1876–77 Governor of Ohio.

1877–81 Nineteenth President of the United States.

1893 (January 17) Died in Fremont, Ohio.

Leading Officials in
Hayes' Administration

Office	Name	Years Served
Chief Justice	Morrison R. Waite	1874-1888
Vice-President	William A. Wheeler	1877-1881
Secretary of State	William M. Evarts	1877-1881
Secretary of War	George W. McCrary	1877-1879
	Alexander Ramsey	1879-1881
Secretary of the Treasury	John Sherman	1877-1881
Attorney General	Charles Devens	1877-1881
Postmaster General	David M. Key	1877-1880
	Horace Maynard	1880-1881
Secretary of the Navy	Richard W. Thompson	1877-1881
	Nathan Goff, Jr.	1881
Secretary of the Interior	Carl Schurz	1877-1881

The people elected Democrat Samuel J. Tilden of New York President in 1876, but in perhaps the most flagrant misuse of power in the nation's history, the politicians agreed to give the office to Ohio Republican Rutherford B. Hayes. Paradoxically enough, the beneficiary of this political bargain was one of the most high-minded and deeply religious men to occupy the White House. He and his wife—called "Lemonade Lucy" because she forbade the serving of alcohol in the Executive Mansion—began each day by kneeling at morning prayers and closed each day by singing hymns.

As part of the deal that gave him the presidency, Hayes ended the Reconstruction of the South by withdrawing federal troops. As a congressman ten years earlier, Hayes had helped vote the Reconstruction Acts into law over President Johnson's veto and had also voted for Johnson's impeachment.

From a standpoint of background, the red-haired, blue-eyed Hayes had the makings of a great President. He was the only Chief Executive to have been both a dashing military-hero general and an elected state governor. Moreover, he was a well-educated lawyer. But, as in the case of John Quincy Adams, the circumstances under which Hayes came to the presidency made it impossible for him to obtain wide support.

Although little was accomplished politically during Hayes' administration, technological advances moved the nation forward. Alexander Graham Bell installed the first telephone in the White House; Thomas Edison perfected the electric light and at Hayes' invitation came to the Executive Mansion to demonstrate the newly invented phonograph.

The birthplace of Rutherford B. Hayes in Delaware, Ohio.

Rutherford Hayes as a young man practicing law in Fremont, Ohio.

RUTHERFORD BIRCHARD HAYES was born in Delaware, Ohio, October 4, 1822. His merchant father died nearly three months before his birth, but left a large estate which permitted his widow to give a good education to the future President and his brothers and sisters.

Young "Rud," as the boy was called, was regarded by his acquaintances as a rather stuffy fellow who "never had any wild oats to sow." He attended schools in Ohio and Connecticut before enrolling at Kenyon College, from which he graduated at the age of twenty. He studied law under the tutelage of a family friend in Ohio, and rounded out his education with three years of law school at Harvard.

Hayes practiced law for several years in Lower Sandusky (now Fremont), Ohio, then moved to Cincinnati in 1849. Within a few years he gained a reputation as a defender of fugitive slaves. He became a friend of various abolitionists who later helped form the Republican party in Ohio.

When Hayes was thirty, he married twenty-one-year-old Lucy Ware Webb, the daughter of a doctor. As a graduate of Cincinnati's Wesleyan Female College, she later became the first college-educated mistress of the White House and a symbol for such militant women's organizations as the Woman's Christian Temperance Union. The Hayeses had eight children, of whom four sons and a daughter grew to adulthood.

Hayes entered public life for the first time in 1858, when the city council of Cincinnati elected him city solicitor to fill a vacancy. The next year he ran for the office in the regular election and won, but was defeated for re-election in 1861.

With the outbreak of war, Hayes was elected captain of a drilling organization formed by a literary club to which he belonged. He then

Lawyer, Soldier, and Politician

Mrs. Rutherford Hayes, the first college-educated mistress of the White House, and a crusader for temperance and abolition of slavery.

helped organize the 23d Ohio Volunteers and was commissioned major. His regiment soon moved into action in West Virginia, and by November he had been promoted to lieutenant colonel.

The war brought out qualities that Hayes had never before discovered in himself. He repeatedly distinguished himself, leading charges and joining in hand-to-hand combat. At the battle of South Mountain, in Maryland, he continued leading his men up the mountain in the face of enemy fire even after his arm had been shattered by a bullet and nearly a third of his force had been killed or wounded. Shortly thereafter he was promoted to colonel.

Rutherford Hayes and his two sons, Webb (left) and Birchard.

In the campaigns of 1864 and 1865 in Virginia, Hayes was wounded four times and had four horses shot out from under him. He received a battlefield promotion to brigadier general in October 1864, and to brevet major general in March 1865.

While Hayes was busy fighting, his admirers at home nominated him for Congress in 1864. When one wrote to him urging that he come home to campaign for votes, he answered tersely: "Thanks. I have other business just now. Any man who would leave the army at this time to electioneer for Congress ought to be scalped." This patriotic sentiment very likely won him more votes than if he had gone home. Elected, he finally took his seat in Congress in December 1865. Re-elected in 1866, he voted as a party regular with the Radical Republicans in their determination to punish the South and squelch President Johnson's efforts toward a soft peace.

When Ohio Republicans nominated Hayes for governor in August 1867, he resigned from Congress and conducted a vigorous campaign that carried him to victory with a majority of about 3000. After demonstrating his capabilities as a successful state administrator, he was re-elected to a second term in 1869.

Upon leaving the governorship, he ran unsuccessfully for Congress in 1872, and then retired to his estate, Spiegel Grove, near Fremont, Ohio, believing that he was through with public life. However, three years later, in 1875, the Republicans again nominated him for governor, and he became the first man in the state's history to win a third gubernatorial term.

The Hayes residence in Fremont, Ohio, located on twenty-five acres—now a memorial and museum.

Hayes and his devoted wife, a very religious woman, who insisted that a chapter of the Bible be read by the family at breakfast every morning.

Hayes taking the oath of office — an artist's drawing from a photograph by Brady.

The Most Controversial Presidential Election

WHEN Ohio Republicans put Hayes forward as their favorite son at the party's National Convention in Cincinnati in 1876, the national leaders paid little attention. James G. Blaine of Maine, who had been Speaker of the House throughout most of Grant's administration seemed to have the nomination sewed up. But Blaine's reputation had been compromised by corruption, and on the seventh ballot the convention gave the presidential nomination to Hayes—an upright teetotaler about whom there never had been and never would be a breath of scandal.

The Democrats chose as their presidential candidate Governor Samuel Jones Tilden of New York, who had won a national reputation as a reformer through his work in overthrowing the notorious Tweed Ring.

The campaign was a bitter one with each party freely accusing its opponents of corruption. Doubting that he could win, Hayes was not surprised by the headlines on the morning after the election that announced Tilden's victory. The popular votes showed 4,284,265 for Tilden and 4,033,295 for Hayes, while the electoral votes stood 203 for Tilden to 166 for Hayes.

But the newspaper headline writers had not reckoned with the determination of the Republican party leaders to hold onto their power. Claiming that Negroes had been prevented from going to the polls in South Carolina, Florida, and Louisiana, the Republicans challenged the returns from these states, and those from Oregon as well. By claiming the electoral votes of all four states, the Republicans could muster enough electoral votes to give Hayes a 185 to 184 margin of victory. But who was to decide the issue? If it were left to Congress, the prospect was for a deadlock between the Democratic House and the Republican Senate.

While the country seethed for more than three months over the issue, the leaders of the two parties met in secret. They decided to put special legislation through Congress appointing an Electoral Commission of fifteen men to arbitrate the problem—five from the House, five from the Senate, and five from the Supreme Court. On the surface this seemed nonpartisan, with five Democrats, five Republicans, and five impartial justices. In actuality, three of the justices were Republicans, so the Commission's findings were a foregone conclusion. Nevertheless, the Democratic leadership agreed to House approval of the plan—upon assurance that Hayes would withdraw troops from the South, leaving local government in the hands of Southern whites, and perhaps paving the way to future Democratic election victories. The deal was made. And the House formally approved Hayes as the winner just fifty-six hours before the inauguration was scheduled to take place.

THE fifty-four-year-old Hayes had left Ohio for Washington on March 1 not knowing whether he really would become President. Upon leaving Columbus he remarked that he might be back as governor within a week. But, on Inauguration Day, March 5, 1877, he happily took the oath of office and attempted to soothe the country in his address:

"The President of the United States of necessity owes his election to office to the suffrage and zealous labors of a political party, the members of which cherish with ardor and regard as of essential importance the principles of their party organization; but he should strive to be always mindful of the fact that he serves his party best who serves the country best. . . .

"The fact that two great political parties have in this way settled a dispute in regard to which good men differ as to the facts and the law no less than as to the proper course to be pursued in solving the question in controversy is an occasion for general rejoicing.

"Upon one point there is entire unanimity in public sentiment—that conflicting claims to the Presidency must be amicably and peaceably adjusted, and that when so adjusted the general acquiescence of the nation ought surely to follow.

"It has been reserved for a government of the people, where the right of suffrage is universal, to give to the world the first example in history of a great nation, in the midst of the struggle of opposing parties for power, hushing its party tumults to yield the issue of the contest to ad-

Mrs. Hayes in a formal gown of that era.

Hayes' Administration

Reception by President and Mrs. Hayes at their home in Fremont, Ohio.

Celebration on Pennsylvania Avenue in Washington, D. C., the night of Hayes' inauguration.

justment according to the forms of law."

Hayes tried hard to be a good President, but was unable to overcome the stigma of the political bargain that had seated him in the White House. He made good on the bargain by withdrawing troops from the South, leaving Southern Negroes effectively disfranchised for a long time to come.

The Democrats controlled the House during the first two years of Hayes' administration, and they also captured the Senate during his last two years in office. So Hayes had little chance to obtain passage of any legislation that he wanted.

The continuing economic depression helped bring on the first great national strike—that of railroad workers in 1877. Riots broke out along the railroads and Hayes forcefully responded to calls from the state governors by ordering federal troops to help restore order in West Virginia, Maryland, Pennsylvania, and Illinois.

When Congress attempted to ease the depression by passing legislation to issue "cheap" silver dollars, Hayes vetoed the law in the belief that

An excellent artist's drawing of the Capitol and the city of Washington, D. C., in 1877, showing the partially completed Washington Monument in the background.

A social scene at the White House, with Carl Schurz of Watertown, Wisconsin, Secretary of the Interior, playing the piano to entertain the Hayes family.

sound money was the basis of the American economic system. Congress passed the measure over his veto, but relatively few of the new silver dollars were issued. Nevertheless, the economy began to improve, though Hayes had to call a special session of Congress in 1877 to get enough money to pay the soldiers and sailors in the armed forces.

Both Democrats and Republicans turned a deaf ear to Hayes' repeated pleas for a reform of the civil service. He proceeded to infuriate members of his own party by trying to free many jobs from partisan control, especially those having to do with tax collection. He raised a particular storm when he authorized the firing of the Collector of the Port of New York, never dreaming that this man, Chester A. Arthur, would within a few years be presiding in the White House.

Although railroads now ran from coast to coast, Indian fighting still continued in the West. A major war came in 1877 when Chief Joseph tried to lead the Nez Percé tribe to freedom in Canada, but was stopped by federal troops. In an effort to quell further uprisings, Hayes issued an executive order banning the sale of firearms to Indians.

In his inaugural address, Hayes had recommended a constitutional amendment expanding the presidential term to six years and barring re-election. The proposal attracted little support, but when it became apparent in 1880 that he had no chance of obtaining a second-term nomination, Hayes could at least say that he had never wanted it.

When Hayes sent his last annual message to Congress in December 1880, he enumerated a long catalog of forward-looking legislation that he knew had little likelihood of passage. He called for Congress to appropriate money to supplement the educational budgets of the states "to promote free popular education." He again asked for a reform of the civil service to eliminate patronage. He called for a reorganization of the Territory of Utah, warning that the Mormons were becoming too powerful and were spreading polygamy. And he called for a host of improvements that ranged from a building for the Library of Congress to the completion of the Washington Monument.

Perhaps to please his wife, Hayes' last executive order, on February 22, 1881, banned the sale of intoxicating liquor at army camps and forts.

After leaving the White House, Hayes lived in quiet retirement, spending most of his time working on charitable enterprises. His wife preceded him in death by four years, and the seventy-year-old former President's last words in his home in Fremont on January 17, 1893, were: "I know I am going where Lucy is."

President Hayes and his Cabinet in session at the White House.

Ulysses S. Grant

The Eighteenth President of the United States
1869–77

1822 (April 27) Born in Point Pleasant, Ohio.

1839–43 Attended West Point.

1843–53 Served as officer in U.S. Army, rising to captain.

1848 (August 22) Married Julia Dent.

1854–58 Farmed near St. Louis, Missouri.

1860–61 Clerked in store at Galena, Illinois.

1861–65 Rose to command all Union Armies in Civil War.

1867–68 Secretary of War *ad interim* under President Johnson.

1869–77 Eighteenth President of the United States.

1880 Unsuccessful candidate for Republican presidential nomination.

1885 (July 23) Died at Mount McGregor, New York.

Leading Officials in
Grant's Administration

Office	Name	Years Served
Chief Justice	Salmon P. Chase	1864-1873
	Morrison R. Waite	1874-1888
Vice-President	Schuyler Colfax	1869-1873
	Henry Wilson	1873-1875
Secretary of State	Elihu B. Washburne	1869
	Hamilton Fish	1869-1877
Secretary of War	John A. Rawlins	1869
	William T. Sherman	1869
	William W. Belknap	1869-1876
	Alphonso Taft	1876
	James D. Cameron	1876-1877
Secretary of the Treasury	Alexander T. Stewart	1869
	George S. Boutwell	1869-1873
	William A. Richardson	1873-1874
	Benjamin H. Bristow	1874-1876
	Lot M. Morrill	1876-1877
Attorney General	Ebenezer Rockwood Hoar	1869-1870
	Amos T. Akerman	1870-1871
	George H. Williams	1871-1875
	Edwards Pierrepont	1875-1876
	Alphonso Taft	1876-1877
Postmaster General	John A. J. Creswell	1869-1874
	James W. Marshall	1874
	Marshall Jewell	1874-1876
	James N. Tyner	1876-1877
Secretary of the Navy	Adolph E. Borie	1869
	George M. Robeson	1869-1877
Secretary of the Interior	Jacob D. Cox	1869-1870
	Columbus Delano	1870-1875
	Zachariah Chandler	1875-1877

The log cabin that was once the home of Ulysses S. Grant.

There are but few important events in the affairs of men brought about by their own choice," Ulysses S. Grant observed philosophically in his memoirs. In his own life he seemed marked for quiet obscurity when the outbreak of the Civil War suddenly flung the door open to his talents. As a result of his victorious leadership of the Union Armies, he inherited the presidency almost as a right.

But his military background was not enough to equip him for the complexities of governing a large and swiftly growing nation, and historians have judged him a failure as a President. The common-sense approach that worked so well on the battlefield proved naive in the world of sharpers and intriguers who frequented the White House during his administration.

In his later years, when he waged a courageous struggle against cancer and bankruptcy, Grant won new sympathy and affection from his countrymen.

Farmboy to Career Officer to Storeclerk

"IN JUNE, 1821, my father, Jesse R. Grant, married Hannah Simpson," Grant says in his *Personal Memoirs*. "I was born on the 27th of April, 1822 at Point Pleasant, Clermont County, Ohio. In the fall of 1823 we moved to Georgetown. This place remained my home, until at the age of seventeen, in 1839, I went to West Point.

"The schools were very indifferent. . . . They were all supported by subscription, and a single teacher—who was often a man or woman incapable of teaching much, even if they imparted all they knew—would have thirty or forty scholars, male and female, from the infant learning the ABC's up to the young lady of eighteen and the boy of twenty, studying the highest branches taught—the three R's, 'Reading, 'Riting, 'Rithmetic.' I never saw an algebra, or other mathematical work higher than the arithmetic, in Georgetown, until after I was appointed to West Point. I then bought a work on algebra in Cincinnati; but having no teacher it was Greek to me."

Grant's father operated both a tannery and a farm, though young 'Lyss, as he was nicknamed, preferred farm chores to working in the tannery. From the time he was eleven he did most of the plowing. Yet despite the shortcomings of the local education system, he won an appointment to West Point, where a clerical error resulted in a change in his name. Named Hiram Ulysses at birth, he found at the military academy that he had been misregistered as Ulysses Simpson Grant. He did not call the mistake to anyone's attention, preferring the new name because the initials of his old one lent themselves to the nickname "Hug." Instead, his fellow-cadets began calling him "Uncle Sam" and later "Sam."

At West Point, Grant numbered among his friends and acquaintances fifty cadets who later served as generals in the Civil War. He later remarked that knowing the weaknesses and strengths of these men, both friend and foe, helped him in battle. An average student, Grant graduated twenty-first in his class of thirty-nine. Because he particularly liked mathematics, he hoped eventually for assignment as a math instructor at West Point, but meanwhile was sent to join an infantry company in St. Louis.

The Mexican War began while Grant was serving as a second lieutenant with his regiment in Texas in 1846. He fought first under Zachary Taylor and later under Winfield Scott, rising to first lieutenant and winning a brevet—temporary promotion—to captain for gallantry at the capture of Mexico City. The war over, Grant obtained a leave of absence and returned to St. Louis, where on August 22, 1848, he married Julia Dent, the sister of one of his West Point classmates. Grant and his wife had three sons and a daughter.

During the early 1850s Grant was assigned to military posts on the West Coast. He left his wife and children in St. Louis, feeling he could not afford to take them West on his low army pay. Grant received his commission as captain, but living the life of a bachelor on a dull army post he began drinking heavily. Finally, in 1854, he was forced to resign his commission.

He was only thirty-two, but his career seemed finished. Returning to St. Louis, Grant moved his family to a small piece of land given to his wife by

The farm in Georgetown, Ohio, built by Grant's father and used as a tannery, where Grant spent his boyhood learning to farm and to handle horses.

Mrs. Grant (Julia Dent) with Jesse and Nellie.

her father as a wedding present. He built a log cabin for them to live in, and named the farm "Hard Scrabble." Continued drinking and illness combined to bring failure to the venture, and in 1858 he sold the farm at auction. He tried to sell real estate in partnership with a cousin of Mrs. Grant, but this, too, proved a failure. In hopes of straightening out his problems his younger brothers offered him a job as clerk in a store they were operating in Galena, Illinois, and he moved there in May 1860.

Recall to Arms

WHEN Lincoln's call for volunteers to defend the Union came in April 1861, the thirty-nine-year-old Grant saw his opportunity. Quitting his job as a storekeeper, and donning his shabby old army overcoat, he helped raise a company of volunteers in Galena, but he declined election as their captain because he hoped for something better. He wrote a modest letter to the governor, mentioning his military experience, and went to Springfield, where he worked for several weeks as a $3-a-day clerk helping organize Illinois' volunteer regiments. When one of these proved unruly, the governor turned it over to Grant. Demonstrating an immediate aptitude for command, he whipped his regiment into shape and took it into successful combat in a diversionary action. In August he received a commission as brigadier general.

With the aid of America's first ironclad gunboats, he captured Forts Henry and Donelson in Tennessee, taking prisoner more than 20,000 Confederate troops. When the Confederate general in command of Fort Donelson (a former fellow-cadet at West Point) asked Grant's terms for the surrender, Grant replied: "No terms except an unconditional and immediate surrender can be accepted." This won Grant a nickname—"Unconditional Surrender" Grant. He also was promptly promoted to major general.

Two months later Grant was in command at Shiloh in southern Tennessee. Although surprised by a massive Confederate attack—some said he was off on a drinking bout—he hung on grimly and finally beat off the enemy in what was the bloodiest battle fought on the American continent up to that time. Temporarily Grant fell under a cloud as the home front gasped at the casualty figures, but failure of his superiors to achieve progress brought a restoration of his position in October, when he was given command of all Union forces in Tennessee.

He set about at once to capture the powerful Confederate stronghold of Vicksburg, protected by nearly insuperable geographic barriers in the form of bayous, swamps, and its own towering Mississippi River bluffs. The campaign was arduous and frustrating, but in it Grant demonstrated a skill and daring to match his stubbornness. When Vicksburg surrendered unconditionally on July 4, 1863, Grant was hailed throughout the North. Given command of all the Western armies, he organized a counter-offensive against a major Confederate thrust into central Tennessee, decisively defeating Confederate General Bragg at the battle of Chattanooga and opening the way for an invasion of Georgia.

Summoned to Washington by President Lincoln in March 1864, Grant was given the highest rank in the Army, lieutenant general, and placed in command of all the armies in the field. He at once planned the final campaign against the Confederacy, assigning William T. Sherman to the Western armies and establishing his own headquarters with the Army of the Potomac. Sherman's mission was to invade the heart of the Confederacy, capture Atlanta, and bring devastation to the South's "store-house" of Georgia. While Sherman was carrying out his orders to the letter, Grant turned his personal attention to the South's main army, commanded by the renowned Robert E. Lee.

General U. S. Grant at City Point, Virginia, during the Civil War.

295

Ignoring criticisms for heavy losses, Grant boldly attacked Lee and pushed him rapidly back into the fortifications of Richmond. Through the winter of 1864–65 Grant applied unremitting pressure. On April 2, 1865, Lee was forced to abandon Richmond and retreat west. One week later the end came at Appomattox Court House. In the moment of triumph Grant proved unassuming and magnanimous, appearing in a mud-spattered uniform to accord generous terms of surrender.

Grant was a national hero. His home town of Galena, Illinois, built him a house, Philadelphia presented him with a mansion, and New York made him a cash gift, raised by popular subscription, of $105,000. Congress honored him with the creation of the new rank of general of the armies.

Reproduction of a wood engraving showing the major battles in which Grant was commander.

General Grant (center) with two of his aides.

Not surprisingly, the leaders of the Republican party soon fixed their eyes on Grant as a presidential possibility. Though at first he seemed to side with President Johnson in his feud with Congress, he acted with the Radicals in turning the post of Secretary of War, to which Johnson had appointed him, back to Stanton. When the Republican Convention met in May 1868, Grant was unanimously nominated on the first roll call. His acceptance message that contained the sentence, "Let us have peace," led many persons to believe he favored milder Reconstruction policies for the South. He easily swept to victory in the November election over the Democratic candidate, former Governor of New York Horatio Seymour. Grant received 214 electoral votes to Seymour's 80, although the popular vote was much closer—3,013,421 to 2,706,829.

A pencil sketch of Grant whittling, the afternoon of the first day's fighting in the Wilderness campaign.

Grant's Administration

WHEN the forty-six-year-old Grant took the oath of office on March 4, 1869, he was the youngest man so far to become President. Vigorous and at the height of his popularity, he seemed to be just what the troubled country needed. In his inaugural address, he declared:

"The responsibilities of the position I feel, but accept them without fear. The office has come to me unsought; I commence its duties untrammeled. I bring to it a conscious desire and determination to fill it to the best of my ability to the satisfaction of the people. . . .

"I shall on all subjects have a policy to recommend, but none to enforce against the will of the people. Laws are to govern all alike—those opposed as well as those who favor them. I know no method to secure the repeal of bad or obnoxious laws so effective as their stringent execution."

Unfortunately, the "bad or obnoxious laws" to which Grant gave the most "stringent execution" were the Reconstruction Acts that had been passed over Johnson's veto. The Southerners against whom they were enforced had no legal power to repeal them, but in retaliation had formed the Ku Klux Klan, a secret terror society that undertook to restore white rule by killings, burnings, and floggings. In the end Radical Reconstruction proved a failure and left a bitter legacy to future generations.

Grant revealed his political ineptitude with his initial cabinet appointments. He chose two old friends from Galena as Secretaries of State and War—one of whom resigned and the other of whom died during the first year of the administration. He appointed as his Secretary of the Treasury a millionaire war contractor who was forced out of office within a few days because of conflict of interest with government business. And as his Secretary of the Navy he named a millionaire banker who resigned within three months because the cabinet position took too much of his time.

The scene at the inaugural ball at the time of the arrival of President Grant and Mrs. Grant.

A Currier and Ives campaign poster featuring Grant and Wilson, the Republican ticket.

The Radical Republicans in Congress who had helped bring Grant into the White House treated him as a puppet. They ignored his mild recommendations to repeal the Tenure of Office Act and to reform the civil service. His rather naive proposal to annex Santo Domingo as a haven for former Negro slaves was summarily rebuffed.

In 1872 "Liberal"—anti-Radical—Republicans nominated New York newspaper editor Horace Greeley for the presidency, and the Democrats joined them with an endorsement of Greeley in an all-out effort to unseat Grant. But the regular Republicans pressed Grant's campaign for a second term, and he won by 3,596,745 votes to Greeley's 2,843,446, a substantial increase in his margin. The electoral vote was 286 to 66.

Scandal had touched Grant's administration during his first term when his brother-in-law's connivance had helped the financier Jay Gould use inside government information in attempting a spectacular Wall Street coup—"cornering the gold market." By Grant's second term, corruption

President Grant and Mrs. Grant with friends at his cottage by the sea.

seethed and boiled throughout the government. Many congressmen, senators, and other officials were involved in illegal dealing in stock connected with the building of the Union Pacific Railroad, which received enormous federal subsidies. Two members of the Cabinet resigned to avoid impeachment for bribery and fraud, as did five federal judges. Grant's secretary was tried as a member of the Whisky Ring that defrauded the government of millions of dollars in excise taxes, and was saved from conviction only by the President's testimony in his behalf.

The voters reacted strongly to these scandals and to the depression which followed the financial panic of 1873. In the congressional elections of 1874, the Democrats won a majority in the House for the first time since the Civil War. Despite pressure from his supporters, Grant decided he should not run for a third term in 1876. In his last annual message to Congress he frankly accepted a share of blame for the disasters of his administration.

"It was my fortune, or misfortune, to be called to the office of Chief Executive without any previous political training. . . .

"Under such circumstances it is but reasonable to suppose that errors of judgment must have occurred. . . . Mistakes have been made, as all can see and I admit, but it seems to me oftener in the selections made of the assistants appointed to aid in carrying out the various duties of administering the Government—in nearly every case selected without a personal acquaintance with the appointee, but upon recommendations of the representatives chosen directly by the people."

A Triumph Abroad

AFTER leaving the presidency, Grant went abroad for nearly three years on a tour of Europe and Asia. Everywhere he was greeted with honor, respect, and huge crowds, as the hero of the war for freedom. Newspaper reports of his triumphant trip helped regain some popularity at home, and a faction of the Republican party pushed for his nomination for President in 1880. The effort ended in a convention deadlock between Grant and James G. Blaine, and the ultimate selection of a dark-horse candidate, James Garfield.

Grant and his wife lived quietly for a few years at the house that had been given to them in Galena, and then moved to New York. He invested all his savings, about $100,000, in a banking firm in which one of his sons was a partner. But the head of the firm, Ferdinand Ward, turned out to be a swindler. The firm went bankrupt in 1884, Grant lost all his money, and Ward was sent to prison.

"I have made it a rule of my life to trust a man long after other people gave him up," the sixty-two-year-old Grant commented bleakly, "but I don't see how I can ever trust any human being again."

Not only was Grant left destitute, but he was suffering from a fatal cancer. His courage, however, had not abandoned him. To provide for his family, he undertook to write his memoirs for magazine serialization. From the start the accounts he wrote of his campaigns—clear, simple, straightforward—were a popular success, and remain to this day one of the classics of military literature.

Sticking to his task with all his old-time tenacity, he managed to complete it only weeks before his death at his home in Mount McGregor, New York, on July 23, 1885. Mark Twain had the memoirs published in book form and turned over a half million dollars' profit to the Grant family.

In the concluding chapter, Grant commented on the war that had brought him fame and the presidency:

"It is probably well that we had the war when we did. We are better off now than we would have been without it, and have made more rapid progress than we otherwise should have made."

The Grant residence in Galena, Illinois, in 1866.

302   ANDREW JOHNSON

Andrew Johnson

The Seventeenth President of the United States
1865–69

1808 (December 29) Born in Raleigh, North Carolina.

1822–24 Worked as a tailor's apprentice.

1827 (May 17) Married Eliza McCardle.

1828–30 Alderman of Greeneville, Tennessee.

1830–33 Mayor of Greeneville, Tennessee.

1835–37; 1839–41 Member of Tennessee house of representatives.

1841–43 Member of Tennessee senate.

1843–53 U.S. representative from Tennessee.

1853–57 Governor of Tennessee.

1857–62 U.S. senator from Tennessee.

1862–64 Military governor of Tennessee.

1865 Vice President of the United States.

1865–69 Seventeenth President of the United States.

1874–75 U.S. senator from Tennessee.

1875 (July 31) Died at Carter Station, Tennessee.

Leading Officials in
Johnson's Administration

Office	Name	Years Served
Chief Justice	Salmon P. Chase	1864-1873
Secretary of State	William H. Seward	1861-1869
Secretary of War	Edwin M. Stanton	1862-1867
	Ulysses S. Grant	1867-1868
	Lorenzo Thomas	1868
	John M. Schofield	1868-1869
Secretary of the Treasury	Hugh McCulloch	1865-1869
Attorney General	James Speed	1864-1866
	Henry Stanbery	1866-1868
	William M. Evarts	1868-1869
Postmaster General	William Dennison	1864-1866
	Alexander W. Randall	1866-1869
Secretary of the Navy	Gideon Welles	1861-1869
Secretary of the Interior	John P. Usher	1863-1865
	James Harlan	1865-1866
	Orville H. Browning	1866-1869

Impeached because he refused to let Congress usurp presidential rights, Andrew Johnson missed conviction and removal from office by one senatorial vote. His fortitude in the face of overwhelming congressional pressure strengthened the presidency and helped preserve the separation of powers among the legislative, executive, and judicial branches of the government.

A former tailor, who had never been to school a day in his life, Johnson forged his way upward in politics by supporting the common man and speaking out his mind even when it was unpopular to do so. As a Tennessee Democrat, he was the only Southern senator who refused to follow his seceding state. Elected Vice President on the National Union ticket in 1864, and thrust into the White House by Lincoln's assassination, he won the enmity of the Republicans because he believed the South should be treated more as a wayward friend than as a conquered enemy. Leaving

Mrs. Andrew Johnson (Eliza McCardle) who was helpful to Johnson in improving his writing and reading.

the presidency a disgraced man in 1869, he triumphantly returned to Washington six years later as the only former President ever elected to the Senate.

ANDREW JOHNSON was born in poverty in Raleigh, North Carolina, on December 29, 1808. His father, Jacob Johnson, a laborer, died when Andrew was three. His mother, Mary McDonough Johnson, worked as a seamstress and washerwoman to support Andrew, his three brothers, and herself; but she was unable to afford to send the boys to school.

When he was nearly fourteen, Andrew was apprenticed to a tailor. As he sat cross-legged sewing, one of his fellow-workers taught him to read, but he still did not know how to write. After a boyhood prank for which he feared his master would punish him, he ran away to Laurens Court-House, South Carolina, where he worked as a journeyman tailor.

Although still wanted by his master as a fugitive, Johnson returned briefly to Raleigh when he was seventeen. He talked his mother and step-father—his mother having remarried—into going west with him to start a new life. They traveled across North Carolina in a two-wheeled cart drawn by a blind pony and settled in Greeneville, Tennessee, just across the border. There Johnson opened his own tailor shop.

A year after coming to Greeneville, Johnson married sixteen-year-old Eliza McCardle, the daughter of a shoemaker. Because she had more education than Johnson, she was able to teach the future President how to write and how to do simple arithmetic. They had five children, including one son who was later killed serving as a Union soldier in the Civil War.

The hard-working young tailor impressed the townspeople with his seriousness, and in 1828, at the age of nineteen, he was elected to the village council. After serving as an alderman for two years, the twenty-one-year-old Johnson received the highest honor his fellow townsmen could bestow, by being elected mayor. A naturally gifted public speaker, Johnson polished his oratory during his three years as mayor by taking an active part in a debating society at Greeneville College.

A follower of Andrew Jackson, Johnson became known as a defender of the rights of the laboring man. In 1835 he was elected to the legislature, was defeated when he ran for re-election in the depression year of 1837, but was returned as a state representative in 1839. Two years later the fast-rising young politician was elected to the state senate where he made a name for himself as an enemy of the state's slave-holding aristocracy.

Johnson was thirty-four when he was first elected to Congress in 1843. Re-elected as a U.S. representative four times, he helped President Polk press the Mexican War, voted for the Compromise of 1850, and tried to win passage of a homestead law to make it easier for poor farmers to obtain western land.

When a redistricting of the state by the Whigs made it impossible for Johnson to be re-elected to Congress, he returned to Tennessee and won election as governor in 1853. Known as the "Mechanic Governor," Johnson still tailored his own clothes and made a suit for the governor of Kentucky as a gesture of friendship. Denouncing the anti-Catholic Know-Nothing movement, he won a second term as governor by a large majority in 1855.

"I have reached the summit of my ambition," Johnson said when the Tennessee legislature elected him to the U.S. Senate in 1857. He again took up the cudgels for a homestead law that eventually was passed in 1862.

In the Democratic National Convention of 1860, Johnson was proposed for the presidential nomination by Tennessee, but he withdrew his name

From Tailor's Apprentice to Vice President

and campaigned for the election of John Breckinridge. Many assumed he was a secessionist. But after Lincoln was elected, Johnson forthrightly denounced the secessionist movement and declared his intention to remain loyal to the Union. Of the secessionists he said:

"I would have them arrested and tried for treason, and, if convicted, by the eternal God, they should suffer the penalty of the law at the hands of the executioner."

When Tennessee joined the Confederacy, Johnson made good on his word, remaining in Washington to be hailed as a patriot in the North and reviled as a traitor in the South.

After Northern troops had seized western and central Tennessee in 1862, Lincoln appointed Johnson military governor of the state. He proved a fair-minded, able administrator, granting amnesty to former Confederate sympathizers but also pushing for an amendment to the state constitution to outlaw slavery in the state. Tennessee, specifically exempted from the Emancipation Proclamation, was the only seceding state to end slavery by its own action.

At the National Union Convention in Baltimore in June 1864, the delegates chose Johnson as the vice-presidential running mate of President Lincoln. The presence of a Jackson Democrat on the Union ticket helped Lincoln run up a large majority over his Democratic opponent, General George McClellan. But at the inauguration on March 4, 1865, Johnson embarrassed himself and his friends by appearing drunk. When some persons suggested to Lincoln that he should ask for the Vice President's resignation, the President good-humoredly silenced them with the remark: "I've known Andy a great many years, and he ain't no drunkard."

Johnson's Administration

ON THE NIGHT Lincoln was shot, the conspirators had also planned to kill Vice President Johnson, but their plans went awry. Awakened by a friend with the news of the assassination, Johnson hastened to his stricken chief's bedside. After the agonizing night-long vigil, Johnson was sworn in as Chief Executive by Chief Justice Salmon P. Chase. The members of the Cabinet assembled in the parlor of his hotel.

". . . I feel incompetent to perform duties so important and responsible as those which have been so unexpectedly thrown upon me, . . ." Johnson told them. "The course which I have taken in the past in connection with this rebellion must be regarded as a guaranty of the future. . . . The best energies of my life have been spent in endeavoring to establish and perpetuate the principles of free government, and I believe that the Government in passing through its present perils will settle down upon principles consonant with popular rights more permanent and enduring than heretofore. . . . I have long labored to ameliorate and elevate the condition of the great mass of the American people. Toil and an honest advocacy of the great principles of free government have been my lot. Duties have been mine; consequences are God's. This has been the foundation of my political creed, and I feel that in the end the Government will triumph and that these great principles will be permanently established. . . ."

However despite Johnson's humble tone he was a fearless, even reckless fighter for what he believed in. As a result he became embroiled in the bitterest intragovernmental conflict this nation has ever seen. The problem was the "reconstruction" of the ex-Confederate states. Johnson, like Lincoln, favored a "mild" reconstruction, in effect turning the state governments over to the white citizens, with only the main leaders of the Confederacy disfranchised. But the Republican congressional leaders favored a "radical" reconstruction, enfranchising the former Negro slaves and barring most of the former Confederates from government. This

The home of Andrew Johnson in Greeneville, Tennessee.
—H. Milhollen photograph

solution had special appeal to the Republicans because it promised to permit a continued hold on the federal government for their party, which even in 1860 had been a minority.

At first the Radical Republicans were pleased with the prospect of Johnson's presidency. They mistakenly regarded him as a weak man who would be easier to control than Lincoln. Moreover, they counted on his past antagonism to leaders of the Southern aristocracy as assurance that he would be congenial to their plans for severe treatment of the defeated South.

"By the gods! there will be no trouble now in running the government!" This was the sentiment expressed by Republican Senator Benjamin F. Wade of Ohio. But two years later this same Wade, as President of the Senate, had become so confident that he could evict Johnson from the White House and succeed him that he was said to have written an inauguration speech and to have chosen his Cabinet in preparation for the event.

But the new President soon made it clear that he intended to carry out Lincoln's plan to grant a soft peace to the South. He ended the blockade of Southern ports and declared a general amnesty except for officials and high officers of the Confederacy and the wealthy Southern aristocrats. By the middle of June, Johnson had issued a series of proclamations enabling the Southern states to begin setting up civil governments. And by the time Congress met in December 1865, the former states of the Confederacy had elected governors, legislatures, and congressmen. Though they had given formal approval to the Thirteenth Amendment outlawing slavery, they had passed "Black Codes" binding the ex-slaves to the land.

". . . It has been my steadfast object," Johnson said in his first annual message to Congress, "to escape from the sway of momentary passions and to derive a healing policy from the fundamental and unchanging principles of the Constitution. . . . I know very well that this policy is attended with some risk; that for its success it requires at least the acquiescence of the States which it concerns; that it implies an invitation to those

States, by renewing their allegiance to the United States, to resume their functions as States of the Union. But it is a risk that must be taken."

But the Northern Republicans had no intention of welcoming back the Democratic congressmen and senators from the seceding states. Instead, Congress passed legislation to re-institute military government throughout the South and establish a powerful Freedmen's Bureau to assist the four million freed slaves. Through this means the most radical congressional leaders hoped to revolutionize the Southern way of life. Johnson promptly vetoed the measure.

"It is plain that an indefinite or permanent exclusion of any part of the country from representation must be attended by a spirit of disquiet and complaint. It is unwise and dangerous to pursue a course of measures which will unite a very large section of the country against another section of the country, however much the latter may preponderate."

For the time being the Radical Republicans were not strong enough to override Johnson's veto. But by April 1866, they had gained sufficient strength to pass over his veto a civil rights law granting citizenship to the former slaves, a measure Johnson considered unnecessary.

In an effort to rally the people behind his mild reconstruction policies, Johnson went on a national speaking tour in the summer and fall of 1866. But the subsequent elections went against him, and the Radical Republicans increased their majority in Congress.

Now able to ignore Johnson's vetoes, the Radicals pushed into law in the spring of 1867 a series of harsh Reconstruction Acts. Military governments replaced the civil governments set up by Southern Democrats. "Carpetbaggers"—immigrant Northerners—and "scalawags"—renegade white Southerners—joined forces with freed Negroes to seize control of Southern state legislatures. Some of the laws passed by these Reconstruction legislatures were enlightened, such as those providing free public education. But corruption and waste of public funds were common.

Johnson warned that the course upon which Congress had embarked "would engender a feeling of opposition and hatred between the two races, which, becoming deep rooted and ineradicable, would prevent them from living together in a state of mutual friendliness." He termed the Reconstruction Acts "legislation which, looking solely to the attainment of political ends, fails to consider the rights it transgresses, the law which it violates, or the institutions which it imperils."

The Radical Republicans slashed back at Johnson by passing over his veto in the spring of 1867 the Tenure of Office Act, which forbade the President to remove from office any federal official who had been appointed with the advice and consent of the Senate. Sure that the act was unconstitutional (and the Supreme Court ultimately so ruled fifty-nine years later), Johnson removed from office in August 1867 his Secretary of War, Edwin M. Stanton, a Radical Republican who had been an obstructionist in his Cabinet. In Stanton's place he appointed General Ulysses S. Grant. In defiance of the President, Grant turned the office back to Stanton in February 1868. Enraged, Johnson again removed Stanton on February 21 and in his place appointed Major General Lorenzo Thomas. Three days later the House of Representatives voted to impeach Johnson on eleven counts, the most important of which was violation of the Tenure of Office Act.

The trial of the President began in the Senate on March 13 and lasted more than two months. It soon became apparent that the Radical Republican leaders were seeking to get rid of the President's opposition to their political plans. Suspense built as the public speculated whether the Republican leadership could hold in line the necessary 36 votes to provide

Senator Benjamin Butler delivering the opening speech at the impeachment proceedings against Andrew Johnson. —*Frank Leslie's Illustrated Newspaper*

a two-thirds majority needed to convict and remove Johnson from office. If seven Republicans decided to vote with the Democrats, Johnson would be adjudged not guilty. By the time a vote was taken on May 16, six Republicans had indicated they would switch, and one, Senator Edmund Ross of Kansas, had refused to say how he would cast his vote. When it came time for him to vote, Ross cast his ballot as "not guilty." The final tally was 35 guilty and 19 not guilty, one short of conviction. On May 26 the roll was called on two more charges, and again Johnson was saved by a single vote.

After the trial, the deadlock between the President and Congress resumed. Johnson, who had been elected Vice President on the Republican or "National Union" ticket in 1864, entertained some hopes of receiving a presidential nomination from the Democrats in 1868, but he was disappointed. In his last annual message to Congress in December 1868, he bitterly denounced the legislators' repeated violations of the Constitution:

"Our own history, although embracing a period of less than a century, affords abundant proof that most, if not all, of our domestic troubles are directly traceable to violations of the organic law and excessive legislation. The most striking illustrations of this fact are furnished by the enactments of the past three years upon the question of reconstruction. After

Taking a vote on the impeachment of Andrew Johnson in the Senate Chamber, May 16, 1868.   —*Frank Leslie's Illustrated Newspaper*

A facsimile of the ticket of admission to the impeachment trial of President Johnson.
—*Harper's Weekly*

a fair trial they have substantially failed and proved pernicious in their results, and there seems to be no good reason why they should longer remain on the statute book."

Perhaps the most valuable achievement of the Johnson administration was the acquisition of Alaska. Scoffed at as "Seward's Folly" and "Seward's Icebox," the vast northern territory proved worth far more than its purchase price of $7.2 million.

Return to Washington

FULL of fire, fight, and determination to prove he was right in his actions as President, Johnson returned to Tennessee and ran for Congress in 1869. Beaten in this attempt, he tried and lost again in 1872. Finally, in 1874, the Tennessee legislature elected him to his old office as U.S. senator.

When Johnson took his seat in the Forty-fourth Congress in March 1875, the Democrats had won control of the House for the first time since the Civil War and had greatly increased their strength in the Senate. Johnson made only one speech in the Senate, reaffirming his belief in the milder reconstruction policies he had attempted to institute and denouncing the punitive policies that had been forced on the nation by the Radical Republicans. He felt vindicated by the applause that broke out in the very chamber that had tried to convict him seven years earlier.

Johnson did not have long to enjoy his revitalized reputation. On July 31, 1875, while visiting his daughter at Carter Station, Tennessee, the sixty-six-year-old former President died of a stroke.

Abraham Lincoln on April 9, 1865, five days before his assassination.   —*Gardner*

Abraham Lincoln

The Sixteenth President of the United States
1 8 6 1 – 6 5

1809 (February 12) Born near Hodgenville, Kentucky.

1816 Moved with parents to Indiana.

1830 Moved to Illinois.

1832 Served as volunteer in Black Hawk War, but saw no fighting.

1834–42 Member of the Illinois legislature.

1836 Licensed to practice law.

1842 (November 4) Married Mary Todd.

1847–49 U.S. representative from Illinois.

1856 Unsuccessful candidate for Republican vice-presidential nomination.

1858 Won national prominence debating slavery issue with Stephen A. Douglas in unsuccessful campaign for U.S. senator.

1861–65 Sixteenth President of the United States.

1865 (April 14) Wounded by assassin John Wilkes Booth.

1865 (April 15) Died in Washington, D.C.

Leading Officials in Lincoln's Administration

Office	Name	Years Served
Chief Justice	Roger B. Taney	1835-1864
	Salmon P. Chase	1864-1873
Vice-President	Hannibal Hamlin	1861-1865
	Andrew Johnson	1865
Secretary of State	William H. Seward	1861-1869
Secretary of the Treasury	Salmon P. Chase	1861-1864
	William P. Fessenden	1864-1865
	Hugh McCulloch	1865-1869
Secretary of War	Simon Cameron	1861-1862
	Edwin M. Stanton	1862-1867
Attorney General	Edward Bates	1861-1864
	James Speed	1864-1866
Postmaster General	Montgomery Blair	1861-1864
	William Dennison	1864-1866
Secretary of the Navy	Gideon Welles	1861-1869
Secretary of the Interior	Caleb B. Smith	1861-1863
	John P. Usher	1863-1865

Given his lack of education and scant public service, Abraham Lincoln seemed less likely to succeed as President than most of his predecessors. Yet his innate wisdom and humanity made him one of the greatest of the nation's Chief Executives.

Entering the White House at a time when many of the Southern states already had seceded from the Union, Lincoln offered them the hand of friendship in his inaugural address. "We must not be enemies," he said, after assuring them that he had no intention of interfering with the institution of slavery and that he would uphold the rights of slave-owners to recover fugitive slaves from other states. But he also firmly warned that "the Union of these States is perpetual."

After hotheaded Southern leaders disregarded Lincoln's inaugural plea for peace, he resolutely mobilized for war. The death and destruction of the ensuing fight between North and South made Lincoln's heart bleed, yet his sorrowing bearded face and gaunt black-garbed figure became a symbol of the North's determination to preserve the Union. His Emancipation Proclamation ordering freedom for slaves in the rebelling states crystallized the central issue of the conflict and moved the nation a great step forward toward realizing Jefferson's dream of equality for all men. And finally his assassination in the moment of victory struck the conscience of both North and South and epitomized the hatreds that must be quelled if the nation were once again to be welded together.

Lincoln's natural humility and lack of pretension are strikingly revealed in a short autobiography that he wrote in 1859 when he was a candidate for the Republican presidential nomination:

"I was born Feb. 12, 1809, in Hardin County, Kentucky. My parents were both born in Virginia of undistinguished families—second families perhaps I should say. My mother, who died in my tenth year, was of a family of the name of Hanks, some of whom now reside in Adams, some others in Macon counties, Illinois. My paternal grandfather, Abraham Lincoln, emigrated from Rockingham County, Virginia, to Kentucky, about 1781 or 2, where, a year or two later, he was killed by Indians . . .

"My father . . . grew up literally without education. He removed from Kentucky to what is now Spencer County, Indiana, in my eighth year. It was a wild region, with many bears and other wild animals. There were some schools, so called, but no qualification was ever required of a teacher beyond 'reading, writing, and ciphering' to the Rule of Three. The little advance I now have upon this store of education, I have picked up from time to time under the pressure of necessity.

"I was raised to farm work, which I continued till I was twenty-two. At twenty-one I came to Illinois, and passed the first year in Macon County. Then I got to New Salem, at that time in Sangamon, now in Menard County, where I remained a year as a sort of clerk in a store. Then came the Black Hawk war and I was elected a Captain of Volunteers—a success which gave me more pleasure than any I have had since. I went the campaign, was elected, ran for the Legislature the same year (1832), and was beaten—the only time I ever have been beaten by the people. The next, and three succeeding biennial elections, I was elected to the Legislature. I was not a candidate afterwards. During this Legislative period I had studied law, and removed to Springfield to practice it. In 1846 I was elected to the lower House of Congress. Was not a candidate

Lincoln photographed by Mathew Brady February 27, 1860.

for reelection. From 1849 to 1854, both inclusive, practiced law more assiduously than ever before . . . I was losing interest in politics, when the repeal of the Missouri Compromise aroused me again. What I have accomplished since then is pretty well known.

"If any personal description of me is thought desirable, it may be said, I am, in height, six feet, four inches, nearly; lean in flesh, weighing, on an average, one hundred and eighty pounds; dark complexion, with coarse black hair, and grey eyes—no other marks or brands recollected—"

LINCOLN's parents were typical of thousands of American frontier families of the nineteenth century who spent their lives in an endless struggle against poverty and the wilderness. They were barely able to keep a roof over their heads, barely able to keep warm in winter, and barely able to keep fed from one day to the next. Both his father, Thomas Lincoln, and his mother, Nancy Hanks, had come from Virginia—genealogists since have traced the origin of the family in America to a Samuel Lincoln who came to Massachusetts from England in 1637.

Born in a crude log cabin near Hodgenville, Kentucky, on February 12, 1809, young Abe knew few of the comforts of civilization before he

On the Frontier

The earliest known photograph of Lincoln, taken in 1848.

was a man. He had a sister, Sarah, who was about two years older, and a younger brother, Thomas, who died as a baby, before the family moved to Indiana.

When Abe was eight his father moved the family west to Indiana where he took possession of 160 acres of forest land in Spencer County. The new Lincoln home was a three-sided lean-to with only a fire to keep out the winter cold. The next year Lincoln's mother died of what was called "the milk sickness."

In 1819 Lincoln's father married Sarah Bush Johnston, a Kentucky widow with three children of her own. The new Mrs. Lincoln improved the family's standard of living with a wagonload of furniture from her previous marriage. More important, she brought Abe affection and instilled in him a desire to better himself.

Although Lincoln went to school no more than a year in all the time he was growing up, he developed a love of books. Since his family was too poor to buy any other books than the Bible, he sometimes walked several miles to borrow one from a neighbor. In later years he recalled that he was particularly impressed with one of these borrowed books, Parson Weems' *Life of Washington*, that gave him insight into the struggles of the Founding Fathers who established the United States.

Tall and strong by the time he was sixteen, Abe began hiring out as a laborer at twenty-five cents a day. He worked as a grocery-store clerk, as a farmhand, as a ferryboat rower on the Ohio River, and in countless other odd jobs that called for a strong back. He also won local renown as a wrestler and for his humorous imitations of some of the eccentric members of the community.

When he was nineteen, Abe had his first look at a city—New Orleans. He floated down the Ohio and Mississippi as a deck hand on a flatboat loaded with farm produce. He made a similar flatboat journey to New Orleans three years later, and it was on this second trip that he is reputed to have acquired his hatred of slavery. One of his companions on the journey, John Hanks, said:

"We saw Negroes chained, maltreated, whipped, and scourged. Lincoln saw it; his heart bled, said nothing much, was silent from feeling, was sad, looked bad, felt bad, was thoughtful and abstracted. I can say, knowing it, that it was on this trip that he formed his opinions of slavery. It run its iron in him then and there—May, 1831. I have heard him say so often and often."

In 1830, after Lincoln had turned twenty-one, his father again decided to seek his elusive fortune by moving west—this time to Illinois. Abe helped move the family to a new farm west of Decatur, put in the first crop, then decided to leave home for good and strike out on his own.

IN the spring of 1831 young Lincoln settled down in the tiny frontier village of New Salem in Illinois. He became a clerk in a store, and won instant popularity with the backwoods people of the community. He proved he could out-wrestle the biggest bullies, could tell funnier stories than anyone, and could be depended on to help out whenever a strong worker was needed.

Life in New Salem

When a militia company was organized in 1832 to fight Chief Black Hawk, Lincoln volunteered. The men of the company elected him captain, giving him his first taste of winning an election. After a month's service the company was discharged, but Lincoln re-enlisted as a private. In the three months that he served he took part in no battles, "but I had a good many bloody struggles with the mosquitoes; and . . . I was often very hungry."

Before joining the militia, the twenty-three-year-old Lincoln had made an important decision—to run for the state legislature. His military service prevented his doing any campaigning, and by the time he returned to New Salem the election was only a few days away. He was not surprised when he was defeated, and counted the experience a valuable one.

With politics temporarily out of the way, Lincoln went into partnership in a general store in New Salem, but being a better storyteller than businessman, he went broke in a few months. It took him seventeen years to pay off his debts.

After his disastrous experience as a merchant, Lincoln decided to improve himself by studying law, walking twenty miles back and forth to Springfield to borrow books, as there were no law books in New Salem. To support himself, he worked as an assistant surveyor, then from 1833 to 1836, served as postmaster of New Salem. Because there was no post office, Lincoln carried the mail "in his hat," which was not too difficult since mail arrived only once a week.

In 1834 the twenty-five-year-old Lincoln again ran for the legislature as a member of the new Whig party. This time he won handily, leading the ticket in his legislative district. He promptly went further in debt by borrowing two hundred dollars to purchase a new outfit so as not to disgrace his constituents with his appearance at the state capital.

The story is told that about this time Lincoln fell deeply in love with Ann Rutledge, the blonde, blue-eyed daughter of a New Salem tavern-keeper, and he was so grief-stricken when she died in 1835 that his friends feared he might do away with himself. Modern historians discount the story somewhat because there is no evidence of it in Lincoln's writings, but many people who knew him well declared that Lincoln still spoke fondly and sadly of Ann Rutledge nearly thirty years after her death. One quoted Lincoln as saying, "I loved the woman dearly. She was a handsome girl; would have made a good, loving wife; was natural and quite intellectual, though not highly educated. I did honestly and truly love the girl, and think often, often, of her now."

Lincoln and his son, Tad, at the White House, April 9, 1865. *—Gardner*

A year after Ann Rutledge's death, Lincoln agreed sight unseen to marry Mary Owens, a well-to-do Kentucky spinster who was the sister of one of his New Salem friends. He later described his consternation upon seeing her, "I knew she was oversize, but she now appeared a fair match for Falstaff. I knew she was called an 'old maid,' and I felt no doubt of the truth of at least half of the appelation; but now, when I beheld her, I could not for my life avoid thinking of my mother; and this, not from withered features, for her skin was too full of fat to permit of its contracting into wrinkles, but from her want of teeth, weather-beaten appearance in general, and from a kind of notion that ran in my head that *nothing* could have commenced at the size of infancy and reached her present bulk in less than thirty-five or forty years; and, in short, I was not at all pleased with her. But what could I do? I had told her sister that I would take her for better or for worse; and I made a point of honor and conscience in all things to stick to my word, especially if others had been induced to act on it, which in this case I had no doubt they had; for I was now fairly convinced that no other man on earth would have her, and hence the conclusion that they were bent on holding me to my bargain."

But over a period of a year and a half, Lincoln worked at convincing Miss Owens that life with him would not be easy. He finally was overjoyed when she decided in 1838 not to marry him.

LINCOLN was re-elected to the state legislature in 1836, and that same year received his license to practice law. He and the other representatives from Sangamon County had their greatest legislative triumph in the session of 1836–37 when they succeeded in having a bill passed to move the state capital from Vandalia to Springfield. When the move was finally carried out in 1839, Lincoln decided to move his permanent residence there. He became a law partner with John T. Stuart, who had loaned him the law books that he walked from New Salem to borrow.

In 1839 Lincoln met twenty-year-old Mary Todd, a Lexington, Kentucky, girl who was living in Springfield at the home of a married sister. They became engaged and arranged to be married in 1840. But suddenly Lincoln decided that he had fallen in love with another girl who lived at the same house, a Matilda Edwards. His friends were convinced that Lincoln had become "as crazy as a loon." They took him to Kentucky to recover, and he stayed there missing the 1841–42 session of the state legislature.

After Lincoln returned to Springfield in 1842, he resumed seeing Mary Todd. In the fall of 1842 Mary wrote some politically satirical newspaper articles about a prominent Democratic politician, James Shields. Thinking that Lincoln was the author of the articles, Shields challenged him to a duel. Lincoln accepted the challenge, and they were about to settle the issue with broadswords when Shields backed down. Shortly thereafter, on November 4, 1842, Lincoln married Mary Todd. Their first home was at the Globe Tavern in Springfield. A year and a half later they moved into the frame house that remained their home until Lincoln became President. The Lincolns had four sons, but one died in 1850, another in 1861, and a third a few years after Lincoln's death. The surviving son, Robert Todd Lincoln, later served as Secretary of War under Presidents Garfield and Arthur.

Lincoln unsuccessfully sought the Whig nomination for Congress in 1843, but three years later, in 1846, won both nomination and election, becoming the only Whig in the Illinois delegation to Congress.

Lincoln was thirty-eight when he took his seat in Congress. As a con-

A reproduction of an artist's sketch of the crowd in Springfield, Illinois, giving Lincoln an enthusiastic send-off as he left for Washington.

gressman he denounced President Polk for having started the Mexican War, but supported bills to supply the Army and applauded the generals for winning battles. As a delegate to the Whig National Convention in 1848, he voted for the nomination of Mexican War hero Zachary Taylor for President. But Lincoln's outspoken criticism of the war had lost him support in Illinois, and Whig leaders decided not to renominate him for Congress.

No longer an office-holder, Lincoln settled down in Springfield to improve his law practice and provide for his growing family. His reputation as a lawyer continued to grow. Judge David Davis, who presided over the circuit court where Lincoln most often appeared, had this to say of Lincoln's legal abilities:

"He seized the strong points of a cause, and presented them with clearness and great compactness. His mind was logical and direct, and he did not indulge in extraneous discussion. Generalities and platitudes had no charms for him. An unfailing vein of humor never deserted him; and he was always able to chain the attention of court and jury, when the cause was the most uninteresting, by the appropriateness of his anecdotes.

"His power of comparison was large, and he rarely failed in a legal discussion to use that mode of reasoning. The framework of his mental and moral being was honesty, and a wrong cause was poorly defended by him. The ability which some eminent lawyers possess, of explaining away the bad points of a cause by ingenious sophistry, was denied him. In order to bring into full activity his great powers, it was necessary that he should be convinced of the right and justice of the matter which he advocated. When so convinced, whether the cause was great or small, he was usually successful . . .

"He hated wrong and oppression everywhere; and many a man whose fraudulent conduct was undergoing review in a court of justice has writhed under his terrific indignation and rebukes. He was the most simple and unostentatious of men in his habits, having few wants, and those easily supplied. To his honor be it said, that he never took from a client, even when the cause was gained, more than he thought the service was worth and the client could reasonably afford to pay. The people where he practised law were not rich, and his charges were always small."

In 1844 Lincoln had gone into law partnership with William H. Herndon, who was nine years his junior. Herndon was an ardent abolitionist, and he continually sought to persuade Lincoln to adopt a more vigorous attitude against slavery. As early as 1837, while a state legislator, Lincoln had made his position clear: he did not believe the federal government had any right to interfere with slavery within any of the states, and he equally felt that the abolitionists were causing more harm than good with their agitation to free the slaves. As a congressman, Lincoln had introduced a bill to free the slaves in the District of Columbia, but the bill had not been brought to a vote.

AT the age of forty-five, Lincoln was almost unknown nationally and had lost much of his political influence in Illinois. But the passage of the Kansas-Nebraska Act in 1854, sponsored by Illinois Democratic Senator Stephen A. Douglas, roused Lincoln to action and gave him his golden opportunity. Lincoln believed that the Act's repeal of the Missouri Compromise would permit the introduction of slavery into northern territories, and he blamed Douglas for trying to win the Democratic presidential nomination with Southern votes by promoting the measure.

Lincoln vs. Douglas

In the fall of 1854 Douglas attempted to explain to his Illinois constituents in a speech at the state fair at Springfield that he had sponsored the Kansas-Nebraska Act only to further the cause of democracy by allowing "popular sovereignty" to decide the slavery issue in the territories. Lincoln, chosen to reply to Douglas, made such an effective speech denouncing the "humbuggery" of the legislation that he at once became leader of the state's anti-Nebraska-Act forces. When Douglas again spoke in defense of the Act in Peoria a few days later, Lincoln followed him there and again debated him. Douglas tacitly conceded defeat on the issue by making no more speeches on the subject in Illinois.

Lincoln was once more elected to the legislature in 1854, but resigned shortly after to become a candidate for the U.S. Senate. Senators, of course, were elected not by the people but by the state legislature. To obtain the support of abolitionist legislators, Lincoln pledged to try to bar slavery from all the Western territories. But the legislature was too firmly in control of the Democratic party to permit the combination of Whigs and abolitionists to win Lincoln the senatorial seat.

Meantime the new, anti-slavery Republican party had come into being. Lincoln embraced the principles of the new party, and helped organize in Illinois. When the first national Republican Convention was held in Philadelphia in June 1856, the Illinois delegation supported Lincoln for the vice-presidential nomination, which, however, went to William L. Dayton. Lincoln, who did not attend the convention, was amazed when he received news that his name had been put in nomination for the nation's second highest office, and exclaimed: "No, it couldn't be: it must have been the *great* Lincoln from Massachusetts." (He was referring to Levi Lincoln, who had been governor of Massachusetts.)

When the Illinois Republican Convention in June 1858 nominated Lincoln to run for the U.S. Senate against Douglas, Lincoln won national attention with his acceptance speech. In it he declared:

". . . 'A house divided against itself cannot stand.' I believe this Government cannot endure permanently half slave and half free. I do not expect the Union to be dissolved,—I do not expect the house to fall; but I do expect it will cease to be divided. It will become all one thing, or all the other. Either the opponents of slavery will arrest the further spread of it, and place it where the public mind shall rest in the belief that it is in course of ultimate extinction, or its advocates will push it forward till it shall become alike lawful in all the States,—old as well as new, North as well as South."

A procession in front of Lincoln's Springfield home, probably during the 1858 campaign. (Note Lincoln in white at right of doorway.)

Abraham Lincoln and President Buchanan on the way to the partially completed Capitol for Lincoln's inauguration.

Lincoln's friends and supporters were dismayed by this forthright declaration of a position much stronger than that advocated by conservative members of the Republican party. They feared the speech would be a millstone around Lincoln's neck and would sink him into political oblivion. Informed of these apprehensions, Lincoln said:

"If I had to draw a pen across, and erase my whole life from existence, and I had one poor gift or choice left, as to what I should save from the wreck, I should choose that speech, and leave it to the world unerased."

The famous Lincoln-Douglas debates then ensued, with the two candidates battling all around Illinois. Douglas portrayed Lincoln as an out-and-out abolitionist, while Lincoln accused Douglas, as the author of the Kansas-Nebraska Act, of re-opening the slavery issue and threatening the country with disunion. So important were these debates that they drew national attention, and members of the legislature ran largely on their support of Lincoln or Douglas.

In the election, candidates who supported Lincoln received a majority of votes over Douglas's supporters. But because of inequitable districting of the state more Democratic candidates were elected, and so the legislature chose Douglas for senator.

In the winter of 1858–59 more and more people began to discuss the possibility of running Lincoln for President, but in the spring of 1859, Lincoln still was replying to inquirers that he was "not fit to be President." Nevertheless, in October he went on a speaking tour of Ohio and in December he traveled to Kansas.

Winning the Presidency

Early in 1860 he journeyed East, New York making Lincoln's acquaintance in February 1860. In his speech there he contended that only one thing would satisfy the South: "This, and this only: cease to call slavery *wrong*, and join them in calling it *right*." The day after the speech, the influential New York *Tribune* reported: "No man ever before made such an impression on his first appeal to a New York audience." After leaving New York, Lincoln went to visit his son Robert at Harvard, and made a series of speeches before Republican clubs in Connecticut, Rhode Island, and New Hampshire.

When the Republican state convention met in Decatur, Illinois, on May 9 and 10, 1860, Lincoln's followers tagged him with the nickname of "The Rail-splitter"—bringing to the convention two rails that he supposedly had made with his ax many years before.

The Republican National Convention opened in Chicago later the same month with New York Senator William H. Seward having the largest following among the delegates. On the first ballot Seward received 173½ votes to Lincoln's 102, with several other candidates trailing. To win Lincoln the nomination, Lincoln's friends promised cabinet posts to the leaders of the Pennsylvania, Indiana, and Ohio delegations. Although Lincoln, who was home in Springfield, had told his managers, "I authorize no bargains and will be bound by none," the promises were made, and as a result Lincoln passed Seward on the third ballot, after which the delegates nominated him by acclamation. Hannibal Hamlin of Maine was chosen as the vice-presidential nominee.

Meanwhile, the Buchanan-Douglas split within the Democratic party deepened into a Northern-Southern break. The Northern Democrats nominated Douglas for President, while the Southern Democrats nominated Vice President John C. Breckinridge. The remnants of the Whigs and Know-Nothings formed a new "Constitutional Union" party, nominating John Bell of Tennessee for the presidency.

Confident that the split among the Democrats would assure him of

The inauguration of Abraham Lincoln, March 4, 1861, showing part of the scaffolding on the roof of the Capitol for constructing the dome.

victory, Lincoln remained in Springfield throughout most of the campaign. When the votes were counted, Lincoln received more popular votes than any other candidate, although far from a majority. The election figures were as follows:

	Popular votes	Electoral votes
Lincoln	1,865,593	180
Douglas	1,382,713	12
Breckinridge	848,356	72
Bell	592,906	39

Shortly after his election Lincoln had a disturbing vision. He described the experience to his secretary, young John Hay:

"It was just after my election . . . I was well tired out, and went home to rest, throwing myself upon a lounge in my chamber. Opposite to where I lay was a bureau with a swinging glass upon it; and, in looking in that glass, I saw myself reflected nearly at full length; but my face, I noticed, had two separate and distinct images, the tip of the nose of one being about three inches from the tip of the other. I got up and looked in the glass; but the illusion vanished. On lying down again, I saw it a second time,—plainer, if possible, than before; and then I noticed that one of the faces was paler than the other. I got up, and the thing melted away; and I went off, and in the excitement of the hour forgot all about it,—nearly, but not quite, for the thing would once in a while come up, and give me a little pang, as though something uncomfortable had happened. When I went home, I told my wife about it; and a few days after I tried the experiment again, when, sure enough, the thing came back again; but I never succeeded in bringing the ghost back after that, though I once tried very industriously to show it to my wife, who was worried about it somewhat. She thought it was 'a sign' that I was to be elected to a second term of office, and that the paleness of one of the faces was an omen that I should not see life through the last term."

In the interval before assuming the office of President, Lincoln appointed his Cabinet. He made good on the political promises of his campaign managers by appointing the Republican leaders of Pennsylvania, Indiana, and Ohio, despite warnings by many persons that these men were not statesmen enough to help him meet the problems of the federal government.

A letter that he received from a little girl in New York caused him to change his appearance. She wrote that she thought he should grow a beard. The hitherto clean-shaven Lincoln decided to honor her request, perhaps feeling that the beard would add dignity. On his way to Washington, Lincoln invited the little girl to visit his train, showed her his beard, and gave her a kiss.

The political aspects of Lincoln's cabinet appointments and the incident with the beard and the little girl made many persons feel that the President-elect was too much a small-town politician to cope with the growing

President Lincoln and his Cabinet (left to right) Edward Bates, Attorney General; Gideon Welles, Secretary of the Navy; Montgomery Blair, Postmaster General; William H. Seward, Secretary of State; Salmon P. Chase, Secretary of the Treasury; President Lincoln; Lieutenant General Winfield Scott; Caleb B. Smith, Secretary of the Interior; and Simon Cameron, Secretary of War.

Grand ball in honor of the inauguration of President Lincoln in the hall especially erected for the occasion, March 4, 1861.

national crisis. In talks that he made in the various towns his train passed through en route to Washington, Lincoln called the crisis an "artificial" one that did not call for a warlike solution. Warned of a supposed plot against his life in Baltimore, Lincoln left his special train in Philadelphia and with one companion slipped through Baltimore at night to arrive unannounced in Washington.

Lincoln's Administration

THE four years and six weeks that Lincoln served as President were more critical than any faced by a previous President. In many ways the events of the time controlled Lincoln's actions and by their results made him a great figure. As he himself said in 1864:

"I claim not to have controlled events but confess plainly that events have controlled me. Now at the end of three years' struggle, the nation's condition is not what either party or any man devised or expected. God alone can claim it."

By the time Lincoln took office seven Southern states had left the Union and others were preparing to do so. Most federal forts in the South had been taken over by the secessionists, but Fort Sumter in the harbor of Charleston, South Carolina, still remained in federal hands. Lincoln decided to make it a symbol of his determination, ordering supplies sent to the beleaguered federal troops in the fort. When the federal supply ships arrived at Charleston, Confederate forces bombarded the fort, forcing its surrender.

The Moment of Decision

TAKING the fall of Fort Sumter as the signal that only force could preserve the Union, Lincoln promptly called for 75,000 volunteers to "suppress" the rebellion, and summoned a special session of Congress. On April 19 he ordered a blockade of Southern ports to cut them off from war supplies.

President Lincoln's visit to the Army of the Potomac, as his train arrived at the station in Frederick, Maryland.

Lincoln at the headquarters of the Army of the Potomac.

Council of War, May 21, 1864, including in the group General Grant, General Meade, and Assistant Secretary of War Charles Dana.

An artist's sketch of the cavalry of the Army of the Potomac passing in review before President Lincoln.

A historic photograph of President Lincoln with General McClellan and Allan Pinkerton, who later became noted for his private detective agency.

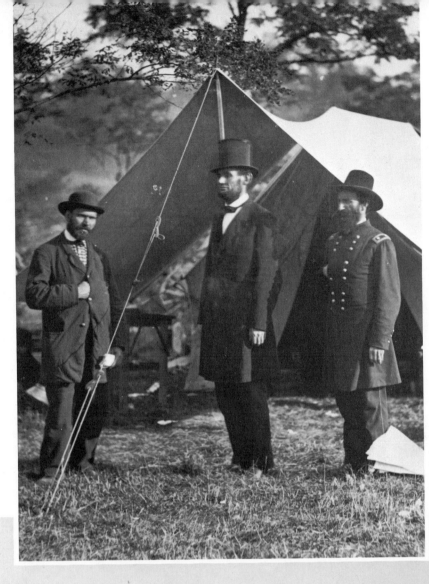

The crowd at Gettysburg awaiting the beginning of the ceremony dedicating the cemetery—the ceremony that became immortal through the address given by Lincoln.

The second inaugural address, delivered by President Lincoln in March, 1865—a notable photograph because the conspirators who committed the assassination were later discovered to be clearly identifiable in the audience.

Hundreds of thousands of volunteers answered Lincoln's call to arms, and Northerners hoped for an early end to the struggle. This optimism was extinguished in July by the disastrous battle of Bull Run.

By the summer of 1862, as Lincoln later explained, "Things had gone from bad to worse, until I felt that we had reached the end of our rope on the plan we had been pursuing; that we had about played our last card, and must change our tactics or lose the game."

The change of tactics that Lincoln devised was the Emancipation Proclamation. On September 22, 1862, Lincoln issued a proclamation warning that unless the rebelling states returned to the Union by January 1, 1863, he would issue an order freeing their slaves. When that day came and the war continued, Lincoln issued the Emancipation Proclamation.

In July 1863 Union troops turned back Confederate General Robert E. Lee's invasion of the North in the great battle of Gettysburg. Late that year Lincoln dedicated the cemetery at Gettysburg with his famous resolve "that these dead shall not have died in vain—that this nation, under God, shall have a new birth of freedom—and that government of the people, by the people, for the people, shall not perish from the earth."

Throughout the early years of the war Lincoln had searched in vain for a commanding general who could seize the initiative and crush the South. Early in 1864 he found the right man in Ulysses S. Grant, who had been winning battles in the West. With Grant in command and with Northern superiority in troops and supplies it became only a matter of time until the war would be ended.

In the election of 1864 the Democrats put up as their candidate for President one of Lincoln's former generals, George B. McClellan. As the election neared, one Union victory after another reinforced the people's faith in Lincoln, and he was re-elected with the huge majority of 212 electoral votes to McClellan's 21. In the popular vote Lincoln received 2,206,938 to his opponent's 1,803,787. In his second inaugural address Lincoln again spoke with unforgettable eloquence, this time on the theme of reconciliation:

"With malice toward none, with charity for all, with firmness in the right as God gives us to see the right, let us strive on to finish the work we are in, to bind up the nation's wounds, to care for him who shall have borne the battle and for his widow and his orphan, to do all which may achieve and cherish a just and lasting peace among ourselves and with all nations."

Final victory came a little over a month later when Lee surrendered to Grant at Appomattox Court House on April 9, 1865. But five days later the North's exultation was cut short. A brooding Southern sympathizer,

Second Term and Assassination

Ford's Theatre in Washington, the scene of the assassination, draped in mourning.

The funeral train that carried President Lincoln from Washington to his final resting place, Springfield, Illinois.

The Lincoln funeral procession in New York City.

Huge crowds entering the courthouse in Springfield, Illinois, to honor Lincoln, as he lay in state.

actor John Wilkes Booth, had long meditated an assassination conspiracy. Even though the Confederacy was beyond all help by the time Booth got his plot to the active stage, he pushed it through with the determination of a fanatic. Extraordinary bad luck and careless guards permitted the assassin to penetrate the presidential box at Ford's Theatre and fatally wound Lincoln with a pistol shot from behind. Booth temporarily escaped by a theatrical flourish, leaping from the box to the stage and fleeing through the wings to a waiting horse. Within a few days he was overtaken and slain. But Lincoln was dead—a tragic loss, as events proved, to the South as well as the North.

His body lay in state at the White House and Capitol, and was borne across the country to Springfield in a train draped in black. Millions of mourners lined the route of the 1700-mile journey, their sorrow finding an echo in Walt Whitman's lines:

> Oh Captain! my Captain! our fearful trip is done,
> The ship has weather'd every rack, the prize we sought is won,
> The port is near, the bells I hear, the people all exulting,
> While follow eyes the steady keel, the vessel grim and daring;
>   But O heart! heart! heart!
>   O the bleeding drops of red,
>   Where on the deck my Captain lies,
>   Fallen cold and dead.

−*Mathew B. Brady*

334 JAMES BUCHANAN

James Buchanan

The Fifteenth President of the United States
1857–61

1791 (April 23) Born near Mercersburg, Pennsylvania.

1809 Graduated from Dickinson College.

1812 Began to practice law in Lancaster, Pennsylvania.

1814–16 Member of the Pennsylvania legislature.

1821–31 U.S. representative from Pennsylvania.

1832–33 U.S. minister to Russia.

1834–45 U.S. senator from Pennsylvania.

1845–49 Secretary of State under President Polk.

1853–56 U.S. minister to England.

1857–61 Fifteenth President of the United States.

1868 (June 1) Died at his home, Wheatland, near Lancaster, Pennsylvania.

Leading Officials in Buchanan's Administration

Office	Name	Years Served
Chief Justice	Roger B. Taney	1836-1864
Vice-President	John C. Breckinridge	1857-1861
Secretary of State	Lewis Cass	1857-1860
	Jeremiah S. Black	1860-1861
Secretary of the Treasury	Howell Cobb	1857-1860
	Phillip F. Thomas	1860-1861
	John A. Dix	1861
Secretary of War	John B. Floyd	1857-1861
	Joseph Holt	1861
Attorney General	Jeremiah S. Black	1857-1860
	Edwin M. Stanton	1860-1861
Secretary of the Navy	Isaac Toucey	1857-1861
Postmaster General	Aaron V. Brown	1857-1859
	Joseph Holt	1859-1861
	Horatio King	1861
Secretary of the Interior	Jacob Thompson	1857-1861

Wheatland, near Lancaster, Pennsylvania, the residence of James Buchanan.

Last of the weak, compromising Presidents elected by a divided country in the years before the Civil War, James Buchanan was, like Pierce, a Northern Democrat, more sympathetic to Southern slave-owners than to Northern abolitionists. When Buchanan unsuccessfully tried to push through the admission of Kansas as a slave state, he infuriated the North and shattered the Democratic party. As the Southern states seceded from the Union one by one in the last months of his administration, Buchanan helplessly stood by, unable to take resolute action.

The only President who never married, Buchanan devoted his life to public service as congressman, senator, diplomat, and Secretary of State before coming to the White House. A friend facetiously said of Buchanan that ever since he had been old enough to marry he had been "wedded to the Constitution."

Legislator, Diplomat, and Cabinet Member

THE eldest son in a family of eleven children, James Buchanan was born in a tiny one-room log cabin in the Blue Mountain country near Mercersburg, Pennsylvania, on April 23, 1791. His father was an Irish immigrant who developed a small frontier trading post into a thriving business. Working in his father's store, young Jimmie learned arithmetic and bookkeeping, which he used to keep meticulous personal accounts throughout his life.

As a youth, he showed a rebellious streak, being expelled from Dickinson College in Carlisle, Pennsylvania, at the end of his first year because of insubordination to his teachers. He was reinstated at the college when he pledged to settle down and work hard. Keeping his promise, he was graduated the next year at the age of eighteen. After studying law for the next three years, he began practice in 1812 in Lancaster, Pennsylvania, where he also bought a part-interest in a tavern.

Volunteering for the War of 1812, he helped defend Baltimore from British attack, then returned to Lancaster and won election to the state legislature in 1814 as a member of the Federalist party. After two terms in the legislature, Buchanan left politics to build a law practice. He proved an able attorney, winning case after case, until at twenty-seven, his income was $8000 a year—a substantial amount in those days. He lived frugally, slowly accumulating a sizable fortune.

In 1818 Buchanan fell in love. The object of his affections was Ann Coleman, daughter of an extremely wealthy iron-mill owner of Lancaster.

This was reaching high. The girl's parents evidently disapproved, believing that Buchanan was a fortune hunter. Ann broke the engagement, writing to Buchanan that she believed he loved her money more than he did her. Shortly thereafter she died under mysterious circumstances, rumors saying that she had committed suicide from grief. The Colemans refused to let Buchanan attend the funeral. He wrote, "I feel that happiness has fled from me forever," and never again became engaged, although he carried on many flirtations.

Resuming his interest in politics, Buchanan won election to Congress in 1820 as a candidate of the Federalist party, but did not take office until December 1821. Buchanan became a supporter of Andrew Jackson in 1824, and personally tried to swing Henry Clay to Jackson's side in the disputed presidential election of that year. Four years later he switched to the new Democratic party, winning election to the House of Representatives for the fifth time.

For his services to Jackson, Buchanan was rewarded by appointment as U.S. minister to Russia. Well-received at the Russian court in 1832, he succeeded in negotiating the first trade treaty between the United States and Russia. But the politically ambitious Buchanan did not wish to remain away from the United States for too long for fear he would be forgotten, and returned home in 1833.

He was elected by the state legislature to the U.S. Senate in 1834, and served in that body for the next eleven years under Presidents Jackson, Van Buren, Harrison, and Tyler. He became a leading member of the conservative wing of the Democratic party, holding the important chairmanship of the Senate Foreign Relations Committee. A Northern supporter of the slave interests, Buchanan backed legislation curbing the activities of abolitionists. During this period he declined offers of appointment by Van Buren as Attorney General and by Tyler as an associate justice of the Supreme Court.

After campaigning for Polk in the presidential election of 1844, Buchanan received appointment as Secretary of State. Much of the credit for Polk's successful territorial expansion program was due to Buchanan's effort, but the two men often fought, as Polk feared the Pennsylvanian was using his cabinet post as a stepping-stone to the presidency. Buchanan complained to a friend: "My life is that of a galley slave."

When he failed to win the Democratic presidential nomination in 1848, Buchanan retired to Wheatland, an estate near Lancaster, Pennsylvania.

A sketch of the slaughter of wild horses in the West during the middle 1800's.

The "Sage of Wheatland," as he became known, narrowly missed the Democratic nomination in 1852, and at the age of sixty-two was once more given a diplomatic mission abroad, this time as U.S. minister to Great Britain. There he gained unexpected notoriety by joining with his ministerial colleagues to France and Spain, both militant pro-slavery Southerners, in writing the "Ostend Manifesto." Pushing "manifest destiny" to its rashest limits, the three diplomats advocated purchase of Cuba from Spain and asserted that if Spain refused to sell "we shall be justified in wresting" the island from its owners. Widely denounced by anti-slavery Northerners, the Ostend Manifesto was cheered in the South.

At the Democratic National Convention in Cincinnati in June 1856, both the Ostend Manifesto and Buchanan's recent absence from the country stood him in good stead. His two chief rivals, President Pierce and Senator Stephen A. Douglas, were tainted by their espousal of the pro-slavery cause in Kansas, where a bitter little civil war had broken out. Possessing the indispensable attributes of being unconnected with "bleeding Kansas" and yet fully acceptable to the South, Buchanan won the nomination.

Against him in the election were arrayed two new parties, fragmented off the now defunct Whigs. The anti-slavery Republican party nominated John C. Frémont, while the more conservative Whigs, calling themselves "Know-Nothings," picked former President Millard Fillmore. Buchanan won easily, though outpolled by the combined totals of his opponents, in an election which clearly showed the depth of division within the nation:

Buchanan	1,832,955 popular votes	174 electoral votes
Frémont	1,339,932	114
Fillmore	871,731	8

This fascinating inaugural scene shows the Buchanan parade featuring a ship model to commemorate Admiral Peary's contact with Japan, opening that area to trade.
—*Frank Leslie's Illustrated Newspaper*

Ornate uniforms and gowns are in evidence at this Presidential reception.

Frémont carried eleven free states, Buchanan only five. Buchanan carried every slave state except Maryland, which went to Fillmore.

SIXTY-FIVE years old, Buchanan had finally achieved his lifelong ambition. In his inaugural address he sought to place himself above party conflict by announcing that he would not be a candidate for re-election in 1860, but in so doing only succeeded in sacrificing the leadership of his own party, which passed to Stephen A. Douglas. Discussing the bitter Kansas dispute, Buchanan called upon the nation to regard it as a judicial question to be settled by the Supreme Court, saying, "To their decision, in common with all good citizens, I shall cheerfully submit, whatever this may be . . ." Actually Chief Justice Roger Taney had already informed the President-elect that the Court was about to hand down a pro-slavery decision in the Dred Scott case, holding that Congress did not have power to prohibit slavery in the territories and thereby nullifying the Missouri Compromise of 1820. When the Court's decision was announced, angry Northerners accused Buchanan of double-dealing in trying to make the country accept in advance a decision that could so decisively extend slavery.

Buchanan also announced his intention to try to purchase both Cuba and Alaska, but negotiations with Spain and Russia to these ends did not succeed.

In his inaugural he also boasted that "Our present financial condition is without parallel in history," thanks to the large surplus in the federal treasury. Within a few months Buchanan was embarrassed by the Panic of 1857 and the depression following it, which drove many businessmen into bankruptcy, threw thousands out of work, and swiftly converted the surplus in the treasury into a deficit of $27 million.

With the Democrats holding a majority in both houses, Buchanan decided to try to put an end to the Kansas agitation by obtaining the territory's admission as a slave state. But when he submitted the pro-slavery Lecompton Constitution to Congress, Northern Democrats revolted, joining Republicans in the House of Representatives to defeat the bill. Buchanan forces revived the bill with an additional feature, amounting to a bribe of several million acres to finance the new state government. But Kansans voted down the Lecompton Constitution, and in the elections of

Buchanan's Administration

339

1858 anti-Lecompton candidates won victories throughout the North. Stephen A. Douglas, who had led the fight against Lecompton in the Senate, triumphed over a Buchanan-backed candidate and over the Republican candidate, Abraham Lincoln. The memorable Lincoln-Douglas debates, filled with attacks on the Buchanan administration's program, helped solidify Northern opinion against the President.

During his remaining two years in office Buchanan slipped more and more into the role of figurehead. John Brown's raid on Harpers Ferry, in an attempt to stir up a slave insurrection, convinced many Southerners that secession from the Union was their only means of protecting themselves from Northern abolitionists. Secession was openly discussed throughout the South, and several Southern legislatures passed resolutions pledging secession and co-operation in case of the election of a "Black Republican" in 1860. In South Carolina, Mississippi, and a few other states, appropriations for military preparedness were passed.

Buchanan believed secession was unconstitutional, but he also believed that it was unconstitutional for the federal government to use force against secession. He was unwilling to stretch the Constitution by taking into his own hands powers that might have halted the spreading conflagration, and he did little but wait in vain for Congress to act. Meantime the fatal split in the Democratic party, in good part the result of Buchanan's inept handling of the Kansas issue, assured the election of Lincoln, the "Black Republican" the Southern firebrands had warned against. South Carolina at once set in motion steps to secede. Buchanan warned of an impending "open war by the North to abolish slavery in the South," and called futilely for amendments to the Constitution to compromise the issues. His one firm resolve was to postpone fighting until he was out of office, so that the onus of civil war would fall on the Republicans.

Breathing a sigh of relief when March 4, 1861, finally arrived, Buchanan turned the government over to Lincoln with the comment: "If you are as happy in entering the White House as I shall feel on returning to Wheatland, you are a happy man indeed."

But Buchanan's remaining years were not as happy as he had anticipated. Though he supported the Union during the war, he spent much of his time defending himself from accusations that his unwillingness to act had helped cause the war. Shortly before his death in 1868, at the age of seventy-seven, he asserted: "I have always felt and still feel that I discharged every public duty imposed on me conscientiously. I have no regret for any public act of my life, and history will vindicate my memory."

A painting of a party of dignitaries who were sent by Japan in 1860 to visit Washington, D.C. to make a trade treaty with the United States, arriving by lorry with tons of luggage and gifts.

In May, 1860, the Japanese trade mission arrived in Washington, D. C., with a full retinue of officials, servants and cooks, plus eighty tons of luggage, which the servants sorted out in the ballroom of the Willard Hotel.

A special kitchen was fitted out in the Willard Hotel for use by the Japanese cooks.

The curiosity of the Japanese was aroused by the sight of a maid operating a sewing machine at the Willard Hotel, where they stayed in Washington.

—Frank Leslie's Illustrated Newspaper

Members of the first Japanese Treaty Commission to the United States in the Washington Navy Yard in 1860.

341

342 FRANKLIN PIERCE

Franklin Pierce

The Fourteenth President of the United States
1853–57

1804 (November 23) Born in Hillsboro, New Hampshire.

1824 Graduated from Bowdoin College.

1827 Admitted to the bar to practice law.

1829–33 Member of New Hampshire state legislature.

1833–37 U.S. representative from New Hampshire.

1834 (November 10) Married Jane Means Appleton.

1837–42 U.S. senator from New Hampshire.

1846–48 Served as a brigadier general in the Mexican War.

1850 President of state constitutional convention.

1853–57 Fourteenth President of the United States.

1869 (October 8) Died in Concord, New Hampshire.

Leading Officials in Pierce's Administration

Office	Name	Years Served
Chief Justice	Roger B. Taney	1836-1864
Vice-President	William R. D. King	1853
Secretary of State	William L. Marcy	1853-1857
Secretary of the Treasury	James Guthrie	1853-1857
Secretary of War	Jefferson Davis	1853-1857
Attorney General	Caleb Cushing	1853-1857
Secretary of the Navy	James C. Dobbin	1853-1857
Postmaster General	James Campbell	1853-1857
Secretary of the Interior	Robert McClelland	1853-1857

A Northern Democrat who supported the extension of slavery, Franklin Pierce was chosen as a dark horse presidential nominee by his party in order to win both Northern and Southern votes. He praised the Compromise of 1850 and promised to prevent slavery from again becoming a national issue, and as a result, swept into office with the greatest electoral landslide since Monroe.

A politician's politician, the dark, curly-haired Pierce never lost an election. He was a master at knowing how to get along with people—evidenced by the fact that he is the only President in history who served out a complete term in office without having to make a single change in his Cabinet.

But he misjudged the temper of the times. He regarded the abolitionists as a lunatic fringe who should be ignored. And, when he signed the Kansas-Nebraska Act and the repeal of the Missouri Compromise of 1820, he unwittingly let loose a storm that made slavery a greater national issue than ever before.

Politician and Mexican War General

ONE of a family of nine children, Franklin Pierce was born in Hillsboro, New Hampshire, on November 23, 1804. His father, Benjamin Pierce, was a Revolutionary War veteran, a farmer, a tavern-keeper, and a leader of the Democratic-Republican party in New Hampshire. Young Frank was given a good education in private schools, and at fifteen was

The boyhood home of Franklin Pierce in Hillsboro, New Hampshire.

Law office first occupied by General Pierce.

sent off to Bowdoin College, where his college mates included Henry
Wadsworth Longfellow and Nathaniel Hawthorne. At his graduation in
1824, the nineteen-year-old Pierce ranked third in his class.

Pierce next began studying law, and in 1827, the same year his father
was elected governor of New Hampshire, he was admitted to the bar
and opened a law office in Hillsboro. Two years later when his father successfully ran for re-election, the twenty-four-year-old Frank also was on the
ticket, winning a seat in the legislature. He was re-elected three times, and
at the age of twenty-six was chosen speaker of the lower house, an office
he held for two sessions.

In 1833, when Pierce was twenty-eight, he was elected to Congress as
a Jackson Democrat. He voted consistently for administration-supported
measures, achieving a reputation as a loyal party man and easily winning
re-election in 1835.

On November 10, 1834, just before his thirtieth birthday, Pierce married Jane Means Appleton, daughter of the late president of Bowdoin
College. They honeymooned en route to Washington and did not set
up housekeeping in Hillsboro until the next spring. His wife, who suffered
from tuberculosis and did not like the national capital, did not accompany
him on his return to Washington in 1835. Pierce proceeded to live a
boisterous life with other bachelor congressmen, often drinking more than
he could hold—a problem that he fought for the rest of his life.

Pierce's political fortunes received a new boost in 1836 when the state
legislature elected him to the U.S. Senate. As the youngest senator in
Washington, the thirty-two-year-old Pierce was overshadowed by such
giants as Clay, Calhoun, and Webster, and, although he was a persuasive
orator in his own right, he had few opportunities to demonstrate his
ability. His wife constantly nagged him to give up his political career and
return to New Hampshire, which he finally did by resigning from the
Senate in 1842.

Pierce left Washington, but he did not give up politics. As state chairman of the Democratic party he became the political boss of New Hampshire. In 1845 he accepted appointment as U.S. district attorney for New

The building in Concord, New
Hampshire, where Pierce had his
law office (to the left of the book
store on the corner).

345

Hampshire, but the following year turned down an offer by President Polk to join the Cabinet as Attorney General of the United States.

Although Pierce had had no other military experience than a nominal appointment as a militia colonel, he received a commission from Polk in February 1847 as a colonel in the volunteer army to fight in the Mexican War. Less than a month later he was promoted to brigadier general. Late in June, Pierce and his New England brigade joined Winfield Scott in the invasion of central Mexico, where in the battle of Contreras in August, Pierce was injured when his horse fell, and fainted from the pain. While pursuing the enemy the next day, he again fainted in front of his troops. These fainting incidents later brought political charges that he was a coward.

Back in New Hampshire in 1848, Pierce resumed his position as head of the Democratic party in the state. He declined nomination as governor in 1848, but two years later presided at a convention to revise the state constitution.

When Pierce and his friends began scheming to obtain the Democratic presidential nomination at Baltimore in 1852, they did not let Mrs. Pierce know about it for fear she would squelch the plan. In any case the choice of the convention seemed to lie entirely between James Buchanan and Lewis Cass. But in ballot after ballot the two main contenders fought each other to a standstill, neither mustering the needed two-thirds majority. On the thirty-fifth ballot Pierce's friends entered his name. By the forty-ninth ballot the entire convention agreed on Pierce as the dark horse who could pull together the warring factions of the party. Pierce's wife collapsed when she heard the news, and Pierce denied to her that he had sought the nomination. Their eleven-year-old son Benjamin added fuel to the flames of family discord when he wrote to his mother: "I hope he won't be elected for I should not like to be at Washington and I know you would not either."

The ensuing campaign was particularly dirty, with unwarranted calumnies thrown both at Pierce and at his Whig opponent, Lieutenant General Winfield Scott. But the Whig party was in a state of disintegration, and Pierce won the election easily. He received a comfortable margin in the popular vote—1,601,117 to Scott's 1,385,453; and a landslide in the electoral vote—254 to 42, carrying all but four states.

Pierce's Administration

PIERCE entered the White House bearing the marks of a personal tragedy that historians believe significantly contributed to destroying his confidence in himself. While President-elect, Pierce had been traveling from Boston to Concord by train with his wife and only son (two other Pierce children had died as infants). Suddenly the railroad car in which the Pierces were riding toppled off the tracks. Pierce and his wife were only slightly injured, but eleven-year-old Benjamin was killed before their eyes. In the days that followed, the deeply religious Mrs. Pierce came to the conclusion that it had been God's will that the boy should die so that concern for the boy's welfare could not distract Pierce from his presidential duties. Pierce suffered a sense of guilt for his son's death, and his sorrowing wife did not attend his inaugural or take part in White House social affairs for the next two years.

Using his most practiced courtroom oratory, the forty-eight-year-old Pierce broke precedent by committing to memory his inaugural address and delivering it without notes. He began it with the words:

"It is a relief to feel that no heart but my own can know the personal regret and bitter sorrow over which I have been borne to a position so suitable for others rather than desirable for myself."

"No North, no South, no East, no West under the Constitution; but a sacred maintenance of the common bond, and a true devotion to the common brotherhood." One of the principles enunciated by Franklin Pierce in 1852 that could well be repeated today.

Referring to the slavery issue, Pierce said:

"I believe that involuntary servitude, as it exists in different States of this Confederacy, is recognized by the Constitution. I believe that it stands like any other admitted right, and that the States where it exists are entitled to efficient remedies to enforce the constitutional provisions. I hold that the laws of 1850, commonly called the 'compromise measures,' are strictly constitutional and to be unhesitatingly carried into effect. . . . I fervently hope that the question is at rest, and that no sectional or ambitious or fanatical excitement may again threaten the durability of our institutions or obscure the light of our prosperity."

The President's Ball at the White House during the Pierce administration.

During the first half of Pierce's administration the Democrats controlled both houses of Congress, but they were so divided that it was difficult for Pierce to get legislation enacted. However, he exerted great effort in helping Illinois Senator Stephen A. Douglas push through the pro-slavery Kansas-Nebraska Act in 1854, which repealed the Missouri Compromise of 1820, enabling Kansas to become a slave state if the settlers voted for it. "Border ruffians" promptly infiltrated from the slave state of Missouri and set up a pro-slavery government, with Pierce upholding their right to do so despite the outcries of anti-slavery Kansans and Northerners everywhere.

It was a serious mistake. The outrages being committed in Kansas contributed to the formation of the new Republican party. At the mid-term congressional elections in 1854, several Democratic congressmen lost seats to Republicans and Know-Nothings.

Pierce had hoped to be another Polk, and in his inaugural address had rattled the saber of "manifest destiny," saying:

". . . the policy of my Administration will not be controlled by any timid forebodings of evil from expansion. Indeed, it is not to be disguised that our attitude as a nation and our position on the globe render the acquisition of certain possessions not within our jurisdiction eminently important for our protection, if not in the future essential for the preservation of the rights of commerce and the peace of the world."

Endeavoring to follow through on his promise of expansion, Pierce offered $50 million to Mexico for much of the northern area of that country and for lower California. But these negotiations resulted only in the Gadsden Purchase of 1854, in which $10 million was paid for a strip of land across southern Arizona and New Mexico to be used as the right of way for a new railroad to the Pacific Coast.

Pierce also made unsuccessful efforts to acquire Cuba, largely because the Southern states feared that Spain was about to free the Negro slaves on that island, and that this in turn might lead to Negro uprisings in the South.

When Hawaii applied for admission to the Union on the condition that it be allowed immediately to become a state, Pierce rejected the proposal.

Following the precedent of previous Democratic Presidents, Pierce disapproved of using federal funds to pay for internal improvements. The resulting economies enabled him to reduce the national debt from $60 million to $11 million during his four years in office.

Pierce endeavored to win popularity in the West and in the North by favoring land grants to railroads being pushed toward the Pacific. He also made available federal funds to begin construction on the Atlantic cable to provide better communication with Europe.

Through negotiation of many trade treaties with other countries, Pierce did much to encourage the expansion of trade. One of the most far-reaching of these treaties was that negotiated by Commodore Matthew Perry, opening the ports of Japan.

When the Democratic National Convention met in Cincinnati in June 1856, Pierce anticipated renomination. But his close association in Northern minds with the Kansas issue damaged his value as a candidate, and to his great disappointment the nomination went to James Buchanan.

Bitter Last Years

PIERCE and his wife had lived in the White House with New England frugality, managing to save about half of his $25,000-a-year salary. They were able to retire comfortably on this and money he had saved from his law practice, making two long trips abroad before settling down in Concord.

Refusing all suggestions from friends that he again seek the presidential nomination in 1860, he proposed instead that his former Secretary of War, Jefferson Davis, would be the best candidate that the Democrats could choose.

Even with the onset of the Civil War, Pierce maintained his unpopular stand, privately and publicly opposing the use of force by the North and denouncing the Emancipation Proclamation as unconstitutional. He came to be regarded as a traitor of sorts and was shunned by former friends. Following the death of his wife in 1863, he began to drink more heavily. Feelings remained so bitter toward him in his native state that more than half a century went by after his death in 1869 before a statue was erected in his honor.

His close friend Nathaniel Hawthorne sought to explain Pierce in these words:

". . . it would ruin a noble character (though one of limited scope) for him to admit any ideas that were not entertained by the fathers of the Constitution and the Republic. . . . There is a certain steadfastness and integrity with regard to a man's own nature (when it is such a peculiar nature as that of Pierce) which seems to me more sacred and valuable than the faculty of adapting one's self to new ideas, however true they may turn out to be."

Mrs. Franklin Pierce (Jane Means Appleton), a very religious woman who never wanted to live in Washington.

350 MILLARD FILLMORE

Millard Fillmore

The Thirteenth President of the United States
1850-53

1800 (January 7) Born in Cayuga County, New York.

1815-19 Apprenticed to a cloth-maker.

1823 Admitted to the bar to practice law in New York.

1826 (February 5) Married Abigail Powers.

1828-31 Member of New York state legislature.

1833-35; 1837-43 U.S. representative from New York.

1848 Comptroller of the state of New York.

1849-50 Vice President of the United States.

1850-53 Thirteenth President of the United States.

1856 Defeated for election as President as candidate of the
    American and Whig parties.

1858 (February 10) Married Caroline McIntosh.

1874 (March 8) Died in Buffalo, New York.

Leading Officials in
Fillmore's Administration

Office	Name	Years Served
Chief Justice	Roger B. Taney	1836-1864
Vice-President	*None*	
Secretary of State	Daniel Webster	1850-1852
	Edward Everett	1852-1853
Secretary of the Treasury	Thomas Corwin	1850-1853
Secretary of War	Charles M. Conrad	1850-1853
Attorney General	John J. Crittenden	1850-1853
Secretary of the Navy	William A. Graham	1850-1852
	John P. Kennedy	1852-1853
Postmaster General	Nathan K. Hall	1850-1852
	Samuel D. Hubbard	1852-1853
Secretary of the Interior	T. M. T. McKennan	1850
	A. H. H. Stuart	1850-1853

S ix feet tall, with blue eyes and a handsome face, Millard Fillmore was more impressive in appearance than he was in accomplishment. He came to the presidency by the only road available to a man of his limited ability—by succeeding to the office upon the death of President Zachary Taylor. Although, as President, Fillmore did everything that he was told to do by the leaders of the Whig party, they refused to give him a chance to run for office on his own at the next election.

From Cloth-Maker's Apprentice to White House

MILLARD FILLMORE was born on January 7, 1800, in Cayuga County, New York, the son of a poor frontier farmer. As a small boy he helped his father clear the land and raise the crops. But with nine children in the family, there was hardly enough food to go around, so at fourteen Millard was apprenticed to a cloth-maker.

At nineteen he fell in love with Abigail Powers, a schoolteacher, two years older than himself. Under her inspiration he purchased his freedom from apprenticeship for $30, bought a dictionary, and obtained a job teaching school.

Presently he won the friendship of a county judge who took the boy into his office to study law. By the time he was twenty-three, Fillmore had learned enough to be admitted to the bar and opened a law office in East Aurora, New York. The youthful lawyer had slow going building his practice, but by 1826 he felt sufficiently established to marry Abigail.

Entering politics in 1828, Fillmore won election to the state legislature. Re-elected twice, he made his most important contribution by sponsorship of legislation to end imprisonment of debtors. In 1830 Fillmore moved to the rapidly growing town of Buffalo where he established a profitable law partnership with Nathan K. Hall, who later served as Postmaster General in Fillmore's Cabinet.

The rising young politician next was elected to Congress in 1832 as a member of the newly formed Whig party. Defeated for re-election in 1834, he regained his congressional seat in 1836 and was re-elected three successive times after that. When the Whigs controlled Congress under President Tyler, Fillmore became chairman of the powerful House Ways and Means Committee. In that post he pushed through protective tariff bills that twice were vetoed by Tyler, and authored the tariff bill finally approved in 1842.

After retiring from Congress in 1843, Fillmore unsuccessfully sought the Whig vice-presidential nomination in 1844. He accepted his party's nomination for governor of New York, but was defeated by the Democratic candidate, Silas Wright. After three years devoted to his law practice and to mending his political fences, he returned to public office with his election in 1847 as state comptroller.

At the Whig National Convention in 1848, Fillmore was chosen as the vice-presidential candidate, and aided in winning New York's crucial electoral vote for the Whig ticket. After assuming office as Vice President in 1849, Fillmore presided over the debates in the Senate that led to the Compromise of 1850.

Fillmore's Administration

THE fifty-year-old Fillmore took the oath of office as President on July 10, 1850, the day after Taylor's death. A supporter of the Compromise, despite his own anti-slavery views, he believed the members of Taylor's Cabinet

Abigail Powers Fillmore, first wife of President Fillmore.

had influenced the late President against it. He accepted the resignations of all the department heads and appointed an entirely new Cabinet —the first and only time that a Vice President succeeding to the Presidency has made such a sweeping change upon assuming office.

In September, Fillmore signed into law the group of measures that made up the Compromise of 1850: admission of California as a free state; establishment of territories in Utah and New Mexico with the provision that neither could pass legislation with respect to slavery; annulment of Texas' claim to New Mexico with payment to Texas of an indemnity of $10 million, prohibition of the slave trade, but continuance of slavery, in the District of Columbia; and finally, a new Fugitive Slave Law that made federal officials responsible for recovering runaway slaves.

Not recognizing that he had signed his own and his party's political death warrant with these measures, more a capitulation to Southern slave

CONGRESSIONAL SCALES,
A TRUE BALANCE.

interests than a compromise, Fillmore in his first annual message to Congress said:

"I believe that a great majority of our fellow-citizens . . . in the main approve and are prepared in all respects to sustain these enactments . . . The series of measures . . . are regarded by me as a settlement in principle and substance—a final settlement of the dangerous and exciting subjects which they embraced."

But the new Fugitive Slave Law caused Northern abolitionists to become even more militant. The underground railway came into being to help slaves escape from the South. Mobs attacked federal marshals to free runaway slaves from custody. And Harriet Beecher Stowe's *Uncle Tom's Cabin,* inspired by the law, aroused hatred for slavery throughout the North.

Fillmore continued to stand firm in his belief in the Compromise, however, and in his second annual message to Congress in December 1851, he reiterated his belief that the Compromise represented a "final settlement" of the differences between North and South.

In June 1852, the Whig party met in national convention at Baltimore. The main contenders for the presidential nomination in order of their strength on the first ballot were Fillmore, General Winfield Scott, and Secretary of State Daniel Webster. Fifty-three ballots later, with the party irretrievably torn by dissension, the Whigs had decided to dump Fillmore and stake their chances on the only kind of candidate who had ever won for them—a war hero—General Scott. But the convention hung a millstone around Scott's neck by adopting a platform that echoed Fillmore's praise of the Compromise of 1850 and pledged strict enforcement of the Fugitive Slave Law. The deaths of Henry Clay and Daniel Webster within the next few months and the landslide defeat of Scott in the national election in November brought an end to the political effectiveness of the Whig party.

Mary Abigail Fillmore, daughter of President Fillmore.

Fillmore's Last Years

His wife died less than a month after Fillmore had turned the government over to his Democratic successor, Franklin Pierce, in March 1853. The ex-President retired to Buffalo and resumed his law practice.

In 1856 Fillmore accepted the presidential nomination of the anti-Catholic, anti-immigrant American party, whose followers were called the Know-Nothings, and he also received the nomination of what was left of the Whig party. But Fillmore ran a poor third behind the Democratic candidate James Buchanan and the Republican candidate John Frémont, carrying only the state of Maryland.

Fillmore then receded into obscurity. In 1858 he married a wealthy widow, Mrs. Caroline McIntosh, thirteen years younger than himself. He continued to make his views known on national politics, but few listened. When the seventy-four-year-old Fillmore died in Buffalo on March 8, 1874, President Grant's eulogy was perfunctory:

"The long-continued and useful public service and eminent purity of character of the deceased ex-President will be remembered beyond the days of mourning in which a nation will be thrown by the event which is thus announced."

Caroline Carmichael McIntosh, who became the second wife of Millard Fillmore.

—*Mathew B. Brady*

356 ZACHARY TAYLOR

Zachary Taylor

The Twelfth President of the United States
1849–50

1784 (November 24) Born in Orange County, Virginia.

1808–48 Served in U.S. Army, rising from lieutenant to major general.

1810 (June 21) Married Margaret Smith.

1847 (February 22–23) Won the battle of Buena Vista.

1849–50 Twelfth President of the United States.

1850 (July 9) Died in Washington, D.C.

Leading Officials in
Taylor's Administration

Office	Name	Years Served
Chief Justice	Roger B. Taney	1836-1864
Vice-President	Millard Fillmore	1849-1850
Secretary of State	John M. Clayton	1849-1850
Secretary of the Treasury	W. M. Meredith	1849-1850
Secretary of War	G. W. Crawford	1849-1850
Attorney General	Reverdy Johnson	1849-1850
Secretary of the Navy	William B. Preston	1849-1850
Postmaster General	Jacob Collamer	1849-1850
Secretary of the Interior	Thomas Ewing	1849-1850

Zachary Taylor was the first President elected to office with no previous political experience. As a result, he was ill-prepared for the politics and problems involved. Like William Henry Harrison, Taylor was chosen by the Whigs as their presidential candidate solely because he was a war hero. And, like Harrison, he died in the White House before he really had an opportunity to prove whether or not he might have coped more effectively than his successors with the issues that were carrying the nation toward civil war.

Taylor spent forty years in the Army—fighting Indians, commanding frontier posts, and winning glory in the Mexican War by the victory of Buena Vista, where his troops were outnumbered four to one. He was called "Old Rough and Ready" by his men because of his frontier bluntness and his disregard of dress—he preferred civilian clothes to a uniform even in battle. Short and plump, he had none of the appearance of a military hero and had to be given a leg-up by his orderly when he mounted a horse.

A Frontier Soldier

THE youngest of three sons in a family of nine children, Zachary Taylor was born on November 24, 1784, on a farm in Orange County, Virginia. When less than a year old, he was taken west by his family to settle near Louisville, Kentucky, on several thousand acres of land that his father, Colonel Richard Taylor, had received as a bonus for his services in the Revolutionary War. Because there were no schools on the Kentucky frontier, the boy grew up with only a rudimentary education provided by tutors that his father hired from time to time.

When Taylor was twenty-three, he received a commission as a first lieutenant in the U.S. Army through the influence of his relative, James Madison, who was then Secretary of State. Two years later, in 1810, he was promoted to captain.

Also in 1810 Taylor married Margaret Smith, who shared the hardships of life in frontier military posts, and who, like Mrs. Andrew Jackson, enjoyed smoking a corncob pipe. The Taylors had six children. Their only son, Richard, later became a lieutenant general in the Confederate Army. In 1835, against her father's wishes, one of their daughters, Sarah, married Lieutenant Jefferson Davis, the future President of the Confederacy. Sarah died three months after the marriage. Taylor and Davis were not reconciled until twelve years later at the battle of Buena Vista where Davis, then a colonel, distinguished himself.

In the War of 1812, Taylor was promoted to the temporary rank of major for his skill in the defense of Fort Harrison, Indiana, from attacks by the Shawnee Chief Tecumseh. At the end of the war, when his rank was reduced to captain, he resigned from the Army, but resumed his military career a year later when his commission as a major was restored. In 1819, Taylor was advanced to lieutenant colonel, but thirteen years went by before he was made a full colonel in 1832 at the time of the Black Hawk War. Taylor led his regiment, the 1st Infantry, to victory, personally accepting the surrender of Chief Black Hawk. Five years later he was sent to Florida to fight the Seminole Indians, and after defeating them on Christmas Day in 1837, was promoted to brigadier general and given command of all the troops in Florida. In 1841 he was made commander of the southern division of the Army; he established a home at Baton

General Zachary Taylor, as drawn by a member of his army unit.

Rouge, Louisiana, and acquired a large plantation with many slaves.

After the annexation of Texas in 1845, Taylor was ordered to defend the territory against any efforts by Mexico to reconquer it, and was given command of troops on the Rio Grande when the Mexican War began. Promoted to major general, he invaded and swiftly conquered the northeastern states of Mexico.

As Taylor's popularity increased with his victories, President Polk became jealous, and many of Taylor's troops were withdrawn from his command and sent to join an army being assembled by Major General Winfield Scott for an invasion of central Mexico. Taylor was left with a small force of about 5000 men. Polk's plan to prevent Taylor from gaining more public acclaim backfired when Taylor and his small army gallantly withstood an attack by about 20,000 troops led by Mexico's President Santa Anna at Buena Vista in February 1847. Shortly thereafter, Taylor, angered by the maneuvers of Polk's administration, took a leave of absence from the Army and returned to his home in Louisiana.

When news of Buena Vista reached the United States, the Whig party immediately set the ball rolling to nominate Taylor for President, even though no one, including Taylor, knew how he stood on the issues of the day. The Whig National Convention in Philadelphia in June 1848 nominated him and named Millard Fillmore of New York as its vice-presidential candidate. To oppose Taylor, the Democratic party nominated Lewis Cass, senator from Michigan. Martin Van Buren also made an attempt to regain the presidency by running as the anti-slavery candidate of the Free Soil party.

Despite Taylor's popular appeal as a war hero, the election of 1848 was close. Taylor won by 1,360,967 popular votes to 1,222,342 for Cass, and by 163 electoral votes to 127. It was Van Buren's candidacy, which split New York's Democratic party and threw that state's 36 electoral votes to Taylor, that provided "Old Rough and Ready" with his margin of victory.

Taylor's Administration

BECAUSE March 4, 1849, fell on a Sunday, Taylor postponed his inauguration to the next day. In one of the shortest inaugural addresses of any incoming President, Taylor said nothing of his plans for the nation, noting only that he would look to Congress "to adopt such measures of conciliation as may harmonize conflicting interests and tend to perpetuate that Union which should be the paramount object of our hopes and affections." Even if Taylor had had a substantial program in mind, it is unlikely that he could have carried it out, since both houses of Congress were controlled by the Democrats.

A new controversy between North and South erupted during Taylor's administration over whether the new territories acquired from Mexico should be free or slave. The Southern states became particularly bitter when Californians late in 1849 adopted a constitution as a free state and asked admission to the Union, threatening to upset the balance in the Senate between free and slave states. Although a Southerner by birth, Taylor urged California's admission. But Congress refused to act.

In an effort to prevent the same thing from happening in New Mexico, the slave state of Texas claimed that territory. Taylor disputed this claim on grounds that the United States had purchased New Mexico and that it therefore should be administered as a federal territory.

In special messages to both houses of Congress late in January of 1850, the President called on Congress to allow the people of California and New Mexico to determine their own status "upon the principles laid down in our own Declaration of Independence." He asked Congress "to avoid any unnecessary controversy" that could endanger the Union.

When debate in Congress became more acrimonious, Southern leaders

The inauguration of General Zachary Taylor, as portrayed by the "Rough and Ready" clubs of the Union.

"The Late General Taylor, President of the United States," as depicted in the *Illustrated London News* following his death in July, 1850.

threatened to drive federal troops out of the disputed territory of New Mexico. With a military bluntness reminiscent of Andrew Jackson, Taylor declared:

"I will command the army in person and hang any man taken in treason."

Senators Clay, Webster, and Calhoun set about constructing the elaborate Compromise of 1850 in an effort to smooth over the problem, but Taylor scorned compromise. If his death had not intervened, he quite likely would have vetoed the compromise measure. Daniel Webster was convinced that Taylor's death prevented the outbreak of civil war in 1850.

On July 4, 1850, at the laying of the cornerstone of the Washington Monument, the sixty-five-year-old Taylor remained out in the hot sun for many hours and became ill from the heat. He had a fever when he returned to the White House, and five days later, on the evening of July 9, he died. In announcing the President's death to Congress, his successor, Millard Fillmore, reported that Taylor's last words were:

"I have always done my duty. I am ready to die. My only regret is for the friends I leave behind me."

General Taylor at Monterey, from an engraving by Wellstood after a painting by Chappel.

362   JAMES KNOX POLK

James Knox Polk

The Eleventh President of the United States
1845–49

1795 (November 2) Born in Mecklenburg County, North Carolina.

1818 Graduated from the University of North Carolina.

1820 Admitted to the bar to practice law in Tennessee.

1823–25 Member of state legislature of Tennessee.

1824 (January 1) Married Sarah Childress.

1825–39 U.S. representative from Tennessee.

1835–39 Speaker of the U.S. House of Representatives.

1839–41 Governor of Tennessee.

1845–49 Eleventh President of the United States.

1849 (June 15) Died in Nashville, Tennessee.

Leading Officials in
Polk's Administration

Office	Name	Years Served
Chief Justice	Roger B. Taney	1836-1864
Vice-President	George M. Dallas	1845-1849
Secretary of State	James Buchanan	1845-1849
Secretary of the Treasury	Robert J. Walker	1845-1849
Secretary of War	William L. Marcy	1845-1849
Attorney General	John Y. Mason	1845-1846
	Nathan Clifford	1846-1848
	Isaac Toucey	1848-1849
Secretary of the Navy	George Bancroft	1845-1846
	John Y. Mason	1846-1849
Postmaster General	Cave Johnson	1845-1849

The home of James K. Polk in Columbia, Tennessee.

—*Hirst Milhollen photograph*

Called "Young Hickory" by his supporters, James Knox Polk came to the presidency as the protégé of Andrew Jackson. Although he did not have the glamour of "Old Hickory," Polk was an astute politician who knew what the people wanted and gave it to them. In the 1840s the United States was in an expansionist mood as huge numbers of settlers flowed West by covered wagon, railroad, and steamboat, and the majority of people believed it was the "manifest destiny" of the country to fill the continent from coast to coast. Polk fulfilled these wishes by pushing the frontier all the way to the Pacific Coast, increasing the size of the United States more than any President since Jefferson, even though it brought war with Mexico and the threat of war with Britain.

Polk, a strait-laced Methodist, and his wife, a strict Presbyterian, banished drinking, dancing, and card-playing from the White House. Sam Houston once commented that the only thing wrong with Polk was that he drank too much water. Tart-penned John Quincy Adams found other faults: "He has no wit, no literature, no point of argument, no gracefulness of delivery, no elegance of language, no philosophy, no pathos, no felicitous impromptus; nothing that can constitute an orator, but confidence, fluency, and labor."

In his inaugural address, Polk enunciated a lofty view of the presidency:

"Although . . . the Chief Magistrate must almost of necessity be chosen by a party and stand pledged to its principles and measures, yet in his official action he should not be the President of a part only, but of the whole people of the United States. While he . . . faithfully carries out in the executive department of the Government the principles and policy of those who have chosen him, he should not be unmindful that our fellow-citizens who have differed with him in opinion are entitled to the full and free exercise of their opinions and judgments, and that the rights of all are entitled to respect and regard."

Frontier Beginnings

BORN of Scotch-Irish parents on a farm on the North Carolina frontier on November 2, 1795, James K. Polk was the oldest of a family of ten children. When he was ten, the boy moved west with his family to central Tennessee, where in time his father became one of the largest land-holders in the region. At nineteen, young James was sent back across the mountains to the University of North Carolina, from which he was graduated with honors three years later.

Returning to Tennessee, Polk began studying law under Congressman Felix Grundy, a friend of Jackson's and later U.S. Attorney General under Martin Van Buren. Admitted to the bar at the age of twenty-four, he began practicing law in Columbia, Tennessee.

Polk entered politics in 1823 as a successful candidate for the state legislature, and because of his small stature, earned the nickname "Napoleon of the Stump." While serving in the legislature, Polk married twenty-year-old Sarah Childress on New Year's Day, 1824. They had no children.

At the age of thirty, Polk was elected to Andrew Jackson's old seat as U.S. representative from Tennessee. He swiftly rose to prominence in

Mrs. James K. Polk (Sarah Childress).

Congress, serving as chairman of the powerful Ways and Means Committee and as majority leader for the Democratic party. He won Jackson's support by helping steer the administration's legislation through the House of Representatives. He was elected Speaker of the House during the last two years of Jackson's administration and the first two years of Van Buren's—the only Speaker of the House ever to become President.

In 1839 the forty-three-year-old Polk left Congress to run for and win the governorship of Tennessee. That same year the Tennessee legislature nominated him for Vice President to run with Van Buren, but after the Democratic National Convention failed to choose a vice-presidential candidate, he declined his state's nomination. His political star seemed to have waned when he twice lost bids for re-election as governor, in 1841 and 1843.

But another chance came when the 1844 Democratic National Convention in Baltimore deadlocked between Van Buren and Lewis Cass of Michigan. Several ballots failed to produce a decision. Then Polk's friends began spreading the word that "Young Hickory" was Jackson's choice and that he could bring harmony to the party. After the eighth ballot, the New York delegation withdrew Van Buren's candidacy, and on the ninth ballot Polk became the unanimous choice of the convention—the first "dark horse" presidential candidate of a major party. When word of Polk's nomination was flashed from Baltimore to Washington by Samuel F. B. Morse's telegraph—the first official use of the new communication system—Washington observers were sure the instrument had failed because they could not believe the news.

Henry Clay, the Whig nominee for President, upon hearing of the Democratic nomination, sarcastically commented: "Who is James K.

James K. Polk taking the oath of office at his inauguration—from a wood engraving in the Illustrated London News.

James Knox Polk as a young man.

Polk?" The Whigs adopted this as a campaign slogan, but it was highly ineffective compared to the Democratic expansionist cries of "Reannexation for Texas and Oregon!" and "54-40 or Fight!" (the latter referring to the northern boundary of the Oregon Territory). Polk was further aided when Jackson used his influence to get President Tyler to withdraw as an independent candidate for re-election, thus preventing a split in the Democratic vote.

The election results were closer than any since 1824. Polk barely squeezed by in the popular vote with 1,338,464 to Clay's 1,300,097 and received 170 electoral votes to Clay's 105. Polk won New York's 36 electoral votes by only a 5000-vote margin—if he had lost this crucial state the election would have gone to Clay.

THE forty-nine-year-old Polk—the youngest man ever to become President up to that time—took office on a rainy March 4, 1845, delivering his inaugural address "to a large assemblage of umbrellas" (in the words of John Quincy Adams). Although he did not mention it in the address, the "Napoleon of the Stump" already was planning to take New Mexico and California, as well as make good on his campaign promises of Texas and Oregon.

Two days after Polk took office, the Mexican minister to Washington filed a protest calling the annexation of Texas, voted by Congress in the last days of February, "an act of aggression." By the end of the month the

Polk's Administration

Mrs. James Polk (left) and her adopted daughter.

United States and Mexico had broken diplomatic relations. The threat of
war was in the air, but no hostile acts occurred during the remainder of
the year. By December 29, 1845, Congress had approved the admission of
Texas as a state, and Polk now pushed forward his plans to acquire New
Mexico and California from Mexico. He made offers to Mexico to purchase the territory, but soon concluded that force would be required to
obtain his ends. A dispute over the Texas-Mexico boundary helped bring
on hostilities. Polk had already prepared a message for Congress calling
for a declaration of war when word came on May 9, 1846, that Mexican
troops had crossed the Rio Grande and fired on American army units.
Polk added this information to his congressional message, and on May 13
Congress declared war on Mexico.

American troops advanced at once into Mexican territory, and by the
end of the year U.S. forces held all of New Mexico and California. In
February 1847, Major General Zachary Taylor won the brilliant victory

of Buena Vista. Two weeks later Major General Winfield Scott landed an army of about 10,000 men near Vera Cruz and fought his way to Mexico City by September 1847. Although Polk was tempted to take all of Mexico for the United States, he approved a peace treaty signed in February 1848, in which Mexico ceded to the United States more than half a million square miles for a payment of $15 million.

While Polk was successfully carrying out his expansionist plans in the Southwest, he was simultaneously negotiating with Britain concerning the Oregon Territory in the Northwest. When Britain balked at U.S. claims to the entire area, he agreed to compromise on a boundary at the 49th parallel of latitude. Many Northerners were angry at this settlement, feeling that the pro-slavery Polk was willing to spill blood to add territory that would extend slavery in the Southwest but was unwilling to fight for added territory in the Northwest that would be free.

Polk made one further but unsuccessful effort to expand the United States. He offered Spain $100 million for Cuba, but Spain rejected the proposition.

Not immodestly, Polk summarized his achievements in adding to the size of the United States:

"The acquisition of California and New Mexico, the settlement of the Oregon boundary and the annexation of Texas, extending to the Rio Grande, are results which, combined, are of greater consequence and will add more to the strength and wealth of the nation than any which have preceded them since the adoption of the Constitution."

During Polk's first two years in office the Democrats controlled both houses of Congress, enabling Polk to obtain passage of almost any legislation he wanted to implement his domestic program, which he called the "New Democracy." At the President's urging, Congress passed a new tariff act in July 1846 that substantially reduced import duties on such basic materials as coal and steel. Shortly after, Congress revived Van Buren's independent treasury system for control of the nation's money, a system which had been repealed in 1841 under President Tyler. But in the mid-term congressional elections, the Whigs won a majority of seats in the House, largely because of the unpopularity of the Mexican War in the Northern states—thus Polk received little co-operation from Congress in the latter part of his administration.

In the field of foreign relations Polk made another important long-range gain for the United States in a Latin American treaty signed in 1847 that gave the United States the right of passage across the Isthmus of Panama for a future railroad or canal.

In his last annual message to Congress in December 1848, Polk helped set off the California gold rush of 1849 with his glowing account of the "abundance of gold" that had been discovered in the newly acquired territory.

Although Polk had made no effort to run for a second term, he was discouraged by the defeat of the Democrats in the 1848 election, feeling that it was a reflection on his administration. After the inauguration of Zachary Taylor, Polk returned to Tennessee, a man made old before his time by the cares of office. Three months later he was stricken with cholera and died in Nashville on June 15, 1849. James Buchanan, his Secretary of State, said of him:

"He was the most laborious man I have ever known; and in a brief period of four years had assumed the appearance of an old man."

370 JOHN TYLER

John Tyler

The Tenth President of the United States
1 8 4 1 – 4 5

1790 (March 29) Born in Charles City County, Virginia.

1807 Graduated from William and Mary College.

1809 Admitted to the bar to practice law.

1811–16 Member of Virginia legislature.

1813 (March 29) Married Letitia Christian.

1813 Captain of militia in War of 1812.

1816–21 U.S. representative from Virginia.

1823–25 Member of Virginia legislature.

1825–27 Governor of Virginia.

1827–36 U.S. senator from Virginia.

1838–40 Member of Virginia legislature.

1841 Vice President of the United States.

1841–45 Tenth President of the United States.

1844 (June 26) Married Julia Gardiner.

1861 President of Peace Conference in Washington, D.C.

1862 Member of Congress of the Confederate States.

1862 (January 18) Died in Richmond, Virginia.

Leading Officials in Tyler's Administration

Office	Name	Years Served
Chief Justice	Roger B. Taney	1835-1864
Vice-President	*None*	
Secretary of State	Daniel Webster	1841-1843
	Hugh S. Legaré	1843
	Abel P. Upshur	1843-1844
	John C. Calhoun	1844-1845
Secretary of the Treasury	Thomas Ewing	1841
	Walter Forward	1841-1843
	John C. Spencer	1843-1844
	George M. Bibb	1844-1845
Secretary of War	John Bell	1841
	John C. Spencer	1841-1843
	James M. Porter	1843-1844
	William Wilkins	1844-1845
Attorney General	John J. Crittenden	1841
	Hugh S. Legaré	1841-1843
	John Nelson	1843-1845
Secretary of the Navy	George E. Badger	1841
	Abel P. Upshur	1841-1843
	David Henshaw	1843-1844
	Thomas W. Gilmer	1844
	John Y. Mason	1844-1845
Postmaster General	Francis Granger	1841
	Charles A. Wickliffe	1841-1845

The nation's first "President by act of God," John Tyler shocked many persons by taking over the presidential title along with the duties upon the death of William Henry Harrison. This was the first of a number of shocks he administered, particularly to the Whig party that had elected him Vice President, but rapidly disowned him as President. Tyler described his administration as "a bed of thorns . . . which has afforded me no repose."

The fifty-one-year-old Tyler was a headstrong slave-holding Virginia planter who had broken with the Democrats over Jackson's vigorous stand against nullification. But in the White House with a Whig Congress in power he used the veto time after time in support of his low-tariff Democratic principles. A friend commented, "When he thinks he is right he is obstinate as a bull, and no power on earth can move him."

Sixteen years after quitting the White House, Tyler had an opportunity to play an even greater role as president of a Peace Convention called in an attempt to head off the Civil War, but he was unable to lead the delegates to a workable compromise. He died a member of the Confederate Congress, denounced in the North as a traitor.

A Southern Aristocrat   TYLER was born on March 29, 1790, in Charles City County, Virginia— the same county where William Henry Harrison had been born seventeen years earlier. Like Harrison, Tyler was the son of a planter-politician who served as governor of the state.

After graduation from William and Mary College at seventeen, Tyler studied law and was admitted to the bar at nineteen. Two years later he launched his political career by winning election to the Virginia legislature. In 1813 he served briefly as a captain of militia, and on his twenty-third birthday, married Letitia Christian. They had eight children and enjoyed a marriage that lasted for nearly thirty years, until Mrs. Tyler's death during her husband's presidency.

Virginia's voters bestowed every honor at their disposal on the likable young lawyer, who for relaxation played the violin and wrote poetry. At the age of twenty-six he was elected to Congress, at thirty-five he became governor, and at thirty-six a U.S. senator.

Although Tyler supported Andrew Jackson in the elections of 1828 and 1832, he broke with Jackson in 1833 over the issue of nullification and secession. He was the only senator to vote against the Force Bill that gave the President authority to use military force, if necessary, to collect federal revenues—a threat aimed at the South Carolina nullifiers. Later that year Tyler voted with a majority of senators to censure Jackson for withdrawing federal deposits from the Bank of the United States.

In 1836 the Virginia legislature, controlled by Jackson supporters, sent instructions to Tyler that he was to vote for a resolution expunging the censure of Jackson from the Senate record. Rather than comply, Tyler resigned as senator. The Whigs promptly seized on the disaffected Democrat as a strong candidate for Vice President on their ticket. Although the Whigs lost the national election of 1836, Tyler made a good showing, gathering 47 electoral votes.

Winning election to the Virginia legislature in 1838 as a Whig, Tyler received the additional honor of being chosen speaker of the lower house. The next year he was unsuccessful in his bid for re-election to the U.S.

Mrs. John Gardiner Tyler, the second wife of John Tyler, with whom he had seven children, although she was thirty years younger than he.

—From a painting by Francesco Anelli

Senate; the voting in the legislature ending in a temporary deadlock with no one chosen to fill the vacancy.

In December 1839, at the Whig National Convention in Harrisburg, Pennsylvania, Tyler was again nominated for Vice President, this time as running mate for William Henry Harrison. The "Tippecanoe and Tyler Too" victory made Tyler Vice President, and within a month, to his own

JOHN TYLER OF VIRGINIA,
10TH PRESIDENT,
April 6, 1841 to March 4, 1845.

The original of this painting of John Tyler by G. P. A. Healy is in the House of Representatives.

astonishment no less than to everyone else's, he was President. After Harrison's inauguration, Tyler had left Washington for his home in Williamsburg. He took no part in discussions about cabinet appointments, and prepared to play an unobtrusive role in the government. These plans were short-lived. Roused out of bed at dawn on April 5, he learned the startling news of Harrison's death.

Tyler rode to Washington the next day and was sworn in as President at noon. He retained all the members of Harrison's Cabinet, but made it clear at once who was boss. He refused to accept the suggestion that all decisions be put to a majority vote. "I can never consent to being dictated to," he warned Secretary of State Daniel Webster and his colleagues.

Yet Henry Clay and the other Whig leaders in Congress were confident they could control Tyler by the majority they held in both houses. As soon as a special session convened in May to deal with the national economic crisis, Clay set about pushing through legislation for a new national bank, even though Tyler warned that he did not believe it was constitutional. When Tyler vetoed the measure in August, Clay was purple with rage, because he did not have enough votes to override the veto. Clay then put through a similar measure, called the Fiscal Corporation Bill, which Tyler also vetoed.

On September 11, 1841, two days after the second veto, all the members of Tyler's Cabinet except Daniel Webster resigned. And two days after that the Whig party officially expelled Tyler. The beleaguered President quickly filled out his Cabinet with conservative Democrats, starting a chain of cabinet appointments that gave Tyler the dubious distinction of having more cabinet changes than any other single-term executive.

Congress continued to pass legislation that it knew Tyler would not accept. In the summer of 1842 he twice vetoed bills that called for higher tariffs, bringing cries from the Whigs that he should be impeached. Finally, when the public treasury was almost empty, he signed a tariff measure in August 1842 to raise needed revenue. This did not stop the impeachment attempt, which was brought to a vote in the House in January 1843, but was defeated 27 to 83.

Tyler's administration achieved more success in the field of foreign relations than in domestic affairs. Daniel Webster remained in the Cabinet long enough to conclude the Webster-Ashburton Treaty, settling a longstanding dispute over the boundary between Maine and Canada. And a treaty with China in 1844 opened that country to trade with American merchants.

An unusual tragedy struck Tyler's administration in February 1844. The President and a large party of friends were on a cruise down the Potomac River on the new steam-powered warship *Princeton* when one of the ship's guns exploded. Several of the guests were killed, including Secretary of State Abel B. Upshur and Secretary of the Navy Thomas W. Gilmer.

Tyler, a widower, gave Washington gossips something to talk about when he married Julia Gardiner, a New York socialite thirty years his junior. Although Tyler's enemies laughed at the May-December marriage, it was a long and happy one. Tyler had seven children by his second wife.

The election year of 1844 found Tyler in the odd position of having no party willing to nominate him for re-election, so he organized a new states-rights Democratic-Republican party and campaigned on the issue of obtaining the annexation of Texas, which was opposed both by Clay, the Whig nominee, and Van Buren, who seemed likely to be the Democratic nominee. But when the Democrats nominated James K. Polk, who

Priscilla Cooper Tyler, daughter-in-law of John Tyler.

favored Texas annexation, Tyler withdrew at the urging of Andrew Jackson in order to insure Clay's defeat.

After Polk had been elected, Congress passed a joint House-Senate resolution approving the annexation of Texas, and Tyler signed it on March 1, 1845. On his last day in office, March 3, he signed legislation admitting Florida as the twenty-seventh state. On the same day Congress mustered enough votes (two-thirds in each house) to override one of Tyler's vetoes on a minor piece of legislation concerning the building of revenue cutters—the first time in history a presidential veto had been overridden.

Immediately after Polk's inauguration on March 4, Tyler and his family left for Virginia.

Tyler's Last Years   FOR more than a dozen years Tyler enjoyed the pleasant life of a Southern planter with a growing young family on his Sherwood Forest estate on the James River in Virginia. Although plagued with the ailments of

Sherwood Forest, the Tyler home.

A portrait of President Tyler in his earlier years.

—*From a painting by J. R. Lambdin*

age, he maintained an active interest in politics, and even entertained the hope that the Democrats would nominate him for President again.

As bitterness between North and South threatened to burst into flame after Lincoln's election in 1860, Tyler proposed that a Peace Convention of border states be called to try to head off civil war. The Virginia legislature indorsed the idea and called for delegates not only from the border states but from North and South as well to meet in Washington. Tyler, a member of Virginia's delegation and special emissary from Virginia to President Buchanan, was unanimously elected president of the convention, which met in February. But he found it impossible to lead the delegates to agreement on a workable compromise. In the end he openly sided with the Southern secessionists, and the Peace Conference ended in failure.

Tyler hurried home to a state convention where he urged Virginia to join the other seceding states. In November 1861, Tyler was elected a Virginia representative to the Confederate Congress. While attending the first session of this Congress in Richmond, the seventy-one-year-old former President died in his hotel room a few minutes after midnight on January 18, 1862.

378 WILLIAM HENRY HARRISON

William Henry Harrison

The Ninth President of the United States
1 8 4 1

1773 (February 9) Born in Charles City County, Virginia.

1791–98 Served in U.S. Army, rising to rank of captain.

1795 (November 25) Married Anna Symmes.

1799–1800 Delegate to Congress from Northwest Territory.

1800–12 Governor of Indiana Territory.

1811 Defeated Shawnee Indians in battle of Tippecanoe.

1812–14 General in the War of 1812.

1817–19 U.S. representative from Ohio.

1819–25 Member of Ohio state senate.

1825–28 U.S. senator from Ohio.

1828–29 U.S. minister to Colombia.

1841 Ninth President of the United States.

1841 (April 4) Died in the White House in Washington, D.C.

Leading Officials in Harrison's Administration

Office	Name	Years Served
Chief Justice	Roger B. Taney	1835-1864
Vice-President	John Tyler	1841
Secretary of State	Daniel Webster	1841-1843
Secretary of the Treasury	Thomas Ewing	1841
Secretary of War	John Bell	1841
Attorney General	John J. Crittenden	1841
Secretary of the Navy	George E. Badger	1841
Postmaster General	Francis Granger	1841

S erving the shortest presidential term in American history, William Henry Harrison never had the opportunity to demonstrate his ability as Chief Executive. Like Jackson, he was elected largely on the basis of his reputation as an Indian fighter and successful major general in the War of 1812. In the presidential campaign and in his inaugural address, Harrison carefully avoided taking a stand on important national issues in order to help hold together the loose confederation of conflicting interests that made up his Whig party.

Soldier and Politician

BORN on February 9, 1773, in Charles City County, Virginia, William Henry Harrison was the youngest of seven children of Benjamin Harrison, a wealthy planter and politician who signed the Declaration of Independence and was governor of Virginia at the end of the Revolutionary War. Young William entered Hampden-Sydney College at the age of fourteen, but left before graduation to take up the study of medicine under Dr. Benjamin Rush in Philadelphia.

After his father's death in 1791, the eighteen-year-old Harrison gave up his medical studies to join the U.S. Army with a commission as ensign. Assigned to duty on the northwest frontier, he became an aide-de-camp to General Anthony Wayne and fought in a number of battles against the Indians.

By the time Harrison was twenty-two, he had risen to the rank of captain and was placed in command of Fort Washington (now Cincinnati), Ohio. While there, he married Anna Symmes, daughter of a well-to-do landowner. In the ensuing years they had ten children. Their son, John Scott Harrison, became the father of the twenty-third President, Benjamin Harrison.

In 1798 Harrison was appointed secretary of the Northwest Territory by President Adams. The next year, at the age of twenty-six, he was elected the territory's first delegate to Congress. When the western half of the Northwest Territory was reorganized in 1800 as the Indiana Territory, Adams appointed Harrison the first territorial governor, an office that he held for the next dozen years.

Harrison won his first national fame in 1811 when he successfully led his territorial militia against the Shawnee Indian Chief Tecumseh and his brother The Prophet in the battle of Tippecanoe. This battle made good the territory's claim to about three million acres of land that had been taken from the Indians.

On the outbreak of the War of 1812, Harrison was commissioned brigadier general and given command of the northwest frontier. Promoted to major general the next year, he led 3000 troops into Canada, where, on October 5, 1813, he defeated a combined British-Indian force in the battle of the Thames River.

Harrison resigned his commission in 1814 and retired to his farm at North Bend, Ohio, but was elected to Congress in 1816. Defeated for re-election, he entered the Ohio state senate, serving six years. In 1825 the state legislature elected him to the U.S. Senate, where he succeeded Andrew Jackson as chairman of the committee on military affairs.

Harrison resigned as a senator in 1828 to accept an appointment by President John Quincy Adams as the first U.S. minister to Colombia, but the next year, after Jackson became President, Harrison was recalled.

A reproduction of a water-color portrait of Mrs. William Henry Harrison (Anna Tuthill Symmes).

General William Henry Harrison, commander of the Army of the Northwest in the War of 1812, and Tecumseh, the great Shawnee Chief who resisted Harrison's efforts to barter land from various Indian tribes, raising his tomahawk against Harrison after being refused the return of land taken from the Indians.

Throughout the rest of Jackson's administration, Harrison lived on his farm. From 1834 he held office as clerk of the court of common pleas of Hamilton County, a position that paid him about $10,000 a year in fees.

IN the confused national campaign of 1836 Harrison was one of several presidential candidates put up by the new Whig party against Martin Van Buren. He made a surprisingly good showing, winning 73 electoral votes and demonstrating national popularity. Four years later the Whig party united behind Harrison and his running mate, John Tyler of Virginia, with a catchy slogan: "Tippecanoe and Tyler Too." With the country still suffering from the economic depression following the Panic of 1837, the Whigs had a good chance. Harrison ran largely on his military record, keeping silent about national problems.

In the middle of the campaign a Van Buren supporter disparaged Harrison with the assertion "Give him a barrel of hard cider and settle a pension of two thousand a year on him and, my word for it, he will sit the remainder of his days in a log cabin." The Whigs pounced on the remark, and turned it in their candidate's favor. Overnight the country blossomed with log cabins and barrels of hard cider as "Tippecanoe" was played up as a rugged frontiersman and man of the people while Van Buren was painted as a New York plutocrat. The campaign song became:

Presidential Campaigns
and Administration

381

Scene at North Bend.

THE PATRIOTS HOME

Senator and Statesman.

Battle of the Thames.

Defence of Fort Meigs.

Treating with Indians.

Pardoning the assassin.

Quelling a mutiny at Fort Defiance.

Harrison at Wayne's Victory.

Welcome of a fellow Soldier.

BATTLE OF TIPPECANOE

Making hard Cider.

382 WILLIAM HENRY HARRISON

Benjamin Harrison, a signer of the Declaration of Independence and father of William Henry Harrison.

As a young officer, General Benjamin Harrison of Berkeley plantation on the James River in Virginia, father of William Henry Harrison.

The inauguration of William H. Harrison in March, 1841, with the Capitol in the background.

Daniel Webster, the eloquent Senator from Massachusetts who served as Secretary of State under Harrison and Tyler.

"What has caused this great commotion, motion
    Our country through?
    It is the ball a-rolling on,
For Tippecanoe and Tyler too, Tippecanoe and Tyler too.
And with them we'll beat little Van, Van, Van;
    Van is a used-up man."

In many ways it was the first modern presidential election. Almost a million more persons went to the polls in 1840 than in 1836. It was the first election in which any candidate received over a million votes. Harrison had 1,275,017 popular votes to Van Buren's 1,128,702, and swamped the New York Democrat with 234 to 60 electoral votes.

Inauguration Day, March 4, 1841, was cold and blustery. But the weather did not chill the ardor of Harrison's supporters, who gave him, in the words of John Quincy Adams, "demonstrations of popular feeling unexampled since that of Washington in 1789." Standing bareheaded on the east steps of the Capitol, the sixty-eight-year-old Harrison—the oldest man ever elected President—read a long, meandering inaugural address that had been edited by his new Secretary of State, Daniel Webster. In it Harrison pledged he would "under no circumstances" run for a second term, and indicated that he was going to leave the direction of the government up to Congress.

Although harassed by Whig office-seekers, Harrison refused to be

A campaign handkerchief of 1840 depicting Harrison, scenes from his life—his log cabin, Harrison plowing a field—and, in each corner, a United States shield with the American eagle, over which floats a spot of red, white and blue and a streamer with the slogan "Harrison and Reform."

Living room in the Harrison home at North Bend, Ohio.

pressured into dismissing government officials purely on a basis of party loyalty. Senator Clay, who had believed he could treat Harrison as a pawn, insisted that some of his friends be appointed to positions. But Tippecanoe kicked Clay out of the White House, warning him by note: "You are too impetuous." Clay left for Kentucky in a rage.

Fatigued and ill with a cold, Harrison took to his bed on March 27. The next day his physicians diagnosed his illness as pneumonia, and, at a half hour past midnight on April 4, 1841, Harrison became the first President to die in office. His last words to one of his cabinet members who was present were:

"Sir, I wish you to understand the true principles of the Government. I wish them carried out. I ask nothing more."

386 MARTIN VAN BUREN

Martin Van Buren

The Eighth President of the United States
1837–41

1782 (December 5) Born in Kinderhook, New York.

1803 Admitted to the bar to practice law.

1807 (February 21) Married Hannah Hoes.

1812–20 Member of New York state senate.

1816–19 Attorney general of New York.

1821–28 U.S. senator from New York.

1829 Governor of New York.

1829–31 Secretary of State of the United States.

1831–32 U.S. minister to England.

1833–37 Vice President of the United States.

1837–41 Eighth President of the United States.

1862 (July 24) Died in Kinderhook, New York.

Leading Officials in Van Buren's Administration

Office	Name	Years Served
Chief Justice	Roger B. Taney	1835-1864
Vice-President	Richard M. Johnson	1837-1841
Secretary of State	John Forsyth	1834-1841
Secretary of the Treasury	Levi Woodbury	1834-1841
Secretary of War	Joel R. Poinsett	1837-1841
Attorney General	Benjamin F. Butler	1833-1838
	Felix Grundy	1838-1840
	Henry D. Gilpin	1840-1841
Secretary of the Navy	Mahlon Dickerson	1834-1838
	James K. Paulding	1838-1841
Postmaster General	Amos Kendall	1835-1840
	John M. Niles	1840-1841

The residence of Martin Van Buren in Kinderhook, New York.

Although Martin Van Buren was the carefully chosen political heir of Andrew Jackson, his personality was vastly different from that of his predecessor. Nicknamed "the Magician" because of his political adroitness in behind-the-scenes maneuvers, he lacked Old Hickory's ability to win popular support for himself or his policies. However, he did achieve the unique distinction of holding, within a span of a dozen years, the offices of U.S. senator, governor of New York, Secretary of State, Vice President, and President.

The country's first major economic depression, the Panic of 1837, ruined Van Buren's popularity, even though he could hardly be held responsible for it—an experience that another President, Herbert Hoover, was to suffer nearly a century later.

That acidulous observer and political rival John Quincy Adams summed up Van Buren in unflattering terms:

"There are many features in the character of Mr. Van Buren strongly resembling that of Mr. Madison—his calmness, his gentleness of manner, his discretion, his easy and conciliatory temper. But Madison had none of his obsequiousness, his sycophancy, his profound dissimulation and duplicity."

Lawyer and Politician

THE FIRST President born an American citizen, rather than a British subject, Martin Van Buren curiously enough grew up speaking Dutch better than English. His ancestors came from the Netherlands as indentured servants, and he grew up in the old Dutch Community of Kinderhook, New York. After attending local schools until he was fourteen, Martin began studying law, first in Kinderhook, and then in New York City. Admitted to the bar in 1803, when he was twenty, he began practicing law in Kinderhook.

In 1807 Van Buren married a distant cousin, Hannah Hoes. They had four sons, but Mrs. Van Buren died twelve years later, in 1819. Van Buren never remarried.

When he was twenty-nine, he won election to the New York state senate as a member of the Democratic-Republican party. Learning the ins and outs of complicated New York State politics, he swiftly rose to leadership of the "Albany Regency," a political machine that dominated the state government by means of the "spoils system."

Continuing to hold office as state senator, Van Buren served as state attorney general from 1816 to 1819. He helped his friend Rufus King, the former Federalist presidential candidate, win election to the U.S. Senate in 1820, and the next year, two days before his thirty-ninth birthday, he joined King as the junior U.S. senator from New York.

Van Buren supported the unsuccessful presidential candidacy of W. H. Crawford in the election of 1824. Four years later, he won election to the governorship, and even more important, helped swing 20 of the state's 36 electoral votes to Andrew Jackson for President.

AFTER serving only two months as governor, Van Buren resigned to accept appointment by Jackson as Secretary of State. Competing with Vice President John C. Calhoun to win control of the Democratic-Republican party, Van Buren ingratiated himself with Jackson, even taking up horseback riding so that he could accompany the President on daily rides about the nation's capital. He particularly won Jackson's favor by his ostentatious friendship with the Eatons during the scandal that rocked Washington in Jackson's first administration. On New Year's Eve of 1829, Jackson wrote a political will, so that his choice of successor would become known if he died. In it Jackson wrote:

"Permit me to say here of Mr. Van Buren that I have found him everything that I could desire him to be, and believe him not only deserving of my confidence but the confidence of the Nation. Instead of his being selfish and intriguing, as has been represented by some of his opponents, I

*Secretary of State and
Vice President*

Hannah Hoes Van Buren, wife of Martin Van Buren, who died just twelve years after her marriage leaving a family of four sons.

A campaign poster during the Van Buren years.

have found him frank, open, candid, and manly. As a Counsellor he is able and prudent, . . . and one of the most pleasant men to do business with I ever saw. He . . . is well qualified . . . to fill the highest office in the gift of the people. . . . I wish I could say as much for Mr. Calhoun. You know the confidence I once had in that gentleman. However, of him I desire not now to speak."

Assured of Jackson's support for his presidential ambitions, Van Buren resigned as Secretary of State in 1831 to make it easier for Old Hickory to clear his Cabinet of Calhoun adherents. Jackson rewarded Van Buren with appointment as minister to England. But, after Van Buren arrived in London, Calhoun succeeded in having the Senate reject the appointment, with himself casting the deciding vote and then triumphantly proclaiming: "It will kill him, sir; kill him dead. He will never kick, sir; never kick."

To Calhoun's chagrin, however, Jackson succeeded in obtaining the 1832 Democratic-Republican vice-presidential nomination for his friend even before Van Buren had returned from Europe.

While Vice President from 1833 to 1837, Van Buren resumed his role as Jackson's closest adviser. He also enjoyed the neat revenge of presiding over the same Senate that had rejected his diplomatic appointment. After an assassination attempt was made on Jackson in 1835, Van Buren regularly carried two pistols with him to the Senate.

Under the mantle of Jackson's prestige, Van Buren easily captured the Democratic presidential nomination for the election of 1836. The party's Baltimore convention, at Jackson's urging, gave the vice-presidential nomination to Kentucky Congressman Richard M. Johnson, a colorful character who claimed to have killed the Indian chief, Tecumseh, at the battle of the Thames and who angered the Southern aristocracy by claiming social equality for his part-Negro daughters. Opposition to the Van Buren-Johnson ticket was widespread but divided. The Whigs, remnants of the old Federalist party and of Clay's National Republican party, nominated William Henry Harrison of Ohio for President; Massachusetts nominated Senator Daniel Webster; and Tennessee revolted against Jackson's rule by nominating Senator Hugh L. White.

Against this divided opposition Van Buren won easily, even though his 765,483 popular votes barely topped the total of 739,795 of his opponents. He received 170 electoral votes to the opposition's combined total of 124. No vice-presidential candidate received a majority of the electoral votes, so for the first and only time in history the election of a Vice President was left to the Senate, which chose Johnson.

AT Van Buren's inauguration Jackson stole the cheers of the crowd, just as Washington had at John Adams' inauguration and as Jefferson at James Madison's. In his address the fifty-four-year-old Van Buren made it frankly clear that he intended to continue to work in Jackson's shadow, saying:

"In receiving from the people the sacred trust twice confided to my illustrious predecessor, and which he has discharged so faithfully and so well, I know that I can not expect to perform the arduous task with equal ability and success. But united as I have been in his counsels, a daily witness to his exclusive and unsurpassed devotion to his country's welfare, agreeing with him in sentiments which his countrymen have warmly supported, and permitted to partake largely of his confidence, I may hope that somewhat of the same cheering approbation will be found to attend upon my path."

As further evidence of the caretaker role he intended to play, Van

Van Buren's Administration

Buren reappointed all the members of Jackson's Cabinet.

Although in his inaugural address Van Buren had described the United States as representing "an aggregate of human prosperity surely not elsewhere to be found," two months later the economic storm clouds of the Panic of 1837 darkened the entire nation as banks suspended the payment of gold or silver for paper money.

Van Buren called a special session of Congress in September 1837 and asked that an independent treasury system be established, so that the government could retain control of the money collected in taxes, rather than deposit it in private banks. He also proposed that the government begin issuing paper money in the form of treasury notes. Van Buren warned Congress that it was not within its constitutional rights to provide "specific aid to the citizen to relieve embarrassments arising from losses by revulsions in commerce and credit." His reasoning was orthodox for the time:

"All communities are apt to look to government for too much. Even in our own country, where its powers and duties are so strictly limited, we are prone to do so, especially at periods of sudden embarrassment and distress. But this ought not to be. The framers of our excellent Constitution and the people who approved it with calm and sagacious deliberation acted at the time on a sounder principle. They wisely judged that the less government interferes with private pursuits the better for the general prosperity. It is not its legitimate object to make men rich or to repair by direct grants of money or legislation in favor of particular pursuits losses not incurred in public service. This would be substantially to use the property of some for the benefit of others."

Congress was slow in adopting the measures that Van Buren requested, and it was not until July 1840 that the independent treasury system went into effect. Although prosperity returned temporarily in the winter of 1839–40, bad times recurred at the end of Van Buren's administration and persisted until 1845.

Van Buren was responsible for one of the first widespread improvements in labor conditions when, after a protest meeting by government laborers outside the White House, he reduced the work day for federal employees to ten hours.

Seeking to maintain the status quo between North and South, Van Buren only succeeded in angering both sections of the country. Antislavery forces opposed his support of a war against the Seminole Indians in Florida, believing it presaged the admission of Florida as a slave state. And pro-slavery forces denounced him for not promoting the annexation of Texas as another slave state.

In the field of foreign affairs, Van Buren's administration was troubled with sporadic outbreaks of warfare along the Canadian border, but the President succeeded in averting full-scale war with Britain or Canada over the issues.

Although Van Buren was unanimously chosen by the Democratic Convention to run for a second term in the election of 1840, the delegates could not agree on a vice-presidential candidate, deciding to leave the choice open to the electors. This extraordinary decision left Van Buren with the unusual handicap of not having a popular running mate to bring him support. Moreover, all the forces that opposed him united behind the Whig party's candidate, William Henry Harrison. The Whigs portrayed Harrison as a man of the people who could live in a log cabin and enjoy hard cider, while denouncing Van Buren as "the Fox of Kinderhook" who ate his meals off gold plate. The strategy worked, and Van Buren was defeated.

Angelica Singleton Van Buren, daughter-in-law of President Van Buren.

A portrait of President Van Buren in his later years.

Van Buren counted on receiving the Democratic presidential nomination again in 1844, but made a fatal blunder that lost him his chance. He reached an apparent agreement with Henry Clay, the prospective Whig presidential candidate, to rule out the annexation of Texas as a campaign issue—both gave out announcements denouncing annexation on the same day, April 27, 1844. This "bargain" between Clay and Van Buren so angered Jackson, a proponent of annexation, that he threw his weight against Van Buren and succeeded in winning the presidential nomination for James K. Polk.

Four years later Van Buren again tried to return to power, accepting the presidential nomination of the new anti-slavery Free Soil party. He failed to win a single electoral vote in the election of 1848, but his candidacy had the important effect of splitting New York State's Democratic vote, assuring the victory of the Whigs' presidential candidate, Zachary Taylor.

The aging Van Buren made a two-year trip to Europe in the 1850s and then retired to an estate, Lindenwald, that he had purchased near his birthplace in Kinderhook, New York. He died there at the age of seventy-nine, on July 24, 1862.

—*From a painting by George P. A. Healy*

394 ANDREW JACKSON

Andrew Jackson

The Seventh President of the United States
1829–37

1767 (March 15) Born in Waxhaw, South Carolina.

1780–81 Member of militia in Revolutionary War.

1787 Admitted to bar to practice law in North Carolina.

1791 Married Rachel Donelson Robards.

1795 Member of Tennessee state constitutional convention.

1796–97 U.S. representative from Tennessee.

1797–98 U.S. senator from Tennessee.

1798–1804 Judge of Tennessee Superior Court.

1812–15 Major general in the War of 1812.

1817–18 Commanded U.S. troops in Seminole War in Florida.

1821 Provisional governor of the Territory of Florida.

1823–25 U.S. senator from Tennessee.

1829–37 Seventh President of the United States.

1845 (June 8) Died at the Hermitage near Nashville, Tennessee.

Leading Officials in Jackson's Administration

Office	Name	Years Served
Chief Justice	John Marshall	1801-1835
	Roger B. Taney	1835-1864
Vice-President	John C. Calhoun	1825-1832
	Martin Van Buren	1833-1837
Secretary of State	Martin Van Buren	1829-1831
	Edward Livingston	1831-1833
	Louis McLane	1833-1834
	John Forsyth	1834-1841
Secretary of the Treasury	Samuel D. Ingham	1829-1831
	Louis McLane	1831-1833
	William J. Duane	1833
	Roger B. Taney	1833-1834
	Levi Woodbury	1834-1841
Secretary of War	John H. Eaton	1829-1831
	Lewis Cass	1831-1836
	Benjamin F. Butler	1836-1837
Attorney General	John M. Berrien	1829-1831
	Roger B. Taney	1831-1833
	Benjamin F. Butler	1833-1838
Secretary of the Navy	John Branch	1829-1831
	Levi Woodbury	1831-1834
	Mahlon Dickerson	1834-1838
Postmaster General	John McLean	1823-1829
	William T. Barry	1829-1835
	Amos Kendall	1835-1840

About the only thing that Andrew Jackson had in common with the scholarly Puritan whom he succeeded as President was their year of birth. Born in a frontier log cabin, Jackson grew up as a poorly educated orphan, fought as a boy-militiaman in the Revolutionary War, dissipated a small inheritance as a wild teen-ager, and then settled down as a backwoods lawyer. The hotheaded Jackson fought countless duels, won and lost thousands of dollars on horse races, speculated in land, and became a slave-holding plantation owner. By the time he was thirty, he had achieved great political power in the newly formed state of Tennessee, rising from prosecuting attorney to U.S. representative to U.S. senator. The hawk-eyed Jackson achieved undying fame in the War of 1812 first as an Indian fighter and then as victor in the battle of New Orleans—the biggest battle fought on the continent to that time.

Like George Washington, Jackson uniquely combined the art of a seasoned politician with the decision-making ability of a successful general. His tenacious loyalty toward his friends was matched by an equally unquenchable enmity for anyone who insulted or betrayed him. And the common people loved him as their fathers and grandfathers had loved George Washington.

As President, Jackson brooked no opposition by politicians in or out of his party because he was confident that the people would follow him wherever he led. He neatly summarized his own views on the presidency when he said: "It was settled by the Constitution, the laws, and the whole

The first residence of Andrew Jackson, in South Carolina near Lancaster, one mile from the Waxhaw Creek.

practice of the government that the entire executive power is vested in the President of the United States . . ."

A contemporary described Jackson as follows:

"In person he was tall, slim and straight . . . His head was long, but narrow, and covered with thick grey hair that stood erect, as though impregnated with his defiant spirit; his brow was deeply furrowed, and his eye was one 'to threaten and command.' His nose was prominent and indicated force. His mouth displayed firmness. His whole being conveyed an impression of energy and daring."

BORN on March 15, 1767, at the settlement of Waxhaw on the border between North and South Carolina, Andrew Jackson was the son of Andrew and Elizabeth Hutchinson Jackson, who had immigrated from Ireland only two years earlier. Because his father died a few days before Andrew's birth, the boy and his two older brothers were reared by their mother. She earned their keep by helping care for the eight children of her sister, Mrs. James Crawford.

Boyhood of an Orphan

A brighter than ordinary child, Andrew learned to read by the time he was five, attending a small country school in Waxhaw. Because many of the older citizens of Waxhaw could not read, those who could, including Andy, took turns as public readers when newspapers erratically reached the backwoods community. In later years he could recall the drama of reading aloud, as a boy of nine, the ringing words of the Declaration of Independence when a copy of that document first reached Waxhaw in the summer of 1776.

At the age of thirteen, Andy and his brother Robert joined the militia company of his uncle, Major Robert Crawford. His oldest brother, Hugh, already had died fighting in the Revolution. Andy and his brother were captured in 1781. When a British officer ordered Andy to clean his boots, the boy haughtily refused, on grounds it was unfit treatment for a prisoner of war. The angry officer struck at the boy with his sabre, leaving scars on the boy's arm and head that he carried the rest of his life. After the boys became ill with smallpox in the British prison at Camden, South Carolina, they were released to the care of their mother. Robert died and so did his mother, leaving Andy in the hands of his numerous Crawford relatives.

At sixteen he unexpectedly received an inheritance of between £300 and £400 from his grandfather, a well-to-do merchant who had died in Ireland. But, instead of purchasing a farm or going to college, the boy squandered the money on clothes, horse races, dice, and the gay life of the taverns of Charleston, South Carolina.

The next year, 1784, found young Jackson visiting friends in Salisbury, North Carolina, where he took up the study of law—that is, he studied when he could take time from his activities as "head of the rowdies" of the town. The dashing, six-foot, hawk-eyed Jackson captivated the hearts of the Salisbury girls with his Irish brogue. But their mothers were happy when he was admitted to the bar in September 1787 and left town to seek his fortune by following the circuit court.

JACKSON was only twenty when his friend John McNairy, a fellow law student in Salisbury, was appointed judge of North Carolina's Western District, as Tennessee then was called. Seeing a chance to go west and be paid for it, Jackson persuaded McNairy to name him attorney general for the district.

Frontier Lawyer and Politician

On the way, Jackson paused to take some cases in the local law court in Jonesborough. Feeling himself insulted by an opposing attorney, he

Rachel Donelson Robards Jackson, Andrew Jackson's beloved wife, who died soon after he was elected President and before the inauguration.

promptly challenged the man to a duel. On the field of honor, friends urged that no blood be shed, and both participants fired in the air, but Jackson had established his reputation as a man not to be trifled with.

When the Cumberland Road opened in September 1788, Jackson joined the first party of settlers moving west. Several members of the party were killed by Indians, but Jackson reached the frontier capital of Nashville unscathed.

There he swiftly established a reputation as a fearless attorney who would help a creditor collect his debts both in and out of the courtroom. Clients flocked to his office. Because land was the currency of the frontier, Jackson soon became a large landowner, collecting fees at the rate of an acre for ten cents of service.

In Nashville, Jackson lived at the boardinghouse of a widow, Mrs. John Donelson, whose dark-haired, pipe-smoking daughter caught his eye. The girl, Mrs. Rachel Donelson Robards, was the estranged wife of Lewis Robards of Kentucky. Robards came to Nashville, patched up his problems with Rachel, and took her home to Kentucky in June 1790. But the next month, Jackson followed her there and she ran away with him to Nashville. Robards threatened to come to Nashville and carry his wife home by force, so Jackson and Rachel hurried south to Natchez, where Jackson owned some land.

Believing that Robards had obtained a divorce, Jackson and Mrs. Robards were married in August 1791. They lived for a time in a log house near Natchez and returned to Nashville later that year. When news came from Kentucky that Robards had delayed getting his divorce until September 1793, Jackson and his wife were remarried on January 7, 1794. Jackson loved his wife dearly and for the rest of his life was ready to fight at any hint of slander regarding the circumstances of their courtship and marriage. Although they never had any children of their own, both Jackson and his wife loved children and adopted several on whom they lavished their affection.

In 1795 Jackson traveled for the first time to the nation's capital, Philadelphia, where he sold several thousand acres of land to speculators, using the money to purchase supplies for a trading post on the Cumberland River. Upon his return home, he was elected a member of a constitutional convention called to organize the new state of Tennessee—a name some have said was suggested by Jackson.

After Tennessee was admitted to the Union as the sixteenth state in 1796, Jackson was elected, with no opposition, as the state's first representative to Congress. There he voted with Thomas Jefferson's Democratic-Republicans and was disappointed in John Adams' victory over Jefferson in the election of 1796. Returning to Tennessee in 1797, he refused to run for re-election.

But that year Senator William Blount of Tennessee was impeached by the House of Representatives and expelled by the U.S. Senate for conspiring to take the Louisiana Territory from Spain with British asssistance. Because most land-hungry Tennesseeans favored Blount's plan, he was greeted as a hero upon his return to the state, and his friend, thirty-year-old Andrew Jackson, was elected by the state legislature to succeed him.

Serving in the Senate for only a few months, Jackson did little more in the nation's capital than establish a lasting friendship with Senator Aaron Burr of New York. He resigned from the Senate in 1798 to devote his attention to his plantation and improve his personal financial affairs. But later that same year he was elected a judge of the state's superior court at an annual salary of $800—an office he held for six years, meting out swift justice with no written decisions.

JACKSON won an honor in 1802 that was to be more important than any other he had received so far—the officers of the Tennessee militia elected him their commander with the rank of major general, a post that at the time was largely honorary.

A Political General

Two years later when some of his business enterprises failed, Jackson resigned as judge, sold most of his possessions to pay his debts, and moved to an undeveloped plantation, the Hermitage, near Nashville. His fortunes were at low ebb, but at this point he borrowed money to buy a racehorse named Truxton. After training the horse, he bet and won $6500 on him in a match race against a horse called Greyhound. With his winnings he purchased Greyhound, and from then on the bets and stakes he won on his racing stable formed a large part of Jackson's income. Even much later, as President, he kept racehorses in the White House stable.

Meanwhile, Jackson kept alive his reputation as a hotheaded duelist.

While still a judge in 1803, he had attacked Governor John Sevier on the courthouse steps in Knoxville for a slurring remark about Rachel. A duel followed, but friends prevented the two most important men in Tennessee from killing each other. In 1806 the same cause led to more serious consequences. This time it was a Nashville lawyer, Charles Dickinson, who cast aspersions on Mrs. Jackson's past. Though Dickinson had the reputation of being the best shot in Tennessee, Jackson instantly challenged him. When the two met, Dickinson fired first, hitting Jackson squarely in the chest. Despite his wound, Jackson took careful aim and killed his opponent before collapsing. Dickinson's bullet was too close to Jackson's heart to be removed, and he carried it in his body for the rest of his life.

When former Vice President Aaron Burr came west in 1805 seeking recruits for his scheme to set up an empire in the Louisiana Territory and Mexico, he twice stayed at Jackson's home. And he won Jackson's support for his plans, which supposedly had the blessing of President Jefferson's administration. In September 1806, Jackson was sufficiently recovered from his dueling wound to play host to a reception in Burr's honor. Jackson ordered his Tennessee militia to stand ready to march against Spanish troops in the Louisiana Territory, and, with money supplied by Burr, he began building riverboats for the transport of his troops.

Jackson was unaware that the federal government had moved to indict Burr for treason in Kentucky, but he learned from one of Burr's confidants that the plan involved attacking U.S. forces at New Orleans. Jackson immediately wrote to President Jefferson and to the governor of the Louisiana Territory warning them of Burr's scheme. "I would delight to see Mexico reduced," Jackson wrote, "but I will die in the last ditch before I would . . . see the Union disunited."

A Kentucky grand jury refused to indict Burr for treason, and Jackson received new assurances by mail from Burr that the plan was not against the interests of the federal government. Then, late in December 1806, before Jackson learned that Jefferson had issued an order for Burr's arrest, Burr slipped into Nashville, obtained two riverboats from Jackson, and hurried off down the Cumberland River. After Burr's arrest, Jackson was subpoenaed as a witness at the trial in 1807 at Richmond, Virginia, but was not called to testify after he made it clear that he had a lower opinion of Jefferson than he did of Burr.

A Fighting General WHEN news came in 1812 that the United States had declared war on England, Jackson at once volunteered to lead his division of 2500 militiamen to Canada to capture Quebec. But, because he was in disfavor with President Madison owing to his involvement in the Burr conspiracy, he was not given permission to carry out his plan. When Detroit surrendered to the British, Jackson offered to recapture it—and this time his offer was ignored completely. He and his militiamen were ordered instead to Mississippi to prepare for an attack on Florida. When they arrived, after a hard march in the winter of 1813, he received orders to disband his troops. Instead, the forty-six-year-old Jackson marched them back to Tennessee, walking all the way so that sick soldiers could ride the available horses. His tough discipline and willingness to share the privations of his troops won from his men the nickname "Old Hickory."

In the summer of 1813 Jackson got involved in a feud with Jesse Benton and his brother Thomas Hart, the future senator from Missouri. Jackson had acted as second for a friend in a duel with Jesse. This angered Thomas Hart Benton, then an army lieutenant colonel, who made some unrecorded but apparently intemperate remarks about Jackson. In turn, Jackson declared he would horsewhip Benton if he ever showed his face in

General Andrew Jackson with Chief Weatherford, Creek Indian.

During his campaigns against the Creeks, Jackson had to put down two mutinies caused by a lack of supplies.

Jackson's headquarters in New Orleans from which he issued his order declaring New Orleans under martial law during his defense of the city.

Nashville again. Soon after, the Bentons came to town heavily armed. In a hotel hallway Jackson waylaid Thomas Hart Benton with a whip in one hand and a pistol in the other. Before he could use either, Jesse Benton appeared behind him and opened fire, hitting Jackson in the shoulder. As Jackson fell, Thomas Hart Benton pumped more bullets into his body. For several days Jackson lay near death with doctors urging him to have his shattered left arm amputated. But the strong-willed Jackson refused to allow it, and slowly began to recover. He carried these bullets in his arm for the next nineteen years, until they were removed while he was President.

While still in bed recovering from this affray, Jackson received word that the Creek Indians under Chief Red Eagle had massacred 200 settlers in the Mississippi Territory. With his wounded arm in a sling, Jackson called his militia to arms and marched south. During the first week of November 1813, he twice defeated small groups of Creeks. Deep in the wilderness of what is now Alabama, Jackson's troops failed to receive any supplies. Cold, hungry, ill-clothed, and homesick, hundreds of Jackson's volunteers and militia began leaving for home at the end of their agreed terms of active service. But Jackson angrily declared that he personally would never retreat: "I will perish first."

After more supplies and fresh troops reached Jackson, he led about 2000 men against 8000 Creeks in the battle of Horseshoe Bend on March 27,

1814. "Arrows, and spears, and balls were flying," wrote Sam Houston, who was a young officer in the battle, "swords and tomahawks gleaming in the sun." The fighting ended at nightfall with more than 750 Indians and 49 of Jackson's troops dead. A few days later Chief Red Eagle surrendered and the war with the Creeks was over. As punishment for their uprising, Jackson forced the Creeks to give up 23 million acres of their land. They also gave Jackson a personal present of three square miles of land.

Returning home a hero, Jackson was rewarded by President Madison with appointment as a major general in the Regular Army and was given command of the entire southwestern part of the United States. Mistrustful of the Spanish in Florida, Jackson sent a scout to Pensacola to find out what was going on. When the scout returned with word that the British were using Pensacola as a naval base, Jackson launched a lightning raid on the Florida port and captured it after a brief fight in November 1814.

Moving his headquarters west to New Orleans, Jackson arrived just in time to learn of an impending attack by a huge British fleet and army. On December 23, the British made a successful surprise landing only a few miles east of New Orleans. Jackson attacked at night, halting the British advance, then withdrew to a defensive line along an abandoned canal four miles from the city. As the British brought up reinforcements until their army numbered 10,000 disciplined veterans, Jackson's forces of only about half as many men—including Jean Laffite's pirates—threw up a mud and log rampart that stretched from the Mississippi River to a swamp.

The British first tried to attack the line on December 28, but were driven back by cannonfire. After bringing up cannon from their warships, the British launched a huge bombardment on New Year's Day, but again were unable to crack the defenses.

Then, in a cold, foggy dawn on January 8, 1815, the British attacked in force. As the redcoats advanced in unbroken lines, Jackson's expert frontier riflemen picked them off one by one. The result was one of the worst British defeats in history, with losses of more than 2600 dead, wounded, or captured—including the death of their commanding general—while Jackson had only eight men killed and thirteen wounded!

As news of the battle of New Orleans spread across the nation, the forty-seven-year-old Jackson was hailed as the hero of the war. More than two months later official word finally reached New Orleans that the War of 1812 was over, with a peace treaty negotiated by John Quincy Adams before the battle of New Orleans had been fought.

AFTER James Monroe's election as President, Jackson declined appointment as Secretary of War, confident that as long as the Spanish held Florida work remained for him to do on the frontier. In 1818 he was given command of an army to put down an uprising of the Seminole Indians, with orders to pursue them into Florida, if necessary. Jackson proposed to Monroe that he be given unofficial authorization to seize Florida from Spain. Proceeding with his plans, Jackson captured the Spanish forts in Florida, appointed one of his colonels as military governor of the area, and returned in triumph to Tennessee.

In the ensuing uproar, Spain threatened to declare war if its Florida forts were not given back. In secret cabinet meetings John Quincy Adams defended Jackson's actions, while Secretary of War John Calhoun urged that Jackson be arrested—facts that were revealed to Jackson more than a dozen years later when he was President and Calhoun was his Vice President.

A Period of Trials and Triumphs

Early in 1819, the House of Representatives, led by its Speaker, Henry Clay, prepared resolutions condemning Jackson's actions in Florida. Jackson hurried to Washington to defend himself, while Clay made allusions to Caesar crossing the Rubicon. Jackson's friends beat down the House resolutions at the same time Adams negotiated a treaty acquiring Florida from Spain for five million dollars.

Jackson accepted appointment as the first territorial governor of Florida in 1821. But he remained there only long enough to organize the government, then retired to plantation life in Tennessee.

As the presidential campaign of 1824 approached, President Monroe offered Jackson the post of minister to Mexico. When Jackson refused, it was taken as an indication of his willingness to run for President. He made even more clear his desire to return to politics when he accepted election by the Tennessee legislature in October 1823 as U.S. senator. When he took his seat in the Senate Chamber, the adjacent desk was that of Missouri Senator Thomas Hart Benton, with whom he had fought almost to the death ten years earlier. But now both men shook hands, and Benton ultimately became one of Jackson's firmest supporters.

Jackson's presidential candidacy received its biggest boost when a political convention in the key state of Pennsylvania nominated him for President in February 1824. Holding himself aloof from the campaign, as was the custom of candidates in those days, Jackson left the electioneering to his friends.

Although Old Hickory won the largest number of popular and electoral votes in the election, he did not receive a majority, so the selection of the next President fell to the House of Representatives. There, Clay engineered the choice of second-place John Quincy Adams as the nation's next Chief Executive.

Though he had not been an enthusiastic presidential candidate in 1824, Jackson now felt he had been cheated and resolved to revenge himself on Adams and Clay. The Tennessee legislature promptly, in 1825, nominated him for President for 1828, and he resigned as senator to devote his full attention to the campaign.

Presidential electioneering sank to new lows. Jackson could scarcely restrain himself from seizing his dueling pistols when Adams-Clay newspapers raked over details of his courtship and marriage. In 1828 Jackson made one of the first "campaign tours" of a presidential candidate, traveling to New Orleans for the thirteenth anniversary celebration of his victory. When the votes were counted, Jackson beat Adams by a clear majority with an electoral vote of 178 to 83 and a popular vote of 647,276 to 508,064.

But in his moment of vengeful glory, Jackson was plunged into sorrow. His wife, Rachel, now a middle-aged, home-loving frontierswoman who enjoyed smoking a corncob pipe as much as did her husband, and had no desire to become First Lady, died just as she and Jackson were preparing to leave for Washington. One of her last remarks was: "I had rather be a door-keeper in the house of God than to live in that palace." The sorrowing President-elect blamed her death both on his political enemies and on himself.

Jackson's First Term

LOOKING older than his sixty-one years, Jackson was in poor shape to assume the burdens of the presidency in 1829. He was racked by tuberculosis, and the bullets he still carried in his body contributed to his poor health. Moreover, with Rachel dead he felt he had little to live for. Many of his friends believed he would never live to complete his first term. And, if he had died during his first two or three years in office, he might well have gone down in history as one of our least successful Presidents, for the first years of his presidency were chaotic and unproductive.

Washington swarmed with job-hunting Jackson supporters on the day of his inauguration. They had come in the belief he would make a "clean sweep" of all the federal officials appointed by Adams. And, although Jackson instituted a greater job-housecleaning than had President Jefferson, the "spoils system" that he was said to have introduced replaced only about a sixth of federal office holders during his years in the White House. Many job-hunters went home disappointed.

Upon Jackson's inauguration—a ceremony that the bitter President Adams avoided attending—the new President called for "extinguishment of the national debt" to "counteract that tendency to public and private profligacy which a profuse expenditure of money by the Government is but too apt to engender." He promised "reform" to remove federal offices from "unfaithful or incompetent hands." And he reassured those who feared the ascendancy of a general to the White House by voicing his conviction that the "military should be held subordinate to the civil power."

From his strong sense of personal loyalty to a friend, President Jackson devoted a disproportionate amount of time and effort during his first term to a social contretemps that became known as the "Affair of Mrs. Eaton." For several years Tennessee Senator John Eaton, Jackson's presidential campaign manager, had been carrying on a dalliance with the pretty, married daughter of the owner of a Washington boardinghouse where Eaton resided. Jackson had lived there, too, while he was a senator, and was fond of the flirtatious girl. When the girl's husband, a Navy officer, died at sea in 1828 (some said he killed himself because of her affair with Eaton), Jackson privately urged Eaton to marry her as quickly as possible to silence the tongues of scandalmongers. Eaton followed Jackson's advice and married her two months before Jackson took office.

But, after Jackson appointed Eaton Secretary of War, many of Washington's society leaders began snubbing Mrs. Eaton. Secretary of State Martin Van Buren and Vice President John Calhoun, who both aspired

Howard Pyle's concept of Andrew Jackson en route to Washington from his home in Tennessee.

Emily Donelson (wife of Rachel Jackson's nephew, Major A. J. Donelson, Jackson's private secretary), who lived in the White House during Jackson's two terms and gave birth to three daughters there.

to the presidency, used the affair of Mrs. Eaton to promote their own political futures. Van Buren, a widower, insinuated himself with Jackson by promoting Mrs. Eaton's social position. On the other hand, Calhoun, whose wife refused to have anything to do with Mrs. Eaton, set himself up as the leader of morality and protector of womanhood.

Because the wives of most of Eaton's fellow cabinet members refused to receive Mrs. Eaton in their homes, Jackson took the highly unusual step of calling a cabinet meeting and asking for the resignation of any whose wives would not treat Mrs. Eaton with respect. The cabinet members blandly said they were unable to control the actions of their wives and refused to resign. Jackson must have felt there was some force in their argument, because even his own official White House hostess, Mrs. Emily Donelson, wife of one of Jackson's adopted nephews and private secretary, refused to help Mrs. Eaton win social success.

Barely on speaking terms with most of the members of his Cabinet, Jackson began to rely for advice on a "kitchen cabinet" made up of loyal political supporters. In a new effort to solve the problem, Jackson had Eaton send his wife to Tennessee to live, and likewise banished Mrs. Donelson to his home state. But it was too late to heal the political split among administration officials.

In 1831 Jackson broke completely with Calhoun, and gave Van Buren assurances he would help him become the next President. Now secure in his position, Van Buren proposed to break the cabinet deadlock by resigning as Secretary of State. This apparent self-sacrifice caused Eaton to resign as Secretary of War. Jackson then demanded the resignations of the three Calhoun supporters in his Cabinet. Shortly after, Eaton challenged each of the three to duels, but all declined. The appointment of five new cabinet members in 1831 closed the "Affair of Mrs. Eaton" and gave Jackson's administration a new lease on life.

Jackson gave Van Buren a recess appointment as minister to England in 1831. When the appointment came up for consideration by the Senate in January 1832, the foes of Jackson and Van Buren decided this would be a good time to embarrass both. The conspirators arranged a tie vote on the appointment, giving Vice President Calhoun the pleasure of casting the deciding vote against Van Buren. But the plot backfired by winning Van Buren national sympathy and making it easier for Jackson to obtain his party's vice-presidential nomination for his friend.

An issue that smouldered and occasionally burst into flame during Jackson's first administration was that of nullification. Calhoun had made himself the leader of the movement that declared that a state had the right to decide which federal laws it wished to observe and which it wished to reject. Calhoun and his followers also felt that a state had the right to secede from the Union. Jackson had made clear his feeling about secession by publicly declaring: "Our Federal Union, it must be preserved." But he had done nothing to uphold decisions by the Supreme Court that rejected the principle of nullification in regard to the rights of federally-protected Indians in Southern states—as an old Indian-fighter Jackson had little regard for any rights for Indians.

But it was not on the issue of nullification that the election of 1832 was to be decided—the main issue was to be the re-chartering of the Bank of the United States. This was decided by Henry Clay, who in December 1831 won the presidential nomination of a new political party called the National Republicans. The new party's vice-presidential nomination went to John Sergeant, the chief lawyer of the Bank. From the outset of his administration, Jackson had declared his hostility to renewing the twenty-year charter of the Bank when it expired in 1836, believing that the control of the nation's monetary system should not be left in the hands of a private corporation. On the other hand, Clay believed that so many people owed money to the Bank, himself included, that they would fear having to repay these loans at once if the Bank were forced to close.

When Congress, at Clay's urging, passed a bill to re-charter the Bank in the summer of 1832, Jackson, as expected, vetoed the measure. But Jackson's veto message was such a clarion call to popular imagination that it overturned Clay's schemes. Jackson said of the Bank: ". . . when the laws undertake . . . to make the rich richer and the potent more powerful, the humble members of society, the farmers, mechanics, and laborers, who have neither the time nor the means for securing like favors to themselves, have a right to complain of the injustice of their government." Clay and his supporters could not muster enough support to override the veto. And, when the returns in the presidential election of 1832 were counted, Jackson and his Democrats, as his party members had begun to be called, won a smashing victory with 219 electoral votes to Clay's 49. The popular vote stood at 687,502 to 530,189.

Shortly after the election, South Carolina's legislature voted to nullify federal tariff laws and prepared to secede from the Union if efforts were made to collect federal tariffs after February 1, 1833. In the face of this ultimatum by Calhoun's home state, Jackson began preparing for civil war. In December 1832, he issued a Proclamation on Nullification, warning: "Disunion by armed force is treason."

Calhoun resigned as Vice President to take a seat as senator from South Carolina, expecting that the issue would be thrashed out in Congress. But Old Hickory began mobilizing thousands of troops and let it be known that he planned to hang Calhoun if South Carolina went through with its

BORN TO COMMAND.

OF VETO MEMORY.

HAD I BEEN CONSULTED.

KING ANDREW THE FIRST.

A cartoonist's concept of Andrew Jackson in 1832.

threat. Everyone, including Calhoun, knew Jackson too well to think he was bluffing. South Carolina backed down by postponing its secession deadline. Congress supported Jackson by passing the Force Bill that authorized the President to use troops to collect federal taxes, but it also threw a bone to South Carolina by passing legislation calling for a gradual reduction of tariffs. The crisis ended when South Carolina rescinded its nullification legislation on Jackson's sixty-sixth birthday—a historic birthday present.

Jackson's Second Term

In his second inaugural address on March 4, 1833, Jackson declared: "In the domestic policy of this Government there are two objects which especially deserve the attention of the people and their representatives, and which have been and will continue to be the subjects of my increasing solicitude. They are the preservation of the rights of the several States and the integrity of the Union." He concluded by calling upon God to aid him "that we may be preserved from dangers of all kinds and continue forever a united and happy people." As long as Old Hickory remained President, there was no more serious talk of secession.

To solidify his popularity, Jackson made an extensive trip through the Middle Atlantic and New England states in the spring of 1833. As part of this journey, Jackson became the first President to ride on a railroad train—a twelve-mile run on the new Baltimore & Ohio Railroad. He also received an honorary doctorate from Harvard—despite the disapproval of one of its most distinguished alumni, John Quincy Adams, who muttered that Jackson could hardly write his own name.

Early in his second term, Jackson determined to crush "the Monster," as he called the Bank of the United States. As a first step, he planned to transfer federal funds from it to state banks. However, he did not have the full support of his Cabinet, and particularly not the support of his Secretary of the Treasury, William J. Duane. In September 1833, when Duane refused to carry out Jackson's plan, the President removed him and appointed Attorney General Roger Taney to take over the treasury post. Taney then carried out the plan to transfer federal deposits to the state banks.

In retaliation, Nicholas Biddle, who headed the Bank of the United States, tightened up credit, recalled loans, and generally slowed down the American economy. When delegations came to Washington to ask the President to ease the economic hard times, Jackson replied: "Go to Nicholas Biddle." In this way, Jackson brought home to the people the immense financial power of Biddle and the Bank. The Senate, controlled by Henry Clay, voted to censure Jackson for his actions against the Bank, but the House of Representatives overwhelmingly passed resolutions supporting Jackson and calling for an investigation of the Bank. Clay maneuvered another harassment of Jackson by having the Senate reject Taney's appointment as Secretary of the Treasury—the first time a presidential appointment to the Cabinet had ever been turned down.

Jackson more than made good on the pledge of his first inauguration to reduce the national debt. On January 8, 1835—the twentieth anniversary of the battle of New Orleans—the federal government completely paid off the national debt for the first time in its history. The country zoomed into a period of prosperity, prices rose, and paper money flowed. And because the federal government was collecting more in taxes than it was

A sketch by an eyewitness of the attempted assassination of Andrew Jackson, January 30, 1835, at the funeral of Senator Warren R. Davis, at the moment when the assailant leaped out of the crowd and misfired two pistols.

The Lafayette bedroom in the Hermitage, Jackson's home in Nashville, Tennessee.

The Hermitage was known for its hospitality, fine horses, which Andrew Jackson raced, and a successful plantation operation.

spending, Jackson approved, in 1836, an act to distribute surplus federal funds to the states. To curb the speculation in public land caused by the abundance of paper money, Jackson issued orders that henceforth only gold and silver would be accepted as payment for public land.

The greatest crisis in foreign relations came with France in 1835–36 over demands by Jackson that payments be made by the French for damages to American shipping during the Napoleonic wars. Diplomatic relations were broken off, and Jackson prepared for military action. But the French had no wish to tangle with the frontier general, so in 1836 Jackson received four past due installments from the French and good relations were resumed.

Jackson left a black record in Indian affairs. He did not honor the terms of treaties that even he himself had drawn with the Indians. During his administration he forced most of the eastern Indian tribes to give up their lands to white settlers and move west of the Mississippi into Indian Territory, now Oklahoma.

In 1836 word came of the fantastic exploit of Jackson's friend Sam Houston, who at the head of a small army had unbelievably defeated and taken prisoner the Mexican President Santa Anna, winning independence for Texas. Soon Texas applied for annexation to the United States. Jackson hesitated to accept the new state because of the growing Northern opposition to the extension of slavery, but, on the last day of his term of office he recognized Texan independence, setting the stage for future annexation.

The next day, the sick, tired Jackson gladly turned over the reins of government to his hand-picked successor, Martin Van Buren. Two days later he left Washington by train to return to his beloved Hermitage.

ALTHOUGH old, in ill health, and plagued by the debts of his spendthrift adopted son, Andrew Jackson, Jr., the aging general maintained a stronger position in the councils of his party and the administration of the government than any other former President.

When the country plunged into depression in 1837, Jackson's enemies blamed his fiscal policies. He repeatedly urged President Van Buren to stiffen his resolve and told him that prosperity would return. As the depression continued, Biddle's Bank of the United States (that had been re-chartered by Pennsylvania) closed its doors in failure, and Jackson felt that his opposition to it had been vindicated.

Jackson played an important role in secret negotiations with Sam Houston to achieve the annexation of Texas. When Van Buren came out against annexation, Jackson sent word to the 1844 Democratic Convention that Van Buren should be dumped as a presidential candidate. Jackson then helped his friend James K. Polk win the Democratic presidential nomination and the election.

At the age of seventy-eight, the old hero who had defied bullets, swords, arrows, and tomahawks died in his bed at the Hermitage. His last words, addressed to all the members of his household surrounding his bedside were: "I hope to see you all in Heaven, both white and black, both white and black."

Poet and editor William Cullen Bryant said of Jackson:

"Faults he had, undoubtedly; such faults as often belong to an ardent, generous, sincere nature—the weeds that grow in rich soil. Notwithstanding, he was precisely the man for the period, in which he well and nobly discharged the duties demanded of him."

Last Years at the Hermitage

412 JOHN QUINCY ADAMS

John Quincy Adams

The Sixth President of the United States
1825–29

1767 (July 11) Born in Braintree (now Quincy), Massachusetts.

1787 Graduated from Harvard.

1790 Began practicing law in Boston.

1794–1801 U.S. diplomatic representative in several European countries.

1797 (July 26) Married Louisa Catherine Johnson.

1803–08 U.S. senator from Massachusetts.

1806–09 Professor of oratory and rhetoric at Harvard.

1809–14 First U.S. minister to Russia.

1814 Led negotiators that drew up the Treaty of Ghent, which ended the War of 1812.

1815–17 U.S. minister to England.

1817–25 U.S. Secretary of State.

1825–29 Sixth President of the United States.

1830–48 U.S. representative from Massachusetts.

1848 (February 23) Died in the U.S. Capitol in Washington, D.C.

Leading Officials in Adams' Administration

Office	Name	Years Served
Chief Justice	John Marshall	1801-1835
Vice-President	John C. Calhoun	1825-1832
Secretary of State	Henry Clay	1825-1829
Secretary of the Treasury	Richard Rush	1825-1829
Secretary of War	James Barbour	1825-1828
	Peter B. Porter	1828-1829
Attorney General	William Wirt	1817-1829
Postmaster General	John McLean	1823-1829
Secretary of the Navy	Samuel L. Southard	1823-1829

The only man ever to win the presidency both with fewer electoral votes and fewer popular votes than his opponent, John Quincy Adams was also the only son of a President ever to succeed to the nation's highest office. Outwardly a Puritanical scholar who found it difficult to bend to public popularity, Adams revealed himself as a man of strong, though hidden, emotions in the voluminous diaries that he kept all his life. He aptly described himself: "I am a man of reserved, cold, austere, and forbidding manners: my political adversaries say, a gloomy misanthropist, and my personal enemies, an unsocial savage. With a knowledge of the actual defect in my character, I have not the pliability to reform it."

Deeply religious, Adams made it a point to read through the entire Bible at least once each year. He perused several chapters each morning before breakfast, first from an English Bible, then from one in French, and from one in German—only a few of the languages he read with ease. He loved books so much that he once wrote: "To live without having a Cicero and a Tacitus at hand seems to me as if it was a privation of one of my limbs."

A man of middle height—he was five feet seven inches tall—he believed in strenuous physical exercise as the key to fitness. He walked for several miles each day, and in the summer swam in the Potomac River—on one such occasion when a sudden squall came up, he lost his clothes and had to make his way half naked back to the White House.

A Revolutionary Boyhood

THE ELDEST of three sons of John and Abigail Adams, John Quincy Adams was born on July 11, 1767, in Braintree, Massachusetts, while his father was a struggling young lawyer. One of his earliest recollections as a boy was standing on a hilltop on "the awful day" of Bunker Hill listening to the thunder of the cannon and watching the smoke of battle.

When Adams was only ten years old, he accompanied his father on a diplomatic mission to France. As the elder Adams was assigned one diplomatic post after another, young Johnny attended schools in France and the Netherlands. At fourteen he won his father's permission to go to Russia for two years as private secretary to Francis Dana, the first American diplomat assigned to the Russian court.

Returning to America in 1785, he enrolled in Harvard and was graduated two years later at the age of nineteen. He immediately took up the study of law and began his own practice in Boston in 1790. Like most young lawyers, he had few clients, so he filled his time by writing political articles for newspapers, defending the Federalist policies of the national government in which his father was then Vice President.

When he was twenty-seven years old, Adams was appointed by President Washington as United States minister to the Netherlands, where he arrived in January 1795 to find the country occupied by an invading French army. The next year he was appointed minister to Portugal, but before he could leave the Netherlands, he received word that his father had been elected President, and that he was re-assigned as minister to Prussia.

Before traveling to Berlin, Adams married twenty-two-year-old Louisa Catherine Johnson, the daughter of an American diplomat. Their long

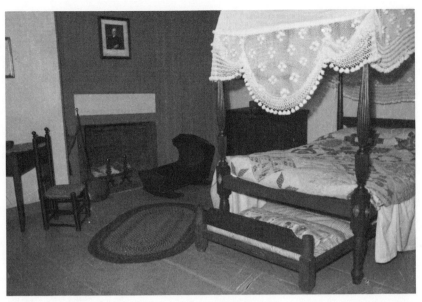

Bedroom where John Quincy Adams was born. —*Doris S. Oberg photograph, Quincy Historical Society*

and happy marriage lasted to Adams' death more than fifty years later. They had four children of whom the youngest, Charles Francis Adams, won the greatest distinction, as U.S. minister to Great Britain during the Civil War.

After spending four years in Berlin, Adams returned to the United States in 1801 when Thomas Jefferson became President. The next year Adams won election to the Massachusetts state senate, and in 1803 the legislature elected him to the United States Senate.

Considering his long training as a diplomat, Adams exhibited little tact as a senator. He had been elected to that office as a member of the Federalist party, but he refused to vote on party lines, studying each issue in light of his own conscience. As he wrote in his diary:

". . . if I cannot hope to give satisfaction to my country, I am at least determined to have the approbation of my own reflections."

In 1807 he broke completely with the Federalists, supporting President Jefferson's embargo act. As a rebuke, the Federalist-controlled Massachusetts legislature chose a successor for Adams six months earlier than was necessary. In anger, he resigned as senator in June 1808, and devoted the next year to his law practice and to teaching oratory and rhetoric at Harvard.

Two days after James Madison's inauguration as President in 1809, Adams was rewarded by the Democratic-Republicans with an appointment as the first U.S. minister to Russia. He was accompanied on the long journey by his wife, youngest son, two servants, and three secretaries. While in Russia, he turned down an appointment in 1811 as a justice of the Supreme Court of the United States. In a moment of reflection, he wrote in his diary on his birthday in 1812:

"I am forty-five years old. Two-thirds of a long life are past, and I have done nothing to distinguish it by usefulness to my country or to mankind. I have always lived with, I hope, a suitable sense of my duties in society, and with a sincere desire to perform them. But passions, indolence, weakness, and infirmity have sometimes made me swerve from my better knowledge of right and almost constantly paralyzed my efforts of good. I have no heavy charge upon my conscience, for which I bless my Maker, as well as for all the enjoyments that He has liberally bestowed upon me.

I pray for his gracious kindness in future. But it is time to cease forming fruitless resolutions."

Adams was in St. Petersburg during Napoleon's invasion of Russia. Becoming good friends with Czar Alexander I, he accepted the Russian ruler's offer to help mediate the War of 1812. This led to his appointment as chief U.S. negotiator at Ghent, where a treaty was concluded on Christmas Eve in 1814. Adams then traveled to Paris, where he witnessed Napoleon's dramatic return from Elba in 1815. From 1815 to 1817 he served as U.S. minister to London, a post once filled by his father.

Secretary of State and Presidential Candidate

APPOINTED Secretary of State by President James Monroe, Adams returned to the United States in 1817, taking office in September. The success of Monroe's administration in the field of foreign policy has been attributed largely to Adams' skill. He wrote that he felt "the most important event of my life" was the successful conclusion of a treaty with Spain acquiring the territory of Florida. He also played an influential role in drafting the Monroe Doctrine.

—From a painting by C. B. King

Louisa Catherine Adams, wife of John Quincy Adams.

Despite the prevailing "Era of Good Feeling," Adams noted in his diary as early as December 1818: ". . . political, personal and electioneering intrigues are intermingling themselves with increasing heat and violence. This Government is indeed assuming daily more and more a character of cabal, and preparation, not for the next Presidential election, but for the one after—that is, working and counter-working, with many of the worst features of elective monarchies. Jackson has made himself a multitude of friends, and still more enemies. The course pursued by the Administration has satisfied neither party, but neither can find much to attack it." The only electoral vote cast against Monroe for a second term in 1821 was given to Adams.

Among those preparing for the election of 1824 was Adams himself. He had four rivals; all Southerners: Secretary of War John C. Calhoun of South Carolina, Secretary of the Treasury W. H. Crawford of Georgia, Congressman Henry Clay of Kentucky, and General Andrew Jackson of Tennessee. Adams expressed private opinions of his opponents in his diary: Calhoun—"very sanguine in his expectations of succeeding to the presidency"; Crawford—"There has never been a man in our history, who has risen so high, of so corrupt a character or upon so slender a basis of service"; Clay—"half-educated" and "his morals, public and private, are loose"; and Jackson—"quarrelsome." Calhoun finally decided to withdraw from the presidential race, settling on the vice presidency as a sure thing by becoming the running mate of both Adams and Jackson.

In the election of 1824 none of the candidates ran with a party label. When the votes were counted, none had received a clear majority, so by the terms of Article II of the Constitution the House of Representatives had the function of choosing the President. The electoral and popular votes stood as follows:

Jackson	99 electoral votes	153,544 popular votes
Adams	84 electoral votes	108,740 popular votes
Crawford	41 electoral votes	46,618 popular votes
Clay	37 electoral votes	47,136 popular votes

Because Clay had the fewest electoral votes, he was forced to drop out of the race; but, by throwing his support to either Jackson or Adams, he could determine the victor. On the evening of January 9, 1825, Clay visited Adams for a "confidential interview," the details of which Adams did not report, even in his diary. But shortly thereafter Clay's supporters swung their votes to Adams, while partisans of Jackson and Crawford screamed that a "corrupt bargain" had been made.

When the House of Representatives voted for President on February 9, 1825, Adams received the votes of 13 states, Jackson 7, and Crawford 4. "May the blessing of God rest upon the event of this day!" Adams wrote in his diary. Significantly, when he announced the appointments to his Cabinet, Clay headed the list as Secretary of State.

Presidential Administration

FULLY cognizant that there were "two-thirds of the whole people adverse to the actual result" of his selection as President, Adams pledged in his inaugural address to do his best under the trying circumstances:

"Less possessed of your confidence in advance than any of my predecessors, I am deeply conscious of the prospect that I shall stand more and oftener in need of your indulgence. Intentions upright and pure, a heart devoted to the welfare of our country, and the unceasing application of all the faculties allotted to me to her service are all the pledges that I can give for the faithful performance of the arduous duties I am to undertake."

John Quincy Adams as he appeared in later years.

418 JOHN QUINCY ADAMS

Nine months later in his first message to Congress, Adams called for a broader interpretation of the Constitution than that held by his three Virginia predecessors, urging that wide-ranging public improvements be financed by Congress for "the benefit of the people." He asked Congress to establish a national university in Washington, to build an astronomical observatory, and to construct more roads and canals. "The spirit of improvement is abroad upon the earth," he said.

With little support from Congress or the people, Adams was unable to achieve his program. Discouraged, he wrote in 1827: "What retirement will be I cannot realize, but have formed no favorable anticipation. It cannot be worse than this perpetual motion and crazing cares. The weight grows heavier from day to day."

Badly defeated by Jackson in his bid for re-election in 1828, Adams noted: "The sun of my political life sets in the deepest gloom. But that of my country shines unclouded."

An Ex-President in Congress

DEEP in despair, Adams remained in Washington after leaving the presidency. His thoughts turned to death, writing in his diary: "I have no plausible motive for wishing to live, when everything that I foresee and believe of futurity makes death desirable." Then, with no campaigning on his part, the people of his home district in Massachusetts elected him in 1830 as their representative in Congress. "No election or appointment conferred upon me ever gave me so much pleasure," he wrote.

As the only former President to return to public office as a member of Congress, Adams won increasing respect as an elder statesman in the more than seventeen years he continued in this office. Although he "abhorred slavery" he labored diligently to cool the passions on this issue that constantly threatened to split the Union between North and South. During much of this time he fought for the removal of the "gag rule" in the House of Representatives that prevented the discussion of the slavery question, finally succeeding in having it abolished in 1845.

After serving in public office through the administrations of the first eleven Presidents of the United States, the eighty-year-old Adams was at his desk in the chamber of the House when he suddenly became ill. Carried to the office of the Speaker of the House, he lay in a coma for more than two days, dying on February 23, 1848. "Where could death have found him," asked Senator Thomas Hart Benton of Missouri, "but at the post of duty?"

420   JAMES MONROE

James Monroe

The Fifth President of the United States
1817–25

1758 (April 28) Born in Westmoreland County, Virginia.

1776–80 Fought in Revolutionary War, rising to rank of lieutenant colonel.

1782 Member of Virginia legislature.

1783–86 Member of Virginia's delegation in Congress.

1786 (February 16) Married Elizabeth Kortright.

1786–90 Member of Virginia legislature.

1790–94 U.S. senator from Virginia.

1794–96 U.S. minister to France.

1799–1802 Governor of Virginia.

1803 Helped negotiate the Louisiana Purchase.

1803–07 U.S. minister to Great Britain.

1811 Governor of Virginia.

1811–17 U.S. Secretary of State.

1814–15 U.S. Secretary of War.

1817–25 Fifth President of the United States.

1829 Co-chairman of Virginia state constitutional convention.

1831 (July 4) Died in New York City.

Leading Officials in
Monroe's Administration

Office	Name	Years Served
Chief Justice	John Marshall	1801-1835
Vice-President	Daniel D. Tompkins	1817-1825
Secretary of State	John Quincy Adams	1817-1825
Secretary of the Treasury	William H. Crawford	1816-1825
Secretary of War	John C. Calhoun	1817-1825
Attorney General	Richard Rush	1814-1817
	William Wirt	1817-1829
Secretary of the Navy	B. W. Crowninshield	1814-1819
	Smith Thompson	1819-1823
	Samuel L. Southard	1823-1829
Postmaster General	Return Meigs, Jr.	1814-1823
	John McLean	1823-1829

Ash Lawn, the home Monroe built in Charlottesville, Virginia, near Monticello, Jefferson's home.

Bringing the country such peace, prosperity, and growth that his administration won the nickname of the "Era of Good Feeling," James Monroe became so popular with voters and politicians that he was unopposed for his second term as President—an honor accorded only one other Chief Executive, George Washington. A hero of the Revolutionary War, described by Thomas Jefferson as "a man whose soul might be turned wrong side outwards without discovering a blemish to the world," he left the country in political turmoil largely because he did not want to hurt the feelings of any of his friends by supporting only one of them as his presidential successor.

Monroe did much to expand the size of the United States. He made the key on-the-spot decision that resulted in the Louisiana Purchase, and as President succeeded in negotiating the acquisition of Florida. His approval of the Missouri Compromise that admitted Missouri as a slave state helped postpone the crisis over slavery between the North and South. And his conclusion of a treaty demilitarizing the boundary between the United States and Canada insured history's first continuing peace between two large neighboring countries.

His most remembered act, the Monroe Doctrine, conceived as a warning to the European powers to keep hands off the new Latin American republics, became an abiding cornerstone of American foreign policy.

A contemporary description of Monroe by William Wirt, who served under him as Attorney General, follows:

"In his stature, he is about the middle height of men, rather firmly set, with nothing further remarkable in his person, except his muscular compactness and apparent ability to endure labor. His countenance, when grave, has rather the expression of sternness and irascibility; a smile, however (and a smile is not unusual with him in a social circle), lights it up to a very high advantage, and gives it a most impressive and engaging air of suavity and benevolence. His dress and personal appearance are those of a plain and modest gentleman. He is a man of soft, polite, and even assiduous attentions . . . there is often in his manner an inartificial and even an awkward simplicity, which, while it provokes the smile of a more polished person, forces him to the opinion that Mr. Monroe is a man of a most sincere and artless soul."

LIKE Washington, Jefferson, and Madison, James Monroe was the son of a Virginia planter. He was born on April 28, 1758, in Westmoreland County, the eldest of five children of Spence and Elizabeth Jones Monroe. When he was sixteen, young Monroe was sent to attend the College of William and Mary at Williamsburg, where one of the other undergraduates at the time was John Marshall, a future Chief Justice of the United States.

A Revolutionary War Hero

With the outbreak of the Revolution, Monroe quit college to join a Virginia regiment of the Continental Army, receiving a commission as lieutenant at the age of eighteen. His regiment joined Washington's troops in New York, where he fought in the battles of Harlem and White Plains. While leading the advance guard in the battle of Trenton, he was wounded in the shoulder, and for his bravery was promoted to captain by Washington. During 1777 and 1778 he took part in the battles of Brandywine, Germantown, and Monmouth. Commissioned a lieutenant colonel in 1778, he undertook to recruit a new Virginia regiment, but was unable to raise enough volunteers. In 1780 he carried out an assignment by Jefferson, then governor of Virginia, to report on the condition of the southern army.

The war ending, Monroe became a protégé of Jefferson, studied law under the older man's guidance, and won election to the state legislature in 1782. The next year he was elected with Jefferson as a member of Virginia's delegation to Congress. During his three years in Congress, he helped write the Northwest Ordinance with Rufus King, whom he was to defeat thirty years later in the 1816 presidential election, and made two trips into the Ohio Valley to gain first-hand information on conditions on the western frontier. Believing that the Articles of Confederation needed strengthening, Monroe drew up an amendment that would have given Congress the power to regulate commerce between the states, but he was unable to win its acceptance.

While serving in Congress, Monroe fell in love with and married Elizabeth Kortright, the daughter of a New York businessman. When his term of office expired in 1786 he temporarily retired from politics and established a law practice at Fredericksburg, Virginia. Later, he built Ash Lawn, near Jefferson's Monticello, where he and his wife reared their two daughters.

Monroe did not take part in the Constitutional Convention of 1787, and he vigorously opposed ratification of the Constitution at the Virginia convention until he received assurances that a Bill of Rights would be adopted. After ratification of the Constitution, he ran for Congress against Madison, but was defeated. In 1790, through the political influence of Patrick Henry, the thirty-two-year-old Monroe won appointment as a U.S. senator to fill a vacancy caused by the death of William Grayson.

In the Senate, Monroe became a leader of the Democratic-Republican party, and helped fight the Federalist policies of Alexander Hamilton. He formed a low opinion of Hamilton's motives, and when he made his views public a few years later he was almost forced into a duel with Hamilton.

BECAUSE Monroe's sympathies for the French revolutionists were well known, President Washington appointed him in 1794 to soothe relations with France. In Paris, Monroe quickly won the friendship of the French and became the only ambassador of a foreign power invited to sit in their national legislature. In an address to the French national assembly he enthusiastically committed himself to aiding the French cause; but when word of his speech reached America he was severely reprimanded for jeopardizing United States neutrality in the war between France and the European coalition. When word of the Jay Treaty with Britain reached Monroe, he denounced it as ". . . the most shameful transaction I have ever known of the kind." Washington ordered the recall of his outspoken ambassador in 1796. Returning to the United States, Monroe published a 500-page book, *A View of the Conduct of the Executive,* in which he attempted to vindicate his conduct in France and blamed Washington's administration for damaging relations with America's former ally.

Late in 1799, the Virginia legislature elected Monroe governor. During the three years that he served in this office, he became closer friends with Madison, who served in the legislature during the first part of this time.

In 1803 Monroe again was sent to France, this time by Jefferson, who needed a special envoy to help negotiate the purchase of New Orleans. When he arrived in Paris, he learned from Robert Livingston, the regular U.S. minister to France, that Napoleon already had indicated the desire to sell all of the Louisiana Territory to the United States. Although he and Livingston were not authorized to agree to such a large transaction, Monroe enthusiastically took the responsibility on himself and helped negotiate a treaty that doubled the size of the United States at a cost of $15 million.

From Paris, Monroe was sent to London where for the next several years he tried to negotiate a treaty that would end the friction between Britain and the United States over freedom of the seas. During this time he also spent several months in Madrid trying to bargain with the Spanish

The original of this Benjamin West portrait of Mrs. James Monroe (Elizabeth Kortright) is in the White House.

for the purchase of Florida. Unsuccessful on both scores, he returned to the United States in 1807 and again resumed the private practice of law in Virginia. Some of his friends urged him to run for President, but a congressional caucus of the Democratic-Republican party overwhelmingly chose Madison.

The Virginia legislature for the second time elected Monroe governor in 1811, but when Madison offered him an appointment as Secretary of State he resigned the governorship. Monroe helped draft the recommendations to Congress that led to a declaration of war on Britain in 1812. As American defeats mounted during the war, Monroe urged Madison to appoint him as Secretary of War. Madison agreed to this appointment after the fall of the city of Washington, and for the rest of the war Monroe held both cabinet posts. He instilled new enthusiasm in the Army, and American troops began to win victories. His vigor and energy are exemplified by a message to Western governors before the battle of New Orleans: "Hasten your militia to New Orleans; do not wait for this government to arm them; put all the arms you can find into their hands; let every man bring his rifle with him; we shall see you paid."

With the end of the war and the expanding prosperity of the country in the last years of Madison's administration, Monroe was held in high esteem throughout the country. With Madison's support, Monroe won the Democratic-Republican presidential nomination when a congressional caucus chose him by a 65 to 54 vote over Secretary of the Treasury William H. Crawford. He then went on to win the 1816 presidential election over Federalist candidate Senator Rufus King of New York, receiving an electoral vote of 183 to King's 34.

Daniel D. Tompkins, who served as Vice-President under James Monroe.

TAKING office at a time when the United States faced no unusual problems, the fifty-eight-year-old Monroe commented in his inaugural address:

"Never did a government commence under auspices so favorable, nor ever was success so complete. If we look to the history of other nations, ancient or modern, we find no example of a growth so rapid, so gigantic, of a people so prosperous and happy. In contemplating what we have still to perform, the heart of every citizen must expand with joy when he reflects how near our Government has approached to perfection; that in respect to it we have no essential improvement to make; that the great object is to preserve it in the essential principles and features which characterize it, and that that is to be done by preserving the virtue and enlightening the minds of the people . . ."

Appointing one of the strongest and most stable Cabinets in presidential history, Monroe helped end sectional discord by choosing John Quincy Adams of Massachusetts as Secretary of State and John C. Calhoun of South Carolina as Secretary of War. Monroe also strengthened his popular support with a three-and-a-half-month tour in 1817 that took him through the New England States and as far west as Detroit—a trip that his critics called a "political jubilee," but one that was so successful that he followed it up with a similar tour of the Southern states in 1819. By the time he ran for re-election in 1820, the Federalist party was dead, and Monroe received 231 of the Electoral College's 232 votes—one elector having cast his ballot for John Quincy Adams, supposedly to preserve for Washington the honor of having received the only unanimous vote.

THE greatest successes of Monroe's administration occurred in the field he knew best—foreign relations. The Rush-Bagot Agreement with Britain in 1817 eliminated fortifications along the Canadian border. Two years later

Monroe's Administration

The Monroe Doctrine

425

President Monroe's desk and clock.

successful negotiations were concluded to acquire Florida from Spain. But the proclamation of the Monroe Doctrine in 1823 has lived on as his most monumental achievement.

Fearing that European powers might attempt to intervene in Latin America, where various countries had just won their independence from Spain, Monroe wrote to Jefferson asking his advice as to what course to take. The elder statesman replied to his protégé: "Our first and fundamental Maxim should be, never to entangle ourselves in the broils of Europe. Our second, never to suffer Europe to intermeddle with cis-Atlantic affairs." Following this advice, Monroe established the doctrine that bears his name in his annual message to Congress on December 2, 1823, in which he said in part:

". . . we should consider any attempt on their part (that of European powers) to extend their system to any portion of this hemisphere as dangerous to our peace and safety. With the existing colonies or dependencies of any European power we have not interfered, and shall not interfere. But with the governments who have declared their independence and maintained it, and whose independence we have, on great consideration and on just principles, acknowledged, we could not view any interposition for the purpose of oppressing them, or controlling in any other manner their destiny, by any European power, in any other light than as the manifestation of an unfriendly disposition toward the United States."

In domestic affairs, Monroe made no effort to lead Congress. He followed the precepts of Jefferson and Madison in denying the constitutionality of federal financing of such public improvements as roads and canals. However, he indicated his support by calling for a constitutional amendment to allow such federal action, and by approving the Survey Act of 1824, which provided for planning of future public works. Several acts increasing protective tariffs were also approved by Monroe. He held himself largely aloof from the congressional debates that led to the Missouri Compromise, but let it be known that he favored admitting Missouri as a slave state.

Last Years

AFTER completing his second term as President, Monroe retired to Virginia, where he resumed at closer hand his friendships with Jefferson and Madison. He served with them as a regent of the University of Virginia, and acted as co-chairman with Madison of the Virginia state constitutional convention of 1829. But in his last years he suffered financial distress and spent much time trying to collect money from the government that he said was owed him for expenses during his long public service. Finally, forced to sell his property in Virginia, he moved to New York to live with one of his married daughters. He died there on July 4, 1831—the third President to die on the anniversary of independence. Upon learning of Monroe's death, John Quincy Adams noted in his diary:

"James Monroe, a man whose life has been marked with vicissitudes as great as have befallen any citizen of the United States since the beginning of our national existence . . . His life for the last six years has been one of abject penury and distress, and they have brought him to a premature grave, though in the seventy-third year of his age. His Administration, happening precisely at the moment of the greatest tranquility which has ever been enjoyed by this country . . . was a time of great prosperity, and his personal popularity was unrivalled. Yet no one regretted the termination of his Administration, and less of popular veneration followed him into retirement than had accompanied all his predecessors. His last days have been much afflicted, contrasting deeply with the triumphal procession which he made through the Union in the years 1817 and 1819."

A painting of James Monroe by Thomas Sully which emphasizes his compact, muscular body.

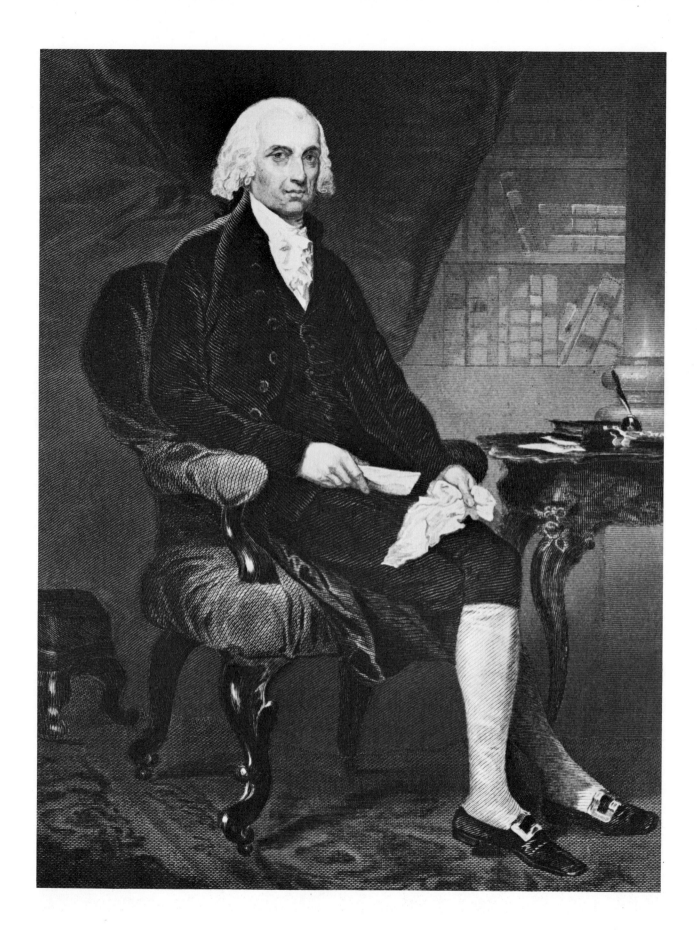

428 JAMES MADISON

James Madison

The Fourth President of the United States
1809–17

1751 (March 16) Born at Port Conway, Virginia.

1771 Graduated from College of New Jersey at Princeton.

1776 Helped write Virginia state constitution.

1776–77 Member of Virginia legislature.

1778–79 Member of Virginia governor's advisory council.

1780–83 Delegate to Congress.

1784–86 Member of Virginia legislature.

1786 Delegate to Annapolis Convention.

1787 Delegate to Constitutional Convention.

1787–88 Member of Congress of the Confederation; wrote many of *The Federalist* essays.

1789–97 U.S. representative in Congress.

1794 Married Dolley Payne Todd.

1799–1800 Member of Virginia legislature.

1801–09 Secretary of State under Thomas Jefferson.

1809–17 Fourth President of the United States.

1826 Succeeded Jefferson as rector of the University of Virginia.

1829 Co-chairman of Virginia state constitutional convention.

1836 (June 28) Died at Montpelier, Orange County, Virginia.

Leading Officials in Madison's Administration

Office	Name	Years Served
Chief Justice	John Marshall	1801-1835
Vice-President	George Clinton	1805-1812
	Elbridge Gerry	1813-1814
Secretary of State	Robert Smith	1809-1811
	James Monroe	1811-1817
Secretary of the Treasury	Albert Gallatin	1802-1814
	George W. Campbell	1814
	Alexander J. Dallas	1814-1816
	William H. Crawford	1816-1825
Secretary of War	William Eustis	1809-1813
	John Armstrong	1813-1814
	James Monroe	1814-1815
	William H. Crawford	1815-1817
Attorney General	Caesar A. Rodney	1807-1811
	William Pinkney	1811-1814
	Richard Rush	1814-1817
Secretary of the Navy	Paul Hamilton	1809-1813
	William Jones	1813-1814
	B. W. Crowninshield	1814-1819
Postmaster General	Gideon Granger	1801-1814
	Return Meigs, Jr.	1814-1823

The last of the Founding Fathers to serve as President, James Madison served two terms in the White House, but his greatest contributions to American history already lay behind him in the Constitution and the Bill of Rights. In many ways his career, as well as his political philosophy, paralleled that of his friend and mentor, Thomas Jefferson. Their mutual political adversary, John Quincy Adams, regarded Madison as "in truth a greater man."

Shorter than average height in a time of short men, Madison relied more upon his brilliant mind than on a commanding presence to lead others to his way of thinking. As a co-founder, with Jefferson, of the Democratic-Republican party, he was vilified by the Federalists, whose chief spokesman, his former friend Alexander Hamilton, said of him: "Mr. Madison, co-operating with Mr. Jefferson, is at the head of a faction . . . subversive of the principles of good government and dangerous to the Union, peace, and happiness of the country."

A Rising Young Virginian

THE SON of a Virginia planter, James Madison was born at his grandparents' home in Port Conway, Virginia, on March 16, 1751. He grew up at his family's plantation, Montpelier, becoming, in Jefferson's words, "the best farmer in the world." At the age of eighteen, he went to the College of New Jersey at Princeton, graduating two years later.

Returning home from college in 1771, he plunged into the political storm that was gathering. When Virginia declared itself independent of Great Britain in 1776, the twenty-five-year-old Madison served as a delegate to the patriotic convention called to form a new state government and helped write the Virginia constitution. Elected to the first state legislature, he met the already-famous Jefferson, just returned from writing the Declaration of Independence in Philadelphia. A lifelong friendship began on the spot. Madison was not re-elected to the legislature because he refused to follow the custom of providing free rum for voters, but Governor Patrick Henry appointed him to the council of state. On this advisory council Madison continued to serve in the following administration of his friend Jefferson.

As a member of Virginia's delegation to Congress from 1780 to 1783, he helped organize the national government under the newly adopted Articles of Confederation. Despite his affinity for Jefferson's democratic ideals, Madison found himself attracted to one of the principal doctrines of Alexander Hamilton, a man of his own age. That was the need for a strong central government. The two young men—Madison was in his early thirties, Hamilton even younger—agreed to work together. It was one of the most fruitful collaborations in United States history.

A little later Madison was able to bring his views on a federal government to the attention of George Washington. Washington was impressed with his young fellow Virginian and applauded his election as a delegate to the Annapolis Convention in 1786. This was a meeting of several states to study inter-state commercial problems. Few delegates appeared, but two —Madison and Hamilton—made the unsuccessful conference a turning point in the nation's history. They prevailed upon the meeting to call for a convention of states to revise the Articles of Confederation. Washington approved, writing to Madison: "Without some alteration in our political creed, the superstructure we have been seven years raising at the expense of so much blood and treasure, must fall."

A portrait of Mrs. James Madison (Dolley Payne Todd), a famous White House hostess.
—From a painting by Gilbert Stuart

As A delegate to the Constitutional Convention in Philadelphia, the thirty-six-year-old Madison played a major role. He took it upon himself to keep a complete record of the debates during the secret meetings of the convention, stationing himself at the front of the room near the chair of the presiding officer, Washington. Further, he had drafted a complete plan for a new national government. Madison's "Virginia Plan," as it was called, became the main basis for the Constitution, ultimately approved four months later. Throughout the convention Madison repeatedly spoke out on the necessity of providing a democratic basis for the government with election of congressmen directly by the people. As a member of the committee on style, Madison helped write the final version of the Constitution that was signed on September 17.

Father of the Constitution and the Bill of Rights

At the close of these sessions, Madison set to work on a series of essays designed to explain the new Constitution to the people. These brilliant tracts, along with others written by Hamilton and John Jay, are collectively known as *The Federalist* and continue to this day to provide an unequaled interpretation of a federated national government. At the time, they were invaluable in winning support for the new Constitution.

Fearing that the opposition of Patrick Henry, Virginia's political boss, might cause their home state to reject the Constitution, Washington appealed to Madison to run for election to the state ratification convention and lead the floor fight there. He wrote: "Explanations will be wanting, and none can give them with more accuracy and propriety than yourself."

Madison attended the convention and helped win ratification by a narrow 89 to 79 vote. In doing so he also won the lasting enmity of Henry. When Madison's name was proposed as one of the state's new U.S. senators, Henry declared that Madison's election would bring a revolution with "rivulets of blood throughout the land." Defeated for senator, Madison ran for U.S. representative. Again Henry tried to thwart him by redistricting, and by putting up the young, well-liked James Monroe to oppose him; but, after a hard-fought campaign, Madison was elected by a small margin.

Congressman and Secretary of State

In Congress, Madison distinguished himself by preparing the Bill of Rights amendments to the Constitution and much of the legislation forming various departments of the new government. He also acted as an adviser to Washington, helping prepare both his Inaugural Address and his Farewell Address.

In 1794 Madison married a pretty widow, Dolley Payne Todd, seventeen years younger than himself. Her social charm aided him immeasurably in his later career as Secretary of State, when she often acted as hostess for the widowed President Jefferson, and as President, when she sustained him during the difficult war years. They had no children of their own, but reared her son by a previous marriage.

When Federalist John Adams became President, Madison retired from Congress, returning to plantation life at Montpelier. But when the Federalist administration threatened the freedoms guaranteed in the Bill of

The room at Harewood, near Charles Town, West Virginia, in which James and Dolley Madison were married in 1794, when he was a Congressman.

A retouched reproduction of an 1848 daguerreotype of Dolley Madison at the age of 80.

Rights, Madison angrily wrote the Virginia Resolutions, denouncing the unconstitutionality of the Alien and Sedition Acts. To further his fight for the defense of civil liberties, Madison again won election to the state legislature, serving from 1799 to 1800.

Madison campaigned for Jefferson's election in 1800, and afterwards accepted appointment as Secretary of State. During the next eight years the two worked together so closely on foreign policy that it is difficult to separate their individual contributions in helping to preserve American neutrality in the European wars and in negotiating the Louisiana Purchase.

As Jefferson's choice to succeed to the presidency, Madison easily won the election of 1808, defeating the Federalist candidate, Charles Cotesworth Pinckney, with 122 electoral votes to 47.

MADISON came to the nation's highest office at a time of crisis in foreign relations. Both Great Britain and France were riding roughshod over American rights as they fought the Napoleonic wars, and American public opinion was sharply divided. The Federalists and the North favored Great Britain while the Democratic-Republicans and the South and West sympathized with France. Jefferson and Madison tried to steer a course of neutrality. One of Jefferson's last decisions as President was to sign the repeal of the Embargo Act, substituting for it the new Non-Intercourse Act, which permitted trade with any countries except France and Britain.

Madison's Administration

A sketch of the James Madison plantation home, Montpelier, in Orange County, Virginia.

The new act failed to influence the warring powers, and friction with Britain was augmented by a major Indian uprising, widely blamed on the British. The Indians were crushed by William Henry Harrison in the battle of Tippecanoe.

Another element making for war was a coterie of American expansionists who dreamed of the annexation of Canada. In Congress the leaders of the "war hawks," as Jefferson called them, were Henry Clay of Kentucky and John Calhoun of South Carolina. This group also hoped that Florida could be wrested from Britain's ally, Spain.

Bowing to external and internal pressures, Madison asked Congress on June 1, 1812, for a declaration of war on Britain. On June 18 the measure passed by the narrow margin of 19 to 13 in the Senate and 79 to 49 in the House. Ironically, two days earlier the British had repealed a set of blockade orders which had been a major provocation to war, but word did not reach America until the war was well under way.

The military and naval forces of the United States were hardly prepared for what became known by the Federalists as "Mr. Madison's War." The Army had only about 10,000 troops and the Navy less than two dozen ships. Campaigns against Canada and Florida failed, and New England actually threatened secession. When the Napoleonic wars ended in Europe, Britain was free to send forces which invaded Chesapeake Bay, drove Madison and Congress from Washington, and set fire to the Capitol, the White House, and other public buildings.

The two sides signed the Treaty of Ghent on December 24, 1814, which called for each side to give up any territory it had occupied. Again, the grim irony of slow communications prevented news of peace from crossing the Atlantic in time to stop the war's biggest battle, at New Orleans on January 8, 1815, in which General Andrew Jackson won a major victory over the British.

During the war, Madison decisively won a second term over the fusion presidential candidate, De Witt Clinton, achieving an electoral vote of 128 to 89. Clinton, a disaffected New York Democratic-Republican, had been chosen as their best hope by the dying Federalist party.

With the end of the war, the westward movement of settlers resumed, bringing the country new prosperity and Madison new popularity. He now accepted in large measure the economic principles of the Federalist party, putting his signature to a law chartering a new United States Bank and calling for higher tariffs to protect American manufacturers.

Although he revised his economic thinking, Madison refused to change his belief that the Constitution should be strictly interpreted. He demonstrated this forcibly on his last day before leaving office, March 3, 1817, when he vetoed John Calhoun's "Bonus Bill" that would have used federal funds to help build a "perfect system of roads and canals" for the nation. Madison explained his veto by saying he believed "the permanent success of the Constitution depends on a definite partition of powers between the General and State governments" and that he could find no provision in the Constitution that called on the federal government to build roads and canals.

Retiring at the end of his second term, Madison left the presidency in the hands of James Monroe, whom he had designated as his successor, and whose overwhelming victory over the Federalist candidate, Rufus King, was taken by Madison as a personal tribute.

SURVIVING all his old colleagues of the Constitutional Convention, Madison lived on to the age of eighty-five, seeing the transportation revolution that came with railroads and steamboats and the expansion of the United States to twenty-five states stretching to the Mississippi. After Jefferson's death in 1826, Madison carried on his friend's work in education by assuming the office of rector of the University of Virginia. He also maintained his interest in constitutional affairs to the end of his life, serving as co-chairman of a Virginia convention in 1829 that revised the state constitution he had helped write more than fifty years earlier. After his death on June 28, 1836, at Montpelier, his wife sold to the government his invaluable, and until then secret, notes on the Constitutional Convention of 1787. In the introduction to these notes, Madison wrote perhaps his own best eulogy:

". . . whatever may be the judgment pronounced on the competency of the architects of the Constitution, or whatever may be the destiny of the edifice prepared by them, I feel it a duty to express my profound and solemn conviction, derived from my intimate opportunity of observing and appreciating the views of the Convention, collectively and individually, that there never was an assembly of men, charged with a great and arduous trust, who were more pure in their motives, or more exclusively or anxiously devoted to the object committed to them, than were the members of the Federal Convention of 1787, to the object of devising and proposing a constitutional system which should best supply the defects of that which it was to replace, and best secure the permanent liberty and happiness of their country."

A Ripe Old Age

435

436 THOMAS JEFFERSON

Thomas Jefferson

The Third President of the United States
1801–09

1743 (April 13) Born at Shadwell in Albemarle County, Virginia.

1762 Graduated from College of William and Mary.

1767 Began practicing law.

1769–79 Served in Virginia legislature.

1772 (January 1) Married Martha Wayles Skelton.

1775–76 Member of Virginia's delegation to Congress; wrote Declaration of Independence.

1779–81 Governor of Virginia.

1783–84 Member of Virginia's delegation to Congress.

1784–85 Diplomatic commissioner of Congress in Europe.

1785–89 U.S. diplomatic minister to France.

1789–93 Secretary of State under George Washington.

1797–1801 Vice President under John Adams.

1801–09 Third President of the United States.

1816–25 Founder and first rector of the University of Virginia.

1826 (July 4) Died at Monticello in Albemarle County, Virginia.

Leading Officials in Jefferson's Administration

Office	Name	Years Served
Chief Justice	John Marshall	1801-1835
Vice-President	Aaron Burr	1801-1805
	George Clinton	1805-1812
Secretary of State	James Madison	1801-1809
Secretary of the Treasury	Samuel Dexter	1801-1802
	Albert Gallatin	1802-1814
Secretary of War	Henry Dearborn	1801-1809
Attorney General	Levi Lincoln	1801-1805
	Robert Smith	1805
	John Breckinridge	1805-1807
	Caesar A. Rodney	1807-1811
Secretary of the Navy	Robert Smith	1801-1809
Postmaster General	Joseph Habersham	1795-1801
	Gideon Granger	1801-1814

I have sworn upon the altar of God eternal hostility against every form of tyranny over the mind of man."

This quotation from Thomas Jefferson, carved on his memorial in Washington, D.C., epitomizes the philosophy to which he dedicated his life, his mind, and his eloquent pen.

Master of any talent or profession to which he turned his hand, the red-haired Jefferson won undying fame at the age of thirty-three as author of the Declaration of Independence. His public service spanned forty years as a legislator, governor, congressman, diplomat, Secretary of State, Vice President, President, and university founder; but he also found time to achieve success as a lawyer, farmer, philosopher, writer, architect, scientist, musician, and inventor.

Denounced as a radical and an atheist by his conservative political opponents, Jefferson became the first leader of an opposition political party to wrest control of the national government from the party in power. Despite grim prophecies by the outgoing Federalists that the Constitution would be overthrown by Jefferson's Democratic-Republicans, he proved to the world the strength and staying power of the American republic and its democratic system under a changing political philosophy. Jefferson believed that the United States should remain an agricultural country of small farms with a national government that interfered as little as possible in the lives of its people; but as President he, in his own words, "stretched the Constitution till it cracked," in using the presidential treaty-making powers to double the size of the nation with the Louisiana Purchase. He established the right of an in-coming President to discharge major political appointees of his predecessor, but was restrained by Chief Justice John Marshall from applying the same principle to federal judges.

Jefferson believed his presidential accomplishments were among the least of his contributions. This was evidenced by the epitaph he wrote, asking that "not a word more" than the following be engraved on his monument at Monticello:

Here was buried
Thomas Jefferson
Author of the Declaration of American Independence,
Of the Statute of Virginia for Religious Freedom,
And Father of the University of Virginia.

A Virginia Plantation Owner

THE SON of Peter Jefferson, a planter and surveyor, Thomas Jefferson was the third child in a family of ten. His mother, Jane, was a member of the Randolph family, one of the oldest and most distinguished in Virginia. He was born at his father's farm, Shadwell, in Albemarle County, Virginia, on April 13, 1743 (April 2 by the Old Style Calendar).

Jefferson, as a boy, took easily to learning. He knew Latin and Greek by the age of fourteen, when his father died, leaving him, as the eldest son, the head of the family with an estate of about 2500 acres and thirty slaves. Two years later he enrolled at the College of William and Mary in Williamsburg.

While attending William and Mary, young Jefferson was stimulated by the hustle, bustle, and culture of the Virginia capital. He became a friend of Governor Francis Fauquier and of two scholars: William Small, profes-

A Thomas Sully painting of Martha Jefferson Randolph, one of two daughters who survived childhood.

sor of mathematics at the college, and George Wythe, a learned lawyer and judge. Jefferson played violin with a chamber music group organized by the governor, and was treated as an equal at intimate dinners with the three older men, later writing that "at these dinners I have heard more good sense, more rational and philosophical conversations, than in all my life besides."

After graduation from William and Mary in 1762, the nineteen-year-old Jefferson took up the study of law, which he continued for five years under Wythe's direction, until being admitted to the Virginia bar in 1767. Often attending sessions of Virginia's House of Burgesses, Jefferson became acquainted with the great Virginia lawmakers of the day, including Patrick Henry. He was particularly impressed with Henry's famous "Give Me Liberty" speech denouncing the British Stamp Act in 1765, saying that Henry's forensic talents were "such as I have never heard from any other man."

All was not seriousness and study for the redheaded young bachelor. Much of his time was occupied with romances, fox hunts, shooting matches, violin-playing, and theater-going. To a friend who wrote suggesting that he marry, he replied: "No, thank ye; I will consider of it first. Many and great are the comforts of a single state."

But like many young bachelors, Jefferson presently changed his mind. In 1772 he married a well-to-do widow, Martha Wayles Skelton, whose fortune practically doubled Jefferson's already sizable estate. His birthplace, Shadwell, had burned down two years earlier, and he had begun building his handsome mansion, Monticello. While awaiting its completion the young couple moved into a one-room cottage. The marriage was a congenial one, but darkened by the loss of four of the six children born in the next ten years, and tragically ended in 1782 by Martha's own death. Jefferson never remarried.

In 1769, when he was only twenty-six, he had already entered politics, winning election to the Virginia colonial legislature. For the next ten years he was regularly re-elected, adding steadily to a reputation for patriotic views and skill in expressing them in writing.

In 1773 he was appointed by the Virginia legislature as a member of the Committee of Correspondence to keep in touch with patriotic leaders in the other colonies. When the governor of Virginia dissolved the colonial legislature because of its patriotic activities, Jefferson wrote a strongly-worded pamphlet for a Virginia convention of legislators called to meet in August 1774. Entitled *A Summary View of the Rights of British America, Set Forth in some Resolutions Intended for the Inspection of the Present Delegates of the People of Virginia, now in Convention,* it won fame for its author as "Mr. Jefferson's Bill of Rights."

Declaration of Independence

BARELY two years later the gifted pen of the tall young Virginian was drafted for the most important piece of writing in American history. The Continental Congress, which had gathered in Philadelphia in 1775 to the sound of the guns of Lexington and Concord, had moved steadily toward a final break with the British monarchy. A five-man committee, including

An early sketch of Monticello.

Roger Sherman, Robert Livingston, Benjamin Franklin, John Adams, and Thomas Jefferson, was chosen to write a suitable "Declaration of Independence" from the crown.

His older colleagues, although noted for their literary skill, promptly deferred to Jefferson, possibly feeling that if written by a Southerner it more likely would be approved by Congress. Seating himself at the portable writing desk he himself had invented, Jefferson "turned to neither book nor pamphlet" for inspiration. From its stirring opening, "When in the course of human events," to its end, the Declaration bears the stamp of a remarkable originality. The three-day debate and extensive editing that followed its presentation irritated the author, but in the end the most important of his ringing words survived. They were finally approved on July 4, making "Life, Liberty and the pursuit of Happiness" a lasting proclamation of the rights of man.

Less than two months later Jefferson resigned to return to Virginia and take his seat in the state legislature. It was supremely important to him that the new laws of his state provide adequate safeguards for the rights of its citizens. As he explained it: "I knew that our legislation under the regal government had many very vicious points which urgently required reformation, and I thought I could be of more use in forwarding that work."

Within a week after returning to Virginia, Jefferson drew up legislation establishing a new system of state courts. Next, he introduced bills to abolish entail and primogeniture, the feudal hereditary restrictions on property. Although himself a slave-owner, he endeavored to abolish slavery, but succeeded only in outlawing further importation of slaves. Tirelessly writing bill after bill, he drew up plans for a system of free public schools, a state library, and many other measures, some of which were not adopted by the legislature until years later.

But Jefferson regarded his greatest accomplishment during this time to be the establishment of religious freedom in Virginia. The Church of England had always been the state church of the colony, established as such in the original land grant to Sir Walter Raleigh; and expenses had been paid by taxation of both members and non-members. Jefferson fought for three years, from 1776 to 1779, to disestablish the church, taking part, in his own words, in "the severest contests in which I have ever been engaged." The statute for religious freedom that he wrote said in part: ". . . no man shall be compelled to frequent or support any religious worship, place or ministry whatsoever, nor shall be enforced, restrained, molested or burdened in his body or goods, nor shall otherwise suffer, on account of his religious opinions or beliefs; but that all men shall be free to profess and by arguments to maintain their opinions in matters of religion, and that the same shall in no wise diminish, enlarge or affect their civil capacities." This Virginia statute later became the basis for the First Amendment to the Constitution.

At thirty-six, Jefferson was elected by the legislature to succeed Patrick Henry as governor of the state. He served for two years, from 1779 to 1781, during the most desperate period of the Revolutionary War in Virginia, when British forces under Lord Cornwallis ravaged the countryside, plundering, looting, and killing. Jefferson himself barely escaped capture at Monticello, where the British burned his barns, ate his livestock, and carried off his slaves.

Most of Jefferson's energies as governor were devoted to raising troops and supplies for Washington's Continental Army, while at the same time trying to organize the defense of Virginia. During this time he wrote:

"The nakedness of the militia on service near Williamsburg and want of shoes is such as to have produced murmurings almost amounting to mutinies . . ." Jefferson declined re-election, recommending that the legislature choose a soldier, General Thomas Nelson, to replace him.

Temporarily retiring from public service, he devoted considerable time to writing *Notes on Virginia,* a book on natural history that won him a reputation in Europe as a scholar and scientist. For the French edition of his book he drew a new map of Virginia.

The death of his wife in 1782 threw Jefferson into such desolation that his family feared he might never recover. He destroyed all the letters they had written each other, and for weeks remained in what he later described as a "stupor of mind which had rendered me as dead to the world as she was whose loss occasioned it."

Congressman and Diplomat

RETURNING to public life in 1783, with his election to Congress by the state legislature, Jefferson again began to utilize the great resources of his mind for his country's benefit. He served as chairman of the committee handling the peace treaty with Great Britain and recommended ratification. He invented the decimal system of coinage adopted by the national government. He also wrote a bill for organizing the Northwest Territory which was later largely adopted. The bill prohibited slavery in the future new states (Michigan, Ohio, Indiana, Illinois, Wisconsin). Jefferson sought to bar slavery from *all* future new states, a measure which, had it been passed, might have prevented the Civil War. This sweeping proposal was defeated by one vote. Jefferson, who was keenly disappointed, wrote:

"The voice of a single individual . . . would have prevented this abominable crime from spreading itself over the new country. Thus we see the fate of millions unborn hanging on the tongue of one man, and Heaven was silent in that awful moment! But it is to be hoped that it will not always be silent, and that the friends to the rights of human nature will in the end prevail."

Deploring the national government's weakness under the Articles of Confederation, Jefferson wrote to George Washington in 1784: "The crippled state of Congress is not new to you. We have only nine states present, eight of whom are represented by two members each, and of course on all great questions not only a unanimity of states but of members is necessary—a unanimity which can never be obtained on a matter of any importance. The consequence is that we are wasting our time and labor in vain efforts to do business."

In July 1784, Jefferson sailed to Europe as a special envoy of Congress, remaining there for the next five years. He first joined Benjamin Franklin and John Adams in negotiating trade treaties for the new United States government and afterwards became United States minister to France.

"Behold me at length on the vaunted scene of Europe!" Jefferson wrote exuberantly. He enjoyed the culture of France and traveled extensively on the Continent, visiting John Adams, United States minister to Great Britain, in London. He was presented to King George, against whom The Declaration of Independence had been directed scarcely a decade earlier, and about whom he did not alter his views on this occasion, describing him afterward as a "mulish being" with a "narrow mind."

Jefferson was intrigued with the invention of phosphorus matches and with the experiments he observed in the use of balloons to carry men. He also noted the first use of mass production methods by the French in

Monticello, Jefferson's home, in 1897—seventy-one years after his death.

1785, the making of muskets with parts that were interchangeable from one gun to another. He himself invented a small hand-printing press, and drew the designs for the new Virginia capitol to be built in Richmond.

Because he was in Europe, Jefferson took no part in the writing of the new United States Constitution, but he welcomed the reorganization of the government, writing: "I approved, from the first moment, of the great mass of what is in the new Constitution." But he was dismayed by the absence of a Bill of Rights guaranteeing the freedoms of the people, and disapproved the provision that permitted a President to be re-elected, fearing it could lead to monarchy. His views on the Bill of Rights later prevailed when the first ten amendments were added to the Constitution.

Living in Paris during the early stages of the French Revolution, Jefferson heartily endorsed its democratic principles and followed its progress with hope. "I was much acquainted with the leading patriots of the Assembly," he wrote. "Being from a country which had successfully passed through a similar reformation, they were disposed to my acquaintance, and had some confidence in me." He was present at the first clash between a French mob and troops of the king on July 11, 1789, and closely followed the events that led to the storming of the Bastille three days later. By the time he left France to return home in the autumn of 1789, Jefferson had acquired a fondness for the French people that was to influence his judgment in international relations for the rest of his life.

Secretary of State

ON HIS return trip, Jefferson received a letter from President Washington asking him to serve as first Secretary of State under the Constitution. He accepted the appointment in December 1789, and arrived in New York, then the national capital, in March of 1790. The political atmosphere of the capital discouraged him. He later wrote: "Here, certainly, I found a state of things which, of all I had ever contemplated, I the least expected. I had left France in the first year of her revolution, in the fervor of natural rights and zeal for reformation. . . . But I cannot describe the wonder and mortification with which the table conversations in New York filled me. Politics were the chief topic, and a preference of kingly over republican government was evidently the favorite sentiment. . . . I found myself for the most part the only advocate on the republican side of the question."

Shortly after joining Washington's administration, Jefferson took part in a "deal" with Alexander Hamilton in which he later claimed that he was "duped" and "made to hold the candle." Hamilton's plan that the national government should assume the war debts of the states had been defeated by a close vote in the House of Representatives, so the Secretary of the Treasury came to Jefferson and asked his aid in switching the votes of some of the Southern congressmen. Jefferson agreed to assist on the condition that Hamilton would help him win congressional approval of a plan to move the national capital to Philadelphia temporarily, and then to Georgetown, Virginia, permanently. With Jefferson and Hamilton in accord, both measures passed.

But Jefferson soon fell out with Hamilton, when the latter proposed and won approval of a Bank of the United States, which Jefferson believed was an evil instrument of power not authorized by the Constitution. Because Hamilton spoke favorably of the British system of government, Jefferson concluded that Hamilton "was not only a monarchist but for a monarchy bottomed on corruption." Jefferson became the acknowledged leader of the Democratic-Republican party and Hamilton the leader of the Federalist party, the members of which Jefferson described as "monarchists in principle" and a "mercenary phalanx."

As Secretary of State, Jefferson was occupied with moving the infant nation's foreign policy along a path in which it would not be endangered by the power politics of Great Britain, France, or Spain, and sought to establish peaceful relations with the Indians on the southern and western frontiers. At the same time he continued to pursue his many other interests. In 1791 he took time off for a trip to Lake George in New York with his friend James Madison, communing with nature, fishing, and collecting botanical specimens. He helped plan the new federal city that was to become Washington, D.C., insisting on streets at least 100 feet wide and suggesting that eight-acre parks be located every 200 yards along the avenues. He corresponded with Eli Whitney about buying one of the inventor's new cotton gins for Monticello. And he drew up a plan for a decimal system of weights and measures that he tried to have ratified in Congress.

When news came in March 1793 that the French had guillotined the king and had established a republic, Jefferson commented that "should the present foment in Europe not produce republics everywhere, it will at least soften the monarchical governments by rendering monarchs amenable to punishment like other criminals." With American recognition of the new French Republic, an important precedent was set: the American government would deal with any new government based on the will of its people. In this regard, he wrote to Gouverneur Morris, the American representative in Paris, "We surely cannot deny to any nation that right whereon our own government is founded, that every one may govern itself according to whatever form it pleases, and change these forms at its own will."

When Great Britain and the other monarchies of Europe went to war with the new French Republic, Jefferson felt that the United States should aid France in accordance with the treaty signed between the two countries during the American Revolution. However, Washington, at Hamilton's urging, decided that because the treaty had been made with the royal government of France it no longer was binding. Jefferson reluctantly went along with Washington's decision to proclaim the neutrality of the United States, but noted in the discussions that led to this decision, "Hamilton and myself were daily pitted in the Cabinet like two cocks."

After the French sent Citizen Edmond Genet as their ambassador to the United States, Jefferson was further embarrassed in his efforts to win support for France. The hotheaded Genet disregarded all rules of diplomacy in trying to stir up war between the United States and Great Britain. "He renders my position immensely difficult," Jefferson wrote. In July 1793, Washington requested that France recall Genet. The neutrality crisis then subsided somewhat.

For more than a year Jefferson made repeated efforts to resign his cabinet post, but each time was persuaded by Washington to remain. Finally, on the last day of 1793, he prevailed on Washington to accept his resignation, and immediately set off for his beloved Monticello in the belief that he was retiring forever from public office.

ALTHOUGH he turned enthusiastically to farming and the invention of a new plow, Jefferson could not disregard politics. When the terms of the Jay Treaty with Great Britain were revealed in 1794, Jefferson led the Democratic-Republicans in denouncing it as an "execrable thing" and an "infamous act." He inveighed against the Federalists as "an Anglican monarchical aristocratical party . . . whose avowed object is to draw over us the substance, as they have already done the forms, of the British government."

In the presidential election of 1796, Jefferson did little to promote his candidacy against that of John Adams, but, as the electoral votes were counted, it was discovered that he had lost to Adams by only three votes—71 to 68. Because he had received the second largest number of electoral votes, Jefferson became Vice President. "A more tranquil and unoffending station could not have been found for me," he commented. "The second office of the government is honorable and easy, the first is but a splendid misery."

At the outset of his term as Vice President, Jefferson received overtures from Adams suggesting that the two old friends could work closely together. But the Federalist Cabinet that Adams inherited from Washington quickly put a stop to any such co-operation. As time went by, the breach widened between the President and Vice President as Jefferson became more and more convinced that Adams wanted war with France.

With the Federalists firmly in control of the government, Jefferson's role as Vice President was largely that of a frustrated and disapproving spectator. The passage of the Alien and Sedition Acts convinced Jefferson that the Federalists had no regard for the Bill of Rights. He wrote that he next expected them to pass "another act of Congress declaring that the President shall continue in office during life, reserving to another occasion the transfer of the succession to his heirs, and the establishment of the Senate for life." In an effort to counter the Alien and Sedition Acts, Jefferson secretly wrote the Kentucky Resolutions, which declared that the acts were unconstitutional and a violation of states' rights—he would have been horrified had he known that these principles would later be used as arguments for nullification and secession in the slavery issue.

As the presidential election of 1800 approached, the attacks on Jefferson by the Federalists increased in fury and intemperance, for it was

Vice President under Adams

One of the most respected portraits of Thomas Jefferson, by Gilbert Stuart.

Monticello after restoration, as it appears today, a national memorial.

evident that he would be the Anti-Federalist candidate. To his good friend James Monroe, Jefferson wrote: "As to the calumny of atheism, I am so broken to calumnies of every kind . . . that I entirely disregard it. . . . It has been so impossible to contradict all their lies that I have determined to contradict none, for while I should be engaged with one they would publish twenty new ones."

On the day of Democratic-Republican victory, Jefferson visited Adams at the White House and later described their conversation as follows: "He (Adams) was very sensibly affected, and accosted me with these words:

"'Well, I understand that you are to beat me in this contest, and I will only say that I will be as faithful a subject as any you will have.'

"'Mr. Adams,' said I, 'this is no personal contest between you and me. Two systems of principles on the subject of government divide our fellow-citizens into two parties. With one of these you concur, and I with the other. As we have been longer on the public stage than most of those now living, our names happen to be more generally known. One of these parties, therefore, has put your name at its head, the other mine. Were we both to die today, tomorrow two other names would be in the place of ours, without any change in the motion of the machinery. Its motion is from its principle, not from you or myself.'

"'I believe you are right,' said he, 'that we are but passive instruments, and should not suffer this matter to affect our personal dispositions.'"

When the electoral votes were counted, Jefferson had indeed defeated Adams, but a curious defect in the wording of the Constitution was uncovered. All 73 electors favoring Jefferson wrote down two names, in accordance with the directive of Article II. The names they wrote down were those of Jefferson and Aaron Burr, a New York Anti-Federalist. It was clear that the popular mandate was for Jefferson to be President and Burr Vice President, but according to the terms of the Constitution the decision was now turned over to the House of Representatives. The House, owing to another quirk of the Constitution, was controlled by the outgoing Federalists, who hoped to extract concessions from Jefferson. Various Federalists, including President Adams, told Jefferson they would swing the election to him if he would give assurances that Federalist officials would not be turned out of office, that he would not disband the new Navy, and that he would not erase the public debt. Jefferson later wrote that he replied "that I should certainly make no terms; should never go into the office of President by capitulation, nor with my hands tied by any conditions which should hinder me from pursuing the measures which I should deem for the public good." Finally, fearing the opportunistic Burr more than Jefferson, the Federalists granted the presidency to the sage of Monticello on the thirty-sixth ballot.

JEFFERSON was fifty-seven years old when he was sworn in as President on March 4, 1801, at a simple ceremony in Washington, D.C.—the first President to take office in the new capital, then a city of about 6000 population. Aware of the drama in being the first Democratic-Republican President and of widespread apprehension that he would destroy the Constitution, he endeavored to allay fears in an eloquent inaugural address.

Jefferson's Administration

"Let us restore to social intercourse that harmony and affection without which liberty and even life itself are but dreary things," he said. "And let us reflect that having banished from our land that religious intolerance under which mankind so long bled and suffered, we have yet gained little if we countenance a political intolerance as despotic, as wicked, and capable of as bitter and bloody persecutions."

Moving immediately to correct the Federalist abuses of power, he freed all persons who were imprisoned or under prosecution by the Alien and Sedition Acts, "without asking what the offenders had done, or against whom they had offended." He ordered reductions in the size of the Army, the Navy, and the diplomatic service, and pushed Congress "to the uttermost in economizing" and in the reduction of taxes.

When Jefferson learned in 1802 that Spain had turned over to France the vast Louisiana Territory, he wrote to Robert Livingston, the American minister in Paris, that this event "reverses all the political relations of the United States." He warned that "the day France takes possession of New Orleans fixes the sentence which is to restrain her forever within her low-water mark. . . . From that moment, we must marry ourselves to the British fleet and nation." He then asked Livingston to urge the French to sell New Orleans to the United States. He also dispatched James Monroe to France to aid in the negotiations.

To Jefferson's amazement, his commissioners reached agreement with Napoleon to purchase the entire Louisiana Territory for $15 million (about three cents an acre). Because the Constitution made no provision for incorporating foreign territory into the United States, Jefferson believed that a constitutional amendment was needed to insure the legality of the agreement; but fearing it would take so much time to amend the Constitution that Napoleon might change his mind, he urged Congress to approve the treaty quickly and appropriate the necessary money. "The less

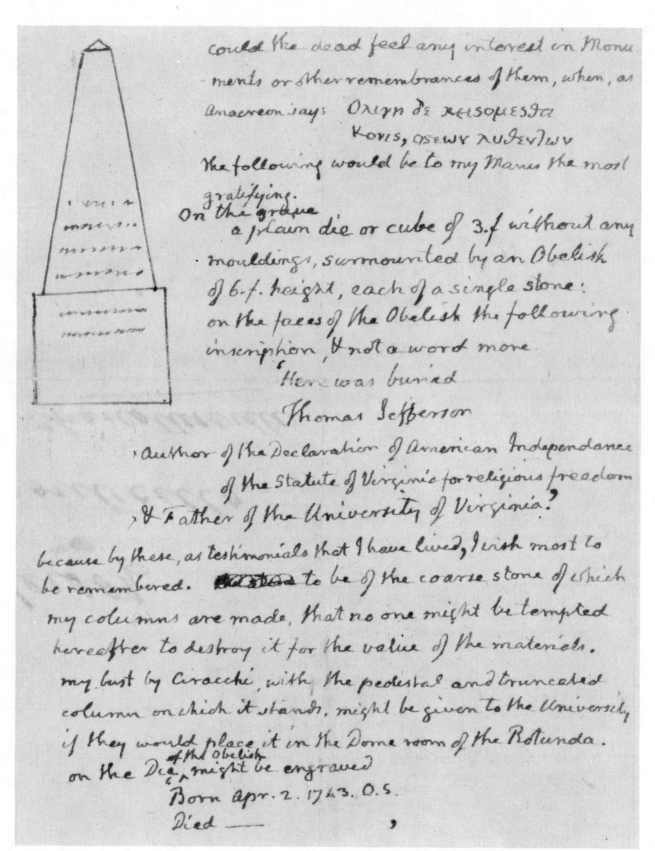

could the dead feel any interest in Monu -ments or other remembrances of them, when, as Anacreon says: Ολιγη δε κεισομεσθα Κονις, οςεων λυθεντων the following would be to my Manes the most gratifying.
On the grave a plain die or cube of 3.f without any mouldings, surmounted by an Obelisk of 6.f. height, each of a single stone: on the faces of the Obelisk the following inscription, & not a word more

    Here was buried

    Thomas Jefferson
    Author of the Declaration of American Independance
        of the Statute of Virginia for religious freedom
    & Father of the University of Virginia.

because by these, as testimonials that I have lived, I wish most to be remembered. ~~~~~~~ to be of the coarse stone of which my columns are made, that no one might be tempted hereafter to destroy it for the value of the materials. my bust by Ciracchi, with the pedestal and truncated column on which it stands, might be given to the University if they would place it in the Dome room of the Rotunda. on the Die, of the Obelisk, might be engraved
    Born apr. 2. 1743. O.S.
    Died ——   .

Detailed instructions left by Jefferson regarding the shape of his gravestone and the inscription he wanted on it.

said about any constitutional difficulty, the better," he wrote. With a minimum of discussion Congress approved the purchase in the autumn of 1803. Soon Jefferson sent Meriwether Lewis, his private secretary, and William Clark on their famous expedition to explore the new territory.

The peace, prosperity, and expansion of the country during Jefferson's first term helped win him an overwhelming victory in the 1804 election. He received 162 electoral votes to 14 for the Federalist candidate, Charles Cotesworth Pinckney.

The Aaron Burr treason scandal rocked the nation during Jefferson's second term. Burr, who had killed Alexander Hamilton in a duel in July 1804, was dropped from the Democratic-Republican national ticket in the 1804 election. After leaving Washington, Burr became involved in a scheme to lead a private army in an attack on Mexico, and then to force the western states to secede from the Union and join Burr's new empire. Jefferson ordered Burr's arrest for treason, and considered it a direct slap at himself when Chief Justice John Marshall, a Federalist, acquitted Burr.

The forcible impressment of American seamen into the British Navy brought a new threat of war in 1807. In an effort to preserve neutrality, Jefferson persuaded Congress to pass an embargo act that forbade the shipping of American products to any foreign country and outlawed the sailing of American ships to foreign ports, describing the act as "the last card we have to play, short of war." Despite opposition by New England merchants, the act remained in force to the end of Jefferson's administration, and war was avoided.

Refusing all pleas that he run for a third term, Jefferson supported his friend and Secretary of State, James Madison, as his successor. When Madison won the election, Jefferson was gratified both at his friend's success and at his own approaching retirement. He wrote: "Never did a prisoner released from his chains feel such relief as I shall on shaking off the shackles of power. . . . I thank God for the opportunity of retiring from them without censure, and carrying with me the most consoling proofs of public approbation."

FOR the remaining seventeen years of his life, Jefferson lived as a farmer-philosopher at Monticello, corresponding prolifically with statesmen, scientists, inventors, and old friends. When the Library of Congress was destroyed by the burning of Washington in 1812, he turned over his own large collection of books as the nucleus of a new national library. But the greatest accomplishment of his old age—one of the three achievements that he asked to be remembered for—was the founding of the University of Virginia at Charlottesville, near Monticello. He designed the school's buildings, planned the courses of study, employed the academic staff, and acted as rector, or head of the governing body of the school. In the year before he died he saw the University open its doors to its first classes.

After an illness of about a month, Jefferson died at the age of eighty-three on the fiftieth anniversary of the adoption of the Declaration of Independence—July 4, 1826.

Philosopher and College President

450   JOHN ADAMS

John Adams

The Second President of the United States
1797–1801

1735 (October 30) Born in Braintree (now Quincy), Massachusetts.

1755 Graduated from Harvard College.

1758 Started practicing law.

1764 (October 25) Married Abigail Smith.

1774–77 Attended Continental Congress as delegate from Massachusetts.

1779 Wrote constitution for state of Massachusetts.

1778–88 U.S. diplomat in Europe.

1789–97 First Vice President of the United States.

1797–1801 Second President of the United States.

1826 (July 4) Died in Quincy, Massachusetts.

Leading Officials in Adams' Administration

Office	Name	Years Served
Chief Justice	Oliver Ellsworth	1796-1800
	John Marshall	1801-1835
Vice-President	Thomas Jefferson	1797-1801
Secretary of State	Timothy Pickering	1795-1800
	John Marshall	1800-1801
Secretary of the Treasury	Oliver Wolcott, Jr.	1795-1800
	Samuel Dexter	1801-1802
Secretary of War	James McHenry	1796-1800
	Samuel Dexter	1800
Attorney General	Charles Lee	1795-1801
Postmaster General	Joseph Habersham	1795-1801
Secretary of the Navy	Benjamin Stoddert	1798-1801

John Adams' birthplace, home of his father, Deacon John Adams, in Quincy, Massachusetts. —*Doris S. Oberg photograph, Quincy Historical Society*

Because he lived in an age of very great men, John Adams, despite extraordinary accomplishments, stood second in almost everything he did. As a patriot in Massachusetts in the days before the Revolutionary War, he was overshadowed by his fiery cousin, Sam Adams. In the Continental Congress when he was assigned to the committee to write the Declaration of Independence, he had to bow to Thomas Jefferson's greater literary ability. As a diplomat in Europe during the Revolutionary War, he was outshone by Benjamin Franklin. And, finally, as the first Vice President and second President of the United States, he worked in the shadow of George Washington.

A scholar and proficient writer in the theory of government, Adams brought to the presidency a greater knowledge of political science than any other President, with the possible exception of Woodrow Wilson. He regarded himself as a strong President but was handicapped by his obligation to carry on his predecessor's Cabinet, a group of men who not only were not devoted to him, but who actually worked to defeat him in his bid for re-election.

Adams' most important accomplishment as President was his avoidance of war with France. But, in preserving peace, he broke with his own party's policy, causing a rupture that destroyed his career.

A short, plump New Englander, Adams believed in plain clothes and plain talk. He tried to do what he believed was right for his country, rather than what was politically expedient. His blunt frankness sometimes lost him friends, but he was respected for his honesty even by his political enemies. His diaries and letters are livelier and more entertaining than was his personality, which often was rude and irascible.

An Adams of Massachusetts   A FIFTH-GENERATION American, John Adams was born the son of a farmer and part-time shoemaker on October 30, 1735 (October 19 by the Old Style Calendar). The small frame house where he was born still stands in Quincy (then Braintree), Massachusetts.

His father was a Harvard graduate who believed in education, and John entered Harvard at the age of sixteen. He was regarded as one of the best students in his class of twenty-four, but was ranked fourteenth in the class according to his social position.

After graduation, Adams taught school for a year in Worcester, Massachusetts, and then decided to become a lawyer. He studied for two years in the office of a Worcester attorney, James Putnam, and in October 1758 was admitted to the bar. Shortly after, he began law practice in Braintree.

While still a struggling small-town lawyer of twenty-nine, he married Abigail Smith, the daughter of a clergyman. Ten years his junior, Abigail matched Adams in wit and love of books. In later years when they were often separated for long periods by his public duties, she kept him informed of happenings at home in clever, perceptive letters that are a treasure house to historians. John and Abby, as he called her, had five children; their eldest son, John Quincy Adams, became the sixth President of the United States.

When the British Parliament passed the Stamp Act in 1765, John and his older cousin Sam Adams took active roles in urging opposition to it. Sam Adams helped organize the Sons of Liberty, a patriotic organization that stirred up mob action against the British, while John Adams prepared resolutions against the tax that were approved by Braintree and other Massachusetts towns. John also wrote a series of anonymous articles in the Boston *Gazette* urging the people to defend America's liberties.

Lawyer, Legislator, and Patriot

In 1766 Adams moved his family to Boston in order to improve his law practice. His most famous case came with the defense of a British captain and eight soldiers who fired into a mob in the Boston Massacre of March 5, 1770. In taking the case, Adams realized that it might lose him popularity; but he felt strongly that the British authorities who had stationed the troops in Boston were more guilty of the murder of Boston citizens than the soldiers who actually fired the shots. Adams and his associate, Josiah Quincy, succeeded in winning the acquittal of the British captain and six of his soldiers. Two were convicted of the lesser charge of manslaughter. Although many Boston patriots, including Sam Adams, denounced John for defending the British soldiers, he also won wide respect for the sense of justice that had led him to take the case. He was elected late in 1770 to the Massachusetts legislature, the General Court.

John Adams did not happen to be in Boston on the night of December 16, 1773, when Sam Adams helped organize the Boston Tea Party, protesting a British tax on tea; but he rejoiced in the action, noting in his diary: "This destruction of the tea is so bold, so daring, so firm, intrepid and inflexible, and it must have so important consequences, and so lasting, that I can't but consider it as an epoch in history!" Subsequent events bore him out, for the British soon retaliated by closing the port of Boston, which in turn led to the convening of the first Continental Congress in Philadelphia in 1774.

Both John and Sam Adams were elected as delegates from Massachusetts to the Continental Congress. Both were eager to unite the colonies to fight Great Britain, but they soon learned at the convention that many delegates from other colonies were too conservative to support strong measures. They had to be satisfied with such mild actions as an appeal to the British king to grant the colonies the right to determine their own taxation and the creation of an association to boycott trade with Great Britain. John Adams vented his irritation by writing in his diary:

Apostle of Independence

"In Congress, nibbling and quibbling as usual. There is no greater mortification than to sit with a half a dozen wits, deliberating upon a petition, address or memorial. These great wits, these subtle critics, these refined geniuses, these learned lawyers, these wise statesmen, are so fond of showing their parts and powers, as to make their consultations very tedious."

After returning home from the Congress, Adams contributed articles to the Boston *Gazette,* over the signature *Novanglus* (New England), in which he detailed the legal position of the American patriots in their controversy with Britain. But the articles were interrupted by the battles of Lexington and Concord.

At the second Continental Congress in May 1775, Adams expected the other delegates to be as fired with zeal for independence as he was; but days dragged into weeks as the Congress talked and did little. Fearing that an irreparable split was developing between North and South that might leave Massachusetts to fight alone, Adams thought of a solution that might anger some New England generals but would help unite the country. On June 14 he nominated a Virginia militia colonel, George Washington, to be commander in chief of an army to be formed with troops from all the colonies. Sam Adams enthusiastically seconded the nomination. The next day the delegates unanimously elected Washington to the post, and the fighting became the American Revolution instead of the Massachusetts Rebellion.

For the next several years Adams worked tirelessly in Congress, noting in his diary that he "unquestionably did more business than any other member of the house." Throughout 1775 and into the spring of 1776, he was particularly concerned with efforts to get the Congress to declare independence from Great Britain. Finally, in June, while Washington's

The Charter room where John Adams, his second cousin Samuel Adams, and James Bowdoin worked over the draft of the Constitution for Massachusetts. *—Doris S. Oberg photograph, Quincy Historical Society*

troops were preparing to defend New York City from an imminent British invasion, Congress elected a committee, with Adams as a member, to write the Declaration of Independence. Although Adams was noted for his writing, he deferred the authorship of the Declaration to Thomas Jefferson, later giving his reasons in his *Autobiography*: "(1) that he was a Virginian and I a Massachusettensian. (2) that he was a Southern Man and I a northern one. (3) that I had been so obnoxious for my early and constant Zeal in promoting the Measure, that any draught of mine, would undergo a more severe Scrutiny and Criticism in Congress, than one of his composition. 4thly and lastly, and that would be reason enough if there were no other. I had a great opinion of the Elegance of his pen, and none at all of my own."

But when the time came in the first week in July for the final debate on whether the colonies would declare themselves independent, Adams stepped to the fore to lead the argument for freedom, speaking—as Jefferson later described—"with a power of thought and expression that moved us from our seats." When the Congress finally did vote for independence, with only New York abstaining, Adams wrote jubilantly to his wife that the event "ought to be solemnized with pomp and parade, with shows, games, sports, guns, bells, bonfires, and illuminations, from one end of this continent to the other, from this time forward, forevermore."

In Adams' last year in Congress, 1777, he presented the resolution establishing the United States flag with thirteen red and white stripes and a union of thirteen white stars on a blue field "representing a new constellation."

Diplomat in Europe

ALTHOUGH more noted for his bluntness than his diplomacy, Adams was appointed by Congress as one of its commissioners to France to try to negotiate military and monetary aid. He arrived in Paris in 1778 to discover that a treaty already had been negotiated by Benjamin Franklin. While awaiting a decision from Congress on his next assignment, he remained in France for about a year with few other duties than sightseeing with his ten-year-old son, John Quincy Adams, who had accompanied him.

Returning home for a few months in 1779, he did most of the work in writing a new state constitution for Massachusetts, sections of which were widely copied by other states; then he returned to France in 1780 as one of the commissioners to negotiate a peace treaty with Great Britain. Because the British were not yet ready to talk about peace, Adams spent most of the next two years in the Netherlands, where he persuaded the Dutch to recognize and loan money to the United States. Late in 1782 he took part in discussions with the British that resulted in the peace treaty ending the Revolutionary War, but Benjamin Franklin won most of the credit for the agreement.

Adams remained in Europe until 1788, spending the last three years as minister to Great Britain, where he was received with cool politeness and a rebuff to all his efforts toward obtaining a trade treaty. During this period Adams helped fill his time by writing an erudite three-volume work of political science entitled *The Defence of the Constitutions of Government of the United States of America*. He sailed back to the United States in the spring of 1788.

Vice President under Washington

As the states prepared for the first presidential election under the new Constitution, it was clear that no one but George Washington had any chance of being named to the nation's highest office, so Adams' friends pushed him as a vice-presidential candidate to represent the North. Under the Constitutional provision as it then stood, each elector cast two votes. When the Electoral College met in February 1789, all sixty-nine electors named Washington. Second choices were numerous, and Adams barely squeaked into office with 34 of the 69 votes cast.

In performing his official duties as presiding officer of the new United States Senate, Adams took part in discussions and tried to guide the deliberations of the body. His ten years abroad in the capitals of kings had led him to respect pomp and protocol, but his efforts to introduce in the new government what he regarded as a proper ceremoniousness merely won him an undeserved reputation as a monarchist. "My office," he wrote, "requires rather severe duty, and it is a kind of duty which, if I do not flatter myself too much, is not quite adapted to my character—I mean it is too inactive and mechanical." Adams used his tie-breaking vote in the Senate to support the President and to strengthen the powers of the presidency, most notably the presidential right to remove from office appointees who had been confirmed by the Senate.

Somewhat bored by the vice presidency, which he described as "the most insignificant office that ever the invention of man contrived or his imagination conceived," Adams again turned to writing, publishing a number of articles called *Discourses on Davila,* which upheld the advantages of the United States' governmental structure as opposed to that set up in France by the French Revolutionists. These articles offended Thomas Jefferson, an enthusiastic supporter of the French Revolution, and led to a break in friendship between the two patriots.

By the time of the second presidential election, the country was clearly divided into two political parties, the Federalists and the Democratic-Republicans, or Anti-Federalists. The Democratic-Republicans, recognizing that it was impossible to overcome Washington's prestige, concentrated their fire on Adams in an effort to defeat his bid for a second term as Vice President. The opposition ridiculed Adams' rotund figure and excoriated him for his supposed monarchial views; but when the electoral votes were tallied in February 1793, Adams won easily with 77 votes to 50 for the opposition candidate, Governor George Clinton of New York.

Throughout his second term as Vice President, Adams stood solidly in support of President Washington, particularly as the attacks of the Democratic-Republicans increased in fury with ratification by the Senate of the Jay Treaty with Great Britain.

The publication of Washington's Farewell Address in September 1796 set off the first real contest in American history for the nation's highest office. As Washington's heir-apparent, Adams was accepted at once by the Federalists as their candidate, while the Democratic-Republicans pressed the candidacy of Jefferson. Neither candidate took an active part in the campaign, in which the Democratic-Republicans accused Adams of desiring to set up an hereditary monarchy in the United States and the Federalists denounced Jefferson as an advocate of overthrowing the Constitution. Adams was particularly angered when his cousin Sam Adams, now governor of Massachusetts, opposed his candidacy and supported Jefferson. Even after the presidential electors were chosen, the election remained in doubt. At this date the custom of electors voting for their party's candidate was not yet an ironclad tradition. Alexander Hamilton, the acknowledged leader of the Federalist party, plotted to get certain electors to switch their votes in an effort to win the presidency for the more tractable Thomas Pinckney, the Federalist candidate for Vice President. The maneuver almost lost the election for the Federalists. The count of the

Living room of
John Adams' birthplace.

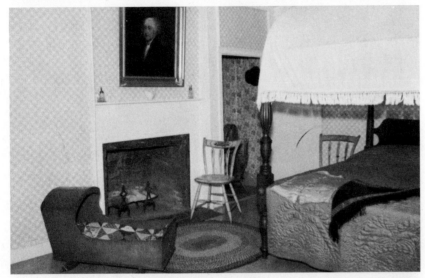

Bedroom in which
John Adams was born.

Fireplace in
the original kitchen
of the John Adams house.

*—Doris S. Oberg **photographs**, Quincy Historical Society*

electoral vote gave Adams the presidency by the narrow margin of three votes—71 for Adams to 68 for Jefferson.

WHEN the sixty-one-year-old Adams was sworn in as President in Philadelphia on March 4, 1797, the ceremony notified the world that the republican form of government had successfully carried out a peaceful and orderly change in Chief Executives. Most of the crowd's cheers were for Washington. Because Abigail Adams had been unable to get to Philadelphia for the inauguration, John wrote to her describing it, commenting that Washington "seemed to enjoy a triumph over me. Methought I heard him say, 'Ay! I am fairly out and you fairly in! See which of us will be the happiest!'"

Adams carried over into his administration all the members of Washington's Cabinet—a grave mistake because these men were not of his choosing nor he of theirs, and behind his back they wrote to Alexander Hamilton for guidance on the nation's affairs. Not until after the death of Washington in 1799 did Adams feel free to rid himself of them.

More seriously yet, from the moment he assumed office he was confronted with a crisis in relations with France that dominated his entire administration. The leaders of the French Revolution wanted the United States to join them in their war with Great Britain. They imperiously refused to recognize the American diplomats sent to them and threatened to hang any American seamen they captured on British ships. Adams called a special session of Congress in May and in a ringing address asserted his intent to prove that the United States would not permit itself to be "humiliated under a colonial spirit of fear and a sense of inferiority." He called for the support of Congress in preparation for national defense.

Early in 1798, Adams received dispatches from the new commissioners he had sent to France revealing that agents of the French government, referred to simply as X, Y, and Z, had demanded a bribe before the American envoys would be received by the foreign minister, Talleyrand. At first inclined to call for a declaration of war, Adams restrained himself, keeping the dispatches secret, and asking Congress instead to revoke Washington's policy of neutrality only enough to permit American merchant ships to arm themselves. When his request was met with violent opposition by the Democratic-Republicans, Adams made the dispatches of the XYZ affair public. The country soon took up the cry, "Millions for defense, but not one cent for tribute."

Preparations for war moved ahead rapidly. Adams called Washington back to active duty as commander in chief of a new United States Army, and, at Washington's insistence, appointed Alexander Hamilton as second in command. When Congress established a Department of the Navy, Adams named Benjamin Stoddert as the first Secretary of the Navy. The frigates *United States, Constitution,* and *Constellation* were the first warships of a new United States Navy that grew to a fleet of forty-nine vessels by 1799.

As part of the war scare, the Federalist-controlled Congress in 1798 passed the Alien and Sedition Acts that gave the government unusual powers to imprison aliens and citizens who threatened or opposed the federal government. These acts were used by the Adams administration to shut down opposition newspapers and silence opponents in a manner that threatened the Bill of Rights.

Dropping a bombshell on both his Federalist supporters and his Democratic-Republican opponents, Adams proposed early in 1799 a new attempt to establish diplomatic relations with France. When Federalist senators told him they would refuse to go along with the plan, Adams threatened to resign and leave the presidency in the hands of Vice President Jefferson. In the end, three commissioners were dispatched to France, and the threat of war abated.

As the presidential election of 1800 approached, the Federalist party was split over Adams' actions in avoiding war with France. Hamilton, who had become commander in chief of the Army after Washington's death, had fancied that he would attain military glory in such a war. Now he sabotaged Adams' chances for re-election by circulating a letter to party leaders declaring that Adams was unfit to continue in office and utilizing secret information about Adams' actions that he had obtained from the treacherous members of the Cabinet. Not surprisingly, Adams was defeated by Jefferson and his running mate, Aaron Burr, who each won 73 electoral votes to Adams' 65.

The last few months of Adams' administration were conducted from Washington, D.C., the new federal capital. The Executive Mansion was still unfinished, but Adams and his wife moved into it while they waited for the House of Representatives to decide whether Jefferson or Burr was to be the next President. During this time, Adams had the satisfaction of receiving a peace agreement with France and seeing it approved by the Senate.

On the last night of his presidency, Adams spent some time signing the commissions of a number of eleventh-hour appointments of federal judges, and then early next morning left Washington for his home in Massachusetts. Historians are not sure whether he refused to attend Jefferson's inauguration from bitterness, or whether he simply had not been invited to the ceremony.

Although toothless, palsied, and old beyond his sixty-five years, Adams lived on to attain the greatest age of any man who ever has served as President—ninety years and eight months. A year before his death Adams had the satisfaction of having his son, John Quincy Adams, become the nation's sixth President. After Jefferson's retirement from the presidency, he and Adams resumed a cordial correspondence, and on his deathbed Adams' last words were of his old friend: "Thomas Jefferson still survives." But by an extraordinary quirk of fate, Jefferson died the same day, July 4, 1826—the fiftieth anniversary of the Declaration of Independence for which they had both struggled so hard.

—From a painting by Charles Willson Peale in 1787
Philadelphia Academy of Fine Arts

460 GEORGE WASHINGTON

George Washington

The First President of the United States
1789–97

1732 (February 22) Born on Pope's Creek Farm in Westmoreland County, Virginia.

1747 Became a surveyor after leaving school at fourteen or
fifteen.

1753 Took oath as major in Virginia militia.

1753–54 Carried message to French in western Pennsylvania warning them to leave Ohio Valley.

1754 (July 4) Forced to surrender Fort Necessity to French
attackers.

1754–58 Fought in French and Indian War, rising to rank
of colonel in command of Virginia militia.

1759 (January 6) Married Martha Dandridge Custis.

1774–75 Member of Virginia's delegation to First and Second Continental Congresses.

1775–83 Commander of Continental Army throughout Revolutionary War.

1787 President of Constitutional Convention that drew up
Constitution of the United States.

1789–97 First President of the United States.

1798 (July 4) Commissioned lieutenant general and commander in chief of the United States Army when war
threatened with France.

1799 (December 14) Died at Mount Vernon, Virginia.

Leading Officials in
Washington's Administration

Office	Name	Years Served
Chief Justice	John Jay	1790-1795
	*John Rutledge	1795
	Oliver Ellsworth	1796-1800
Vice-President	John Adams	1789-1797
Secretary of State	Thomas Jefferson	1789-1793
	Edmund Randolph	1794-1795
	Timothy Pickering	1795-1800
Secretary of War	Henry Knox	1789-1795
	Timothy Pickering	1795
	James McHenry	1796-1800
Secretary of the Treasury	Alexander Hamilton	1789-1795
	Oliver Wolcott, Jr.	1795-1801
Attorney General	Edmund Randolph	1789-1794
	William Bradford	1794-1795
	Charles Lee	1795-1801
Postmaster General	Samuel Osgood	1789-1791
	Timothy Pickering	1791-1795
	Joseph Habersham	1795-1801

*Senate refused to confirm appointment.

George Washington at the age of twenty-five.

Elected by the unanimous vote of his countrymen, George Washington brought to the newly created office of United States President such enormous prestige that he easily set lasting precedents that made it the most powerful elective office in the world.

Although reluctant to leave retirement at his beloved Mount Vernon, he felt it was his duty to guide the first steps of the new Republic, whose struggle for independence he had led. Later insinuations by political enemies that he had accepted the office to please his vanity sent him into a rage, for he knew, as did his associates, that a single hint from him at the end of the Revolutionary War would have caused him to be crowned King of America.

His sense of destiny had led him to accept the hazardous command of the Continental Army in 1775 and hold together his troops through every hardship until freedom had been won. In 1787, when he saw that the new nation was threatened by discord under the weak Articles of Confederation, he brought together and inspired the delegates who wrote the Constitution.

Washington was a towering figure, both in physique and accomplishments. The aristocratic bearing of his six-foot-two-inch figure and the calm nobility of his face created awe in those who saw him. His presence, coupled with the battlefield miracle he had accomplished, made him an idol among his contemporaries. But idolatry brought with it a difficulty. People both then and now refused to accept the truth that Washington was mortal, a man with normal appetites and frailties—a man who loved women, enjoyed gambling, liked to dance all night, and prided himself on his fine horses. They interpreted as a god-like coldness his self-conscious determination not to make any blunders that would reveal the background of a poorly educated orphan who had achieved success and riches by a combination of luck, ingenuity, and resolution. Legends about his strength and honesty won more ready acceptance as fact than understanding of the human qualities that both hindered and helped him on his path to immortality.

No man knew Washington's strengths and weaknesses better than Thomas Jefferson, who served as his first Secretary of State. Fifteen years after Washington's death, Jefferson wrote:

"His mind was great and powerful, without being of the very first order; his penetration strong, though not so acute as that of a Newton, Bacon, or Locke; and as far as he saw, no judgment was ever sounder. It was slow in operation, being little aided by invention or imagination, but sure in conclusion. . . .

"Perhaps the strongest feature in his character was prudence, never acting until every circumstance, every consideration, was maturely weighed; refraining when he saw a doubt, but, when once decided, going through with his purpose whatever obstacles opposed. His integrity was most pure, his justice the most inflexible I have ever known, no motives of interest or consanguinity, of friendship or hatred, being able to bias his decision. He was indeed, in every sense of the words, a wise, a good and a great man. . . .

"On the whole, his character was, in its mass, perfect, in nothing bad, in few points indifferent; and it may truly be said, that never did nature and fortune combine more perfectly to make a man great, and to place him in the same constellation with whatever worthies have merited from man an everlasting remembrance. . . ."

THE eldest child of a second marriage, George Washington was born on February 22, 1732 (February 11 by the Old Style Calendar). When he was two, his family moved from his birthplace, Pope's Creek Farm in Westmoreland County, Virginia, to a new farm about fifty miles north along the broad, curving Potomac River. This new plantation, later to become part of the huge estate of Mount Vernon, was called Little Hunting Creek Farm. During Washington's childhood there was neither the wide expanse of meticulously trimmed lawn nor the gleaming white-pillared colonial mansion. There was only a rustic tobacco farm with few neighbors in the surrounding countryside.

When Washington was six, his father, Augustine, decided to move again, to be closer to an ironworks in which he had a part interest. This time the move was to the 260-acre Ferry Farm on the east bank of the Rappahannock River. There young George grew up enjoying hunting, fishing, and horseback riding.

Washington's father died when the boy was eleven, leaving a substantial estate of about 10,000 acres of land and about fifty slaves. The largest share of the inheritance went to Lawrence Washington, the eldest son of Augustine's first marriage; George was to receive Ferry Farm as his share when he reached the age of twenty-one. George and his five younger brothers and sisters were left to grow up under the guidance of their widowed mother, Mary Ball Washington.

Little is known of Washington's formal education. Historians have speculated that he may have gone to school in the small town of Fredericksburg, which lay just across the Rappahannock from Ferry Farm, or he may have been tutored by an indentured servant. In either case, it is certain that what little education he received was closely supervised by his possessive mother, who was determined to keep her eldest son as close to her as possible. Perhaps the learning that had the most effect upon him was his copying, as a schoolboy of thirteen, of 110 "Rules of Civility and Decent Behaviour in Company and Conversation." All his later behavior as a man seems to have been guided by these principles, a few of which are listed below as he wrote them:

Use no Reproachful Language against any one neither Curse nor Revile.

Every Action done in Company ought to be with some Sign of Respect to those that are Present.

While you are talking, Point not with your Finger at him of whom you Discourse nor Approach too near him to whom you talk especially to his face.

Strive not with your superiors in argument, but always submit your Judgment to others with Modesty.

Be not Curious to Know the Affairs of Others neither approach those that Speak in Private.

Washington was never a scholar. Even in his latter years he seldom read books unless they could serve some practical purpose, such as helping him learn more about farming methods. But he had respect for books and once wrote: "I conceive a knowledge of books is the basis upon which other knowledge is to be built." Throughout his life Washington wrote extensively in diaries and letters, leaving a wealth of material that gives historians much information about his life and his beliefs.

Young George Washington hero-worshipped his stepbrother Lawrence, fourteen years his senior. He spent as much time as his mother would allow visiting Lawrence at the handsome new mansion at Mount Vernon, which Lawrence had built and named for a British admiral under whom he had served in a brief war with Spain in the 1740s. Lawrence encouraged George to join the British Navy, but Mary Washington refused to give her consent.

When George was fifteen, he decided he must find some way of bringing more money into his household—under his mother's management Ferry Farm was accumulating more debts than income. So he dusted off an old set of surveying instruments that his father had owned, and began work as an assistant surveyor. When he was sixteen, he made his first trip into the wilderness of western Virginia to help survey the huge landholdings of Lord Fairfax, a relative of Lawrence Washington's wife. By 1749, when he had established enough of a reputation to be appointed official surveyor of Culpeper County, he began using his income to buy land, a practice he continued throughout his life, gradually becoming one of the largest landholders in the country.

When Washington was nineteen, he accompanied Lawrence on a trip to Barbados that his brother undertook for his health. It was the only time he ever left America's shores. But in Barbados, Washington contracted smallpox. He noted in his diary: "Was strongly attacked with the small Pox: sent for Dr. Lanahan whose attendance was very constant till my recovery, and going out which was not 'till thursday the 12th of December."

After returning from Barbados, George fell deeply in love with a pretty sixteen-year-old by the name of Betsy Fauntleroy. But she rejected his marriage proposals, even though George enlisted the help of her father "in hopes of a revocation of the . . . cruel sentence."

Lawrence Washington died of tuberculosis in 1752. His will provided that the Mount Vernon estate should go to George if his only daughter, Sarah, died without having any children—an event that came to pass two years later.

In an effort to emulate his beloved Lawrence, George applied to the governor of Virginia for an appointment as adjutant in the militia, a post Lawrence had held. After considering the matter, the governor decided to apportion the position among four persons, and chose George as adjutant for the southern part of the colony. Accordingly, on February 1, 1753, George was sworn in as a major in the Virginia militia, a twenty-year-old with great ambition but little more knowledge of military affairs than had the men he was to command.

In the autumn of 1753, George read reports in the Virginia newspapers that French troops had invaded the Ohio Valley near Lake Erie, an area claimed by Virginia. When he learned from a friend that Governor Robert Dinwiddie was planning to send a warning message to the French commander, he realized that this might be the chance of a lifetime to have a look at the western frontier. Hurrying to the capital at Williamsburg, Washington volunteered his services as messenger and was gladly accepted.

Setting out from Williamsburg on October 31, 1753, Washington collected supplies, horses, and a party of six frontiersmen. In the teeth of extreme cold, much snow, and unfriendly Indians, he made the hazardous 800- to 1000-mile round-trip journey to the French Fort Le Boeuf on Lake Erie. It took two and a half months. Once he had to swim for his life

George Washington was active in the Masonic Lodge, as a number of other Presidents were.

amid chunks of ice in a flooded river; he was shot at by an Indian; and he had to walk hundreds of miles when his horses grew too weak to go farther. In his report on the journey he wrote: "From the first Day of December to the 15th, there was but one Day on which it did not rain or snow incessantly: and throughout the whole Journey we met with nothing but one continued Series of cold wet Weather . . ."

The message that Washington brought back from the French rejected Dinwiddie's request that they leave the Ohio Valley, and Dinwiddie immediately set about raising money and troops to push them out.

Four months after returning from his journey as a messenger, the twenty-two-year-old Washington commanded a British force in the first engagement of the French and Indian War. Promoted to lieutenant colonel, and leading a small body of Virginia troops, he ran into a French scouting party in southern Pennsylvania on May 27, 1754. Washington and his men captured twenty-one of the enemy and killed ten in the skirmish, losing only one man. He later wrote that he "heard the bullets whistle" and felt that there was "something charming in the sound."

Early in June, Washington was promoted to colonel in command of all Virginia troops in the field. Expecting a retaliatory attack from the French, he prepared for it by building Fort Necessity, near the site of present-day Uniontown, Pennsylvania. True to his predictions, several hundred French and Indians surrounded the fort on July 3, forcing Washington and his 400 troops to surrender on the early morning of July 4. He and his men were allowed to return to Virginia with their arms and ammunition.

Shortly after his return, the British government ordered all militia officers commissioned by the colonial government reduced in rank so that none would outrank captains commissioned by the British king. Washington resigned as colonel in October 1754 and returned to Mount Vernon. But the next spring, he volunteered to serve as aide-de-camp to British Major General Edward Braddock, who was planning to attack the French at Fort Duquesne (now Pittsburgh). Although Washington warned Braddock about Indian ambush tactics in frontier fighting, the British army marched toward the fort as though on parade before the king in London. On July 9, 1755, the French and Indians fell on the British troops with murderous war whoops, and the terrified redcoats broke and ran. Almost a thousand British soldiers were killed and Braddock was fatally wounded. Washington later wrote: "I had four bullets through my coat, and two horses shot under me, yet escaped unhurt, altho' death was levelling my companions on every side!"

With mounting fear of a French and Indian attack on Virginia's western settlements, Governor Dinwiddie appealed to Washington to resume command of the Virginia militia with the rank of colonel. At first Washington rejected the offer, but after persistent urging he agreed. He continued in this command until the end of the war.

Planter and Legislator

In the meantime, Washington proposed to and was accepted in marriage by Mrs. Martha Dandridge Custis. But at the same time he apparently was involved with his neighbor's wife, Mrs. Sally Fairfax. A letter to Sally from the frontier in September 1758 reads: "The world has no business to know the object of my love, declared in this manner to you, when I want to conceal it." No reply has ever been found, and the affair remains a mystery. Relations between the Fairfaxes and the Washingtons continued to be cordial, and Washington duly married Martha Custis on January 6, 1759. She brought to the marriage a fortune in land and money as well as two children by her first marriage. The Washingtons never had children of their own.

Meantime, he had been elected to the Virginia House of Burgesses. After a short honeymoon, Martha accompanied him to Williamsburg for the session. In the following years he was regularly re-elected, gaining a fine schooling in representative government.

During these same years, Washington acquired more and more land, traveling deep into the Ohio Valley in 1770 looking for sites to purchase for future development. He rented thousands of acres to tenant farmers, but he devoted his greatest attention to the management of Mount Vernon. He enjoyed experimenting in agriculture, trying new crops, and breeding better livestock, and took pleasure in the social life and recreation of the plantation—the dances, games, fox hunts, and sports.

George Washington's marriage to the young widow, Martha Dandridge Custis, mother of two small children, Patsy and Jack, and owner of vast farmlands and forests in Virginia.   *—From a painting by H. A. Ogden*

A Currier and Ives print of George Washington before the Continental Congress, accepting the appointment as Commander-in-Chief of all forces raised for the defense of the Colonies.

The Revolutionary War

BECAUSE he was a military man, it was natural that Washington's thoughts turned to the use of force when actions of the British government interfered with the rights of colonists. When the governor of Virginia disbanded the House of Burgesses in 1769 because its members protested the British Stamp Act, Washington wrote privately to a friend of his conviction that the colonists must "maintain the liberty which we have derived from our ancestors" even if it meant resorting to arms.

As a delegate to the First Continental Congress in Philadelphia in 1774, Washington impressed his colleagues from other colonies with his assurance and wisdom. When Patrick Henry was asked to name the greatest man in the Congress, he replied: ". . . if you speak of solid information and sound judgment, Colonel Washington is unquestionably the greatest man on that floor."

When the Second Continental Congress opened in May 1775, just after Lexington and Concord, the forty-three-year-old Washington wore his bright colonel's uniform to the sessions to dramatize his belief in the necessity of concerted military action by all the colonies. On June 15 the delegates unanimously elected him commander in chief of the armed forces. He accepted with modesty, rejecting any pay for the position, and expressed his willingness to accept only repayment of his expenses.

By July 2, 1775, Washington had taken command of the troops in Massachusetts at headquarters in Cambridge. He organized the siege of the British forces in Boston, despite a serious shortage of ammunition, and succeeded in forcing the British to sail away from Boston in March 1776, leaving the city in the hands of American forces.

Guessing that the British probably would attack New York City in an effort to drive a wedge between the northern and southern colonies, Washington was there to meet them when they landed in force in July. Lack of supplies, undisciplined troops, and inexperienced officers brought defeat, forcing Washington to retreat into New Jersey by November.

Desertions and the refusal of "sunshine patriots" to re-enlist weakened Washington's army to a total of about 5000 men by December, and many began to fear the war was lost. Hope revived with Washington's brilliant surprise attack on Hessian troops at Trenton the day after Christmas, 1776. He followed this victory with another at Princeton the first week of January 1777.

Washington spent the summer of 1777 anticipating a British land assault on Philadelphia from New York. But the British used their superior naval power to bypass the American army and land troops south of Philadelphia. Washington, hurrying south to oppose them, was defeated at the battle of Brandywine Creek in September, losing Philadelphia to the British. The American cause was strengthened in October when General Horatio Gates won a major victory at Saratoga, New York, capturing the British General John Burgoyne and about 5000 British troops.

Washington and his men spent the bitterly cold winter of 1777–78 at Valley Forge, Pennsylvania. Their misery was made doubly hard with the knowledge that the British were wintering in comfort in Philadelphia. Washington's steadfastness to the American cause and his closeness to his men held the army together, even while some of the leaders of Congress were wondering whether he should be replaced. Of his troops, Washington wrote: "Naked and starving as they are, we cannot sufficiently admire the incomparable patience and fidelity of the soldiers."

Good news came in the spring of 1778. The kingdom of France had decided to join in open alliance with the Americans and would send money, troops, and a fleet. When they learned of the French alliance, the British decided to consolidate their position, quitting Philadelphia to march across New Jersey to New York. Washington planned an attack on the British column for June 28 at Monmouth, but the cowardice and insubordination of his second in command, Major General Charles Lee, lost him the opportunity. Lee was found guilty of disobedience by a court-martial and was discharged from the army.

From the summer of 1778 through the summer of 1781, Washington kept the main part of the British army sealed in New York City. During

A poster of General Washington reviewing troops at Fort Cumberland.

The importance of Lafayette's contribution to the success of the Revolutionary Army was great. Here Currier and Ives depict the first meeting of Generals Washington and Lafayette, in 1777.

The winter of 1777 at Valley Forge found the Continental Army at its lowest ebb, and tested Washington's mettle to the fullest extent, as shown in this early painting of Washington and Lafayette visiting the Army. —*From a painting by A. Gibert*

these years he faced and overcame one discouragement after another as inaction led to grumbling and desertions by his soldiers, while a weak Congress had to be continuously prodded to supply necessary money and supplies. Late in 1780, Washington wrote:

"We have been half of our time without provision, and are likely to continue so. We have no magazines, nor money to form them; and in a little time we shall have no men, if we had money to pay them. We have lived upon expedients till we can live no longer. In a word, the history of the war is a history of false hopes and temporary devices, instead of system and of economy. . . ."

Washington's patience was rewarded in the summer of 1781 when he received word that the French finally were sending the main part of their fleet, thousands of troops, and a substantial loan to aid the Americans. At once he resolved to take the offensive. When word came that a large British force led by Lord Cornwallis had invaded Virginia, Washington and Count Rochambeau, the French commander, marched their combined armies rapidly to Virginia, where they joined smaller forces under the young Marquis de Lafayette and troops from the French fleet that had sealed off Chesapeake Bay. From the end of September to the middle of

October, Washington besieged Cornwallis at Yorktown. On October 19, 1781, Washington experienced the greatest triumph of his military career when Cornwallis surrendered his entire army of more than 7000 men. The blow was decisive.

The fighting was over, although it took nearly two years for a formal peace treaty to be written and signed. In this interlude between war and peace, Washington had many problems with his army, which was again growing disgruntled with the reluctance of Congress to vote adequate reimbursement. One of his colonels, Lewis Nicola, openly advocated in May 1782 that America should become a monarchy with Washington as king. To this proposal Washington reacted in typical fashion:

"With a mixture of great surprise and astonishment, I have read with attention the sentiments you have submitted to my perusal. Be assured, Sir, no occurrence in the course of the war has given me more painful sensations, than your information of there being such ideas existing in the army, as you have expressed, and I must view with abhorrence and reprehend with severity. . . .

"I am much at a loss to conceive what part of my conduct could have given encouragement to an address, which to me seems big with the greatest mischiefs, that can befall my Country. . . . you could not have found a person to whom your schemes are more disagreeable. . . ."

When the officers of the army were on the verge of overthrowing Congress and setting up their own government, Washington called them together in March 1783 and persuaded them that they must have patience. The emotional climax of his talk came when he put on eyeglasses and commented: "Gentlemen, you must pardon me. I have grown gray in your service and now find myself growing blind."

On the day the British fleet sailed out of New York Harbor, December 4, 1783, Washington met with his few remaining officers in Fraunces Tavern, embraced them individually, and left the city at once in his eagerness to return to Mount Vernon. Each city he passed through on his homeward journey made the event a celebration. At Annapolis, Maryland, where Congress then was meeting, he addressed the representatives on December 23, 1783, turning back to them his commission as commander in chief. At the close of his brief talk, he said:

"Having now finished the work assigned me, I retire from the great theater of action, and bidding an affectionate farewell to this august body, under whose orders I have so long acted, I here offer my commission, and take my leave of all the employment of public life."

Now in his early fifties, Washington happily resumed the life of a Virginia planter confident that his days of public service were concluded. But, as the next few years went by, he became more and more concerned with the inability of Congress to solve national problems because of its lack of authority under the Articles of Confederation. News of Shays' Rebellion in Massachusetts increased his fears that the independence he had so long struggled for might be destroyed unless he took a hand in strengthening the national government. In May 1786, he wrote:

"That it is necessary to revise and amend the articles of Confederation, I entertain no doubt; but what may be the consequences of such an attempt is doubtful. Yet something must be done, or the fabric must fall, for it certainly is tottering."

His friends convinced Washington that he must lend his prestige to the Constitutional Convention called in Philadelphia in 1787, so he reluctantly accepted election by the Virginia legislature as a delegate to the

*Helping Redesign
the Government*

meeting. On May 25, the day the convention opened in Philadelphia, Washington was unanimously elected its president. From a chair with a rising sun painted on its back, he presided over the convention throughout the summer, while the debates that raged were as hot as the weather. He never expressed his own views from the chair; but his continued presence, and his privately stated determination that all obstacles could be overcome, became dominant factors in its success.

On the final day of the convention, September 17, 1787, Washington made his only formal request to the delegates. He asked that they adopt an amendment increasing the number of representatives in Congress to provide a broader base for the democracy. The amendment was quickly written and approved. Washington and most of the other delegates then signed the new Constitution.

In the months that followed, Washington waited anxiously at Mount Vernon as the various states argued the question of whether or not to ratify the Constitution. He did not enter the public debate and issued no statements, but he kept in close correspondence with his friends who were taking an active part in the individual ratification conventions. Within nine months New Hampshire became the ninth state to ratify the Constitution, putting the new government into operation.

Washington's First Term

THROUGHOUT the states there was a general assumption that Washington would be the first President under the Constitution. This belief made it easier for the states to accept the idea of a strong national executive, because they were sure that Washington never would abuse the great powers granted to the office. When the first Electoral College met in New York

—From a painting by J. L. G. Ferris

The gaiety of the Christmas season at Mount Vernon, the Washington plantation home.

An interesting profile of Washington, drawn from life.

City on February 4, 1789, Washington was unanimously elected President. He accepted, although "with more diffidence and reluctance than I ever experienced before in my life."

From the day of his inauguration, April 30, 1789, Washington began setting precedents and traditions that were to be followed by each of his successors. The inauguration took place on a balcony at Federal Hall in New York City, then the capital of the United States. When he took the oath of office, administered by Chancellor Robert Livingston of New York, Washington spontaneously added the words "So help me God" and kissed the Bible on which his right hand had rested. After receiving cheers from the crowd that filled the streets and adjacent rooftops, the new President went inside the building, where he delivered a twenty-minute inaugural address to the assembled members of the Senate and the House of Representatives.

In his address he appealed somewhat indirectly to Congress to amend the Constitution with a Bill of Rights, the lack of which had prevented Rhode Island and North Carolina from approving ratification. In this regard he remarked: ". . . a reverence for the characteristic rights of freemen and a regard for the public harmony will sufficiently influence your deliberations on the question how far the former can be impregnably fortified or the latter be safely and advantageously promoted." He also declared that he would accept nothing more than expenses during his term of office.

Shortly after his inauguration, the fifty-seven-year-old President wrote to a friend concerning his feelings of uncertainty in his new position: "I walk, as it were, on untrodden ground, so many untoward circumstances may intervene in such a new and critical situation, that I shall feel an insuperable diffidence in my own abilities."

The residence of George Washington in New York City while he was serving as President.

Washington faced four major problems upon assuming the presidency. These were: (1) organizing the new government and making the many necessary appointments; (2) straightening out the tangled financial affairs of the nation; (3) obtaining better relations with Great Britain; and (4) negotiating treaties of friendship with the Indian tribes on the frontiers. He successfully achieved solutions to each during the course of his administration.

Nearly five months went by before Congress approved all the legislation necessary to set up the main departments of the federal government. Washington placed great reliance in the advice of his department heads, but it was not until his second term that this group began to be called the Cabinet.

In the realm of finance, Secretary of the Treasury Alexander Hamilton worked out a plan approved by Congress in which the national government took over the debts accumulated by the states during the Revolutionary War. In turn, money was borrowed from foreign countries to meet the debts.

In an effort to improve relations with Great Britain, Washington asked Gouverneur Morris to act as diplomatic representative in London. Washington particularly hoped that Morris could arrange a trade treaty with the British, but this was not accomplished until his second term.

Treaty negotiations with the frontier Indian tribes went on throughout Washington's eight years as President. He insisted on fair treatment of the tribes and won their friendship in return.

Under the leadership of James Madison, then a U.S. representative from Virginia, Congress approved the ten Bill of Rights amendments to the Constitution. After ratification by the states, these amendments became effective in December 1791. Meanwhile, the two states that had held out for more guarantees of freedom joined the Union, North Carolina in November 1789, and Rhode Island in May 1790. Three other states were created during Washington's presidency: Vermont in 1791, Kentucky in 1792, and Tennessee in 1796.

Washington established the presidential veto in April 1792, when for the first time in American history a President turned down legislation passed by Congress. The bill in question was a re-apportionment of Congress based on the census of 1790, which showed that the population of the country was nearly 4,000,000 persons (including close to 700,000 slaves). The measure seemed to give a disproportionate share of new seats in Congress to the northern states, so Washington vetoed it. The House of Representatives failed to override the veto. Several months later new legislation that provided a more equitable apportionment was passed and signed by Washington.

Although Washington believed the President should be a strong leader, he also felt that the three main branches of the government should be as separate as possible. Therefore, he did not personally endeavor to sway Congress to pass legislation that he favored. Instead, he left this to his department heads, particularly Secretary of State Jefferson and Secretary of the Treasury Hamilton.

Because Jefferson represented the agrarian South and Hamilton the commercial North, it was natural that their views were often opposed to each other on important national issues. It distressed Washington to see this division between two men that he admired, and he was deeply concerned that the political parties which they fostered were likely to divide the country. Hamilton and his supporters promoted the Federalist party, while Jefferson and his followers became known as Anti-Federalists or Democratic-Republicans.

Washington's Second Term

ALTHOUGH Washington had planned to retire at the end of his first term and had even begun to prepare his Farewell Address as early as 1792, he bowed to demands that he accept four more years as President. Jefferson told him, "North and South will hang together if they have you to hang on." He was again elected unanimously when the Electoral College met on February 13, 1793. Washington was sixty-one at the time of his second inauguration on March 4, 1793, in Philadelphia, to which the national capital had been transferred in 1790.

Washington's second term was vastly different from his first. He felt betrayed when his two closest advisers resigned from his Cabinet—Jefferson in the summer of 1793 and Hamilton early in 1795. Political invective began to be directed at Washington himself by the Democratic-Republican newspapers—sniping criticisms that wounded him deeply, partly because he had grown so used to universal adulation. The excitement of forming the new government was over, and he found it increasingly difficult to find good men to replace those who retired.

In the area of foreign relations, Washington's task was made exceedingly hard by the general war in Europe, in which Great Britain and the other monarchies fought against the new French republic. Washington proclaimed a policy of "strict neutrality" that was opposed by Jefferson and the Democratic-Republicans who favored aid to the French revolutionaries. Criticism of Washington by the Democratic-Republicans reached a peak in 1795 when he signed the Jay Treaty, a trade agreement with

Martha Custis Washington, wife of George Washington.

Mount Vernon, one of the nation's most revered shrines, in Virginia just outside Washington, D.C., became Washington's home in 1748 and continued to be his home for the remainder of his life.

—*Hirst Milhollen photograph*

George Washington's birthplace in Virginia.

Great Britain that had been negotiated by Chief Justice John Jay. Washington had been strongly influenced to sign the treaty when documents came into his hands that indicated Secretary of State Edmund Randolph had been bribed by the French to speak against the treaty. Randolph denied he had been in the pay of France, but he resigned from the Cabinet.

On the domestic scene, the greatest crisis of Washington's second term was the Whisky Rebellion in Pennsylvania. In the summer of 1794 riots broke out in western Pennsylvania when farmers refused to pay federal excise taxes on the whisky they distilled from their grain. The whisky provided the largest share of their income, and they felt that the federal government had no right to collect taxes on it. To prove that the federal government could enforce its power of taxation, Washington called up 15,000 militia and went with them to Pennsylvania. The leaders of the revolt were arrested and the rebellion ended.

The last year of Washington's administration was relatively quiet and uneventful. Economic conditions improved as a result of the trade stimulated by the Jay Treaty. Attacks on Washington by the Democratic-Republicans diminished both in violence and in frequency. Efforts were under way to persuade him to accept a third term, but he published his eloquent Farewell Address on September 19, 1796, ending talk of his candidacy and setting the important two-term precedent.

Washington's Last Years

AFTER turning the presidency over to John Adams in March 1797, Washington and his wife set off for Mount Vernon as quickly as they could. He wrote of his retirement in May 1797:

"To make and sell a little flour annually, to repair houses (going fast to ruin), to build one for the security of my papers of a public nature, and to amuse myself in agricultural and rural pursuits, will constitute employment for the few years I have to remain on this terrestrial globe. If . . . I could now and then meet the friends I esteem, it would fill the measure and add zest to my enjoyments; but, if ever this happens, it must be under my own vine and fig-tree. . . ."

But Washington was not to be left in the peaceful retirement he had contemplated. In 1798 war threatened with France. As the nation prepared to defend itself, President Adams asked Washington to accept a new commission as lieutenant general and take command of the new United States Army to be raised. For the next several months he was busy helping choose the generals and other officers for the Army. Then, in 1799, the French crisis subsided, and Washington once more relaxed into plantation life.

On the snowy morning of December 14, 1799, he awoke with a throat so sore that he could hardly speak. He had noticed the sore throat the day before, but thought it would quickly pass. Doctors came and employed the traditional remedy of bleeding. Washington quickly grew weaker, and at about 10 P.M. he died. Four days later his body was buried in the family vault at Mount Vernon.

Memorial services were held in scores of towns and cities. On the day after Christmas, one of the most elaborate ceremonies took place in the nation's capital, Philadelphia, where one of Washington's former officers, Henry "Light Horse Harry" Lee, gave the eulogy that contained the famous description of Washington:

"First in war, first in peace and first in the hearts of his countrymen, he was second to none . . ."

What Presidents Have Said About the Presidency

*I Walk on
Untrodden Ground*

All see, and most admire, the glare which hovers round the external trappings of elevated office. To me there is nothing in it, beyond the lustre which may be reflected from its connection with a power of promoting human felicity. In our progress toward political happiness my station is new; and, if I may use the expression, I walk on untrodden ground. There is scarcely any part of my conduct which may not hereafter be drawn into precedent. Under such a view of the duties inherent to my arduous office, I could not but feel a diffidence in myself on the one hand; and an anxiety for the Community that every new arrangement should be made in the best possible manner on the other. If after all my humble but faithful endeavours to advance the felicity of my Country and mankind, I may indulge a hope that my labours have not been altogether without success, it will be the only real compensation I can receive in the closing of life.

—George Washington, January 9, 1790.

★　　★　　★

*An Appeal
to Support the Independence
of Presidents*

People of the United States!—you know not half the solicitude of your Presidents for your happiness and welfare, not a hundredth part of the obstructions and embarrassments they endure from intrigues of individuals of both parties. You must support them in their independence, and turn a deaf ear to all the false charges against them. But, if you suffer them to be overawed and shackled in the exercise of their constitutional powers, either by aristocratical or democratical manoeuvres, you will soon repent of it in bitter anguish. Anarchy and civil war cannot be far off. Whereas, by a steady support of the independence of the President's office, your liberties and happiness will be safe, in defiance of all foreign influence, French or English, and of all popular commotion and aristocratical intrigue.

—John Adams, 1808.

★　　★　　★

*Unceasing Drudgery and
Daily Loss of Friends*

I am tired of an office where I can do no more good than many others, who would be glad to be employed in it. To myself, personally, it brings nothing but unceasing drudgery and daily loss of friends. . . . My only consolation is in the belief that my fellow citizens at large will give me credit for good intentions.

—Thomas Jefferson, 1807.

478

Assuring myself that under every vicissitude the determined spirit and united councils of the nation will be safeguards to its honor and its essential interests, I repair to the post assigned me with no other discouragement than what springs from my own inadequacy to its high duties. If I do not sink under the weight of this deep conviction it is because I find some support in a consciousness of the purposes and a confidence in the principles which I bring with me into this arduous service.

—James Madison, March 4, 1809.

★　★　★

The Fear
of Personal Inadequacy

No one knows, and few conceive, the agony of mind that I have suffered from the time that I was made by circumstances, and not by my volition, a candidate for the Presidency till I was dismissed from that station by the failure of my re-election. They were feelings to be suppressed; and they were suppressed.

—John Quincy Adams, November 4, 1830.

★　★　★

The Agony
of the Presidency

The most disagreeable duty I have to perform is the removals, and appointments to office. There is great distress here, and it appears, that all who possess office, depend upon the emolument for support, and thousands who are pressing for office to it upon the ground, that they are starving, and their families, and must perish without they can be relieved by the emolument of some office. These hungry expectants, as well as those who enjoy office, are dangerous contestants over the public purse, unless possessed by the purest principles of integrity, and honesty, and when any and every man can get recommendations of the strongest kind, it requires great circumspection to avoid imposition, and select honest men.

—Andrew Jackson, May 20, 1829.

★　★　★

The Most
Disagreeable Duty

Urgent and dangerous emergencies may have arisen, or may hereafter arise in the history of our country, rendering delay disastrous, such as the bombardment of Fort Sumter by the Confederate Government, which would for the moment justify the President in violating the Constitution, by raising a military force without the authority of law, but this only during a recess of Congress. Such extreme cases are a law unto themselves. They must rest upon the principle that it is a lesser evil to usurp, until Congress can be assembled, a power withheld from the Executive, than to suffer the Union to be endangered, either by traitors at home or enemies from abroad. In all such cases, however, it is the President's duty to present to Congress, immediately after their next meeting, the causes which impelled him thus to act, and ask for their approbation . . .

—James Buchanan, 1867.

The Usurpation
of Emergency Powers

**The Struggle
to Maintain the Government**

I am struggling to maintain the government, not to overthrow it. I am struggling, especially, to prevent others from overthrowing it. I therefore say that if I shall live I shall remain President until the 4th of next March; and that whoever shall be constitutionally elected therefor, in November, shall be duly installed as President on the 4th of March; and that, in the interval, I shall do my utmost that whoever is to hold the helm for the next voyage shall start with the best possible chance to save the ship.

—*Abraham Lincoln*, October 19, 1864.

★　　★　　★

The Vials of Wrath

Notwithstanding a mendacious press; notwithstanding a subsidized gang of hirelings who have not ceased to traduce me, I have discharged all my official duties and fulfilled my pledges. And I say here tonight that if my predecessor had lived, the vials of wrath would have poured out upon him.

—*Andrew Johnson*, September 3, 1866.

★　　★　　★

**The Difference
Between a President
and a King**

To me there is something fine in the American theory that a private citizen can be chosen by the people to occupy a position as great as that of the mightiest monarch, and to exercise a power which may for the time being surpass that of Czar, Kaiser, or Pope, and that then, after having filled this position, the man shall leave it as an unpensioned private citizen, who goes back into the ranks of his fellow citizens with entire self-respect, claiming nothing save what on his own individual merits he is entitled to receive. But it is not in the least fine, it is vulgar and foolish, for the President or ex-President to make believe, and, of all things in the world, to feel pleased if other people make believe, that he is a kind of second-rate or imitation king. . . . The effort to combine incompatibles merely makes a man look foolish. The positions of President and King are totally different in kind and degree; and it is silly, and worse than silly, to forget this. It is not of much consequence whether other people accept the American theory of the Presidency; but it is of very much consequence that the American people, including especially any American who has held the office, shall accept the theory and live up to it.

—*Theodore Roosevelt*, October 1, 1911.

★　　★　　★

**The Personal Inconvenience
of Being President**

I am constantly reminded as I go about, as I do sometimes at the week end, of the personal inconvenience of being President of the United States. If I want to know how many people live in a small town all I have to do is to go there and they at once line up to be counted. I might, in a census-taking year, save the census takers a great deal of trouble by asking them to accompany me and count the people on the spot. Sometimes, when I am most beset, I seriously think of renting a pair of whiskers or of doing something else that will furnish me with an adequate disguise, because I am sorry to find that the cut of my jib is unmistakable and that I must sail under false colors if I am going to sail incognito.

—*Woodrow Wilson*, May 15, 1916.

★ ★ ★

The White House is a prison. I can't get away from the men who dog my footsteps. I am in jail.

—*Warren G. Harding*, 1922.

The White House as a Prison

★ ★ ★

I learn more each day as to the relation of the Presidential office to the press. It appears to expect me to perform two separate duties, which occasionally in some degree seem to conflict. One duty is to help the people of the United States to get along peacefully and prosperously without any undue commotion or trouble over their affairs—that is, not to start anything that will occasion conflict and dissension. The other duty, which is almost every day borne in powerfully upon me, is that I should provide the press with exciting news of something about to happen. These are duties difficult at times to perform simultaneously.

—*Herbert Hoover*, April 13, 1929.

On Pleasing the Press

★ ★ ★

It is not by any means the sole task of the Presidency to think about the present. One of the chief obligations of the Presidency is to think about the future. We have been, in our one hundred and fifty years of constitutional existence, a wasteful nation, a nation that has wasted its natural resources and, very often, wasted its human resources. One reason why a President of the United States ought to travel throughout the country and become familiar with every State is that he has a great obligation to think about the days when he will no longer be President, to think about the next generation after that.

—*Franklin D. Roosevelt*, September 27, 1937.

The Importance of Thinking of the Future

★ ★ ★

Our Government is made up of the people. You are the Government. I am only your hired servant. I am the Chief Executive of the greatest nation in the world, the highest honor that can ever come to a man on earth. But I am the servant of the people of the United States. They are not my servants. I can't order you around, or send you to labor camps, or have your heads cut off if you don't agree with me politically.

—*Harry S Truman*, September 26, 1948.

The Hired Servant of the People

★ ★ ★

I should say or remind you, sir, that in the many months, indeed the many years that I talked about such a prospect—even in those days when I thought I had removed it forever by a letter that I wrote—I

Upon Being Asked: How Do You Like Being President?

never said I would like it. It is not a job that I suppose it is intended one should like.

I merely say this: like everything else there are compensations. It is an inspiration to deal with people that believe in America, that want to do right by a country and by a people, rather than merely selfishly seeking their own welfare. I honestly believe that in Government today I find the selfless class really far overwhelming what I would call the strictly selfish group. So to that extent, at least, there is a very great satisfaction. Now the confinement, and all the rest—those of you that have gone with me for years, you know the degree in which I like informality, my own individual freedom to do as I please. Those things are what you pay.

—*Dwight D. Eisenhower,* February 25, 1953.

★   ★   ★

*The President
as a Decision-Maker*

I think sometimes we overstate the administerial difficulties of the Presidency. I think really, in many ways, it's a judicial function, where alternatives are suggested which involve great matters, and finally the President must make a decision. That is really the most onerous and important part of the burdens of being President.

—*John F. Kennedy,* April 19, 1961.

★   ★   ★

*No Place
for a Timid Soul*

The Presidency of this Nation is no place for a timid soul or a torpid spirit. It is the one place where a petty temper and a narrow view can never reside. For the Presidency is both a legacy from the past and a profusion of hope for the future. To those who cry havoc and shout for war, we must give them understanding. To those who advocate retreat or appeasement by whatever new names they use, we modestly suggest that they re-read history, for there on history's face the blotch of Munich is still visible.

—*Lyndon B. Johnson,* February 27, 1964.

★   ★   ★

The Privacy of Advice

Unless a President can protect the privacy of the advice he gets, he cannot get the advice he needs.

—*Richard M. Nixon,* April 29, 1974.

★   ★   ★

*The Right to
Face-to-Face Discussion*

I think the American people have the right to see their President and to have him discuss face-to-face with them his views and to get from them, by one means or another, their reactions, their views, their expressions. This is what I think America was built on.

—*Gerald R. Ford,* November 2, 1974.

★   ★   ★

Some Highlights of White House History

THE WHITE HOUSE stands on eighteen landscaped, tree-shaded acres at 1600 Pennsylvania Avenue. The main building, the original President's mansion, has had two large wings added in this century to provide office space for the enlarged presidential staff. Each wing is joined to the main building by a one-story terrace. The architectural effect is one of spacious elegance, mellowed by the passing of a century and a half.

The "Palace for the President," a part of the plan for the city of Washington conceived by French engineer Pierre L'Enfant, was designed by Irish-born architect James Hoban in the taste of the Georgian country houses of the 1700s. George Washington was present at the cornerstone ceremony on October 13, 1792, but the mansion was not ready for occupancy until late in John Adams' administration. President Adams moved into what was then a gray sandstone building on November 1, 1800. Almost alone in the sparsely furnished mansion the following evening, he wrote a letter to his wife, voicing the prayer that Franklin D. Roosevelt later caused to be carved on the mantel of the State Dining Room: "I pray Heaven to bestow the best of Blessings on this House and all that shall hereafter inhabit it . . . May none but honest and wise men ever rule under this roof."

Both exterior and interior have changed under the varying influences of the long succession of Presidents and First Ladies. Three times the mansion has undergone major repair and renovation—first after the fire set by the British in 1814, a second time under Theodore Roosevelt, when it was about a hundred years old, and a third time under President Truman

The White House staff around 1890.

beginning in 1948. Nearly every First Family has left its enriching imprint on landscaping, building, furniture, or furnishings, making the house as it stands today a priceless historic museum and one of America's great national treasures.

The first additions to the still unfinished building were made by Thomas Jefferson when he assumed office in 1801. Aided by Benjamin Latrobe, his Surveyor of Public Buildings, Jefferson developed one-story East and West Terraces, which included servants' quarters, a henhouse, woodsheds, and a wine cellar. He also began to furnish the main building, importing French furniture and décor. Probably his greatest contributions to the livability of the mansion were a well and cistern. The Adamses had been forced to get their water hauled from a spring down the road.

In 1814 a British expedition, carrying out a reprisal for the burning of York, Canada, attacked the ill-defended capital and burned all the public buildings, including the presidential mansion. President and Mrs. Madison were forced to flee, Dolley Madison rescuing the silver plate and Gilbert Stuart's portrait of Washington.

James Hoban, the original architect, was commissioned to carry out reconstruction of the gutted mansion. Because the gray exterior sandstone was blackened by the flames, Hoban decided to paint it white, and at a stroke the "White House" was born.

To Madison's successor, James Monroe, fell the task of completing the refurnishing, for which he obtained a generous congressional appropriation and contributed some of his own French furniture and silver. A large suite of gilt furniture was created for the Blue Room by Paris cabinetmaker Pierre-Antoine Bellangé. Three marble busts, of Columbus, Amerigo Vespucci, and George Washington, bought for $100 each, were probably the work of the Italian sculptor Ceracchi. Monroe also commissioned Benjamin Latrobe to add the North Colonnade in 1824, the year in which the North Portico was finished.

Monroe's successor, J. Q. Adams, contributed little to White House growth, owing largely to his unpopularity with Congress. But in 1829 Andrew Jackson recalled Benjamin Latrobe to work on the Porch, completed that same year. In the French tradition of Jefferson, Madison, and Monroe, Jackson furnished the spacious East Room, where Abigail Adams had hung her wash thirty years before.

Jackson's successor Van Buren added a domestically valuable though politically hazardous improvement—a water tank in the basement to supply hot bath water. Van Buren's opponents seized on the innovation as proof of the decadent luxury which they accused the President of enjoying. Polk's administration saw the installation of gas lighting, though the first time the new illumination was used it suddenly failed, plunging a presidential reception into darkness. Luckily Mrs. Polk had kept the East Room equipped with candles.

Not until 1850, when the Fillmores moved in, did the White House Kitchen receive that important nineteenth-century improvement, the stove. Until then cooking was done over an open fireplace. The new stove, made of cast iron, proved so baffling a contraption that President Fillmore had to inspect the original model in the Patent Office before he could brief his kitchen staff on its proper use. The Fillmores were responsible for another innovation—the first White House Library, established by Mrs. Fillmore in the Oval Room.

The Pierces put in the building's first central heating plant, a hot-water and hot-air system with a coal furnace which at last supplied heat to some of the corners remote from fireplaces—corners that Andrew Jackson had declared hell itself could not warm.

Both the Buchanans and the Lincolns carried out much repair and replacement work, though no significant new additions were made. Mrs. Lincoln was especially tireless in petitioning Congress for funds needed for maintenance and restoration. Perhaps her most important original contribution was the portrait of Lincoln she had painted by G. P. A. Healy, which remains the most popular picture in the White House collection.

The post-Civil War White House stood in need of considerable maintenance because of troops quartered in the East Room, damage by souvenir-hunters at Lincoln's Second Inauguration, and wear and tear from an exceptionally busy administration. Furthermore, age itself was beginning to take toll. Finally, the rapid addition of executive functions brought pressure for more office space. Andrew Johnson established his Cabinet Room in Lincoln's former office, today the Treaty Room, on the second floor. The Grants carried out extensive renovation, particularly in the East Room where the soldiers had bivouacked.

President Hayes, who had taken part in one of Alexander Graham Bell's earliest demonstrations of his remarkable new invention, enthusiastically installed the first telephone in the White House in 1877. The original lone operator was succeeded by a switchboard staff that has since grown to a dozen, capable of handling calls round the clock at a rate of 10,000 a day.

Hayes also acquired a celebrated piece of furniture, a desk made from the timbers of an icebound British ship that an American expedition had salvaged and returned to Britain as a good-will gesture. The desk, a return gift from Queen Victoria, was later discovered in a utility room by the Kennedys and stands today in the Executive Office.

The sophisticated Chester A. Arthur, complaining that the White House looked like a barracks, commissioned Louis Tiffany of New York to execute a fresh renovation. The greenhouse and conservatories were rebuilt and a new tone lent to many rooms by Tiffany's rococo *"art nouveau,"* including a huge stained-glass screen placed in the entrance hall. Another new gadget made its appearance: the elevator.

The East Room about 1893.

A bedroom about 1890.

Both Presidents Cleveland and Harrison sought funds for office expansion, and Mrs. Harrison had an architect make several designs that would have added enormous wings virtually dwarfing the original structure. But Congress, with what was probably fortunate parsimony, rejected the proposal. President McKinley caused the plans to be scaled down, but still had no luck with Congress.

Two important improvements were nevertheless carried out in the nineties. President Harrison ordered the old gas lights replaced with Thomas Edison's new electric illumination. A young man named Ike Hoover supervised the installation, and at President Harrison's request stayed on to make sure nothing went wrong. Hoover, who recalled in his memoirs that the Harrisons "were afraid to turn the lights on and off for fear of getting a shock," stayed forty-two years, mostly as Chief Usher.

The second improvement in the nineties was not to the house itself but to its atmosphere. Since the Potomac had begun silting up in the 1840s, mud flats had formed in front of the White House, turning the area into an unwholesome swamp. Once these swamps had been drained, lawn entertaining became popular, possibly reaching a climax with a night garden party at which President and Mrs. Taft regaled four thousand guests at their silver wedding in 1911.

By 1901 the need for office space was so pressing that Congress could no longer procrastinate. To undertake both expansion and large-scale remodeling President Theodore Roosevelt engaged the leading architectural firm in the country, McKim, Mead and White. Under their plan a whole new building, the Executive Wing, rose on the west lawn, connecting with the main building by an open colonnade. Jefferson's west pavilion was absorbed into the new structure. Extensive remodeling was also carried out on the main building. The second-floor area formerly occupied by offices was turned into private rooms, at last separating executive from living quarters. A new boiler room was dug in the basement, and the old plumbing, heating and electrical systems entirely replaced. Throughout, the décor took on a new look. Out went Chester Arthur's gaudy stained-glass screen, and in came a set of Teddy Roosevelt's hunting-trophy heads for the State Dining Room.

The 1902 alteration solved the major White House problems for half a century. In 1909 President Taft added an oval office for the President to the new West Wing. The first Mrs. Woodrow Wilson turned the attic—which the Theodore Roosevelt children had used as a vast playroom—into guest rooms for the growing White House list of distinguished visitors. A more unusual touch during the Wilson administration was the addition

Carriages and drivers parked outside the White House during the gaslight
era, with an enormous gas fixture visible in the front hall.

of a flock of sheep grazing on the White House lawn, to free manpower from the lawn-mowing job for military service.

In 1927, under the Coolidge occupancy, the old attic on the third floor of the main building was enlarged and finished to provide additional guest rooms and servants' quarters, as well as a sun room over the rounded South Portico—a room Grace Coolidge called the "sky parlor."

The Hoovers brought a touch of the exotic when they moved in in 1929. Veteran world travelers, they had collected art objects, rugs, and bamboo furniture that brightened the second floor. Mrs. Hoover filled the fan-shaped window at the west end of the corridor with an enormous cageful of canaries.

The President's Oval Office in the West Wing of the White House during President Kennedy's administration.

Despite a fire that swept the Executive Wing and forced the Hoovers to vacate the house for a few weeks, no further extensive structural changes took place until the advent of President Franklin D. Roosevelt, whose New Deal turned the White House into a humming beehive of activity. The Executive Wing had to be enlarged to house the rapidly proliferating presidential staff. The expansion was largely concealed from the exterior by the ingenious trick of adding space underground. A noteworthy feature of the second Roosevelt renovation was the addition of a swimming pool, paid for by popular subscription so the polio-crippled

President could enjoy his favorite exercise. When the war brought demands for yet more office space, a reconstruction of the East Wing provided it.

But it was during the postwar administration of President Harry S Truman that the last truly major alteration came about. For decades the various structural changes and the addition of conduits, pipes, and wiring had weakened walls and floors of the venerable main building. The groanings of the ancient timbers gave rise to newspaper feature stories of ghosts in the White House.

Truman had already drawn considerable press attention by putting a balcony in the South Portico in 1947 to shade the windows of the Blue Room below. That teapot-tempest controversy was forgotten in 1948 when it became evident that something far more serious was wrong with the mansion. Not only did floors creak and ceilings crack, but the President's bathtub appeared to be sinking into the floor. One day Margaret Truman's piano thrust a leg down into the family dining room below. When the crystal chandelier in the Blue Room began shivering ominously during a reception a thorough study was ordered, resulting in the shocking revelation that the White House was threatened with imminent collapse. W. E. Reynolds, Commissioner of Public Buildings, said the family floor was staying in place "purely from habit." The Trumans moved bag and baggage across the street to Blair House, normally reserved for presidential guests. Then a reconstruction commission went to work.

Bulldozers rumbled in to dig a new basement and sub-basement to house the service core of what was to become a thoroughly modern, if unique, home-office building, complete with air conditioning. The entire interior of the mansion was removed from inside the shell of the outer walls, which were underpinned with concrete piers. Inside the walls a steel skeleton was erected. The whole job was carried out with the most painstaking caution. Irreplaceable chandeliers, mantelpieces and ornamental woodwork were removed and stored. Even the ornamental plasterwork was diagrammed before being removed.

When the three-year-long reconstruction job was finished in 1952, visitors discovered a subtly transformed mansion. The new décor was one of simple elegance, with many of the ornate and rococo touches of an earlier era giving way to softer, lighter, and more modern tones. Theodore Roosevelt's trophy heads vanished from the walls of the State Dining Room, no longer dark oak but soft green. The crystal chandeliers of the East Room reappeared, but in a simpler, more graceful form.

The Truman reconstruction was calculated to last. Since its completion, alterations in the mansion have been scarcely discernible. When under President Eisenhower the old need for more room for the Executive staff revived, an effective answer was found that did not touch the White House itself. A new Executive Office Building was constructed across Pennsylvania Avenue, connected to the mansion by a tunnel. Neither the Kennedys nor the Johnsons, both notably sensitive to the historic importance of their temporary residence, did more than add decorative touches. Mrs. Kennedy followed in the footsteps of Mrs. Coolidge, Mrs. Hoover, and Mrs. Eisenhower in the recovery and restoration of authentic presidential and other period pieces. She also successfully sought more appropriate art for the walls. President Kennedy followed the Fillmores and Trumans in pressing the project of a White House Library. That of Mrs. Fillmore had been replaced, in the Truman reconstruction, by a new library in the Ground Floor (originally the basement). A commission appointed by President Kennedy, under the chairmanship of James T. Babb, Librarian of Yale University, chose 2780 titles, mostly by American authors.

Today the hundred-plus-room mansion (Mrs. Eisenhower pointed out that a figure of "one hundred and two" was problematical because it is not easy to say which storerooms and other auxiliaries should be counted) is comfortable but not oversized. The scale of formal entertaining has grown steadily, and that of informal entertaining even more. Even the sightseers outside the picket fence were sometimes turned into a sort of receiving line under President Johnson, who interrupted strolls on the grounds to shake hands through the fence.

Not a palace or a fortress, but an attractive and livable dwelling, the White House stands today in cheerful contrast to the gloomy grandeur of most of the great European official residences. Yet it has its own air of majesty as America's shrine—the mansion of democracy.

The Diplomatic Reception Room in the White House.

Biographies of the Defeated Nominees

The role of the also-ran, the principal defeated candidate for the Presidency, has varied considerably in American politics. In some cases the candidate has run again and lost again.

In the case of Henry Clay and William Jennings Bryan, each lost three times, and each time by a larger margin. One candidate, Samuel Jones Tilden, had a clear majority of both the popular vote and the electoral vote in the election of 1876, but had the office of President stolen from him by political maneuvering in the electoral vote.

This group of biographies includes only the main defeated candidates, and not the third or fourth party losers.

George Stanley McGovern

The prairie-flat voice of George McGovern made even his most fiery political speeches sound like the Sunday sermons he once preached as a student minister. When, during the election campaign of 1972, he called President Nixon's administration "the most corrupt in history," he was unable to stir moral indignation in more than a small percentage of voters. Partly because of this, McGovern suffered one of the worst defeats ever experienced by a Democratic Presidential nominee.

The second oldest of four children of a Methodist minister, George Stanley McGovern was born July 19, 1922, in Avon, South Dakota, only about 150 miles from the birthplace of Hubert Humphrey, McGovern's immediate predecessor as a Democratic Presidential candidate. When George was six, his family settled in Mitchell, South Dakota, where his father became minister of a newly built Wesleyan Methodist church.

After graduation from high school in Mitchell, McGovern attended Dakota Wesleyan University, only a few blocks from his home. Both in high school and college, he made high marks in his studies. Debate and oratory became his major hobby, one in which he won many awards, including first prize in the 1942 South Dakota Peace Oratory Contest for an oration called "My Brother's Keeper."

While in college, McGovern took flying instruction and received his pilot's license. In February 1943, while still in his junior year, he was called to active duty in World War II in the Army Air Corps.

On his first leave from the Army in the spring of 1943, he returned home to marry Eleanor Stegeberg, his college sweetheart, whom he had first met when she and her twin sister, Ila, were members of a rival high school debating team from Woonsocket, South Dakota. George's father performed the marriage.

After receiving his commission as a lieutenant, McGovern was sent overseas to join the 15th Air

George S. McGovern

Force's 455th Bomb Group in Italy as a B-24 bomber pilot. During his tour of duty, he flew thirty-five combat bombing missions, and was awarded the Distinguished Flying Cross for his courage and ability.

When the war was over in 1945, McGovern returned to Mitchell, resuming his studies at Dakota Wesleyan under the GI Bill. After graduation from DWU, he attended Garrett Theological Seminary in Evanston, Illinois. There he was assigned as a student minister to Diamond Lake, a resort community northwest of Chicago. McGovern did not find his life as a minister as satisfying as he had hoped it would be.

Late in 1947, he decided to give up the ministry, entering graduate school at Northwestern University. While still a graduate student, McGovern got his first taste of national politics, actively supporting the left-wing Progressive party candidacy of Henry Wallace for President in 1948. After receiving his master's and doctor's degrees in history at Northwestern, McGovern returned to Mitchell, where he joined the faculty of Dakota Wesleyan.

The 30-year-old McGovern decided in 1952 to leave the teaching profession and enter politics. He became executive secretary of the nearly defunct state Democratic party, which at that time held only two of the 105 seats in the two-house state legislature. Within four years he rebuilt the party to the point that he felt confident that he should run for office himself. In 1956 he defeated an incumbent Republican Congressman to take a seat in the U.S. House of Representatives.

The McGoverns, who by this time had four daughters and a son (Ann, Susan, Terry, Mary, and Steven), moved to the Washington suburb of Chevy Chase, Maryland, where their next-door neighbors turned out to be the family of Hubert Humphrey, then the junior Senator from Minnesota. McGovern and Humphrey developed a close friendship that only later became strained over the issue of the Vietnam War and their rivalry for the Presidency.

After easily winning re-election to Congress in 1958, McGovern tried unsuccessfully two years later to win a seat in the U.S. Senate. Newly-elected President John Kennedy, whom McGovern had supported in the campaign, rewarded him with the post of director of the Food for Peace Program, distributing food to needy nations around the world.

McGovern again ran for the U.S. Senate in 1962. This time he won by a margin of 100 votes out of more than 240,000 cast. A recount later increased his margin to 504 votes.

As the United States became more deeply involved in the Vietnam War in the years that followed, Senator McGovern became one of the most outspoken opponents of the war. In 1968 he supported Robert Kennedy's antiwar bid for the Democratic Presidential nomination. When Kennedy was assassinated in June, McGovern was persuaded to wage a last-minute campaign for the nomination. His efforts, however, were too little, too late. Hubert Humphrey won nomination on the first ballot at the Democratic convention, with McGovern receiving only 146½ votes. While Humphrey was defeated for the Presidency, McGovern was re-elected to a second term in the U.S. Senate.

After continuing to speak out against the Vietnam War during President Nixon's first years in office, McGovern announced his candidacy for the 1972 Democratic Presidential nomination in January 1971, a year and a half before the next Democratic national convention.

The other major contenders for the nomination were Humphrey and Senator Edmund Muskie of Maine. Although few persons thought McGovern had a chance for the nomination, he worked doggedly, entering eighteen primaries. With the support of young voters and liberals, he called for an end to the Vietnam War and an end to poverty, with a guaranteed annual income to all Americans. By the time of the Democratic national convention in July 1972, he had succeeded in collecting enough votes to win easily on the first ballot, despite opposition of most of the party's regular politicians.

For his running mate as the Vice-Presidential candidate, McGovern chose Senator Tom Eagleton of Missouri. However, when it was revealed a few days after the convention that Eagleton had a previous medical history of hospitalization for treatment of "nervous exhaustion," McGovern asked Eagleton to withdraw from the ticket. He replaced him with Sargent Shriver, President Kennedy's brother-in-law. Many voters interpreted McGovern's unprecedented action as a sign of weakness. His popularity dropped in the public opinion polls.

The Republicans in the ensuing campaign portrayed McGovern as a man who repeatedly changed his mind like a weather vane and as a radical who would put half the nation on the welfare rolls.

Hubert Horatio Humphrey

A voluble speaker, Hubert Humphrey could talk rings around most other men when he was inspired by a liberal cause. Lyndon Johnson said Humphrey could "prepare a speech in the time it took to draw

Hubert H. Humphrey —*Harris & Ewing*

age of 28 in 1939. The next year he taught at Louisiana State University, where he received a master's degree in political science. He then returned to Minnesota where he worked for two federal agencies, the Works Progress Administration and the War Manpower Commission.

Distressed by corruption in the city government of Minneapolis, Humphrey entered politics in 1943 to run for mayor. He was beaten. The next year he helped form the Democratic-Farmer-Labor party. With its backing he again ran for mayor in 1945 and won at the age of 34. A reformer, he quickly cleaned out the city's racketeers and then was re-elected in 1947. While he was mayor he helped form the Americans for Democratic Action, an organization dedicated to the election of liberals throughout the nation.

Humphrey first came to wide attention at the Democratic National Convention in 1948, where he fought for and obtained adoption of a platform plank calling for greater civil rights for Negroes. Adoption of the plank caused Southern Democrats to bolt the party and run Governor Strom Thurmond of South Carolina for President on the States Rights ticket.

Later in 1948 the 37-year-old Humphrey won election as U.S. Senator from Minnesota—the first Democrat to win this office from his state since the Civil War. He was re-elected to the Senate in 1954 and 1960. He sponsored more than a thousand bills and resolutions—some of the better-known include the Peace Corps and the National Defense Education Act. The first bill he introduced as a freshman Senator was for Medicare, medical care for the aged —legislation he kept reintroducing until it finally was approved sixteen years later. During his final term in the Senate he served as assistant majority leader.

At the age of 49, in 1960, Humphrey ran a strong campaign against John Kennedy in an effort to win the Democratic presidential nomination. But when he lost a hard-fought primary in West Virginia to Kennedy, he withdrew from the race.

President Johnson in an unprecedented action went to the floor of the Democratic National Convention in Atlantic City, New Jersey, in 1964 to tell the delegates personally that he wanted Humphrey as his vice-presidential running mate. After the Johnson-Humphrey ticket was elected in a landslide, Johnson gave the 53-year-old Vice President many additional responsibilities. These included direction of the enforcement of the new civil rights laws and coordination of the anti-poverty programs. However, Humphrey came in for considerable criticism from former friends in the liberal wing of the

a deep breath." But he was unable to talk the nation into giving him enough votes to win the presidency.

He lost the presidential election of 1968 to Richard Nixon by one of the closest margins in history—only one-half of one percent of the popular vote. Many voters felt Nixon and Humphrey were equally well qualified for the office. Both had served as Vice President. And each had been a U.S. Senator.

The son of a druggist, Hubert Horatio Humphrey, Jr. was born in Wallace, South Dakota, on May 27, 1911. The family moved to Doland, South Dakota, and later to Huron, South Dakota. He was attending the University of Minnesota in 1929 when hard times caused by the Great Depression forced him to drop out of school to help in his father's store. In 1933 he got a pharmacist's degree from the Denver (Colorado) College of Pharmacy. He continued working for his father for the next four years. He married Muriel Fay Buck in 1936. They had a daughter and three sons.

Anxious to receive more education, Humphrey returned to college in 1937 while his wife worked to help pay the expenses. He was graduated *magna cum laude* from the University of Minnesota at the

Democratic party for not speaking out against the President's policy of escalating the Vietnam War.

With Johnson's assistance, Humphrey won the Democratic presidential nomination in 1968. But the party was too torn with arguments over Johnson's Vietnam War policy to pull itself together behind Humphrey's campaign. After the vote was in, Humphrey conceded the election to Nixon, saying, "I shall continue my personal commitment to the cause of human rights, of peace, and to the betterment of man."

Two years later Humphrey resumed his public career by winning election in 1970 as U.S. Senator from Minnesota.

Barry Morris Goldwater

The most conservative members of the Republican party had been forced for nearly three decades to accept the nomination of presidential candidates who they believed were too liberal. Each time after the defeats of Landon, Willkie, Dewey, and Nixon, these conservatives set up a cry that if only the candidate had been farther to the right he would have attracted conservative voters from both parties and would have won.

Finally, in 1964, the Republican conservatives of the West and South wrested control of the party from the more liberal Eastern Republicans and obtained the presidential nomination of Barry Goldwater, who offered "a choice, not an echo." But "Mr. Conservative," as Goldwater was called, succeeded in losing the election to President Johnson by nearly as large a margin as Alf Landon did to President Roosevelt in 1936.

Born in Phoenix, Arizona, on January 1, 1909, Goldwater was the son of a well-to-do department store owner. At 19 he graduated from Staunton (Virginia) Military Academy, and then attended the University of Arizona. But he dropped out of college when his father died in 1929 to go to work in the family store. Eight years later at the age of 28 he became president of the department store company.

A lieutenant in the Army reserve, Goldwater was called to active duty in 1941 even before the United States had been drawn into World War II. He transferred from the infantry to the Army Air Corps and became a transport pilot in 1943. By the time of his discharge from active duty in 1945 he had risen to the rank of lieutenant colonel. After the war he remained in the Air Force reserve and rose to the rank of major general.

Goldwater became active in politics in 1949 when at the age of 40 he was elected to the city council of Phoenix. Three years later in 1952, Goldwater was elected to the U.S. Senate, defeating the Democratic incumbent, and was re-elected in 1958.

As a U.S. Senator Goldwater often voted against legislation proposed by President Eisenhower because he thought it was too liberal. He made hundreds of speeches throughout the country raising funds for the Republican party and espousing his views on conservatism. He particularly opposed civil rights legislation and expansion of the social security system. He attracted the support of extreme right wing conservatives.

In his acceptance speech after receiving the Republican presidential nomination in San Francisco, Goldwater shocked liberals with his statement that ". . . extremism in the defense of liberty is no vice . . . and moderation in the pursuit of justice is no virtue." This was taken by most persons as meaning that he welcomed the support of right wing groups such as the John Birch Society, an organization that believed that even President Eisenhower was pro-communist.

During the campaign that followed, the Democrats played on people's fears that Goldwater was likely to be "trigger-happy" if he became President and could make the ultimate decision on when to use atomic warfare. On the other hand, Goldwater accused the Democrats of being "soft on communism." In the election Goldwater carried only his home state of Arizona and five Southern states.

As an aftermath of the election, Goldwater sued for libel *Fact* magazine which had published a survey of psychiatrists that concluded that Goldwater was mentally unfit to serve as President. Four years after the election, in 1968, Goldwater was awarded damages of $75,000 in the suit.

Barry M. Goldwater

494

Adlai Ewing Stevenson

Born to politics, Adlai E. Stevenson was named for his grandfather, who was Vice-President of the United States from 1893 to 1897 under President Grover Cleveland. But, unfortunately for Stevenson, in his two efforts to win the presidency in 1952 and 1956 he was no match for the popularity of war hero Dwight D. Eisenhower.

Stevenson was born on February 5, 1900, in Los Angeles, California, but grew up in Bloomington, Illinois, where his family owned a newspaper, the *Daily Pantagraph*. In 1922 he graduated from Princeton University. He attended law school at Harvard University for two years, and then completed his law degree at Northwestern University in 1926. For the next fifteen years he practiced law in Chicago.

In 1941 Stevenson became a special assistant to the Secretary of the Navy. During the last years of World War II he went to Italy in charge of an American economic aid mission. He next became an assistant to the Secretary of State and served as the department's press spokesman at the founding of the United Nations in San Francisco in 1945. Then he became a member of the U.S. delegation to the UN for the next two years.

Stevenson returned to Illinois to run for governor on the Democratic ticket in 1948, carrying the state by a larger majority than President Truman did in the same election. As governor he compiled an excellent record, reforming many abuses in the state government.

When Truman decided not to run for another term in 1952, he attempted to persuade Stevenson to enter the race for the Democratic presidential nomination. Stevenson said he would only accept the nomination if the delegates drafted him, refusing to campaign for the honor. Stevenson's reluctance won him many friends, and when the convention met he was drafted as the presidential nominee on the third ballot.

Stevenson's campaign speeches were polished and witty. Many thought they were too intellectual to be easily understood by the man in the street. But, more important in contributing to his defeat in the election, were the people's dissatisfaction with the Korean War and the people's admiration for Dwight D. Eisenhower, the Republican presidential nominee. In the end Stevenson lost disastrously, winning the electoral votes of only eight states—even losing his home state of Illinois.

During the next four years Stevenson kept himself in the public eye as the leader of the Democratic

Adlai E. Stevenson

party, writing books, lecturing, and traveling extensively, both in the United States and throughout the world. He easily won the 1956 Democratic presidential nomination on the first ballot, and again faced Eisenhower as his rival. His second presidential campaign was even harder than his first for Stevenson, because the United States was enjoying its greatest prosperity in history under Eisenhower. In the election he received over a million fewer votes than he got in 1952, and he carried only six states.

After his second defeat Stevenson returned to his Chicago law practice and indicated he had given up all hope of attaining the White House. However, his most ardent supporters made another effort to win the 1960 Democratic presidential nomination for him, giving up only when the party leaders threw their support to John F. Kennedy.

President Kennedy appointed Stevenson as ambassador to the UN with cabinet rank, a post he continued to hold under President Johnson. As the chief American spokesman at the UN, Stevenson exercised his wit and urbanity to strengthen U.S. ties with other countries. A heart attack brought his unexpected death at the age of 65 while he was walking on a street in London on July 14, 1965.

Thomas Edmund Dewey

The first Republican presidential candidate to lose two national elections in a row, Thomas E. Dewey—like other also-rans before him — was doubly disappointed because he had been assured he was bound to win. A short, dapper lawyer, Dewey had a cold personality which failed to appeal to a majority of the nation's voters, and was described by one political observer as having the appearance of "the bridegroom on a wedding cake."

Thomas E. Dewey was born on March 24, 1902, in Owosso, Michigan. His father was the local postmaster and also owned the local Republican newspaper. In high school he was a good student, a debater, and a singer. He graduated from the University of Michigan in 1923, helping earn his way through college by singing in churches. He then went to New York, where he continued to take voice lessons while attending law school at Columbia University.

After completing his studies at Columbia, Dewey gave up the possibility of a singing career and was admitted to the bar. Dewey spent several years as a

Thomas E. Dewey

corporation lawyer. Then in 1931 he was appointed as the chief assistant to the U.S. district attorney in New York, and two years later, at the age of 31, he was appointed U.S. district attorney. In this office he successfully convicted one of New York City's chief gangsters, Waxey Gordon. In 1935 Dewey was appointed as a special prosecutor to a grand jury investigating New York's gangsters. He convicted gangster Lucky Luciano, who controlled the city's prostitution, and scores of other underworld figures. In 1937 he was elected as the city's district attorney, and continued his vigorous prosecution of racketeers.

In 1938 the Republicans nominated the 36-year-old Dewey for governor. He was defeated in the election by a narrow margin—but in the Roosevelt Era Republican defeats were common, and Dewey became a Republican hero because he almost won. Therefore, he became the leading contender for the Republican presidential nomination in 1940, but lost out to the popular groundswell for Wendell Willkie.

Then in 1942 Dewey ran again for governor of New York, and this time won by a large majority. As governor he built a smooth running political machine that enacted into law legislation favoring the business community. At the 1944 Republican national convention in Chicago Dewey was given the nomination on the first ballot to oppose President Roosevelt's try for a fourth term. The 42-year-old Dewey criss-crossed the country campaigning on the basis that World War II was nearly over and that the people should elect a Republican administration to get the country onto a sound business basis when the war was over. But Dewey was no match for Roosevelt and lost by more than three-and-a-half million votes, obtaining the electoral votes of only 10 states.

Dewey was re-elected governor of New York in 1946, and immediately began preparing for the next presidential election. In 1948 he again won the Republican presidential nomination handily. This time he was confident that he would win against President Truman—just as he had won the governorship of New York on his second try. Dewey, along with most of the nation's newspapers and the poll takers, was lulled into overconfidence. He misjudged the effect of his cold personality compared to the down-to-earth touch of Truman. When the final results were in, Dewey received fewer votes in 1948 than he had in 1944.

Dewey was re-elected governor again in 1950. He helped Dwight D. Eisenhower attain the Republican presidential nomination in 1952, and then retired from public life in 1955 at the end of his third term, resuming the private practice of law. At the age of 68, he died March 16, 1971, in Bal Harbour, Florida.

Wendell Willkie

Wendell Lewis Willkie

The third of four Republican presidential candidates to be defeated by Franklin D. Roosevelt, Wendell Willkie received more popular votes than any of the other three. If he had defeated Roosevelt in 1940, he would have been President when the United States was drawn into World War II. It is difficult to know what sort of wartime President he might have been because throughout his life he had a habit of suddenly shifting his thinking from one side to the other. He never held any elective political office.

Willkie was born on February 18, 1892, in Elwood, Indiana. His mother was the first woman admitted to practice law in the state, and she and Willkie's father ran a law office together. Wendell was the youngest of six children. At 17 he enrolled in the University of Indiana. He refused to join a fraternity and became an active campus politician, fighting the fraternities for his first few years; then, pulling a switch, he joined a fraternity. After graduating with a degree in law in 1913, he returned to Elwood and entered the family law firm.

During World War I he went to France as a lieutenant in the artillery, but did not take part in any battles. After briefly rejoining the family law firm, he decided he did not like small town life, and moved to Akron, Ohio, to take a position in the law department of the Firestone Rubber Company. A short time later he left this job to become a member of an Akron law firm. During the 1920's he established a reputation as one of the best lawyers in Akron. At the same time he was active in the Dem-

ocratic party, fighting the Ku Klux Klan and attending the 1924 Democratic national convention where he supported Al Smith's candidacy.

When he was 36 years old in 1929, Willkie moved to New York City as the legal counsel for a large electric utility holding company, Commonwealth and Southern. He continued to be active in the Democratic party, supporting the election of Franklin D. Roosevelt in 1932.

In 1933 Willkie became president of Commonwealth and Southern. He now switched sides politically, becoming an opponent of Roosevelt's New Deal and the most active spokesman against public ownership of electric power facilities, such as the Tennessee Valley Authority. During the next several years he wrote dozens of magazine articles, made countless lecture appearances, and appeared on popular radio shows, using humor as well as statistics to make his point that the public had more to fear from "big government" than it did from "big business."

In the spring of 1940 admirers of Willkie began a movement to help win him the Republican presidential nomination. Soon Willkie Clubs sprang up throughout the nation, financed by businessmen who saw Willkie as a shining hope to prevent Roosevelt from winning a third term. At the Republican party's national convention in Philadelphia in June, the galleries were packed with his followers, who chanted, "We want Willkie!" until the professional politicians threw in the sponge and gave him the nomination on the sixth ballot.

Willkie campaigned hard from one end of the country to the other. A big, genial, tousle-haired man, Willkie presented himself as a plain-spoken fellow from Indiana. But the Democrats caustically labeled him "a simple barefoot Wall Street lawyer." Many of Willkie's campaign statements were contradictory from one day to the next, confusing the voters as to exactly where he stood. Moreover, the impending fate of the world overshadowed domestic issues, with Hitler's troops having overrun France and Hitler's air force waging the Battle of Britain. Many voters feared that Willkie just was not soundly enough grounded in international affairs to take over the White House in such a critical period. But up to Election Day it appeared that Willkie had at least a 50-50 chance to win. When the votes were counted he had received 45 percent to Roosevelt's 55 percent.

Following his defeat, Willkie endeavored to maintain his leadership of the Republican party while supporting Roosevelt's policies as the United States was plunged into World War II. As Roosevelt's special envoy, Willkie toured the world. He then wrote a book in 1943, *One World,* which called for inter-

497

national cooperation in the postwar era. He mounted a campaign to again win the Republican presidential nomination in 1944, but withdrew after being defeated in the Wisconsin primary by Thomas Dewey. The 52-year-old Willkie had a heart attack in August, 1944, and died in New York City on October 8, 1944. Some said that, like Horace Greeley, he had died of a broken heart.

Alfred Mossman Landon

No major party presidential candidate in a two-way race ever was so badly defeated, either before or since, as Alfred M. Landon in the 1936 election. It was not that the voters particularly disliked this mild-mannered governor of Kansas, it was just that the majority of people felt that President Roosevelt was solving the problems of the Great Depression and they were not about to turn the destiny of the country over to anyone else.

Born on September 9, 1887, in West Middlesex, Pennsylvania, Alf Landon moved to Kansas with his father and mother when he was a teen-ager. At the age of 20 he was graduated from the University of Kansas law school, and became a bookkeeper in a bank in Independence, Kansas. But he soon gave up

Alfred M. Landon

banking to follow in the footsteps of his father, who was a wildcat oil prospector. During World War I he served briefly as a lieutenant in the army, but did not see overseas duty. He then returned to his work as an oil promoter and by the time he was 40 he was a millionaire.

Landon began to take an active interest in politics. In 1928 he ran the campaign of Republican Clyde Reed, who was elected governor of Kansas. Then in 1932 he himself ran for the governorship and gained national attention because he was the only Republican west of the Mississippi to win election as chief executive of a state. Two years later he became the only Republican governor in the nation to win re-election. As governor he followed a liberal program and supported the national policies of President Roosevelt. While doing so, he performed a minor miracle by balancing the state budget, while most other states were going deeply into debt.

As about the only Republican who could win any office, the 48-year-old Landon had little competition at the 1936 Republican national convention and won the presidential nomination on the first ballot. With a Kansas sunflower as a campaign symbol, Landon barnstormed the country, growing more and more vociferous against Roosevelt's New Deal. Landon was confident that he was going to win. He was reinforced in this thinking by a national poll by the magazine *Literary Digest,* which forecast a Republican victory. But in the election Landon received only 37.5 percent of the popular vote and carried only Maine and Vermont.

After his defeat Landon returned to his private business. He continued to take an active interest in politics, but was seldom heard of on the national scene.

Alfred Emanuel Smith

If Alfred E. Smith had been elected President in 1928 instead of Herbert Hoover, he almost surely would have launched a program of government controls and social reforms that might have saved the nation and the world much of the suffering and unrest of the era of the Great Depression. And, if this had occurred, it is possible that Adolf Hitler would not have risen to power in Germany and brought on World War II.

Born in an East Side New York City tenement on December 30, 1873, Smith grew up with a first-hand knowledge of big city poverty. After the death of his father when Alfred was 13, the boy dropped out of school and went to work to help support his widowed mother. As a teen-ager he cleaned and sold fish in the Fulton Fish Market for wages of $12 a week. As a hobby he acted in amateur plays put on by a theatrical club sponsored by his parish church.

Smith obtained his first political job when he was 22, as a jury process server—a position he held for six years. Then in 1901, when he was 28, he became an assistant to the Democratic party leader of his slum neighborhood. His loyalty and hard work were repaid when his Democratic party friends helped the 29-year-old Smith win election to the state legislature in 1903.

In his early years in the legislature it was hard for the young man who had never attended high school to understand the legislation he was voting on. But he made the legislature his school and read and re-read the legislation until he understood it. His district repeatedly re-elected him, and when the Democrats won control of the legislature in 1911 Smith was elected majority leader. Two years later he was elected Speaker of the House. In 1915, when Smith served as a delegate to the state constitutional convention, the chairman of the convention, Elihu Root, described Smith as "the best-informed man on the business of the state of New York."

Smith was elected to the lucrative position of sheriff of New York County in 1915, and two years later was elected President of the New York City Board of Aldermen. He was now one of the most popular figures in the state, so it was logical that his party chose him to run for governor in 1918—an election in which the 44-year-old Smith defeated the Republican incumbent.

In his first term as governor Smith had many difficulties because the Republicans controlled both houses of the legislature and refused to support his legislative program. But he managed to get the state's Sunday blue laws relaxed to permit baseball and motion pictures on Sundays, and he called a special session of the legislature to ratify the woman suffrage amendment to the United States Constitution.

The Harding landslide of 1920 defeated Smith's bid for re-election as governor. But he came back in 1922 to again defeat the incumbent Republican governor. And he was re-elected governor in 1924 and 1926. During his administration as governor, Smith obtained passage of much liberal legislation to improve conditions for laboring people and to protect the rights of women and children. Because the legislature often opposed his reform measures, Smith regularly appealed to the people to bring pressure on their representatives, who then grudgingly responded to his requests.

Alfred E. Smith

Smith's name was placed in nomination for the presidency at the Democratic national convention in 1920, but he was not a serious candidate. Four years later, in 1924 Smith's reputation as governor of New York made him the leading candidate for his party's presidential nomination, but because he was a Roman Catholic and was in favor of repealing Prohibition his candidacy was blocked by delegates controlled by the powerful Ku Klux Klan and by the Anti-Saloon League.

Tired of losing national elections, the delegates to the Democratic national convention in 1928 in Houston, Texas, overcame their prejudices and nominated "the Happy Warrior," as he was called by his friend, Franklin Delano Roosevelt, because he had the best record for winning elections of any party leader. But the nation, fat with prosperity, was not overly interested in turning the national government over to the Democrats. Moreover, the anti-Catholics and anti-saloon groups attacked Smith so hard that in the final count of votes he even lost such solidly Democratic states as Virginia and Texas.

After his defeat by Herbert Hoover, Smith entered private business. He headed a group that financed the construction of the Empire State Building, the world's tallest skyscraper, which was completed in 1931. He then became president of the corporation that operated the building.

Smith hoped that the Democratic party would again nominate him for President in 1932, when it seemed likely that any Democrat could win over Hoover. He became embittered when the party turned instead to his protégé, Franklin D. Roosevelt, who had succeeded Smith as governor of New York. He supported Roosevelt's campaign in 1932, but by 1936 he was urging Roosevelt's defeat and the election of Republican candidate Alfred Landon. In his later years Smith lost all touch with the common people whose champion he once had been, and was no longer of any consequence in politics by his death at the age of 70 on October 4, 1944.

John William Davis

If John W. Davis had defeated Calvin Coolidge in 1924, it is likely that because of his liberal background he would have curbed the excesses of the financiers and corporations that led to the Great Depression.

Born in Clarksburg, West Virginia, on April 13, 1873, Davis was the son of a Congressman. When he was 16, John entered Washington and Lee University. He was graduated three years later. For two years he worked as a tutor and then as a clerk in his father's law office. He returned to Washington and Lee for a year of law school, then at the age of 21 entered law practice with his father in Clarksburg.

In 1898 the 25-year-old Davis was elected to the state legislature, the first Democratic state representative his county had elected in twenty years. But Davis preferred behind-the-scenes politics to public office, and after a short term in the legislature he became Democratic chairman of his county, a post he held for a dozen years. Meanwhile, his law practice grew as he represented both unions and corporations of the region.

When Davis was 37, in 1910, he was elected to Congress, where he worked on the judiciary committee, helping draft the Clayton Antitrust Act and other progressive measures. He was re-elected to Congress in 1912, but resigned the next year to accept President Wilson's appointment of him as Solicitor General of the United States, an office he held for five years, in which he defended the constitutionality of much of the Wilson administration's progressive legislation.

In 1918 Davis was appointed ambassador to Great Britain, and the next year, while still serving in this post, he was called to Versailles to help draft the peace treaty with Germany and the Central Powers. He continued to serve in Britain until the end of Wilson's administration.

Upon returning to the United States in 1921, Davis accepted a partnership in one of New York City's most influential corporation law firms. In this position he was now retained by many of the firms that he had opposed while he was Solicitor General.

Davis had received some votes at the 1920 Democratic national convention, but as the 1924 convention approached, a stronger campaign was mounted by his West Virginia friends to obtain the presidential nomination for him. Davis was nominated as West Virginia's favorite son, but the majority of delegates were pledged to William G. McAdoo or Alfred E. Smith. It soon developed that neither McAdoo nor Smith could muster enough votes to win, and the convention was deadlocked. Voting went on day after day for weeks. Finally, to save the Democratic party both McAdoo and Smith withdrew, and Davis won the nomination on the 103rd ballot. This convention was the first Democratic convention broadcast by radio, and it left a bad impact on listeners.

Not only was Davis handicapped in the ensuing campaign by the bitter aftermath of the convention within his party, but he also was faced by a third party movement led by Senator Robert La Follette of Wisconsin which endeavored to capture the progressive independent and Democratic voters. Davis was portrayed by his opponents as a Wall Street lawyer and a tool of the big corporations. When the election votes finally were counted, Davis went down to defeat, carrying only one more state than Cox had

John W. Davis

four years earlier, and even losing his home state of West Virginia.

Davis returned to the practice of law, winning a reputation as the country's foremost constitutional lawyer, and argued more cases before the Supreme Court than any other lawyer up to his time. At the age of 80 he lost his last case before the Supreme Court, a defense of the school segregation laws of South Carolina. Davis died the next year, on March 24, 1955, at Charleston, South Carolina.

James M. Cox

James Middleton Cox

Although he was defeated by the greatest popular vote margin in any presidential election—more than 27.6 per cent, James Middleton Cox undoubtedly would have been a better President than the man who beat him in 1920—Warren G. Harding.

Born in a farmhouse on March 31, 1870, near Jacksonburg, Ohio, Cox became a newspaperman as a teen-ager when he worked part-time for his brother-in-law's weekly newspaper while attending school in Middleton, Ohio. He taught school for a few years, then gave it up to become a full-time newspaperman at the age of 20. He worked as a reporter for the Cincinnati *Enquirer.* Then a wealthy Congressman, Paul Sorg, invited Cox to come to Washington with him as his private secretary.

After Sorg completed his term in Congress, he loaned the 28-year-old Cox enough money to buy the Dayton *News,* a Democratic newspaper. As new industries were attracted to Dayton, the paper grew and Cox prospered, partly because the corporations gave the newspaper blocks of their stock to insure that they got good publicity.

At the age of 38, in 1908, Cox ran for Congress and was elected. Two years later he was re-elected to a second term. In 1912 he was elected governor of Ohio, was defeated for re-election in 1914, and then won two more terms as governor in 1916 and 1918. As governor, Cox brought many reforms to the Ohio state government. He particularly spearheaded improvements in the public school system, helping consolidate rural school districts to improve the education of farm children.

Cox was in the midst of his third term as governor when the Democratic national convention met in San Francisco in 1920. The Republicans had already nominated Harding, who also was an Ohio newspaperman and politician. The Democrats were badly divided and altogether sixteen presidential contenders were put before the delegates. The convention voted day after day for a total of 44 ballots before finally giving the nomination to Cox. For his running mate the Democrats chose Franklin D. Roosevelt as the vice-presidential candidate.

Cox and Roosevelt campaigned hard for the United States to join the League of Nations. But the American people were weary of world affairs and believed the Republicans would return things to the way they were before World War I. In the election Cox did not carry a single state outside the South.

After finishing his term as governor of Ohio early in 1921, Cox dropped out of politics. He returned to public life briefly in 1933 when his former running mate, now President Roosevelt, appointed him to the U.S. delegation to the World Monetary and Economic Conference in London. Cox published his autobiography, *Journey Through My Years,* in 1946. At the age of 87, Cox died in Dayton on July 15, 1957.

Charles Evans Hughes

Like Democrat Alton B. Parker, Republican Charles Evans Hughes discovered that being a highly respected judge was not enough to guarantee his

Charles E. Hughes

election as President. However, Hughes came much closer to winning in 1916 than Parker did in 1904, so close in fact that he went to bed after the election thinking that he had won. It wasn't until the next day that Hughes learned that California had gone Democratic for the first time since the Civil War, insuring Woodrow Wilson's re-election to a second term.

The son of a Baptist minister, Hughes was born on April 11, 1862, in Glens Falls, New York. He attended a variety of schools as his father moved from one pastorate to another. At the age of 14 he entered Colgate University (then called Madison University), attended two years, then transferred to Brown University, from which he graduated at 19. He spent a year teaching school, then attended law school at Columbia University, graduating in 1884 at the age of 22.

He became a law clerk in a New York City law firm and four years later married one of the partners' daughters and was made a member of the firm. When he was 29 he dropped the practice of law to accept a law professorship at Cornell University, but returned to his New York law practice after two years.

Hughes first came to wide public notice in 1905 at the age of 43 when he was appointed counsel of committees that uncovered corruption in gas and insurance companies. The Republican party nominated him for governor the next year and he defeated the Democratic candidate, publisher William Randolph Hearst. He was re-elected in 1908.

At the end of his four years as governor of New York, Hughes was appointed by President Taft as an associate justice of the United States Supreme Court. For the next six years Hughes added to his reputation by his record as a progressive member of the Supreme Court. When Republicans began to talk of nominating him for President, Hughes declared publicly, "The Supreme Court must not be dragged into politics, and no man is as essential to his country's well-being as is the sustained integrity of the courts."

But at the Republican national convention in 1916 the delegates ignored Hughes' repeated denials that he would run and nominated him on the third ballot. Hughes decided it was his duty to accept the nomination and announced his decision by sending a telegram to President Wilson with his resignation from the Supreme Court.

Hughes waged a hard-hitting campaign that was critical of Wilson's first term. When the votes were counted on the evening of the election, Hughes had carried most of the Northern states, including Wilson's home state of New Jersey. Hughes' election seemed assured. But the next day word came that California had been carried by Wilson, and that state's electoral vote was just enough to defeat Hughes.

Having resigned from the Supreme Court, Hughes resumed his law practice in New York City. He served on the city's draft appeals board during World War I and at the request of President Wilson conducted an investigation of the nation's fledgling aircraft industry. When Warren Harding became President in 1921, the 58-year-old Hughes was appointed Secretary of State, an office he continued to hold until 1925 under Harding's successor, Calvin Coolidge. In 1928 he was appointed to the Permanent Court of International Justice.

In 1930 President Hoover appointed Hughes as Chief Justice of the United States to succeed William Howard Taft, who as President first had appointed Hughes to the Supreme Court twenty years earlier. In the early years of President Roosevelt's New Deal, the Supreme Court under Hughes' leadership threw out much of the New Deal legislation as unconstitutional. This led to a battle between Roosevelt and the "nine old men" on the Supreme Court in which the President sought the power to appoint additional members to the court. Age finally forced a majority of the members of the Hughes' Court to resign between 1938 and 1941, and Hughes himself retired as Chief Justice in 1941 at the age of 79. He died seven years later at Osterville, Massachusetts, on August 27, 1948, having outlived five of the six Presidents under which he had served.

William Jennings Bryan

Equaling the record of Henry Clay, William Jennings Bryan ran three times as the Democratic candidate for President and lost each time by a larger and larger margin in 1896, 1900, and 1908. When Bryan ran for the first time against William McKinley he was only 36—the youngest man ever to be the presidential candidate of a major party. He was one of the greatest speakers of his day and was nicknamed "The Boy Orator of the Platte."

Bryan was born in Salem, Illinois, March 19, 1860, the son of a judge. He was graduated from Illinois College and Union College of Law. At the age of 23 he began practicing law in Jacksonville, Illinois, but he was unable to attract enough clients to make a living. So, after four years, in 1887, he moved to Lincoln, Nebraska, hoping for better luck there.

Solidly Republican Nebraska had never elected a Democrat to Congress, so Bryan seized the opportunity in 1890 of obtaining the Democratic nomination for Congress that no one else wanted. He saw it as a fine opportunity to make himself known, even if he couldn't win the election. But the 30-year-old Bryan surprised himself and the politicians by winning the election as the result of a vigorous door-to-door and farm-to-farm handshaking campaign. And by the same tireless tactics he won re-election in 1892. Two years later he was defeated in an effort to be elected to the U.S. Senate, and then became editor of the Omaha *World-Herald*.

At the Democratic national convention in 1896, Bryan was invited to address the delegates. Using the powers of his magnificent voice, he seemingly hypnotized his listeners with his famous "Cross of Gold" speech that concluded: "Having behind us the producing masses of this nation and the world, supported by the toilers everywhere, we will answer to their demand for a gold standard by saying to them: You shall not press down upon the brow of labor this crown of thorns, you shall not crucify mankind upon a cross of gold." The convention went wild with acclaim for Bryan, swept aside the previous leading contenders for the presidential nomination and gave the nomination to Bryan on the fifth ballot.

Running on a platform that promised to bring prosperity back to the country by coining silver at a ratio of 16 to 1 for gold, Bryan embarked on the most extensive whistle-stop campaign tour that any presidential candidate had undertaken up to that time. On the other hand, his opponent, William McKinley stayed at home conducting a front-porch campaign. But Bryan's energy was no match for the millions of dollars that the Republicans were able to spend on McKinley's campaign.

After losing the election, Bryan supported himself by going on lecture tours and by writing magazine articles. When the Spanish-American War began, Bryan raised a regiment of Nebraska volunteers who elected him colonel, but he saw no action in the war.

Bryan again was nominated for President by the Democratic national convention in 1900. He again emphasized the free silver issue and condemned the McKinley administration as imperialistic for having taken over the Philippines. But prosperity had returned to the country under McKinley, and fewer people voted for Bryan this time than had in 1896.

Bryan passed up the presidential nomination in 1904, figuring that Theodore Roosevelt was too formidable an opponent. But in 1908 he again sought and won the Democratic nomination. Now 48 years old, Bryan had seen Theodore Roosevelt put into action most of the liberal ideas that he had previously campaigned for, so in this campaign he attacked his opponent, William Howard Taft, on religious grounds, pointing out that Taft was a Unitarian and regarded Christ as a "cunning imposter." Although his words stirred the fundamentalists of the Bible belt, Bryan again went down to defeat by a greater margin than ever before.

In 1912 Bryan helped swing the Democratic presidential nomination to Woodrow Wilson. As a re-

William J. Bryan

ward Wilson appointed him as Secretary of State. But he resigned in 1915 when he felt that Wilson was taking too war-like an attitude toward Germany over the sinking of the liner *Lusitania*.

Bryan moved to Florida in 1920 and was sent by that state as a delegate to the Democratic national convention in 1924. He was hopeful that he would again be named as his party's presidential candidate, but in the end settled for the nomination of his brother, Charles W. Bryan, as the vice-presidential candidate running with John W. Davis.

In 1925 Bryan went to Dayton, Tennessee, to aid in the prosecution of John T. Scopes in the famous "Monkey Trial," in which Clarence Darrow acted as defense lawyer. As a fundamentalist Bryan agreed vehemently with the Tennessee law that forbade the teaching of evolution and believed the young teacher, Scopes, should be punished for breaking the law. The trial took place in July and the heat in the courtroom sapped the aging Bryan's strength. Five days after the conclusion of the trial, in which Scopes was convicted, the 64-year-old Bryan died.

Alton Brooks Parker

The Democrat who ran against and lost to Teddy Roosevelt in 1904, Alton B. Parker, was so overshadowed by the personality of his opponent that he lost by a greater margin than any other major party candidate up to that time. However, most historians are agreed that if he had been elected he most likely would have been as successful a President as Roosevelt.

Born on May 14, 1852, in Cortland, New York, Alton Parker was the son of a farmer. When he was 18 the low state of the family's finances forced him to drop out of school and take up teaching in village schools. He then clerked in a law office for a year, saving enough money to attend Albany Law School, from which he was graduated in 1873 at the age of 21.

Parker established himself in law practice in Kingston, New York, and almost at once began to take an active part in politics. He was elected to the office of surrogate in 1877 and was re-elected regularly thereafter. He soon became the leader of the Democratic party in Ulster County.

In 1880 and 1884 he was a delegate to the Democratic national conventions, and in 1885 successfully managed the election campaign of Governor David B. Hill. As a reward Hill appointed the 33-year-old Parker as a justice of the state supreme court.

He moved up to the state court of appeals in 1888, and nine years later was elected chief justice of the court of appeals.

Democratic party leaders had urged Parker to run for governor and for U.S. Senator, but he had turned down these invitations because he preferred to pursue his career as a judge. But his reputation was such that at the 1904 Democratic convention he was

Alton B. Parker

chosen as the party's presidential nominee on the first ballot, largely because the conservative elements of the party feared that his major contender for the nomination, William Randolph Hearst, was too liberal. Upon receiving the nomination, Parker sent a telegram to the convention declaring himself an advocate of the gold standard and offering to withdraw if the convention believed the party should continue to support the old platform of free silver that had been Bryan's major plank in the two previous campaigns.

Because Parker was more conservative than Teddy Roosevelt, the Wall Street tycoons who feared Roosevelt's trust-busting turned their pockets inside out to contribute to Parker's campaign expenses. But Parker believed that it was beneath the dignity of a judge to traipse about the country making speeches as

Bryan had done, so he left most of the campaign effort to local politicians and made few public appearances. When the votes were counted, Parker received only 40 per cent to Roosevelt's 60 per cent.

Having resigned from his court post, Parker was unable to return to the bench. So he entered the practice of law in New York City. For the next twenty years he was one of the city's most influential lawyers and handled many of the important cases of the time. He died in New York City on May 10, 1926, just four days before his 74th birthday.

James Gillespie Blaine

The first Republican candidate to fail to win the presidency since the Civil War, James G. Blaine lost the election of 1884 when New York went Democratic largely because Blaine failed to correct a supporter who tagged the Democrats as the party of "rum, Romanism and rebellion."

Blaine was born in West Brownsville, Pennsylvania, on January 31, 1830. After he was graduated from Washington College, he became a teacher, first at a military academy in Kentucky and then at the Philadelphia Institute for the Blind. At the age of 24, in 1854, he moved to the state of Maine where he became a newspaper editor, first of the *Kennebec Journal* and then of the *Portland Advertiser*.

Taking an active part in state politics, young Blaine became a delegate to the first Republican national convention in 1856. He was elected to the Maine legislature in 1858, and two years later at the age of 30 he became speaker of the lower house of the legislature.

Blaine moved onto the national scene in 1862, winning election to Congress. He was re-elected to six successive terms, serving as Speaker of the House from 1869 to 1875 under President Grant. When the Democrats won control of the House they started an investigation of the corruption during the Grant administration and Blaine became one of their chief targets.

In 1876 a witness before a House investigating committee revealed the "Mulligan letters" which had been written by Blaine to a railroad contractor while he was Speaker of the House. The letters seemed to implicate Blaine in questionable dealings with the railroads, but Blaine appeared before the committee and defended himself so brilliantly that no action was taken against him. However, the letters were a factor in preventing him from winning the Republican presidential nominations in 1876 and 1880.

The Maine legislature in 1876 showed its faith in Blaine by electing him as a U.S. Senator, an office he held until 1881 when President Garfield appointed him Secretary of State. During Garfield's short administration most persons considered him as little more than a puppet of Blaine, who was regarded as the most powerful man in the government. But with Garfield's assassination Blaine lost his power and he resigned from President Arthur's cabinet late in 1881.

During the next several years Blaine laid the groundwork to assure himself of winning the Republican presidential nomination in 1884. He also wrote and published the first volume of his work *Twenty Years of Congress, from Lincoln to Garfield.*

In the 1884 election campaign Blaine's supporters praised him as the "Plumed Knight from the State of Maine." But mud-slinging in the campaign reached a new low, and Blaine lost to Grover Cleveland.

When the Republican nominating convention met in 1888, Blaine again was a leading candidate for the nomination. The convention deadlocked and Blaine, who was traveling in Scotland, cabled instructions for his supporters to switch to Benjamin Harrison, who won the nomination and then the election. To repay his political debt, Harrison appointed Blaine as his Secretary of State.

Still hopeful of becoming President, Blaine resigned from Harrison's cabinet in 1892 again to seek his party's nomination. But his fellow Republicans would not give Blaine another chance and Harrison was renominated.

The next year, on January 27, 1893, Blaine died of Bright's disease just a few days short of his 63rd

James G. Blaine

birthday, a disappointed man who had devoted the last twenty years of his life to pursuing but never attaining the presidency.

Winfield S. Hancock

Winfield Scott Hancock

After Andrew Jackson the Democrats were never able to elect a general as President and Winfield Scott Hancock's attempt to win the presidency in 1880 was no exception to the rule, although he came within 10,000 votes of winning a popular majority.

Hancock was a regular army officer all his adult life. He was born at Montgomery Square, Pennsylvania, on February 14, 1824, and twenty years later he was graduated from West Point. He fought in the Mexican War and during the 1850's served in various frontier outposts in the western states. At the outbreak of the Civil War, he was stationed in Los Angeles, California, and held the rank of captain.

With the rapid expansion of the Federal army at the beginning of the Civil War, Hancock was advanced to brigadier general in 1861 and given command of a brigade in the Army of the Potomac. As a general he was noted for his immaculate dress and his lurid swearing, as well as his bravery in battle. In November, 1862, he was promoted to major general and given command of a division. After distinguishing himself at the Battle of Chancellorsville, he was given command of the II Corps.

Before the arrival of General George Meade, Hancock was in command of Union forces in the Battle of Gettysburg. On July 3, 1863, he was in command of the troops that held Cemetery Ridge against Pickett's charge, and was himself shot from his horse and seriously wounded but refused to be carried from the scene until the battle had been won. After a slow recovery he returned to regular duty in 1864 and fought in the battles of the Wilderness and Spotslvania Courthouse.

During the Reconstruction Era Hancock commanded occupation forces in various Southern states, winning praise for the fairness with which he treated his conquered foes. In December, 1867, President Andrew Johnson cited Hancock to Congress for his distinguished service, saying:

"It will be perceived that General Hancock announces that he will make the law the rule of his conduct; that he will uphold the courts and other civil authorities in the performance of their proper duties, and that he will use his military power only to preserve the peace and enforce the law. He declares very explicitly that the sacred right of the trial by jury and the privilege of the writ of *habeas corpus* shall not be crushed out or trodden under foot . . . When a great soldier, with unrestricted power in his hands to oppress his fellow-men, voluntarily foregoes the chance of gratifying his selfish ambition and devotes himself to the duty of building up the liberties and strengthening the laws of his country, he presents an example of the highest public virtue that human nature is capable of practicing . . ."

The Democrats chose Hancock in 1880 to oppose the Republican candidate James Garfield. Tariffs were the major issue of the campaign with the Republicans favoring a high protective tariff and the Democrats calling for lower tariffs. The election was close, and if Hancock had been able to carry New York he would have won.

Upon Hancock's death on February 9, 1886, at the age of 61, President Grover Cleveland's order calling for a period of mourning described Hancock as: "A patriotic and valiant defender of his country, an able and heroic soldier, a spotless and accomplished gentleman, crowned alike with the laurels of military renown and the highest tribute of his fellow-countrymen to his worth as a citizen . . ."

Samuel Jones Tilden

Samuel Jones Tilden was the only man ever elected President who was not allowed to serve in the office. Although he had a clear majority of both the popular vote and the electoral vote in the election of 1876, Tilden had the office stolen from him and presented to Rutherford B. Hayes.

Born in New Lebanon, New York, on February 9, 1814, Tilden went to college both at Yale University and the University of the City of New York, being graduated from the latter in 1837. He studied law and was admitted to the bar in 1841, at the age of 27. A bachelor, he devoted himself intensively to his practice as a corporation lawyer and soon made himself a multi-millionaire.

He first took an active part in politics when he was elected as a Democratic representative to the state legislature in 1845. He then became a member of the state constitutional convention the next year. He aligned himself with the anti-slavery Free Soil wing of the Democratic party and was a delegate to the party's national convention in 1848.

From the Mexican War through the Civil War Tilden did not hold political office, but in 1866 he became chairman of the state committee of the Democratic party and the following year was chairman of the state constitutional convention.

In the early 1870's Tilden achieved national prominence as a reformer, heading a committee that helped bring an end to the domination of New York City government by the corrupt "Tweed Ring."

At the age of 60 Tilden was elected governor of New York, in 1874. In this office he continued his role as a reformer, exposing corruption in the building of the state's canal system.

Because of the public indignation at the corruption existing in the national administration of President Grant, it was natural that the Democrats turned to Tilden as their champion in the election of 1876.

Even after the Republican power-play of the Electoral Commission and the ratification of Hayes' being given the presidency by the U.S. House of Representatives, Tilden's friends continued to call him President Tilden. And to his death at the age of 72 on August 4, 1886, he stood by his statement:

"Everybody knows that . . . the men who were elected by the people as President and Vice President were counted out; and the men who were not elected were counted in and seated."

Samuel J. Tilden

Horace Greeley

The most tragic of all the men who have run for and lost the presidency, Horace Greeley lost his mind and died less than a month after being defeated by President U. S. Grant in the election of 1872. If Greeley had been elected President, he likely would have prevented the corruption that marked Grant's second term and would have ended the oppression of the South then going on in the Reconstruction Era.

Born on a farm near Amherst, New Hampshire, on February 3, 1811, Horace Greeley was the third of seven children of Zaccheus Greeley, a poor farmer. A child prodigy, he learned to read by the time he was two and began going to school at the age of three. When Horace was ten his father fled to Vermont to avoid being imprisoned for debt. The Greeley family was reunited in Westhaven, Vermont, where the father worked as a handyman. Horace continued in school only to the age of thirteen, when his teacher informed the Greeleys that Horace already knew more than he did.

At fourteen, young Greeley apprenticed himself to a printer in East Poultney, Vermont. He worked there until he was nineteen, earning $40 a year and his room and board. His apprenticeship ended when the East Poultney printer closed his shop. For a time he found work as a journeyman printer in Erie, Pennsylvania, and then decided to go to New York City to seek his fortune.

Greeley worked as a typesetter for several years, carefully saving his money until he had enough to join with a partner in opening a small printing shop. At the same time he began writing short articles for various newspapers. Soon writing and journalism became more important to him than printing. In 1834 he started the newspaper, *The New Yorker*, in which he printed his famous advice, "Go west, young man." In 1838 he became editor of a Whig weekly, the *Jeffersonian*. Then in 1840 Greeley started a weekly Newspaper called the *Log Cabin*, which supported the presidential campaign of William H. Harrison.

But all his early excursions into journalism were merely preparatory for the launching by Greeley on April 10, 1841, of the daily *Tribune*, a penny daily newspaper dedicated to the principles of the Whig party. The *Tribune* was an immediate success. Greeley was a crusader, and he made the *Tribune* a lively, fighting newspaper. He promoted a kind of socialism called Fourierism, while at the same time he supported the most conservative captains of industry. And he became a leading voice in the anti-slavery movement.

In 1848 Greeley was elected to Congress to complete the three-month term of a Congressman who had died. During his brief stay in Washington, Greeley stirred considerable controversy by exposing many dishonest practices by the other members of Congress and by proposing that Congressmen should not be paid for days that they were absent from the House.

As a hobby, Greeley purchased a 50-acre farm in Chappaqua, New York, in the 1850's. He visited the farm each Saturday and took great pride in winning prizes with his turnips and corn.

Greeley helped found the Republican party in 1854 and four years later helped Abraham Lincoln win the presidential nomination. However, during the Civil War Greeley did not fully trust Lincoln and believed that the President was not doing everything that he could to end the war. Greeley unsuccessfully tried to arrange an end to the war by meeting with Confederate leaders in 1864. When the war finally ended, Greeley called for a policy of universal amnesty for Southerners, and personally signed the bail bond for the former President of the Confederacy, Jefferson Davis. But, with the Radical Republicans, Greeley called for the impeachment of President Andrew Johnson.

The choice of U. S. Grant as the Republican party's nominee in 1868 did not please Greeley, and during Grant's first term the New York editor became increasingly disturbed by the signs of corruption in the national government. Therefore, when Liberal Republicans split off from the national party in 1872 and met in convention in Cincinnati, Ohio, Greeley was happy to accept their nomination of him for the presidency. Subsequently the Democratic party also named Greeley as its candidate.

Throughout the campaign Greeley was ridiculed from one end of the country to the other as a man who had opposed the Democratic party all his life and now accepted its nomination. He exhausted himself in a vigil at the bedside of his wife of forty years who died of consumption on October 30, a few days before the election. When the votes were counted after the election, Greeley carried only six states, all in the South.

The effect of his wife's death and the result of the election were too much for Greeley to bear, and he became mentally deranged. Friends forcibly placed him in a mental institution near Pleasantville, New York, where he died on November 29, 1872.

Horace Greeley

Horatio Seymour

Despite U. S. Grant's overwhelming popularity as the winning general of the Civil War, Democratic candidate Horatio Seymour came close to beating him in the presidential election of 1868. A shift of only

Horatio Seymour

155,000 votes would have given the Democratic governor of New York a majority in the popular vote, even though hundreds of thousands of Democratic voters in the South had been disenfranchised by Reconstruction.

There is little doubt that Seymour would have made a better President than Grant because he had amply demonstrated his administrative abilities in his many years of public service in New York. But it is difficult to calculate what effect he would have had on the history of the United States with his more liberal attitude toward the Southern leaders of the Confederacy.

Horatio Seymour was born at Pompey Hill in Onondaga County, New York, on May 31, 1810. He was educated at a military school and then studied law in Utica, New York. He was admitted to the bar to practice law at the age of 22. Nine years later he was elected to his first public office, as a member of the state legislature, and the following year, when he was 32, he was elected mayor of Utica.

After completing a term as mayor, Seymour was again elected to the state legislature, and in 1845 became speaker of the house.

In 1850 Seymour was named the Democratic candidate for governor of New York but was defeated in the election. However, he ran again in 1852, and this time was elected to the office. During his term as governor the state legislature passed a prohibition law, and when Seymour vetoed it as being unconstitutional he was denounced by temperance leaders. When he ran for re-election in 1854, he was defeated, and retired to private life.

In 1862 Seymour returned to public life as a "Peace Democrat," calling for an end to the Civil War. He was elected to a new term as governor from 1863 to 1865. In 1864 he became national chairman of the Democratic party and helped manage the unsuccessful presidential campaign of George McClellan. In 1868 he again ran for the governorship of New York, but was defeated. He then became the Democratic party's presidential standard bearer in the 1868 election, but lost to U. S. Grant.

After losing his bid for the presidency, Seymour retired from public life. He died at Utica on February 12, 1886, at the age of 75.

George Brinton McClellan

George McClellan was only 37 years old when he was defeated by Abraham Lincoln in the election of 1864. When the Democrats nominated "Little Mac," as McClellan was called, he seemed a sure-thing winner, because the Civil War had been going badly for the Union under Lincoln's leadership. Even Lincoln confided to one of the members of his cabinet in August that it seemed "exceedingly probable" that he would be defeated, and that he planned to cooperate with his successor in an effort to save the Union. But Lincoln was saved from defeat when the tide of war turned for the Union in September with the capture of Atlanta by the forces of General William Tecumseh Sherman.

If McClellan had been elected President, it is possible that Lincoln might have gone down in history as a bungler while McClellan would have been hailed as the leader who saved the Union. It is also likely that if McClellan had become President slavery might have been allowed to continue in the South, because he had said he was not opposed to slavery although he intended to continue the war to preserve the Union.

Born in Philadelphia, Pennsylvania, on December 3, 1826, McClellan attended the University of Pennsylvania before receiving an appointment to the U.S. military academy at West Point. He graduated from West Point at the age of 19, ranking as the second man in his class. He served in the Mexican War,

George McClellan

winning two battlefield promotions. After the war he served as a teacher at West Point, writing a textbook on the use of the bayonet, and then was appointed to a military commission to study the armies of Europe.

In 1857 McClellan resigned from the army to become a railroad executive. By the time he was 33 he had become president of the eastern division of the Ohio and Mississippi Railroad.

When the Civil War began in 1861, McClellan was appointed major general in command of Ohio's volunteer troops. His forces drove Confederate troops out of western Virginia, and because of this success Lincoln called him to the nation's capital in July, 1861, to take command of the Union army defending Washington, D.C. He began training the raw recruits and whipping them into the well-organized Army of the Potomac. In November, 1861, he was appointed commander of all the Union armies.

However, McClellan did not believe his army was well enough trained and supplied to attack the Confederate forces. This caused Lincoln to lose faith in him, and early in 1862 he was relieved as commander of all Union forces but left in command of the Army of the Potomac. In the spring of 1862 McClellan advanced his army on Richmond, Virginia, but was driven off by Confederate General Robert E. Lee. In

September, 1862, McClellan stopped Lee's advance in Maryland at the Battle of Antietam, but failed to follow up his victory with pursuit of the defeated Confederate army. In disgust, Lincoln relieved McClellan of his command and replaced him with Major General Ambrose Burnside. This ended McClellan's active military career although he continued to retain his commission in the army.

As the war dragged on many people, and particularly the members of the Democratic party, became increasingly critical of Lincoln's conduct of the war. In 1864 the critics were particularly upset by Lincoln's appointment of Grant as commander of Union forces and believed that McClellan was a far superior general, who should have been reinstated in command. McClellan was flattered when his supporters obtained the Democratic presidential nomination for him. He waited until election day in November, 1864, before resigning his army commission.

Disappointed by his unexpected defeat by Lincoln, McClellan left the United States and traveled abroad for three years. After returning to the United States, he worked for several years as an engineer for the government of New York City. In 1878 he was elected to a term as governor of New Jersey. Four years after retiring from that office he died in Orange, New Jersey, on October 29, 1885, at the age of 58.

Stephen Arnold Douglas

If Stephen A. Douglas had been elected President in 1860 instead of Abraham Lincoln, the Civil War quite possibly might not have taken place when it did. A Northern Democrat who was not opposed to slavery, Douglas quite likely would have found some way to reach a political compromise with Southern leaders that would have at least postponed the outbreak of fighting.

The 5-foot Douglas, called the "Little Giant" because of his stature, was born in Brandon, Vermont, on April 23, 1813. His father, a doctor, died when Douglas was a baby, but his widowed mother struggled to make sure he received a good education. After graduating from Canandaigua Academy at Rochester, New York, the 20-year-old Douglas went west in 1833 to seek his fortune.

He settled in Illinois where he taught school while studying law for a year, and then was admitted to the bar to practice law at Jacksonville, Illinois, in 1834. After becoming active in the Democratic party, the 22-year-old Douglas was elected prosecuting attorney of Morgan County in 1835. The next year he was elected to the state legislature, and by the time he was 28 he was appointed as one of the judges on the Illinois Supreme Court.

Douglas stepped onto the national stage at the age of 29 when he was elected to Congress in 1842. After serving two terms as a Representative, he was elected by the state legislature as U.S. Senator in 1847, an office that he held for the rest of his life.

Stephen A. Douglas

The ambitious Douglas was one of the contenders for the Democratic presidential nomination in 1852, but was passed over when his party chose Franklin Pierce as the candidate.

Determined to win the support of Southern Democrats for his political future, Douglas helped push through Congress the Kansas-Nebraska Act of 1854 which nullified the Missouri Compromise and opened up the possibility of slavery being permitted in northern territories by leaving the decision to "squatter sovereignty." But by the time the Democratic presidential nominating convention rolled around in 1856, The Kansas-Nebraska Act had resulted in the outbreak of fighting between slavery and anti-slavery proponents in Kansas. Douglas was a main contender

for the 1856 presidential nomination, but again his party passed him over to choose instead James Buchanan.

When Douglas campaigned for re-election to the Senate in 1858 he was opposed by Abraham Lincoln and the famous Lincoln-Douglas debates ensued. Although Lincoln's supporters won more popular votes in the 1858 election than those of Douglas, more Douglas supporters were elected to the legislature because of Illinois' gerrymandered election districts. So Douglas was re-elected to the Senate.

Douglas rang the death knell for his presidential hopes when he opposed President Buchanan's efforts to obtain the admission of Kansas as a slave state. Angered Southern Democrats refused to support him when Northern Democrats finally nominated him for the presidency in 1860. Instead the Southern Democrats nominated Vice-President John C. Breckinridge. With the Democratic vote split, Douglas could not win and Lincoln was elected President with a minority of the popular vote. The disappointed Douglas died of typhoid fever at the age of 48 on June 3, 1861—just short of three months after he would have taken office as President if he had been elected.

John Charles Fremont

At the age of 43, John Charles Frémont, the conqueror of California and the most famous explorer of the times, lost the election of 1856 as the first Republican presidential candidate. Had he won, the Civil War might have been precipitated four years earlier, or, more possibly, the strong-willed Frémont might have snuffed secession in the bud by using federal troops to jail Southern leaders.

Frémont was born on January 21, 1813, in Savannah, Ga. His father, Jean Frémon, was a French immigrant school teacher, and his mother, Mrs. Anne Whiting Pryor, was a Virginia belle who ran away from a wealthy, but elderly, husband to live with the poor, but handsome, Frenchman. His father died when John was six, so he was brought up by his mother in Charleston, S.C. He attended Charleston College, but was expelled for neglecting his studies.

After working several years as a mathematics teacher and as a surveyor, the 25-year-old Frémont received an appointment as a lieutenant in the army in 1838. He immediately was sent as a member of an expedition to explore the Dakotas and Minnesota.

Fortune smiled on him when he married 17-year-old Jessie Benton, daughter of Missouri Senator

Thomas Hart Benton, for his father-in-law used influence to obtain Frémont command of an expedition that explored the Rocky Mountains in 1842. Leading a second expedition in 1843-1844, Frémont crossed the Rockies, mapped the Great Salt Lake, explored the Oregon Territory, then traveled south and scaled the Sierra Nevada mountains for the first time to reach California. The books that he and his wife wrote about these expeditions sold thousands of copies and made him a national hero.

Before the outbreak of the Mexican War he led a third expedition west, and in 1846 helped American settlers in northern California revolt against Mexico to set up the independent Bear Flag Republic. After news of the declaration of war by the United States on Mexico reached him, he joined Navy Commodore Robert F. Stockton in conquering Mexican forces in southern California. Stockton promoted Frémont to lieutenant colonel and appointed him as the first American governor of the California territory. When Major General Stephen W. Kearney arrived in 1847 with orders to set up a government in California, Frémont refused to recognize Kearney's authority, was arrested, and carried back to Washington, D.C., for court-martial. Found guilty on several charges, including mutiny, he received an offer of a pardon by President Polk, but angrily refused it and resigned from the army.

In 1848 he led a privately-financed expedition seeking a railroad route across the Rockies, but met disaster when he lost a third of his party in a mountain blizzard. Upon reaching California he learned that gold had been discovered on property that he bought in 1847, and almost overnight he became a multi-millionaire.

Upon California's admission to the Union, Frémont served a short term from 1850 to 1851 as one of the state's first two Senators. In Washington he made a name for himself as an opponent of slavery by voting for a bill to outlaw slavery in the District of Columbia.

The newly-formed Republican party nominated Frémont as its candidate for President in 1856. Although Frémont's supporters waged a rip-roaring campaign on the promise to prevent the expansion of slavery, he lost largely because the South solidly supported James Buchanan while the vote in the North and the West was split by Millard Fillmore's third party candidacy.

At the beginning of the Civil War, Frémont was appointed major general in charge of the western department. Without authority from Washington, he ordered the emancipation of slaves owned by rebels in Missouri in the summer of 1861. But this act angered many slave owners in the border states, so Lincoln removed Frémont from his command and transferred him to the mountain department of western Virginia. When his command was made part of the Army of the Potomac under John Pope, an officer junior to him, he resigned.

The radical wing of the Republican party offered him the presidential nomination in 1864, but he declined in order to prevent a party split that might have defeated Lincoln's election to a second term. After the war he lost his fortune in various bad investments. He then served for three years as governor of the Arizona territory from 1878 to 1881. Retiring to New York City, he died there at the age of 77 on July 13, 1890.

John C. Fremont

Winfield Scott

If Lieutenant General Winfield Scott had won the Whig party's nomination in 1848, he undoubtedly would have become President. But, unfortunately for "Old Fuss and Feathers," as he was called because of

Winfield Scott

his flamboyant uniforms, the Whig party already was beginning to break up when he did get his chance to run for the nation's highest office in 1852, and he lost disastrously to Franklin Pierce.

If Scott had been elected President, it is doubtful that he would have been much more successful than Pierce; but his election undoubtedly would have prevented the formation of the Republican party in 1854, and thus would have changed the course of the struggle between North and South.

Born near Petersburg, Va., on June 13, 1786, Scott attended the College of William and Mary, and then at 20 was admitted to the bar to practice law. Two years later, in 1808, he joined the U.S. Army as a captain—beginning a military career that lasted more than fifty years.

The 6-foot 5-inch Scott made a striking figure as an officer in the War of 1812, winning particular fame at the Battle of Lundy's Lane where he was severely wounded and had two horses shot out from under him. By the end of the war, the 28-year-old Scott had risen to the rank of major general.

In 1841 Scott was appointed as commanding general of the U.S. Army, and three years later was promoted to lieutenant general—the first man since George Washington to attain that rank.

Scott distinguished himself in the Mexican War, planning and carrying out the successful campaign that captured Mexico City and ended the war. But he fell into a dispute with President Polk, and was called home to face a court of inquiry which exonerated him of any wrong-doing.

After his defeat by Franklin Pierce in the presidential election of 1852, Scott remained as commanding general of the army. Although he was 75 years old at the outbreak of the Civil War, he directed military operations until relieved by President Lincoln in November, 1861, and assigned as superintendent of the U.S. Military Academy. Scott died at West Point at the age of 79, on May 29, 1866.

Lewis Cass

Defeated by Zachary Taylor in the presidential election of 1848, Lewis Cass lost his bid for the nation's highest office because of the split in the Democratic party engendered by Martin Van Buren's third-party Free Soil movement. Although much better grounded in the art of government than Taylor, it is doubtful that if elected Cass would have vastly changed the course of history. In the crucial issue of the day, he favored the Compromise of 1850 and voted for it as a Senator from Michigan.

The son of a Revolutionary War officer, Lewis Cass was born on October 9, 1782, in Exeter, N.H. He was educated at Phillips Exeter academy, where he was a schoolmate of Daniel Webster. When his family went west to seek its fortune in Ohio in 1799, young Cass went along. He studied law in Marietta, Ohio, in the office of Return J. Meigs, who later served as Postmaster General under James Madison. At the age of 20, Cass was admitted to the bar to practice law.

Like many other young lawyers, he entered politics by winning election first as a county prosecutor and then as a state legislator. His promising career as a lawyer and politician was interrupted by the War of 1812. Elected a colonel of the Ohio militia, he raised a regiment and marched to Detroit to serve under Major General William Hull, but Hull surrendered Detroit and his army to the British without firing a shot. The angry Cass later testified at the court-martial that convicted Hull of cowardice and neglect of duty. Cass then raised another Ohio regiment and advanced to the rank of brigadier general.

In 1813 President Madison appointed Cass to succeed Hull as territorial governor of Michigan, a post that Cass held for eighteen years. During this time he demonstrated great ability as an administrator, brought representative government to the territory, and laid much emphasis on the founding of a sound educational system.

From 1831 to 1837 Cass served as Secretary of War under President Jackson. Then from 1837 to 1842 he was minister to France under Van Buren, Harrison, and Tyler. He returned home from Paris to become an unsuccessful candidate for the Democratic presidential nomination in 1844, losing to dark horse James K. Polk.

Cass became Senator from Michigan in 1845, an office that he held until 1857, except for the period in 1848 when he unsuccessfully ran for President as the Democratic nominee. Cass was the leading contender for the Democratic presidential nomination in 1852, but again lost to a dark horse—this time Franklin Pierce.

His last public service came as Secretary of State under James Buchanan from 1857 to 1860. But he resigned from the Cabinet in protest against Buchanan's unwillingness to take a firm stand against South Carolina secessionists, commenting:

"I saw the Constitution born, and I fear I may see it die."

Lewis Cass

But Cass lived to see the Union preserved in the Civil War. He died at the age of 83 in Detroit on June 17, 1866.

Henry Clay

Losing three times as a presidential candidate, Henry Clay once complained: "I am the most unfortunate man in the history of parties, always run by my friends when sure to be defeated . . ." But it was his own tricky scheming, rather than his friends, that led to his defeats. The nation was fortunate that he lost. Clay wanted power for power's sake, supporting whichever side of any question best seemed to serve his own ends at the moment.

Unable to attain the nation's highest office by hook or by crook, Clay used his great abilities as an orator and political manipulator to dominate Congress for nearly half a century. By repeatedly compromising the issues between North and South, Clay won the nickname of "the Great Pacificator." But these compromises were not lasting, and, in the long view of history, may have done more harm than good in leading to the ultimate catastrophe of the Civil War.

Born on April 12, 1777, in Hanover County, Virginia, Clay was one of a family of twenty children. His father died when Henry was only 4 years old, and by the time he was 15 the boy was earning his own living—first as a grocery clerk, and then as a court assistant. He studied law under George Wythe, who had taught Jefferson, and was admitted to the bar at the age of 20.

Moving to the frontier town of Lexington, Ky., the ruggedly handsome 6-feet-1-inch Clay achieved instant success, using his oratory to defend criminals, to help creditors collect debts, and to win a seat in the state legislature for himself. He acquired a fortune by accepting land in payment for his fees and by marrying a wealthy heiress. As attorney for Aaron Burr in 1806, he temporarily saved the former Vice-President from disgrace by arguing a Kentucky grand jury out of indicting Burr for treason.

Although the Constitution provides that Senators must be at least 30 years old, Clay took his seat as a U.S. Senator from Kentucky at the age of 29, because no one thought to question his age. After several years in the Senate, he shifted to the House of Representatives in 1811, where he won election as Speaker.

As a leader of the War Hawks, he helped bring about the War of 1812. Then he went to Europe to help John Quincy Adams negotiate the peace that

Henry Clay

to the nation's capitol as a Senator again in 1831. That same year he became the presidential candidate of the conservative National Republican party, opposing Andrew Jackson's try for a second term. But Clay was no match for Jackson. Campaigning for a re-chartering of the Bank of the United States—an issue he learned too late was unpopular—Clay was overwhelmingly defeated by Old Hickory in the election of 1832.

At the age of 67, Clay came closest to winning the presidency when he ran as the candidate of the Whig party against James K. Polk in 1844. But, again, Clay lost because he chose the wrong side of the most important issue of the campaign—he opposed the annexation of Texas.

Senator Clay's last major contribution to American history was his preparation of the Compromise of 1850—another futile effort to steer a middle course between the pro-slavery South and the anti-slavery North.

Ill with tuberculosis, the 75-year-old Clay died in a hotel room in Washington, D.C., on June 29, 1852.

"I had rather be right than President," Clay had said. But no one believed him.

ended the war—during which period, Adams complained to his diary that Clay disturbed his sleep with all-night drinking and gambling parties in his adjacent hotel room.

Believing that being Secretary of State was the sure road to the White House because Jefferson, Madison, and Monroe had all held that office, Clay was angered when Monroe chose Adams instead of himself for the premier Cabinet post. He took his vengeance by thwarting legislation favored by President Monroe and by promoting his own "American System" that called for a powerful national bank, federal expenditures for roads and canals, and high tariffs. He also was a principal architect of the Missouri Compromise of 1820 that maintained the balance between free and slave states.

Defeated for the presidency in 1824, he helped "steal" the White House for Adams, even though he disliked him, in order to achieve his own ill-starred ambition to become Secretary of State. In defense of his "corrupt bargain" he fought a notorious, though bloodless, duel with Senator John Randolph of Virginia.

His presidential aspirations temporarily crushed by the defeat of Adams in 1828, Clay bounced back

Rufus King

The last Federalist party candidate for President, Senator Rufus King of New York might have drastically changed the history of the United States if he had defeated James Monroe in the election of 1816. A strong opponent of slavery, he fought the Missouri Compromise that admitted Missouri to the Union as a slave state, and, if he had been President, he might well have precipitated a crisis between North and South that could have brought about the Civil War 40 years sooner.

Born on March 24, 1755, in Scarboro, Massachusetts (now in Maine), King graduated from Harvard, served briefly in the Revolutionary War, and then took up the practice of law.

As a member of the Massachusetts delegation to the Congress of the Confederation from 1784 to 1787, King helped write the Northwest Ordinance that outlawed slavery in the new states to be formed from the Northwest Territory. He also represented Massachusetts at the Constitutional Convention of 1787 where he fought against continuance of the importation of slaves. He signed the Constitution, voted for it in Congress, and helped achieve its ratification at the Massachusetts convention in 1788.

Rufus King

When the Massachusetts legislature refused to elect him as a U.S. Senator in the new Congress of the United States, King moved to New York, won election to the state legislature, and then was chosen as one of New York's first U.S. Senators in 1789. In the Senate he worked diligently to help carry out Alexander Hamilton's Federalist program, and helped Hamilton write a series of newspaper articles signed "Camillus" that supported the Jay Treaty with Great Britain in 1794.

From 1796 to 1803 King served as U.S. Minister to Great Britain under Presidents Washington, Adams, and Jefferson, working hard to preserve American neutrality during this difficult period. Upon his return to the United States, he ran unsuccessfully as Charles Cotesworth Pinckney's vice-presidential running mate in the national elections of 1804 and 1808.

Again elected a U.S. Senator from New York in 1813 and in 1820, King led northern efforts to prevent Missouri's admission as a slave state. He proposed that all the slaves should be freed, with the government paying restitution to the slave owners.

Under President John Quincy Adams, he again served as U.S. Minister to Great Britain from 1825

to 1826, but became ill and returned home to die on April 29, 1827, on his farm at Jamaica, Long Island, New York.

De Witt Clinton

His fame as the builder of the Erie Canal still lay ahead of him when De Witt Clinton ran and lost against James Madison in the presidential election of 1812. Even if he had been elected, it is unlikely that he could have brought the War of 1812 to any more satisfactory or quicker conclusion, but, because of his dedication to western expansion and canal building, he almost surely would have approved John Calhoun's "Bonus Bill" and have speeded the process of putting the federal government into the business of financing large scale public works projects.

Clinton was born on March 2, 1769, at Little Britain, N.Y. His father, James Clinton, was a brigadier general in the American army during the Revolutionary War. Young Clinton graduated from Columbia College, studied law, and then in 1790 became private secretary to his uncle, George Clinton, who was then governor of New York and later Vice-President of the United States under both Jefferson and Madison.

Entering politics as a Democratic-Republican, Clinton had a meteoric rise, winning election as a state senator in 1798, as a U.S. Senator in 1802, and then as mayor of New York City in 1803, at the age of 34. It was while holding the latter office that a group of

De Witt Clinton

dissident Democratic-Republicans in New York nominated him for the presidency in the election of 1812 and a convention of Federalists subsequently also endorsed his candidacy. His running-mate for Vice-President was Jared Ingersoll, a signer of the United States Constitution, who at the time was attorney general of Pennsylvania and head of the Federalist party in that state.

After losing the presidential election to Madison, Clinton continued to serve as mayor of New York City until 1815, and then became president of a commission to build a canal from the Hudson River to Lake Erie. Winning state-wide popularity for the project, he ran successfully three times for governor of New York, serving from 1817 to 1823, and from 1825 to his death in Albany on February 11, 1828. The crowning achievement of his career came during his last term as governor when he officially opened the completed 363-mile Erie Canal on October 26, 1825, linking the Great Lakes and New York City.

Charles Cotesworth Pinckney

Leader of the Federalist party after the retirement of John Adams and the death of Alexander Hamilton, Charles Cotesworth Pinckney twice was his party's losing presidential candidate—in 1804 against Thomas Jefferson and in 1808 against James Madison. If he had been elected President, it is possible that the War of 1812 might not have been fought with Great Britain. Pinckney favored the British more than the French in the wars then raging in Europe, and, although the United States still might have been dragged into the conflict, under Pinckney the odds would have been that the United States would have sided with Great Britain against France.

A good friend of George Washington and a signer of the United States Constitution, Pinckney was one of the most highly educated and respected lawyers of his day. He repeatedly rejected offers by Washington to join his Cabinet or take a seat on the Supreme Court, pleading the press of his law practice which brought him an annual estimated income of $20,000 a year—a fortune in those times. When the new United States Army was organized during John Adams' administration, Pinckney was appointed major general and third in command after Washington and Hamilton.

Charles C. Pinckney

Born in Charleston, S.C., on February 25, 1746, he was the son of the chief justice of the colony. He was educated at Oxford University, studying law under Sir William Blackstone, and received military training at the Royal Military Academy in France. An officer in the Revolutionary War, he was captured by the British during the siege of Charleston, S.C., and then after his release was advanced to the rank of brigadier general.

As one of the United States commissioners to France during the XYZ affair in 1797, he won fame for his reply to the French request for a bribe: "It's no, no! Not a sixpence!"

When Adams ran for a second term as President in 1800, Pinckney was chosen by the Federalists as the vice-presidential candidate. Hamilton's maneuvers to have Pinckney elected President in place of Adams resulted in a Federalist defeat.

For the last twenty years of his life, Pinckney was president of the Society of Cincinnati, the association of officers who had served in the Revolutionary War. He lived to the age of 79, dying at Charleston on August 1, 1825.

How the Presidency Was Created

THE office of President of the United States was created by the Founding Fathers during the Constitutional Convention of 1787. The delegates from the various states assembled in Philadelphia in May, planning only to revise the existing Articles of Confederation that had been written in 1777—ten years earlier—and had been ratified and became effective in 1781. Under the Articles of Confederation all the powers of the national government—including executive powers—were delegated to Congress.

There had been a president of the Congress under the Articles of Confederation, but he had been only a presiding officer with little or no power in his own right. The office was given only passing mention in the Articles of Confederation:

"The united States in congress assembled shall have authority . . . to appoint such other committees and civil officers as may be necessary for managing the general affairs of the united states under their direction—to appoint one of their number to preside, provided that no person be allowed to serve in the office of president more than one year in any term of three years . . ."

The Virginia Plan

THE first formal proposal that a chief executive be provided for the new federal government was contained in the Virginia Plan presented by Governor Edmund Randolph of Virginia on May 29, 1787:

"Resolved that a National Executive be instituted; to be chosen by the National Legislature for the term of _____ years, to receive punctually at stated times, a fixed compensation for the services rendered, in which no increase or diminution shall be made so as to affect the Magistracy, existing at the time of increase or diminution, and to be ineligible a second time; and that besides a general authority to execute the National laws, it ought to enjoy the Executive rights vested in Congress by the Confederation.

The residences of George Washington (*left*) and Robert Morris in Philadelphia.

519

John Rutledge
—From a painting by John Trumbull

"Resolved that the Executive and a convenient number of the National Judiciary, ought to compose a Council of revision with authority to examine every act of the National Legislature before it shall operate, and every act of a particular Legislature before a Negative thereon shall be final; and that the dissent of the said Council shall amount to a rejection, unless the Act of the National Legislature be again passed, or that of a particular Legislature be again negatived by _____ of the members of each branch."

The Pinckney Plan

On the same day Charles Pinckney of South Carolina presented his "Plan of a Federal Constitution." The Pinckney Plan did not figure in the debates during the Convention, but it was one of the documents later used by John Rutledge's committee of detail in drafting a complete constitution. Although the original of Pinckney's Plan was lost, he produced a copy of it for the national archives in 1818. Its Article VIII called for the establishment of the office of President in the following words:

"The executive power of the United States shall be vested in a President of the United States of

Charles Pinckney
—From a painting attributed to Gilbert Stuart
American Scenic and Historic Preservation Society Collection.
Frick Art Reference Library.

America, which shall be his style; and his title shall be His Excellency. He shall be elected for __years; and shall be re-eligible.

"He shall from time give information to the Legislature, of the State of the Union, and recommend to their consideration the measures he may think necessary. He shall take care that the laws of the United States be duly executed. He shall commission all the officers of the United States; and except as to ambassadors, other ministers, and judges of the Supreme Court, he shall nominate, and, with the consent of the Senate, appoint, all other officers of the United States. He shall receive public ministers from foreign nations; and may correspond with the Executives of the different States. He shall have power to grant pardons and reprieves, except in impeachments. He shall be Commander-in-Chief of the army and navy of the United States, and of the militia of the several States; and shall reeive a compensation which shall not be increased or diminished during his continuance in office. At entering on the duties of his office, he shall take an oath faithfully to execute the duties of a President of the United States. He shall be removed from his office on impeachment by the House of Delegates, and conviction in the Supreme Court, of treason, bribery, or corruption. In case of his removal, death, resignation, or disability, the President of the Senate shall exercise the duties of his office until another President be chosen. And in case of the death of the President of the Senate, the Speaker of the House of Delegates shall do so."

Madison Establishes the President's Authority

THE Constitutional Convention began studying the parts of the Virginia Plan concerned with the chief executive on Friday, June 1, and continued to debate them for the next several days. On the first day of the debate the Convention adopted a motion by James Madison of Virginia to fix the extent of the chief executive's authority by changing the Resolution to read: "Resolved that a National Executive be instituted with power to carry into effect the national laws, to appoint to offices in cases not otherwise provided for . . ."

Next, the Convention began studying the question of how long the chief executive should serve. James Wilson of Pennsylvania and Roger Sherman of Connecticut proposed that the term of office be for three years. But Charles Pinckney of South Carolina and George Mason of Virginia spoke out for a term of seven years. Five states voted aye, four voted no, and one, Massachusetts, was divided. The president of the Convention, George Washington, decided that the motion for a term of seven years had carried.

The Delegates at first Reject an Electoral College

THE Constitutional Convention delegates then turned their attention to deciding whether the chief executive should be elected by the people or be appointed by the Congress. James Wilson proposed the establishment of a system of presidential electors to be chosen by the people. But on June 2 this proposal was turned down by a vote of 8 to 2 and by the same number of votes it was decided that the chief executive should be elected by Congress.

Benjamin Franklin of Pennsylvania made an impassioned plea that the chief executive not be paid a salary, arguing that a higher caliber of man would be found for the office if there was no question of personal gain on his part. His motion was seconded by Alexander Hamilton of New York, but the Convention postponed debate or voting upon it, rather than hurt the old man's feelings by abruptly voting it down.

John Dickinson of Delaware, who had written the Articles of Confederation, moved "That the Executive be made removable by the National Legislature on the request of a majority of the Legislatures of individual States." He believed this would keep the states in a controlling position over the chief execu-

tive. But his moton was defeated, with all states except Delaware voting against it. The Convention then voted to make the chief executive ineligible for re-election after seven years in office.

Hugh Williamson of North Carolina moved to add that the executive "be removable on impeachment and conviction of malpractice or neglect of duty." This was approved by the delegates.

Should the Executive Be One Man or Three?

TOWARD the close of the session on Saturday, June 2, John Rutledge of South Carolina, who later was to be appointed Chief Justice by George Washington but be rejected by the U.S. Senate, moved that the blank for the number of persons to serve as Executive be filled with the words, "one person." Rutledge said that the reasons were so obvious and conclusive in favor of a single chief executive that he believed no one would oppose the motion.

However, Edmund Randolph, who later was to be the first Attorney General of the United States under President Washington, spoke out against the single chief executive. He said he believed the people would regard the establishment of a chief executive as resembling a monarchy. Instead, he proposed that the Executive be made up of three men on equal footing

James Madison

—From a painting by Charles Willson Peale
Thomas Gilcrease Institute of American History and Art, Tulsa, Oklahoma.
Frick Art Reference Library.

An early sketch of one of the ideas for the official seal.

to be chosen from different parts of the country. The Convention adjourned that day before a vote could be taken on the matter.

After considering the matter over Sunday, the Convention resumed debate on the question of the single chief executive on Monday, June 4. James Wilson of Pennsylvania, who later was to be appointed by President Washington as one of the first associate justices of the Supreme Court, argued eloquently for a single chief executive. He said that with a triumvirate holding the executive power he foresaw "nothing but uncontrolled, continued and violent animosities." He said these quarrels would "diffuse their poison through the other branches of government, through the states, and at length through the people at large."

Finally, the delegates agreed upon a single chief executive, although three states opposed the resolution—New York, Delaware, and Maryland.

Establishment of the Veto Power

THE Convention then turned its attention to a discussion of the part of the Virginia Resolutions that called for the establishment of a "Council of revision."

Elbridge Gerry of Massachusetts, who later was to serve as Vice-President under President James Madison, moved that instead of considering the "Council of revision," the delegates should adopt a proposal "that the National Executive shall have a right to negative any legislative act, which shall not be afterwards passed by __ parts of each branch of the National Legislature."

James Wilson and Alexander Hamilton made an effort to obtain an absolute veto for the chief executive, eliminating any possibility of Congress overriding a presidential veto. Benjamin Franklin strongly opposed this, pointing out that the chief executive could use such a power to extort money from the legislature. He commented that "The Executive will be always increasing here, as elsewhere, till it ends in a monarchy."

The delegations unanimously voted down the idea of giving the chief executive an absolute veto, and agreed to fill the blank in Gerry's resolution with the word "two-thirds." In a final vote on the entire resolution giving the chief executive a limited veto that could be overridden by a two-thirds vote of each house of Congress, eight states voted for the resolution and two opposed—Connecticut and Maryland.

On Wednesday, June 6, Wilson and Madison made an effort to revive the idea of a "Council of revision" that would include representatives of the judicial branch in the exercise of veto over legislation. But their resolution was voted down, with only Connecticut, New York, and Virginia voting aye.

The question of how the chief executive was to be chosen was again brought up for debate on Saturday, June 9. Elbridge Gerry of Massachusetts proposed that the chief executive be elected by the governors of the states, instead of by Congress as had been previously agreed upon. He said he believed that the governors, being executives themselves, would be more likely to choose an able chief executive than would the legislature. However, the delegates voted down his idea.

The Revised Virginia Plan Resolutions

ON Wednesday, June 13, after the delegates had completed their initial debates on the Virginia Plan, the wording of the two resolutions concerned with the chief executive stood as follows:

"Resolved, that a National Executive be instituted, to consist of a single person; to be chosen

The State House of Philadelphia in 1774.

Thomas Jefferson

by the National Legislature, for the term of seven years; with power to carry into execution the national laws; to appoint to offices in cases not otherwise provided for; to be ineligible a second time; and to be removable on impeachment and conviction of malpractices or neglect of duty; to receive a fixed stipend by which he may be compensated for the devotion of his time to the public service, to be paid out of the National Treasury.

"Resolved, that the national Executive shall have a right to negative any legislative act, which shall not be afterwards passed by two-thirds of each branch of the National Legislature."

The New Jersey Plan

SEVERAL of the smaller states had been becoming increasingly concerned that the Convention was moving toward too strong a centralized government. So on Friday, June 15, William Paterson of New Jersey, who later was to serve as an associate justice of the Supreme Court, presented what became known as the "New Jersey Plan." Its provisions for the executive branch were as follows:

"Resolved, that the United States in Congress be authorized to elect a Federal Executive, to consist of ___ persons, to continue in office for the term of ___ years; to receive punctually, at stated times, a fixed compensation for their services, in which no increase nor diminution shall be made so as to affect the persons composing the Executive at the time of such increase or diminution; to be paid out of the Federal treasury; to be incapable of holding any other office or appointment during their time of service, and for ___ years thereafter: to be ineligible a second time, and removeable by Congress, on application by a majority of the Executives of the several States; that the Executive, besides their general authority to execute the Federal acts, ought to appoint all Federal officers not otherwise provided for, and to direct all military operations; provided, that none of the persons composing the Federal Executive shall, on any occasion, take command of any troops, so as personally to conduct any military enterprise, as General, or in any other capacity."

Alexander Hamilton's Plan

As the Convention began to debate the respective merits of the New Jersey Plan versus the Virginia Resolutions, Alexander Hamilton spoke out against both, saying that neither provided for a strong enough central government. In turn, he presented his own plan. In Hamilton's plan the provision for the chief executive was as follows:

"The supreme Executive authority of the United States to be vested in a Governor, to be elected to serve during good behaviour; the election to be made by Electors chosen by the people in the Election Districts aforesaid. The authorities and functions of the Executive to be as follows; to have a negative on all laws about to be passed, and the execution of all laws passed; to have the direction of war when authorized or begun; to have, with the advice and approbation of the Senate, the power of making all treaties; to have the sole appointment of the heads or chief officers of the Departments of Finance, War, and Foreign Affairs; to have the nomination of all other officers (ambassadors to foreign nations included), subject to the approbation or rejection of the Senate; to have the power of pardoning all offences except treason, which he shall not pardon without the approbation

Robert Livingston

Alexander Hamilton

Chief Justice John Jay

of the Senate.

"On the death, resignation, or removal of the Governor, his authorities to be exercised by the President of the Senate till a successor be appointed."

The delegates voted to postpone discussion of the New Jersey Plan and ignored Hamilton's Plan. For the next month the delegates devoted their consideration almost entirely to the provisions for the legislative branch of the government. It was not until Tuesday, July 17 that the resolutions concerning the executive branch again came up for discussion.

Rejection of Direct Election by the People

GOUVERNEUR Morris of Pennsylvania, who later became a U.S. Senator, moved that the chief executive be elected by the citizens of the United States, instead of by the National Legislature. He said: "If the people should elect, they will never fail to prefer some man of distinguished character, or services . . . If the Legislature elect, it will be the work of intrigue, of cabal, and of faction . . ."

The proposal for direct election by the people was opposed by Roger Sherman of Connecticut, Charles Pinckney of South Carolina, George Mason of Virginia, and Hugh Williamson of North Carolina.

Mason said he believed "it would be as unnatural to refer the choice of a proper character for Chief Magistrate to the people, as it would, to refer a trial of colors to a blind man."

When Morris' resolution was put to a motion, only his own state of Pennsylvania voted for it. All the other states voted no.

By a vote of 6 to 4, the delegations voted to strike out the words "to be ineligible a second time." Gouverneur Morris in supporting the motion pointed out that if the chief executive was ineligible for re-election it would tend to "destroy the great motive to good behaviour, the hope of being rewarded by a re-appointment. It was saying to him, make hay while the sun shines."

Delegates Fear Development of a Monarchy

THE Convention next spent considerable time discussing whether or not to change the chief executive's term of office from seven years to "during good behaviour." Gouverneur Morris and James Madison were among the chief supporters of this proposed change. They saw this as a further way to free the chief executive from dependence on the national legislature. George Mason of Virginia made the main speech against the motion, declaring that "an Executive during good behaviour" was "a softer name only for an Executive for life." He said he believed the next easy step was to a hereditary monarchy. The delegates decided by a vote of 6 to 4 to retain the seven-year term for the chief executive.

Establishment of an Electoral System for Choosing the Chief Executive

ON Thursday, July 19, the Convention again took up the question of how the chief executive should be elected. James Madison made an impassioned address calling upon the delegates to free the chief executive from any dependence on the national legislature. He said, "If it be a fundamental principle of free government that the Legislative, Executive and Judiciary powers should be *separately* exercised, it is equally so that they be *independently* exercised."

Oliver Ellsworth of Connecticut, who later was to become the second Chief Justice of the United States, moved to strike out the provision for election of the chief executive by the national legislature and substitute, "to be chosen by Electors, appointed by the Legislatures of the States in the following ratio; to wit: one for each State not exceeding two hundred thousand inhabitants; two for each above that number and not exceeding three hundred thousand; and three for each State exceeding three hundred thousand." The Convention voted to accept this motion,

Gouverneur Morris

but deferred action on the ratio of number of electors for each state.

On motion of Oliver Ellsworth, the Convention decided to reduce the length of the chief executive's term from seven years to six years.

On Friday, July 20, Elbridge Gerry moved that the Electors for the chief executive be alloted to the states in the following ratio: New Hampshire, one; Massachusetts, three; Rhode Island, one; Connecticut, two; New York, two; New Jersey, two; Pennsylvania, three; Delaware, one; Maryland, two; Virginia, three; North Carolina, two; South Carolina, two; Georgia, one. Despite opposition by the smaller states, the Convention adopted Gerry's proposal by a vote of 6 to 4. It was further agreed, "that the Electors of the Executive shall not be members of the National Legislature, nor officers of the United States, nor shall the Electors themselves be eligible to the supreme magistracy."

That same day the delegates spent a substantial amount of time discussing whether the chief executive should be made liable to impeachment and removal from office. Benjamin Franklin, James Madison, and Edmund Randolph led the arguments for preserving the right of impeachment. Franklin pointed out that without impeachment the only recourse for removal of a corrupt chief executive was assassination. The Convention retained the impeachment clause by a vote of 8 to 2, with only Massachusetts and South Carolina opposing.

Attempt to Modify the Presidential Veto

On Saturday, July 21, James Wilson of Pennsylvania revived the idea that members of the judiciary should be associated with the chief executive in exercising the veto power over legislation. James Madison supported the proposition on the basis that it would give the judicial branch "an additional opportunity of defending itself against Legislative encroachments."

Elbridge Gerry opposed Wilson's motion because he felt that it would lead to a "combining and mixing together" of the executive and judiciary. And Nathaniel Gorham, also of Massachusetts, opposed the measure, pointing out that since there would be only one chief executive and several judges the proposal would have the effect of taking the veto power "entirely out of the Executive hands, and, instead of enabling him to defend himself, would enable the Judges to sacrifice him."

John Rutledge of South Carolina also opposed the proposition saying that of all men judges were the most unfit to be given the veto power on legislation. He said, "Judges ought never to give their opinion on a law, till it comes before them."

The inclusion of the judiciary in the executive veto power narrowly missed being added to the Constitution. Four states opposed the measure—Massachusetts, Delaware, North Carolina, and South Carolina; three states voted in favor—Connecticut, Maryland, and Virginia; two states were divided—Pennsylvania and Georgia; and New Jersey was absent.

The Convention next began considering a motion by James Madison that the chief executive should nominate the members of the judiciary and that these nominations should become appointments unless two-thirds of the Senate disagreed. But several delegates objected to taking the power of appointment away from the National Legislature, so the motion went down to defeat by a vote of 3 for and 6 against.

Choosing of the President Returned to Congress

AFTER several days debating other aspects of the Constitution, the delegates on Tuesday, July 24, again took up the question of how the chief executive was to be elected. William C. Houston of New Jersey moved that, instead of having the chief executive chosen by special electors as had already been agreed to, the National Legislature should be given the task. He said he believed the use of electors would cause extreme inconvenience and considerable expense. He also said he believed that capable men would not agree to serve as electors, particularly in the more distant states.

When the delegations were polled on the question they reversed their previous stand, and by a vote of 7 to 4 agreed to put the election of the chief executive back into the hands of the National Legislature. Then they fell to arguing about all aspects of the chief executive, the length of his term of office, and whether or not he should be eligible for re-election. After two days of wrangling, the Convention decided on Thursday, July 26, by a vote of 7 to 3 to limit the chief executive's term to seven years and make him ineligible for a second term. Later that same day the Convention turned all the resulting resolutions over to a Committee of Detail headed by John Rutledge of South Carolina to write them up into the form of a Constitution. In addition the Convention passed along to the Committee the New Jersey Plan and the Pinckney Plan and adjourned for ten days.

Draft by the Committee of Detail

WHEN the Convention reconvened on Monday, August 6, Rutledge presented the delegates with a draft of the Constitution which had drawn heavily upon the Pinckney plan for its wording concerning the chief executive. Its Article X read as follows:

"Section 1. The Executive power of the United States shall be vested in a single person. His style shall be, "The President of the United States of America," and his title shall be, "His Excellency." He shall be elected by ballot by the Legislature. He shall hold his office during the term of seven years; but shall not be elected a second time.

"Section 2. He shall, from time to time, give information to the Legislature of the state of the Union. He may recommend to their consideration such measures as he shall judge necessary, and expedient. He may convene them on extraordinary occasions. In case of disagreement between the two Houses, with regard to the time of adjournment, he may adjourn them to such time as he thinks proper. He shall take care that the laws of the United States be duly and faithfully executed. He shall commission all the officers of the United States; and shall appoint officers in all cases not otherwise provided for by this Constitution. He shall receive Ambassadors, and may correspond with the supreme executives of the several States. He shall have power to grant reprieves and pardons, but his pardon shall not be pleadable in bar of an impeachment. He shall be Commander-in-chief of the army and navy of the United States, and of the militia of the several States. He shall, at stated times, receive for his services a compensation, which shall neither be increased nor diminished during his continuance in office. Before he shall enter on the duties of his department, he shall take the following oath or affirmation, "I _____ solemnly swear, (or affirm) that I will faithfully execute the office of President of the United States of America." He shall be removed from his office on impeachment by the House of Representatives, and conviction in the Supreme Court, of treason, bribery, or corruption. In case of his removal, as aforesaid, death, resignation, or disability to discharge the powers and duties of his office, the President of the Senate shall exercise those powers and duties, until another President of the United States be chosen, or until the disability of the President be removed."

In the new Constitution prepared by the Committee of Detail, the provision for a presidential veto was moved to Article VI, which dealt with the procedures of the two houses of Congress.

The Convention did not take up Article X, relating to the President, until Friday, August 24, and the debate on the provisions extended until Monday, August 27. Most efforts to change the Article, whether by those trying to strengthen the office or by those trying to weaken it, were voted down. On August 31, the Convention turned over to a Committee of Eleven (with one delegate from each state) such knotty problems as how the chief executive should be elected.

Report by the Committee of Eleven

On Tuesday, September 4, the Committee of Eleven reported back to the Convention their solutions for the various problems surrounding the office of the President. They recommended creating a Vice-President and the establishment of a four-year term of office for both President and Vice-President. And the Committee solved the problem of how the President and Vice-President should be chosen by drawing up plans for an elaborate electoral system that would leave the method of choosing presidential electors up to the legislatures of the various states. The Committee established the qualifications for being President —a natural-born citizen, at least 35 years old, and a resident within the United States for at least 14 years. Another important change by the Committee gave the President the power to make treaties with the advice and consent of the Senate and to appoint judges of the Supreme Court.

For the rest of the first week of September the Convention debated the changes in the article dealing with the office of the President, making some minor but few major changes. Then on Saturday, September 8, a five-man Committee of Revision was

Rufus King

529

John Marshall

appointed to revise the style and arrangement of the articles that had been agreed to. The Committee included James Madison, Gouverneur Morris, Alexander Hamilton, Rufus King, and William Samuel Johnson.

Final Version in the Constitution

THE Committee of Revision submitted its report on Wednesday, September 12. In the new Constitution prepared by the Committee, the provisions concerning the President became Article II. The wording was approved with a few minor changes on Saturday, September 15. And on Monday, September 17, 1787, the delegates approved and signed the final version of the Constitution of the United States. The wording of Article II follows:

Article II

"Section 1. The executive Power shall be vested in a President of the United States of America. He shall hold his Office during the Term of four Years, and, together with the Vice President, chosen for the same Term, be elected as follows:

"Each State shall appoint, in such Manner as the Legislature thereof may direct, a Number of Electors, equal to the whole Number of Senators and Representatives to which the State may be entitled in the Congress: but no Senator or Representative, or Person holding an Office of Trust or Profit under the United States, shall be appointed an Elector.

"The Electors shall meet in their respective States, and vote by Ballot for two Persons, of whom one at least shall not be an Inhabitant of the same State with themselves. And they shall make a List of all the Persons voted for, and of the Number of Votes for each; which List they shall sign and certify, and transmit sealed to the Seat of the Government of the United States, directed to the President of the Senate. The President of the Senate shall, in the Presence of the Senate and House of Representatives, open all the Certificates, and the Votes shall then be counted. The Person having the greatest Number of Votes shall be the President, if such Number be a Majority of the whole Number of Electors appointed; and if there be more than one who have such Majority, and have an equal Number of Votes, then the House of Representatives shall immediately choose by Ballot one of them for President; and if no Person have a Majority, then from the five highest on the List the said House shall in like manner choose the President. But in choosing the President, the Votes shall be taken by States, the Representation from each State having one Vote; A quorum for this Purpose shall consist of a Member or Members from two-thirds of the States, and a Majority of all the States shall be necessary to a Choice. In every Case, after the Choice of the President, the Person having the greatest Number of Votes of the Electors shall be the Vice President. But if there should remain two or more who have equal Votes, the Senate shall choose from them by Ballot the Vice President.

"The Congress may determine the Time of choosing the Electors, and the Day on which they shall give their Votes; which Day shall be the same throughout the United States.

"No Person except a natural born Citizen, or a Citizen of the United States, at the time of the Adoption of this Constitution, shall be eligible to the Office of President; neither shall any Person be eligible to that Office who shall not have attained to the Age of thirty five Years, and been fourteen Years a Resident within the United States.

"In Case of the Removal of the President from Office, or of his Death, Resignation, or Inability to discharge the Powers and Duties of the said Office, the Same shall devolve on the Vice President, and the Congress may by Law provide for the Case of Removal, Death, Resignation or Inability, both of the President and Vice President, declaring what Officer shall then act as President, and such Officer shall act accordingly, until the Disability be removed, or a President shall be elected.

"The President shall, at stated Times, receive for his Services, a Compensation, which shall neither be increased nor diminished during the Period for which he shall have been elected, and he shall not receive within that Period any other Emolument from the United States, or any of them.

"Before he enter on the Execution of his Office, he shall take the following Oath or Affirmation:— "I do solemnly swear (or affirm) that I will faithfully execute the Office of President of the United States, and will to the best of my Ability, preserve, protect and defend the Constitution of the United States."

"Section 2. The President shall be Commander in Chief of the Army and Navy of the United States, and of the Militia of the several States, when called into the actual Service of the United States; he may require the Opinion, in writing, of the principal Officer in each of the executive Departments, upon any Subject relating to the Duties of their respective Offices, and he shall have Power to grant Reprieves and Pardons for Offences against the United States, except in Cases of Impeachment.

"He shall have Power, by and with the Advice and Consent of the Senate, to make Treaties, provided two thirds of the Senators present concur; and he shall nominate, and by and with the Advice and Consent of the Senate, shall appoint Ambassadors, other public Ministers and Consuls, Judges of the supreme Court, and all other Officers of the United States, whose Appointments are not herein otherwise provided for, and which shall be established by Law: but the Congress may by Law vest the Appointment of such inferior Officers, as they think proper, in the President alone, in the Courts of Law, or in the Heads of Departments.

"The President shall have Power to fill up all Vacancies that may happen during the Recess of the Senate, by granting Commissions which shall expire at the End of their next Session.

"Section 3. He shall from time to time give to the Congress Information of the State of the Union, and recommend to their Consideration such Measures as he shall judge necessary and expedient; he may, on extraordinary Occasions, convene both Houses, or either of them, and in Case of Disagreement between them, with Respect to the Time of Adjournment, he may adjourn them to such Time as he shall think proper; he shall receive Ambassadors and other public Ministers; he shall take Care that the Laws be faithfully executed, and shall Commission all the Officers of the United States.

"Section 4. The President, Vice President and all civil Officers of the United States, shall be removed from Office on Impeachment for, and Conviction of, Treason, Bribery, or other high Crimes and Misdemeanors."

Amendments Bearing on the Presidency

SINCE the Constitution went into effect in 1789, five amendments have been adopted that have modified Article II. These are as follows:

Amendment 12
(proclaimed September 25, 1804)

This amendment was adopted to prevent from happening again the crisis that developed in 1800-01 when Jefferson and Burr each received an equal number of electoral votes and the House of Representatives had to decide which should become President, because the Constitution had not provided for the electors to vote separately for President and Vice President. The text of Amendment 12 follows.

"The Electors shall meet in their respective states, and vote by ballot for President and Vice-President, one of whom, at least, shall not be an inhabitant of the same state with themselves; they shall name in their ballots the person voted for as President, and in distinct ballots the person voted for as Vice-President, and they shall make distinct lists of all persons voted for as President, and of all persons voted for as Vice-President, and of the number of votes for each, which lists they shall sign and certify, and transmit sealed to the seat of the government of the United States, directed to the President of the Senate;—the President of the Senate shall, in the presence of the Senate and House of Representatives, open all the certificates and the votes shall then be counted;—The person having the greatest number of votes for President, shall be the President, if such number be a majority of the whole number of Electors appointed; and if no person have such majority, then from the persons having the highest numbers not exceeding three on the list of those voted for as President, the House of Representatives shall choose immediately, by ballot, the President. But in choosing the President, the votes shall be taken by states, the representation from each state having one vote; a quorum for this purpose shall consist of a member or members from two-thirds of the states, and a majority of all the states shall be necessary to a choice. And if the House of Representatives shall not choose a President whenever the right of choice shall devolve upon them, before the fourth day of March next following, then the Vice-President, as in the case of the death or other constitutional disability of the President. The person having the greatest number of votes as Vice-President, shall be the Vice-President, if such number be a majority of the whole number of Electors appointed, and if no person have a majority, then from the two highest numbers on the list, the Senate shall choose the Vice-President; a quorum for the purpose shall consist of two-thirds of the whole number of Senators, and a majority of the whole number shall be necessary to a choice. But no person constitutionally ineligible to the office of President shall be eligible to that of Vice-President of the United States."

Amendment 20
(proclaimed February 6, 1933)

This amendment was adopted to shorten the period between the November election and the time the President and the new Congress would take office. It was called the "Lame Duck" amend-

Designs for the Great Seal of the United States as submitted by the second committee.

ment because it was intended to end the practice of so-called "lame-duck" post-election sessions of Congress, often controlled by a party that had been defeated at the polls. The amendment was adopted at the height of the Great Depression when the people were eager for President Franklin D. Roosevelt to take office so that his new administration could get to work on solving the nation's economic ills. The text follows:

"Section 1. The terms of the President and Vice-President shall end at noon on the 20th day of January, and the terms of Senators and Representatives at noon on the third day of January, of the year in which such terms would have ended if this article had not been ratified; and the terms of their successors shall then begin.

"Section 2. The Congress shall assemble at least once in every year, and such meeting shall begin at noon on the third day of January, unless they shall by law appoint a different day.

"Section 3. If, at the time fixed for the beginning of the term of the President, the president elect shall have died, the Vice-President elect shall become President. If a President shall not have been chosen before the time fixed for the beginning of his term, or if the President elect shall have failed to qualify, then the Vice President elect shall act as President until a President shall have qualified; and the Congress may by law provide for the case wherein neither a President elect nor a Vice-President elect shall have qualified, declaring who shall then act as President, or the manner in which one who is to act shall be selected, and such person shall act accordingly until a President or Vice-President shall have qualified.

"Section 4. The Congress may by law provide for the case of the death of any of the persons from whom the House of Representatives may choose a President whenever the right of choice shall have devolved upon them, and for the case of the death of any of the persons from whom the Senate may choose a Vice-President whenever the right of choice shall have devolved upon them.

"Section 5. Sections 1 and 2 shall take effect on the 15th day of October following the ratification of this article.

"Section 6. This article shall be inoperative unless it shall have been ratified as an amendment to the Constitution by the legislatures of three fourths of the several States within seven years from the date of its submission."

Amendment 22
(proclaimed February 27, 1951)

This amendment, limiting a President to being elected only twice, was adopted largely at the urging of Republicans who still were smarting from having lost four elections in a row to President Franklin D. Roosevelt. Text of the amendment follows.

"Section 1. No person shall be elected to the office of the President more than twice, and no person who has held the office of President, or acted as President, for more than two years of a term to which some other person was elected President shall be elected to the office of the President more than once. But this article shall not apply to any person holding the office of President, or acting as President, during the term within which this article becomes operative from holding the office of President or acting as President during the remainder of such term.

"Section 2. This article shall be inoperative unless it shall have been ratified as an amendment

533

to the Constitution by the legislatures of three fourths of the several States within seven years from the day of its submission to the States by the Congress."

Amendment 23
(proclaimed April 3, 1961)

Prior to this amendment, only residents of the states could vote for President, and so residents of Washington, D.C., could not vote for the nation's chief executive. This amendment gave them the right to vote for President and Vice President. Its text follows.

"Section 1. The District constituting the seat of Government of the United States shall appoint in such manner as the Congress may direct: A number of electors of President and Vice-President equal to the whole number of Senators and Representatives in Congress to which the District would be entitled if it were a State, but in no event more than the least populous State; they shall be in addition to those appointed by the States, but they shall be considered, for the purposes of the election of President and Vice-President, to be electors appointed by a State; and they shall meet in the District and perform such duties as provided by the twelfth article of amendment.

"Section 2. The Congress shall have power to enforce this article by appropriate legislation."

Amendment 25
(proclaimed February 10, 1967)

This amendment was adopted to establish a means of filling the office of Vice President if it becomes vacant, and to prevent a break-down in government if a President becomes physically or mentally incapacitated. Amendment 25 was first used when Vice President Spiro Agnew resigned in 1973 and Gerald R. Ford was nominated by President Nixon and confirmed by Congress to fill the vacancy. It again came into use in 1974 following Nixon's resignation when Ford became President and named Nelson A. Rockefeller as Vice President. The text of Amendment 25 follows.

"Section 1. In case of the removal of the President from office or his death or resignation, the Vice-President shall become President.

"Section 2. Whenever there is a vacancy in the office of the Vice President, the President shall nominate a Vice President who shall take the office upon confirmation by a majority vote of both houses of Congress.

"Section 3. Whenever the President transmits to the President pro tempore of the Senate and the Speaker of the House of Representatives his written declaration that he is unable to discharge the powers and duties of his office, and until he transmits to them a written declaration to the contrary, such powers and duties shall be discharged by the Vice-President as Acting President.

"Section 4. Whenever the Vice-President and a majority of either the principal officers of the executive departments or of such other body as Congress may by law provide, transmit to the President pro tempore of the Senate and the Speaker of the House of Representatives their written declaration that the President is unable to discharge the powers and duties of his office, the Vice-President shall immediately assume the powers and duties of the office as Acting President.

"Thereafter, when the President transmits to the President pro tempore of the Senate and the Speaker of the House of Representatives his written declaration that no inability exists, he shall resume the powers and duties of his office unless the Vice-President and a majority of either the principal officers of the executive department or of such other body as Congress may by law provide, transmit within four days to the President pro tempore of the Senate and the Speaker of the House of Representatives their written declaration that the President is unable to discharge the powers and duties of his office. Thereupon Congress shall decide the issue, assembling within 48 hours for that purpose if not in session. If the Congress, within 21 days after receipt of the latter written declaration, or, if Congress is not in session, within 21 days after Congress is required to assemble, determines by two-thirds vote of both houses that the President is unable to discharge the powers and duties of his office, the Vice-President shall continue to discharge the same as Acting President; otherwise, the President shall resume the powers and duties of his office."

Index

Chiang Kai-shek, 107
China: Boxer Rebellion, 132, 228; communism, 84, 92, 107; Cuba, 66, 69; Formosa, 84; Hoover, 129, 132; immigration (to U.S.), 264; Korean War, 107; Nixon, 17-18; U.S., 92, 228; treaty (1844), 375; UN, 18; Vietnam, 30
Chou En-lai, 17
Churchill, Winston, 123, 126; Potsdam, 96, 98; Truman, 93
Civilian Conservation Corps (CCC), 121
Civil rights: Acts (1866), 307; (1964), 37; Eisenhower, 80; Johnson, L. B., 35, 37; Kennedy, 58, 66; Madison, 433; Truman, 92, 98-9; Wilson, 185-6
Civil Service, 299; Commission, 193; Pendleton Act, 264; politics, 263; reform, 236, 264, 274-5, 288
Civil War, 176, 326, 330-1, 336, 349, 415, 442, 506; Arthur, 259, 261; Buchanan, 340; Garfield, 267, 270; generals, 292; Grant, 291, 292, 293, 295, 301; Harrison, 249, 251, 254; Hayes, 220, 277, 279, 280; Johnson, Andrew, 305; McKinley, 219, 220; Peace Convention (1861), 371; Republican presidential candidates, 253; veterans, 254 (see GAR)
Clark, Champ, 181
Clark, William, 449
Clay, Henry, 337, 345, 361, 367, 375-6, 391, 403-4, 407-8, 417, 434; Adams, J. Q., 404; death, 355; Harrison, 385; Missouri Compromise, 361; presidential candidate, 366-7, 406-7, 491, 503, 514-15; Secretary of State, 417; Van Buren, 393
Clayton Antitrust Act, 186, 500
Cleveland, Grover, 231-47, 495, 505, 506; appearance, 232; birth, 231, 232; characteristics, 232-3, 235, 242; death, 231, 232, 247; education, 231, 232-3; governor, 231, 233; health, 242, 245; McKinley, 224-5, 229; marriage, 231-2, 238; President, 231, 235, 241-6, 253, 264-5; Wilson, 178
Clinton, DeWitt, 435, 516-17
Clinton, George, 456, 516
Cold War, 4, 6, 18, 19, 50, 72, 81, 92
Colgate University (Madison University), 502
College of William and Mary, 371, 423, 438, 513
Colson, Charles W., 23
Columbia College, 516
Columbia University, 109; Eisenhower, 71, 78; Law School, 111, 112, 203, 496, 502
Committee of Correspondence, 440
Communism, 6, 7, 8, 9, 39, 92, 106; China, 106; Cuba, 72; "Eisenhower Doctrine," 84. See McCarthy, Joseph
Compromise of 1850, 305, 344, 347, 513, 515. See Missouri Compromise
Concord, battle of, 440, 454, 468
Confederate Congress, 330, 371
Confederate States, 330, 347; Reconstruction (see Reconstruction)
Conkling, Roscoe, 261, 273
Connally, John B., 26, 68
Conrad, Charles, Jr., 12
Constitutional Convention, 429, 431, 435, 461, 471-2, 519-34
"Constitutional Union" party, 323
Continental Army, 423, 441, 461, 469-71
Continental Congress: Adams, J., 451,

452-3; First, 440-1, 453, 468; Second, 454, 468, 470-1; Washington, 461
Conventions (national), first (1832), See under name of party
Coolidge, Calvin, 46, 122, 145-57, 500, 502; appearance, 146; birth, 145, 146; Boston police strike, 149, 165; Cabinet, 171; characteristics, 146, 147, 149, 150, 152, 155; death, 145, 156; education, 145, 147; governor, 149-50, 165; Hoover, 129, 130, 134; marriage, 145, 147, 149; nickname: "Silent Cal," 146; President, 140, 145, 150, 152, 155, 157, 171; Vice President, 150, 165
Cooper-Church Amendment, 15
Cornell University, 502
Cornwallis, Lord, 441, 470
Corruption: Blaine, 284; Grant, 299; Harding, 160; politician, synonym, 260; Tilden, 507. See Scandals
Cox, Edward, 5
Cox, James M., 114, 165, 189, 501
Coxey, Jacob S., 245
Cramer, Charles F., 167
Crawford, Robert, 397
Crawford, William H., 389, 417, 425
CREEP, 20, 21, 23
"Cross of Gold" Speech, 503
Cuba, 86, 195, 339, 349, 369; Bay of Pigs invasion, 63; communism, 63, 66, 72, 86; missile crisis, 50-1, 63, 66; Spanish-American war, 226-8. See Ostend Manifesto
Curtis, Charles, 134
Custis, Martha Dandridge, 461. See Washington, Martha
Czolgosz, Leon F., 229

Dakota Wesleyan University, 491, 492
Dana, Francis, 414
"Dark horse," 299, 300, 344, 346, 367
Daugherty, Harry, 161, 162-3; Attorney General, 150, 166-7, 171, 172
Davis, James J., 166
Davis, Jefferson, 176, 349, 358, 508
Davis, John W., 152, 500-1, 504
Dawes, Charles G., 152, 167
Dean, John W., III, 22, 23
Debs, Eugene, 245
Declaration of Independence, 451, 459; Adams, J., 455; Jackson, 397; Jefferson, 437, 438, 440-2, 449, 455; signers, 251, 380
Defeated Nominees, 491-517
Democratic Farmer Labor party, 493
Democratic National Conventions: (1836), 391; (1840), 392; (1844), 366-7, 411; (1848), 359; (1852), 346; (1856), 338, 349; (1860), 305-6, 323; (1884), 233, 235; (1888), 241; (1892), 241; (1896), 246, 503; (1900), 93, 503; (1912), 181-2, 199, 216; (1920), 117, 165, 497, 500; (1924), 117, 152, 500, 504; (1928), 117; (1932), 117, 497; (1940), 122; (1944), 95; (1948), 99, 493; (1956), 52, 57-8; (1960), 35, 57-8; (1964), 39, 42, 493; (1968), 11, (1972) 21
Democratic party, 228-9, 336, 337, 349, 355, 369, 407, 509; Roosevelt, F. D., 111; split, 323, 340. See Democratic National Conventions
Democratic-Republican party, 375, 388, 433, 456, 475, 516; founders, 403; Jefferson, 444; Monroe, 423
Denby, Edwin, 150, 165

Denver College of Pharmacy, 493
Depressions. See under Economic conditions
Dewey, George, 228
Dewey, Thomas E., 7, 79, 95, 100, 102, 126, 494, 496
Dickinson, Charles, 400
Dickinson, John, 521
Dickinson College, 335, 336
Dinwiddie, Robert, 464, 466
Disarmament: Eisenhower, 86, 87, 88, 89; Washington Conference (1921), 166
District of Columbia, slavery, 321, 353
Doheny, E. L., 171
Domestic politics. See under name of policy; President; Civil rights
Dominican Republic, 30, 45, 213
Donelson, Emily, 406
"Do-Nothing Congress," 6, 102
Douglas, Helen Gahagan, 7
Douglas, Stephen A., 321, 339, 348, 510-11; -Lincoln debates, 313, 321, 323, 340, 511
Douglas, William O., xxvi
Draft (military), 45, 233
Dred Scott case, 339
Duane, William J., 409
Duke University, 3, 5
Dulles, John Foster, 7, 84

Eagleton, Thomas F., 20, 492
Eaton, John, 389, 405-7; "Affair of Mrs. Eaton," 404-7
Economic conditions, 17, xxxiv, xxxviii, 63, 81, 201, 232, 236, 238, 241-2, 245-6, 254, 287-8, 349, 409, 411, 435, 474; "bank holiday," 118; business, 182; federal controls, 238; depressions, 282, (1820's), 132, (1837), 305, 381, 388, 392, 409-11, (1857), 339, (1873), 300, (1893), 224, 242, 245, 254, (1897), 225, (1907), 214, Coolidge, 155, Great, 112, 117, 118, 121, 132, 140-2, 155; farmers, 155; Fiscal Corporation Bill, 375; free silver, 246, 247; gold standard, 118, 225, 246; gold vs. silver, 225, 228; Hoover, 134; muckrakers, 213-14; Roosevelt, F. D., 122; stock market crash (1929), 117, 132, 140, 156; tariffs (see Tariffs); Truman, 98; trusts, 196, 209, 212, 213; Wilson, 183-6; post-World War I, 140; post-World War II, 92. See also Labor; Railroads; Unions
Edison, Thomas, 278
Egypt, 82
Ehrlichman, John D., 22, 23, 26, 27
Eisenhower, Arthur, 93
Eisenhower, David, 5
Eisenhower, Dwight D., xxv, 8, 9, 10, 34, 53, 71-89, 93, 100, 482, 495; appearance, 73; birth, 71, 72; characteristics, 74, 78; Cuba, 63; "Doctrine," 84; education, 71, 72-3; farewell address, 86-9; health, 9, 82; hero, 72, 78, 495; Hoover, 129, 143; Kennedy, 57; MacArthur, 71, 74; marriage, 71, 73-4; NATO, 71, 79, 106; popularity, 82, 495; President, 5, 10, 35, 71, 72, 78-89, 109; summit meeting (1955), 81; U-2 incident, 86; World War II, 72, 74, 78, 79, 126-7
Elections: first modern, 384; major candidates popular and electoral vote, 480; most controversial, 278, 284-5; radio returns, 160; (1796), 399; (1824),

Picture Credits

Key to position of photograph:
T(top)—C(center)—B(bottom)—L(left)—R(right).
Numbers refer to page numbers.

ACME
101(TR), 106, 127, 496, 497, 498, 499

PHOTOGRAPHY UNDER THE DIRECTION OF OLLIE ATKINS,
PERSONAL PHOTOGRAPHER TO PRESIDENT RICHARD NIXON
2, 18(T), 18(B), 24

FRANK DEMENTI'S COLONIAL STUDIO
78

HARRIS & EWING
73, 168(T), 174, 190, 492, 500

INDEPENDENCE NATIONAL HISTORICAL PARK COLLECTION
450

INTERNATIONAL NEWS
79 (R), 80(L), 81, 85(T), 97(TL), 101(CR), 101(B),
104(T), 104(B), 105(TR), 108(TL)

THE LYNDON BAINES JOHNSON LIBRARY
46(B), 47(T), 47(B)

LIBRARY OF CONGRESS
v, vi, xv(BL), xv(BC), 32, 48, 53, 65(T), 70, 75(TL) U.S.
Army, 75(TR) Bureau of Publications, War Department,
75(B) U.S. Army, 76(TL), 76(TR), U.S. Army, 76(BL),
76(BR), 77(T), 77(B), 84, 88(L), 96, 97(TR), 110 Perskie,
113, 114(T), 114(B) Clinedinst, 115(T), 115(B), 116(TL),
116(B), 116(TR), 117, 118(T), 118(B), 120(T), 120(B),
121, 122, 124(T), 124(LB), 126(T), 126(B), 130, 132(L),
132(R), 133 Herbert French, 135(T), 135(B), 136, 138(T),
139(B), 140(T), 140(B), 141(T), 141(B), 142 National
Photo, 143(T), 144 Ruband, 146, 147 Keystone, 148, 149,
151(T), 151(B), 152, 153(T), 153(BR) National Photo,
154(T), 154(B), 155(TL), 155(R), 156(T), 156(B), 157,
158 Grady, Seattle, 161, 162, 163, 164(T), 164(B), 166,
168(BL), 170, 172, 173, 176, 177, 178 Marceau, 179,
180(TL), 180(TR), 181, 182, 183(T), 183(B), 184, 185,
186, 187, 188(T), 188(B), 189, 192, 193, 194, 195, 196 Bain
Collection, 197(T), 197(B), 198(T), 198(BL), 198(BR),
199, 200, 203, 204, 205, 206, 207, 208, 209, 210(all), 211(T),
211(B), 212(T), 212(B), 213, 214(T), 214(B), 215 Bain
Collection, 216(T), 216(B), 217, 218, 220, 221, 222(T),
222(B), 223, 224, 225(T), 225(B), 226(T), 226(B), 227,
228, 229, 230, 232, 233, 234, 237, 238, 239, 240, 241, 242,
243, 244(T), 244(B), 245, 246, 247, 248, 250, 252, 255,
256(T), 256(B), 257, 258, 261, 262, 263, 265(T), 265(C),
266, 268, 270, 271, 272(T), 272(B), 273, 274 George Prince,
275, 276, 278, 279, 280, 281, 282, 283, 284, 285, 286(T),
286(B), 287, 288, 289, 290, 292, 293, 294, 295, 296, 297(T),
297(B), 298, 299, 300, 301, 302, 304, 307, 309, 310, 311, 312,
315, 316, 318 Meserve, 320, 322(T), 322(B), 324, 325, 326,
327(T), 328(B), 328(T), 328(B), 329(T), 329(B), 330
Meserve, 331, 332(T), 332(B), 333 S. M. Fossett, 334, 336,
337, 338, 339, 340, 341(all), 342, 344, 345(T), 345(B), 347,
348, 349, 350, 353, 354, 355(T), 355(B), 356, 359, 360,
361(T), 361(R), 362, 364, 365, 366, 367, 368, 370, 373, 374,
375, 376, 377, 378, 380, 381, 382, 383(all), 384(B), 385, 386,
388, 389, 390, 392, 393, 394, 396, 398, 401(T), 401(B), 402,
405, 406, 408, 409, 410(T), 410(B), 416, 418, 420, 422, 424,
425, 426, 427, 428, 431, 432, 433, 434, 436, 439, 440, 443,
445, 446, 448, 460, 465, 467, 468, 469, 470(T), 470(C), 472,
473, 474, 476(all), 483, 484, 485, 486, 487(T), 487(B), 502
Campbell Studios, 503 Lumiere Studio, Omaha, 504 George
Prince, 505 N. Sorony, 506, 507, 508, 509, 510, 511, 512, 513,
514, 515, 516(T), 516(B), 517

RUSSELL MANUEL, COMMERCIAL PHOTOGRAPHER
101(TL)

SENATOR GEORGE S. MC GOVERN
491

NATIONAL AERONAUTICS AND SPACE ADMINISTRATION
13, 62(B)

NATIONAL GALLERY OF ART
412

NATIONAL PARK SERVICE, U.S. DEPARTMENT OF THE INTERIOR
28, Four-color section following p. 32 (all), 38, 39, 40(BL),
41(T), 41(BR), 44, 45(T), 58(T), 60(T), 61(B), 62(TL),
62(TR), 63, 65(B), 67(T), 67(B), 68, 80(R), 85(B), 87,
88(R), 89, 90, 93, 95, 97(B), 98, 99, 100, 105(TL), 105(BL),
105(BR), 108(TR), 119(T), 124(BR), 488

DORIS S. OBERG, QUINCY HISTORICAL SOCIETY
415, 452, 454, 457 (all)

THE HARRY S. TRUMAN LIBRARY
107, 109(T), 109(B)

UNDERWOOD & UNDERWOOD
128, 131, 134, 137(T), 137(B), 138(C), 138(B), 139(T),
139(C), 153(BL), 167, 168(BR), 169(T), 169(B), 269

UNITER PRESS INTERNATIONAL
xv(BR), xvi(BR), xx, xxi(T), xxi(R), xxii(all), xxiii, xxiv,
xxv(T), xxv(B), xxvi(T), xxvi(L), xxvii(T), xxvii(B),
xxviii(all), xxix(all), xxx, xxxi(T), xxxi(R), xxxii(all),
xxxiii, xxxviii, xl(T), xl(B), 4, 5, 6(T), 6(B), 7(T), 7(B),
8(T), 8(B), 9, 10, 11(T), 11(B), 12, 14, 15, 16, 17, 20(T),
20(B), 21(T), 21(B), 22(T), 22(B), 23(T), 23(B), 25, 26,
27, 31, 33, 34(T), 34(B), 35, 36, 37(T), 37(B), 40(T),
40(BR), 41(BL), 42(T), 42(B), 43(BL), 43(BR), 45(B),
46(T), 50, 54(all), 55(all), 56(T), 56(B), 57, 58(B),
59(TL), 59(TR), 59(B), 60(B), 61(T), 64(T), 64(C),
64(B), 66, 69(T), 69(B), 79(L), 82, 83(T), 83(B), 94,
102, 103(T), 103(B), 108(B), 119(B), 123, 125(T), 125(B),
143(B), 494, 495, 501

THE WHITE HOUSE 1974–75
xviii, xxxiv, xxxv(all), xxxvi(T), xxxvi(B), xxxvii(all),
xxxix, 490